D0242055

56

EU Environmental Law

EU Environmental Law

Editor

Professor Dr Ludwig Krämer
Former Judge at Landgericht in Kiel, LL.D.
Former Head of the Unit for Governance in DG Environment of the European
Commission

SWEET & MAXWELL   **THOMSON REUTERS**

First Edition   1992   by Professor Dr Ludwig Krämer
Seventh Edition   2011   by Professor Dr Ludwig Krämer

Published in 2011 by Sweet & Maxwell, 100 Avenue Road, London NW3 3PF part of
Thomson Reuters (Professional) UK Limited (Registered in England & Wales, Company No
1679046.
Registered Office and address for service: Aldgate House, 33 Aldgate High Street, London
EC3N 1DL)

For further information on our products and services, visit *www.sweetandmaxwell.co.uk*

Typeset by Letterpart Ltd, Reigate, Surrey

Printed and bound by CPI Group (UK) Ltd, Croydon, CR0 4YY.

No natural forests were destroyed to make this product; only farmed timber was used and
re-planted.

A CIP catalogue record of this book is available for the British Library.

ISBN: 978-0-41404-299-5

Preface

This book on European Union environmental law is the result of almost 40 years of occupation with this topic. Indeed, in the early 1970s, as young judge at the Landgericht Kiel (Germany), I was delegated to the European Commission in Bruxelles and worked, since its very beginnings, in the newly established environment protection service which became later the Directorate General for the environment. Thus, I had the privilege to live the evolution of European environmental law from the first hour, and as my delegation to the Commission continued until 2004, I was able to participate in the elaboration and the monitoring of this law for decades. As I had started, for personal reasons, also an academic career, I lectured on EU environmental law since 1985 in some twenty European universities and in six languages. After 2004, I continued lecturing, while acting at the same time as a private consultant. I tried to insert this experience as judge, European official, lecturer and private consultant into the different chapters of this book.

It is obvious that European environmental law has evolved, these last 40 years, in a spectacular manner. In numerous Member States of the Union, it is the first source of national environmental law which is almost at 100 per cent derived for EU environmental law. In the other Member States, it exercised a very strong influence on national environmental law and continues to do so: there is no section of the environment, where EU law did not considerably influence the elaboration and application of national environmental law.

While thus the balance of these 40 years is largely positive, the perspectives for European environmental law do not incite optimism: EU environmental law slowly moves towards a cumulation of good intentions—a high level of protection, the polluter and not the taxpayer shall pay for pollution, a sustainable development the integration of environmental requirements into other policies, the utilisation of the best technique, etc.—which are later on forgotten or bypassed when concrete rules are elaborated and in particular, when rules are to be applied and enforced. In the conflict of environmental interests and economic interests, in 999 out of 1,000 cases, the environment loses. The main raison for this is that the environment has no voice, does not vote and has no important social group behind it—such as agricultural law the farmers, fisheries law the fishermen, competition law the competitors or transport law the transporters (or the transported). To this has to be added that in all Member States of the EU and also at European level, the protection of the environment has been laid into the hands of the administration: it is the administration which grants permits, plans and realises large and less large infrastructure projects, monitors, controls and examines pollution, the use of resources and which soles conflicts of interests. However, the administration is neither the owner of the environment nor necessarily its best defendant. And in times of economic or financial crisis, the administrations are looking for solutions, even at the price of environmental protection.

Four problems appear to put at risk European environmental law: the first is the obvious lack of political will of the institutions, in particular of the Commission, to keep the promise, often given and lastly repeated in the Lisbon Treaties, to ensure a high level of environmental protection in Europe and therefore conceive, elaborate and apply effective provisions in order to ensure this protection. European environmental law is more and more reduced at general terms which are hardly applicable and the application of which is hardly controlled, neither by the European Commission nor by the European Parliament nor by the national, regional or local administrations in the Member States.

The second problem which goes hand in hand with the first one is the effective application of European environmental law. The Commission which practically has a monopoly in the monitoring of this application, limits itself more and more to oversee the legal transposition of the European provisions into national law, but does not really look at the effective application of these provisions in concrete, specific situations. The Commissions argues that the Member States shall ensure the implementation of EU environmental law, though it knows quite well—it had publicly stated that itself in 2001—the European (environmental) law is treated, at national level as a foreign law: you cannot always avoid having to deal with foreigners, but it is better to try to avoid them.

Nothing undermines the credibility of a State more that laws which are not applied. The Commission did not develop structures or mechanisms to improve the control of environmental law application, for example by transferring tasks to the European Environmental Agency, or granting to civil society representatives the right of standing in order to defend EU environmental law, or be it the setting up of a European inspection service. This passivity contributes so largely to the fact that EU environmental law is no longer altogether taken seriously. One may dare the comparison with the ten commandments: of high moral value, almost never openly disputed, used in Sunday speeches or in the introduction to solemn treaties, but of limited practical application.

This lack of practical application is clearly demonstrated by the fact that the state of the environment within the European Union diverges very considerably from one Member State to the other, even when the European provisions apply everywhere. This difference is explained by the more or less determined national policy to protect the environment. The EU institutions decreasing integrative capacity finds its reflection—and this is the third problem—at global level. Confronted with worldwide problems—climate change, the loss of biodiversity, the omnipresence of chemical substances, the use of natural resources and the fight against poverty—the European Union is not able to present itself as a union. It does not offer a model for the third world how to reconcile economic growth and protection of the environment. Whether it is a system of fair trade, fisheries agreements which care for the environment, a climate change agreement with the Cotonou countries of Africa, the Caraibes and the Pacific, provisions on corporate social and environmental responsibility of European undertakings, agreements with other regions in the world of the "Aarhus Convention type"—the foreign environmental policy of the European Union lacks concrete initiatives. The EU wants to play at the same level as the USA and China, and forgets that it has a specific vocation.

The last problem, again linked to the previous one, concerns the fight against poverty. The European Union is the only region in the world which had fixed itself the objectives of economic growth and sustainable development which ensures the protection of the environment. However, it has still not elaborated and put into practice a policy of sustainable development towards the third world, systematically supported by the development of policies in the areas of water, waste, soil protection, nature conservation, etc. The EU development policy continues to be marked by some mercantilistic spirit. And there are few signs that the EU would re-orient itself—despite the fact that scientists think that there might be some 200 to 250 environmental refugees by 2050. An environmental policy towards and with the third world is thus more necessary than ever.

Environmental law is the attempt to protect the environment with the means of the law. "Between the strong and the weak, it is the law which makes free and it is freedom which oppresses". In modern society, it is the environment which is, without doubt, the weak part. Environmental law can play its part in the efforts for protection—if it were taken seriously by its authors and by its addressees. I hope that this book will contribute to a better knowledge of law and to a better protection of the environment, in Europe and elsewhere.

Legislation and jurisprudence were taken into consideration until end of March 2011; later texts were only partly considered.

Ludwig Krämer
July 2011

TABLE OF CONTENTS

ix

ALPHABETICAL TABLE OF CASES

NUMERICAL TABLE OF CASES

TABLE OF EUROPEAN CONVENTIONS AND TREATIES

TABLE OF REGULATIONS

TABLE OF DIRECTIVES

TABLE OF DECISIONS

TABLE OF INTERNATIONAL CONVENTIONS AND TREATIES

BIBLIOGRAPHY

Aburatne, R., "Aircraft noise-legal and regulatory issues and trends", *Environmental Policy and Law*, 2001, p.51.

Adams, C., "Die Kennzeichnung lebender Wirbeltierarten nach der EG-Durchführungsverordnung", Natur und Recht, 1998, p.14.

Addink, G., et al., *Europees milieurechtspraak* (Zwolle, 1996).

Alcovér Sampedro, A., "*La protección del medio atmosferico*". In M. Campins i Eritja and I. Pont i Castejón (eds), *Perspectives de dret comunitari* (Bellaterra, 1997), p.239.

Alonso García, E., *Derecho ambiental de la Comunidad Europea* (Madrid, 1993), Vols I and II.

Alvarez Baquerizo, C. and Gonzalez Vela, V., "*La directiva de habitats*", *Revista de Derecho Ambiental*, 1992, p.57.

Anselmann, N., "Die Bezugnahme auf harmonisierte technische Regeln im Rahmen der Rechtsangleichung". In P. Müller-Graff (ed.), Technische Regeln im Binnenmarkt (Baden-Baden, 1991).

Aubin, A., La Communauté européenne face à la pollution atmosphérique (Rennes, 1993).

Aubin, A., L'impact du droit communautaire de l'environnement en France (Nantes, 1995).

Auvret-Finck, J., "L'avis 2/91 relatif à la Convention no 170 de l'OIT", Cahiers de droit européen, 1995, p.443.

Bache, I. and McGillivray, D., "Testing the extended gatekeeper: the law, practice and politics of implementing the Drinking Water Directive in the United Kingdom". In J. Holder (ed.), *The impact of E.C. environmental law in the United Kingdom* (Chichester, 1997), p.147.

Baldock, D., "The legal status of Special Protection Areas for the protection of wild birds", *Journal of Environmental Law*, 1992, p.139.

Ballosteros, M., "The Habitats Directive: pressure on governments essential", *Metamorphosis, The EEB Newsletter*, 1998, 10, p.3.

Bandi, G. and others, The environmental jurisprudence of the European Court of Justice (Budapest 2008).

Bär, S. and Kraemer, R., *Amsterdam and the environment* (Berlin, 1997).

Barents, R., "Milieu en de interne markt", Tijdschrift voor Europees en Economisch Recht, 1993, p.5.

Bartaire, G., "*Nociones de contaminación atmosferica*". In L. Parejo Alfonso and L. Krämer (eds), *Derecho medioambiental de la Unión Europea* (Madrid, 1996), p.297.

Bartlsperger, R., "Die Entwicklung des Abfallrechts in den Grundfragen von Abfallbegriff und Abfallregime", Verwaltungsarchiv, 1995, p.32.

Basse M., "Environment impact assessment (EIA)". In B. Wenzel (ed.), *First Nordic Conference on E.U. Environmental Law* (Copenhagen, 1994).

Baziadoly, S., Le droit communautaire de l'environnement depuis l'Acte Unique européen jusqu'à la Conférence Intergouvernementale (Brussels, 1996).

Bechmann, P. and Mansuy, V., *Le principe de précaution* (Paris, 2002).

Becker, U., Der Gestaltungsspielraum der EG-Mitgliedstaaten im Spannungsfeld zwischen Umweltschutz und freiem Warenverkehr (Baden-Baden, 1991).

Behrens, P. and Koch, H. (eds), Umweltschutz in der Europäischen Gemeinschaft: Spannungsfelder zwischen nationalem und europäischem Gemeinschaftsrecht (Baden-Baden, 1991).

Beijen, B., De kwaliteit van milieurichtlijnen (Utrecht, 2010).

Bennett, G., (ed.), Air pollution control in the European Community (London, 1991).

Bennett, G. (ed.), De uitvoering van EG-milieurichtlijnen toegespitst op milieugevaarlijke stoffen (Zwolle, 1989).

Bennett, G., The internal market and environmental policy in the Federal Republic of Germany and the Netherlands (Arnhem, 1989).

Berggren, E. and Taams, R., "De Cockerill-zaak: de betekenis van een vergunning en een Europees richtlijn voor lozingen in de Maas", Tijdschrift voor Milieu-Aansprakelijkheid, 1995, p.46.

Bergkamp, C.L., "The proposed environmental liability directive", *European Environmental Law Review*, 2002, p.294.

Bernauer, T., "Protecting the Rhine river against chloride pollution" in R. Keohane (ed.), *Institutions for environmental aid: pitfalls and promise* (Cambridge, Mass., 1996).

lxv

Betlem, G., "Being 'directly and individually concerned', the Schutznorm doctrine and Francovich liability" in H. Micklitz and N. Reich (eds), *Public interest litigation before European courts* (Baden-Baden, 1996), p.319.

Betlem, G., "Enforcement of E.C. environmental law in the light of the 5th action programme". In N. Reich and R. Heine-Mernik (eds), *Umweltverfassung und nachhaltige Entwicklung in der Europäischen Union* (Baden-Baden, 1997), p.119.

Beurier, J., "Le droit de la biodiversité", Revue juridique de l'environnement, 1996, p.5.

Biezeveld, G.: Onze ecologische voetafdruk. Hoe het milieurecht kan helpen die te verkleinen (Groningen ,2009).

Birnie, P., "The case of the Convention on Trade in Endangered Species". In R. Wolfrum (ed.), Enforcing environmental standards: economic mechanisms as viable means? (Berlin, etc., 1996), p.233.

Birnie, P., "The European Community and preservation of biological diversity". In M. Bowman and C. Redgwell (eds), *International law and the conservation of biological diversity* (London, 1995), p.71.

Bleckmann, A. and Koch, T., "Zu den Funktionen und Wirkungen der Querschnittsklausel des Art.130r Abs.2S.3 des EG-Vertrages", Jahrbuch des Umwelt- und Technikrechts, 1996, p.33.

Bocken, H. and Ryckbost, D. (eds), L'élaboration et l'application des directives européennes en matière d'environnement (Ghent, 1990).

Bodiguel, M., La qualité des eaux dans l'Union européenne—pratiques d'une réglementation commune (Paris, 1996).

Bouckaert, J., "Artikel 130s EEG als juridische basis voor de afvalrichtlijn", Tijdschrift voor Milieu en Recht, 1993, p.226.

Boudant, J., "La préservation communautaire des oiseaux et la chasse en France: le temps des recours", Recours de droit rural, 1990, p.373.

Bowman, M., "The protection of animals under international law" *Connecticut Journal of InternationalLaw*, 1989, p.487.

Bowman, M., "The Ramsar Convention comes of age", *Netherlands International Law Review*, 1995, p.1.

Boye, M. and Ege, C., EU Environmental Policy. Can free trade and environment go together? (Copenhagen, 1999).

Brans, E., "EC proposals for an environmental liability directive: standing and assessment for damages", *Environmental Liability*, 2002, p.135.

Breier, S., "Das Schicksal der Titandioxid-Richtlinie", Europäische Zeitschrift für Wirtschaftsrecht, 1993, p.315.

Breier, S., "Die Bedeutung der umweltrechtlichen Querschnittsklausel des Art.130r Abs.2 S.2 EWG-Vertrag für die Verwirklichung des Europäischen Binnenmarktes", Natur und Recht, 1992, p.174.

Breier, S., "Die öffentliche Beschaffung umweltfreundlicher KFZ und Kraftstoffe aus europarechtlicher Sicht", Umwelt- und Planungsrecht, 1995, p.128.

Breier, S., "Die Organisationsgewalt der Gemeinschaft am Beispiel der Errichtung der Europäischen Umweltagentur", Natur und Recht, 1995, p.516.

Breier, S., "Umweltschutz in der Europäischen Gemeinschaft—eine Bestandsaufnahme nach Maastricht", Natur und Recht, 1993, p.457.

Breuer, R., "Der Entwurf einer EG-Wasserrahmenrichtlinie", Neue Zeitschrift für Verwaltungsrecht, 1998, p.1001.

Breuer, R., "EG-Richtlinien und deutsches Wasserrecht", Wirtschaft und Verwaltung, 1990, p.79.

Breuer, R., Entwicklungen des europäischen Umweltrechts—Ziele, Wege und Irrwege (Berlin and New York, 1993).

Breuer, R., "Umweltrechtliche und wirtschaftslenkende Abgaben im europäischen Binnenmarkt", Deutsches Verwaltungsblatt, 1992, p.485.

Brinkhorst, L., Subsidiariteit en milieu in de Europese Gemeenschap. Doos van Pandora of Panacee? (Leiden, 1992).

Burgi, M., "Das Schutz- und Ursprungsprinzip im europäischen Umweltrecht", Natur und Recht,1995, p.11.

Calliess, C., "Ansatzpunkte für eine umweltverträgliche Verkehrspolitik im europäischen Binnenmarkt—unter besonderer Berücksichtigung der Querschnittsklausel des Art.130r Abs.2 S.3 EGV", Zeitschrift für angewandte Umweltforschung, 1994, p.322.

Calliess, C., "Die Umweltkompetenzen der EG nach dem Vertrag von Nizza – zum Handlungsrahmen der europäischen Umweltgesetzgebung", Zeitschrift für Umweltrecht, 2003, p.129.

Calliess, C., "Perspektiven für die Weiterentwicklung der Europäischen Union zu einer ökologischen Rechtsgemeinschaft", Kritische Justiz, 1995, p.284.

Calliess, C. and Wegener, B. (eds), Europäisches Umweltrecht als Chance: die Umweltpolitik der EG und die Einflussmöglichkeiten der Umweltverbände (Taunusstein, 1992).

Cameron, J., "Introduction of group action on the European level: how can interest groups use E.C. law to protect the environment". In M. Führ and G. Roller (eds), *Participation and litigation rights of environmental associations in Europe* (Frankfurt/Main, 1991), p.141.

Campins Eritja, M., La gestion de los residuos peligrosos en la Comunidad Europea (Barcelona, 1994).

Campins Eritja, M. (ed.), *Sustainability labelling and certification* (Madrid-Barcelona, 2004).

Campins i Eritja, M. and Pont i Castejón, I. (eds), *Perspectives de dret comunitari ambiental* (Bellaterra, 1997).

Capria, A., "Direttive ambientali CEE", Stato di attuazione in Italia 2nd edn (Milan, 1992).

Cashman, L., "Compliance promotion and enforcement in the field of the environment". In *Journal for European Environmental & Planning Law,* 2006, p.385.

Caspari, S., Die Umweltpolitik der Europäischen Gemeinschaft, Eine Analyse am Beispiel der Luftreinhaltepolitik (Baden-Baden, 1995).

Cassese, S. (ed.), *Diritto ambientale communitario* (Milan, 1995).

Castanon i Garcia-Alix, O., *"Aplicació del dret comunitari per les Comunitats Autònomes"*. In M. Campins i Eritja and I. Pont i Castejón (eds), *Perspectives de dret ambiental* (Bellaterra, 1997), p.449.

Chalmers, D., "Environmental protection and the Single Market: an unsustainable development. Does the E.C. Treaty need a Title on the environment?", *Legal Issues in European Integration,* 1994, p.I-65.

Charbonneau, S., Droit communautaire de l'environnement (Paris, 2003).

Cheyne, I. and Purdue, M., "Fitting definition to purpose: the search for a satisfactory definition of waste", *Journal of Environmental Law,* 1995, p.149.

Cheyne, I., "The definition of waste in EC law", *Journal of Environmental Law,* 2002, p.61.

Chiti, M., *"Ambiente e 'costituzione' europea: alcuni nodi problematici"*. In S. Grassi, M. Cecchetti and A. Andronio (eds), *Ambiente e diritto* (Milan, 1999), p.131.

Christoforou, T., "The precautionary principle, risk assessment and the comparative role of science in the European and the US legal systems". In N. Vig and M. Faure (eds), *Green Giants?* (Cambridge/Mass., 2004) p.17.

Christiansen, P., "Waste—a national aspect". In B. Wenzel (ed.), *First Nordic conference on EU environmental law* (Copenhagen, 1994), p.79.

Christoforou, T., "The regulation of genetically modified organisms in the European Union: the interplay of science, law and politics", *Common Market Law Review,* 2004, p.637.

Churchill, R., and Kütting, G., "International environmental agreements and the free movement of gods in the EC: the case of the Montreal Protocol", *European Environmental Law Review,* 1995, p.329.

Clair, V., La lutte contre le bruit en droit communautaire (Paris, 1997).

Clement, K., "Economic development and environmental gain" (London, 2000).

Clinton-Davis, S., "Enforcing E.C. environmental law: a personal perspective". In H. Somsen (ed.), *Protecting the European environment: enforcing E.C. environmental law* (London, 1996), p.7.

Coffey, C. (ed.), Implementing the Habitats Directive in marine and coastal areas (Luxembourg, 1998).

Collier, U., Deregulation in the European Union: environmental perspectives (London and New York, 1997).

Comte, F., "Criminal environmental law and Community competence", *European Environmental Law Review* (2003), p.147.

Comte, F. and Krämer, L., *Environmental crime in Europe* (Groningen, 2004).

Cross, G., "Subsidiarity and the environment", *Yearbook of European Law* (1996), p.107.

Davies, P. and Goh, J., "E.C. law on aircraft noise: recent developments", *European Environmental Law Review,* 1993, p.229.

Dawkins, K., Ecolabelling: consumers' rights to know or restrictive business practices? (Minneapolis, 1995).

de Benito, J., "Nuevas orientaciones en la protección de la naturaleza en Espana por imperativos del derecho comunitario" in M. Campins i Eritja and I. Pont i Castejón (eds), Perspectives de dret comunitari ambiental (Bellaterra, 1997), p.315.

de Lange, F., "Beyond Greenpeace—courtesy of the Aarhus Convention", *Yearbook of European Environmental Law,* 2003, p.227.

de Sadeleer, N., "EC law and biodiversity". In R. Macrory (ed.), *Reflections on 30 years of EU environmental law* (Groningen, 2006).

de Sadeleer, Environnement et marché intérieur (Bruxelles, 2010).

de Sadeleer, N., *Environmental principles* (Oxford, 2002).

de Sadeleer, N., "Habitats conservation in EC law—from nature sanctuaries to ecological networks", *Yearbook of European Environmental Law*, 2005, p.215.

de Sadeleer, N., "La directive 92/43 concernant la conservation des habitats naturels ainsi que de la faune et de la flore sauvages: vers la reconnaissance d'un patrimoine naturel de la Communauté européenne", Revue du Marché Commun et de l'Union Européenne, 1993, p.24.

de Sadeleer, N., "Les conflits d'intérèts portant sur la protection des milieux naturels en droit communautaire", Revue juridique de l'environnement, 1993, p.351.

de Sadeleer, N., *"Pollution des eaux: protection des eaux intérieures"*. In M. Campins i Eritja and I. Pont i Castejón (eds), *Perspectives de Dret Comunitari Ambiental* (Barcelona, 1997), p.215.

de Sadeleer, N. and Born, H., *Le droit international et communautaire de la biodiversité* (Paris, 2004).

de Sadeleer, N., Roller, G. and Dross M. (eds), *Access to justice in environmental matters and the role of NGOs: empirical findings and legal appraisal* (Groningen, 2005).

de Silguy, R., *"Les oiseaux migrateurs et l'Europe"*, Gazette du Palais, 1993, p.30.

de Silguy, R., *"Migrateurs et Europe; évolution juridique récente"*, Gazette du Palais, 1995, p.4.

de Villeneuve, C., *"Les mouvements transfrontières de déchets dangereux"*, Revue du Marché Commun, 1990, p.568.

Decaesteker, J., *"Les instruments financiers de la Communauté Européenne en matière d'environnement"*. In M. Campins and I. Pont (eds), *Perspectives de dret comunitari ambiental* (Bellaterra, 1997), p.57.

Dejeant-Pons, M. and Pallemaerts, M., *Human rights and the environment* (Strasbourg, 2002).

Delbeke, J. and Bergman, H., "Environmental taxes and charges in the E.U.". In J. Golub (ed.), *New instruments for environmental policy on the E.U.* (London and New York, 1998), p.242.

Dell'Anno, P., *"L'attuazione del diritto communitario ambientale tra supremazia delle fonti e disapplicazione amministrativa: spunit di riflessione"*, Rivista trimesteriale di diritto pubblico, 1994, p.615.

Delwing, P., *Umsetzungsprobleme des EG-Wasserrechts. Dargestellt für das Abwasserrecht der Bundesrepublik Deutschland* (Baden-Baden, 1995).

Demaret, P., "Trade-related environmental measures (TREMs) in the external relations of the European Community". In M. Maresceau (ed.), *The European Community's commercial policy after 1992: the legal dimension* (Deventer, 1993), p.315.

Demey, T., Hannequart, J. and Lambert, K., *Packaging Europe. A directive standing up to transposition into 15 national laws* (Brussels, 1996).

Demmke, C., *Die Implementation von EG-Umweltpolitik in den Mitgliedstaaten. Umsetzung und Vollzug der Trinkwasserrichtlinie* (Baden-Baden, 1994).

Demmke, C. (ed.), *Europäische Umweltpolitik und nationale Verwaltungen* (Maastricht, 1998).

Demmke, C., *"Nationale Verwaltung und europäische Umweltpolitik—die Umsetzung und der Vollzug von EG-Umweltrecht"*. In C. Demmke (ed.), *Europäische Umweltpolitik und nationale Verwaltungen* (Maastricht, 1998), p.85.

Demmke, C., *"Umweltpolitik im Europa der Verwaltungen"*, Die Verwaltung, 1994, p.49.

Devos, J., "Legal Aspects" in *Ullmann's Encyclopedia of Industrial Chemistry* (Weinheim, 1995), Vol.B7, p.299.

Dhondt, N., "Environmental Law Principles and the EC Law of the Court of Justice". In M. Sheridan and L. Lavrysen (eds), *Environmental Law Principles in Practice* (Brussels, 2002), p.141.

Dhondt, N., *Integration of environmental protection into other EC policies* (Groningen, 2003).

Dibout, P., *"Fiscalité européenne et environnement"*, Revue des affaires européennes, 1995, p.31.

Dieckmann, M., *Das Abfallrecht der Europäischen Gemeinschaften* (Baden-Baden, 1994).

Dietrich, B., Au, C. and Dreher, J., *Umweltrecht der Europäischen Gemeinschaften* (Berlin, 2003).

Díez de Vellasco Vallejo, M., *Aspectos juridicos de la protección del medio ambiente en la Comunidad Europea y en especial la contribución de su Tribunal de Justicia* (Granada, 1991).

Douma, W., "Wallooon waste import ban", *European Business Law Review*, 1993, p.32.

Driessen, B., "New opportunities or trade barriers in disguise? The EC eco-labelling scheme", *European Environmental Law Review*, 1999, p.5;

Durner,W., "Zehn Jahre Wasserrahmenrichtlinie in Deutschland. Erfahrungen und Perspektiven". In W.Köck and K.Fassbender (eds): *Implementation der Wasserrahmenrichtlinie in Deutschland—Erfahrungen und Perspektiven* (Baden-Baden 2011), p.17.

Ebbesson, J., *"Lex pernix apivorus: an experiment of environmental law methodology"*, Journal of Environmental Law, 2003, p.153.

Ebbesson, J. and Langlet, D. (eds), *Koll paa kemikalier? Rättsliga förändringar, möjligheter och begränsninger* (Stockholm, 2010).

Eiderström, E., "Ecolabels in E.U. Environmental Policy". In J. Golub (ed.) *New instruments for environmental policy in the E.U.* (London and New York, 1998), p.190.

Elsworthy, S., "Crated calves and crazy cows: live animals and free movement of goods". In J. Holder (ed.), *The impact of E.C. environmental law in the United Kingdom* (Chichester, etc., 1997), p.303.

Emonds, S., "*Die neue EG-Artenschutzverordnung und das geltende nationale Artenschutzrecht. Drohender Verstoß gegen EG-Recht?*", *Natur und Recht*, 1997, p.26.

Engelsberger, C., *Der Vollzug europarechtlicher Vorschriften auf dem Gebiet des Umweltschutzes* (Berlin, 1998).

Epiney, A., "*Dezentrale Durchsetzungsmechanismen im gemeinschaftlichen Umweltrecht—dargestellt am Beispiel der UVP-Richtlinie*", *Zeitschrift für Umweltrecht*, 1996, p.229.

Epiney, A., "*Die Massstabsfunktion des Art: 30 EGV für nationale umweltpolitische Massnahmen*", *Zeitschrift für Umweltrecht*, 1995, p.24.

Epiney, A., "*Die umweltpolitischen Handlungsprinzipien in Art.130r EGV: politische Leitlinien oder rechtsverbindliche Vorgaben? Zu den Urteilen des EuGH in den Rs C–284/95, C–341/95 (Safety Hi-Tech) vom 14.7.1998*", *Natur und Recht*, 1999, p.181.

Epiney, A., "*Einbeziehung gemeinschaftlicher Umweltschutzprinzipien in die Bestimmung mitgliedstaatlichen Handlungsspielraums*", *Deutsches Verwaltungsblatt*, 1993, p.93.

Epiney, A., "Sustainable use of freshwater resources*", *Zeitschrift für ausländisches und öffentliches Recht und Völkerrecht*, 2003, p.377

Epiney, A., "*Umweltrechtliche Querschnittsklausel und freier Warenverkehr: die Einbeziehung umweltpolitischer Belange über die Beschränkung der Grundfreiheit*", *Natur und Recht*, 1995, pp.497, 498.

Epiney, A., *Umweltrecht in der Europäischen Union* 2nd edn (Köln, Berlin, München, 2005).

Epiney, A., *Verkehrspolitik und Umweltschutz in der Europäischen Union: zur Einbeziehung ikologischer Aspekte im Bereich des Strassen- und Schienenverkehrs* (Fribourg, 1997).

Epiney, A., "*Vogel- und Habitatschutz in der EU. Mitgliedstaatliche Beurteilungsspielräume bei der Ausweitung von Schutzgebieten und der Anwendung der Schutzregime*", *Umwelt- und Planungsrecht*, 1997, p.293.

Epiney, A., "*Zu den Anforderungen der Aarhus-Konvention an das europäische Gemeinschaftsrecht*" *Zeitschrift für Umweltrecht*, 2003, 176.

Epiney, A. and Furrer, A., "*Umweltschutz nach Maastricht. Ein Europa der drei Geschwindigkeiten?*", *Europarecht*, 1993, p.369.

Epiney, A. and Gruber, R., *Verkehrsrecht in der EU* (Baden-Baden, 2001).

Epiney, A. and Pfenninger, H., "*Auswirkungen eines Beitritts zur europäischen Union auf das schweizerische Umweltrecht—das Problem der Umweltnormung*". In T. Cottier and A. Kopse (eds) *Der Beitritt der Schweiz zur Europäischen Union* (Zürich, 1998) p.649.

Epiney, A. and Sollberger, K., *Zugang zu Gerichten und gerichtliche Kontrolle im Umweltrecht* (Berlin, 2002).

Erbguth, W. and Stollmann, F., "*Die Bindung der Verwaltung an die Vorgaben der FFH-Richtlinie*", *Deutsches Verwaltungsblatt*, 1997, p.45.

Ermacora, F., "Community legislation and jurisprudence in the area of waste management: recent developments", *Review of European Community and International Environmental Law*, 1998, p.274.

Esty, D. and Geradin, D., "Environmental protection and international competitiveness", *Journal of World Trade*, 1998, 3, p.5.

Everling, U., "*Durchführung und Umsetzung des Europäischen Gemeinschaftsrechts im Bereich des Umweltschutzes unter Berücksichtigung der Rechtsprechung des EUGH*", *Neue Zeitschrift für Verwaltungsrecht*, 1993, p.209.

Everling, U., "*Umsetzung von Umweltrichtlinien durch normkonkretisierende Verwaltungsanweisungen*", *Recht der Internationalen Wirtschaft*, 1992, p.392.

Everling, U., "*Umweltschutz durch Gemeinschaftsrecht in der Rechtsprechung des EUGH*". In P. Behrens and H. Koch (eds), *Umweltschutz in der Europäischen Gemeinschaft* (Baden-Baden, 1991), p.29.

Fajardo del Castello, T., "Revisiting the external dimension of the environmental policy of the European Union: some challenges ahead", *Journal for European Environmental & Planning Law*, 2010, p.365.

Fallon, M., "Les ecotaxes et le droit communautaire" in CEDRE (ed.), *L'introduction des ecotaxes en droit belge* (Brussels, 1994), p.33.

Falke, J., "Standardisation by professional organisations". In G. Winter (ed.), *Sources and Categories of European Union Law* (Baden-Baden, 1996), p.147.

Falke, J. and Schlacke, S. (eds), *Neue Entwicklungen im Umwelt-und Verbraucherrecht* (Berlin, 2004).

Faulks, J. and Rose, L., "Common interest groups and the enforcement of European environmental law". In H. Somsen (ed.), *Protecting the European environment: enforcing E.C. environmental law* (London, 1996), p.195.

Faure, M. and de Smedt, K., "Should Europe harmonise environmental liability legislation?". In *Environmental Liability*, 2001, p.217.

Feddersen, C., "Recent E.C. environmental legislation and its compatibility with WTO rules: free trade or animal welfare trade", *European Environmental Law Review*, 1998, p.207.

Fehr, H. and Van der Stelt-Scheele, D., "The E.C. environmental policy in relation to the E.C. structural funds: a critical analysis of its application", *European Environmental Law Review*, 1992, pp.121, 143.

Fenelly, N., "The role of Community law in controlling the transposition and execution of environmental regulations". In A. García Ureta (ed.), *Transposición y control de la normativa ambiental comunitaria* (Basauri, 1998), p.15.

Fernández de Casadevante, C., "*El incumplimiento del derecho comunitario en las Marismas de Santona*", *Revista de Instituciones Europeas*, 1994, p.137.

Fernández Sánchez de Gatta, D., "*Politica Ambiental Comunitaria en el Tratado de la Unión Europea*", *Revista de Derecho Ambiental*, 1994, p.73.

Fisahn, A., "*Die Konvention über die biologische Vielfalt und die Flora-Fauna- Habitat-Richtlinie der EU*", *Zeitschrift für Umweltrecht*, 1996, p.3.

Fischer, K. and Freytag, E., *Österreich und das Umweltrecht der Europäischen Union* (Vienna, 1995).

Fluck, J., "*Zum Abfallbegriff im europäischen, im geltenden und im werdenden deutschen Abfallrecht*", *Deutsches Verwaltungsblatt*, 1993, p.590.

Fluck, J., "*Zum EG-Abfallrecht und seiner Umsetzung in deutsches Recht*", *Europarecht*, 1994, p.71.

Forster, M., "Enforcing the Drinking Water Directive", *Land Management and Environmental Law Report*, 1991, p.56.

Frees, C., "*Massnahmen und rechtliche Möglichkeiten der EG zur Bekämpfung und Verhütung von Öltankerunfällen vor ihren Küsten*", *Natur und Recht*, 1992, p.16.

Freestone, D., "The enforcement of the Wild Birds Directive". In H. Somsen (ed.), *Protecting the European environment: enforcing E.C. environmental law* (London, 1996), p.229.

Freestone, D., "The Leybucht Dikes case", *Water Law*, 1991, p.153.

Freestone, D. and Somsen, H., "The impact of subsidiarity". In J. Holder (ed.), *The impact of E.C. environmental law in the United Kingdom* (Chichester, 1997), p.87.

Freestone, D. and Streck, C. (eds), *Legal aspects of implementing the Kyoto Protocol mechanisms: Making Kyoto work* (Oxford, 2005).

Frenz, W., *Europäisches Umweltrecht* (München, 1997).

Frenz, W., "*Subjektiv-öffentliche Rechte aus Gemeinschaftsrecht vor deutschen Verwaltungsgerichten*", *Deutsches Verwaltungsblatt*, 1995, p.408.

Freytag, C. and Iven, K., "*Gemeinschaftsrechtliche Vorgaben für den nationalen Habitatschutz*", *Natur und Recht*, 1995, p.109.

Fuchs, W. and Rapsch, A., "*Das deutsche Gentechnikrecht im Lichte quantitativer Vorgaben europarechtlicher Provenienz*", *Die öiffentliche Verwaltung*, 1991, p.873.

Führ, M., "*Betriebsorganisation als Element proaktiven Umweltschutzes*", *Jahrbuch des Umwelt- und Technikrechts*, 1993, p.145.

Führ, M., *Reform der europäischen Normungsverfahren* (Darmstadt, 1995).

Führ, M., "*Von Rio nach Brüssel über 15 europäische Hauptstädte—Entwicklungstendenzen im Europäischen Umweltrecht*", *Kritische Vierteljahresschrift für Gesetzgebung und Rechtswissenschaften*, 1995, p.335.

Führ, M. and Roller, G. (eds), *Participation and litigation rights of environmental associations in Europe: current legal situation and practical experience* (Frankfurt/Main, 1991).

Furrer, A. and Bölscher, V., "*Technische Normen im Spannungsfeld zwischen Umweltschutz und freiem Binnenmarkt*", *Zeitschrift für Umweltrecht*, 1998, p.3.

Gale, L., "Citizen and NGO participation in policymaking and enforcement of environmental Community law". In M. Campins i Eritja and I. Pont i Castejón (eds), *Perspectives de dret comunitari ambiental* (Bellaterra, 1997), p.515.

Gallas, A., "*Aspekte der Luftreinhaltepolitik*". In P. Behrens and H. Koch (eds), *Umweltschutz in der Europäischen Gemeinschaft: Spannungsfelder zwischen nationalem und europäischem Gemeinschaftsrecht* (Baden-Baden, 1991), p.98.

Garcia Burgués, J. and Insausti Muguruza, M., "Trade and the environment in the WTO: the European Community's participation in the Committee on Trade and Environment", *Review of European Community and International Environmental Law*, 1997, p.163.

García Ureta, A., *Derecho europeo de la biodiversidad: aves silvestres, habitats y especies de flora y fauna* (Madrid 2010).

García Ureta, A., *"En busca de la línea divisoria entre los artículos 100a y 130s del Tratado CE: reflexiones a la luz de los asuntos C–300/89, C–155/91 y C–187/93"*, *Revista vasca de administracion publica*, 1995, p.607.

García Ureta, A., *"La protección del ambiente a la luz del Tratado de la Unión Europea"*, *Revista Vasca de Administración Publica*, 1992, p.85.

García Ureta, A., *Protección de hábitats y de especies de flora y fauna en derecho comunitario europeo* (Basauri, 1997).

García Ureta, A. (ed.), *Transposición y control de la normativa ambiental comunitaria* (Basauri, 1998).

Garzia, G., *"L'attuazione delle direttive CEE mediante regolamenti ed il diritto dell'ambiente"*, *Rivista giuridica edilizia*, 1993, 2, p.159.

Gaskin, F., "The implementation of E.C. environmental law", *Review of European Community and International Environmental Law*, 1993, p.335.

Gebers, B. and Jendroska, J. (eds), *Environmental control of products and substances* (Düsseldorf, 1989).

Gebers, B. and Robesin, M. (eds), *Licensing procedures for industrial plants and the influence of E.C. procedures* (Frankfurt/Main, 1993).

Gellermann, M., *Beeinflussung des bundesdeutschen Rechts durch Richtlinien der EG—dargestellt am Beispiel des europäischen Umweltrechts* (Cologne, etc., 1994).

Gellermann, M., *"Rechtsfragen des europäischen Habitatschutzes"*, *Natur und Recht*, 1996, p.548.

Gellermann, M. and Szczekalla, P., *"Gemeinschaftskonforme Umsetzung von Umweltrichtlinien der EG"*, *Natur und Recht*, 1993, p.54.

Geradin, D., "The Belgian waste case", *European Law Review*, 1993, p.144.

Geradin, D., "Trade and environmental protection: Community harmonisation and national environmental standards", *Yearbook of European Law*, 1993, p.151.

Geradin, D., *Trade and the environment—a comparative analysis of E.C. and U.S. law* (Cambridge, 1997).

Giesberts, L., *"Die CO2-/Energiesteuer der EG. Anmerkungen zum geänderten Richtlinienvorschlag der Europäischen Kommission"*, *Recht der Internationalen Wirtschaft*, 1995, p.847.

Giesbert, L., *"Erweiterung des Herstellerbegriffs in der AltfahrzeugV als verstärkte Schutzmassnahme nach Art. 176 EG?"* *Deutsches Verwaltungsblatt*, 2003, p.94.

Ginzky, H., *Saubere Produkte, schmutzige Produktion. Eine Untersuchung zu Importbeschränkungen wegen umweltschädigender Produktionsnormen* (Düsseldorf, 1997).

Ginzky, H., *"Umweltschutz und der internationale Handel mit Waren"*, *Zeitschrift für Umweltrecht*, 1997, p.124.

Ginzky, H., *"Vermarktungs- oder Verwendungsbeschränkungen von Chemikalien— Verfahren, materielle Anforderungen und Reformüberlegungen"*, *Zeitschrift für Umweltrecht*, 2000, p.129.

Gisbert Pi, I., *"Instrumentos fiscales y reforma ecológica de la fiscalidad en la Unión Europea"*. In M. Campins and I. Pont (eds), *Perspectives des dret comunitari ambiental* (Bellaterra, 1997), p.73.

Glim, M., *European environmental legislation, what does it really mean?* (Delft, 1990).

Godt, C., "Enforcement of environmental law by individuals and interest groups: reconceptualising standing", *Journal of Consumer Policy*, 2000, p.79.

Goebel, B., *"Gemeinschaftsrechtlich begründete Staatshaftung—ein Beitrag zum Vollzug des Gemeinschaftsumweltrechts?"*, *Umwelt und Planungsrecht*, 1994, p.361.

Goldenmann, G., "Transboundary transfer of goods". In G. Winter (ed.), *European environmental law. A comparative perspective* (Aldershot, Brooklyn, Sydney and Singapore, 1996), p.341.

Golub, J. (ed.), *Global competition and E.U. environmental policy* (London, 1998).

Golub, J. (ed.), *New instruments for environmental protection in the E.U.* (London, 1998).

Götz, V., *"Agrarumweltrecht der Europäischen Gemeinschaft"*. In H. Rengeling (ed.), *Umweltschutz und andere Politiken der Europäischen Gemeinschaft* (Cologne, Berlin, Bonn and Munich, 1993), p.173.

Grabitz, E. and Zacker, C., "Scope for action by the EC Member States for the improvement of environmental protection under EEC Law: the example of environmental taxes and subsidies" (1989) C.M.L.R. 423.

Grawe, J., *"Umweltschutz und Energiepolitik"*. In H. Rengeling (ed.), *Umweltschutz und andere Politiken der Europäischen Gemeinschaft* (Cologne, Berlin, Bonn and Munich, 1993), p.87.

Grohs, S., "Commission infringement procedure in environmental cases". In M. Onida (ed.), *Europe and the environment* (Groningen 2004), p.63.

Gröpl, C., *"Die Euratom auf dem Weg zu einer Umweltgemeinschaft"*, *Deutsches Verwaltungsblatt*, 1995, p.322.

Grube, C., "Decision-making in E.C. environmental law" in B. Wenzel (ed.), *First Nordic conference on E.U. environmental law* (Copenhagen, 1994), p.45.

Habley, A. and Blackmore, S., "Greenhouse gas emissions trading in the United Kingdom and EU compared: the same destination, different routes", *Environmental Liability*, 2002, p.55.

Hager, G., *"Europäisches Umwelthaftungsrecht"*, *Zeitschrift für europäische Politik*, 1997, p.9.

Haigh, N. (with G. Bennett, P. Kromarek and T. Lavoux), *Comparative report: water and waste in four countries* (London, 1986).

Haigh, N., et al., *Manual of environmental policy: the E.C. and Britain* (London) (looseleaf).

Hailbronner, K., *Umweltrecht und Umweltpolitik in der Europäischen* Gemeinschaft (Linz, 1991).

Hailbronner, K., *"Verkehrspolitik und Umweltschutz"*. In H. Rengeling (ed.), *Umweltschutz und andere Politiken der Europäischen Gemeinschaft* (Cologne, Berlin, Bonn and Munich, 1993), p.149.

Hancher, L., "Energy and the environment: striking a balance?" *Common Market Law Review*, 1989, p.669.

Handl, G. and Lutz, R. (eds), *Transferring hazardous technologies and substances: the international legal challenge* (London, Dordrecht and Boston, 1989).

Hannequart, J., *European waste law* (London, The Hague and Boston, 1998).

Hannequart, J., *"Le règlement européen sur les mouvements de déchets"*, *Aménagement-Environnement*, 1993, p.67.

Hansjürgens, B.(ed.), *Emissions trading for climate policy. Constructing the climate change regime* (London, 2005).

Hansmann, K., *"Schwierigkeiten bei der Umsetzung und Durchführung des Europäischen Umweltrechts"*, *Neue Zeitschrift für Verwaltungsrecht*, 1995, p.320.

Harrems, N., "The leghold trap regulation and potential pitfalls during the Dutch Presidency of the E.U.", *European Environmental Law Review*, 1998, p.7.

Hart, D. and Marcos, R., *"Mesquer and the new waste framework directive"*, *Environmental Liability*, 2008, p.195;

Harte, J., "Nature conservation: the rule of law in European Community law", *Journal of Environmental Policy*, 1997, p.168.

Hattan, E., *"The Environmental Liability Directive"*, *Environmental Liability*, 2002, p.3.

Hattan E., *"The implementation of EU environmental law"*, *Journal of Environmental Law*, 2003, p.273.

Hedemann-Robinson, M., "Defending the consumer's right to a clean environment in the face of globalisation", *Journal of Consumer Policy*, 2000, p.25.

Hedemann-Robinson, M., "E.C. law, the environment and consumers: addressing the challenge of incorporating an environmental dimension to consumer protection at Community level", *Journal of Consumer Policy*, 1997, p.1.

Hedemann-Robinson, M., *Enforcement of European environmental law* (London, New York, 2007).

Heikkilä, M., "Une nouvelle ère en matière de réglementation sur les substances chimiques: le règlement REACH est entré en vigueur", *Revue du Droit de l'Union européenne*, 2007, p.839.

Heim, S., *Unmittelbare Wirkungen von EG-Richtlinien im deutschen und französischen Recht am Beispiel des Umweltrechts* (Baden-Baden, 1999).

Hendler, Reinhard (ed.): *Umwelthaftung nach neuem EG-Recht* (Berlin,2005)

Henke, J., *"EUGH und Umweltschutz"*, *Die Auswirkungen der Rechtsprechung des Gerichtshofs der Europäischen Gemeinschaften auf das Umweltschutzrecht in Europa* (Munich and Florence, 1992).

Henshaw, L., Aalders, M. and Molander, P., "Implementation of the E.C. Directive on integrated pollution prevention and control (96/61): a comparative study", *Environmental Liability*, 1998, p.39.

Hession, M. and Macrory, R., "Balancing trade freedom with the requirements of sustainable development" in N. Emiliou and D. O'Keeffe (eds), *The European Union and world trade law* (Chichester, 1996), p.181.

Hession, M. and Macrory, R., "Maastricht and the environmental policy of the Community: legal issues of a new environment policy". In D. O'Keeffe and P. Toomey (eds), *Legal issues of the Maastricht Treaty* (London and New York, 1994), p.151.

Heuser, I., *Europäisches Bodenschutzrecht* (Berlin, 2005).

Hey, C. and Jahns-Böhm, J., *Ökologie und freier Binnenmarkt* (Freiburg and Frankfurt/M., 1989).

Hey, C. and Taschner, K. (eds), *EEB Industry Handbook* (Brussels, 1998).

Hey, C., "The European Community's courts and international environmental agreements", *Review of European Community and International Environmental Law*, 1998, p.4.

Heyvaert, V., "Balancing trade and environment in the European Union: proportionality substituted" *Journal of Environmental Law*, 2001, p.392.

Hilf, M., *"Umweltabgaben als Gegenstand von Gemeinschaftsrecht und-politik"*, *Neue Zeitschrift für Verwaltungsrecht*, 1992, p.105.

Hilson, C., "Community rights in environmental law: rhetoric or reality". In J. Holder (ed.), *The impact of E.C. environmental law in the United Kingdom* (Chichester, 1997), p.51.

Hoffmann-Riem, W. and Schneider, J. (eds), *Umweltpolitiche Steuerung in einem liberalisierten Strommarkt* (Baden-Baden, 1995).

Holder, J., "A dead end for direct effect? Prospects for enforcement of European Community environmental law by individuals", *Journal of Environmental Law*, 1996, p.313.

Holder, J., "Safe science? The precautionary principle in U.K. environmental law". In J. Holder (ed.), *The impact of E.C. environmental law in the United Kingdom* (Chichester, 1997), p.123.

Holder, J. (ed.), *The impact of E.C. environmental law in the United Kingdom* (Chichester, 1997).

Holtwisch, C., Fajardo de Castillo, T. and Tichá, T. (eds), *Strengthening European environmental law in an enlarged Union* (Aachen, 2004).

House of Lords, Select Committee on the European Communities, *Implementation and enforcement of environmental legislation* 9th report (London, 1992).

House of Lords Select Committee of the European Communities, *Protection of wild birds 1993/94*, 11th report (London, 1994).

Howarth, W. and Somsen, H., "The E.C. Nitrates Directive", *Water Law*, 1991, p.149.

Howarth, W., *"Umweltrecht und Vollzug des Umweltrechts in England und Wales"*. In G. Lübbe-Wolff (ed.), *Vollzug des europäischen Umweltrechts* (Berlin, 1996), p.37.

Hubschmid, C. and Moser, P., "The co-operation procedure in the E.U.: why was the European Parliament influential in the decision on car emission standards?", *Journal of Common Market Studies*, 1997, p.225.

Huglo, J., *"L'application par les Etats membres des normes communautaires en matière d'environnement"*, *Revue trimestérielle de droit européen*, 1994, p.451.

Hunter, R., "Standardization and the environment", *International Environmental Reporter*, 1993, p.185.

IJlstra, T., *"L'action communautaire dans les Commission de Paris et d'Oslo"*. In J. Lebullinger and D. Le Morvan (eds), *La Communauté et la mer* (Paris, 1990), p.381.

Ingelaere, F., Lavrysen, L. and Vanden Bilcke, C., *Inleiding to het internationaal en europees milieurecht* (Brussels, 1992).

Iven, K., *"Schutz natürlicher Lebensräume und Gemeinschaftsrecht"*, *Natur und Recht*, 1996, p.373.

Jacobs, F., "The role of the European Court of Justice in the protection of the environment", *Journal of environmental Law*, 2006, p.185.

Jans, J., "Legal protection in European environmental law: an overview". In H. Somsen (ed.), *Protecting the European environment: enforcing E.C. environmental law* (London, 1996), p.49.

Jahns-Böhm, J., *"Güterkraftverkehrspolitik und Umweltschutz im EWG-Vertrag"*, *Europäische Zeitschrift für Wirtschaftsrecht*, 1991, p.523.

Jacobs, F., "The role of the European Court of Justice in the protection of the environment" *Journal of Environmental Law*, 2006, p.185.

Jadot, B., *"Mesures nationales de police de l'environnement, libre circulation des marchandises et proportionnalité"*, *Cahiers du droit européen*, 1990, p.408.

Jahns-Böhm, J., *"Güterkraftverkehrspolitik und Umweltschutz im EWG-Vertrag"*, *Europäische Zeitschrift für Wirtschaftsrecht*, 1991, p.523.

Jahns-Böhm, J., *Umweltschutz durch Europäisches Gemeinschaftsrecht am Beispiel der Luftreinhaltung* (Berlin, 1994).

Jans, J., Vedder, H., *European environmental law* 3rd edn (Groningen, 2008).

Jans, J., Vedder, H., *"Europeesrechtelijke grenzen aan nationaal milieubeleid"*, *Sociaal-economische wetgeving*, 1989, p.217.

Jans, J., "Self-sufficiency in European waste law?". In B. Wenzel (ed.), *First Nordic conference on EU environmental law* (Copenhagen, 1994), p.71.

Jans, J., "State aid and Articles 92 and 93 of the E.C. Treaty. Does the polluter pay?", *European Environmental Law Review*, 1995, p.108.

Jans, J., "The rule of law and European environmental policy: legal protection against acts of the European institutions". In L. Krämer (ed.), *Recht und Um- Welt*, essays in honour of Prof. Dr Gerd Winter (Groningen, 2003), p.301.

Jans, J., "Waste policy and European Community law: does the EEC Treaty provide a suitable framework for regulating waste?", *Ecology Law Quarterly*, 1993, p.165.

Jans, J. and Scott, J., "The Convention on the future of Europe: an environmental perspective", *Journal of Environmental Law*, 2003, p.323

Jans, J., Mortelmans, K., Sevenster, H. and Temmink, H., *Zo sterk als de zwakste schakel: Nederlands produktgericht milieubeleid in Europees en internationaalrechtelijk verband* (Amsterdam, 1993).

Jansen, B., "*Ökologische Steuern in der Europäischen Gemeinschaft*", *Zeitschrift für Umweltrecht*, 2003, p.257.

Jarass, H., *Grundfragen der innerstaatlichen Bedeutung des EG-Rechts* (Cologne, Berlin, Bonn and Munich, 1994).

Jarass, H., "*Die Beschränkung der Abfallausfuhr und EG-Recht*", *Natur und Recht*, 1998, p.397.

Jarza Bandarra, N., "*La protection de l'espace et politiques agri-environnementales*", *Revue du Marché Commun et de l'Union Européenne*, 1994, p.444.

Jendroska, J. and Stec, S., "The Kyiv Protocol on strategic environmental assessment", *Journal of European Environmental & Planning Law*, 2003, p.105.

Jessurun d'Oliveira, H., "*Die EWG und die Versalzung des Rheins*", European University Institute, Florence, Working Paper 88/334 (San Domenico, 1988).

Joerges, C., Falke, J., Micklitz, H. and Brüggemeier, G., *Die Sicherheit von Konsumgütern und die Entwicklung der Europäischen Gemeinschaft* (Baden-Baden, 1988).

Joerissen, J., *Möglichkeiten und Probleme bei der Verfolgung und Sicherung nationaler und EG-weiter Umweltschutzziele im Rahmen der europäischen Normung. (Büro für Technikfolgen-Abschätzung beim Deutschen Bundestag)* (Bonn, 1996).

Joerissen, J., *Produktbezogener Umweltschutz und technische Normung* (Berlin, 1997).

Joseph, T., "Preaching heresy: permitting Member States to enforce stricter environmental laws than the European Community", *Yale Journal of International Law*, 1995, p.227.

Juin, D., *L'application de la législation communautaire de l'environnement en France* (Paris, 1992).

Kahl, W., "*Der EUGH als 'Motor des europäischen Umweltschutzes'?*", *Thüringer Verwaltungsblätter*, 1994, pp.225, 256.

Kahl, W., "*Der Vollzug des europäischen Umweltrechts*", *Die öffentliche Verwaltung*, 1995, p.860.

Kahl, W., "*Stellung und Funktion von Umweltagenturen—eine rechtsvergleichende Typologie*", *Jahrbuch des Umwelt- und Technikrechts*, 1996, p.119.

Kahl, W., *Umweltprinzip und Gemeinschaftsrcht* (Heidelberg, 1993).

Kamminga, M. and Klatte, E., "*Twintig jaar EG milieubeleid en het integratiebeginsel*", *Milieu en Recht*, 1994, p.2.

Khalastchi, R. and Ward, H., "New instruments for sustainability: an assessment of environmental agreements under Community law", *Journal of Environmental Law*, 1998, p.257.

Kiel, T., "Ten years of European environmental management and audit system; future perspectives", *Yearbook of European Environmental Law*, 2006, p.61.

Kirchsteiger, C., "*Il rischio industriale nell'Unione europea*", *Rivista giuridica dell'ambiente*, 2000, p.123.

Klemm, A., *Klimaschutz nach Marrakesch.* (Köln, Berlin, Bonn, München, 2002).

Klett, W. and Enders, R., "*Gefährliche Abfälle—Umsetzungsdefizite europarechtlicher Vorgaben*", *Betriebsberater*, 1997, *Beilage* 4.1.

Klocke, U., *Klimaschutz durch ökonomische Instrumente* (Baden-Baden, 1995).

Kloepfer, M. et al., *Leben mit Lärm? Risikobeurteilung und Regulation des Umgebungslärms im Verkehrsbereich* (Berlin, Heidelberg, New York, 2006).

Klösters, A., *Kompetenzen der EG-Kommission im innerstaatlichen Vollzug von Gemeinschaftsrecht* (Cologne, 1994).

Koch, H., "*Luftreinhalterecht in der Europäischen Gemeinschaft*", *Deutsches Verwaltungsblatt*, 1992, p.124.

Koch, H., "*Luftreinhalterecht in der Europäischen Gemeinschaft*". In P. Behrens and H. Koch (eds), *Umweltschutz in der Europäischen Gemeinschaft, Spannungsfelder zwischen nationalem und europäischem Gemeinschaftsrecht* (Baden-Baden, 1991), p.75.

Köck, W. and Fassbender, K. (eds), *Implementation der Wasserrahmenrichtlinie in Deutschland—Erfahrungen und Perpektiven* (Baden-Baden 2011).

Köck, W., "*Vollzugsaspekte des Öko-Audit-Systems*". In N. Reich and R. Heine-Marnik (eds), *Umweltverfassung und nachhaltige Entwicklung in der Europäischen Union* (Baden-Baden, 1997), p.149.

Kolkmann, J., *Die EG-Trinkwasserrichtlinie: die Nitrat- und Pestizidgrenzwerte im deutschen Umweltrecht* (Berlin, 1991).

Koller, P. and Cashman, L., "Implementing EC environmental law. Compliance promotion and enforcement by the European Commission", *Journal for European Environmental & Planning Law*, 2009, p.1.

Konzak, O., "*Inhalt und Reichweite des europäischen Abfallbegriffs*", *Natur und Recht*, 1995, p.130.

Koppen, I., "The role of the European Court of Justice in the development of the European Community environmental policy", *European University Institute Working Paper 92/18* (Florence, 1993).

Köster, V., "Le comité d'examen du respect des dispositions de la Convention d'Aarhus: un panorama des procédures et de la jurisprudence" *Revue Européenne du Droit de l'Environnement*, 2007, p.326.

Köster, V., *The five global biodiversity-related conventions: a stocktaking*, RECIEL, 2000, p.96.

Krämer, L., "Access to environmental information in an Open European Society—Directive 2003/4", *Yearbook of European Environmental Law*, 2005, p.1.

Krämer, L., "Access to letters of formal notice and reasoned opinions in environmental law matters" *European Environmental Law Review*, 2003, p.197.

Krämer, L., *Casebook on EU environmental law* (Oxford, 2002); German text, *Europäisches Umweltrecht in der Rechtsprechung des EuGH; dargestellt anhand von 50 Urteilen* (Vienna, 2002).

Krämer, L., "*Das 'hohe Schutzniveau' im EG-Vertrag*", *Zeitschrift für Umweltrecht*, 1997, p.303.

Krämer, L., "Deficits in application of E.C. environmental law and its causes". In L. Krämer, *Focus on European environmental law* (London, 1997), p.1.

Krämer, L., "*Die Europäische Union und der Export von Abfällen in die Dritte Welt*", *Kritische Justiz*, 1998, p.345.

Krämer, L., "*Die Integrierung umweltpolitischer Erfordernisse in die gemeinschaftliche Wettbewerbspolitik*". In H. Rengeling (ed.), *Umweltschutz und andere Politiken der Europäischen Gemeinschaft* (Cologne, Berlin, Bonn and Munich, 1993), p.47.

Krämer, L., "*Die Rechtsprechung der EG-Gerichte zum Umweltrecht 1995 bis 1997*", *Europäische Grundrechte Zeitschrift*, 1998, p.309.

Krämer, L., "*Die Rechtsprechung des Gerichtshofs der Europäischen Gemeinschaften zum Umweltrecht 1992 bis 1994*", *Europäische Grundrechte Zeitschrift*, 1995, p.45.

Krämer, L., "Direct effect of E.C. environmental law". In H. Somsen (ed.), *Protecting the European environment: enforcing E.C. environmental law* (London, 1996), p.99.

Krämer, L., "*Droit à l'environnement et installations de déchet*". In M. Prieur and C. Lambrechts (eds), *Mankind and the environment; études en hommage à Alexandre Kiss* (Paris,1998), p.353.

Krämer, L., *E.C. Environmental Law* 6th edn (London, 2006).

Krämer, L., "Environmental judgments by the Court of Justice and their duration", *Journal of European Environmental & Planning Law*, 2008, p.263.

Krämer, L., "Environmental protection and Article 30 EEC Treaty" (1993) C.M.L.R. 111.

Krämer, L., *European Environmental Law Casebook* (London, 1993).

Krämer, L., *Focus on European Environmental Law* (London, 1992).

Krämer, L., *Focus on European Environmental Law* (London, 1997).

Krämer, L., "*Grundlagen (Grundfragen) der E.U.-Umweltverfassung, Ziele, Kompetenzen, Durchführung*". In N. Reich and R. Heine-Mernik (eds), *Umweltverfassung und nachhaltige Entwicklung in der Europäischen Union* (Baden-Baden, 1997), p.11.

Krämer, L., "*Le déversement des déchets en mer et le droit communautaire*", *Revue du Marché Commun*, 1988, p.328.

Krämer, L., "*Mieux légiférer et déréglementation du droit de l'environnement européen*", *Revue du Droit de l'Union Européenne*, 2007, p.801.

Krämer, L., "Participation of environmental organisations in the activities of the EEC". In M. Führ and G. Roller (eds), *Participation and litigation rights of environmental associations in Europe* (Frankfurt/Main, 1991), p.129.

Krämer, L., "Protection of the marine environment in Community law". In L. Krämer, *Focus on European environmental law* (London, 1997), p.259.

Krämer, L., "Public interest litigation in environmental matters before European courts", *Journal of Environmental Law*, 1996, p.1.

Krämer, L., "The environmental complaint in EU law", *Journal of European Environmental & Planning Law*, 2009, p.13.

Krämer, L., "The implementation of environmental laws by the European Economic Communities", *German Yearbook of International Law*, 1991, p.9.

Krämer, L., "The interdependency of Community and Member State activity on nature protection within the European Community", *Ecology Law Quarterly*, 1993, p.25.

Krämer, L., "Thirty years of EC environmental law: perspectives and prospectives", *Yearbook of European Environmental Law*, 2002, Vol.2, p.155.

Krämer, L., "Zehn Jahre Wasserrecht-Rahmenrichtlinie in Europa—Erfahrungen und Perspektiven". In W. Köck and K. Fassbender (eds), *Implementation der Wasserrahmenrichtlinien in Deutschland—Erfahrungen und Perspektiven* (Baden-Baden 2011), p.45.

Krings, M., "*Der Abfallbegriff nach geltendem und künftigem Abfallrecht aus europäischer und nationaler Sicht*", *Wirtschaftsverwaltung*, 1995, p.103.

Kromarek, P., "*La Cour de Justice des Communautés européennes et l'environnement*", *Jurisclasseur-environnement*, Fasc. 1120 (Paris, 1992).

Kummer, K., "The international regulation of transboundary traffic in hazardous wastes: the 1989 Basel Convention", *International and Comparative Law Quarterly*, 1992, p.530.

Ladeur, K., "*Die Europäische Umweltagentur und die Perspektiven eines europäischen Netzwerks der Umweltverwaltungen*", *Natur und Recht*, 1997, p.8.

Larssen, C. (ed.), *Ten years of access to environmental information in international, European and Belgian law: stock-taking and perspectives* (Bruxelles, 2003).

Lavrijsen, L., "*De Europese reglementering betreffende de verbranding van huishoudelijke en gevaarlijke afvalstoffen*". In *Brussels Instituut voor milieubeheer* (ed.), *De laatste ontwikkeling van de Europese reglementering inzake afvalstoffen* (Brussels, 1995), p.89.

Lavrysen, L., "Recent developments in EC policy and law relating to chemicals", *Europarättslig Tidskrift*, 1999, p.285.

Layard, A., "The 1994 Directive on the incineration of hazardous waste, 'substitute fuels' and trans-scientific choices", *European Environmental Law Review*, 1997, p.16.

Leclerc, S., *Politique agricole commune et environnement* (Rennes, 1993).

Lee, M., *EU Environmental Law* (Oxford and Portland, 2005).

Lee, M., "Public participation, procedure and democratic deficit in EC environmental law", *Yearbook of European Environmental Law*, 2003, p.193.

Lefevre, J., "Greenhouse gas emission allowance trading in the EU: a background", *Yearbook of European Environmental Law*, 2003, p.149.

Lefevre, J., "State liability for breaches of Community law", *European Environmental Law Review*, 1996, p.237.

Lemke, M., *Gentechnik-Naturschutz-Ökolandbau*. (Baden-Baden, 2003).

Lenaerts, K., "The principle of subsidiarity and the environment in the European Union: keeping the balance of federalism". In F. Abraham, K. Deketelaere and J. Stuyck (eds), *Recent economic and legal developments in European environmental policy* (Leuven, 1995), p.11.

Levis, L., "The European Community's internal regime on trade in hazardous wastes: lessons from the U.S. regime", *Review of European Community and International Environmental Law*, 1998, p.283.

Lewis, C., "The role of the ECJ in the development and enforcement of environmental law". In B. Wenzel (ed.), *First Nordic conference on EU environmental law* (Copenhagen, 1994), p.161.

Lindemann, H. and Delfs, S., "*Vollzug des europäischen Umweltrechts. Lösungsansätze zurÜberprüfung und Verbesserung*", *Zeitschrift für Umweltrecht*, 1993, p.256.

Loibl, G., "The role of the European Union in the formation of international environmental law", *Yearbook of European Environmental Law*, 2002, Vol.2, p.223.

London, C., "*Instruments économiques et droit communautaire*", *Revue Juridique de l'Environnement*, 1998, p.31.

London, C. and Llamas, M., *E.C. law on protection of the environment and the free movement of goods* (London, Dublin and Edinburgh, 1995).

Lübbe-Wolff, G., "*Der britische Emissionshandel—Vorbild für Deutschland?*", *Energiewirtschaftliche Tagesfragen*, 2001, p.342.

Lübbe-Wolff, G. (ed.), *Der Vollzug des europäischen Umweltrechts* (Berlin, 1996).

Lübbe-Wolff, G., "*Die Bedeutung des EG-Rechts für den Grundwasserschutz*". In J. Behrens and H. Koch (eds), *Umweltschutz in der Europäischen Gemeinschaft* (Baden-Baden, 1991), p.127.

Lübbe-Wolff, G., "*Präventiver Umweltschutz—Auftrag und Grenzen des Vorsorgeprinzips im deutschen und europäischen Recht*". In J. Bizer and H. Koch (eds), *Sicherheit, Vielfalt, Solidarität. Ein neues Paradigma des Verfassungsrechts?* (Baden-Baden, 1998), p.47.

Lübbe-Wolff, G., "*Stand und Instrumente der Implementation des Umweltrechts in Deutschland*". In G. Lübbe-Wolff (ed.), *Vollzug des europäischen Umweltrechts* (Berlin, 1996), p.77.

Macrory, R., *Environmental citizenship and the law: repairing the European road* (London, 1996).

Macrory, R., "European Community water law", *Ecology Law Quarterly*, 1993, p.119.

Macrory, R. (ed.), *Principles of European Environmental Law*(Groningen, 2004).

Macrory, R., *Regulation, enforcement and governance in environmental law* (London, 2008).

Macrory, R. and Turner, S., "Participatory rights, transboundary environmental governance and EC law", *Common Market Law Review*, 2002, p.489.

Mahmoudi, S., "*EG-medlemskap och strängere nationella miljöutgärder*", *Svensk Juristtidning*, 1993, p.419.

Mahmoudi, S., *E.U.:s miljörätt* 2nd edn (Stockholm, 2003).

Malafosse, J., "*Législation sur la chasse et application de la directive de la CEE sur les oiseaux sauvages*", *Environmental Policy and Law*, 1981, p.7.

Marburger, P. and Enders, R., "*Technische Normung im Europäischen Gemeinschaftsrecht*", *Jahrbuch des Umwelt- und Technikrechts*, 1994, p.333.

Maresceau, M. (ed.), *The European Community's commercial policy after 1992: the legal dimension* (Deventer, 1993).

Markus, T., *European fisheries law: from promotion to management* (Groningen, 2009).
Markus, T., "Making environmental principles work under the Common Fisheries Policy",
  European energy and Environmental Law Review, 2010, p.132.
Markus, T. and Schlacke, S., "Die Meeresstrategie-Rahmenrichtlinie der Europäischen
  Gemeinschaft", *Zeitschrift für Umweltrecht,* 2010, p.464.
Marocco, T., "La direttiva IPPC e il suo recepimiento in Italia" *Rivista Giuridica dell'Ambiente,*
  2004, p.35.
Martín Mateo, R., *"La protección de la fauna y la flora",* Revista Vasca de Administración Publica,
  1995, p.647.
Martín Mateo, R., *Nuevos instrumentos para la tutela ambiental,* Madrid, 1994.
Martín Mateo, R., *Protección del medio ambiente en la Europa de los ciudadones* (Valladolid,
  1993).
Martínez Aragón, J., *"El control del a aplicación de la normativa comunitaria en materia de medio
  ambiente por parte de la Comisión y los procedimientos de infracción contra el Estado
  espanol".* In M. Campins i Eritja and I. Pont i Castejón (eds), *Perspectives de dret comunitar
  ambiental* (Bellaterra, 1997), p.497.
Marx, A., "Towards sustainability? The case of tourism and the E.U.", *European Environmental
  Law Review,* 1997, p.181.
Mathews, G., *The Ramsar convention on wetlands. Its history and development* (Gland, 1992).
Mayr, C., *"Vierzehn Jahre EG-Vogelschutzrichtlinie. Bilanz ihrer Umsetzung in der Bundesrepublik
  Deutschland",* Berichte zum Vogelschutz, 1993, p.13.
McIntyre, O., "Proportionality and environmental protection in E.C. law". In J. Holder (ed.), *The
  impact of E.C. environmental law in the United Kingdom* (Chichester, 1997), p.101.
McManus, F., "The EC Green Paper on future Noise Policy and its impact on the UK", *European
  Public Law,* 1999, p.125.
McManus, F. and Burns, T., "The impact of E.C. law on noise law in the United Kingdom". In J.
  Holder (ed.), *The impact of E.C. environmental law in the United Kingdom* (Chichester, 1997),
  p.183.
Michaelowa, A. and Butzengeiger, S. (eds), *EU emissions trading scheme* (London, 2005).
Micklitz, H., "International regulation and control of the production and use of chemicals and
  pesticides", *Michigan Journal of International Law,* 1992, p.653.
Micklitz, H., Roethe, T. and Weatherhill, S. (eds), *Federalism and responsibility—a study on
  product safety and practice in the E.C.* (London, 1994).
Middeke, A., *"Der Kompetenznormenkonflikt umweltrelevanter Gemeinschaftsakte im
  Binnenmarkt",* Deutsches Verwaltungsblatt, 1993, p.769.
Middeke, A., *Nationaler Umweltschutz im Binnenmarkt* (Berlin, 1992).
Möbs, H., *"Gewässerschutz in Deutschland und der Europäischen Gemeinschaft—divergierende
  Zielsetzungen?".* In P. Behrens and H. Koch (eds), *Umweltschutz in der Europäischen
  Gemeinschaft* (Baden-Baden, 1991), p.112.
Moench, C., *"Der Einfluss des europäischen Rechts auf das deutsche Umweltrecht",* Kritische
  Vierteljahreszeitschrift, 1996, p.214.
Möllers, T., *"Qualitätsmanagement, Umweltmanagement und Haftung",* Der Betrieb, 1996, p.1455.
Morena Molina, A., *"La empresa y el derecho de la Unión Europea en el medio ambiente.
  Autorisación. Evaluación de impacto ecologico. Prevention de accidentes. Control integrado de
  la contaminación. Eco-etiqueta".* In L. Parejo Alfonso and L. Krämer (eds), *Derecho
  medioambiental de la Unión Europea* (Madrid, 1996), p.169.
Moreno Molina, A., *"Los 'sanciones' al estado incumplidor del derecho ambiental europeo: Espana
  y sus aguas de bano",* Revista Interdisciplinar de Gestión Ambiental, 2004, p.1.
Moreno Molina, A., *"Productos chimicos, biotechnologia, acuerdos voluntarios".* In L. Parejo
  Alfonso and L. Krämer (eds), *Derecho medioambiental de la Unión Europea* (Madrid, 1996),
  p.273.
Morena Molina, A., *"Puest en foniconamento del derecho comunitario del medio ambiente. Acceso
  a la información. Acceso a la justicia".* In L. Parejo Alfonso and L. Krämer (eds), *Derecho
  medioambiental de la Unión Europea* (Madrid, 1996), p.141.
Moreno Molina, M., *Derecho comunitario del medio ambiente*(Madrid, 2006).
Morgan de Rivery, E., *"Réglementation communautaire des déchets",* (Paris) Juris-Classeurs (1995),
  Fasc. 805.
Morrow; K., "Public participation in the assessment of the effects of certain plans and programmes
  on the environment – Directive 2001/42, the UN/ECE Espoo Convention and the Kiev
  Protocol", *Yearbook of European Environmental Law,* 2005, p.49.
Mortelmans, K., *EG-milieuwetgeving* 2nd edn (Deventer, 1993).

Müller, B., *Die Öffentlichkeitsbeteiligung im Recht der Europäischen Union und ihre Einwirkungen auf das deutsche Verwaltungsrecht am Beispiel des Immissionsschutzrechts* (Baden-Baden 2010).

Müller-Graff, P. (ed.), *Technische Regeln im Binnenmarkt* (Baden-Baden, 1991).

Narbona Ruiz, C., *"Aplicación de la normativa comunitaria en materia de medio ambiente por parte del Estado espanol"*. In M. Campins i Eritja and I. Pont i Castejón (eds), *Perspectives de dret comunitari ambiental* (Bellaterra, 1997), p.463.

Nespor, S., *Il governo dell'ambiente* (Milano, 2009).

Nettesheim, M., *"Die völkerrechtlichen Vertragsschlusskompetenzen der Europäischen Gemeinschaft und ihrer Mitgliedstaaten im Bereich des Umweltschutzes"*, *Europarecht*, 1993, p.340.

Newell, P. and Grant, W., "Environmental NGOs and EU environmental law", *The Yearbook of European Environmental Law*, 2001, p.225.

Nicolas, F. (with J. Repussard), *Common standards for enterprises* (Luxembourg, 1995).

Nicklas, C., *Implementations probleme des EG-Umweltrechts* (Baden-Baden, 1997).

Nijman, M., *Le développement du principe de subsidiarité, avec une étude de cas sur la politique de l'environnement dans la Communauté européenne et le principe de subsidiarité* (Amsterdam, 1991).

Noble, D., "Enforcing E.C. environmental law: the national dimension". In H. Somsen (ed.), *Protecting the European environment: enforcing E.C. environmental law* (London, 1996), p.37.

Nollkaemper, A., "Habitat protection in European Community law: evolving conceptions of a balance of interests", *Journal of Environmental Law*, 1997, p.271.

Nollkaemper, A. "Improving compliance with the international law of marine environmental protection: the role of the European Union". In J. Golub (ed.), *Global competition and E.U. environmental policy* (London and New York, 1998), p.85.

Offermann-Clas, C., *"Das Luftreinhalterecht der Europäischen Gemeinschaft—Fortschritte seit dem Jahre 1983"*, *Neue Juristische Wochenschrift*, 1986, p.1388.

Oluoch-Wauna, L., "EMAS and ISO 14001: a comparaison", *Environmental Policy and Law*, 2001, p.237.

O'Neill, M., "Agriculture, the E.C. and the WTO: a legal critical analysis of the concepts of sustainability and multifunctionality", *Environmental Law Review*,2002, p.144.

Ong, D., "The Convention on international trade in endangered species (CITES, 1973): implication of recent developments in international and E.C. environmental law", *Journal of Environmental Law*, 1998, p.291.

Onida, M., "Challenges and opportunities on EC waste management: perspectives on the problem of end-of-life vehicles", *The Yearbook of European Environmental Law*, 2000, p.253.

Onida, M. (ed.), *Europe and the environment* (Groningen, 2004).

Onida, M., "Plaidoyer pour une politique communautaire des montagnes: l'exemple à prendre de la Convention alpine" *Revue du Droit de l'Union européenne*, 2008, p.739.

Organisation for Economic Co-operation and Development, "Trade measures in multilateral environmental agreements: synthesis report of three case studies", COM/ENV/TO (98) 127 (Paris, 1998).

OSPAR Commission, *Quality Status Report 2010* (London, 2010).

Pagh, P., *"E.U.'s beskyttelse af vilde fugle og fisk: indgribende betydning for arealanvendelsen"*, *Ugeskrift for Retsvaesen*, 1997, p.511.

Pagh, P., *E.U. miljoeret* 2nd edn (Copenhagen, 1996).

Pagh, P., *"Farlige stoffer og EF-retten"*, *Ugeskrift for Retsvaesen*, 1991, p.B353.

Pagh, P., *"Luftforurenigsbekaempelsen i retlig belysning"*, *Ugeskrift for Retsvaesen*, 1992, p.B361.

Pagh, P., *"Miljoegarantien efter PCP.dommen"*, *Ugeskrift for Retsvaesen*, 1994, p.B276.

Pagh, P., "The 'direct effect doctrine' in E.C. environmental law", *Nordic Journal of International Law*, 1995, p.23.

Pagh, P., *"Unionstraktaten og milioeet"*, *Juristen*, 1992, p.225.

Pallemaerts, M. and others, *Drowning in process? The implementation of the EU's 6th environmental action programme* (London 2006).

Pallemaerts, M. (ed.), *EU and WTO law: how tight is the legal straitjacket for environmental product regulation?* (Brussels, 2006).

Pallemaerts, M. (ed.), *The Aarhus Convention at ten: interactions and tensions between conventional international law and EU environmental law* (Groningen 2011).

Pallemaerts, M., *Toxics and Transnational Law* (Oxford, 2003).

Pallemaerts, M., *"Van de stranden van Blackpool tot de moerassen van Santona: plaatsgebonden verplichtingen in het milieurecht"*, *Tijdschrift voor Milieurecht*, 1994, p.19.

Palme, C., *Nationale Umweltpolitik in der EG. Zur Rolle des Art. 100a IV im Rahmen einer europäischen Umweltgemeinschaft* (Berlin, 1992).

Parejo Alfonso, L. and Krämer, L. (eds), *Derecho medioambiental de la Unión Europea* (Madrid, 1996).

Pâques, M. and Renaudière, P., *"Agriculture et environnement dans le droit communautaire, quelques questions"*, *Aménagement*, 1992, special issue on "agriculture", p.44.

Peeters, M., "Towards a European system of tradable pollution permits", *Tilburg Foreign Law Review*, 1993, p.117.

Peine F.-J., *"Neue Literatur über die Probleme der Umsetzung des europäischen Naturschutzrechts in nationales Recht"*, *Natur und Recht*, 2003, p.11.

Pernice, I., "Environment and trade in the field of waste: a legal assessment", *Jahrbuch des Umwelt- und Technikrechts*, 1995, p.135.

Pernice, I., *"Kriterien der normativen Umsetzung von Umweltrichtlinien der EG im Lichte der Rechtsprechung des EUGH"*, *Europarecht*, 1994, p.325.

Pernice, I., *"Umweltschutz und Energiepolitik"*, *Recht der Energiewirtschaft*, 1993, p.45.

Pernice, I. and Rodenhoff, V., *"Die Gemeinschaftskompetenz für eine Richtlinie über den Zugang zu Gerichten in Umweltangelegenheiten"*, *Zeitschrift für Umweltrecht*, 2004, p.149.

Picheral, C., *"L'ambivalence de la notion de déchet dans la jurisprudence de la CJCE"*, *Revue juridique de l'environnement*, 1995, p.559.

Pieper, S., *"Gemeinschaftsrechtliche Anforderungen an Umweltsonderabgaben unter Berücksichtigung ihres Aufkommens"*, *Die Öffentliche Verwaltung*, 1996, p.232.

Pillitu, P., *Profili costituzionali della tutela ambientale nell'ordinamento comunitario europeo* (Perugia, 1992).

Pluge, W., *"Die Politik der Europäisierung auf dem Gebiet der Gas- und Wasserwirtschaft"*, *Universität des Saarlandes, Vorträge, Reden und Berichte aus dem Europa-Institut*, no.278 (Saarbrücken, 1993).

Pocklington, D., "An assessment of the proposed European legislation for end-of- life vehicles", *European Environmental Law Review*, 1998, p.138.

Poostchi, B., "The 1997 Treaty of Amsterdam—implications for European Union environmental law and policy making", *Review of European Community and International Environmental Law*, 1998, p.76.

Prat, J., "The role and activities of the European Communities in the protection and the preservation of the marine environment of the North Sea" in D. Freestone and T. IJlstra (eds), *The North Sea: perspectives on regional environmental co-operation*, London, 1990, p.101.

Prechal, S. and Hancher, L., "Individual environmental rights: conceptual pollution in EU environmental law?", *Yearbook of European Environmental law*, 2002, Vol.2, p.89.

Pridham, G. and Cini, M., "Enforcing environmental standards in the European Union: is there a Southern problem?" in M. Faure, J. Vervaele and A. Weale (eds), *Environmental standards in the European Union in an interdisciplinary framework* (Anvers and Appeldoorn, 1994), p.251.

Purdue, M., "The impact of E.C. environmental law on planning law in the United Kingdom". In J. Holder (ed.), *The impact of E.C. environmental law in the United Kingdom* (Chichester, etc., 1997), p.231.

Quick, R., *"Der Gemeinschaftsrahmen für staatliche Umweltschutzbeihilfen"*, *Europäische Zeitschrift für Wirtschaftsrecht*, 1994, p.620.

Raum-Degrève, R. and de Hemptinne, F. (eds), *Le droit communautaire de l'environnement; problèmes de mise en oeuvre nationale* (Luxembourg, 1995).

Redman, M., "European Community planning law", *Journal of Planning and Environmental Law*, 1993, p.999.

Rehbinder, E., *"Das Konzept des anlagen- und produktbezogenen EG-Gentechnikrechts"*, *Zeitschrift für Umweltrecht*, 1999, p.6.

Rehbinder, E., "Environmental regulation through fiscal and economic incentives in a federalist system". In H. Somsen (ed.), *Protecting the European environment: enforcing E.C. Environmental Law* (London, 1996), p.151.

Rehbinder, E., "Take-back and recovery obligations in the light of the E.C. Treaty" in M. Prieur and C. Lambrechts (eds), *Mankind and the environment; Études en hommage à Alexandre Kiss* (Paris, 1998), p.367.

Rehbinder, E. and Stewart, R., *Environment protection policy* (Berlin and New York, 1985).

Reich, N., *Bürgerrechte in der Europäischen Union* (Baden-Baden, 1999).

Reich, N., *"Der Schutz subjektiver Gemeinschaftsrechte durch Staatshaftung"*, *Europäische Zeitschrift für Wirtschaftsrecht*, 1996, p.709.

Reich, N. and Heine-Mernik, R. (eds), *Umweltverfassung und nachhaltige Entwicklung* (Baden-Baden, 1997).

Reid, C., "Nature conservation law". In J. Holder (ed.), *The impact of E.C. environmental law in the United Kingdom* (Chichester, etc., 1997), p.199.

Renaudière, P., "De nouveaux instruments: la taxe CO2-énergie et l'écofiscalité". In P. Renaudière and P. van Pelt (eds), Développements récents du droit communautaire de l'environnement (Diegem, 1995), p.29.

Renaudière, P., "Le cinquième programme d'action communautaire à mi-parcours", Aménagement-Environnement, 1996, p.65.

Renaudière, P., "Le droit communautaire de l'environnement apràs Maastricht", Aménagement-environnement, 1992, p.70.

Renaudière, P. and Van Pelt, P. (eds), Développements récents du droit communautaire de l'environnement (Diegem, 1995).

Rengeling, H. (ed.), Handbuch zum europäischen und deutschen Umweltrecht, Vol.1, Vol.2, 2nd edn (Cologne, etc., 2002).

Rengeling, H.-W. (ed.), "Klimaschutz durch Emissionshandel", (Köln, Berlin, Bonn, München, 2001).

Rengeling, H. (ed.), Umweltnormung (Berlin, 1998).

Rengeling, H. (ed.), Umweltschutz und andere Politiken der Europäischen Gemeinschaft (Cologne, Berlin, Bonn and Munich, 1993).

Rengeling, H. and Gellermann, M., "Gestaltung des europäischen Umweltrechts und seine Implementation im deutschen Rechtsraum", Jahrbuch des Umwelt- und Technikrechts, 1996, p.1.

Renson, A. and Verdure, C., "Déchets et sous-produits à l'aune de la directive 2008/98", Revue du Droit de l'Union Européenne 209, p.733.

Rhode, B. (ed.), Air pollution in Europe, Vol.1, Western Europe (Vienna, 1988).

Riechenberg, K., "La directiva sobre la protección de las aves salvajes: un hito en la política comunitaria del medio ambiente", Revista de Instituciones Europeas, 1990, p.369.

Robinson, J., "Environmental impact assessment and Community law", in M. Campins and I. Pont (eds), Perspectives de dret comunitari ambiental (Bellaterra, 1997), p.371.

Rodenhoff, V., "The Aarhus Convention and its implications for the 'institutions' of the European Community", Review of European Community and International Environmental Law, 2002, p.343.

Roethe, T., "Management von Gefahrstoffrisiken in Regelungsausschüssen der Europäischen Gemeinschaft". In G. Winter (ed.), Risikoanalyse und Risikoabwehr im Chemikalienrecht (Düsseldorf, 1995), p.115.

Romi, R., Droit europien et international de l'environnement (Paris, 2005).

Rossnagel, A., "Europäische Techniknormen im Lichte des Gemeinschaftsrechts", Deutsches Verwaltungsblatt, 1996, p.1181.

Rossnagel, A., "Lernfähiges Europarecht—am Beispiel des europäischen Umweltrechts", Neue Zeitschrift für Verwaltungsrecht, 1997, 122.

Ruffert, M., Sujektive Rechte im Umweltrecht der Europäischen Gemeinschaft (Heidelberg, 1996).

Ryland, D., "The European Environmental Agency", European Environmental Law Review, 1994, p.138.

Sakse, D., "Environmental legislation in Member States. Notification and 'standstill' obligations in Community law", in B. Wenzel (ed.) First Nordic Conference on E.U. Environmental Law (Copenhagen, 1994), p.53.

Sander, A. and Küppers, P. (eds), Environmentally sound waste management (Frankfurt/M., 1993).

Sands, P., "Danish bottles and Mexican tuna", Review of European Community and International Environmental Law, 1992, p.18.

Sands, P., "The European Court of Justice: an environmental tribunal?" In H. Somsen (ed.), Protecting the European environment: enforcing E.C. environmental law (London, 1996), p.23.

Sands, P. and Blatch, C., "Estuaries in European Community law: defining criteria", International Journal of Marine and Coastal Law, 1998, p.1.

Schäfer, E., Individualrechtsschutz im Umweltrecht (Vienna, 1998).

Schenek, M., Das Gentechnikrecht der Europäischen Gemeinschaft (Berlin, 1995).

Scherer, J., "Grenzen und Schwächen der legislatorischen Rechtsvereinheitlichung im europäischen Umweltrecht", Kritische Vierteljahresschrift für Gesetzgebung und Rechtswissenschaft, 1995, p.197.

Scherer, J., "Umweltrecht: Handelshemmnis im EG-Binnenmarkt", Umweltrecht in der Praxis, 1992, p.H.1, 76.

Scheuer, S. (ed.), EU environmental policy. A critical analysis of EU environmental legislation (Bruxelles, 2005)

Scheuing, D., "Instrumente zur Durchführung des Europäischen Umweltrechts", Neue Zeitschrift für Verwaltungsrecht, 1999, p.475.

Schink, A., "Die Deponie-Richtlinie der EU und die Abfallentsorgung in der Bundesrepublik Deutschland", Abfallrechtliche Praxis, 1999, p.3.

Schliessner, U., *"Entwurf einer EG-Richtlinie über Verpackungen und Verpackungsabfall"*, *Europäische Zeitschrift für Wirtschaftsrecht*, 1993, p.52.

Schmidt, A., "Transboundary movements of waste under E.C. law. The emerging regulatory framework", *Journal of Environmental Law*, 1992, p.61.

Schmitz, S., *"Habitatschutz für Vögel? Zur unmittelbaren Wirkung der FFH- Richtlinie der EU"*, *Zeitschrift für Umweltrecht*, 1996, p.12.

Schmidt-Räntsch, A., *"Besitz und Vermarktung von geschützten Tieren und Pflanzen nach der Vollendung des EG-Binnenmarktes"*, *Natur und Recht*, 1992, p.49.

Schram, F., "Public access to EU environmental documents – Regulation (EC) 1049/2001", *Yearbook of European Environmental Law*, 2005, p.23.

Schreurs, M., "The climate change divide: the European Union, the United States and the future of the Kyoto Protocol". In N. Vig and M. Faure (eds), *Green giants?* (Cambridge-London, 2004), p.207.

Schröder, M., *"Die Berücksichtigung des Umweltschutzes in der gemeinsamen Agrarpolitik der Europäischen Union"*, *Natur und Recht*, 1995, p.117.

Schröder, M., *"Aktuelle Konflikte zwischen europäischem und deutschem Abfallrecht"*, *Die öffentliche Verwaltung*, 1991, p.910.

Schröder, M., *"Die steuernde und marktbegrenzende Wirkung umweltschutzrelevanter Prinzipien des EG-Vertrages am Beispiel des Abfallexportes"*, *Neue Zeitschrift für Verwaltungsrecht*, 1996, p.833.

Schröder, M., *"Instrumente zur Bekämpfung der neuartigen Waldschäden nach deutschem und europäischem Recht"*, (UPR, 1989), p.49.

Schröder, M., *"Zusammenwirken von Gemeinschaftsrecht und nationalem Recht auf dem Gebiet der Umweltabgaben"* in P. Kirchhoff (ed.), *Umweltschutz im Abgaben- und Steuerrecht* (Cologne, 1993), p.87.

Schröer, T., *Die Kompetenzverteilung zwischen der europäischen Wirtschaftsgemeinschaft und ihren Mitgliedstaaten auf dem Gebiet des Umweltschutzes* (Berlin, 1992).

Schweitzer, M., *"Alpentransit und Europäische Verkehrspolitik"*, *Zentrum für Europäisches Wirtschaftsrecht*, Bonn no.47 (1995).

Schweizer, R. and Calame, T., *"Das Gentechnikrecht der EG"*, *Recht der Internationalen Wirtschaft*, 1997, p.34.

Scott, J., "Environmental compatibility and the Community's structural funds: a legal analysis", *Journal of Environmental Law*, 1996, p.99.

Scott, J., "Flexibility in the implementation of EC environmental law", *The Yearbook of European Environmental Law*, 2000, p37.

Seidl-Hohenveldern, I., "LKW-Transit durch Österreich und die EG" (Saarbrücken, 1996).

Serrano Lozano, R., *El regimén jurídico de los residuos de envases* (Madrid 2007).

Sevenster, H., *Milieubeleid en Gemeenschapsrecht* (Deventer, 1992).

Sevenster, H., "The environmental guarantee after Amsterdam: does the emperor have new clothes?" *The Yearbook of European Environmental Law*, 2000, p.291

Simon, D. and Rigaux, A., *"Les contraintes de la transcription en droit français des directives communautaires: le secteur de l'environnement"*, *Revue juridique de l'environnement*, 1991, p.269.

Sioutis, G., *"Die Implementation der Umweltgesetzgebung der EG in Griechenland"*. In G. Lübbe-Wolff (ed.), *Vollzug des europäischen Umweltrechts* (Berlin, 1996).

Sobczak, C., *Normung und Umweltschutz im Europäischen Gemeinschaftsrecht* (Berlin-Bielefeld-München, 2002).

Sobotta, C., "Artenschutz in der Rechtsprechung des Europäischen Gerichtshofs" *Natur und Recht*, 2007, p.642.

Sommer, J., *"Les déchets, de l'autosuffisance et de la libre circulation des marchandises"*, *Revue du Marché Commun et de l'Union Européenne*, 1994, p.246.

Somsen, H., "E.C. water directives", *Water Law*, 1990, p.93.

Somsen, H., "Francovich and its application to E.C. environmental law". In H. Somsen (ed.), *Protecting the European environment: enforcing E.C. environmental law* (London, 1996), p.135.

Somsen, H., "Member States' obligations under Directive 79/409", *Water Law*, 1993, p.209.

Somsen, H. (ed.), *Protecting the European environment: enforcing E.C. environmental law* (London, 1996).

Somsen, H., "The private enforcement of Member States' compliance with EC environmental law: an unfulfilled promise?", *The Yearbook of European Environmental Law*, 2000, p.311.

Stede, B., *"Grenzüberschreitendes Umweltrecht: warum die natürlichen Lebensgrundlagen weiter zerstört werden, obwohl jeder Umweltschutz für nötig hält"*, *Kritische Justiz*, 1999, p.456.

Steinberg, R., *"Probleme der Europäisierung des deutschen Umweltrechts"*, *Archiv des öffentlichen Rechts*, 1995, p.549.

Steinberg, R., "*Zulassung von Industrieanlagen im deutschen und europäischen Recht*", *Neue Zeitschrift für Verwaltungsrecht*, 1995, p.209.
Steinberg, R. and Britz, G., "*Die Energiepolitik im Spannungsfeld nationaler und europäischer Regelungskompetenz*", *Die öffentliche Verwaltung*, 1993, p.313.
Stockholm Environmental Institute (ed.), *Study of costs for measures in the environmental area* (Stockholm, 1999).
Stuyck, J., "*Le traitement des déchets dans la (non-) réalisation du marché intérieur*", *Journal des tribunaux—droit européen*, 1994, p.10.
Suman, D., "Regulation of ocean dumping by the European Economic Community", *Ecology Law Quarterly*, 1991, p.559.
Temmink, H., "From Danish bottles to Danish bees: the dynamics of free movement of goods and environmental protection—a case analysis", *The Yearbook of European Environmental Law*, 2000, p.61
Thieffry, P., *Droit de l'environnement de l'Union Europiennce* (Bruxelles, 2008).
Thiel, J., *Umweltrechtliche Kompetenzen in der Europäischen Union* (Bochum, 1995).
Thomson, G., "*La Communauté européenne et le paysage*", *Revue juridique de l'environnement*, 1993, p.541.
Uebersohn, G., *Effektive Umweltpolitik—Folgerungen aus der Implementations- und Evaluationsforschung* (Frankfurt/M., 1990).
Uitenboogaart,Y., Van Kempen, J. and Van Rijswick, H. (eds), *Dealing with complexity and policy discretion. A comparison of the implementation process of the European water framework directive in five Member States* (Den Haag 2009).
Untermaier, J., "*Des petits oiseaux aux grands principes*", *Revue juridique de l'environnement*, 1988, p.466.
Untermaier, J., "*La politique et le droit communautaires de protection de la nature et de la vie sauvage*". In M. Campins i Eritja and I. Pont i Castejón (eds), *Perspectives de dret comunitari ambiental* (Bellaterra, 1997), p.303.
Vacca, M., *La politica communitaria dell'ambiente e la sua attuazione negli stati membri* (Milan, 1992).
Van Calster, G., "E.C. noise legislation and policy", *European Environmental Law Review*, 1997, p.174.
Van Calster, G., "The legal framework for the regulation of waste in the European Community", *The Yearbook of European Environmental Law*, 2000, p.161.
Vanden Bilcke, C., *The Stockholm Convention on Persistent Organic Pollutant* (RECIEL, 2002), p.328.
Vandermeersch, D., "*Het vrije verkeer van afvalstoffen binnen de Europese Gemeenschap*", *Tijdschrift voor Milieurecht*, 1992, p.78.
Vandermeersch, D., "*Twintig jaar EG-milieurecht in retrospectief: van casuistiek naar modern beleid?*", *Sociaal Economisch Wetgeving*, 1992, p.532.
Van der Mensbrugghe, Y., "*Les frontières maritimes de la CE (observations à propos de la directive 84/631 sur les transferts transfrontaliers de déchets dangereux*", *Revue du Marché Commun*, 1989, p.360.
Van der Zwiep, K. and Backes, C., *Integrated system for conservation of marine environments* (Baden-Baden, 1994).
Von Köller, H., Klett, W. and Konzak, O., *EG-Abfallverbringungsverordnung* (Berlin, 1994).
Van Hoorick, G., *Beschrijving van de EG-Richtlijnen inzake de bescherming van het leefmilieu en de stand van implementatie in het Vlaamse Gewest* (Ghent, 1993).
Vara Arribas, G., *La révision de la directive aux emballages et aux déchets d'emballages: une mesure prématurée?*, EIPASCOPE (Maastricht, 2000), no.1 p.12.
Veldkamp, A., *Overbrengen van afvallstoffen; (trans) nationale uitvoering en handhaving* (Utrecht, 1998).
Vennekens-Capkova, J., "Dangerous substances: chameleons in water policy". In D. Freestone and T. IJlstra (eds), *The North Sea: perspectives on regional environmental co-operation* (London, 1990), p.150.
Verschuuren, J., "EC environmental law and self-regulation in the member States: in search of a legislative framework", *The Yearbook of European Environmental Law*, 2000, p.103.
Verschuuren, J., "Effectiveness of nature protection legislation in the EU and the US: the birds and habitats directives and the endangered species act", *Yearbook of European Environmental Law*, 2003, p.305.
Verschuuren, J., "Participation regarding the elaboration and approval of projects in the EU after the Aarhus Convention", *Yearbook of European Environmental Law*, 2005, p.29.
Vieweg, K., "*Technische Normen im EG-Binnenmarkt*". In C. Müller-Graff (ed.), *Technische Regeln im Binnenmarkt* (Baden-Baden, 1991), p.57.

Vig, N. and Faure, M. (eds), *Green giants? Environmental policies of the United States and the European Union*(Cambridge (Ms.), London, 2004).

Vitzthum, W. and Imperiali, C. (eds), *La protection régionale de l'environnement marin* (Paris, 1992).

Vitzthum, W. and Schenk, M., *"Die Europäisierung des Gentechnikrechts"*. In R. Hrbek, T. Oppermann and J. Starbatty (eds), *Integration Europas und Ordnung der Weltwirtschaft* (Baden-Baden, 1993), p.47.

Vogel, D., "Trade and environment in the global perspective: contrasting European and American perspectives". In N.Vig and M. Faure (eds), *Green Giants?* (Cambridge (Ms.), London, 2004), p.231.

Vogelgezang-Stoute, E.: *Bestrijdingsmiddelenrecht* (Deventer 2004);

Vohrer, M. (ed.), *Ökologische Marktwirtschaft in Europa* (Baden-Baden, 1992).

Von Wilmowsky, P., *"Abfall und freier Warenverkehr: Bestandsaufnahme nach dem EUGH-Urteil zum wallonischen Einfuhrverbot"*, *Europarecht*, 1992, p.414 (English version: *Common Market Law Review*, 1993, p.541).

Von Wilmowsky, P., *"Das Nähe- und Optimierungsprinzip des europäischen Abfallrechts"*, *Neue Zeitschrift für Verwaltungsrecht*, 1999, p.467.

Von Wilmowsky, P., *"Grenzüberschreitende Abfallentsorgung: Ressourcenkonflikte im gemeinsamen Markt"*, *Neue Zeitschrift für Verwaltungsrecht*, 1991, p.1.

Vorwerk, A., *Die umweltpolitischen Kompetenzen der Europäischen Gemeinschaft und ihrer Mitgliedstaaten nach Inkrafttreten der Einheitlichen EuropäÑischen Akte* (Munich, 1990).

Voss, U., *"Die Rechtsprechung des Europäischen Gerichtshofes zum Umweltschutz"* in C. Demmke (ed.), *Europäische Umweltpolitik und nationale Verwaltungen* (Maastricht, 1998), p.163.

Wägenbaur, R., "The European Community's policy on implementation of environmental directives", *Fordham International Law Journal*, 1990–1991, p.455.

Wägenbaur, R., *"Zwölf Thesen zum Thema 'Umweltvereinbarungen'"*, *Europäische Zeitschrift für Wirtschaftsrecht*, 1997, p.645.

Ward, A., "Judicial review of environmental misconduct in the European Community: problems, prospects and strategies", *The Yearbook of European Environmental Law*, 2000, p.137.

Ward, A., "The right to an effective remedy in E.C. law and environmental protection", *Journal of Environmental law*, 1994, p.331.

Ward, H., "Trade and Environmental Issues in Voluntary Eco-labelling and Life-cycle-analysis", *Review of European Community and International Environmental Law*, 1997, p.131.

Warren, L., "The impact of E.C. environmental law on law and practice relating to marine and coastal waters". In J. Holden (ed.), *The impact of E.C. environmental law in the United Kingdom* (Chichester, 1997), p.167.

Wasmeier, M., *"Die Integration des Umweltschutzes als allgemeine Auslegungsregel des Gemeinschaftsrechts"*, *Europäisches Wirtschafts- und Steuerrecht*, 2000, p.47.

Wasmeier, M., *Umweltabgaben und Europarecht* (Munich, 1995).

Wegener, B., *"Rechte des Einzelnen"*, *Die Interessentenklage im europäischen Umweltrecht* (Baden-Baden, 1998).

Wegener, B., *"Vollzugskontrolle durch Klagerechte vor mitgliedstaatlichen Gerichten"*. In G. Lübbe-Wolff (ed.), *Vollzug des europäischen Umweltrechts* (Berlin, 1996), p.145.

Wendenburg, H., *"Die Umsetzung des europäischen Abfallrechts"*, *Neue Zeitschrift für Verwaltungsrecht*, 1995, p.833.

Wenneraas, P., "Fog and acid rain drifting from Luxemburg over Art.95(4): case C-3/00 Denmark v. Commission", *European Environmental Law Review*, 2003, p.169

Wenneraas, P., *The enforcement of EC environmental law* (Oxford, 2007).

Wenzel, B. (ed.), *First Nordic Conference on E.U. environmental law* (Copenhagen, 1994).

Werner, J., *"Das EU-Netzwerk für Umsetzung und Vollzug von Umweltrecht"*. In G. Lübbe-Wolff (ed.), *Vollzug des europäischen Umweltrechts* (Berlin, 1996), p.131.

Wiegand, B., *"Bestmöglicher Umweltschutz als Aufgabe der Europäischen Gemeinschaften"*, *Deutsches Verwaltungsblatt*, 1993, p.533.

Wiers, J., *Trade and environment in the EC and the WTO* (Groningen, 2002).

Wiggers-Rust, L., "Is waste law still only a national affair?", *European Business Law Review*, 1991, p.282.

Wilkins, A., *Animal welfare in Europe* (London, 1997).

Williams, R., "Enforcing European environmental law: can the European Commission be held to account?", *Yearbook of European Environmental Law*, 2002, p.271.

Williams, R., "The European Commission and the enforcement of environmental law: an invidious position", *Yearbook of European Law*, 1995, p.351.

Wils, W., *"La protection des habitats naturels en droit communautaire"*, *Cahiers de droit européen*, 1994, p.398.

Wils, W., "The Birds Directive 15 years later: a survey of the case law and a comparison with the Habitats Directive", *Journal of Environmental Law*, 1994, p.220.

Winter, G., "*Constitutionalizing Environmental Protection in the European Union*", Yearbook of European Environmental Law, 2002, Vol.2, p.67.

Winter, G., "*Das Umweltrecht der Europäischen Union unter dem Druck der globalen Konkurrenz*". In N. Reich and R. Heine-Mernik (eds), *Umweltverfassung und nachhaltige Entwicklung in der Europäischen Union* (Baden-Baden, 1997), p.33.

Winter, G., "*Der Säbelschnäbler als Teil fürs Ganze*", *Natur und Recht*, 1992, p.21.

Winter, G., "Die Dogmatik der Direktwirkung von EG-Richtlinien und ihre Bedeutung für das EG-Naturschutzrecht" *Zeitschrift für Umweltrecht*, 2002, p.313.

Winter, G. (ed.), *European environmental law* (Brookfield USA, Singapore and Sydney, 1995).

Winter, G., "*Kompetenzen der Europäischen Gemeinschaft im Verwaltungsvollzug*" in G. Lübbe-Wolff (ed.), *Vollzug dees europäischen Umweltrechts* (Berlin, 1996), p.107.

Winter, G., "*Massstäbe der Chemikalienkontrolle im deutschen Recht und im Gemeinschaftsrecht*". In G. Winter (ed.), *Risikoanalyse und Risikoabwehr im Chemikalienrecht* (Düsseldorf, 1995), p.1.

Winter, G., "*Notifizierung und Andienung bei grenzüberschreitender Verbringung von gefährlichen Abfällen zur Verwertung*", *Natur und Recht*, 1998, p.233.

Winter, G., "On the effectiveness of E.C. administration: the case of environmental protection", *Common Market Law Review*, 1996, p.689.

Winter, G., "*Rechtsschutz gegen Behoerden, die Umweltrichtlinien der EG nicht beachten*", *Natur und Recht*, 1991, p.453.

Winter, G., "*Regelungsmasstäbe im Gefahrstoffrecht*", *Deutsches Verwaltungsblatt*, 1994, p.913.

Winter, G. (ed.), *Risk Assessment and Risk Management of Toxic Chemicals in the European Community* (Baden-Baden, 2000).

Winter, G., "Risks, costs and alternatives in EC environmental legislation: the case or REACH". RECIEL, 2006, p.56.

Winter, G., "The GATT and environmental protection: problems of construction", *Journal of Environmental Law*, 2003, p.113.

Woolley, J., "The enforcement of E.C. environmental law and the role of local government". In H. Somsen (ed.), *Protecting the European environment: enforcing E.C. environmental law* (London, 1996), p.167.

Zetter, J., "Environment impact assessment: has it had an impact?". In J. Holder (ed.), *The impact of E.C. environmental law in the United Kingdom* (Chichester, 1997), p.257.

Ziegler, A., *Trade and environmental law in the European Community* (Oxford, 1996).

Zierock, K. and Salomon, N., "*Die Umsetzung des Artikels 16 Abs.2 der Eg-IVU- Richtlinie auf internationaler und nationaler Ebene*", *Zeitschrift für Umweltrecht*, 1998, p.27.

Zils, H., *Die Wertigkeit des Umweltschutzes in Beziehung zu anderen Aufgaben der Europäischen Gemeinschaft* (Heidelberg, 1994).

Zittl, J., *Integrierter Umweltschutz in der neuesten Rechtsentwicklung* (Baden-Baden, 1998).

Zuleeg, M., "*Umweltschutz in der Rechtsprechung des Europäischen Gerichtshofs*", *Neue Juristische Wochenschrift*, 1993, p.31.

CHAPTER 1

Objectives, Principles and Conditions

1. The environment in European Union law

The Lisbon Treaty on European Union (TEU) which entered into effect on   **1–01**
December 1, 2009,[1] fixes in art.3(3) TEU as one of the objectives of the
European Union "a high level of protection and improvement of the quality of the
environment". In the same paragraph, sustainable development is fixed as one of
the aims of the Union, and both the protection of the environment and the
sustainable development are also mentioned in Recital 9 of the Treaty on
European Union. The objectives of art.3(3) TEU are completed by the specific
environmental objectives in art.191 of the Treaty on the functioning of the Union
(TFEU) which are a high level of protection, a prudent use of natural resources, a
contribution to human health and the promotion of environmental protection at
international level.

Neither of these provisions, though, define "environment"; nor do the other
provisions of the Treaties contain any definition. It follows from arts 191(1) and
192(2) TFEU that the environment includes human beings, natural resources,
land use, town and country planning, waste and water. These categories include
practically all areas of the environment, in particular fauna and flora, which are
part of the natural resources, and climate. The inclusion of issues concerning
town and country planning underlines that the environment is not limited to
natural elements, but also includes the man-made environment.

Article 177(2) TFEU provides for the setting up of a Cohesion Fund which
shall provide a financial contribution to transport infrastructure projects of the
trans-European networks and to the environment. Regulation 1084/2006 on the
Cohesion Fund provides[2] that energy and transport projects which "clearly
present environmental benefits" shall be considered to be environmental projects;
this concerns projects on energy efficiency and on renewable energies,
furthermore transport projects on rail, river and sea transport, intermodal
transport systems and their interoperability, the management of road, sea and air
traffic, clean urban transport and public transport. Such an interpretation of the
notion "environment" is too large: indeed, the management of traffic and, for
example, the organisation on the transport of containers or of petrol by sea has
not much to do with the environment.

When the section "environment" was first included in the EC Treaty in 1987,   **1–02**
there was already extensive secondary European legislation adopted on the basis
of three environmental action programmes and this was generally perceived as

---

[1] [2008] OJ C115/1.
[2] [2006] OJ L210/79.

legislation on the environment. This secondary legislation covered water and air, noise and chemicals, nature conservation, waste and some measures of a general character. Furthermore, in June 1990, shortly before the commencement of the negotiations on the Maastricht Treaty on European Union, the Community Heads of State and Government adopted a "Declaration on the Environment",[3] where they proclaimed a right to a healthy and clean environment, which included, in particular:

> "... the quality of air, rivers, lakes, coastal and marine waters, the quality of food and drinking water, protection against noise, protection against contamination of soil, soil erosion and desertification, preservation of habitats, flora and fauna, landscape and other elements of the natural heritage, the amenity and quality of residential areas."

It must be assumed that by using the concept "environment" in this legal, political, economic and ecological context, the authors of the Treaties have given to the term the emphasis which it had at that time in EU law. The term "environment" is thus all-embracing and includes economic, social and aesthetic aspects, the preservation of natural and archaeological heritage, and the man-made as well as the natural environment.

1–03   "Environment" in arts 3 TEU and 4, 191 to 193 TFEU is different from the "working environment" used in arts 114 and 153 TFEU, which obviously concerns the conditions at the workplace, such as air pollution, noise, risk of accidents, etc. The specific conditions of the workplace justify a different treatment of "environment" and "working environment", although in the early 1970s, EU environmental policy did not make this distinction[4] and some directives do not really differentiate between worker protection and environmental protection.[5] Working environment provisions come, therefore, under art.153 or, as the case may be, under art.114 TFEU.

Doubts were sometimes raised as to whether "environment" also includes animal welfare. However, wild animals are part of the natural environment; thus protection measures for wild animals—not only as a threatened species, but as living creatures—are environmental measures. The Amsterdam Treaty on European Union added a protocol to the EC Treaty, according to which the Union's policies on agriculture, transport, the internal market and research had to pay "full regard to the welfare of animals".[6] The TFEU took this up and inserted a new art.13 which declared that "since animals are sentient beings", full regard had to be paid to the welfare requirements of animals. It is obvious, though, that this provision refers to domestic, not wild, animals and therefore does not contradict the interpretation given here.

The uncertainty of how to classify (wild) animal welfare became obvious when the Commission made a proposal for a directive on the protection of zoo animals. In view of the subsidiarity debate, the Commission repealed this proposal and replaced it by a proposal for a recommendation. However, the

---

[3] European Council Resolution of June 15, 1990 (1990) *Bulletin of the European Communities*, para.1.36.
[4] See first environmental action programme [1973] OJ C112/1, p.43.
[5] See Dir.96/82 on the prevention of industrial accidents [1997] OJ L10/13.
[6] [1997] OJ C340/110.

Council rearranged the text so as to be a text that was mainly concerned with protecting animals as endangered species and adopted, on that basis, a directive in 1999.[7]

Geographically, the environment mentioned in the Treaty is not limited to the European Union's environment, as is clear from the mention of "measures at international level and regional or worldwide environmental problems" in art.191(1) TFEU. Consequently, the European Union can—and did—take measures to protect the environment outside the territory covered by the Treaties, such as measures to protect the ozone layer, combat climate change, protect endangered species in the Third World or ban the export of waste to non-industrialised countries. The question of whether the Union should deal with matters of a purely local nature, is something to be answered under the general principle of subsidiarity. In the past, the Commission has sometimes rejected requests to take initiatives on a specific environmental problem, arguing that such matters could be better solved at local or regional level; such questions concerned, for instance, noise from nightclubs and discothèques, bicycle facilities in urban areas or noise in the vicinity of airports. However, it may well be that, for example, in order to ensure equal competition conditions within the European Union and protect, at the same time, the environment, some day the ambient noise level in the neighbourhood of airports will become the subject of an EU regulation, as the Commission had already announced in 1992.[8]

1–04

Furthermore, it may well be argued that the quality of the (local) bathing waters, of drinking water or of urban waste water treatment, are questions of purely local nature and should, therefore, not be regulated at EU level. The EU legislature has, in all three cases, decided that there should be EU-wide minimum standards, and no Member State ever invoked the subsidiarity principle in this regard. The own opinion is that there is a large margin of discretion of the EU legislature whether a specific problem should be dealt with at EU level or not. I consider all three pieces of EU legislation compatible with the subsidiarity principle.

When the Commission made, in 2006, a proposal for a directive on the assessment and management of floods, some Member States suggested to limit this proposal to river basins which affected more than one Member State. However, this suggestion was rejected, probably because also coastal floods were included and because the management of such floods, including any financial assistance from the European Union, would not be made easier; the Directive which was adopted, covered all types of floods.[9]

More generally, there is no EU environment distinguishable from any individual, local, regional or national environment. Therefore, the EU measures need not be and are not restricted to transfrontier environmental problems. Quite rightly, art.5(3) TEU abandoned the notion of a "transfrontier" dimension of a measure which was contained in art.5 EC Treaty, and only refers to the "scale" of the measure as one criterion among others for assessing the application of the subsidiarity principle. As mentioned above, the definition of "environment" is, as regards its content and its geographical extension, very wide and includes human beings, fauna and flora, soil, water, air, climate, landscape, material assets, and

[7] Dir.1999/22 [1999] OJ L94/24, see for more details para.5–38, below.
[8] COM (92) 494 of December 2, 1992.
[9] Dir.2007/60 on the assessment and management of flood risks [2007] OJ L288/7.

natural heritage.[10] Environmental law is the totality of the legal measures which try to prevent, protect and improve parts or all of the environment.

2.   Genesis and development of EU environmental law

1–05   The original EC Treaty of 1957 did not contain any provision on the environment, environmental policy or environmental law. Subsequent to the discussions of the late 1960s, where the Club of Rome described the limits to growth, the European Commission announced in 1970 the necessity of establishing a Community action programme on the environment. In 1971 it submitted a first communication on Community environmental policy,[11] where it suggested the establishment of EU measures for the protection of the environment recurring, if necessary, to the possibilities for action outlined in art.308 EC (now art.352 TFEU). This Communication was soon followed by a proposal for an environmental action programme.[12]

In 1972, the United Kingdom, Denmark and Ireland joined the Union. In the autumn of that year, the Heads of State and Government met for the first time, agreed on the necessity to take action on the environment and asked for an EU environmental action programme.[13] Since this programme was already before the Council, discussions advanced relatively quickly. France in particular considered, however, that EU action should not be based on the EC Treaty provisions, but should instead take place in the form of intergovernmental co-operation, as the EC Treaty did not contain an explicit competence provision. For this reason, the finally adopted programme was agreed in the form of a joint "declaration" by the Community and by the representatives of Member States meeting in Council.[14] In the same way the agreement to inform the Commission of national environmental measures which could have a direct effect on the functioning of the internal market, was made in the form of a non-binding gentleman's agreement[15]; this policy continued throughout 1973 and 1974.[16]

1–06   The first legally binding instruments on environmental issues were adopted in 1975, based on art.94 EC and/or art.308 EC (now arts 115 and 352 TFEU). The choice of measures was determined both by the environmental action programme and by the necessity of selecting areas which did not come under the

---

[10] Enumeration from Dir.85/337 on the assessment of the effects of certain public and private projects on the environment [1985] OJ L175/40, art.3.

[11] Commission, First communication on a Community policy for the environment, SEC (71) 2616 of July 22, 1971.

[12] [1972] OJ C52/1.

[13] Commission Sixth General Report (1972), p.8.

[14] [1973] OJ C112/1.

[15] [1973] OJ C9/1.

[16] See Agreement of July 20, 1974 to complete the 1973 agreement [1974] OJ C86/1; Resolution of March 3, 1974 on energy and the environment [1975] OJ C168/2; Recommendation 75/436 of March 3, 1975 on cost allocation and action by public authorities on environmental matters [1975] OJ L194/1; Resolution of June 24, 1975 on a second group of air pollutants which are to be studied [1975] OJ C168/4; Resolution of July 15, 1975 on adapting Community measures to technical progress [1975] OJ C168/5; Decision of December 8, 1975 setting up a common procedure for an inventory of information sources on the environment [1976] OJ L31/8.

responsibility of the internal market or agricultural services of the Commission. This was the case in particular for measures in the area of water and waste.[17]

The EC Treaty was amended in 1987 to complete, by the end of 1992, the internal market.[18] Majority voting for internal market measures was introduced by inserting a new art.95 (now art.114) into the Treaty. And for the first time, a section was introduced for environmental measures (arts 174–176, now arts 191–193 TFEU). However, such measures had to be adopted unanimously. This led to considerable discussions on the legal basis for environmental measures, which the Commission and the European Parliament often wished to base on the actual art.114, while the Council and Member States preferred the present art.192.

When the Maastricht Treaty on European Union amended the EC Treaty in 1993 it introduced majority decisions in environmental matters (art.192), though some matters remained subjected to unanimous decisions.[19]

The Amsterdam Treaty,[20] which entered into effect on May 1, 1999, introduced the co-decision procedure for environmental matters (art.192(1)) and aligned this provision thus further to that of art.114, though the unanimity clause for some areas (art.192(2)) was not deleted. The Treaty of Nice which came into effect on February 1, 2003, did not significantly change the provisions of arts 191–193. Also the Lisbon Treaty on European Union did not bring changes to these provisions, except that the fight against climate change was inserted into art.191 TFEU as one of the objectives of EU environmental policy.

3.   Sources of community environmental law

The broad definition of objectives of EU environmental policy, as laid down in arts 3 TEU and 191(1) TFEU, hardly leaves any area of environmental policy, as it is perceived in any one of the 27 Member States, outside EU competence. Measures to realise the objectives of the Union's environmental policy may be based on any relevant article of the FEU Treaty, although arts 191 and 192 remain the most relevant provisions for EU environmental action. Thus, measures which concern agricultural aspects of environmental protection will normally be based on art.43 TFEU; an example was Directive 91/414 on the authorisation and marketing of plant protection products.[21] Measures on environmental aspects of transport may be based on art.80 EC [now 91 TFEU]; an example is Directive 99/62 on the charging of heavy good vehicles for the use of certain infrastructures.[22] The choice of the correct legal basis is important because the elaboration of the proposal, the participation of other Union institutions, the

1–07

---

[17] See, in chronological order, Decision 75/437 of March 3, 1975 to adhere to the Paris Convention on marine protection from land-based sources [1975] OJ L194/5; Dir.75/439 of June 16, 1975 on waste oils [1975] OJ L194/23; Dir.75/440 of June 16, 1975 on surface water [1975] OJ L194/26; Dir.75/442 of June 16, 1975 [1975] OJ L194/2 3 on waste; Dir.76/160 of December 8, 1975 on bathing water [1976] OJ L31/1.
[18] Single European Act [1987] OJ L169/1.
[19] [1992] OJ C191/1.
[20] [1997] OJ C340/1.
[21] [1991] OJ L230/51.
[22] [1999] OJ L187/42.

intensity of this participation (see arts 293–294 TFEU) and the residual rights for Member States are different from one provision to another.

The rules of arts 191 and 192 TFEU are not directly applicable: while for instance, art.34 TFEU states that "quantitative restrictions on imports and all measures having equivalent effect shall... be prohibited between Member States", no similar formulation can be found in arts 191 or 192 TFEU, stating that pollution is prohibited or that the polluter shall pay for pollution. Therefore, arts 191 and 192 need to be operationalised and made precise by secondary legislation in order to become applicable for administrative bodies and courts or used for or against polluters.

The most relevant other provisions, on which EU environmental measures can be based are art.114 TFEU for measures aiming at the establishment and the functioning of the internal market, art.43 TFEU for agricultural and fisheries measures, art.91 TFEU for measures concerning transport, art.207 TFEU for commercial measures and art.182 TFEU on research and development. Environmental measures in the energy sector were in the past frequently based on art.192 TFEU, as there was no specific chapter on energy policy in the EC Treaty; an example is Directive 2001/77 on the promotion of electricity produced from renewable energy sources in the internal electricity market.[23] Otherwise, art.352 TFEU was used. The Lisbon Treaty introduced a new provision, art.194 TFEU. This provision is likely to be used in future for energy related environmental measures.

The choice of the correct legal basis for an environmental matter will be further discussed below at paras 2–69 et seq., the rights of Member States under paras 3–41 et seq.

1–08   International conventions to which the European Union has adhered to, are part of EU law, see art.216(2) TFEU. They rank below the primary law of the FEU Treaty, but above secondary legislation and thus prevail over conflicting environmental directives or regulations.[24] The European Union has adhered to a considerable number of international environmental conventions and to numerous protocols, drawn up in pursuance of these conventions. All these conventions are so-called "mixed" conventions: the competence for the subject-matter regulated by the conventions was partly in the hands of the European Union and partly in the hands of Member States. Where exactly the line is drawn between the Union's responsibility and Member States' responsibility inevitably varies from one convention to the other.

As decisions which are based on art.192 TFEU and transpose environmental conventions into EU law have as a consequence that Member States may, under art.193 TFEU, introduce more stringent provisions in that area at national level, such decisions can never establish an exclusive EU competence for the subject-matter regulated by the convention.[25]

---

[23] [2001] OJ L283/33.

[24] See Court of Justice, *IATA and ELFAA* (C–344/04) [2006] E.C.R. I–403, para.35: "Article 300(7) EC [now Article 216(2) TFEU] provides that 'agreements concluded under the conditions set out in this Article shall be binding on the institutions of the Community and on Member States'. In accordance with the court's case-law, those agreements prevail over provisions of secondary Community legislation".

[25] See para.3–50, below, for concrete cases where the question of exclusive competence became relevant at EU level.

In practice, an international environmental convention only plays a significant role in the Union's law where the European Union has adopted a directive or a regulation in order to transpose the content of the convention into EU law. Where there is only a Council decision to adhere to a convention, but no transposing secondary legislation, the Commission omits to enforce the content of the convention against Member States. Member States are left at their discretion to also ratify the convention and to apply it. This practice is well established, although it clearly contradicts art.17 TEU, which assign the task to the Commission to ensure that *all* EU law is applied within the European Union.[26] Indeed, the European Union, by adhering to an international convention, commits itself with regard to the other contracting parties to comply with the convention's requirements throughout the territory of the European Union, independently from the question, whether the EU Member State in question has made, through its own ratification, a commitment that pertains to its national territory.

The European Union has adopted an important number of pieces of environmental legislation in the form of regulations, directives and non-binding recommendations. Their exact number depends on the classification of measures. Thus, for example, since at least the mid-1980s standards for air emissions or noise levels from cars have been set and strengthened in order to better protect the environment; nevertheless, they were based on arts 115 or 114 TFEU, because the two basic directives on air and noise emissions from cars had been adopted, in the 1970s, as part of an EU programme for the elimination of technical barriers to trade in the internal market. The reason for recurrence to art.114 TFEU is the existence of art.193 TFEU: the car industry, EU institutions and probably also Member States have an interest in establishing uniform standards for cars and avoid that different national standards create barriers to the free circulation of cars.

1–09

The different instruments will be further discussed at paras 2–31 et seq., below. Environmental action programmes are, since the end of 1993, regulated by art.192(3); they are now adopted in the form of a legally binding decision.[27] This constitutes a significant difference to the five environmental action programmes which had been adopted between 1973 and 1993. These had been elaborated by the Commission and sent to the other EU institutions. The Council, together with governments from Member States, had normally approved their concept and the approach in the form of a unanimously adopted (political) resolution, but had carefully avoided any statement that it adopted the programme as such.[28]

In future, the content of an EU action programme which was adopted under art.192(3) TFEU will constitute a source of law. Thus, where for example the Sixth Environmental Action Programme,[29] requests in art.7(1) that "chemicals that are dangerous should be substituted by safer chemicals or safer alternative

---

[26] EC Treaty art.17 TEU: "the Commission shall . . . ensure the application of the Treaties and of the measures adopted by the institutions pursuant to them."

[27] See Decision 1600/2002 laying down the Sixth Community Environment Action Programme [2002] OJ L242/1.

[28] See, e.g. Resolution of the Council and the Representatives of the Governments of the Member States, meeting within the Council of February 1, 1993 [1993] OJ C138/1: " . . . approve the general approach and strategy of the programme towards sustainability presented by the Commission; . . ." Against the binding nature of the 5th Action Programme: Court of Justice, *Rovigo v Commission* (C–142/95P) [1996] E.C.R. I–6669, n.32.

[29] See fn.27, above.

technologies not entailing the use of chemicals with the aim of reducing risks to man and the environment", this clearly constitutes the recognition of the substitution principle in EU environmental law, which may influence the interpretation of arts 34, 36, 114, 192 or 193 TFEU.[30] Also, the interpretation of the subsidiarity principle will be influenced by decisions under art.192(3): where a decision under this provision explicitly provides for an EC measure on a specific item, it will normally not be possible to object such an EU measure by invoking the subsidiarity principle—though much depends, of course, on the exact content of the measure.

4. Objectives of environmental policy

General remarks

1–10   Article 3 TEU[31] fixes the general environmental objectives of the European Union, which are completed by the specific objectives fixed in art.191[32]; it is common understanding that the tasks of art.3(3) TEU are not an exhaustive enumeration.

The different objectives of the Treaties are not in a hierarchical order. The European Union has to try to attain all its objectives. Should different objectives conflict in a specific case, then the EU institutions must try to find a compromise (see art.7 TFEU). Conflicts—for instance between the establishment of an internal market for goods and the need to protect the environment via the precautionary principle—are frequent. Article 11 TFEU,[33] which was introduced by the Treaty of Amsterdam, does not lead to a different interpretation. Indeed, any such hierarchy would have needed clearer expression in the Treaty.

The different environmental objectives do not lead to concrete requirements for legislative action. It is not possible, for instance, to deduce from the requirement of a prudent use of natural resources the right to limit land use, e.g. for agricultural purposes. Nor are the objectives, in practice, enforceable. The possibility of an action under art.265 TFEU against the European Union, the Council or the Commission for not pursuing the environmental objectives, is theoretical, since EU institutions have a very large discretion for taking—or not taking—action.

EU action shall *contribute* to achieve the different objectives, as is stated in art.191 TFEU. Next to EU measures there are also national, regional, local or

---

[30] On the substitution principle see also Court of Justice, *Kemikalieinspektionen* (C–473/98) [2000] E.C.R. I–5681.

[31] Treaty on European Union (fn.1, above), art.3(3): "The Union shall work for the sustainable development of Europe, based on . . . a high level of protection and improvement of the quality of the environment."

[32] art.191(1) TFEU: "Union policy on the environment shall contribute to pursuit of the following objectives:—preserving, protecting and improving the quality of the environment; protecting human health;—prudent and rational utilisation of natural resources;—promoting measures at international level to deal with regional or worldwide environmental problems, and in particular combating climate change."

[33] art.11 TFEU: "Environmental protection requirements must be integrated into the definition and implementation of the Union policies and activities, in particular with a view to promoting sustainable development." An almost identical text had been inserted, in 1987, into an earlier version of the present art.191(2.3) TFEU.

international measures which exist to help reach the objectives. The responsibility and competence of the European Union in environmental matters is thus shared with Member States, but is not exclusive. In specific cases the environmental action programmes specify which action is to be undertaken in order to approach or even reach one or several objectives of the EU Treaties; nevertheless, the individual measures still need to be adopted by a formal EC instrument (see art.288 TFEU), for which the relevant decision-making procedure under the different Treaty provisions must be followed.

Sustainable development

The Amsterdam Treaty 1999 introduced the concept of sustainable development into EU law: the Preamble to the TEU, art.3 of that Treaty, as well as art.11 TFEU mention this objective[34] without defining it. Already, art.2 in the version of the Maastricht Treaty, had fixed as one of the Community objectives "sustainable growth", also without defining it. Both notions go back to a report which an ad hoc "World Commission on Environment and Development" chaired by Gro Brundtland (Norway) had made in 1987 to the United Nations and which was entitled *Our Common Future*. In that report, the need for economic development was emphasised which should, however, be "sustainable". Sustainable development was described as a "development which meets the needs of the present without compromising the ability of future generations to meet their own needs". **1–11**

However, even after 30 years of discussions, the precise meaning of the notion is unclear. "It cannot usefully be defined. It seems clear, though, that a policy of economic growth which disregards environmental considerations will not meet the criterion of sustainable development".[35] This, though, was exactly what the Lisbon European Council did in 2000 when it fixed as an objective for the European Union to become, within 10 years, "the most competitive and dynamic knowledge-based economy in the world, capable of sustainable economic growth with more and better jobs and greater social cohesion". In 2001, the Göteborg European Council tried to repair this (deliberate) omission, by adding the environmental aspects to the Lisbon declaration.[36]

In 2005, the Commission declared that sustainability of the EU policy required actions with regard to climate change, clean energy, public health, social exclusion, demography and migration, management of natural resources, global poverty and challenges to development.[37] This was followed by a declaration on

---

[34] art.9 of the Recitals of TEU mentions that sustainable development is a "principle".

[35] P. Birnie and A. Boyle, *International Law & the Environment* 2nd edn (Oxford, 2002), p.45; on sustainable development, see also M.Lee *EU Environmental Law* (Oxford, 2005) and Portland, p.25ss.

[36] See Presidency Conclusions, Göteborg European Council (2001) June, 15 and 16, nos 19 and 20: "Sustainable development—to meet the needs of the present generation without compromising those of future generations—is a fundamental objective under the Treaties. That requires dealing with economic, social and environmental policies in a mutually reinforcing way. The European Council agrees a strategy for sustainable development which completes the Union's political commitment to economic and social renewal, adds a third, environmental dimension to the Lisbon strategy and establishes a new approach to policy making."

[37] Commission, COM(2005)37. See, also Dec 1600/2002 on the Sixth Environmental Action Programme (fn.26, above), Recitals 6 and 7: "A prudent use of natural resources and the protection of the global eco-system together with economic prosperity balanced social development are a condition for sustainable development. The Programme aims at a high level of protection of the environment

guiding principles for sustainable development which the Council approved; these were environmental protection, social equity and cohesion, economic prosperity and the assuming of international responsibility.[38] And in June 2006, the European Council adopted a declaration on a strategy for sustainable development where it fixed seven objectives of sustainable development: climate change and clean technologies, sustainable transport, sustainable consumption and production, conservation and management of natural resources, public health, social inclusion, demography and migration, and global poverty and the challenges of sustainable development. The European Council also fixed ten leading principles and seven main challenges which should be addressed. For each challenge, it fixed a number of actions to be taken by the EU institutions, though it carefully avoided to give them any legally binding form.[39]

In the political practice since 2006, most of the European Union's policy and legislation followed the principle of "business as usual". It is true, though, that the fight against climate change became, for the Union's internal policy, one priority. With regard to the other strategic objectives, it appears that the Union institutions do not pay more than lip-service to the objective of reverting the unsustainable tendencies identified by the Commission and to put the strategy of 2006 into reality.[40]

In secondary legislation, "sustainable development" was only rarely defined; as can be seen such a definition is not really meaningful: "Sustainable development means the improvement of the standard of living and welfare of the relevant populations within the limits of the capacity of the ecosystems by maintaining natural assets and their biological diversity for the benefit of present and future generations".[41] Taken literally, nobody could comply with such requirements.

The basic difficulty of knowing which economic development is sustainable, remains. It might well be argued that the use of nuclear energy, which includes the generation of radioactive waste for which no safe disposal technology exists as yet and which will continue to be hazardous for thousands of years, most certainly affects future generations and is therefore not sustainable. Another example is the gradual, progressive contamination of groundwater, which often shows its effects only decades later, when the groundwater is used. Further examples are the disappearance of fauna and flora species, urbanisation and the construction of motorways. At the end of 2003, the Council approved, by way of Council conclusions and thus in a non-binding form, a list of 14 headline indicators to assess sustainable development, among them three "environmental" indicators, namely greenhouse gas emissions, energy intensity of economy and the volume of transport.[42] Reliable EU-wide data on the last two indicators do not

---

and human health and at a general improvement in the environment and quality of life, indicates priorities for the environment dimension of the sustainable development strategy and should be taken into account when bringing forward actions under the strategy."

[38] Commission COM(2005) 218.

[39] Council, document 10917 of 26 June 2006.

[40] See Eurostat, sustainable development in the EU. 2009 monitoring report on the EU sustainable development strategy. Luxemburg 2009. See also Ch.13, below.

[41] Definition from art.2 of Reg.2493/2000 [2000] OJ L288/1; see also earlier Reg.3062/95 [1995] OJ L327/9, art.2(4).

[42] Council, Conclusions of 8 December 2003 on structural indicators, document 15875/03.

yet exist and it might well be argued that these indicators do not mean anything, e.g. for biodiversity loss, groundwater pollution or noise levels.

Another approach was chosen by Eurostat, the Commission's Statistical Office, which published in 2002 a study where it tried to assess sustainability with the help of 63 social, economic, environmental and institutional indicators; the environmental indicators concerned energy use, total use of resources, water use, land use, need of transport, organic farming and the protection of biodiversity.[43] However, data on these issues and trends which may be deduced from them, do not necessarily allow any conclusion on, the state of the environment and its development towards sustainability.

In view of this contradictory and confusing use of the word "sustainability", it is not surprising that the Union practice shows an inflationary use of the expression "sustainable" which is linked to very different activities—sustainable transport, sustainable tourism, sustainable use of energy or water, sustainable regional development, sustainable production and consumption—in order to give them a green colour [44]; contents are put into the notion of "sustainability", which are later derived from it, and the notion is more and more used as a substitute for "positive, favourable development", thereby losing all its environmental content. Generally, it seems impossible to determine precisely if and when future generations will be able or unable to meet their own needs. For example, the construction of the Via Appia some 2,500 years ago has affected the siting of towns and villages; in the same way, any town siting and road construction today will affect future generations' rights to determine their own needs, i.e. their own town siting or road construction. The different provisions in the Treaty on sustainable development and their practical application thus give more of a guideline to policy action than any meaningful legal concept.

1–12

High level of protection

The objective to reach a high level of environmental protection is now enshrined in the EU Treaty[45] art.3(3) and is repeated in similar terms in art.191(2.1) TFEU.[46] A similar provision is to be found in art.114(3) TFEU.[47] Neither article specifies what is a high level of protection: certainly, it is not the highest level one could think of.[48] A high level can probably best be determined by looking at environmental standards which Member States that normally have a high

1–13

---

[43] Eurostat: Environment and Energy. Topic 8 2/2002 (Luxembourg, 2002).
[44] The Sixth Environmental Action Programme, Dec.1600/2002 (fn.27, above) uses the word, in its different forms (sustain, sustainable, sustainability) not less than 64 times.
[45] See fn.1, above.
[46] art.191(2.1) TFEU: "Union policy on the environment shall aim at a high level of protection taking into account the diversity of situations in the various regions of the Community."
[47] art.95(3) TFEU: "(The Commission, in its proposals concerning environmental protection) will take as a base a high level of protection taking account in particular of any new development based on scientific facts. Within their respective powers, the European Parliament and the Council will also seek to achieve this objective."
[48] See also Court of Justice, *Germany v Parliament and Council* (C–233/94) [1997] E.C.R. I–2405, para.48 for a case of consumer protection where under art.153 EC (now art.169 TFEU) a high level of protection is required: "Admittedly, there must be a high level of consumer protection . . .; however, no provision of the Treaty obliges the Community legislature to adopt the highest level of protection which can be found in a particular Member State. The reduction in the level of protection which may thereby result in certain cases through the application of . . . the Directive does not call into question

standard of environmental protection (Denmark, the Netherlands, Sweden, Finland, Austria, Germany) have set; the practice of other industrial states with a recognised strong environmental policy, such as Switzerland or Norway, may also be considered. Policy declarations, resolutions and targets can be an important indicator, especially in areas where no standards have yet been set at national or international level, or where scientific uncertainty is great. As art.3 TEU expressly declares the improvement of the quality of the environment to be one of the objectives of Union policy, any measure aiming at a high level must therefore aim at improving the existing situation.

The specific reference to a high level of protection no longer permits the adoption of measures which only provide for the lowest common denominator of environmental protection and lets individual Member States, which are in favour of more stringent measures, to adopt such measures by virtue of art.193 TFEU at national level. Indeed, the high level is to be achieved by the Union as a whole, not by national measures. Article 191 TFEU clarifies that the interests of regions which are environmentally lagging behind shall be duly taken into account, allowing them to catch up; this again pleads for a high level, not the highest level of protection.

A high level of environmental protection cannot be enforced in court. This follows from the fact that arts 3 TEU and 191 TFEU refer to the environmental policy as a whole, not to the individual measure adopted under that policy; also, the policy has to "aim at" a high level and can thus always argue that it is on its way towards this attainment. *Epiney* who is of the opinion that the provision is legally binding and can be enforced, practically reaches the same conclusion by emphasising the wide discretion which the EC institutions have in interpreting the notion[49].

1–14   In contrast to art.3 TEU and 191 TFEU, art.114 TFEU requests Commission proposals to be made at a high level of environmental protection; thus, it refers to individual measures, not to the policy in general. Where a Commission proposal is not based on a high level of environmental protection, the European Parliament has a right of action against the Commission[50] under art.263 TFEU. This follows from the procedural provisions of arts 293 and 294 TFEU. Indeed, where the Commission has made a "high level" proposal (case A), the Council can reach a common position and adopt a proposal that lowers the protection, only by unanimity (art.293 TFEU); however, where the Commission has made a "low level" proposal (case B), the Council can reach a common position and finally adopt the proposal by a qualified majority, at a lower level (provided, it conforms to the low level proposal from the Commission) since it does not amend the Commission's proposal. The Council's common position may only be challenged by an absolute majority of the European Parliament. Where the European Parliament's majority opinion is concurrent with the Commission's opinion, the

---

the general result which the Directive seeks to achieve, namely a considerable improvement in the protection of . . . [consumers] within the Community."

[49] A. Epiney, *Umweltrecht in der Europäischen Union* 2nd edn (Köln-Berlin-München, 2005), p.98ss.

[50] The Parliament has no such right against the Council, since art.114(3) TFEU expressly provides that the Council shall only "seek to achieve" a high level of protection.

Council must decide unanimously (case A); where this majority opinion does not concur with the Commission's opinion, the Council may decide by majority (case B).[51]

These considerations are of theoretical character. The European Parliament has, until now, never attempted such a case against the Commission; without doubt, this practice is also due to the difficulties of determining what is in reality a "high level". In all situations—under arts 114 and 192 TFEU—that have occurred up until now, the practice of the Commission and the Council indicates that both institutions use the formula of a high level in its reversed order: whatever is proposed or adopted is considered to be a high level of environmental protection.

The "sanction" for not proposing or adopting measures on a high level of environmental protection is art.193 TFEU for measures under art.192 and art.114(4)–(9) TFEU: in both cases, Member States may, under certain conditions, maintain or introduce more stringent national measures. In theory, one might argue that the lower the level of protection the Union measure is, the greater becomes the pressure from Member States with a high level of protection to opt out of the Union environmental measure and take or maintain national measures. In practice, though, economic operators rather push for lowering the high level also in Member States with more stringent measures than the European Union.

The specific objectives of art.191(1) TFEU

The four specific objectives mentioned under art.191(1) are rather detailed in their description; but these details do not, in fact, add too much to the objective to protect the environment. They clarify that the Union protection measures are not limited to the Union's territory, which, in practice, these measures never were. Measures to protect human health[52] can, as the case may be, pursue an environmental, internal market, agricultural, consumer protection or public health objective and thus be based on other Treaty provisions than arts 191–193. In the context of its examination of national legislative measures under art.114(4–8) TFEU) the Commission does not accept that a national measure is based on health considerations, as that provision only allows considerations to protect the environment; this practice contradicts the provision of art.191 TFEU, according to which environmental measures also aim at the protection of human health.[53] "Natural resources" is a vague term: it probably covers the management of all resources which are found in the environment, fauna and flora, timber, minerals, air, water, soil, oil, natural gas and chemicals. Measures to prevent degradation or impairment of these resources, such as accident prevention and the safe disposal

1–15

---

[51] Jans-Vedder, *European Environmental Law* 3rd edn (Groningen, 2008), are of the opinion that a Commission proposal is not an "act", in the sense of art.263 TFEU, and thus cannot be tackled in court.

[52] The difference between "health of humans" (art.36 TFEU), "human health" (art.191, but also art.169) and "public health" (title of art.168 TFEU) has lost its legal precision; see also Court of Justice, *Biologische Produkten* (C–272/ 80) [1981] E.C.R. 3277, where the Court refers to art.30 EC (now art.36 TFEU) as protecting "public health". See furthermore, Court of Justice, *Standley* (C–293/97) [1999] E.C.R. I–2603, where the Court considered Directive 91/676 on the protection of water from nitrates pollution to be a directive which protects "public health".

[53] See Ch.3, below.

of waste, are included in the term "prudent and rational use". Identifying the objective, eventually the main objective, of a measure is important, because the objective is one of the determining factors of the legal base for the measure; and the decision-making procedure, the content of the measure and Member States' residual rights and obligations vary according to the legal base applicable.

5.   Principles of environmental action

General remarks

1–16   Part one of the TFEU, arts 1–17, is entitled "Principles". It fixes the basics of the TFEU, objectives, institutional and procedural rules and a number of other provisions of a general character. As regards the environment, arts 5 TEU on subsidiarity[54] and 11 TFEU on integration[55] are of relevance. To these general principles, art.191(2.2) TFEU adds some specific environmental principles.[56]

It is doubtful whether all these different provisions have the same legal character. As regards the principles of art.191(2.2) TFEU, they constitute, in my opinion, general guidelines for Union's environmental policy, but not binding rules of law which apply to each individual Community measure. They *allow* the taking of specific measures in favour of the environment, but do not *oblige* the EU institutions to take such measures. Therefore, they could only be enforced by the European Court in very extreme cases where a systematic disregard of the principles in the policy is demonstrated.

1–17   This reasoning is contested. Some authors see the principles of art.191(2.2) TFEU as binding rules of law, which have to be respected in each individual measure.[57] The wide discretion of Union institutions, however, for taking measures could only lead to the illegality of a measure in exceptional cases because the principles had been disregarded. As can be seen, the practical results are not really very different.

The discussion on principles in environmental law and policy is, to a large extent, a spill-over from discussions which take place under the auspices of public international law. In that context, principles may play an important role in contributing to the shaping of international environmental law. However, it should not be forgotten that the essential part of public international environmental law is soft law, which is not really binding on the States. In contrast to that, EU law is binding and capable of fixing provisions that have binding force on Member States and on private persons. In the same way as, e.g. the United Nations' Declaration on Human Rights remains of high value for the international community, but is of secondary importance in Europe, where the

---

[54] art.5(3) TEU: "Under the principle of subsidiarity, in areas which do not fall within its exclusive competence, the Union shall act only if and in so far as the objectives of the proposed action cannot be sufficiently achieved by the Member States, either at central level or at regional and local level, but can rather, by reason of the scale or effects of the proposed action, be better achieved at Union level."
[55] art.11 TFEU (fn.33, above).
[56] art.191(2.2) TFEU: "[Union policy] ... shall be based on the precautionary principle and on the principles that preventive action should be taken, that environmental damage should as a priority be rectified at source and that the polluter should pay."
[57] See the different contributions in R. Macrory (ed.), *Principles of European Environmental Law* (Groningen, 2004).

Council of Europe's Convention on Human Rights established binding, enforceable human rights, the environmental principles in the TFEU are less important for EU environmental law, which has developed a large number of binding provisions that materialise these principles for the actual, concrete situations.

The Court of Justice has in one case interpreted EU law in the light of one of the principles of art.191(2.2) TFEU.[58] In that judgment, the Court had to decide whether a regional ban for waste imports was compatible with the EU provisions on the free circulation of goods, although such waste imports from other Member States were treated differently from imports of waste from other regions of that State. The Court found no discrimination in this case.[59]

1–18

In other cases, the Court frequently recurred to the formula that provisions of EU law could not be interpreted in such a way "as to give rise to results which are incompatible with the general principles of Community law and in particular with fundamental rights".[60] The question is, whether also the environmental principles of art.191(2) TFEU are such principles which EU legislation may not infringe. In my opinion, this is not the case. Rather, they constitute guiding principles for political or legislative decisions and are often used—as a sort of leitmotif—to explain or justify a decision which was taken. But they cannot really be used to declare an EU measure void with the argument that it contradicts one of these principles.

The judgment in the abovementioned case C–2/90 was given under the 1987 version of the present art.191 TFEU, which referred to Community action rather than to Community policy. Under that provision it could be argued that the principles of art.191 TFEU referred to individual measures. By contrast, the present wording of that article considers the EU policy as a whole; it does not require that each individual EU measure take into account all the principles of art.191(2.2) TFEU. Requesting that the principles of art.191 apply to each individual EU measure would mean that numerous measures would contradict, for instance, the polluter-pays principle, since they do not contain any provision about it.[61]

Even where the principles of art.191 TFEU are seen as general guidelines for EU policy only, they have some indirect legal significance. They place an obligation on the Union to base its policy on these principles and to plan policy

---

[58] *Commission v Belgium* (C–2/90) [1992] E.C.R. I–4431.

[59] *Commission v Belgium* (C–2/90) [1992] E.C.R. I–4431, para.34: " ... in order to determine whether the obstacle in question is discriminatory, the particular type of waste must be taken into account. The principle that environmental damage should as a priority be rectified at source—a principle laid down by Art.174(2) E.C. for action by the Community relating to the environment—means that it is for each region, commune or other local entity to take appropriate measures to receive, process and dispose of its own waste ..." See also *R. v Minister of Agriculture* (C–157/ 96) [1998] E.C.R. I–2211 and *United Kingdom v Commission* (C–180/96) [1998] E.C.R. I–2265, where the Court interpreted the prevention principle.

[60] Court of Justice, *Dow Chemical* (Joined Cases 97/87, 98/87 and 99/87) [1989] E.C.R. I–3165, para.9.

[61] The judgment in Case C–2/90 (fn.58, above) seems to have been influenced by some policy considerations which might explain some inconsistencies: the principle of art.191(2.2) TFEU was applied to a national measure, although the article refers to EU policy; the Court did not examine whether the Belgian measure was proportional; the Court transformed the principle into a rule of law; it also justified its finding by reference to the Basel Convention on the shipment of hazardous waste, although the Union was, at the time of the judgment, not a member of that Convention, etc.

and measures accordingly. Moreover, observance of these principles can play an important part in deciding, case by case, whether the objectives of art.191(1) TFEU cannot be sufficiently achieved by the Member States and are therefore capable of being better achieved by the Union (subsidiarity, art.5 TEU). Where, for instance, the Union takes a measure on environmental liability, it could invoke the prevention and the polluter-pays principle to justify the EU action against subsidiarity arguments; this example shows at the same time the limited usefulness of the principles, since Member States which oppose the measure could argue that the subsidiarity principle would not allow action to be taken at EU level.

The principles could also be used to justify the chosen legal basis—art.192 TFEU or another provision—for a specific measure and its content[62] and to interpret secondary EU legislation.

Subsidiarity

1–19   The subsidiarity principle,[63] which is now laid down in art.5 TEU, was first inserted in 1987 into the EC Treaty, but in a different version and limited to environmental matters.[64] The Maastricht Treaty 1993 repealed that provision and inserted a new art.3b—the present art.5 TEU—into the Treaty. The Amsterdam Treaty 1997 added to this, as an annex to the EC Treaty, a "Protocol on the application of the principles of subsidiarity and proportionality",[65] where, in 13 detailed points, rules were laid down on subsidiarity and proportionality. The Lisbon Treaty slightly reworded the principle, placed it at art.5(3) TEU and also took over the Protocol. The style of this Protocol gives the impression that it was drafted less from the perspective of a European Union, but rather with the aim of containing as far as possible the threat of European integration which was perceived as reducing the amount of power that regional or national administration had up until then. Article 5 TEU and its Protocol were probably inspired by the old art.130r(4) EC and a preceding draft from the European Parliament on a general Treaty on European Union.[66] It establishes a general rule for all Union activity, including the environment.

It is not a rule of competence but a principle which concerns the exercise of that competence, and predetermines the activity of the European Union[67]; as such, it has legal force. When taking action, EU institutions will have to demonstrate for each individual measure that the conditions of art.5 TEU and its Protocol are actually complied with. They benefit, however, from a large amount

---

[62] See for the integration principle of art.11 TFEU, European *Parliament v Council* (C–62/88) [1990] E.C.R. I–1527: "[the integration requirement which] reflects the principle whereby all Community measures must satisfy the requirements of environmental protection, implies that a Community measure cannot be part of Community action on environmental matters merely because it takes account of these requirements."

[63] See, for this principle in general (without specific reference to the environment), Commission COM (93) 545 of November 29, 1993; COM (94) 533 of November 25, 1994; SEC (95) 580 of November 24, 1995; SEC (96) 2 of June 14, 1996, SEC (96) 7 of November 27, 1996.

[64] EC Treaty art.130r(4) (1987 version): "The Community shall take action relating to the environment to the extent to which the objectives referred to in paragraph 1 can be attained better at Community level than at the level of the individual Member States."

[65] [1997] OJ C340/105.

[66] [1984] OJ C77/33, arts 55 and 59.

[67] See also Commission SEC (92) 1990 of October 27, 1992.

of discretion on the question of what content a measure would have. In practice, recitals of environmental regulations or directives often contain a clause, that the legislative act in question respects the principle of subsidiarity.

The discussion on subsidiarity is ongoing at EU level, in particular since the **1–20** signature of the Maastricht Treaty, concentrating on the deregulation and simplification of legislation and of the possibility of the national parliaments and the Committee of the Regions to apply to the Court of Justice, when they consider that an EU measure does not comply with the principle of subsidiarity. Political approaches were started in 1992, in the name of subsidiarity, to review existing environmental directives, where Member States felt obliged to undertake financial investments to clean the environment: this discussion has been particularly intense in the water sector. In contrast to that, there is hardly ever a discussion on subsidiarity when questions of EU funding for economically weaker regions are in question, where measures are considered which improve the competitivity of EU economic operators or where financial assistance for small- and medium-sized enterprises is discussed.

For the environment, much depends on the interpretation given to the requirement that the objective of environmental protection cannot be sufficiently achieved by Member States and can thus be *better* achieved at Community level. Probably the best illustration of the practical difficulties is the discussion in the Economic and Social Committee on the proposal for Directive 96/61 on integrated prevention and pollution control.[68] The Committee discussed the pros and cons of fixing Community wide emission limit values for industrial installations and concluded:

> "the subsidiarity principle, properly understood, is not inconsistent with the establishment of limit values at European level. The high level of protection in the Community called for in the EC Treaty can only be achieved if European limit values are set."

A minority view of the Committee (eight members) stated in contrast to that[69]:

> "the subsidiarity principle, properly understood, is consistent with the establishment of limit values at Member State level. The high level of protection in the Community called for in the EU Treaty can only be achieved if Member State limit values are set and implemented."

It is not easy to establish general rules to show when environmental policy **1–21** objectives can be better attained at EU level. Member States with an active environmental policy of their own may well think that measures at the level of individual Member States are a better solution. At present, there is a wide gulf between the individual Member States' national environmental policies and regulations. Member States such as Denmark, the Netherlands, Sweden, Austria and Germany are far more convinced of the need for environmental protection measures than, for instance, Greece, Spain, Portugal or Italy—though the governmental approach to environmental issues also depends on the political party which is in power. In some Member States—Ireland, Greece, Portugal, Spain or the new Member States which acceded in 2004—environmental legislation often consists of not much more than the transposition of measures which had previously been adopted at EU level. Consequently, action at EU level

---

[68] For this Dir. see para.4–41.
[69] [1995] OJ C195/54 and App. II.

is often a means of ensuring that environmental measures are taken in *all* Member States. If, instead, it were left to the Member States to take action, it could not be ensured that all and not only some Member States would adopt provisions on that specific environmental problem. Even if they did, concepts, contents and timing would rarely coincide. Where Member States take action at different times, there is once again a danger for the Union as a whole of imbalances, distortions of competition and of trade patterns, the creation of new barriers to trade, etc.

Furthermore, river and sea water, air pollution, protection of fauna and flora species, climate issues, ozone layer protection, acidification, eutrophication and the management of products which have finished their useful lifetime (waste) cannot seriously be tackled at national level alone. In such cases the efforts of one Member State would easily be frustrated by the passivity of another Member State. This also would have an effect on the location of industrial undertakings, employment and quality of life, for example. Therefore, the objectives of art.191(1) TFEU can normally be attained faster and more effectively by and within the entire European Union, i.e. for the EU ecosystem as a whole. This is the reason why EU legislative activities practically covers all areas of environmental protection.

It must also be borne in mind that some Member States find it difficult, if not impossible, to conceive and implement measures to provide effective protection for the environment in general, and for fauna and flora in particular, since environmental protection measures are perceived as slowing down economic development. The negative effects of environmental impairment normally become more visible and therefore also politically more relevant when economic development is sufficiently advanced. Poverty is the biggest environmental pollutant; in Western Europe there is an element of economic divide between the north and the south, to which new EU Member States of Central and Eastern Europe have to be added. In these countries, environmental awareness and readiness to act are distinctly less prevalent, due to differences in the public discussion of environmental matters, traditions—hunting, bull fighting, fox hunting—education, public and media sensitivity, administrative determination, law enforcement, political priorities, etc. EU discussions on where environmental protection can be better achieved may not leave these considerations aside, although this often happens in Germany or the United Kingdom.

1–22   Precisely what "better" means in art.5 TEU is not at all clear; it could mean quicker, more effective, cheaper, more efficient, closer to the citizen (i.e. not too centralised), more democratic, more uniform, more consistent with measures in other parts of the industrialised world, or the global or the European Union, without these concepts being more precise.[70] It will, therefore, have to be decided on a case-by-case basis, considering all the facts, whether or not it is better to take measures at EU level, in order to attain the Union's environmental objectives. The aim must be to protect and improve the quality of the environment in the whole European Union. Due consideration must be given to the differences in the Member States' environmental legislation, the differing awareness of environmental issues, the environmental infrastructure in Member States, the risk that

---

[70] The European Parliament is of the opinion that the notions in art.5 are deliberately vague in order to increase the legislative discretion of Union institutions, Res.of April, 20, 1994, (1994) OJ C128/190 n.5.

national protection measures might be differently timed or formulated, the danger of relocating industrial undertakings to countries with lower standards, the possible deflection of trade and the potential changes in the competitive position within the European Union and of the European Union towards non-EU countries. The main concern is to improve the quality of the environment, to reach a high level of protection and to ensure sustainable development over the broadest possible area. Article 5 mentions the scale or effects of the proposed action as examples where objectives can be better achieved at Union level.

If one tries to apply all these theoretical issues to the debate as to whether there should be EU legislation on, for example, environmental liability, the following aspects would also have to be considered: there is legislation on liability in all Member States, but this differs as to questions of liability for negligence or strict liability, burden of proof, protected assets and damages; there are differences as to the application of these provisions to damage to the environment itself; environmental damage is differently defined; *locus standi* varies; the number of cases decided by courts varies considerably; costs for economic operators are likely to increase, e.g. due to insurance premiums; the environmental problem is not one of accidental pollution, but the progressive accumulation of pollutants in the environment; many an impairment is caused by a multitude of polluters, not by a single one; where an economic operator respects existing legislation, he should not be liable for environmental impairment, and so on. At the end of such a list of considerations, the conclusion cannot be other than that the question of whether there should be EU legislation on liability for damage to the environment or not and what content such legislation should have, is a political one, not a legal one of subsidiarity.[71]

1–23

Another good example is the discussion on binding EU energy efficiency targets: Member States oppose such binding targets, arguing that under the principle of subsidiarity, questions on energy efficiency are of their competence. Others argue that in order to ensure efficient measures in all 27 Member States which contribute to the fight against climate change, EU action is necessary. The outcome of this discussion will be determined by political, not legal considerations.[72]

There are many other examples of the ambiguous nature of the subsidiarity principle: why should, under subsidiarity auspices, the Union be competent to ban the import of furs from third countries which do not prohibit leg-hold traps[73] but not be competent to stop bullfighting, foxhunting or cockfighting? Why should there be common measures on smog in urban zones,[74] but not on the quality of bathing water in public swimming pools?

It is submitted that at the end of almost any discussion on a specific topic, the lawyer is placed in a position behind the policy-maker, who has to weigh political, economic, social, cultural, legal and environmental aspects as best he can: his decision usually remains a political decision.

---

[71] See Dir.2004/35 on environmental liability with regard to the prevention and remedying of environmental damage (2004) OJ L143/56.

[72] In 2009, EU-wide binding measures were rejected by the Council. The debate continues, though.

[73] See Reg.3254/91 (1991) OJ L308/1.

[74] See Dir.2008/50 (2008) OJ L 152/1.

Integration

1-24 The present art.11 TFEU[75] had antecedents in the environmental chapter of the EC Treaty: the 1987 version of art.174 contained a clause on integration,[76] which was formulated in such a way that it could, using the Court of Justice's doctrine of direct effect, be applied directly. The clause was considered both too precise and too vague and was therefore replaced by a phrase that was similar to the one used now in art.11 TFEU[77]. As it was felt that some other Union policies did not sufficiently integrate environmental considerations into their policies and measures, the discussion prior to the Amsterdam Treaty on European Union focused on the request to incorporate into the chapters on agriculture, transport, competition and so on, a reference to environmental considerations. This was objected by the sectors concerned as being too precise and thus led to the removal and slight reformulation of the provision to the present art.11 TFEU.[78]

The provision states that environmental considerations be fully taken into account in the elaboration and implementation of other Union policies. It is based on the concept that environmental requirements and, subsequently, environmental policy cannot be seen as an isolated green policy which groups specific actions on the protection of water, air, soil, fauna and flora. Rather, the environment is affected by other policies such as on transport, energy and agriculture, for example. art.11 TFEU therefore calls for a permanent, continuous "greening" of all Union policies. As mentioned above, though, art.11 TFEU does not allow priority to be given to environmental requirements over other requirements; rather, the different objectives of the Treaties rank at the same level and the policy must endeavour to achieve all of them; this is also the meaning of art.7 TFEU.

"Union policies and activities" referred to are the different policies listed in arts 3 and 4 TFEU. They include all activities of the Union under the FEU Treaty. Policies under the EURATOM Treaty are not included, as the EURATOM Treaty, essentially a Treaty to promote the use of nuclear energy, is not mentioned in art.11 TFEU. In my opinion the Union has spent, from the beginning, too much EU money on nuclear energy compared with expenses for renewable energy; art.11 TFEU would allow a reversal of this policy, if the political will existed to promote renewable energies. Again, this is a question of policy, not of law: there is no legal obligation to invest increased sums into the promotion of renewable energies.

1-25 "Environmental protection requirements" are first of all the different objectives laid down in arts 3 TEU and 191(1) TFEU. Thus, the objectives of ensuring a sustainable development, of preserving, protecting and improving the quality of the environment shall also have to be considered within the framework of other policies. The principles laid down in art.191(2.2) TFEU also form part of environmental protection requirements. Indeed, it does not make sense to apply the precautionary principle, under the environmental policy, and take action

---

[75] See fn.33, above.

[76] art.130r(2.2) EC (1987 version): "Environmental protection requirements shall be a component of the Community's other policies."

[77] art.130r(2.3) EC (1993 version): "Environmental protection requirements must be integrated into the definition and implementation of other Community policies."

[78] See also arts 167 (culture), 168 (public health) and 169(2) (consumer protection) TFEU, which also contain a requirement of integration; however, these policies are not mentioned in art.11 TFEU.

without the last scientific evidence of a substance's harmfulness, and then take the opposite approach in the context of the internal market policy. The Court of Justice reached the same conclusion when applying the principle of preventive action of art.191(2) TFEU to the BSE ("mad cow disease") case, which had no relationship whatsoever with environmental protection issues.[79]

In the same way, it would be contradictory to provide for preventive measures in environmental policy, but not to do so in other policies, thus limiting EU action to remedial measures which try to repair the environmental damage. Indeed, the greatest damage to the environment is caused by transport, agriculture, energy, industrial development and other policies, not by measures taken within the framework of environmental policy.

The whole debate on how to classify a specific Union measure is rather futile: **1–26** whether the protection of waters from nitrates of an agricultural source is a measure of agricultural or environmental policy should not have any influence on the principles which are to be taken into consideration. The same applies to a ban on asbestos fibres, the use of phthalates, pollution-abatement measures for cars, fuels or industrial installations. It seems rather old-fashioned to classify a specific measure as belonging to a specific policy: art.11 TFEU contributes to progressively overcoming this artificiality. Therefore, its interpretation is wide: wherever a measure is taken under the FEU Treaty, full consideration must be given to protecting the environment. This wide interpretation should not let us forget that environmental requirements should be taken into consideration at the formulation and implementation of policies, not of individual measures: it is true, however, that a specific policy is made operational by individual measures. It is therefore doubtful whether each individual measure in the internal market, agriculture or transport policy must take into consideration the environmental requirements which appears too far-reaching. In any case, EU institutions have a very broad discretion in putting the principle of art.11 TFEU into practice. Since art.11, in contrast to its 1987 version, no longer states a fact but rather propounds the necessity of procedure for EU policy, its application in practice will depend almost entirely on the political will of EU institutions to make this provision operational. Again, only in extreme cases could it be argued that EU policies do not take into account environmental protection requirements in their definition and implementation. Normally, the wide discretion which is available under art.11 TFEU would not make such an action successful.

To give some examples: to what extent transport policy promotes a European network of high-speed trains is a question, for or against which a number of environmental and other arguments can be raised. The promotion of biomass for fuel by agricultural policy would save fossil fuels, but would at the same time promote monocultures, large-scale use of pesticides and reduce biodiversity.

---

[79] *R v Minister of Agriculture* (C–157/96) [1998] E.C.R. I–2211, paras 63–64; *United Kingdom v Commission* (C–180/96) [1998] E.C.R. I–2265, paras 99–100: "Where there is uncertainty as to the existence or extent of risks to human health, the institutions may take protective measures without having to wait until the reality and seriousness of those risks become fully apparent. That approach is borne out by Art.130 r(1) of the EC Treaty, according to which Community policy on the environment is to pursue the objective inter alia of protecting human health. Art.130r(2) provides that that policy is to be based in particular on the principles that preventive action should be taken and that environmental protection requirements must be integrated into the definition and implementation of other Community policies."

Other examples are provisions to ban aeroplane flights at night, the decommissioning of used platforms at sea, development of an electrical windpark in or next to a natural habitat, requirement for an environment impact assessment in all cases where a project is co-financed with EU funds, and so on. The question to what extent such measures are to be taken is in all these cases of a political, not a legal nature. The integration requirement of art.11 TFEU does not provide for a useful solution to these problems.

Until now, the Court of Justice never discussed the question, whether an EU act would have to be annulled, because it did not take into consideration environmental requirements. Some legal writers are of the opinion that such a legal act would, as a matter of law, have to be annulled. An example is Regulation 1954/2003[80] which gave the EU fishing fleet access to the waters around the Azores, without even discussing the impact on the very vulnerable local ecosystems. The Azores brought a case to the General Court[81]; however, their application was considered inadmissible, and the appeal was rejected.[82] In my opinion, the complete lack of even considering the environmental impact of the Regulation constitutes a breach of art.11 TFEU and could lead to the annulment of the Regulation.

Precautionary principle

1–27   The precautionary principle was inserted into art.174(2) EC in 1993, while the prevention principle had already been present in the Treaty since 1987. Origin and content of the precautionary principle are unclear. Since no definition exists in the Treaties, the principle is open to broad interpretation. The Convention on the protection of the marine environment in the North-East Atlantic (OSPAR), to which the European Union adhered,[83] describes the precautionary principle as a principle:

> "by virtue of which preventive measures are taken when there are reasonable grounds for concern that substances or energy introduced directly or indirectly into the environment may bring about damage to human health, harm living resources,... even where there is no conclusive evidence of a causal relationship between the inputs and effects."

The principle was mentioned in the Declaration of the United Nations Conference in Rio de Janeiro in 1992[84] and increasingly it is understood to justify measures also in cases where scientific uncertainty exists as to the cause and extent of environmental impairment. In its reviewed strategy on sustainable development of 2006—mentioned in para.1.11, above—the European Council defined the precautionary principle as follows, clearly going beyond the Rio

---

[80] Reg.1954/2003 [2003] OJ L289/1.

[81] General Court, *Azores v Council* (T–37/04) [2008] E.C.R. II–103.

[82] Court of Justice, *Azores v Council* (C–444/08P), judgment of November 26, 2009.

[83] Dec.98/249 [1998] OJ L104/1.

[84] Rio de Janeiro Declaration on Environment and Development, June 16, 1992, Principle 15: "In order to protect the environment, the precautionary approach shall be widely applied by States according to their capabilities. Where there are threats of serious or irreversible damages, lack of full scientific certainty shall not be used as a reason for postponing cost-effective measures to prevent environmental degradation." The reference to "approach" rather than to "principle" was due to US objections to the use of the word "principle".

Declaration: "In case of scientific uncertainty, use the appropriate assessment procedures and preventive measures in order to avoid damage to human health and the environment".

An example for the application of the precautionary principle is the taking of measures to ban or restrict the circulation of substances or products such as asbestos, cadmium and phthalates: under Regulation 793/93,[85] economic operators asked that for each of these products a risk assessment be made to find out whether the environmental and human risk justifies restrictions. Applying the precautionary principle would mean that EU measures can be taken without waiting for such a risk assessment, which all too often takes several years to be elaborated, is inconclusive or is interpreted differently as to the results. Another example is climate change: the European Union adhered to the United Nations' Convention on Climate Change which undertakes to combat global warming, while the latest scientific evidence of man-made global warming—at least in the eyes of some—still lacks.

Sometimes it is argued that the adoption of the precautionary principle   **1–28** requires a scientific assessment of risks.[86] This argument seems to stem more from political efforts to reduce the field of application of this principle as far as possible; indeed, art.191(2) TFEU does not contain any such condition and the abovementioned examples show the political character of these arguments: if for precautionary measures a scientific risk assessment is necessary, it would be necessary for any measure. However, such a requirement could only be introduced by way of legislation.[87]

Similar considerations apply to other requests to limiting the application of the precautionary principle to cases where there is the possibility of an extreme, irreversible hazard, where there is a need to adopt measures urgently or to limit it to provisional measures only. None of these conditions are found in art.191(2) TFEU, which demonstrates the political rather than legal character of these arguments.

The Court of Justice applied the precautionary principle in the above-mentioned cases C–157/96 and C–180/96,[88] though the English version referred to the prevention principle only, whereas the German and other languages mentioned the precautionary and prevention principles. Of course, the Court did not request that the Commission, before pronouncing an export ban for British beef, should have made a risk assessment.

The General Court considered it a "general principle of Community law".[89]

---

[85] See in detail paras 6–27 et seq.

[86] See, e.g. Dir.1999/39 on baby food [1999] OJ L124/8, 4th recital: "Whereas, taking into account the Community's international obligations, in cases where the relevant scientific evidence is insufficient, the precautionary principle allows the Community to provisionally adopt measures on the basis of available pertinent information, pending an additional assessment of risk and a review of the measure within a reasonable period of time."

[87] See also Court of Justice, *Afton Chemical* (C–343/09) judgment of July 8, 2010, where neither the Commission nor the Court considered a risk assessment to be necessary before the decision on the restriction of use of a chemical substance was taken.

[88] See fn.79, above.

[89] General Court, *Artegodan a.o. v Commission* (Joined Cases T–74/00, T–76/00 and others) [2002] E.C.R. II–4945, n.184: "the precautionary principle can be defined as a general principle of Community law requiring the competent authorities to take appropriate measures to prevent specific potential risks to public health, safety and the environment, by giving precedence to the requirements related to the protection of those interests over economic interests. Since the Community institutions

The Commission adopted in the year 2000 a Communication on the precautionary principle where it stated[90]:

> "whether or not to invoke the precautionary principle is a decision exercised where scientific information is insufficient, inconclusive, or uncertain and where there are indications that the possible effects on the environment, or human, animal or plant health may be potentially dangerous and inconsistent with the chosen level of protection."

Prevention principle

1–29 It is unclear to what extent the prevention principle has content independent from the precautionary principle, although the history of the principles' insertion into the EC Treaty suggests there is none. There seems to be no EU action which would be possible under the precautionary principle, but not under the prevention principle—and vice versa. Since both principles are, in practice, almost always used together and there is no definition for either of them in the TFEU, the added legal value of one to the other is not visible; therefore, they should be used synonymously.[91]

The precautionary/prevention principle is of overriding importance in every serious environmental policy, since it allows or requires action to be taken at an early stage. Measures are no longer primarily meant to repair damage or impairment after it has occurred: instead, measures are to be taken earlier, to prevent impairment or damage occurring. This also makes economic sense since it is normally far more costly to clean up or remedy impairment after it has occurred—if any remedy is possible at all. Article 191(2) TFEU does not specify which form the preventive action should take: it is probably "better" to produce goods without cadmium, but once cadmium-containing products are on the market—batteries, crates, window frames, etc.—should they be recycled, burnt with or without energy recovery, or landfilled? No answer can be found in the prevention/ precautionary principle.

Rectification of damage at source

1–30 The principle that environmental damage[92] should, as a priority, be rectified at source was inserted into the Treaty in 1987. It represents wishful thinking rather than reality. Indeed, to rectify environmental damage from cars—air pollution, land use, noise, traffic congestion, waste generation, etc.—at source would mean that cars would have to be abolished or at the very least absolute priority be given to public transport, the price of fuel be increased in order to reduce the use of

---

are responsible, in all their spheres of activity, for the protection of public health, safety and the environment, the precautionary principle can be regarded as an autonomous principle stemming from the abovementioned Treaty provisions. It is settled case-law that, in the field of public health, the precautionary principle implies that where there is uncertainty as to the existence or the extent of risks to human health, the institutions may take precautionary measures without having to wait until the reality and seriousness of those risks become fully apparent."

[90] Commission, Communication on the precautionary principle COM(2000) 1.

[91] See also Cases C–157/96 and C–180/96 (fn.79, above) where the Court based its reasoning that in order to combat the BSE disease, full evidence of the extent and seriousness of a risk was not required in order to take action on the prevention principle, not on the precautionary principle.

[92] About half of the linguistic versions of the Treaty use the word "damage", the other half "impairment".

cars, restrictions on the making of cars—maximum fuel consumption, maximum speed and so on—be imposed or other measures taken. This would have implications on production, employment and investments for which no country in the world seems to be prepared. The present technology of catalytic converters for cars is clearly an end-of-the-pipe technology, but it is not seriously challenged. Similar examples could easily be given for measures regarding climate change, waste generation, forest decline, acidification or marine pollution.

It is not clear what "rectified" means. Certainly, as in all other cases, EU institutions have a large discretion as to what measures they wish to take, and the time-span and content of these measures. Since environmental damage (impairment) often cannot really be completely rectified, it must be up to the legislature to decide how the damage, once it has occurred, can be minimised, how the environment can be restored—at the same or at a different place—and further damage be prevented.

As mentioned above at para.1–18, the Court of Justice has justified a regional import ban for waste amongst other arguments with this principle, which leads, in the Court's opinion, to the necessity of disposing of waste as close to the place of waste generation as possible. In a similar case, the Court of Justice declared a German provision which required that the disposal of waste take place in Germany to be compatible with the Treaty since it:

> "reflects the pursuit of an objective which is in conformity with the principle laid down in Article 130r(2) of the Treaty that environmental damage should, as a principle, be rectified at source.[93]"

As stated, the judgment in the first case seems more motivated by   **1–31** considerations about the division of responsibilities between the European Union and Member States. It seems impossible to deduce a legal rule that "waste shall be disposed at the closest possible place" from the principle that is discussed here. Legal literature discusses, whether the principle of rectifying damage at source does not lead the European Union to be required, in future, to adopt, as a priority, emission limit values rather than adopt or favour quality standards.[94]

EU practice, though, certainly prefers quality standards for air and water pollution.[95] This tendency has been more pronounced since 1991–1992, when the EU debate on deregulation, subsidiarity and flexibility started.

Using the same reasoning as in the two waste judgments mentioned above, the Court of Justice could, in theory, state that the principle of rectification at source requires EU legislation to be based mainly on emission standards. Also, the Court could come to the conclusion that the catalytic converter approach, which EU law had adopted to minimise car emissions, was not compatible with this principle and that cars and fuels had to be developed which generate fewer pollutants. These examples demonstrate how far the reasoning could go, if the principles of

---

[93] *Commission v Germany* (C–422/92) [1995] E.C.R. I–1097; the judgment referred to a time when EU secondary law did not yet contain a provision which dealt with the export or import of wastes for disposal. The judgment therefore dealt only with primary law. The relevant EU provisions were introduced in 1993.
[94] H. Sevenster, *Milieubeleid en Gemeenschapsrecht* (Deventer, 1992), p.111; Jans-Vedder, *European environmental law* 3rd edn (Groningen, 2008) p.22.
[95] See below, paras 7–01 and 8–01.

art.191(2) TFEU are turned into legal rules—leaving even aside the point that at best they only constitute legal rules for European Union, not for national or regional provisions.

The conclusion is that this principle well *allows* that EU provisions are established which deal with import or export bans on waste, but it does not *require* the elaboration of such provisions. The principle allows EU emission limit values to be preferred over quality standards, but it does not require that such an approach be taken: a ban on waste exports to developing countries[96] may be supported by this principle, but the principle does not impose such a ban to be pronounced. No Member State could bring the Council before the European Court, if the Council were adopting other measures; and it may be added that no Member State would have been entitled, in the absence of a Council measure on the export ban, to pronounce such an export ban unilaterally.

Polluter-pays principle

1–32   This principle was introduced into the Treaty in 1987, though it has existed at EU level since 1973.[97] Its linguistic versions are quite different: while the English version states "the polluter should pay", there are several versions which affirm "the polluter pays" and the German text talks of the principle of causation. As all versions are of equal value and the principle, as any other notion of EU law, must be interpreted autonomously by virtue of EU law and without recourse to national interpretations,[98] its content is difficult to determine: who is a polluter? A person who contaminates the environment or a person who exceeds existing limit values? Is a car driver a polluter, the car manufacturer or the producer or importer of the fuel? Furthermore, who is to pay (or should pay) for emissions or damage that was caused? What about damage in another Member State or in a third country? Should car manufacturers or drivers also pay for the construction of roads? How much should be paid? Is an investment in cleaner technologies also a payment?

The questions demonstrate that the polluter-pays principle is first of all an economic principle and has to be understood as expressing the concept that the cost of environmental impairment, damage and clean-up should not be borne via taxes by society, but that the person who caused the pollution should bear those costs. Its transfer to the EU Treaties has led to all sorts of anomalies which have not much to do with law. First, hardly any Union text contains provisions on who shall pay for what or any other provision which puts the polluter-pays principle into practice: if the principle were legally binding and enforceable, this would be a systematic omission that could hardly be tolerated; however, no one has as yet invoked that principle and claimed damages.

1–33   Secondly, if the polluter and not the taxpayer had to pay for pollution, subventions and state aids would not be in line with this principle and would have to be deleted. However, EU measures have from the very beginning accepted that undertakings and other economic operators may receive state aid and have set up general rules for such aid.[99] The same applies to EU environmental aid, which is

---

[96] Example given by P. Pagh, *E.U.-Miljoeret* 2nd edn (Copenhagen, 1996), p.81.
[97] Rec.75/436 (fn.16, above).
[98] See *Kraaijeveld* (C–72/95) [1996] E.C.R. I–5403.
[99] See Rec.75/436 (fn.16, above).

given to Member States under the Structural Funds, the Cohesion Fund, LIFE+ and other budgetary titles. If the polluter-pays principle were a legally binding principle, the Cohesion Fund[100] would certainly be partly incompatible with it since it also finances clean-up measures. However, no legal writer has ever claimed any enforcement of the polluter-pays principle with regard to state aids.

In reality, in all Member States and at EU level the clean-up of the environment is seen as a task for public authorities which exists independently from the question of whether a polluter can be identified and asked to pay for pollution. Such an identification is practically impossible in cases of groundwater or coastal water pollution, forest decline, soil erosion, desertification, climate change, smog in urban areas and numerous pollution from past activities. Public authorities are thus the only ones to ensure a clean-up or to take other remedial or preventive measures to stop continued contamination.

A rather sad illustration on the application of the polluter-pays principles is found in Directive 2004/35 on environmental liability.[101] The Commission proposal had suggested that in the case, where the polluter of environmental damage could not be identified or was unable to pay, the Member States should be obliged to restore the impaired environment. The final version of the Directive, invoking the polluter-pays principle, provides that in such cases no obligation exists to restore the environment. Thus, it is to be expected that in such cases, the environment is normally not restored, and the high number of contaminated sites within the EU demonstrates that this is part of a deliberate policy.

On the whole, the polluter-pays principle *allows* EU institutions to adopt measures which charge persons who cause environmental pollution to bear the cost of pollution; however, this possibility would also be available to EU institutions without the principle being inserted in art.191(1) TFEU. In its 2006 strategy for sustainable development, mentioned in para.1–11, above, the European Council interpreted the polluter-pays principle as follows:

> "Prices shall reflect the true societal costs of consumption and production and polluters should pay for the damage which they caused to human health and the environment. This, indeed, is far away from a legally binding principle."

6.   Conditions for action

General remarks

Article 191(3) TFEU lists a number of conditions which EU environmental policy should take into account. This obligation refers to the policy as a whole, not to each individual measure adopted at EU level. The provision addresses all EU institutions and bodies. The words "taken into account" indicate that the paragraph does not contain preconditions for EU actions, which is further clarified by the fact that no details are given as to which condition is to be

1–34

---

[100] See Reg.1164/94 establishing a Cohesion Fund [1994] OJ L130/1, art.3: "[The Fund may provide assistance for] projects resulting from measures adopted pursuant to Art.130s of the Treaty.]" Since then, this Regulation was repealed and replaced by Regulation 1084/2006 [2006] OJ L 210/79 which does not contain an equivalent provision.

[101] Dir.2004/35 (fn.72, above).

attained, which level of regional development requires action (or derogations) nor what data would be needed for action. No other sector of EU policy has such conditions laid down in the Treaty.

In EU practice, the four conditions only play a subordinate role. They are rarely mentioned in the preamble of legal texts; references to them are slightly more frequent in explanatory memorandums for legislative proposals. Their legal impact is hardly measurable except for the cost-benefit condition, which is used by economic operators to object to measures that would internalise the environmental costs or make the polluter pay.

Available scientific data

1–35   This criterion states the obvious: it only requires that account be taken of the available data. The European Union need not even order its own studies before shaping its policy or take individual measures, but may simply draw on the available data. Nor is there any need to give scientific evidence that a specific measure would be effective, which is not really possible in any case. In particular, the precautionary/prevention principle allows action without definite scientific proof being available. This principle would lose much of its force if unequivocal data had to be produced before any measure could be taken. In order to improve information on the environment, a European Environment Agency was set up in Copenhagen[102] which has been operational since the end of 1993. The Agency has the task to collect, process and distribute data on the environment in order to improve knowledge of scientific and technical data.

It also has the task of publishing a report, at regular intervals, on the state of the EU environment.[103]

Regional conditions

1–36   The provision that the environmental conditions in the various regions of the Union be taken into account is a reminder that the environment within the European Union is by no means uniform, but that geographical, climatic, soil, water and other conditions vary greatly from one area to another. The provision does not require the taking into account of divergency: for this reason some EU legislation contains specific derogations whilst other does not. Where derogations are given, they are never directly applied to a specific region – though sometimes to small islands, mountainous areas or outermost regions, but instead to a specific

---

[102] Reg.1210/90 on the establishment of the European Environment Agency and the European Environment Information and Observation Network [1990] OJ L120/1.

[103] So far, the Union has published eight reports on the state of the environment: State of the environment, First Report (Brussels, Luxembourg, 1977); State of the environment, Second Report (Brussels and Luxembourg, 1979), The state of the environment in the EEC (Luxembourg, 1986); The state of the environment in the European Community, COM (92) 23, Vol.III of April 3, 1992; European Environment Agency: Environment in the European Union (Copenhagen, 1995); European Environment Agency: Environment in the European Union at the turn of the century (Luxembourg, 1999); European Environment Agency: The European Environment. State and outlook 2005 (Copenhagen, 2005); European Environment Agency, The European environment. State and outlook 2010 (Copenhagen, 2010).

Member State,[104] which well reflects the small direct influence that regions have in the decision-making procedure. Instead of giving a direct derogation for a Member State, EU legislation may provide for indirect derogations, e.g. for less sensitive or mountainous areas or small islands.[105]

Potential benefits and charges

This condition reads "advantages and charges of action or lack of action" in most EU languages but not in English, because it was thought, in 1987 when the provision was inserted, that "costs and benefits" were equivalent to "advantages and charges". This is obviously not the case, at least not in the political debate, where discussion on the advantages and disadvantages of EU environmental measures has been reduced, de facto, to the economic costs and benefits of an EU measure. Also since economists have, up until now, not yet developed a standardised method of how to calculate in monetary terms the environmental benefits of a measure, this debate is all too often reduced to the question of how much the envisaged measure will cost trade and industry. This development has been particularly evident in EU activity since the early 1990s and more specifically in the measures to combat air pollution in the transport sector, where the Commission justified a number of derogations with nothing more than the argument that they were not "cost-effective". The advantages-charges factor suggests that the full range of short-, medium- and long-term measures be considered in an attempt to assess the effect of taking action or failing to do so. This consideration is not to be limited to economic aspects, but has to include social, employment, ecological, human and other aspects. At the end of this appraisal, if doubts still persist as to whether the measures will be sufficiently effective, the precautionary or prevention principle comes into play, together with the express mandate of art.191(1) TFEU that the European Union not only preserve but also improve the quality of the environment.

    The provision gives no details of the ways and means of taking account of the potential charges and advantages. In this respect, the political resolutions adopted by the Council and the decisions on the EU environmental action programmes under art.192(3) TFEU become of importance: where the Union institutions approved or adopted a programme or a number of actions of environmental measures, this will normally be sufficient proof that according to the best knowledge of the EU institutions the advantages of a specific measure outweigh the disadvantages.

1–37

Economic and social development

The condition on the economic and social development of the Union as a whole and the balanced development of its regions is meant to reflect the less-developed Member States' concern that environmental protection provisions should not be

1–38

---

[104] Examples: Dir.88/609 on large combustion plants (1988) OJ L336/1 where Spain, Portugal and Greece obtained special derogations; see also para.8–37; Dir.94/62 on packaging and packaging waste [1994] OJ L365/10 where Greece, Portugal and Ireland obtained derogations; on this Dir. see also para.10–49.

[105] See, e.g. Directive 1999/31 on landfills (1999) OJ L182/1 which provides in art.3(4) for derogations for small islands and isolated settlements.

imposed at the expense of economic growth. This criterion is so broadly drafted that it covers practically all economic and social development. Every EU-wide rule inevitably implies a degree of standardisation and harmonisation and cannot, therefore, take account of every individual region. Similarly, the same scientific and technical data which demonstrate a need for action may not be available in every region; however, this cannot be a decisive factor in differentiating. The European Union also has the task of ensuring environmental improvement in all parts of the Community, although it is obvious that any specific measure will bring greater advantages for some regions more than for others.

The Union institutions must weigh up all these factors and produce an overall assessment. At the end of the day it is up to the Council and the European Parliament to decide to what extent regional differences should lead to specific wording in the final texts adopted at EU level.

EU practice has never taken into consideration the situation of specific regions, but, as already mentioned, has from time to time given derogations to specific Member States—which, until 2004, mainly coincided with the so-called "Cohesion Fund-countries" (Greece, Spain, Portugal, Ireland) that were economically lagging behind. In the area of air pollution, a directive was adopted in 2001 on "national emission ceilings", which fixed a certain quantity of allowed pollution emissions per Member State.[106] As can be seen, this concept has little to do with regional differences (which could be very great between Lombardy and Calabria, Catalunya and Estremadura, Essex and Northern Ireland, Hamburg and Thüringen, etc.) but more to do with a certain renationalisation of environmental policy.

---

[106] Dir.2001/81 [2001] OJ L309/22.

CHAPTER 2

Actors, Instruments, Decision-making Procedures

1. Actors

EU environmental policy is conceived and elaborated by the EU institutions, with of course, considerable input from national governments and other national actors. The EU institutions contribute in differing degrees to the making of EU environmental policy; art.288 TFEU provides for the legal instruments to carry out the Union tasks in the making of EU environmental law. Hereafter, the different actors will be described, followed by the instruments for the making of environmental law and the decision-making procedure.

2–01

The European Commission
The Commission has in particular the following tasks (see also art.17 TEU):

2–02

- make proposals for new environmental legislation;
- ensure that the provisions of the EU Treaties and the measures taken by the institutions pursuant thereto are applied;
- formulate opinions and recommendations; take decisions and "participate in the shaping of measures" where the Treaty so provides.

Administrative structures

Since January 1, 2007, the Commission consists of 27 commissioners—one for each Member State—appointed for five years by the Council.[1] This number will be reduced with the appointment of a new Commission in 2014, unless the European Council unanimously decides otherwise (art.17(5) TEU). The President of the Commission is appointed by the Council acting in its composition of heads of State or Government and with approval of the European Parliament.[2]

2–03

The Commission autonomously divides the general work among its members. Each ordinary member of the Commission has a private office which consists of six members who assist him in his task.

The administrative services of the Commission consist of Directorate-Generals for the different areas (e.g. transport, agriculture and information); at

---

[1] See art.17(5) TEU: "as from 1 November 2014, the Commission shall consist of a number of members, including its President and the High Representative of the Union for Foreign Affairs and Security policy, corresponding to two thirds of the number of Member States, unless the European Council, acting unanimously, decides to alter this number".

[2] For details see art.17(7) TEU.

present there are some 30 Directorate-Generals, some of which, as for instance the Legal Service, are known as "Services". A General Secretariat organises the daily administration of the Commission and the Directorates-General. A member of the Commission may be responsible for several Directorates-General; conversely, one general directorate may, for different parts of its activity, be under the responsibility of several commissioners. Overall, there is a staff of some 32,000 officials, among whom are a number of national officials on secondment with the Commission for up to three years and persons employed on a contractual basis.[3] The Commission works in all the official languages—at present 23 (art.55 TEU)—though in daily practice English and French dominate.

2–04   Environmental matters are mainly, but not exclusively, the responsibility of the Directorate-General for Environment (DG ENV) which, between 2009 and 2014, is placed under the responsibility of the Slovenian member of the Commission, Mr Jan Potocnik. After the establishment of a new Directorate-general for climate change issues, the Directorate-General for the environment comprises about 400 officials, to which a number of persons on secondment and under contract (overall some 50) have to be added; about half of these officials have a university education.[4] The Commission's staff policy tries to ensure that officials change their jobs every three to five years. This policy, introduced under UK influence, favours technocratic behaviour, not expert knowledge. Combined with strong incitements for striving for promotion—annual assessment, increased payment, power and prestige—this leads to officials' attitudes as " his masters voice" rather than to conceive policies, strategies, programmes and legislation which effectively protect the environment; this influence of staff policy is particularly strong for senior officials.

The 2009 budget provides for environmental expenses of about 450 million €[5] compared for example with 55 billion € for agricultural policy and 28 billion € for regional policy. About half of the environment budget is earmarked for the financial instrument LIFE[6]; other important sums are destined for forest management (18 million), civil protection and natural disasters (13 million), marine pollution (4 million), environmental thematic strategies, and a financial contribution to the European Environmental Agency (27 million) and awareness-raising measures (15 million); these last two sections are sailing under the wrong flag of "implementation measures". However, these sums only cover the expenses coming under the management of Directorate-General ENV; they do not include expenses for example on alternative energies, clean transport, agricultural measures, research, etc. In 1992, the Commission estimated the total EU expenses for the environment at 600 million € per year; no new overall

[3] Budget 2009 for the European Union [2009] OJ L69/1, Ch.7.
[4] These figures may be compared to those of national environmental administration (quoted from C. Demmke, *Europäische Umweltpolitik und Nationale Verwaltungen* (Maastricht, 1998), p.98 who collected the data from national departments): Belgium 41 (at central level), Denmark 100 (plus 1,000 in the Environmental Agency), Germany 780 (plus 1,820 in the Environmental Agency), Greece 250, Spain 500, France 2,300 (plus 6,000 in the Environmental Agencies), Ireland 480 (plus 327 in the Environmental Agency), Italy 450 (plus 5,220 in the Environmental Agencies), the Netherlands 1,000, Austria 300 (plus 230 in the Environmental Agency), Portugal 3,500, Finland 300 (plus 500 in the Environmental Agency), Sweden 130 (plus 750 in the Environmental Agency), United Kingdom 3,700 (plus 2,260 in the Environmental Agency).
[5] See Budget 2009(fn.3, above), Ch.7.
[6] Reg.614/2007 concerning the Financial Instrument for the Environment (LIFE+) [2007] OJ L149/1.

estimation has been made since, though this figure might now be considerably higher; all depends on what is considered to be an "environmental" measure.

The structure and working methods of the Commission continue to be considerably affected by the original aim of the EC Treaty to organise a common agricultural policy, to open up national markets and to realise the four fundamental freedoms of the EC Treaty, free movement of goods and services, capital and labour. Environmental policy, which started in the early 1970s without an express legal basis in the Treaty, was considered an illegitimate child, and this perception only gradually began to disappear when, in 1987, the Single European Act "legitimised" it by inserting an environmental chapter in the Treaty. The Commission's environmental activity, orientated towards achieving the objectives laid down in arts 3 and 191(1) TFEU, may be structured for the purpose of presentation into activities initiating new measures, activities of management and monitoring activities. Legal questions of monitoring activities will be discussed in detail in Ch.12.

Commission initiatives

Under the FEU Treaty the Commission has the exclusive right to initiate new environmental legal measures at EU level. As in the early 1970s, when the European Union started an environmental policy, no explicit legal basis for environmental matters existed in the EC Treaty, it was considered opportune to lay down the objectives, principles and priorities of EU action in environmental action programmes. These different environmental action programmes constituted, at least in the past,[7] a frame for initiatives, but never put limits on such actions. Indeed, numerous proposals for directives or regulations which were made had never been previously announced by an environmental action programme, and initiatives which the action programmes announced were not necessarily presented by the Commission.[8] The action programmes are completed by annual working programmes which the Commission publishes every year: the published version, however, only contains the most important new activities. Furthermore, each member of the Commission may have for his area of responsibility, a work programme which directs the work of the administrative services. Whether the Treaty provisions of arts 192(2) and 192(3) TFEU limited the Commission's right of initiative, will be discussed below.[9]

2–05

Next to these general programmes, the Commission submits from time to time action programmes for specific sectors, such as groundwater and biodiversity, for example, for which the environmental Directorate-General is, as for the general environmental action programme, the file-leading department. Under the sixth environmental action programme, the European Union decided to develop thematic strategies for soil protection, urban environment and the marine

---

[7] Since 1993, art.192(3) TFEU provides that general environmental action programmes are adopted in the form of a decision by the European Parliament and the Council jointly. See Dec.1600/2002 laying down the Sixth Community Environment Action Programme [2002] OJ L242/1.

[8] A recent example of a legislative proposal which was not announced in the Sixth Environmental Action Programme is the proposal for a directive on the assessment and management of floods, [2006] OJ C67/38, which later became Directive 2007/60 [2007] OJ L288/27. An example of legislation which was announced, but never proposed until now, is a directive on construction and demolition waste, Sixth Environment Action Programme (fn.7, above), art.8(2)(IV).

[9] See para.2–21, below.

environment, the use of pesticides, the use of natural resources, the recycling of waste and air pollution[10] which constitute, de facto, sectoral action programmes. These thematic strategies were to be submitted to the European Parliament and the Council and were, where appropriate, adopted under art.251 EC.[11] This provision aimed at avoiding a circumvention of art.192(3) TFEU which gives the European Parliament a co-decision right for environmental action programmes.

More general communications which the Commission submits are presented as green papers, white papers, strategy papers or else are given another name, without any specific difference between these communications; normally, they do not provide for specific legislative measures. Examples of recent times concern communications on adapting to climate change,[12] on the halting the loss of biodiversity beyond 2010,[13] on the review of environmental policy[14] and on the prevention of natural and man made disasters.[15]

In view of art.11 TFEU, precursors of which have appeared in similar Treaty provisions since 1987, other initiatives in other areas such as agriculture, industrial or regional policy or transport shall take into consideration the environmental requirements. Initiatives-programmatic initiatives or individual measures-are prepared by the Directorate-General responsible, with generally close participation from the environmental and other interested Directorate-Generals.

2–06 The Commission decides on all drafts as a college (i.e. all Commissioners decide on the drafts). This also leads to situations, where the Commission does not dare to take majority decisions—better: make proposals based on the majority of its members—for fear of appearing not united in the public opinion. Examples are initiatives on climate change (increasing the EU commitment to a 30 per cent reduction of greenhouse gas emissions until 2020) or a clear position of the safety of nuclear installations within the European Union, following the Japanese nuclear incident of March 2011. This clearly appears as lack of leadership in the eyes of the public.

In view of the shortage of staff in all its departments and the often considerable size of these (agriculture, industry, foreign trade and competition) drafts, it remains only theoretical that a proposal, which has been developed for several months or even years by the file-leading department, can still be significantly amended by other departments. The general approach, the structure and most of the detailed provisions are de facto carried in the form proposed by the file-leading department and are only in exceptional cases put into question at the political level of the Commission. The shortage of staff thus makes it extremely difficult to integrate environmental requirements into other policies on an everyday basis. Indeed, identifying the specific environmental interest in the numerous discussions and preparatory meetings for decisions inside the Commission requires time, human and financial resources and efforts, which the present Directorate-General for the environment does not have at its disposal.

---

[10] Sixth Environmental Action Programme (fn.7, above).
[11] Sixth Environmental Action Programme (fn.7, above), art.4.
[12] Commission, COM(2009) 147.
[13] Commission, COM(2010) 4.
[14] Commission, COM(2009) 304.
[15] Commission, COM (2009) 82.

In order to improve the integration of environmental requirements within its own administration, the Commission adopted internal rules in 1993,[16] which were revised in 1997 and 2002[17] and provide that all Commission proposals shall be checked for their economic, social and environmental impact; where such impact is likely, a detailed impact assessment is to be made on all three aspects, including consultations with stakeholders. No agreed method for making such assessments exists and time pressure, political requirements or ambitions, lobby influence and similar aspects limit their usefulness. The economic and social value of the environment is not easily accessible to econometric determination— what is the economic value of a butterfly species, a woodlouse or a mosquito? In practice, therefore, these Commission impact assessments are not too credible and are often used to impede or restrict environmental initiatives which are considered detrimental to economic interests.

Suggestions to take initiatives for new legislative measures come from all sources. Council and European Parliament may, via resolutions, ask for this or that new proposal and the Council may, during the debate over or adoption of a Commission proposal, request another measure to be proposed or an existing proposal to be amended. The Commissioner responsible for the environment may wish a given new proposal to be developed or the environmental Directorate-General may take the initiative. From outside the EU institutions, the initiative for action might be suggested by Member States or it might stem from international activities such as existing or new environmental conventions, or be proposed by lobby groups, researchers, environmental organisations or have other origins. In all cases, however, the college of the Commission will have to formally decide on a text which is submitted to it by its administration before there can be any question of a Commission initiative.   **2–07**

Connected to these legislative initiatives is the possibility of the Commission to initiate new orientations for environmental policy. Recent examples concern soil management, marine environment protection, an integrated product policy or the management of resources. To what extent such political initiatives are, subsequently, followed by policy re-orientations or concrete actions by the Council and/or the Member States is different from one topic to the other. Generally, political statements by the Commission, the Council or the European Parliament have little or no effect, unless they are, later on, followed by binding legislative proposals and their adoption. This is explained by the fact that the European Union is not a State and political interests and priorities in Member States are often too divergent to accept an integrated, joint environment policy.

Administrative activities

The Commission's task to initiate new policies, strategies and individual measures is perceived by the Commission itself as its most important task: managing activity clearly ranks lower. One of the reasons for this is the express provision in art.192(4) TFEU, according to which it is the Member States which shall, as a rule, implement the measures decided at EU level. Since most of the Union's environmental legislation is adopted in the form of directives which are addressed to Member States, it is up to Member States to transpose these   **2–08**

---

[16] Written Question E–649/97(Díez de Rivera) [1997] OJ C367/33.
[17] Commission, Impact Assessment, COM (2002) 276 of June 5, 2002; see also para.4–38, below.

directives into national law and to ensure that these provisions are complied with. The Commission has the task of ensuring that EU environmental directives and regulations are properly applied.[18]

2–09   Besides this, the Commission has a number of tasks attributed to it by the different environmental directives or regulations, which concern the administering of the "Union acquis". These tasks include:

The collection of national legislation which was adopted in pursuance of the EU provisions. Since European environmental legislation dates back to the mid-1970s and Member States' legislation is variously amended, renewed, replaced, and often adopted at a regional level, sometimes even referring to non-environmental, more general legislation, the precise knowledge about the state of environmental legislation within the European Union is at times difficult to obtain. The Commission regularly mandates so-called implementation studies which examine the transposition of environmental directives by Member States. However, it refuses to disclose these studies.

The collection and comparison of national reports on the transposition and implementation of directives and the publication of European implementation reports. Most of European environmental directives and regulations provide for Member States to report regularly on the implementation measures adopted; the Commission is required to establish regular European reports. In view of considerable deficiencies in the national reporting and, subsequently, the Commission's reports, a directive was adopted in 1991 to streamline and improve the reporting.[19] However, this Directive has not brought about the desired improvements. The national and the Commission reports normally continue to be published late or even not at all, their content is frequently incomplete and does not comply with scientific or serious administrative standards. Judgments by the Court of Justice which blamed Member States for not submitting reports[20] had no visible effect

The collection and comparison of national clean-up or other plans for specific sectors or plants. Several directives, for instance on air quality, or nitrate concentrations in water plans, provide for clean-up programmes for regions which are contaminated, where pollutant levels are exceeded or for industrial plants to adapt to new legal requirements. Other directives, such as on the protection of birds, on water or on waste management, provide for management plans.

Member States are regularly obliged to send such plans or programmes to the Commission, which shall align and occasionally also compare them in order to obtain greater coherence. The number of directives asking for planning measures is in continuous increase since the early 1990s, although planning experience in conjunction with EU environmental law matters is anything but a success story. Indeed, the Commission occasionally attacks Member States in court for not having drawn up or submitted plans or programmes. However, the Commission hardly ever evaluates the national plans, compares them, tries to promote planning according to similar criteria or gives an overall assessment of the

---

[18] See paras 12–01 et seq., below.

[19] Dir.91/692 standardising and rationalising reports on the implementation of certain directives relating to the environment [1991] OJ L377/48.

[20] See for example Court of Justice, *Commission v Italy* (C–248/02) judgment of September 16, 2004; *Commission v Ireland* (C–406/03) judgment of October 26, 2004; *Commission v France* (C–191/04) judgment of June 16, 2005.

planning instruments and in particular on their monitoring, implementation and enforcement. In this way, plans give the wrong impression that they improve the protection of the environment, whereas this is often not the case.[21]

Exchange of experience concerning problems with the application of environmental measures. These comprise environmental directives which regularly ask Member States to plan improvements and clean-up, to promote or impose cleaner technologies and reduce pollutant emissions; examples are directives on the prevention of industrial accidents,[22] on permits for industrial installations[23] or for environmental impact assessment[24]. Discussion takes place on these questions as well as on how issues such as "best available technologies", licensing, inspection procedures or the interpretation of provisions in a directive are transposed into administrative practice, and furthermore, on co-operation in frontier regions or with administrations of another Member State. Often such exchanges between Member States' administrations are necessary or useful. Such an exchange also allows a transfer of environmental know-how from one administration to the other.

Information on new scientific and technical developments. EU directives also age over time and might have to be adapted due to scientific and technical developments. Most of this exchange normally takes place in the different committees for adapting directives to scientific and technical progress.

Elaboration of implementation measures. Directives may require that the Commission deal with forms and formulae, establish lists, registers, collect data, take individual decisions on national derogating measures or other technical measures to ensure a smooth application of the legislation. On its own initiative, the Commission may find it necessary to issue guidance or interpretation documents, convey its understanding of specific legislative provisions and inform about its policy following judgments of the Court of Justice.

Administration of funds. The amount of EU funding for environmental measures including in sectors such as energy, transport or research, has considerably increased over the years. These amounts are monitored according to specific regulations which lay out the legal basis for expenditure.[25] The Commission has to collect the national programmes or projects, assess them, select the most appropriate applications and decide on the European Union's financial participation, assisted in this on a regular basis by a committee made up of representatives from Member States.

Exchange of data. Almost all EU decisions require that the Commission collect data on the state of the environment, such as data on air or water pollution and soil contamination. The Commission organises the networks, the co-operation required between different parties and the related practical questions. These tasks are progressively being transferred to the European

---

[21] For more details, see L. Krämer, *Casebook on EU Environmental Law* (Oxford, 2002) pp.177 and 367. Examples of Court judgments on the lack of national programmes: *Commission v Germany* (C–454/01) judgment of June 10, 2004; *Commission v Ireland* (C–282/02) judgment of June 2, 2005; *Commission v Greece* (C–364/03) judgment of July 7, 2005.

[22] Dir.96/82 on the major accident hazards of certain industrial installations, [1997] OJ L10/13.

[23] Dir.2010/75 on industrial emissions, [2010] OJ L334/17.

[24] Dir.85/337 on the assessment of the effects of certain public and private projects on the environment [1985] OJ L175/40.

[25] See, e.g. Reg.614/2007 (LIFE+) (fn.6, above); Reg.1084/2006 establishing a Cohesion Fund [2006] OJ L210/79.

Environmental Agency or the EU's Statistical Office which need, however, assistance from the Commission, certainly in the beginning, combined, if necessary, with formal, binding decisions.

Participation in international discussions. Where environmental issues are discussed at international level, the Commission, beyond participation in the elaboration of conventions, etc., co-ordinates and aligns the position of the Member States and tries to ensure that internationally the Union speaks with one voice.[26]

Information of the wider public. The Commission is not an administrative body that can remain distanced from discussions about the organisation of Europe and its environment. It has to inform about the state of the environment, its policy and its individual measures and try to persuade, publicly, in committees or in bilateral meetings, policy makers, interest groups, environmental organisations, the media and the public of its proposals and the Union's decisions. For this purpose, press releases are made, speeches delivered, articles written, interviews granted, conferences, workshops or encounters organised, and information is placed on the website. In so doing it is fulfilling the objective which is outlined in art.17 TEU: to promote the general interest of the Community in environmental issues.

The Environment Agency and other "satellites"

2–19   During the last decades a number of bodies have been set up to assist the Commission in its work. The most relevant of these are:

- The European Environment Agency, which was created in 1990,[27] but only became operational in 1993 due to Member States' disagreement on its seat which was finally fixed in Copenhagen. The Agency has the task of collecting, processing and distributing information about the EU environment and publishing at regular intervals a report on the state of the environment. Its advice function is not limited to the Commission, but also extends to the other institutions and to Member States. It is headed by an executive director, who is appointed by the management board; this board is composed of Member States' representatives, two Commission representatives and two scientific experts appointed by the European Parliament. Non-EU states, which are members of the Agency, are also represented. The Agency has an annual budget of about 40 million € and a staff of about 120 persons, to which a network of about 2,000 persons in member countries have to be added.

  When the Agency was created there was much debate between the European Parliament and the Council over whether it should also have the function to enforce application of EU environmental law. The compromise reached provided that this question should be decided at a later stage. The amendment of the Agency's statute, adopted in 1999, does not contain anything on law enforcement[28]; as the European Parliament has no historic

---

[26] See for more details art.216 TFEU.

[27] Reg.1210/90 on the establishment of the European Environment Agency and the European Environment Information and Observation Network [1990] OJ L120/1.

[28] Reg.933/1999 amending Reg.1210/90 [1999] OJ L117/1.

memory, this question is no longer discussed. The Agency has to publish, every five years, a report on the state of the environment in the European Union; this delay was shortened to four years by the new Regulation transposing the Aarhus Convention into EU law.

- In 1993, a European Consultative Forum on the environment and sustainable development, was set up by the Commission,[29] consisting of 32 members from business, local and regional authorities, environmental and consumer organisations, trade unions and general environmental experts. The Forum was consulted by the Commission on any problem of European Union environmental policy. The impact of the opinions given by the Forum was rather limited, due mainly to its heterogenious composition. In 2001, it was closed, because the Commission wanted to establish "a sustainable round table which will report directly to the Commission's President"; this body was set up, but does not deploy any visible activity on environmental matters any more.[30]

- IMPEL. The fifth environmental action programme 1992 announced the creation of an implementation network with the primary task of promoting the "exchange of information and experiences and the development of common approaches at practical level, under the supervision of the Commission".[31] This network was set up under the name European Network for the Implementation and Enforcement of Environmental Law (IMPEL) by Member States. Driving force was the intention to avert requests for an EU environmental enforcement body on the one hand, to give in particular to German Länder the possibility of influencing the making of EU environmental legislation. IMPEL was an informal body and acted as an inter-governmental, not an integrated EU co-operation network. It tried to improve implementation of EU legislation and influence new Commission initiatives. In 2008, IMPEL transformed itself into an international association of environmental authorities, in order to obtain EU financing more easily. Overall, its impact is limited.

- The "Environmental Policy Review Group"—also an informal body. Its setting-up was announced by the fifth action programme.[32] It groups the Director-Generals from national central environmental administrations who meet with high officials from the Directorate-General Environment of the Commission to discuss the conception and shaping of the Commission's environmental strategies and initiatives. The Group has no secretariat of its own and its deliberations and conclusions are not made public, contrary to any transparency rules of the Commission.

The European Parliament

The European Parliament has played a prominent role in initiating and strengthening environmental issues at EU level since the early 1970s. Its proposals and suggestions for institutional and administrative structures, for new initiatives or proposals were very often taken up by the Commission, although

2–20

---

[29] Dec.93/701 [1993] OJ L328/53; amended by Dec.97/150 [1997] OJ L58/48.
[30] Dec.2001/704 [2001] OJ L258/20.
[31] Fifth environmental action programme [1993] OJ C138/5, Ch.9.
[32] Fifth environmental action programme [1993] OJ C138/5, Ch.9.

sometimes after some delay. One of the reasons for this is that the European Parliament also decides—along with the Council—on the Commission's budget and thus has a subtle means of pressure at its disposal.

Parliament's opinions on proposals for directives or regulations, obviously considerably influenced by the very active Parliamentary Committee on Environment, Public Health and Food Safety, may be summarised as follows:

- On general environmental questions or on horizontal legislation, Parliament constantly urges the Commission and the Council to do more and provide for even better environmental protection than the Commission had proposed. There seems to be few Commission environmental proposals where Parliament was of the opinion that they were too ambitious, too far-reaching or too protective. Parliament generally opposed soft law, environmental agreements or recommendations, environmental deregulation and other forms or attempts to reduce environmental protection.

- Proposals of a more technical nature are only exceptionally challenged as to the approach chosen by the Commission. The amendments suggested concern the need for more and stricter environmental protection. Parliament not only looked for more progressive and efficient environmental legislation, but also pleaded for greater transparency in environmental matters, better access to information and greater participation of environmental organisations in the decision-making process.

- Parliament gradually managed to introduce environmental requirements into its opinions on proposals for legislative acts in agricultural and regional matters, the internal market or other policies and in this it was more advanced than the Commission or the Council. This aspect is, however, influenced by the majority groups in Parliament: where these groups are conservative, environmental-minded opinions are more difficult to obtain.

2–21   Parliament's influence on the development of environmental legislation has been constantly increased over the years. Article 225(2) TFEU, introduced in the EC Treaty in 1993, gave Parliament the right to require, with the majority of its component members, that the Commission submit a proposal for a directive or regulation. The Commission and the Council are of the opinion that this right does not question the Commission's discretion to decide alone whether it submits a proposal or not. This seems incorrect since the majority requirement in art.225 would not make much sense otherwise: the European Parliament has always had the possibility of asking for a proposal of a legal measure. Thus, the Council's and Commission's interpretation would remove the efficacy of the insertion of art.225(2) into the Treaty. In 1994, the Parliament formally asked for a proposal of a directive on environmental liability: the Commission followed up this request in early 2002 only.[33]

Article 192(3) TFEU provides that general environmental action programmes be adopted by a joint decision of the Council and the European Parliament. Since a decision is "binding in its entirety",[34] the sixth environmental action programme and future programmes will be binding. During the review of the fifth

---

[33] [2002] OJ C151E/132.
[34] art.288 TFEU.

and the discussions of the sixth action programme, the European Parliament's objective therefore was to have concrete provisions laid down; it was the European Parliament that insisted to have the thematic strategies under the sixth programme adopted in the form of legally binding decisions, to have them submitted by the Commission by 2005 and to have an annual progress report on them; it is also true, though, that later on, Parliament did not insist on its position.[35]

The problem with Parliament's policy is that it has no historical memory. It occurs quite often that a conflict with the Council is postponed for some years; and when the matter is discussed anew, the Parliament—normally newly composed after elections—does not defend its previous position any more. For example, the Commission does not submit annual progress reports on the environmental thematic strategies—and the Parliament does not insist on this.

In the past, a considerable part of the Union's legislative activity—in 2004, 2,625 measures were adopted in this way, numerous of them legislative measures—which was subject to the "comitology" procedure (adaptation of existing provisions due to technical or scientific progress) of art.202 EC, was not accessible to the European Parliament, since the procedures for the some 250 different committees (2004), established by the Council,[36] did not provide for its participation. Attempts in the nineties to enable access of the European Parliament to the different technical committees did not prove successful and though the 1999 review of the procedure brought some improvement,[37] the overall situation remained unsatisfactory for the European Parliament. A political compromise of 2006 did not lead to significant changes. Article 290 TFEU now tries to simplify and clarify the procedure. A delegated act now must be titled as such and may enter into force only, if no objection has been expressed by the European Parliament (and the Council). Previous limitations of Parliament's rights to questions of "ultra vires" or subsidiarity were not taken up by art.290 TFEU. It remains to be seen, to what extent the new provision of art.290 TFEU will in practice lead to greater Parliamentary influence on delegated or implementing decisions—these are regulated in art.291 TFEU—by the Commission.

2–22

The European Parliament does not attend meetings of the Council or of its working parties. Overall, its influence on the Council is, in the context of a specific legislative environmental text, limited mainly for two reasons: on the one hand, the Parliament had, until the coming into effect of the Amsterdam Treaty in May 1999, a mainly cooperative role and its resolutions were not binding for the Council. As since May 1999, the co-decision procedure of art.294 TFEU applies in almost all cases, the legislative influence of Parliament is progressively increasing. On the other hand, the Council frequently discusses a proposal from the Commission before the European Parliament has given its opinion. These discussions rather often lead to a political consensus in Council; then only the opinion of Parliament is waited for before the Council formally adopts its common position. Since there is a tacit agreement in Council not to change a common position if at all possible, Parliament's opinions only may change Council's positions in exceptional cases or for less important aspects. This

---

[35] See Dec.1600/2002 (fn.7, above) art.4(1).
[36] Dec.87/373 [1987] OJ L197/33.
[37] Dec.1999/468 [1999] OJ L184/23.

Council practice, which is not limited to the environmental sector, at the very least contradicts the spirit of the EU Treaties which is based on the idea that the opinions of Parliament, the Economic and Social Committee and the Committee of the Regions are available, when the Council discussions begin—not when they are ended.

In the conciliation procedure of art.294 which is, in environmental matters, quite frequently used, the Council's position is regularly prevailing over that of the Parliament. The reasons for this are in particular:

1. the Council secretariat plus the number of environmental attachés from each Member State have greater facilities to liaise with each other and with the different capitals to form an opinion on a specific compromise text;
2. while the Member States have officials at their disposal who are experts of the specific file for years and know all details of the previous Council discussions, the European Parliament and its secretariat do not dispose of the same amount of expertise, as the rapporteur, his assistant(s) and almost all the other deputies normally were in contact with the subject-matter only during the two readings of the Commission proposal in Parliament;
3. Parliament's capacity to organise the necessary European know-how at short-term is smaller than that of the Council.

Generally, these reasons reflect the dominant role which public administration plays in all Member States in the legislative standard-setting for the environment.

The Economic and Social Committee; Committee of the Regions

2–23   The Economic and Social Committee (arts 301 et seq. TFEU) is thought to represent the different non-governmental interests within the European Union, although representatives of the environment are not expressly mentioned in art.302(2) TFEU. At present (2009–2014), only one member of this Committee has indicated that he comes from an environmental organisation. The Committee of the Regions (arts 305 et seq. TFEU) is composed of regional and local authorities. The Committee of the Regions may apply to the Court of justice, where it is of the opinion that an environmental measure interferes with its prerogatives (art.263(3) TFEU) or is against the principle of subsidiarity.[38]

Article 13(4) TEU provides that the Economic and Social Committee and the Committee of the Regions both advise the Council, the European Parliament and the Commission. In reality this advisory function is exercised by both Committees only after the Commission has submitted a proposal or made a communication. Nor does the Commission consult these Committees. The opinions of both Committees in environmental matters have not yet reached the point of having any significant influence on the content of EU directives or regulations.

---

[38] Protocol No 2 on the application of the principle of subsidiarity and proportionality, [2008] OJ C115, p.206, art.8(2).

The Council

The Council, while formally one institution, meets under relatively specific   **2–24**
configurations (e.g. Agricultural Council, Transport Council, Social Affairs
Council). In environmental matters, the Council normally meets three times
under each presidency—which changes every six months—twice formally in
Brussels and once informally at a place which is determined by each presidency.
At the informal meetings issues of environmental policy or environmental
strategy are discussed, without any decisions being made. The ministers
responsible for environmental matters have Council meetings in Brussels or in
Luxembourg, on agenda issues drawn up by the presidency. The Council
meetings are not public except where the Council decides otherwise; however, up
until now such public meetings, introduced after 1993, have been exceptional and
not been dealing with essential matters. Nor does the Council organise public
hearings. Position papers from lobby groups or other organisations are only rarely
distributed within the Council or among Member States. Contacts with media or
with representatives of vested interests are not organised by the Council, though
there is a press release issued after each Council meeting: at best, meetings with
the media are organised by individual Member States immediately before or after
a Council meeting. Normally, however, such contact takes place at the capital of
each Member State. The public is thus informed about a Member State's
viewpoint in the Council or during the preparatory meetings by this Member
State itself. There is no possibility of compelling the Council to debate a proposal
for a directive or a regulation presented by the Commission. The Council,
therefore, can, by not discussing a Commission proposal, let this proposal
become obsolete. An example is the Commission proposal for a directive on
access to justice in environmental matters.[39] The Council did not discuss the
proposal, the official reasons are not known; probably, Member States are of the
opinion that this matter does not come under EC competence.[40] Also a
Commission proposal for a directive to protect the soil[41] was only very shortly
discussed by the Council; again, reasons of subsidiarity were invoked, though it
is known that United Kingdom, Germany, Netherlands and France opposed the
proposal.

Institutional co-operation between the Council and the Commission generally   **2–25**
occurs as regards the organisation of work in Council working groups, since here
the Commission has to explain and defend its proposals for legislation. This
co-operation is, however, limited to organisational questions; if, when, and how
often Commission proposals are discussed in Council and within the different
Council working groups, is decided by each Council Presidency at its discretion.
The Council working groups are normally composed of the environmental
attachés of each Member State's Permanent Representation with the Union, as
well as of a Commission official; officials from Member States—normally from
the environmental department—participate at the discretion of each Member

---

[39] Commission, COM(2003) 624 of October 24, 2003; see also para.4–20, below.
[40] To what extent the Aarhus Convention, which was ratified by the EU and forms thus part of EU
law (art.216(2) TFEU) requires EU-wide measures in order to ensure its application in *all*parts of the
EU, will be discussed below in para.4–19.
[41] Commission, COM(2006) 232.

State, mainly in cases where expert advice is needed. The meetings are presided over by an official of the Member State who holds the presidency.

Institutional co-operation between the Council and other institutions, in particular the European Parliament, practically does not exist in environmental matters, though the increasing number of co-decision procedures has progressively led, during the last years to more organisational contacts between the two institutions, in particular in view of avoiding a second reading of the Commission's proposal or even a conciliation procedure.[42]

The European Courts (Court of Justice and General Court)

2–26   No detailed description needs to be given of the role of the European Courts in ensuring that "the law is observed" in the interpretation and application of the environmental Treaty provisions and secondary legislation (art.19 TEU). The Courts have almost always tried to interpret existing legislation in a way which is favourable to the environment and to formalise the concept of environmental law which has often been rather general and vague. Of course, there have been judgments which have been influenced by political considerations.[43] However, it is usual that judgments from a supreme court will also include policy considerations and are not given in a policy free environment.

The division of work between the Court of Justice and the General Court is decided by the Treaty (art.256 TFEU). At present, the General Court decides in particular on all applications from individual persons (art.263(4) TFEU), and in competition matters.

2–27   For a number of reasons the Commission does not automatically bring cases concerning a breach of EU law before the Court of Justice. The Court has repeatedly stated that the Commission has, under art.258 TFEU a discretion as to whether it wishes to bring an action or not.[44] This may well be but in any case, the clear wording of art.258 indicates that the Commission has no such discretion on the question over whether it begins infringement procedures or not against a Member State. Since, however, the Court of Justice has furthermore stated that the Commission cannot be obliged to begin procedures under that article,[45] the Commission's attitude of not beginning procedures under art.258, and thus not bringing them before the Court of Justice either, remains unchallenged. In my opinion, the Court has, by this jurisdiction, created an area where public power is exercised without being controlled by the judiciary.

One essential difference between the judgments given by the Court of Justice and judgments given by a national supreme court is that the Court of Justice's judgment is given in an area in which different legal cultures exist. Thus, for

---

[42] See, also as one rare example, the *modus vivendi* between the European Parliament, Council and Commission concerning the implementation measures for acts adopted in accordance with the procedure laid down in art.251 EC [1995] OJ C293/1.

[43] This seems to be the case, for instance, with *Commission v France* (C–252/85) [1988] E.C.R. 2243 on traditional hunting; *Commission v Denmark* (C–302/86) [1988] E.C.R. 4607 on a deposit and return system for bottles; *Commission v Belgium* (C–2/90) [1992] E.C.R. I–4431 on import bans for waste; *Commission v Council* (C–155/91) [1993] E.C.R. I–939 on the legal basis for waste legislation.

[44] Cases 416/85 *Commission v United Kingdom* [1988] E.C.R. 3127; C–234/91 *Commission v Denmark* [1993] E.C.R. I–6273.

[45] *Star Fruit Company v Commission* (C–247/87) [1989] E.C.R. 291; *Emrich v Commission* (C–371/89) [1990] E.C.R. I–1555.

example, a judgment which states that one Member State has breached EU law because it has not submitted clean-up plans, not reported on the implementation of a specific directive or not ensured that the quality of drinking water complies with the requirements of the Union's law, is normally not accepted by the administration of all other Member States as obliging them to make sure that the same omission does not occur under their responsibility; and the national courts do often not either take the Court jurisdiction into account in their daily judgments. In fact, Member States do not really pay too much attention to an environmental judgment that was given against another Member State, at least, where this would involve obligations for them. Implementation, application, monitoring and enforcement of EU environmental legislation is thus very different in the different legal cultures.

Non-institutional actors

Professional organisations

The representation of vested interests at Union level is probably even greater than in most capitals of Member States; the number of representatives in Brussels is estimated at 15,000. Economic operators and their professional organisations discovered the common market, globalisation effects and the advantages of economies of scale a long time ago and are also well aware that European Union trade needs EU legal provisions. Their influence on the shaping of European environmental law is considerable, although only with difficulty is it capable of being demonstrated. This influence is not so much exercised by legal papers which argue this or that rule, but rather by influencing the strategic thinking inside the Commission administration. I estimate that even with Directorate-General ENV, out of the 100 contacts or interlocutors which the Directorate-General has outside the national administrations, more than 90 represent vested interests. Such exchange of views is bound to have some long-term repercussions.

2–28

European professional associations are normally relatively lacking in influence, compared to their national member organisations, and the influencing of the EU decision-making persons or bodies is mirrored by similar approaches by national associations or individual members at national level.

Examples where vested interests seem to have significantly influenced the EU policy of environmental law, are in my opinion: the abandoning of integrated emission limit values for industries or sectors of industries[46]; the abandoning, as a rule, of setting emission values from point sources at European level[47]; the omission to establish provisions for environmental taxes and charges at European level; the 15-year delay in fixing limit values for CO^2 emissions from cars[48]; the omission to formalise, in some binding form, the polluter-pays principle; active participation in industrial standardisation; the omission to heavily promote alternative energies and the strong financial support for a nuclear energy policy; the omission to fix air quality standards for heavy metals.[49]

---

[46] See para.4–47ss, below.
[47] See para.4–40ss, below.
[48] See paras 8–22 et seq., below.
[49] Dec.466/2002 [2002] OJ L75/1.

Environmental organisations

2–29 European environmental organisations suffer from a chronic shortage in manpower and financial resources which seriously affects their organisational structures. There is no overall European umbrella organisation which contains all environmental associations. In the mid-1990s, environmental organisations formed a loose co-operation group, Green 10, to pool their forces. Members are: BirdLife International (European Office); Bankwatch Network; Climate Action Network Europe; European Environmental Bureau; European Federation for Transport and Environment; European Public Health Alliance; Friends of the Earth Europe; Greenpeace Europe; International Friends of Nature and World Wildlife Fund (WWF) European Policy Office.

In 2002 the European Parliament and the Council adopted a Decision, based on art.175(1) EC(!) concerning an "action programme promoting non-governmental organisations primarily active in the field of environmental protection".[50] This Decision was repealed by Regulation 614/2007 which included the possibility to support environmental organisations financially. A specific financial amount was not fixed. The attributions to environmental organisations are decided yearly, on the basis of work programmes.

The "Green 10" organisations frequently divide work priorities among themselves, according to their political preferences. With the exception of Greenpeace they all obtain financial support from the Commission, under Regulation 614/2007; it cannot be excluded that this fact also influences the organisation's actions and positions. One might wonder whether it is not time for environmental organisations to pool their limited personal and financial resources and form an EU Institute for environmental organisations or a similar body. The current diversity of environmental organisations is also an obstacle to the professionalisation. For example, an association such as the European Environmental Bureau, the umbrella environmental organisation of some 140 national organisations, has a permanent staff of some ten people in Brussels and is thought to cover all facets of EU environmental policy and law. Other organisations are even smaller. The organisations mainly work to influence the opinions of the European Parliament and the public. Overall, the contribution of environmental organisations to EU environmental law is limited. Their best ally is public opinion, and where they do manage to highlight an issue in the public awareness and find access to the media, they may considerably influence EU environmental policy and the content of some measures. Also, in the cases of catastrophies, such as the mad cow disease, accidents—the *Prestige* tanker accident 2002 or the *Aznalcollar* (Spain) accident 1998—or scandals such as the Brent Spar platform incident 1995, contaminated food, PVC in toys or others, their ability to influence public opinion definitely influences the EU legislature.

Individuals

2–30 The environmental provisions of the EU Treaties do not mention individual persons and, as mentioned, are not set out in such a way that they could be, under the Court of Justice's doctrine of direct effect, interpreted so that individual

---

[50] Reg.614/2007 concerning the Financial Instrument for the Environment (LIFE+), [2007] OJ L149/1.

persons could invoke them in disputes with administrations or courts. The European Court made a major effort in increasing the position of individual persons, by declaring, in a landmark decision of 1990, that environmental measures which also aimed at the protection of human health, were to be interpreted in a way that would allow individuals to invoke these rights before courts.[51] But neither the Commission nor environmental organisations or individual persons have ever pushed this line of thinking further, e.g. by making proposals for introducing a right of action for individuals or their associations against environmental impairment (Commission), or by trying, via an established number of test cases in court, to explore the content and the limits of environmental rights for individuals (environmental organisations) or by trying to bring into action a "right to a clean environment" which is so often referred to by politicians.[52]

EU institutions, and in particular the Commission, start from the premise that the protection of the environment is the task of the public administration—as if the (European Union) administration were the owner of the environment; since the EU administration knows best what is desirable to preserve, protect or improve the quality of the environment, an individual person is, under this concept, rather perceived as a nuisance. This basic concept is the reason why access to environmental information at European level is so much less organised than access to environmental information at national level,[53] why there are no systematic hearings organised for the preparation of environmental legislation in order to overcome the structural imbalance between professional and environmental organisations and why environmental organisations and individuals are simply not given the possibility to contribute to the enforcement of EU environmental provisions. In my opinion, there is a basic difference between an environmental action by a professional organisation and by an environmental organisation: an environmental organisation usually tries to promote not the general interest to protect the environment, whereas a professional organisation usually has in mind specific, vested interests, not the general interest.

It is the European Commission's omission that it does not try to mobilise private individuals who wish to ensure a better protection of the environment, by making people participate in environmental law-making and implementing. The EU citizenship, introduced by arts 20 et seq. TFEU, is lacking a concrete follow-up in the environmental sector, where individual persons remain receivers of EU environmental law and policy, rather than being given the status of instigators and participants.[54]

---

[51] *Commission v Germany* (C–361/88) [1991] E.C.R. I–2567; *Janecek* (C–237/07) [2008] E.C.R. I–6221.

[52] See paras 4–01 et seq., below.

[53] See, on the one hand, Dir.90/313 [1990] OJ L158/56 and Dir.2003/4 [2003] OJ L41/26, on the other hand Reg.1049/2001 on access to documents held by EC institutions [2001] OJ L145/43. It is true, though, that the application of the Aarhus Convention by the EU institutions might slightly improve access to information at EU level.

[54] As regards participation in decision-making, see below, paras 4–10 et seq.

2. Instruments

Legal and political instruments

General remarks

2–31   The following presentation of instruments is limited to the FEU Treaty; the terminology of the EURATOM Treaty corresponds to it—except, of course, the numbers of the articles. The CECA Treaty has expired in July 2002 and no longer exists.

In environmental matters a number of instruments were developed which are not detailed in the central provision of art.288 TFEU. The main reason for this evolution is the absence of an express chapter in the EC Treaty on environmental policy prior to 1987.

Regulations and directives can only be adopted by the European Parliament and the Council jointly, by the Council alone or by the Commission. The Commission has the monopoly of initiating legislative measures in all such cases: environmental regulations and directives may only be adopted upon proposal on the Commission.

2–32   The possibility to have directives and regulations adopted jointly by the European Parliament and the Council has only existed since 1993. As regards the environment, arts 192(1) for environmental measures, 114 for measures which have significance for the internal market and art.192(3) TFEU, for the adoption of environmental action programmes, provide for this joint adoption. In a number of cases the Council alone adopts environment-related regulations and directives, in particular under arts 192(2), 43(3), 113 and 207(3) TFEU. Where the Council adopts measures by a qualified majority, Member States' votes are weighed according to art.3 of Protocol 36[55]: a qualified majority needs 255 of the 343 votes, cast by the majority of Member States.[56] It is important to underline that the Council can only amend a Commission proposal unanimously (art.293 TFEU).

The Commission can adopt regulations or directives only where it has expressly been authorised to do so by the Treaty or by secondary EU law (arts 290 and 291 TFEU). The Commission is frequently authorised under art.290 TFEU to decide on the adaptation of environmental regulations and directives to take account of scientific or technical progress; individual regulations or directives specify how far this authorisation may go. In environmental matters the Commission is normally assisted in such cases by a committee, which has to give an opinion on proposals for adaptation before the Commission can decide. In cases of divergency between the committee and the Commission, the decision is normally taken by the Council. Details were outlined in a Council decision of 1999 which has, since the entry into force of the Lisbon Treaty, not yet been replaced.[57]

Regulations, directives and decisions must "state the reasons on which they are based" (art.296 TFEU). This is the aim of the recitals which precede the

---

[55] Protocol 36 on transitional provisions, [2008] OJ C115/322.

[56] See also, in complement, arts 16 TEU and 238 TFEU.

[57] Dec.1999/468 (fn.37, above); see also for the strengthening of the role of the European Parliament in this Comitology procedure, para.2–22.

different texts and give, in condensed form, the objectives of the legislative act and why the different provisions were adopted in this or that form. The Court of Justice uses the recitals for the interpretation of the provisions; the Court's interpretation is not too severe as regards their content, though it sometimes happens that legal acts are voided because of a lack of reasoning.[58]

Since the entry into effect of the Maastricht Treaty in 1993 the Council, when establishing a common position, publishes, in the Official Journal, in summary the reasons for its common position and also why it has not adopted all the proposals by the Commission or the European Parliament.

Regulations, directives and decisions are published in the Official Journal of the European Community, with the exception of those directives and decisions which are addressed to individual Member States or individual persons (art.297 TFEU).

Regulations

In environmental matters, the Union mainly acts in the form of directives: regulations are exceptional. They are normally adopted when uniform provisions are sought,[59] since regulations are of general application and shall be binding in their entirety and directly applicable to all Member States (art.288 TFEU). A first group is composed of regulations which set up a specific administrative structure, such as the European Environmental Agency,[60] the financial instrument LIFE,[61] or the Cohesion Fund.[62] Furthermore, there are measures which create committees, uniform procedures or structures; examples are the provision on organic agriculture,[63] the procedures for attributing an eco-label,[64] the require-ment for manufacturers or importers to submit data and reports to the Commission[65] and the eco-audit scheme.[66]

A second group is formed by regulations which transpose obligations of international environmental conventions into EU law. They mainly serve to organise international trade, concerning products, waste, fauna and flora species. Examples are the Regulation on ozone-depleting substances,[67] the shipment of waste[68] and the trade in endangered species.[69] Also the regulations on an import

2–33

---

[58] See, e.g. *France v Commission* (C–41/93) [1994] E.C.R. I–1829; *WWF v Commission* (T–105/95) [1997] E.C.R. II–313; Case C–378/00 *Commission v EP and Council* [2003] E.C.R. I–937.
[59] Written Question E–3089 (93) (Arbeloa Muru) [1994] OJ C358/15.
[60] Reg.1210/90 (fn.27, above).
[61] Reg.614/2007 (fn.50, above).
[62] Reg.1084/2006 establishing a Cohesion Fund [2006] OJ L210/79.
[63] Reg.834/2007 on organic production and labelling of organic products [2007] OJ L189/1.
[64] Reg.66/2010 on the EU eco-label [2010] OJ L27/1.
[65] Reg.793/93 on the evaluation and control of the risks of existing substances [1993] OJ L84/1.
[66] Reg.1221/2009 allowing voluntary participation by organisations in a Community eco-management and audit scheme [2009] OJ L342/1.
[67] e.g. Reg.1005/2009 on substances that deplete the ozone layer [2009] OJ L286/1.
[68] Reg.1013/2006 on shipments of waste [2006] OJ L190/1.
[69] Reg.338/97 on the protection of species of wild fauna and flora by regulating trade therein [1997] OJ L61/1.

ban of whale products,[70] on the ban of leg-hold traps and the import of certain furs[71] and the import or export of chemicals[72] belong to this category.

2-34 Regulations do not exist in the water, air and noise sector and there are only a few in the area of nature protection, waste and chemicals. However, these last two sectors show a slowly increasing need for uniform provisions. The reasons for this might lie in the necessity of having uniform provisions before the international state or trade community, but also in the wish to avoid, within an internal market which is still developing, different provisions that could lead to competitive distortions and changes in commercial relationships.

Although regulations are directly applicable in all Member States, not all provisions of environmental regulations have this direct effect. Several regulatory provisions require an action by Member States, such as the licensing and supervision of environmental auditors,[73] the authorisation of imports, the establishment of documents or certificates,[74] the designation of competent authorities, the supervision of plants, activities or transports, the establishment of reports and the transmission of information to the Commission or to other Member States. In these cases, regulations seem to have more the content of a directive. Furthermore, not all provisions of a regulation are of a directly applicable nature: thus, a provision such as "Member States may apply the system provided for in Titles II and VIII within their jurisdiction"[75] is of purely facultative character.

2-35 No environmental regulation outlines details of sanctions which apply in case of non-respect of the regulation. For instance, the Regulation on the shipment of waste provides that Member States[76]:

> "shall lay down the rules on penalties applicable for infringement of the provisions of this Regulation and shall take all measures necessary to ensure that they are implemented. The penalties provided for must be effective, proportionate and dissuasive;"

the Regulation on the assessment of chemicals asks Member States to[77]:

> "establish appropriate legal or administrative measures in order to deal with non-compliance with the provisions of this Regulation."

Whether the sanction is criminal, administrative or civil, is left to the discretion of Member States. The jurisprudence of the Court of Justice only requires that national sanctions are proportional and deterrent and correspond to sanctions which are pronounced in similar cases under national law.[78]

---

[70] Reg.348/81 on common rules for imports of whales or other cetacean products [1981] OJ L39/1.

[71] Reg.3254/91 prohibiting the use of leghold traps in the Community and the introduction into the Community of pelts and manufactured goods of certain wild animal species originating in countries which catch them by means of leghold traps or trapping methods which do not meet international humane trapping standards [1991] OJ L308/1.

[72] Reg.689/2008 concerning the export and import of dangerous chemicals [2008] OJ L240/1.

[73] Reg.1221/2009 (fn.66, above).

[74] Reg.338/97 (fn.69), art.8.

[75] Reg.1013/2006 (fn.68), art.33(3).

[76] Reg.1013/2006 (fn.68), art.50(1); a similar provision is found in Reg.689/2008 (fn.72, above), art.18.

[77] See Reg.793/93 (fn.65, above), art.17.

[78] Court of Justice, *Commission v Greece* (C–68/88) [1989] E.C.R. 2965.

Directives

Directives[79] are the most frequently used instrument in EU environmental policy.   **2–36**
The degree of detail provided for in a directive is less determined by the concept
of a "directive" than by the need to attain the different objectives pursued. Thus,
directives on harmonising motor vehicles rules quite often contain 50–80 pages
of detailed rules, which outline all the details of the composition of products, test
methods and so on.[80] Such detailed directives are frequent for products, but exist
also in the agricultural sector. In contrast to that, environmental directives tend to
be of a general nature. In particular the debate over the last twenty-five years on
subsidiarity and deregulation and the general loss of integration capacity of the
European Union has led to environmental directives which limit themselves to
outline general rules, framework provisions and basic requirements. Provisions
on measuring methods and frequency, emission limit values, quantitative
restrictions and other similar provisions are only laid down in exceptional cases.
Whether this restriction is really capable of contributing to a high level of
environmental protection, is doubtful; such general provisions do not increase the
added value of EU environmental law provisions and, furthermore, perpetuate
differences in the level of protection among Member States: they allow to apply
the EU provisions, if the political will to do so exists, but also allow to avoid full
application of such rules, if such a political will does not exist.

Directives address Member States and normally oblige them to act in a certain
way. Private persons, undertakings or associations cannot be obligated by a
directive; however, they can acquire rights from a directive in those cases where
a provision in a directive is sufficiently concrete, precise and unconditional and
where the Member State has not transposed that directive completely or correctly
into national law (direct-effect doctrine).[81]

Member States have to transpose the provisions of a directive into national   **2–37**
law. It is up to each Member State to decide whether this is done by an Act of
Parliament or a regulation, whether the transposition measure is one piece of
legislation or whether several regional or even local provisions are adopted. It is
only relevant that the directive's provisions are transposed for the whole territory
of the Member State. The transposing measure may be incorporated in one legal
act; more frequently, however, the transposition is ensured by a number of legal
measures, in particular in Member States with a decentralised or federal structure.

Where the definition of a provision is relevant, such transposition also needs
to include the definition in order to establish a common language.[82] For the rest,
at the very least those provisions need to be transposed which are capable of
creating rights or obligations for private persons. In contrast to this, provisions

---

[79] art.288 TFEU: "A directive shall be binding, as to the result to be achieved, upon each Member
State to which it is addressed, but shall leave to the national authorities the choice of form and
methods."

[80] Dir.97/24 on three-wheel cars has a length of 454 pages in the Official Journal [1997] OJ L226/1.
Such a length would not be imaginable for a directive on the environment.

[81] See further at para.12–27, below.

[82] See, e.g. Court of Justice, *Commission v Ireland* (C–354/99) [2001] E.C.R. I–7657, where Ireland
was found in breach of EC law, because it had not transposed a specific definition; *Commission v
Belgium* (C–120/09), judgment of December 9, 2009.

which exclusively address the administration (for instance, requiring it to send reports to the Commission or to designate competent authorities) need not be transposed.

2–38   The provisions of the directive which have been transposed into national law must be actually applied. This follows from the very nature of a directive, which obliges Member States to achieve a certain result. It is not enough to take all practical steps to reach the directive's objectives; indeed, the directive indicates to Member States how to achieve a certain result, but does not leave it at their discretion as to whether they achieve the result or not. It was for this reason that the United Kingdom was not heard before the Court of Justice with its argument that it had taken all reasonable steps to ensure clean drinking water: the Court requested that the requirements of the drinking water Directive be complied with.[83]

Amendments of directives follow the general rules. Normally, they are adopted by the same institutions which adopted the original directive; however, as pointed out, the Commission may be authorised, under art.290 TFEU to amend a directive, in particular to adapt it as a result of technical or scientific progress. Furthermore, the legal basis of a directive is determined by its objective and its content, not by the legal basis of a previous directive; thus, where an environmental directive, based on art.192 TFEU is amended by a directive which has a trade-related objective, art.207 TFEU may become the appropriate legal basis for the amending measure, and the institution which adopts the amendment may be different.[84]

Legally, differentiations such as "umbrella directive", "daughter directive", etc., are not relevant. Such concepts only signal that the specific directive is placed in a close context with a more general directive; however, the specific directive is to be interpreted by itself, including, of course, possible references to other directives.

Directives do not become obsolete with time. Since they are legal acts, they need to be repealed expressly: in EU practice this normally takes place with the adoption of a new directive. No environmental directive has as yet been repealed without the adoption of new provisions, though the Commission's announcement to simplify its legislation might in future lead to more such repeals. The agreement of the Council and the European Parliament will be necessary.

Decisions

2–39   Decisions[85] are rather numerous in EU environmental policy. The most frequent types of decisions are: decisions to establish a committee or another body[86]; to grant financial assistance for environmental projects under the Cohesion Fund or the financial instrument LIFE; in the context of competition policy on agreements (art.101 TFEU); abuse of dominant positions (art.102 TFEU) or on state aid (arts 107 and 108 TFEU); on details of putting into operation specific directives or

---

[83] *Commission v United Kingdom* (C–337/89) [1992] E.C.R. 6103.
[84] See, e.g. Reg.1420/1999 [1999] OJ L166/6 which concerned the shipment of non-hazardous waste and was based on art.133 EC, though the original Regulation 259/93 on the shipments of waste was based on art.175 EC.
[85] art.288 TFEU: "A decision shall be binding in its entirety. A decision which specifies those to whom it is addressed, shall be binding only on them."
[86] See, e.g. Dec.76/431 setting up a committee on waste management [1976] OJ L115/73.

regulations[87] or establishing criteria for the attribution of an eco-label for specific product groups[88]; on the adherence of the European Union to international (environmental) conventions; on environmental action programmes according to art.192(3); and on art.114(4) and (5) TFEU on more stringent national environmental measures.

Recommendations

Commission or Council recommendations have no binding force (art.288 TFEU). They play a limited role in EU environmental policy. Indeed, experience has shown that neither economic operators nor Member States are inclined to respect recommendations, and the example of international organisations—OECD, Council of Europe, United Nations—which largely work with recommendations, demonstrate the very limited effective influence of non-binding environmental measures.   **2–40**

The Council made environmental recommendations on cost allocation,[89] on the cost of pollution control to industry,[90] the reuse of waste paper and the use of recycled paper[91] and coastal zone management.[92] The Commission in particular made recommendations on birds,[93] on environmental agreements[94] and the use of CFCs in industry.[95] Where an environmental agreement is made at EU level, the Commission furthermore issues a recommendation taking up the content of the agreement.[96]

None of these recommendations had, as far as can be seen, any significant influence on European or national environmental policy or law.

Communications

Communications, not expressly provided for in the EU Treaty, are legally not binding. They are sent from the Commission to the other institutions, in particular the Council or the Parliament, and expose the Commission's position on a particular problem, indicate orientations and discuss options which the Commission considers possible. Since the beginning of the 1990s, the number of communications on environmental matters has increased.   **2–41**

Communications appear under different headings, as strategies, green or white papers, reports or communications. Legally, there is no difference. Communications may be accompanied by a draft for a Council resolution, a directive or a regulation.

---

[87] See, e.g. Dec.2000/532 establishing a list of wastes [2000] OJ L226/3.
[88] Under Reg.66/2010 (fn.64,above); see, e.g. Dec.93/430 on ecological criteria for dishwashers [1993] OJ L38; Dec.98/488 on ecological criteria for soil improvers [1998] OJ L219/39; Dec.99/205 on ecological criteria for personal computers [1999] OJ L70/46.
[89] Rec. 75/436 [1975] OJ L194/1.
[90] Rec. 79/3 [1979] OJ L5/28.
[91] Rec. 81/972 [1981] OJ L355/56.
[92] Rec. 2002/413 [2002] OJ L148/24.
[93] Rec. 75/66 [1975] OJ L21/24.
[94] Rec. 96/733 [1996] OJ L33/59.
[95] Rec. 89/349 [1989] OJ L89/56; 90/437 and 90/438 [1990] OJ L227/26 and 30 (CFC).
[96] Rec. 1999/125 [1999] OJ L40/49.

Action programmes

2–42   EU environmental action programmes have been developed since the early 1970s, mainly in reaction to the fact that the EC Treaty did not provide for an express legal basis for environmental measures. When such specific provisions were introduced in 1987, the practice of action programmes was maintained. Action programmes were, legally, communications by the Commission to other EU institutions, which set out for a period of four to five years, the objectives, principles and priorities of EU action which the Commission envisaged. The Court of Justice confirmed that the environmental action programmes did not contain legally binding or enforceable provisions.[97] Action programmes were followed by (political) resolutions by the Parliament and the Council. Between 1973 and mid-1998, five environmental action programmes were agreed at EU level.[98] Their main effect was essentially political. They achieved a large consensus among Member States on objectives and priorities of EU environmental policy, and since the majority of Member States did not have a national environmental policy, the measures agreed and adopted at EU level often influenced environmental policy within Member States. Since the end of 1993, environmental action programmes have to be adopted by way of a joint decision by the European Parliament and the Council (art.192(3) TFEU) which is, of course, binding.

2–43   Action programmes under art.192(3) TFEU must at least outline priority objectives for EU action, provide for measures to achieve these objectives and contain a time period within which the measures are taken. The right for initiative for such a programme rests with the Commission, and no other institution can oblige it to submit a programme.[99]

EU action programmes may oblige the Commission to make proposals for specific measures, with the consequence, in the case of failure to do so, of an action—by the Council and also by the European Parliament—under art.265 TFEU. It is true that the Commission normally has the monopoly for legal initiatives and cannot be compelled to make a proposal. However, primary and secondary law contain a number of exceptions to this rule[100] and there is no provision in EU law which would oppose such an exception. In contrast to this, it does not seem possible to oblige, by virtue of a programme, the Council or even the Member States to adopt specific measures: in such a case, an all too concrete content—such as, for instance, that the use of certain substances or products will be banned from a specific date onwards—would contradict the form of an action programme; such measures would require a directive or a regulation and would be adopted in respect of the procedures foreseen for those instruments.

The provision of art.192(3) TFEU creates new possibilities for the European Parliament to influence the legislative programme of the European Union and to

---

[97] *Rovigo* (C–142/95P) [1996] E.C.R. I–6669.
[98] First environmental action programme 1973–1976 [1973] OJ C112/1; second environmental action programme (1977–1982) [1977] OJ C139/1; third environmental action programme 1982–1986 [1983] OJ C46/1; fourth environmental action programme 1987–1992 [1987] OJ C328/1; fifth environmental action programme 1993–2000 [1993] OJ C138/5.
[99] Argument taken from Court of Justice, *Commission v Belgium* (C–347/97) [1999] E.C.R. I–309.
[100] See, e.g. art.241 TFEU; an example in secondary law was art.1(5) of Dir.91/689 on hazardous waste [1991] OJ L377/20 which requests the Commission to make a proposal on hazardous household waste; Directive 91/689 has now been repealed.

see proposals for legislative measures presented. Parliament's interest must therefore be to have environmental action programmes as concrete as possible, whereas the interests of the Commission and the Council must be to keep the programme as general and loosely drafted as possible. This difference of interest was very notable in the Commission's proposal for a review of the fifth action programme and Parliament's position on it.[101] The final Decision on this review contained objectives and principles, but not actions.[102]

When the sixth action programme was elaborated, Parliament insisted again on precise wording for specific actions. The thematic strategies which first appeared in art.4 of the sixth environmental action programme, do not constitute a specific legal form of instrument. Indeed, they may take the form of a communication, a proposal for a directive or a proposal for a (sectoral) programme, or a combination of such measures.

Resolutions

The Treaty does not contain any provision on resolutions. These are political   **2–44**
statements adopted by the Council, with or without a proposal from the Commission. Following a consensus in the Council which is not laid down in writing, Council (environmental) resolutions are agreed upon unanimously; it is true that no vote is taken, but the Council redrafts the text until a consensus of all Member States is reached.

Resolutions often constitute the Council's reaction on a Commission communication concerning an environmental issue. However, the Council is not obliged to react to such communications. Where it adopts a resolution, this gives political or legal orientation to the Commission, the Parliament, private actors without being legally binding for the Council. Also the European Parliament adopts environmental resolutions, as a reaction to a Commission communication or on its own initiative. These resolutions are adopted by majority vote. Again, they are of political, not of legal nature.

Environmental agreements

Environmental agreements were defined by the Commission as agreements, by   **2–45**
which stakeholders undertake to achieve pollution abatement, as defined in environmental law, or environmental objectives set out in art.191 TFEU.[103]

Such agreements are not mentioned in art.288 TFEU. Since the European Union may only act within the limits of powers conferred upon it (art.5 TEU), agreements are not capable of regulating substantive parts of Community

---

[101] Commission, [1996] OJ C140/5. European Parliament [1996] OJ C362/112.

[102] Dec.2179/98 on the review of the fifth environmental action programme [1998] OJ L275/1.

[103] Commission: Environmental Agreements at Community level, COM(2002)412 of July 17, 2002. Another definition is given in art.3(12) of Dir.94/62 on packaging and packaging waste [1994] OJ L365/10: "'Voluntary agreements' shall mean the formal agreement concluded between the competent public authorities of the Member State and the economic sectors concerned, which has to be open to all partners who wish to meet the conditions of the agreement with a view to working towards the objectives of this Directive". Directive 2004/12 ([2004] OJ L47/26) now inserted a new art.3*bis*, according to which the Directive's recycling targets also could be attained by voluntary agreements. As regards the most prominent "agreement" at EU level, that on the reduction of CO^2 from cars, see also paras 8–18ss.

environmental policy, as this is reserved to the instruments listed in art.288 TFEU. The European Parliament opposed the recourse to environmental agreements which it understood as some form of commitment that was binding for the Commission or the European Union.[104] It invoked in particular that such agreements simply did not conform to the Parliamentary principle. As the European Parliament, the Economic and Social Committee and the Committee of the Regions have institutional rights and guarantees to take part in the EU decision-making procedures, environmental agreements, which set these rights aside, are legally not permissible. For this reason the Commission declared in two communications that it could only make non-binding environmental agreements at EU level and even included this approach in the very definition of "agreement".[105] And in 2002, the Commission stated that "environmental agreements are not negotiated with the Commission".[106]

Even these basic concerns being left aside, procedures for the making of such agreements—who should negotiate in the name of the European Union?— and the follow-up—how and by whom the agreement would be monitored, enforced, sanctioned, applied to free-riders, such as importers and third country producers?—are not clear; nor are they answered by the Commission's communications.[107] Since Member States would have to monitor and enforce agreements, their participation in the negotiation procedure appears inevitable. However, it is then not clear where the advantage is with regard to a directive which is negotiated and decided in Council and the European Parliament.

2–46 The core of the problem is the attempt to obtain a commitment from the legislature—at EU level mainly from the Commission which has the right of initiating legislation—not to adopt binding legislation. In law, the legislature cannot bind itself in this way. Also, problems under competition policy—arts 101 and 102 TFEU—are not really solved. Agreements among competitors may come under art.101, even where public authorities participate in such agreements. As regards measures which have an impact on imports, international trade provisions may also be applicable.

Looking into the experience with environmental agreements in Member States, it seems that EU environmental agreements may contribute to the protection of the environment in those cases where legally binding measures are also effective; however, in those parts of the European Union where environmental directives are almost or not at all effective, environmental agreements are not likely to have a greater effect.

2–47 EU legal policy tries to circumvent these obstacles: in the case of an environmental agreement on CO_2 emissions from cars, negotiations took place in the mid and the end of the 1990s between the Commission and economic operators on what might by an acceptable offer from the car industry; Council and Parliament were informed of the state of negotiations, but did not participate. At the end of these negotiations a statement and a recommendation were issued by the Commission, in the sense that there was no need for binding measures at

---

[104] EP, Resolutions of 17 July 1997, [1997] OJ C 286/254; October 26, 2000, [2000] OJ C197/433; January 18, 2001 [2001] OJ C262/236.

[105] Commission, Communication on Environmental Agreements, COM(96) 561; see also COM(2002)412 (fn.103, above) and Council Resolution of October 7, 1997 [1997] OJ C321/6.

[106] Commission (fn.103, above) p.4.

[107] Commission (fnn.103 and 105, above); Council (fn.105, above); EP (fn.104, above).

EU level, since there was a voluntary commitment by the car industry.[108] It should be noted, though, that the agreement was not made with the car manufacturers themselves, but with their industrial associations. Thus, when the Rover company later left the association, it was no longer bound by the agreement.

A second way consists in negotiations between the Commission and one or more professional organisations on an improvement in environmental performance. At the end of these negotiations, the European professional organisations make a commitment to the Commission. The Commission adopts a recommendation based on art.288 TFEU, which recommends that those environmental commitments be followed, which the professional organisation had agreed to accept. An example of this model which does not contain any form of "agreement" (i.e. some form of a contract) is the use of detergents, where the Commission made a recommendation in 1998.[109]

Underlying both types of environmental "agreements" is the Commission's commitment not to make proposals for a directive or a regulation. The abovementioned statement by the Commission that "the Commission can never, by 'acknowledging' such an engagement, forgo its right of initiative"[110] is legally quite correct. However, politically, an acknowledgment by the Commission is perceived by the economic actors as a commitment not to initiate legislation, and this is, of course, intended.

The main difference to environmental agreements as they are negotiated and concluded, for example, in the Netherlands is that on the one hand the Dutch authorities fix themselves—by way of legislation/regulation or Government decision—the result to be reached, whereas at EU level the result of an agreement to be reached is bargained between the vested interest group and the Commission. On the other hand, the obligation to publicly lay account at regular intervals on progress is normally much stricter and much stricter monitored by the Dutch public authorities.

As regards environmental agreements at national level, Member States are free to act as they consider appropriate. To what extent Member States might feel bound by any agreement that was produced at EU level and abstain from introducing legislation, is a political decision. On general aspects of the implementation of EU environmental legislation through national environmental agreements, the Commission made a communication and a recommendation, in 1996.[111] By end of 2010, only four Directives[112] contained a clause that allowed Member States to implement some of the Directives' provisions by environmental agreements, for which a number of conditions were laid down. Future will show whether the statement in the sixth environmental action programme[113] that "legislation remains central to meeting the environmental challenges and full and

---

[108] See also para.8–22, below.

[109] Rec. 98/480 [1998] OJ L215/73; see also the recommendations on CFCs 89/349, 90/437 and 90/438 (fn.72) which followed the same pattern, but became obsolete because of the evolution in the sector of ozone-depleting substances.

[110] Commission (fn.103, above), p.4.

[111] Commission, COM (96) 561 (fn.105); Rec. 96/733 (n.94).

[112] Dir.2000/53 on end-of-life vehicles [2000] OJ L269/34 art.10(3); Dir.2002/96 on waste electrical and electronic equipment (WEEE) [2003] OJ L37/24 art.5(3); Dir.94/62 on packaging and packaging waste (fn.103, above); Dir.2006/66 on batteries [2006] OJ L266/9.

[113] (113) Dec.1600/2002 (fn.7, above) Recital 12.

correct implementation of the existing legislation is a priority" will have the effect of mitigating the pressure for deregulation through environmental agreements.

Tripartite contracts and agreements

2–48 At the end of 2002, the Commission proposed the use of tripartite contracts and agreements at EC level.[114] Tripartite contracts were defined as contracts between the European Union, a Member State and regional or local authorities "in direct application of binding secondary Community law (regulations, directives or decisions)", tripartite agreements were such contracts "outside a binding Community framework". In the case of tripartite contracts an enabling clause in the legislative instrument is necessary, furthermore a clause in the contract that the Member State alone is responsible for the implementation of EC legislation.

In the environmental sector, tripartite agreements seem in particular useful in the area of local environmental issues such as coastal zone management, urban environment issues or questions of waste management, where legislation does not really reach. To what extent regions or local authorities will seize the opportunity to enter into direct contractual relationship with the EU level, remains to be seen and might also depend on the availability of financial means. Until the end of 2010, this instrument has never been used.

Instruments to influence the behaviour of undertakings and individual persons

2–49 EU law contains a number of provisions which aim at influencing the behaviour of undertakings or individual persons towards a better environment. Since the great majority of EU environmental law is made in the form of directives, these provisions do not directly address these private persons; they normally address instead Member States and ask them to "transmit" these messages via their national provisions, to the addressees. The most important instruments that exist under EU environmental law are the following.

Obligation of notification

2–50 In a number of cases, private persons are obliged to notify the authorities of a Member State of a certain activity or practice. Thus, persons who intend to put new chemical substances on the EU market have to notify public authorities of their intention and submit certain documents referring to the tests of that substance: they may put the substance on the market only 60 days after that notification.[115] Where a chemical, whose use in the European Union is prohibited or restricted, is to be exported into a third country for the first time, this intention must be notified 30 days before the export takes place; the intention behind this

---

[114] Commission: A framework for target-based tripartite contracts and agreements between the Community, the States and regional and local authorities, COM(2002) 709 of December 11, 2002.
[115] Reg.1907/2006 concerning the registration, evaluation , authorisation and restriction of chemicals [2006] OJ L396/1; see further at para.6–60, below.

provision is to inform the third country ("prior informed consent" principle).[116] A notification obligation also exists for the contained use of genetically modified micro-organisms[117] and the deliberate release of genetically modified organisms[118]; sometimes in these two instances, however, the notification is followed by an express authorisation. Directive 86/609 on animal testing[119] detailed notification obligations for experiments on animals or the details of persons conducting such experiments; establishments which use animals had to be registered. In 2010, this Directive was replaced by Directive 2010/63 which introduced authorisation requirements for breeders, suppliers and users, as well as for specific projects which use animals.[120] Also, the production, processing and import of organic agricultural products must be notified.[121]

As regards installations, notification is required for any industrial activity during which certain chemicals are used or produced; notification has to inform the authorities of the substances used, the plant and possible risks of accidents.[122] Furthermore, malfunctions or breakdowns of the functioning of installations sometimes requires notification.[123]

All these obligations for information or notification are intended to inform the authorities responsible in due time, in order to allow them to take appropriate, and if necessary preventive, action.

Authorisation

Authorisation is organised in very different ways in Member States. It is thus usual that EU legislature limits itself to requiring that certain activities have an environmental authorisation[124] (sometimes the word "permit" is used,[125] without there being any legal difference) and to setting out conditions for this authorisation.

2–51

First, a number of new installations need an authorisation for operating. Directive 2010/75[126] has to some extent harmonised the permits and the conditions thereof; however, this Directive only applies to some bigger installations. The authorisation for discharges into water under Directives 76/464 on water discharges,[127] 2001/80 on large combustion plants,[128] 1999/13 on plants

---

[116] Reg.689/2008 on the export and import of certain chemicals [2008] OJ L204/1; see also para.6–64, below.

[117] Dir.90/219 on the contained use of genetically modified micro-organisms [1990] OJ L117/1, arts 8 and 10.

[118] Dir.2001/18 on the deliberate release into the environment of genetically modified organisms [2001] OJ L106/1, arts 6 et seq.

[119] Dir.86/609 on the protection of animals used for experimental and other scientific purposes [1986] OJ L358/1.

[120] Dir.2010/63 on the protection of animals used for scientific purposes, [2010] OJ L276/33.

[121] Reg.834/2007 (fn.63, above).

[122] Dir.96/82 on the control of major accident hazards involving dangerous substances [1997] OJ L10/ 13, art.6.

[123] See, e.g. Dir.2010/75 on industrial emissions [2010] OJ L 334/17, arts 8(2) and 37(2); Dir.2010/75 is a recast of Dir.2008/1 on integrated pollution prevention control [2008] OJ L24/8.

[124] See, e.g. Dir.2010/75 (fn.123, above); Dir.76/464 on the discharge of pollutants into water [1976] OJ L129/23; this Directive will be repealed as of 2013; Dir.2006/118 on the protection of groundwater against pollution and deterioration [2006] OJ L372/19.

[125] See for instance Dir.2008/1 (fn.123, above); Dir.2008/98 on waste [2008] OJ L312/3.

[126] Dir.2010/75 (fn.123, above).

[127] Dir.76/464 (fn.124, above).

using organic solvents,[129] 78/176 on installations producing titanium dioxide,[130] and 2000/76 on waste incinerators[131] are gradually being adapted to the provisions of Directives 2010/75 which will thus become a framework directive. In the waste sector, all installations which recover, collect, treat or dispose of waste, need an authorisation.[132]

2–52 A second area deals with the authorisation to impair the environment. Besides the discharge from installations which are mentioned above, the artificial enrichment of groundwater may be mentioned,[133] or the discharge of waste-water from urban waste-water treatment plants[134]; the discharge of sewage sludge into surface waters is forbidden since 1998.[135] Product-related authorisations concerns the placing on the market of pesticides,[136] biocides[137] and the release of genetically modified organisms into the environment.[138] Also the import and export of ozone-depleting substances[139] and of endangered species of fauna and flora[140] fall into this category.

There is no general rule on the conditions which accompany the authorisation. Early directives established very detailed conditions[141] which were, however, not really controlled. Directive 2010/75 also provides for detailed conditions, such as emission limit values or equivalent parameters, the best available techniques, measurement frequency and methodology, suitable requirements for controlling emissions and measures for other than normal operating conditions. However, the condition requirements are vaguely formulated and leave large discretion to Member States.

2–53 In contrast to earlier directives, Directive 2010/75 does not provide for limited authorisation; it only requires that the authorisation be regularly reconsidered (art.21).

The procedural requirements for authorisations are few and far between. Directive 2010/75 requires a written application with a number of minimal indications and a non-technical résumé of the documentation (art.12). The application has, for an appropriate length of time, to be made available to the public to enable it to comment. An environmental impact assessment is only required for certain specific projects and, since 2004, for spatial planning and

---

[128] Dir.2001/80 on the limitation of emissions of certain pollutants into the air from large combustion plants [2001] OJ L309/1.

[129] Dir.1999/13 on the limitation of emissions of volatile organic compounds due to the use of organic solvents in certain activities and installations [1999] OJ L85/1.

[130] Dir.78/176 on waste from the titanium dioxide industry [1978] OJ L54/19.

[131] Dir.2000/76 on the incineration of waste [2000] OJ L332/91.

[132] Dir.2008/98 (fn.125, above).

[133] Dir.2006/118 (fn.124, above).

[134] Dir.91/271 on urban waste water [1991] OJ L135/40, arts 12 and 14.

[135] Dir.91/271 (fn.134, above) art.14.

[136] Reg.1107/2009 concerning the placing of plant protection products on the market [2009] OJ L309/1.

[137] Dir.98/8 concerning the placing of biocidal products on the market [1998] OJ L123/1.

[138] Dir.2001/18 (fn.118, above).

[139] Reg.1005/2009 on substances that deplete the ozone layer [2009] OJ L286/1.

[140] Reg.338/97 on trade in endangered species [1997] OJ L61/1.

[141] See, e.g. Dir.80/68 on the protection of groundwater against pollution caused by certain dangerous substances [1980] OJ L 20/43 which required methods of discharge, essential precautions, monitoring arrangements and monitoring groundwater to be detailed.

programmes.[142] These Directives provide that the public must be given "the opportunity to express an opinion" on the project, which means that the affected person has a right to be consulted.

Directive 2010/75 furthermore provides that authorisation be made available to the public; most other directives concur with this requirement. No details are set out, and the requirement for checking on whether the conditions for authorisation continue to be complied with or not has been reduced in recent directives. Directive 2003/35 now introduces a right of the public concerned to participate in the authorisation of certain projects, plans and programmes.[143]

While Directive 76/464 and its subsequent different daughter directives outlined detail control requirements, Directive 75/440 on the quality of surface water[144] was even completed by a specific "control" directive[145] and the directives on air quality standards also contained detailed measurement and control provisions.[146] All water and air provisions in this regard are now substituted by more general provisions in the water and air quality framework directives[147] which do not go into much detail. Directive 2010/75 now introduced monitoring requirements for the installations (arts 14 and 16) and the obligation for the authorities to periodically inspect the installations covered by that Directive.

Interdiction and obligation to act

EU environmentally relevant interdictions have been pronounced essentially in the product-related legislation. The most important provision was Directive 76/769[148] which was continuously amended to include further restrictions, but has now been replaced by the new regulation REACH on chemicals.[149] Besides that, every measure which fixes emission limit values, implicitly contains the interdiction on exceeding these values. Other interdictions and restrictions are found in numerous directives, such as the ban on certain heavy metals or other substances in products, on the discharge of sewage sludge into water[150] or on the non-authorised disposal of waste.[151] Most of these interdictions allow that the interdiction is disregarded in extraordinary circumstances. Occasionally, EU law

2–54

---

[142] Dir.85/337 on the assessment of the effects of certain public and private projects on the environment [1985] OJ L175/40; Dir.2001/42 on the assessment of the effects of certain plans and programmes on the environment [2001] OJ L197/30.

[143] Dir.2003/35 providing for public participation in respect of the drawing up of certain plans and programmes relating to the environment; [2003] OJ L56/17.

[144] Dir.75/440 concerning the quality required of surface water intended for the abstraction of drinking water in the Member States [1975] OJ L194/26. This Directive was in the meantime repealed.

[145] Dir.79/869 concerning the methods of measurement and frequencies of sampling and analysis of surface water intended for the abstraction of drinking waters in the Member States [1979] OJ L271/44. This Directive was in the meantime repealed.

[146] Dir.80/779 (SO_2 in the air) [1980] OJ L229/30; 82/884 (lead in the air) [1982] OJ L378/15, 85/203 (NO_x in the air) [1985] OJ L87/1. These directives were in the meantime replaced.

[147] Dir.2000/60 establishing a framework for Community action in the field of water policy [2000] OJ L327/1; Dir.2008/50 on ambient air quality and cleaner air for Europe [2008] OJ L152/1.

[148] Dir.76/769 relating to restrictions on the marketing and use of certain dangerous substances and preparations [1976] OJ L262/201.

[149] Reg.1907/2006 (fn.115, above).

[150] Dir.91/271 (fn.134, above).

[151] Dir.2008/98 (fn.125, above).

itself authorises Member States to establish a ban. General authorisation in this regard are found in arts 114(4) and 193 TFEU.

Further elements exist in secondary law under the so-called safeguard clause: these clauses give the possibility of temporarily prohibiting a product even though it complies with EU requirements. Such a ban provokes an EU control procedure which ends either with an EU-wide prohibition or an invitation to the acting Member State to repeal its ban. Specific authorisations for Member States to issue bans exist for using sewage sludge where certain concentrations of heavy metals are exceeded[152] and for importing/exporting hazardous waste for disposal purposes.[153] EU environmental law only rarely provides for general national derogations of a ban. An example is the possibility of hunting certain birds in specified Member States.[154] Considerably more often it happens that a Member State may grant a derogation of a ban on a case-by-case basis.

2–55   Obligations to act are also rather few and far between. They concern, for instance, obligations to keep registers, to measure emissions, to hand over waste to an authorised undertaker, to discharge air emissions via a chimney, etc. Never are sanctions provided: these are left to national legislation.

Directive 2010/75 sets out "general principles" for the operator of installations that come under that Directive,[155] which probably have a placebo effect because they are hardly enforceable and may be interpreted in many different ways. Also, Directive 96/82 obliges the operator of a plant to take "all necessary measures" to prevent accidents.

Recent waste legislation started to introduce take-back obligations for cars and electrical/electronic equipment.[156] National take-back schemes are allowed under EU law and sometimes required by EU legislation.[157] Deposit and return systems are likewise possible at national level, but have not yet been imposed by EU legislation. Obligations to ensure financial security only exist for the shipment of hazardous waste to another State.[158] No insurance obligation exists against environmental impairment; the Directive on environmental liability left the question whether there should be compulsory insurance for damage to the environment to the national legislation.[159]

2–56   There is no obligation for an undertaking to mandate a person to look into environmental issues. Directive 82/501 contained the obligation for an undertaking coming under that Directive to designate a specific person in charge

---

[152] Dir.86/278 on the use of sewage sludge in agriculture [1986] OJ L181/6, arts 5 and 7.

[153] Reg.1013/2006 (fn.68, above).

[154] Dir.2009/147 on the conservation of wild birds [2010] OJ L20/7, art.7(3) and annex II(2).

[155] Dir.2010/75 (fn.123, above), art.11: For instance: "no significant pollution is caused"; "energy is used efficiently"; "the necessary measures are taken to prevent accidents and limit their consequences" and so on.

[156] Dir.2000/53 (fn.112, above); Dir.2002/96 (fn.112, above) where the obligation is limited to waste from electrical and electronic equipment (WEEE) other than WEEE from private households. For such waste from private households, Member States only have to set up return systems, art.5(2).

[157] Dir.2006/66 on batteries and accumulators [2006] OJ L266/1; Dir.94/62 (fn.103, above), art.7; Dir.96/59 on the disposal of PCB/PCT [1996] OJ L243/31, art.6, furthermore the directives mentioned in fn.156, above.

[158] Reg.1013/2006 (fn.68, above).

[159] Dir.2004/35 on environmental liability with regard to the prevention and remedying of environmental damage [2005] OJ L143/56, art.14.

of security and to implement the accident prevention and evacuation plans.[160] However, Directive 96/82 which replaced Directive 82/501, deleted this provision altogether.[161]

EU environmental law does not expressly require to take the supply of water, electricity or fuel from a specific place, or to deliver waste or waste water to a specific place or installation. However, such an obligation implicitly underlies the Directive on urban waste water.[162] Member States are free to make provisions for such an obligation, however not for waste which may be recovered. Obligations for remedial action, following an action that impaired the environment, were established by Directive 2004/35 on environmental liability.[163] An indirect obligation flows, in my opinion, from art.13 of Directive 2008/98 on waste[164] which ensures that waste disposal does not impair the environment; this provision requires the elimination of illegally disposed waste and the restoration of the impaired environment.[165] Regulation 1013/2006 obliges Member States to take back waste which has been illegally shipped to another Member State.[166]

2–57

Liability obligations only exist, up to now, for damage caused by defective products[167]; this Directive also applies to damage caused by waste, although this is contested.[168] Directive 2005/35 on environmental liability does not contain any financial responsibility of a polluter to compensate a victim, but is limited to environmental restoration obligations under public law.

Information, appeals, warnings

EU environmental law and policy contain numerous addresses and appeals to citizens to behave in a way which is environmentally more beneficial. A good example is the Council resolution on the fifth environmental action programme, where the Council declared that "many current forms of activity and development are not environmentally sustainable" and that "the achievement of sustainable development calls for significant changes in current patterns of development, production, consumption and behaviour"; this implied "a sharing of responsibility at global, Community, regional, local and even personal level".[169] It is impossible to measure the impact of such appeals.

Since 1992, the European Union has tried to re-educate consumers' and users' behaviour towards environmentally "better" products, by establishing an EU eco-label.[170] Since industry associations are not really in favour of a system that classifies some products to be better than others, the work advances very slowly, all the more as the system also has to compete with differing national systems;

[160] Dir.82/501 on accident prevention [1982] OJ L230/5; see also *Commission v Netherlands* (C–190/90) [1992] E.C.R. I–3265.
[161] Dir.96/82 (fn.122 above), art.11.
[162] Dir.91/271 (fn.134 above).
[163] Dir.2004/35 (fn.159, above).
[164] Dir.2008/98 (fn.125, above).
[165] Court of Justice, *Commission v Italy* (C–365/97) [1999] E.C.R. I–2773; on this issue see L. Krämer, *Casebook on EU Environmental Law* (Oxford, 2002) pp.341 and 391.
[166] Reg.1013/2006 (fn.68, above).
[167] Dir.85/374 on product liability [1985] OJ L210/29.
[168] See also para.4–50, below.
[169] [1993] OJ C138/1.
[170] Reg.66/2010 (fn.64, above).

thus, its effects have been up until now very limited.[171] The EU eco-audit scheme[172] has had more success, though it also has to compete with an international ISO-standard which is less ambitious.[173]

The European Union has never issued warnings against environmentally dangerous products. A recommendation to be careful with toys for small children that contain PVC with certain phthalates,[174] obviously aimed more at protecting health than the environment. Under Directive 2008/50,[175] Member States are obliged to warn the population of each individual Member State where certain levels of ozone concentration are exceeded, a way to replace remedial action by warnings.

Generally, the effect of EU appeals and information is not significantly greater than that of corresponding national measures. It is correct that EU institutions have, at least in part, greater credit with the population in environmental matters; however, this is balanced by a greater distance towards the ordinary citizen.

Financial assistance

2–58   Up until now, no EU provision has provided for financial advantages of environmentally "better" products. Member States oppose such rules, since environmental protection is of different importance in the different Member States, and they are afraid of competitive disadvantages. Thus, a Commission proposal to introduce a price differentiation between leaded and unleaded petrol and thereby accelerate the introduction of catalytic converters and lead-free petrol[176] was rejected: such differentiation was subsequently introduced at national level. In the same way the attempt failed to introduce general financial advantages for the introduction of cars with catalytic converters; the final compromise only allowed such encouragement for a limited period of time. Attempts in this direction seem to have been largely abandoned since then, though the idea of "getting the prices right" continues to be mentioned. Attempts to introduce a reduced VAT tax for products which carry an EU ecolabel were discussed, but finally not proposed by the Commission.

Subventions

2–59   National subventions (state aids) are in principle prohibited (art.107 TFEU), but are in practice far-spread in all Member States. The total amount of state aids in 2008 was 67.4 billion €,[177] the amount of environmental aid is not known. Since 1974 the Commission has fixed an EU framework for environmental aids, which was last reviewed in 2008.[178] This framework fixes the conditions under which the Commission normally considers environmental aid compatible with the Treaty. The regular amount is differentiated according to the size of the enterprise

---

[171] See for more details paras 6–56 et seq., below.
[172] Reg.1221/2009 (fn.66, above).
[173] See for more details paras 4–51 et seq., below.
[174] Rec. 98/485 [1998] OJ L217/35.
[175] Dir.2008/50 on ambient air quality and cleaner air for Europe [2008] OJ L152/1.
[176] [1984] OJ C178/5.
[177] Commission, COM(2009)661; if one adds the amounts which were injected into the economy because of the financial and economic crisis in 2008, the amount was 279.6 billion €.
[178] Commission, Community guidelines on State aid for environmental protection [2008] OJ C82/1.

and is normally up to 70 per cent for small enterprises, 60 for medium-sized enterprises and 50 per cent for large enterprises. Financial encouragements to consumers to acquire environmentally "better" products do not fall into this scheme as long as the aid does not advantage individual undertakings.[179]

EU subventions are particularly granted under the Structural Funds and the Cohesion Fund.[180] The Structural Funds aim at balancing the situation of economically disadvantaged regions, including rural areas (art.174 TFEU). The Member States entitled to receive funds establish programmes which are approved by the Commission; the individual projects which come under these agreed programmes are then realised under the responsibility of the Member State. The priorities and the taking of environmental measures are largely left to the discretion of each Member State.

In the past, the Cohesion Fund co-financed individual projects in the environmental and transport sector in those Member States where the gross national product lies below 90 per cent of the EU average. Until 2006 this was the case for Greece, Spain, Portugal and Ireland. The new regional policy system, applicable since 2007, integrates the Cohesion Fund into the general Regional Fund System which means that the sums which are made available are no longer ear-marked for specific projects. Regional funds may thus also co-finance projects which contribute to the implementation of obligations under EU environmental law, such as the construction of sewers, waste-water treatment plants, waste disposal or recovery installations or nature protection projects which is hardly completely compatible with the polluter pays principle as laid down in arts 191 and 192(5) TFEU. There are several other EU aid programmes, in particular in the sectors of energy, research or agriculture.

As mentioned, there have been up until now no fiscal advantages granted by EU measures. Likewise, there are as yet no EU rules on environmental charges.

Tradable certificates; bubbles

Environmental certificates are used as tokens, which, against payment, are issued by the public authorities and give the right to input into the environment the quantity of pollutants indicated by the token. These certificates are tradable.   **2–60**

In 2003, The European Union adopted a directive on tradable emission permits for greenhouse gases.[181] This Directive was elaborated under the auspices of the Kyoto Protocol to the United Nation Convention on Climate Change[182] which required, internationally, the introduction of tradable certificates by 2008. The EU system has been operational since the beginning of 2005. Undertakings which come under the Directive—some 20,000 installations which emit about 45 per cent of all CO^2-emissions—obtain an allowance for emitting CO^2-gases. Where they invest in cleaner technologies which reduce emissions, they may sell those

---

[179] Commission, Community guidelines on State aid for environmental protection [2008] OJ C82/1.

[180] Reg.1083/2006 laying down general provisions on the European Regional Development Fund, the European Social Fund and the Cohesion Fund [2006] OJ L210/25; Reg.1084/2006 establishing a Cohesion Fund [2006] OJ L210/79.

[181] Directive 2003/87 establishing a scheme for greenhouse gas emission allowances trading within the Community [2003] OJ L275/32; for more details see para.9–11, below.

[182] See Dec.2002/358 concerning the approval, on behalf of the Community, of the Kyoto Protocol to the United Nations Framework Convention on Climate Change and the joint fulfilment of commitments thereunder [2002] OJ L 130/1.

allowances which they do not need any more. If, conversely, they need more allowances, they can buy them from other undertakings.

Under Regulation 1005/2009 producers of ozone-depleting substances have the possibility, granted by the Commission, of marketing specific quantities of ozone-depleting substances or to use the quantities themselves. Such rights may be transferred to other EU producers of the same substance; the Commission is to be informed of any such transaction.[183] The essential difference to certificates is the fact that this provision deals with a product for which limitations already exist and that the general objective of all these provisions is to progressively reduce and finally completely end the production of such substances.

The bubble concept requires, within a specific geographical area that total pollution quantities are taken into account. Within this total quantity, the different emittors may emit differing quantities of pollutants. EU law provides for a bubble concept in Directive 2001/80 on emissions from large combustion plants,[184] where total quantities for sulphur dioxides (SO_2), nitrogen oxides (NOx) and dust emissions have been set for each Member State. These total quantities are to be reduced in two or three stages. It is left to Member States to distribute nationally the total quantities for emissions.

Furthermore, Directive 2001/81 on national emission ceilings asked Member States to reduce, by 2010, air emissions of SO_2, NOx, volatile organic compounds and ammonia by a certain percentage.[185] How Member States achieve this reduction target was left to them. As with the Directive on large combustion plants, the main problem with this Directive is the monitoring of its application. It will hardly be possible for any national or EU body to monitor the application of the targets, or for the Commission to take any action under art.258 TFEU. Indeed, the compilation of data to prove the non-respect of the obligations is much too complicated and in the hands of the Member State in question. Therefore, the same remarks as para.2–32, above, apply: where a Member State has the political will to comply with the requirements of Directive 2001/81, it has at its disposal a sufficiently flexible instrument to do so. However, where this political will is absent, almost no enforcement means are available.

A form of bubble concept was incorporated into the Agreement on the transit of the Alps between Austria and the European Union.[186] Trucks which crossed the Alps via Austria were charged with "eco-points"; the number of points varied according to the truck's pollution emissions. Member States obtained a total number of carriages which they had to attribute on the individual trucks. The total number of eco-points was to be reduced by 60 per cent during the 12-year period of the Convention. This agreement became incorporated in the Austrian Accession Treaty when Austria joined the European Union in 1995, but ended in 2003.[187]

---

[183] Reg.1005/2009 (fn.67, above), arts 3(10) and 4(5).

[184] Dir.2001/80 (fn.128, above).

[185] Dir.2001/81 on national emission ceilings for certain air pollutants [2001] OJ L309/22.

[186] Agreement between the European Economic Community and the Republic of Austria on the transit of goods by road and rail [1992] OJ L373/6; Reg.3637/92 on a system of distribution of rights of transit (eco-points) for heavy goods vehicles with a laden weight of over 7.5 tonnes registered in a Member State transiting through Austria [1992] OJ L373/1.

[187] Agreement between the European Economic Community and the Republic of Austria on the transit of goods by road and rail [1992] OJ L373/6; Reg.3637/92 on a system of distribution of rights

3.   Decision-making procedure

Elaboration of a legislative measure

Commission proposal

The Commission has, as mentioned, the monopoly on taking initiatives for legal   **2–61**
action, although there is at least a political, if not a legal, obligation to take such
initiatives under art.225(2) and art.192(3) TFEU.[188] It is at the Commission's
discretion to decide what form, objective and content its proposal for a legislative
act shall take and what preparatory work is undertaken. Normally, a comparative
assessment of national legislation is made as well as one or several studies on the
scientific, technical, economic and environmental aspects of a subject and
estimations about the impact of the planned measures undertaken. Draft proposals
are prepared by the technical units inside the Directorate-General responsible, not
by a central "drafting unit".

Consultations with Member States at an administrative level generally start
with a first draft of a directive, which is frequently accompanied by background
documents which explain the approach chosen, indicate the options and raise
other matters that might be of interest. Practice varies as to whether at this stage
of the drafting a consensus is sought with other departments inside the
Commission before a draft is sent to a wider audience.

Such discussions hardly ever take the form of bilateral discussions with   **2–62**
Member States (which would take place in the different capitals rather than in
Brussels): they are limited to particularly "important" Member States and they
are mainly made to consult on the approach to be taken or the strategy to be
adopted. Multilateral discussions on draft proposals for environmental directives
between the Commission's administration and Member States' officials always
take place. These meetings are convened in Brussels on invitation by the
Commission administration which chairs them. Officials from interested
Commission departments participate. The invitation to these meetings is
addressed to the Permanent Representation of Member States with the European
Union and asks them to designate experts to attend the meeting. The experts need
not come from environmental administration or even administration at all.

As environmental law often is technical and has a limited number of national
rules to take into consideration, only one or two of such multilateral meetings of
experts are usually needed to reach a consensus. In areas where more general
problems are touched upon, discussions inside the Commission and with Member
States' experts may take a long time. Thus, while the Commission services
drafted 23 texts for a proposal on environmental impact assessment[189] before the
text could become an official proposal for a directive and be sent to the Council,
the Directive on liquid beverage containers[190] had almost as many drafts.

Parallel to those meetings with governmental experts, discussions with   **2–63**
organisations from trade and industry and environmental organisations take

---

of transit (eco-points) for heavy goods vehicles with a laden weight of over 7.5 tonnes registered in a
Member State transiting through Austria [1992] OJ L373/1.
[188] See para.2–21, above.
[189] Dir.85/337 [1985] OJ L175/40; for more details see paras 4–29 et seq., below.
[190] Dir.85/339 [1985] OJ L176/18; see also paras 10–49 et seq., below.

place. No systematic consultation is organised, although the Commission services prefer consultation with European organisations over national bodies or even individual companies. The sheer number of professional organisations guarantees them a greater chance of consultation, compared to environmental organisations which are under-represented at EU level and lack resources, know-how and expertise in successful lobbying. Internet consultation became, since several years, more and more frequent; it is almost exclusively done in English.

Since the beginning of 2003, the Commission has established an impact assessment process. For new legislative proposals, an impact assessment is made, which researches the economic, social and environmental implications of the future proposal, including the examination of alternatives, of a zero alternative (not legislating), etc.[191] The impact assessment paper is made available to the public in the form of a Commission working document.

At the end of the consultation and impact assessment process, a draft text emerges which the Directorate-General responsible takes back into the Commission in order to start the formal adoption phase. The draft, together with an explanatory memorandum,[192] is sent to all interested Directorates-General and in all cases to the Legal Service with the request for approval. There will be different positions (which of course are also influenced by outside lobbying) with an attempt to reach a compromise text. The revised text then goes into the approval procedure of the Commission itself. At cabinet level, attempts are made to find, if necessary, a political compromise on outstanding questions.

If the cabinets succeed, the 27 Commissioners normally approve the draft by way of written procedure. Where they do not succeed or where the text is of political importance, the draft is discussed orally: a simple majority of Commissioners is necessary to have a draft adopted as a formal Commission proposal. It may happen that a text is not capable of being approved by the Commission, though this is rather unusual in environmental matters.

The official Commission proposal for a directive or a regulation is published as a COM-document, and only in exceptional cases in the Official Journal of the European Communities, Part C. The explanatory memorandum, which is not an integral part of the proposal, is made available to the public in the form of an official COM-document; in order to avoid lengthy translations, numerous details are put into a SEC-document which is normally also publicly available. The text of the proposed Act is drafted in all official languages, while the explanatory memorandum is usually produced in only English, French and German.

---

[191] Commission, Communication on Impact Assessment COM(2002) 276.

[192] Internal Commission rules have largely standardised the content of the explanatory memorandum, though each text is adapted to the specific subject matter; as an example, the proposal for a directive on end of life vehicles, COM (97) 358 of July 9, 1997, might be quoted which contains the following headings: 1. Introduction; 2. Problems addressed in this proposal; 3. The fifth environmental action programme; 4. Environmental objectives; 5. Internal market and economic objectives; 6. Economic assessment; 7. Situation in Member States; 8. Developments at international level; 9. Subsidiarity and proportionality; 10. Legislative and administrative simplification; 11. Imports from third countries; 12. Consistency with other Community policies; 13. Consultation with stakeholders; 14. Legal basis; 15. Data/scientific bases; 16. Content Article by Article; 17. Impact of the proposal on business with special reference to small and medium-sized enterprises.

European Parliament, ECOSOC and Committee of the Regions

The Commission's proposal is transmitted to the European Parliament and the   **2–64**
Council, which passes the text on to the Economic and Social Committee and the
Committee of the Regions. The Parliament adopts a legislative resolution with
textual amendments, the Committees give opinions on the text. These comments
are prepared within committees, under the responsibility of a rapporteur for the
proposal, who is selected from the committee's members. Commission officials
attend committee meetings, answer questions and explain reasons for the options
taken. Their position is marked by the necessity to "defend", if possible, the
Commission's proposal.

There is no standard practice for how the rapporteurs assemble the necessary
know-how to prepare their report and the draft opinion. Both are mostly prepared
by means of informal contacts with persons or groups which are politically or
professionally close to the rapporteur's political party or group; formal written
consultation with groups or public hearings in the Parliament are exceptional and
almost never take place in the other two bodies.

In Parliament, the Environmental Committee votes on the draft opinion and all
amendments which were presented by members of the Committee. Other
committees also deal with the proposal, according to their responsibilities. Thus,
for example, the Commission's proposal for a directive on environmental liability
was discussed in the Committee on Legal Affairs and Internal Market as the
leading committee, the Environmental Committee, the Industry Committee, the
Economic Affairs Committee and the Petitions Committee. All these committees
may request amendments of the proposed text. Then the text which has been
adapted by the leading committee, goes to Parliament's plenary, where again
amendments to the draft opinion may be tabled. The opinion is voted upon and is,
after adoption, published in the Official Journal. The Committees' reports are
published on the internet.

Since 1979, when the European Parliament became elected by general   **2–65**
elections, there has been agreement between the Commission and the Parliament
that the Commission would take on board amendments suggested by the
Parliament wherever possible. Obviously, such a vague clause which raises
difficulties in practice, does not satisfy Parliament, which is of the opinion that,
as it is an elected body, all amendments to proposals should be accepted by the
Commission. It sometimes uses procedural means (delays or refusals to vote,
extensive discussions between the rapporteur and the Commission's services or
the president of the Environmental Committee and the Commissioner for
environmental issues) in order to compel the Commission to accept its
amendments. The procedure in the Economic and Social Committee and the
Committee of the Regions is similar; also their adopted opinions which generally
do not contain precise drafting proposals, are published in the Official Journal.

Council procedure

At Council level the Commission's proposal is first examined by a working   **2–66**
group, which normally takes up its work without having the opinion of the other
institutions. The frequency of meetings depends on whether the presidency

wishes to get ahead with the proposal[193]; whereas some proposals are immediately taken up, others might wait for years or not be discussed at all. The working party starts with a general discussion and then passes through each individual article. After having revised the proposal and listed all objections to its different provisions in detail, the working group's chair sends the text to the Committee of Permanent Representatives (COREPER). He may also do so when he wishes to receive political instruction on questions which the working group feels unable to solve. The report sent to COREPER contains the new text proposal, accompanied by remarks, reservations, suggested compromise solutions or declarations by Member States.

COREPER meets once a week and deals with practically all questions of EU policy. In environmental matters, COREPER tries to concentrate discussions on Commission proposals in one or two meetings which take place in preparation of Council meetings on environmental matters. After discussion of the environmental proposal as it emerged from the working group the text is either sent back to the working group with further instructions or—where an agreement by the Council seems possible—it is sent to the Environmental Council for decision or for political guidance on basic issues. COREPER prepares the Council agenda, though the final decision on it is made by the presidency of the Council.

2–67   The Council may only take a decision where the opinions of the other institutions, in particular that of the European Parliament, have been given; and in all cases the Council must decide unanimously where it amends a Commission proposal (art.293 TFEU), though the Commission, wanting its proposal to be adopted, hardly ever refuses to agree to amendments in environmental matters. The Council's decision in environmental matters consists in the adoption of the Commission's proposal, where the Parliament has only a consultative function— mainly art.192(2) in environmental matters and 43 TFEU in agricultural-environmental matters—or where Parliament has either not proposed amendments or the Council adopts all amendments proposed by the European Parliament.[194] In other environmental cases, the Council establishes its "position".[195] This position and a short explanation, where it deviates from the Commission's proposal and/or the Parliament's opinion, are published in the Official Journal.

Subsequently, the Council's position is submitted to the European Parliament for a second reading. If Parliament agrees to that position or does not decide, the Council's position is formally adopted as the legislative act; if Parliament rejects the Council's position with an absolute majority, the proposal is rejected. If the Council agrees to all amendments which Parliament has proposed in the second reading the legal act is so adopted. In practice, as mentioned in para.2–21, above, the Parliament only very exceptionally succeeds in substantially changing the Council's position. In recent years, more and more informal agreements were made between the Parliament and the Council to even avoid a second reading and to have the legislative act adopted in the first reading. The negotiations leading to

---

[193] As an example, Dir.96/59 on PCB/PCT (fn.157, above) may be quoted, which took eight years between the Commission's proposal and the adoption by the Council; in contrast to that, Dir.96/61 on integrated prevention and pollution control, which now, after several amendments, has become Directive 2010/75 (fn.123, above) was adopted within two years.
[194] art.294 no.4 TFEU.
[195] art.294 TFEU uses the term "position". Before the entry into force of the Lisbon Treaty, this Council position was called "common position", and this terminology continues to be frequently used.

such agreements are largely influenced by policy and political party considerations; they are not public and open the door to all sorts of bargaining.

Where after the second reading divergencies continue to exist, a Conciliation Committee is convened which consists of 27 members of the Council and the same number of members from Parliament; the Commission participates, but is not a member as such. Also, the Commission is no longer to defend its own proposal, but has the obligation to try to find a compromise between the European Parliament and the Council. Where a compromise is reached, that compromise becomes the adopted legal act. Where no compromise is reached, the proposal is considered rejected. Details of this co-decision procedure, which is the normal procedure in environmental matters since 1999, are laid down in art.294 TFEU.

The co-decision procedure is complicated and can hardly be called a   2–68
legislative procedure in which citizens have much input. It is marked by the effort to place more influence on the legislative procedure to the European Parliament, the only elected EU institution, without significantly reducing the decision-making power of Member States who meet in Council.

The co-decision procedure is the normal procedure for decisions in environmental matters, as follows from art.192(1) TFEU. However, since art.11 TFEU requires that environmental requirements are taken into consideration when measures in other policy sectors are adopted, measures which aim at protecting or improving the environment need not necessarily be based on art.192(1) TFEU. Rather, art.192(2), art.191(4) for international environmental matters, art.43 for agricultural matters, art.90 on transport, art.113 on taxation, art.114 on the internal market, art.207 on commercial matters or art.188 TFEU on research may also be applicable.

The choice of the legal basis

General principles

The choice of a legal basis of a legislative act is of importance, as the   2–69
decision-making procedure and in particular the European Parliament's right to participate in the making of the decision is different under different Treaty provisions. Furthermore, the rights of Member States to adopt legislation at national level after the adoption of the EU Act, vary.

The Council favours art.192 TFEU in environmental matters, but does not hesitate, according to circumstances, to choose a double legal basis[196] or to take another legal basis than art.192, in particular arts 114, 90 or 43 TFEU. Sometimes, such a decision also seems to be influenced by political considerations.

The Court of Justice stated at several occasions that the choice of the legal basis for an EU measure is not left to the discretion of the EU institutions, but has to be based on objective criteria, in particular the stated objective and the content

---

[196] See, e.g. Dec.94/800 on adhering to the Uruguay agreements (WTO provisions) [1994] OJ L336/1,which was based on (old) arts 43, 54, 57, 66, 75, 84, 99, 100, 100a, 113, 235 EC Treaty; Dec. 98/487 on an agreement with the United States on humane trapping methods for animals [1998] OJ L219/24, which was based on (old) arts 113 and 100a EC Treaty.

of the measure.[197] Furthermore, the Court is of the opinion that where a measure pursues two objectives at the same time, which have exactly the same weight in a given context, preference has to be given to the legal basis that ensures greater participation of the European Parliament.

A situation that two policy objectives have exactly the same weight, seems to be very exceptional. The relevant decision in this regard[198] was taken at a time when the European Parliament had greater participation rights under art.114 TFEU (co-decision rights according to art.294 TFEU) than under art.192 TFEU (at that time co-operation procedure under art.252 EC). These differences no longer exist. It seems impossible to base a legislative environmental act on both arts 192 and 114 TFEU, as the residual powers of Member States under arts 193 and 114(4–9) TFEU are very different and a double legal basis would create considerable legal uncertainty. Consequently, and quite rightly neither the Commission nor the Council ever tried to base a legislative act on arts 192 and 114 jointly.[199]

However, in case C–178/03 the Court stated that Regulation 304/2003 on the export and import of dangerous chemicals had to be based on the double legal basis of arts 133 and 175 (now arts 207 and 192 TFEU).[200] It considered, without further discussion, that the co-decision procedure of art.251 EC Treaty (now art.294 TFEU) should apply, though this procedure was foreseen in art.175, but not in art.133 EC Treaty. The Court did not discuss the question of Member States' residual rights; this is problematic, as art.192 TFEU is followed by art.193 TFEU which gives Member States the right to maintain or introduce more stringent environment legislation, whereas art.207 TFEU is not accompanied by a corresponding provision.

May thus a Member State, based on art.193 TFEU, ban the export of a chemical, the export of which was not banned by the Union? It will be interesting to see how this dilemma is finally solved. I plead for an application of art.193 TFEU in such a case, as this would strengthen environmental legislation. The solution which would better correspond to the structure of the Treaty, though, would have been to have opted for art.207 TFEU as the only legal basis: indeed, Regulation 304/2003 which is now replaced by Regulation 689/2008,[201] is a product-related measure and it makes more sense to use, for such product-related provisions, arts 114 (internal market) and 207 (international trade) TFEU.[202]

---

[197] *Commission v Council* (C–155/91) [1993] E.C.R. I–939; *European Parliament v Council* (C–187/93) [1994] E.C.R. I–2857; *European Parliament v Council* (C–164 & 165/97) [1999] E.C.R. I–1139.

[198] Court of Justice, *Commission v Council* (C–300/89) [1991] E.C.R. I–2867.

[199] See as an example on the one hand Dir.2000/53 on end-of-life vehicles (fn.112, above) which also contained a ban of certain substances in cars; this Directive was based on art.175 EC; on the other hand Dir.2002/96 (fn.112, above) and Dir.2002/95 [2003] OJ L37/19 which limited the use of certain substances in electrical and electronic equipment. While Directive 2002/96 was based on art.175, Dir.2002/95 was based on art.95 (now, art.114 TFEU).

[200] Court of Justice, *Commission v Council* (C–178/03) [2006] E.C.R. I–107.

[201] Reg.689/2008 concerning the export and import of dangerous chemicals [2008] OJ L204/1.

[202] See also Court of Justice, *Kemikalieinspektionen* (C–288/08), judgment of November 19, 2009, where the Court decided that a national export ban of mercury exports was not compatible with EU secondary law. In my opinion, the Court wrongly interpreted EU law against the interests of the environment, see for more details Krämer, *JEEPL* 2010, p.124.

Another option was chosen by Regulation 842/2006 on certain fluorinated greenhouse gases[203]: the Regulation was based on the EC Treaty "and in particular, Article 175(1) thereof and Article 95 thereof in relation to Articles 7, 8 and 9 of this Regulation". Thus, within one and the same legislative act, different legal provisions apply. This might help to a certain extent; however, provisions also are to be interpreted in their systematic content (contextual interpretation), which may require subtle ponderations, whether a Member State may deviate from the act's provision or not. It appears doubtful, whether this differentiation will increase legal certainty.

Where two or more objectives of an environmental measure have a different emphasis, the Court applies the theory of the "centre of gravity": it looks at the legislative measure as a whole as well as at its different provisions. Where the measure primarily aimed at the protection of the environment, art.192 TFEU applies; where the main emphasis was placed on ensuring the free movement of goods, art.114 TFEU is the appropriate legal basis, even in cases where the measure also aims, secondly, at the protection of the environment.[204] Similar reasoning is applied when other Treaty provisions such as arts 43 or 207 are considered against art.192 TFEU.   **2–70**

The Court summarised its jurisprudence as follows[205]:

> "it is necessary, in order to determine the appropriate legal basis, to consider whether the measures in question relate principally to a particular field of actions, having only incidental effects on other policies, or whether both aspects are equally essential. If the first hypothesis is correct, recourse to a single legal basis is sufficient …; if the second is correct, it is insufficient and the institution is required to adopt the measure on the basis of both the provisions from which its competence derives … However, no such dual basis is possible, where the procedures laid down for each legal basis are incompatible with each other…"

This theory seems to give good results in most cases. However, its concept raises a number of problems. Whether the objective of a directive or a regulation is the protection of the environment or the achievement of the internal market and the free flow of goods, is not at all clear. It is worth mentioning in this regard that the basic Directive on emission standards for cars was adopted as part of the EU programme to eliminate technical barriers to trade, i.e. with the objective of establishing a common market for cars.[206] The fact that a Member State presses for more stringent environmental standards for cars does not detract from the fact that the EU provision is primarily designed to maintain the free circulation of goods and to lay down stringent environmental standards to prevent a disturbance of the internal market. However, it may equally be the objective of an EU provision to take on board the motives of the environmentally conscious Member State and improve the quality of the environment. These reasons for an EU provision may be supplemented by others, such as protection of consumers, protection of the national or European motor industry, the attempt to restrict imports from third countries, or economic, transport or commercial policy reasons.   **2–71**

The introduction of EU car emission standards, which required the introduction of catalytic converters, was motivated by increased air pollution.   **2–72**

---

[203] Reg.842/2006 on certain fluorinated greenhouse gases [2006] OJ L161/1.
[204] Cases C–164 and 165/97 (fn.197, above), para.14.
[205] Cases C–164 and 165/97 (fn.197, above), para.14.
[206] Dir.70/220 [1970] OJ L76/1.

This was the reason stated in the Directives, which were partly an amendment of Directive 70/220 and partly independent directives[207]; mention was also made of internal market considerations—however, this was in a very accessory way. Directive 91/173 on restrictions of the use of pentachlorophenol (PCP)[208] was constructed in a similar way: the Commission was notified by Germany of restrictions on the use of PCP. On its proposal, the Council adopted Directive 91/173 which severely restricted the use of PCP in the European Union, stating in the Directive that the main objective was to reduce the environmental and human health risk of PCP. Directive 2006/66 limits the content of dangerous substances in batteries and accumulators.[209] Its primary objective, as it appears in the preamble and the text of the Directive, is the reduction of dangerous substances in the environment. The Directive concerning the reduction of lead in petrol and sulphur in diesel[210] was based on art.95 (now art.114 TFEU), the Directive on the reduction of sulphur in diesel alone on art.175 (now art.192 TFEU).[211] The restriction and ban of ozone-depleting substances is based on art.192 TFEU,[212] though the Regulation expressly stated that that its main objective was the need to reduce the environmental and human health risks. The limitation of heavy metals in batteries and accumulators was justified by the need to reduce dangerous substances in the environment; also the other measures of that Directive— separate collection of batteries, specific labelling requirements—had essentially an environmental objective. And yet the Directive was based on art.95, as regards the restriction of substances, the placing on the market of batteries and their labelling, for the rest on art.175 EC Treaty.[213]

If one were taking the theory of the "centre of gravity" seriously, all these directives would have had to be based on art.192 TFEU alone, since their primary objective, as indicated in their recitals and as it appears from their objective and content, was the protection of the environment. In particular, where a substance or a product is banned or its use restricted, it is almost never the case that the primary objective will be the functioning of the internal market.

2–73
The theory of the centre of gravity of a specific measure is not as clear as it might appear. A good example is case C–300/89,[214] relating to Directive 89/428 on the harmonisation of programmes for the reduction of waste from the titanium dioxide industry,[215] where both the Council and the Commission agents based their arguments before the Court of Justice on the primary objective of Directive 89/428. However, while the Commission agent (attorney) saw the primary objective of the Directive as the creation of equal competitive conditions for the titanium dioxide industry and thus wanted to have the present art.114 established as the correct legal basis, the Council agent saw as its primary objective the protection of the environment and pleaded for the present art.192 as the appropriate legal basis. The Court, in that specific case, did not concur with that

---

[207] Dir.88/6 [1988] OJ L36/1; Dir.88/436 [1988] OJ L214/1; Dir. 89/458 [1989] OJ L226/1; Dir.91/441 [1991] OJ L242/1; Dir.93/59 [1993] OJ L186/21; Dir.94/12 [1994] OJ L100/42.
[208] Dir.91/173 [1991] OJ L85/34.
[209] Dir.2006/66 [2006] OJ L266/1.
[210] Dir.98/70 [1998] OJ L350/58.
[211] Dir.1999/32 [1999] OJ L121/13.
[212] Reg.1005/2009 (fn.67, above).
[213] Dir.2006/66 (fn.209, above).
[214] Case C–300/89 (fn.198, above).
[215] Dir.89/428 [1989] OJ L201/56.

theory at all and decided, for other reasons, in favour of art.114. Also in the abovementioned case C–178/03, the Commission, Council and Parliament disagreed on the centre of gravity of Regulation 304/2003; in that case, the Court decided that the double legal basis of arts 133 and 175 was the correct basis.[216]

The conclusion from all this is that the wording of the Preamble and the articles of a legal Act cannot be decisive on their own, particularly as it is an EU institution, namely the Council, in fact, which determines the wording of a legislative act, in cases of co-decisions together with the European Parliament. Recitals are normally adopted without much discussion. However, the Council is also obliged to respect the provisions of the Treaty; it cannot turn away from it just by arranging the wording of a legislative measure.

2–74

The relevant criterion must therefore be, whether—independent from the wording of the measure—uniformity is necessary to achieve the Treaty's objective. Indeed, as follows from art.26 TFEU, the European Union has the objective of achieving the free movement of goods and services as quickly as possible. This objective requires uniform rules. For this reason, EU instruments laying down common product standards must come under art.114 TFEU. This provision also applies when the measure contains common provisions of a restrictive nature, such as bans, restrictions on use, or maximum concentration levels, for example. If such measures were based on art.192 TFEU, the effect arising from art.193 TFEU would be that the European Union's objective of achieving free circulation of goods or, more generally, of completing the internal market, would never be attained. The legal basis of a measure which affects the environment and the circulation of goods should therefore be chosen with a view to permitting achievement of both objectives, namely completion of the internal market (art.26 TFEU) and improvement of the quality of the environment (art.192 TFEU). The better provision for both these objectives is art.114 and, for international measures, art.207 TFEU. Since art.11 TFEU requires that environmental requirements must be integrated into other EU policies, the choice of this legal basis is not really a risk for the environment.

The Council seems, at present, to apply art.192 as a basis for harmonisation of product-related measures, in cases where it does not wish to proceed to total harmonisation under art.114. This approach neglects art.26 TFEU, which expressly requires measures that lead to the achievement of the internal market. Article 26 TFEU is so clear and unambiguous that there is no room for having product-related measures adopted under art.192 TFEU. Article 26 TFEU and, more generally, the whole Treaty is also binding on the Council. It should also be noted that art.114 TFEU also allows the adoption of legislative acts which allow Member States to adopt or maintain more stringent protection measures; a recent example is Directive 2010/63.[217]

In conclusion, therefore, all product-related measures must, under the present FEU Treaty, be based on art.114 TFEU, with the exception, though of art.43, which is lex specialis to art.114, as appears from art.38(2) TFEU.[218] For international product-related measures, art.207 TFEU would be the appropriate legal basis.

---

[216] Case C–178/03 (fn.200, above).

[217] Dir.2010/63 on the protection of animals used for scientific purposes [2010] OJ L276/63.

[218] art.38(2) TFEU: "Save as otherwise provided in Articles 39 to 44, the rules laid down for the establishment and functioning of the internal market shall apply to agricultural products."

Nature protection

2–75   Nature conservation measures are a specific problem. Fauna and flora species are not products under the TFEU, as is obvious from art.36 TFEU: if they were to be treated as products, their mentioning in art.36, which constitutes an exception to art.34 TFEU, would not be justified. It also appears from art.114(4) TFEU that measures for the protection of the health and life of animals and plants are different from product-related measures: under certain conditions, Member States may take such measures, while they are not allowed to do so in order to protect products.

The Council has therefore quite rightly based nature protection measures on art.192(1),[219] including provisions on trade in endangered species. Exceptions are Regulation 3254/91 on the ban of leg-hold traps and the import of certain furs from specified non-EU countries, which the Council based on the present arts 192(1) and 207 TFEU, jointly,[220] and Reg.1007/2009 which introduces a ban on trade in seal products and was based on the present art.114 TFEU.[221]

Measures on biotechnology also belong to nature conservation measures. Genetically modified organisms as well as genetically modified micro-organisms remain organisms, thus living entities. The fact of basing the deliberate release of genetically modified organisms on art.114[222] only indicates that the borderline between life and non-life has been lost. I would not find it shocking to have different provisions on biotechnology from one Member State to the other, as the ethical and environmental opinions about this technology differ so widely within the European Union. The situation is not fundamentally different from that of nuclear technology, waste incineration or the landing and take-off—the "free circulation"—of the *Concorde* airplane, where also each Member State decides whether it wants or not to have this technology on its territory. In 2010, the Commission proposed to allow Member States to prohibit or restrict the cultivation of genetically modified organisms in their territory, for reasons other than the protection of health or the environment.[223] The proposal which was based on art.114 TFEU, is at present under discussion.

Waste

2–76   Another specific problem is the legal basis for waste measures. Wastes are physical objects and as such are capable of being traded between Member States. International legislation has, in the last twenty years, started to differentiate between waste which is destined for recovery and waste which is destined for final disposal. The reason for this is that a buyer might have an interest in acquiring waste which has an economic value; by contrast, the owner of waste which is destined for disposal would normally be willing to pay for such a disposal.

---

[219] Prior to 1987, the Council had used art.308 EC Treaty as the legal basis.

[220] Reg.3254/91 [1991] OJ L308/1; see also paras 5–36 et seq., below.

[221] Reg.1007/2009 on trade in seal products [2009] OJ L286/36.

[222] Dir.2001/18 (fn.118, above).

[223] Commission, COM(2010)375; see also Commission, SEC(2011)184 on a list of possible grounds for Member States to restrict or prohibit GMO cultivation.

The Court of Justice decided that waste comes under art.34 TFEU, whether it was recoverable or not. [224] The Court justified this decision by pointing out that waste was the subject of commercial transactions and that it was in practice impossible to differentiate between recoverable and non-recoverable waste. The Court added, however, that "waste has a special characteristic. The accumulation of waste, even before it becomes a health hazard, constitutes a threat to the environment because of the limited capacity of each region or locality for receiving it".

Although waste is a product, the Court held, in another judgment, that Directive 91/156[225] on waste was rightly based on art.175 EC (now art.192 TFEU).[226] In this judgment, the Court recurred to the theory of the "centre of gravity", to the primary objective of the legislative act: it saw the Directive as aiming primarily at the protection of the environment and only dealing in an ancillary way with aspects of the internal market. This choice of legal basis was further confirmed in case C–187/93,[227] where the Court again recurred to the theory of "centre of gravity" and held that Regulation 259/93 on the shipment of waste[228] was correctly based on the present art.192 TFEU.

2–77

The Council based directives on titanium dioxide waste[229] and on packaging and packaging waste[230] on art.95 EC (now 114 TFEU). This approach seems to suggest that the Council considers arts 192 and 114 as being equally capable of being used for product-related waste standards and that it chooses the legal basis according to the relative emphasis on free circulation or the protection of the environment as it is expressed in each directive. As mentioned, the Treaty provisions are not at the disposal of the Council and the obligation to complete the internal market as quickly as possible excludes having recurrence to art.192 or 114 at the Council's discretion.

A closer look at Directive 94/62 illustrates the problem. The Directive is based on the present art.114. Of the first 12 recitals, 10 deal with environmental objectives and two with environmental and internal market issues; not one recital deals exclusively with internal market issues. Article 1 indicates the objective of the Directive, stating as the first objective the protection of the environment.[231] Articles 9 and 10 provide for essential requirements which packaging has to

2–78

---

[224] *Commission v Belgium* (C–2/90) [1992] E.C.R. I–4431: "waste, whether recyclable or not, should be regarded as a product the movement of which must not in principle, pursuant to Article 30 EEC, be impeded."

[225] Dir.91/156 on waste [1991] OJ L78/32.

[226] *Commission v Council* (C–155/91) [1993] E.C.R. I–939.

[227] *European Parliament v Council* (C–187/93) [1994] E.C.R. I–2857.

[228] Reg.259/93 [1993] OJ L30/1; this Reg. is now replaced by Reg.1013/2006 (fn.68, above).

[229] Dir.89/428 (fn.215, above).

[230] Dir.94/62 on packaging and packaging waste [1994] OJ 365/10).

[231] Article 1 of Directive 94/62: "1. This Directive aims to harmonise national measures concerning the management of packaging and packaging waste in order, on the one hand, to prevent and impact thereof on the environment of all Member States as well as of third countries or to reduce such impact, thus providing a high level of environmental protection, and, on the other hand, to ensure the functioning of the internal market and to avoid obstacles to trade and distortion and restriction of competition within the Community.

2. To this end this Directive lays down measures aimed, as a first priority, at preventing the production of packaging waste and, as additional fundamental principles, at reusing packaging, at recycling and other forms of recovering packaging waste and, hence, at reducing the final disposal of such waste."

comply with. Article 18 stipulates that packaging which satisfies the Directive's provisions shall not be impeded from circulating within the European Union.

It is difficult to see how the main aim of this Directive, according to its objective and content, could be the achievement of the internal market rather than the protection of the environment. All the Court's criteria plead for art.192 TFEU as the legal basis.

Jans is of the opinion that a directive which contains a free-movement clause, such as the one of art.18 of Directive 94/62, leads to the application of art.114 TFEU; where there is no such clause, a product-related environmental measure would normally fall under art.192 TFEU.[232] Advocate-General Tesauro, in his Opinion on case C–155/91,[233] held that waste directives concerning specific items of waste or waste from specific industrial sectors (such as batteries, packaging waste or waste from the titanium dioxide industry) are to be based on art.114 TFEU, since in such cases the competitive element of an act at EU level is dominant. In contrast, waste measures which tackle the problem of waste generally were to be based on art.192 TFEU, since their primary objective was environmental protection.

2–79   It is not quite clear whether the Court of Justice, in case C–155/91, implicitly adhered to that concept. It has the disadvantage that the impact of a "general" directive or regulation on a specific sector of industry might be as great as the impact of a "specific" directive: the borderline between general acts and specific acts is not at all clear, particularly if one remembers that, for instance, "general" Directive 2008/98 is accompanied by Decision 2000/532 which contains a detailed list of wastes which come under that Directive[234]; and that "general" Regulation 1013/2006 on the shipment of waste contains a long list of waste, the shipment of which undergoes different control procedures or the export of which to third countries is banned.[235]

In conclusion there is not yet a clear, convincing way to classify waste-related measures under either art.192 or 114 TFEU. The Council favours art.192, because of the existence of art.193, and because that provision leads to less uniform EU legislation, leaving national administrations more leeway. The Court of Justice generally accepts this approach. It is to be expected that in future most waste legislation will be based on art.192, also because the European Parliament no longer has more participation rights under art.114 than under art.192 and is thus unlikely to push for the application of art.114.

Other environmental measures

2–80   Industrial installations and other production-related standards and environmental production standards concern air emissions or water discharges from installations, conditions for landfill sites and accident-prevention measures in industrial plants.

Installations do not circulate freely within the European Union, but the products produced in them do. Environmental standards for plants may have an

---

[232] J. Jans, *European Environmental Law* 2nd edn (Groningen, 2000). This position appears to have been abandoned by Jans-Vedder, *European Environmental Law* 3rd edn (Groningen, 2008).
[233] C–155/91 (fn.226, above), Advocate Tesauro's Opinion, para.10.
[234] Dec.2000/532 (fn.87, above).
[235] Reg.259/93 (fn.228, above); see also para.10–34, below.

impact on costs and affect the competitive position of a manufacturer. This is therefore relevant for the establishment and functioning of the internal market which also includes competition that is free from distortion (art.114(4)TFEU).[236] The risk of distortion of competition increases as environmental standards become more stringent, unless uniform provisions prevail throughout the Union. If the objectives "completion of the internal market" and "improvement of the quality of the environment" are to be attained simultaneously throughout the Union, provisions relating to production standards or to plants must be based on art.114 TFEU.

The Council instead bases all production-related directives on art.192 TFEU and the Commission now follows the same line in its proposals. Underlying this decision is the concept that production standards within the European Union should, in principle, not be harmonised, a decision which was taken implicitly, when Directive 84/360 was substituted by Directive 96/61,[237] and also Directive 76/464 was repealed by Directive 2000/60.[238] The consequence is that the air or water emission standards from one steel work to the other, from one cement kiln to the other or from one power plant to the other vary within the European Union.

The present practice seems doubtful. Different environmental standards for the production of goods will lead to different competitive situations, the more cost-intensive such standards are, the greater the competitive distortion becomes. It might be acceptable to have differences between one Member State and another of 1 or 2 per cent in the production costs, when the differences are due to different environmental standards. However, where such differences reach 5, 10 or more per cent of the production costs[239] these differences must be eliminated through the adoption of uniform standards, thus by measures based on art.114. In other words, the dividing line between arts 114 and 192 TFEU is not fixed once and for all: it is flexible, and the more stringent the environmental standards are—always bearing in mind the requirement of a high level of environmental protection—the more it is necessary to base the measure on art.114.

Basing production-related environmental measures on art.192 also bears the political risk that Member States who place low priority on environmental issues will inevitably try to ensure that standards fixed at EU level are low, arguing that Member States with a developed environmental policy could always, under art.193, adopt more stringent protective measures. But a tendency towards lower EU environmental standards is bound to increase discrepancies within the Union and will thus be, from an environmental point of view, counterproductive. Indeed, even environmentally conscious Member States will be reluctant to adopt stricter measures as this would lead to a competitive disadvantage of installations on their territory.[240] Finally, it should be mentioned that the debates at EU level on environmental standards such as air emissions or water discharges or even on quality standards, never centre on the issue of how much pollution of the pollutant the environment can tolerate; the discussion instead focuses on the question of what standards can reasonably be imposed on the polluting industries or other polluters. This demonstrates that it is the competitive aspect—which

2–81

---

[236] C–300/89 (fn.198 above).

[237] Dir.96/61 (1996) OJ L257/26; this Dir. was since replaced by Dir.2008/1 and then by Dir.2010/75 (fn.123, above).

[238] Dir.2000/60 (fn.147, above).

[239] In C–300/89 (fn.198, above) these differences reached 20 per cent of the production costs.

[240] Such a trend is already svisible at the discussion on the introduction of a CO_2 tax at national level.

comes under art.114 TFEU—which is in question, not the protection of the environment—which comes under art.192.

2–82   The Council's practice is in the meantime well established. The use of art.192 is in Member States' and the affected industries interest, though not necessarily in the interest of competition and of the environment. However, as the environment has no voice, it cannot be expected that the present practice will change.

The Council's practice as to the choice of the legal basis might be summarised as follows:

1. Measures of a general nature are based on art.192. Examples: access to information, environmental impact assessment, eco-audit, measures related to installations, environmental liability;
2. Nature conservation measures are all based on art.192; Exceptions: ban on leg-hold trap and fur trade: arts 192 and 207 TFEU; ban on trade in seal products: art.114;
3. Products: measures are based on art.114. Exceptions: authorisation for pesticides: art.43; ozone-depleting substances, contained use of genetically modified micro-organisms: art.192;
4. Water measures are all based on art.192;
5. Air pollution measures are based on art.192. Exceptions: emissions from cars and motorcycles, composition of petrol and gas: art.114; emissions from aeroplanes: art.90;
6. Product-related noise measures are based on art.114. Exception: noise from aeroplanes: art.90. Measures on measuring noise levels are based on art.192;
7. Waste measures are based on art.192. Exception: packaging and packaging waste, waste programmes from titanium dioxide industry: art.114.

The different legal bases

Measures under art.192(1) TFEU

2–83   Legal decisions—regulations, directives, decisions or recommendations—under art.192(1) are taken by Council and Parliament jointly, according to the procedure of art.294 TFEU. The consultation of the Economic and Social Committee and of the Committee of the Regions is mandatory. Council and Parliament must be in possession of a proposal by the Commission.

Article 192(1) is completed by art.192(5) TFEU which was introduced in 1993. This provision has its origin in the idea, particularly stressed by the less wealthy Member States, that if the protection of the environment were in the general interest of the Union, then the Union should pay for such measures. The provision stipulates that the Council may, together with the legislative measure which it adopts, decide on either a temporary derogation for a specific Member State or a financial support from the European Union for that State. The following conditions must be fulfilled:

1.   The EU measure must be adopted by virtue of art.192(1) TFEU. This
      condition prevents a single Member State from vetoing the adoption of a
      Union measure until the State has obtained a temporary derogation or a
      financial assistance;
2.   there must be a request from a Member State that costs are disproportion-
      ate. This condition leads to an examination of the request by the Council,
      i.e. by all other Member States, and the Commission; thus, trivial requests
      will more easily be detected.
3.   the costs must be deemed to be inappropriate for the public authorities. It is
      thus not the cost of the measure itself which will be examined, but rather
      the cost impact on public authorities; where these authorities have the
      possibility of charging private undertakings, where they can make the
      polluter pay, in particular, art.192(5) TFEU is not applicable.

The Council decision, which needs a qualified majority, may consist of   **2–84**
temporary derogations or financial support from the Cohesion Fund. The
possibility of granting a temporary derogation to some Member States existed
well before the Maastricht Treaty and was used in a number of cases. This
provision demonstrates that non-compliance with environmental provisions
brings an economic advantage to the non-complying Member State.

The financial support from the Cohesion Fund, which, under art.192(5), is not
limited to the Member States which are normally beneficiary of the Cohesion
Fund,[241] is not further specified. It may consist of a lump sum or in regular
payments over a longer period, or the financing of an investment programme.

Paragraph 5 is introduced by the words "without prejudice to the principle that
the polluter should pay". In view of this wording, it could well be argued that
non-compliance with EU environmental legislation is a breach of the polluter-
pays principle. Until the end of 2010, art.192(5) had not been applied even once
by the Council.

Decisions on programmes, art.192(3)TFEU

Article 192(3) TFEU provides for co-decision majority procedures and also for   **2–85**
the adoption of "general action programmes setting out priority objectives to be
attained". The initiative for art.192(3) lies with the Commission, which cannot
legally be obliged to submit a proposal for a decision on an action programme.[242]
An action programme may be limited to a specific sector of environmental
policy; it need not cover the whole range of activities.[243]

Decisions under art.192(2)TFEU

Article 192(2) provides for the adoption of some measures by unanimous
decisions. The provision is an exception to art.192(1) and has therefore to be

---

[241] At present, until 2013, Greece, Spain, Portugal, Latvia, Lithuania, Poland, Czech Republic,
Hungary, Slovakia, Slovenia, Cyprus, Malta, Romania and Bulgaria.
[242] See also para.2–05, above.
[243] See, e.g. the proposal for a groundwater action programme [1996] O.J. C355/178.

interpreted narrowly. The European Parliament, the Economic and Social Committee and the Committee of the Regions are only to be consulted; the Parliament has no right of a co-decision.

2–86   *Fiscal provisions.* Provisions of a fiscal nature normally come under art.113 TFEU, which expressly provides for unanimous decisions. Article 113 provides for harmonisation of fiscal legislation to the extent that it is necessary for the establishment and functioning of the internal market. Article 192(2) TFEU clarifies that fiscal measures are also permitted in order to achieve the objectives of environmental protection (art.191(1) TFEU). Fiscal measures touch the core of national sovereignty. It is therefore understandable that Member States who did not accept majority decisions under art.113 TFEU were not ready to accept such majority decisions for eco-taxes.

Since the provision only mentions the fiscal character of a measure, acts which provide for environmental charges, environmental fees or an environmental fund for covering damage of the environment do not come under art.192(2) TFEU.[244] For a measure to come under art.192(2), the fiscal content must be the primary objective of the EU measure. Environmental provisions on taxes which form an additional part of another set of rules that are not primarily of a fiscal nature, may be the subject of majority decisions.[245]

2–87   *Town and country planning and land use.* The underlying concept of this provision is that Member States should themselves decide how they want to organise their territory. Therefore, measures for town and country planning and land use also have to be adopted unanimously. The provision in particular leaves infrastructural planning decisions to the autonomous decision of each Member State, since it gives to each State, via the unanimity requirement, a veto against EU planning decisions which affect its territory. It is consistent with this understanding that the provision of the EU Treaty, which deals with planning measures for infrastructures, also requires unanimous decisions: art.172(2) TFEU concerns the planning of trans-European networks for transport, telecommunications and energy infrastructure; it provides for the elaboration of EU (non-binding) guidelines for such networks, which may be adopted only with the approval of the Member State concerned.

Measures on environmental impact assessment for plans and programmes[246] do not concern town and country planning as such, but the way in which this planning is to be organised; such measures therefore come under art.192(1).

2–88   *The quantitative management of water resources or affecting, directly or indirectly, the availability of those resources.* This provision was reformulated by the Treaty of Nice; the previous version of the Treaty only talked of "management of water resources". In its Decision C–203/96, the Court of Justice had, against the wording of the Treaty in all but the Dutch and the French language, clarified that this older version only applied to the quantitative but not the qualitative management of water resources.[247] The Court based its

---

[244] Jans-Vedder (fn.232, above) p.36; P. Pagh, *EU miljoeret* 2nd edn (Copenhagen, 1996), p.120; A. Epiney, *Umweltrecht in der Europäischen Union* 2nd edn (Köln, Berlin, München, 2005), p.58.
[245] See, e.g. the tax provisions in the different directives on car emissions, paras 4–62 et seq., below.
[246] Dir.2001/42 (fn.142, above).
[247] Court of Justice, *Spain v Council* (C–36/98) [2001] E.C.R. I–779.

interpretation on the objective of the provision, arguing that a measure concerning the quality of water would not affect the availability of the water resource.

Land use, with the exception of waste management. Also this provision was reformulated by the Treaty of Nice. The earlier version had, as a supplementary exclusion, "measures of general nature". It is questionable whether this amendment changed the sense of the provision.

2–89

The objective of the exclusion is again to ensure that Member States keep responsibility, if, where and in which dimensions they want to build, e.g. a new airport, a railway line, a port or another infrastructure project. This means in practical terms that, for instance, Directive 91/271 on urban waste water, which requests Member States to build waste-water treatment plants,[248] would not have to be adopted under art.192(2) but under art.192(1) TFEU: indeed, each Member State remains free to decide how many installations are to be built and where they are to be placed.

Whether Directives 2009/147[249] and 92/43[250] principally deal with "land use", is doubtful. Indeed, both Directives aim at the protection of species of fauna and flora and provide for a number of measures in this regard. Directive 2009/147 asks Member States to designate a sufficient number of birds' habitats in order to allow, for all those habitats together, to form a "coherent whole", thus a European network of habitats. The individual decision which habitat is to be designated is up to the Member States. Directive 92/43 requests Member states to establish lists of habitats which might form part of an EU-wide list of habitats. Again, the original choice is thus made by Member states and specific provisions ensure that final, EU-wide designations of a habitat only occur with the agreement of a Member State in question. Furthermore, land use and changes of land use in designated habitats are not prohibited though restrictive assessment criteria apply.[251]

It follows from all this that habitat protection measures in both Directives do not prohibit the land use in designated areas, and that the provisions for the balancing of interests in specific areas allow for a proportionate consideration of diverging interests. As the objective of both Directives is not the regulation of land or of habitats, but of fauna and flora protection, for which comprehensive provisions are made, the centre of gravity of both Directives is not land use, but nature and biodiversity protection. Therefore, art.192(1), not 192(2) TFEU would apply.

Energy matters. Unanimous decisions are finally required for "measures significantly affecting a Member State's choice between different energy sources and the general structure of its energy supply". Measures which come under this provision are, for instance, measures which lead to the abandoning, for environmental reasons, of nuclear energy or of lignite or coal that has too high a sulphur content. Conversely, however, an EU measure not to allow the import of

2–90

---

[248] Dir.91/271 (fn.134, above).

[249] Dir.2009/147 on the conservation of wild birds [2010] OJ 20/7; this Directive replaced Directive 79/409 on wild living birds [1979] OJ L103/1. Article 175(1) (now art.192(1) TFEU) remained the legal basis.

[250] Dir.92/43 on the protection of natural habitats and wild fauna and flora [1992] OJ L206/7.

[251] *Epiney* (fn.244, above) p.59 is of the opinion that Directives 79/409 and 92/43 would now come under art.192(2); in the same sense Frenz, *Europäisches Umweltrecht* (Munich, 1997) para.86; Jans-Vedder (fn.244, above) leave the question open.

petrol from third countries and to rely primarily on nuclear energy throughout EU territory would need unanimity in Council.

In contrast to this, the decision to adhere to the United Nations Convention on Climate Change[252] was rightly based on art.192(1), not on 192(2), TFEU. Indeed, the Convention neither imposes specific measures which affect energy supply nor ask Member States to change their choice of energy sources. Finally, it does not impose the introduction of fiscal measures either, such as the introduction of an energy tax. What measures are taken at EU level in order to comply with the requirements of the Convention need thus to be decided by another measure, but this has not been prejudged by the decision to adhere to the Convention.

When the European Union prepared the adherence to the Kyoto Protocol, a number of Member States were of the opinion that the Council decision would have to be based on art.192(2), as the commitment to reduce greenhouse gas emissions till 2012 by 8 per cent with regard to 1990, significantly affected their energy policy. Only when the environmental Commissioner threatened to submit this question to the Court of Justice, was the resistance abandoned and art.192(1) as the legal basis accepted. As the reduction of 8 per cent does not prescribe how it is to be achieved, there can be hardly any doubt that art.192(1) was the correct legal basis for the Council decision.[253]

While in all these cases of art.192(2), the Council decides unanimously, it may decide to take majority decisions in the future in this area. The provision is of a rather theoretical nature; indeed, it has existed in a different form[254] since 1987, but has not played any significant role: there has not been one single sector in which the Council has introduced majority decisions.

Decisions on international co-operation (art.191(4) TFEU)

2–91   Article 191(4) TFEU gives express competence to the European Union to conclude international environmental agreements (conventions), which are then binding on the institutions of the European Union and on Member States (art.216(2) TFEU). Details are laid down in art.218 TFEU.

Agreements were, prior to the Lisbon Treaty negotiated by the Commission. Article 218(3) TFEU now provides that the Council appoints a "negotiator" which also may be, if it is not the Commission, the Member State that holds the Presidency of the Council. The Council may give, on the proposal of the Commission, but without the participation of the European Parliament, a negotiating mandate which is not published. During the negotiation period, the Commission continuously consults with a special Council committee composed of Member States' representatives. In practice, Member States also participate in the negotiation of agreements at international level, since such agreements also come into the competence of Member States; in fact, the influence of Member States, at least some of them, is often greater than that of the Commission during these negotiations.

The question, whether decisions to adhere to an international environmental convention, agreement or protocol is to be based on art.191(4), 192(1) or even on

---

[252] Dec.94/69 [1994] OJ L33/11.

[253] Dec.2002/358 [2002] OJ L130/1.

[254] Between 1987 and 1993, all environmental measures under art.192 TFEU had to be adopted unanimously.

art.207 TFEU was, for some time, differently answered by the Commission and the Council. While the Commission, following in this a Court judgment in case C–268/94,[255] based its proposals on art.191(4), the Council adopted the proposals on the basis of art.192(1).[256] A clarification in this controversy was brought by the Opinion 2/00 of the Court,[257] where the question was at issue, on which basis the Council decision to adhere to the Protocol of Cartagena[258] should be based. The Commission was of the opinion that arts 207 and 191(4) TFEU constituted the appropriate legal basis, whereas the Council and Member states were in favour of art.192(1) TFEU. The Court examined which the predominant purpose of the Protocol was and concluded that this was an environmental purpose. It excluded the application of art.191(4) TFEU, as the Protocol did not merely establish "arrangements for co-operation in environmental matters", but laid down precise substantive rules; this, it stated, required the Council decision to be based on art.192(1) TFEU.

As practically all international environmental agreements and the accessory protocols go beyond the fixing of arrangements for environmental co-operation, art.191(4) TFEU may thus only be used in rather exceptional circumstances. Following the Opinion of the Court in case 2/00 the Commission abandoned its idea to use, as a rule, art.191(4) as a basis for decisions to adhere to international conventions.

Decisions based on other Treaty provisions

As mentioned, EU acts affecting the environment may be based on Treaty provisions other than arts 191 and 192 TFEU. This applies to those environmental provisions where the "centre of gravity"[259] lies in policy area other than environmental policy. The most relevant provisions are as follows. | **2–92**

Decisions in the agricultural sector (art.43 TFEU). Article 43 provides that the Council, in working out and implementing the common agricultural policy, adopts legislation by a qualified majority. Numerous measures in agricultural policy affect air and soil, water, fauna, flora and the landscape. Examples include the use of fertilisers and pesticides, drainage and irrigation measures, land use, discharge of substances, animal waste, the production and marketing of agricultural products. The objective of the rules adopted by virtue of art.43 is the establishment of a common agricultural policy among Member States, which includes the production of uniform products and unified production and marketing conditions. | **2–93**

Since 1988 it has been accepted that measures under art.43 may also protect human health.[260] Also in 1988, the Court of Justice had to decide on the relationship between art.192 and art.43 and concluded that art.43 also included

---

[255] Court of Justice, *Portugal v Council* (C–268/94) [1996] E.C.R. I–6177; this case concerned the legal basis of art.181 EC which had the same wording as art.174(4) EC.

[256] Dec.2002/628 [2002] OJ L201/48.

[257] Court of Justice, Opinion 2/00 [2001] E.C.R. I–9713.

[258] Protocol on biosafety, specifically focusing on transboundary movement, of any living modified organism resulting from modern biotechnology that may have adverse effects on the conservation and sustainable use of biological diversity, setting out for consideration, in particular, appropriate procedures for advanced informed agreement. [2002] OJ L201/50.

[259] See para.2–69, above.

[260] The landmark decision was Case 68/86 *United Kingdom v Council* [1988] E.C.R. 855.

measures to protect the environment. The case concerned the ban on drift-nets for fishing which the Council had established by Regulation 345/92.[261] Some fishermen contested the legality of that ban, arguing, amongst other things, that the regulations should also have been based on art.192, which required, at that time, unanimous decisions. The Court held that the Regulation's principal objective was the protection of living marine resources and that this was an objective of the common fishery policy; thus, the appropriate legal basis was art.43. According to the Court, the application of art.192 was not necessary because environmental requirements had to be integrated into other policies anyway.[262]

2–94   All legislation on agricultural pesticides is now to be based on art.43 since that provision prevails, as mentioned at para.2–74, above, on art.114. This is accepted for the placing on the market of such pesticides,[263] but there is room for doubt as regards the ban of pesticides. Indeed, Directive 79/117, which first provided for the ban on some pesticides, was based on art.94 EC (now art.115 TFEU). However, this legislation was adopted prior to the abovementioned Court decision in case 68/86. Today, that legal basis would be replaced by art.43, exactly because there is the new Treaty provision that environmental requirements must be integrated into other policies and measures under such policies. The Court's reasoning in case C-405/92 thus also applies in the case of banning pesticides.

Legal debate has taken place over which legal basis should apply to measures that protect forests against fire or against air pollution. The Council originally adopted such measures on the basis of arts 37 and 308 EC Treaty,[264] as there were no environmental provisions in the Treaty in 1986. Amendments of 1989 were based on arts 37 and 175 EC Treaty.[265] In 1997, the Council adopted further amendments, basing them exclusively on art.37 EC Treaty.[266] The European Parliament attacked both Regulations 307/97 and 308/97 before the Court of Justice, arguing among other things that the Council had wished to exclude the co-operation of the European Parliament in the elaboration of these Regulations, which had become mandatory under art.175(1) EC Treaty since 1993. The Court considered art.175 as the appropriate legal basis as it was of the opinion that the protection of forests against fire and atmospheric pollution was primarily an environmental measure and did not establish rules on the production and marketing of agricultural products.[267] This reasoning is all the more convincing, if one considers that the Commission co-financed reforestation projects after fire damage under the Cohesion Fund—which may co-finance environmental, but not agricultural projects.

The question whether environmental measures which are adopted under art.43 TFEU, allow Member States, under art.193 TFEU to take more stringent measures, will be discussed at paras 3–69 et seq., below.

---

[261] Reg.345/92 [1992] OJ L42/15.
[262] Court of Justice, *Mondiet v Islais* (C–405/92) [1993] E.C.R. I–6133.
[263] Dir.91/414 [1991] OJ L230/51; in 2009, this Directive was repealed and replaced by Reg.1107/2009 (fn.136, above), which was based on the present arts 43(2), 114 and 169(4.b) TFEU.
[264] Reg.3528/86 [1986] OJ L326/2.
[265] Reg.1613/89 [1989] OJ L165/8.
[266] Reg.307/97 [1997] OJ L51/9.
[267] Court of Justice, Cases C–164/97 and C–165/97 (fn.197, above).

Decisions in the transport sector (Article 90). The common transport policy, arts 90–100 TFEU, tries to set common conditions for transport within the European Union and beyond: such conditions may have a very considerable impact on the environment.

Both arts 91 and 100 TFEU now provide, as a rule, for majority decisions by virtue of art.294 TFEU. For that reason, the most relevant question is whether art.193 can be applied to measures adopted under art.90; again, this question will be discussed below at paras 3–69 et seq.

Decisions regarding the internal market. Article 114 outlines the fulfilment of the objectives set out in art.26 TFEU,[268] i.e. the progressive establishment of the internal market. Its wording clarifies that it can also be the legal basis for measures aiming at the protection of the environment. Indeed, finding the demarcation line between arts 114 and 192 TFEU was one of the biggest legal problems of the past. The Amsterdam Treaty has brought the two provisions much closer to one another, so that only some differences continue to exist concerning the procedures and consequences of maintaining or introducing more stringent national environmental measures than those agreed at EU level.

The Treaty itself does not contain criteria for making a clear distinction between arts 114 and 192. Article 114 wishes to achieve the internal market. Articles 191 to 193 aim at the protection of the environment at a high level; the provisions do not contain anything explicit that could be described as the "free movement of goods". On the contrary, art.191 explicitly states that different measures are both possible and necessary to protect the environment at a high level.

As art.114 is concerned with goods and services, provisions which affect trade in such goods and services should, as mentioned above, be allocated primarily to art.114. Provisions which contribute to the attainment of one of the objectives specified in art.191 should primarily be assigned to art.192. As a consequence of the arguments on the choice of the legal basis given above, at paras 2–69 et seq. the Council should have based the Regulation on ozone-depleting substances[269] and the Regulation on export and import of certain dangerous chemicals[270] on the present art.114, since they both deal with product standards.

Decisions on commercial matters (Article 207 TFEU). Framework Decisions in the area of commercial policy are taken by the European Parliament and the Council by a qualified majority (art.207(2) TFEU). The Council alone decides, with qualified majority, on the negotiation and conclusion of trade agreements with third countries or international organisations (art.207(4) TFEU); the European Parliament does not participate. The provisions on commercial policy establish exclusive Community competence, which means that there is no longer a Member States' commercial policy. In the past, however, the importance of art.133 EC Treaty for environmental issues was diminished as a result of differences about its meaning. Whereas the Commission considered art.133 EC relevant for all commercial provisions and international agreements, the Council applied art.133 EC only in those cases where the measure in question did not

2–95

2–96

2–97

---

[268] art.26(2) TFEU: "The internal market shall comprise an area without internal frontiers in which the free movement of goods, persons, services and capital is ensured in accordance with the provisions of the Treaties".
[269] Reg.1005/2009 (fn.67, above).
[270] Reg.2455/92 [1992] OJ L251/13. This Reg. is now replaced by Reg.689/2008 (fn.201, above).

pursue any other than a commercial objective. Thus, where a trade-related measure also aimed at the protection of the environment, art.133 was, according to the Council, not relevant; other provisions applied instead, in particular art.175. In practice therefore, art.207 TFEU is not applied to environmental matters, at least not without art.192 TFEU being added.

The respective interpretations have been influenced by the fact that art.133 EC (now art.207 TFEU) gives exclusive competence to the European Union (see art.3(1e) TFEU), whereas, under arts 191–193 TFEU, the competence is shared between the European Union and Member States.

2–98   In recent times, the Court of Justice was consequent to apply its theory of "centre of gravity" to art.133 (now art.207 TFEU); this had for a long time not been the case. Thus, in case C–281/01,[271] the Court decided that art.133 was the appropriate legal basis for the decision to conclude an agreement between the USA and the EC on the co-ordination of energy efficient labelling requirements for office equipment. The Council had based its decision on art.175.[272] The Court held that the "predominant" objective of the Agreement was that to facilitate trade and therefore commercial policy promotion. In contrast to that the Court decided that a decision to ratify the Cartagena Protocol on trade in genetically modified products would have to be based on art.175,[273] as environmental considerations were predominant in this Protocol. The Commission had argued in favour of the application of art.133.

In view of these decisions, it is not likely that the Council practice will change quickly, all the more, as the Court had decided, as mentioned in para.2–69, above, that under certain conditions, the present arts 207 and 192 TFEU could be the double legal basis, without discussion Member States' residual rights. A further Court judgment will be necessary to solve this outstanding issue.

2–99   *Decisions on research matters.* Article 188 TFEU provides that the European Parliament and the Council decide on research measures, such as the establishment of joint undertakings or any other structure for the execution of EU research, technological development, demonstration programmes and on measures for the implementation of multi-annual research programmes. Multi-annual research framework programmes are adopted under art.182 TFEU.

Thus, decisions on research and development programmes in the area of the environment are taken on the basis of art.182. Article 192 does not apply since art.179(3) TFEU has solved this potential conflict by stipulating:

> "All Union activities under the Treaties in the area of research and technological development, including demonstration projects, shall be decided on and implemented in accordance with the provisions of this Title."

Decisions under the provisions on enhanced co-operation

2–100   The Amsterdam Treaty had introduced a new form of decision-making, the so-called "enhanced co-operation" procedure. This procedure which was amended by the Treaty of Nice and the Lisbon Treaty, is laid down both in arts 20 TEU and arts 326–334 TFEU. It is not limited to environmental matters.

---

[271] Court of Justice, *Commission v Council* (C–281/01) [2002] E.C.R. I–11221.

[272] Dec.2001/469 [2001] OJ L172/1.

[273] Opinion 2/00 (fn.257, above).

The underlying rationale of the procedure is that some Member States might wish to advance more rapidly than the European Union as a whole. Nothing currently prevents them from concluding a bilateral or multilateral international convention, which would then be governed by public international law and not constitute EU law—although, of course, such obligations would have to respect the Member States' obligations under the Treaty on European Union.

The flexibility provisions now offer a new possibility to those Member States that want to proceed more quickly: they may, under certain conditions[274] laid down in art.20 TEU, make use of the institutions, procedures and mechanisms laid down by the Treaties.

2–101

For any such enhanced co-operation, the Member States in question need an express authorisation from the Council. The Council may only act on a proposal from the Commission which has its own discretionary power to decide whether it wishes to submit a proposal to the Council or not.[275] The Council shall decide on the authorisation to co-operate by unanimity of those Member States which want to cooperate, after consultation with the European Parliament.

As regards the measure adopted under the enhanced cooperation procedure all the relevant provisions of the Treaty apply. The question once so controversial under art.293 EC (now repealed)—whether the conventions adopted under that provision were part of EU law or were measures of public international law—is answered in the case of the flexibility procedure: they are EU law. Indeed, the Commission, which must make a proposal for an enhanced co-operation measure, has only the competence to propose measures that are mentioned in art.288 TFEU, i.e. a regulation, directive or a decision. As regards the enhanced cooperation procedure, the decision-making in Council, the consultation of or the co-decision with the European Parliament, and the transposition of the measure into national law, its monitoring by the Commission under art. 258 TFEU and the possible judicial control under arts 19 TEU—all follow EU law provisions. This leaves no room for the application of provisions of public international law. Article 20(4) TEU provides, though, that only the Member States which participate in the enhanced cooperation, are bound by the measures adopted under that procedure, and that accession countries are not obliged to take them over, when they accede to the Union.

2–102

In order to illustrate the impact of the flexibility provisions on the environment, the fictitious example of a directive on environmental standards for swimming pools may be given. Under art.20(2) TEU, at least nine Member States could request the Commission to submit a proposal for such a directive. The Commission could then ask the Council to authorise the use of the "institutions, procedures and mechanisms of the Treaty". The Council would normally decide on this proposal by a qualified majority of the Member States which participate in the enhanced cooperation (art.330 TFEU).

2–103

The procedure of substance has to be distinguished from the authorisation procedure. The Commission would make a proposal for a directive on water quality in swimming pools, following the institutional procedures of art.192(1). The Directive would be adopted by a qualified majority of those Member States that participate in the co-operation. If, later, another Member State would like to

---

[274] See art.329(1) TFEU: "In the event of the Commission not submitting a proposal, it shall inform the Member States concerned of the reasons for not doing so."
[275] art.329 TFEU.

be party to the EU enhanced co-operation procedure, the provisions of art.331 TFEU shall apply; the Council shall finally decide, whether the conditions for such a participation are fulfilled.

Nothing would prevent the Commission, during its discussions in Council on a proposal which was intended to cover all Member States, from submitting to the Council a proposal for authorising the enhanced co-operation procedure. Indeed, despite the somewhat unclear wording of art.329 TFEU,[276] the start of the procedure does not depend on the initiative of a majority of Member States. It is up to the Commission to ensure that the flexibility procedure does not put the coherence of the Union at risk.

2–104   Articles 326 et seq. TFEU do not provide for the elaboration of a proposal by Member States. Indeed, the reference to the Treaty provisions also has the consequence that the Council may only act upon a proposal from the Commission, as is also foreseen in art.192(1). In particular, art.293(1) TFEU provides that the Council may only unanimously amend a proposal from the Commission.

This provision would be set aside if the Council could also decide upon a proposal from Member States.

In conclusion, co-operating Member States have the choice to recur either to forms of public international law, or to establish, within the EU framework, EU law.

Since 1999, not one single case occurred, where a Member State, in environmental matters, asked for or suggested the application of the enhanced co-operation procedure. The chances that this situation changes in the future are small, though the enlargement of the European Union might make general decision-making more difficult. Candidates for enhanced co-operation are in particular provisions in the area of climate change. Politically, it is feared that a "Europe at different speed" would rather contribute to the disintegration of the European Union as a whole.

---

[276] art.329 TFEU: "Member States which wish to establish enhanced cooperation between themselves ... shall address a request to the Commission... The Commission may submit a proposal to the Council to that effect."

CHAPTER 3

Union Powers and Member State Powers

1. General aspects on the division of competence in environmental matters

The objective of EU environmental policy and law is the preservation, protection and, over all, the improvement of the quality of the environment within the European Union. This objective, however, is also that of Member States' environmental policy and law. The protection and preservation of the environment is a fundamental part of the general interest of the European Union[1] and of Member States. Because it is in the general interest, the environment, like the non-commercial assets listed in art.36 TFEU, cannot be left unprotected: as long as the Union fails to take action on a given environmental issue, the Member States retain their powers to adopt provisions to protect and preserve the environment, provided, of course, that these measures are compatible with the general rules laid down in the EU Treaties. When the European Union takes action, this by no means removes Member States' powers to take environmental measures, although such powers then no longer apply to the particular subject governed by EU legislation, in so far as this has been regulated.

3–01

Since the protection of the environment is in the general interest of the European Union, the Union is "competent",[2] i.e. responsible for taking legal provisions in order to protect it. In doing so, the European Union has, of course, to take into consideration the principles which the Treaties provides for such action, in particular the subsidiarity principle.[3] Where an EU environmental legal rule conflicts with a national legal rule, EU law prevails, according to the established case law of the Court of Justice.[4] The reason for this is obvious: if the national legal rule prevailed, the EU legal provision would apply only in those Member States which had not taken legal measures. Then, the EU legal rule would not be a rule which applied throughout the Union, but only in those parts of it where no national measures had been taken. Also, the EU measure could at

---

[1] See already *Procureur de la République v Assoc. de Défense de Brûleurs de Huiles Usagées* (Case 240/83) [1985] E.C.R. 531, para.13: "environmental protection . . . is one of the Community's essential objectives".

[2] The notion of "competence" is used in art.191(4) TFEU and, more generally, in arts 3 and 4 TFEU.

[3] EU Treaty, art.4(a) "competences not conferred upon the Union remain with the Member States". Art.5(3): " . . . in areas which do not fall within its exclusive competence, the Union shall act only if and in so far as the objectives of the proposed action cannot be sufficiently achieved by the Member States, either at central level or regional and local level but can rather, by reason of the scale or effects of the proposed action, be better achieved at Union level". 5(2): "Under the principle of conferral, the Union shall act only within the limits of the competence conferred upon it".

[4] *Costa v ENEL* (6/64) [1964] E.C.R. 1265; *Simmenthal* (106/77) [1978] E.C.R. 629; *Factortame* (C–213/89) [1990] E.C.R. I–2466; *Nimz* (C–184/89) [1991] E.C.R. I–297.

any moment be reduced in its application by a subsequent national measure, which would create quite considerable legal uncertainty. Such legal uncertainty would also be created by differences over the question of whether or not the national measure really is applicable in a specific case or not. As the national law would mainly be interpreted by national courts, inevitable discrepancies would follow.

3–02 It is therefore now uncontested that, in the case of conflict, EU (environmental) law prevails over national law. From this it follows that EU environmental law cannot be amended by subsequent national law. In other words, the rule *lex posterior derogat legem anteriorem* (the later legal provision prevails over the earlier provision) does not apply to the relationship between EU law and national law.

Both the European Union and Member States are thus responsible, "competent" or empowered to take action on environmental issues. In view of the almost unlimited scope of the term "environment" in the EU Treaties, this holds true for all environmental issues. The Treaties assign no particular area of environmental legislation exclusively to the European Union or exclusively to Member States. As can be seen from art.193 TFEU, this similarly applies to subjects already covered by EU legislation. Consequently, the inter-relationship between the European Union's and the Member States' competence is flexible, dynamic and complementary.

3–03 It follows from the above-mentioned art.5 TEU that EU environmental action is dependent on certain circumstances which have to be fulfilled. EU institutions decide themselves whether this is the case. In the case of dispute, the matter has to be decided by the EU Court of Justice, which has to ensure, under art.19 TEU that the provisions of the Treaty are respected.[5] The logical consequence of art.5 TEU is that in cases where the European Union has not taken action to protect, preserve or improve the quality of the environment, Member States are free to do so. Their competence to deal with environmental issues is unlimited. They can do whatever they wish in whatever form they wish to ensure environmental protection. Limitations to this right to protect—or not to protect—the environment stem from:

- Member States' own, national rules, such as for instance, rules on local government and rules for regional responsibility in environmental matters;
- rules of international law, such as existing international Conventions or other written or unwritten rules of international law;
- rules of EU law.

The first two limitations are not dealt with in this book, which deals with EU law. As regards the third limitation, the EU Treaties themselves constitute a set of provisions that may limit national environmental measures. Indeed, the EU Treaties contain a number of provisions that limit the Member States' possibilities of action. These different limitations will be discussed below.

---

[5] art.19 TEU: "It [The Court of Justice of the European Union] shall ensure that in the interpretation and application of the Treaties the law is observed."

2.   Member States' measures in the absence of EU measures

National environmental measures that affect imports: arts 34 and 36 TFEU

Article 34 TFEU provides that all "quantitative restrictions on imports and all measures having equivalent effect shall be prohibited between Member States"; art.35 TFEU mirrors this provision by stating that "quantitative restrictions on exports, and all measures having equivalent effect, shall be prohibited between Member States".   **3–04**

From these provisions, art.36 TFEU makes an exception; this provision reads as follows:

> "The provisions of Articles 34 and 35 shall not preclude prohibitions on imports, exports . . . justified on grounds of . . . the protection of health and life of humans, animals or plants; . . . Such prohibitions or restrictions shall not, however, constitute a means of arbitrary discrimination or a disguised restriction on trade between Member States."

Article 36 TFEU thus does allow certain trade restrictions. The Court of Justice has declared, on a number of occasions, that art.36 is an exception to the principle of art.34 and must therefore be narrowly interpreted.[6] In particular, according to the established case law of the Court of Justice, the grounds for restricting trade by virtue of art.36 constitute an exhaustive list and may not be extended.

The protection of the environment is not listed in art.36 TFEU as a possible justification for restrictions to the free circulation of goods of art.34. Therefore, only such national environmental measures that aim at the "protection of health and life of humans, animals and plants" could be justified by art.36. Such measures concern, for instance, provisions on banning or restricting the use of substances or products which are dangerous to health; measures to limit the presence of pollutants in drinking water or in the air; measures to regulate the marketing of pesticides or biocides.

However, there are numerous environmental measures which cannot be considered to protect the health and life of humans, animals or plants. Such measures include environmental label schemes, eco-management systems, environmental taxes and charges, measures to prevent the generation of waste, environmental impact measures, deposit-and-return schemes, environmental liability or environmental information and education. For other measures, it is doubtful whether they can really be considered to protect health and life; such measures are, for instance, provisions to reduce the noise level of cars, the designation of fauna or flora habitats, emission limit values from installations, licensing procedures or measures to protect the ozone layer or to combat global warming.   **3–05**

The criterion that defines whether or not a measure aims at the protection of health or life is the relationship of the measure to health effects, i.e. its "proximity" to health effects. Thus, the Court of Justice decided that the shipment

---

[6] *Marimex* (29/72) [1982] E.C.R. 1309; *Commission v Ireland* (113/80) [1981] E.C.R. 1625; *Commission v Greece* (C–205/89) [1991] E.C.R. I–1361.

of recoverable waste oils did not pose a threat to the life and health of humans that could justify the application of art.36[7].

Another example is the restriction on the use of CFCs and other ozone-depleting substances in order to protect the ozone layer. Damage to the ozone layer may increase skin cancer for humans and may have other health effects on humans, animals and plants. However, this possibility is remote and indirect. Therefore, national measures to restrict the use of ozone-depleting substances cannot really be justified on the basis of art.36 TFEU.

3–06
Fortunately enough, however, this problem of subsuming environmental measures under art.36 TFEU has lost its relevance. Indeed, the Court of Justice in 1979 adopted a landmark decision on art.34.[8] The Court declared that in the absence of EU legislation, a national restriction on the free circulation of goods from other Member States had to be accepted to the extent that it was necessary to satisfy mandatory requirements such as the necessity for fiscal controls, fair trading practices and consumer protection, and added that there might be other mandatory requirements. The Court added further that the national measure taken in order to satisfy such a mandatory requirement had to be non-discriminatory and proportional:

> "in the absence of common rules relating to the marketing of the products in question obstacles to free movement within the Community resulting from disparities between the national laws must be accepted in so far as such rules, applicable to domestic and imported products without distinction, may be recognised as being necessary in order to satisfy mandatory requirements recognised by Community law. Such rules must also be proportionate to the aim in view. If a Member State has a choice between various measures for achieving the same aim, it should choose the means which least restricts the free movement of goods.[9]"

In 1988, the Court recognised that the protection of the environment was such a mandatory requirement which could justify restrictions on the free circulation of goods.[10] In this case the Commission had attacked a Danish national measure, which introduced a deposit-and-return system for drink containers. The Commission considered that the system could not be justified by art.36 TFEU and that it was incompatible with art.34. It was followed in its assessment by the Advocate General, but not by the Court of Justice.

3–07
As regards the application of art.36, there was practically no dispute: it was not really possible to consider a deposit-and-return system to protect the health or life of humans; art.36 was therefore not discussed by the Court. Instead, the Court held that Denmark was entitled to introduce a deposit-and-return system, since such a system aimed at the protection of the environment, which was an objective of general Union interest. Denmark, according to the Court, was entitled to set up an efficient system of waste prevention and such a system required the introduction of a deposit-and-return scheme even though the practical circumstances might make it more difficult for non-Danish producers and traders to comply with the system.

---

[7] *Dusseldorp* (C–203/96) [1998] E.C.R. I–4075, para.47.

[8] *Rewe v Bundesmonopolverwaltung* ("*Cassis de Dijon*") (120/78) [1979] E.C.R. 649.

[9] Wording from *Commission v Denmark* (302/86) [1988] E.C.R. 4607.

[10] Wording from *Commission v Denmark* (302/86) [1988] E.C.R. 4607.

The recognition of the protection of the environment as a mandatory requirement under art.34 was confirmed in later Court judgments[11] without the Court sharply distinguishing between justification under arts 36 (health grounds) and 34 (grounds to satisfy a mandatory requirement). Thus, while national environmental measures may restrict the free circulation of goods on either of these grounds, the limits to such national measures follow from the Treaty provisions and from the limits drawn by the very detailed and sophisticated case law of the Court.

The necessity for action. The first problem is whether a Member State may adopt any trade-restricting measure to protect the environment which seems appropriate or whether it may only adopt some measures, which are "necessary" or, in the Court's words, proportionate. The Court itself has contributed to this debate by not accepting, in case 302/86, a Danish measure which obliged economic operators to use only authorised standardised containers. The Court stated[12]:

> "It is undoubtedly true that the existing system for returning approved containers ensures a maximum rate of reuse and therefore a very considerable degree of protection of the environment. Nevertheless, the system for returning non-approved containers is capable of protecting the environment."

This seems to indicate that the Court is of the opinion that a "very considerable degree" of environmental protection is not necessary—not proportionate—and therefore not allowed, only a "reasonable" degree of environmental protection—whatever that may be—is permitted. In other words, it is not a Member State which decides on the necessary degree of the environmental protection, but EU law (as interpreted by the Court) which determines what is necessary (or proportionate). This proportionality is measured against the interest in free circulation of goods, as there is no other factor to consider.

The underlying principle of this approach is that EU law provides for the free circulation of goods which is of paramount importance. Restrictions on the free circulation of goods are allowed only where they are necessary (proportionate); in other words, measures to protect the environment are possible where their importance is greater than that of free circulation of goods. This leads to the conclusion that the free circulation of goods, in the event of any conflict with environmental (national) measures, will normally prevail, unless it can be proven that environmental interests are more relevant.

This conclusion, however, is not compatible with the division of competence for the protection of the environment. The protection of the environment is of general Union interest. It is expressly mentioned in the Recital 9 and art.3(3) TEU. Nothing indicates that it is less important than other objectives, in particular the free circulation of goods. On the contrary, the rule of art.11 TFEU according to which environmental protection requirements must be integrated into the definition and implementation of all other policies is rather unique in the Treaties; nowhere in the Treaties is the same said of the free circulation of goods. Furthermore, Commission proposals in the area of the internal market must be based on a high level of environmental protection and the European Parliament

3–08

3–09

---

[11] *Commission v Belgium* (C–2/90) [1992] E.C.R. I–4431; *Commission v Germany* (C–131/93) [1994] E.C.R. I–3303.

[12] Case 302/86 (fn.9, above), paras 20 and 21.

and the Council must try to achieve such a high level (art.114(3) TFEU). This is the only provision in the FEU Treaty which contains quality requirements for individual measures that are proposed by the Commission. Finally, art.114(4)–(8) and art.193 TFEU allow Member States, once an EU measure has been taken, to maintain or to introduce more protective environmental measures at national level. Article 114(5)–(8) only applies to environmental measures, not to all non-economic assets of art.36, as is the case with art.114(4) TFEU.

All these provisions clearly show the importance that the Treaties attach to the protection of the environment. In view of this importance, which has been growing continuously and achieved recognition in the different Treaty amendments of 1987, 1993, 1999 and 2003, it cannot be considered that only a reasonable degree of environmental protection is allowed to restrict the free circulation of goods. Rather, it is the Member States which decide on the amount of environmental protection which they wish to ensure.

3–10   There are two other arguments which plead against a limitation for environmental measures to "reasonable" measures. First, art.114(5)–(8) TFEU, which was newly introduced by the Amsterdam Treaty 1997, outlined provisions for the Member States to introduce new environmental measures at national level once an EU harmonisation measure under art.114(1) had been adopted. These measures are not limited to reasonable measures, as will be discussed below; rather, the criteria for the national measures are whether the measure constitutes an arbitrary discrimination, a disguised distortion of trade or whether they hamper the functioning of the internal market. It is not consistent to ask for only reasonable measures under arts 34–36 where no EU measure exists, and not to ask for only reasonable measures under art.114.

3–11   Second, the only instance which could decide what is proportionate is the Court of Justice—and in the pre-litigation stage, the European Commission. But what criteria could be used, if there is no EU legislation? The EU Treaties give no clarification of what is reasonable or not.

To give a specific example: in the early 1990s Denmark limited the noise level from electrical windmills that are used for energy production; the standards are stricter, the closer the windmill is installed to residential areas. France protested against this measure, arguing that the sale and export of French windmills to Denmark would be hampered by the Danish measure. It seems obvious that nobody outside Denmark can really decide whether a noise level of 50 decibels is reasonable for the Danish environment and Danish citizens and whether a noise level of 40 decibels is unreasonable. The environmental conditions are specific in each case. No element in the Treaty allows the establishing of EU criteria for such an assessment. As there is no EU legislation on windmills or on acceptable noise levels for citizens, EU law cannot decide what is reasonable or not in Denmark.

Similar reasons argue in favour of the noise levels for pleasure boats to be allowed, which Sweden introduced in the early 1990s. In view of the thousands of lakes—independently from the endless miles of shoreline—with numerous small islands in Sweden, it would not be possible to allow the marketing of pleasure boats but prohibit their use in all or in parts of Sweden if they exceed a certain noise level. Also the level of permitted noise cannot, in the absence of EU provisions, be determined by a manufacturer or authorising body from another Member State—or by the European Union. The Swedish problem was "solved" by an EU directive of 1994 which fixed common noise levels for new boats, but allowed Member States to adopt provisions concerning navigation on certain waters for the protection of the environment.[13]

Another example is a restriction on the use of Karlstad airport which Sweden   **3–12**
had banned for some noisy aeroplanes, although Directive 92/14[14] provided that these aeroplanes were allowed to be used until 2002. It is clear that not every aeroplane which circulates within the European Union may use any airport that exists. Indeed, Member States implicitly regulate access to airports, for example by regulating the number and length of the runways, the size of the airports, or landing and take-off times. Where the neighbourhood is residential or is an ecologically valuable habitat this may lead to the conclusion that specific aeroplanes may not use specific airports. The most obvious example is the supersonic aeroplane, *Concorde*, which was not allowed to land at most EU airports. In the same way as it is possible to prohibit the use of certain roads for trucks—or indeed for cars generally—without impeding the free circulation of cars, it is possible to prohibit the use of certain airports for certain aeroplanes. It is not clear, who else other than the Swedish authorities could determine whether the local environmental conditions at Karlstad make it necessary or not to restrict the landing or take-off of noisy airplanes at it. Directive 92/14 is not relevant, since aeroplanes which conform to that Directive are allowed to use Swedish airports, except, perhaps, Karlstad airport.

The Commission based its decision against the Swedish restrictions at Karlstad airport not on art.34 TFEU, but on secondary EU legislation, Regulation 2408/92 and Directive 92/14,[15] and decided that these provisions gave any air transport carrier a right to access to any EU airport[16]; Sweden accepted this decision. If that secondary EU legislation indeed went so far—I question this—the abovementioned considerations, which start from the assumption that there is no EU legislation regulating this issue, are obsolete.

For restrictions in the free circulation of goods which affect human health and   **3–13**
therefore come under art.36 TFEU, the Court of Justice has already come to the same decision. In case C–125/88,[17] it was faced with a Dutch measure concerning the use of a pesticide "Improsol"; the question was whether such a national measure did not unduly restrict the free circulation of that pesticide which was used in other Member States. The Court found that pesticides constituted "significant risks to the health of humans and animals and to the environment" and then continued:

> "It is therefore for the Member States, pursuant to Article 36 of the Treaty and in the absence of full harmonization in this matter, to decide at what level they wish to set the protection of the life and health of humans."

---

[13] Directive 94/25 relating to recreational craft, [1994] OJ L164/25; see for the interpretation of this directive Court of Justice, *Mikkelsson and Roos* (C–142/05), judgment of June 4, 2009; *Sandström* (C–433/05), judgment of April 15, 2010. In these cases, the Court assessed the national restriction measures as regards the use of recreational craft against the proportionality principle. It left the final decision, whether this principle had been respected, to the national courts, though it tried to limit those courts, by extensively interpreting the proportionality principle.

[14] Dir.92/14 on the limitation of the operation of aeroplanes covered by Pt II, Ch.2, Vol.1 of annex 16 to the Convention on International Civil Aviation 2nd edn [1992] O.J. L76/21.

[15] Reg.2408/92 [1992] OJ L240/8; Dir.92/14 (fn.14, above).

[16] Commission, Dec. 98/523 [1998] OJ L233/25.

[17] *H. Nijman* (C–125/88) [1989] E.C.R. I–3533.

This judgment has been confirmed by several other judgments on pesticides and Member States' measures to restrict their use.

It is not really imaginable that the Member States themselves set the degree of protection which they wish to ensure for measures to protect the environment which concern the health and life of humans, animals and plants (art.36 TFEU), but that for measures to protect the environment which concern other environmental values and thus come under art.34 TFEU, the Member States are limited to proportionate measures.

3–14   The conclusion is that the freedom to set national environmental standards does not allow protectionist measures to be taken or measures to be taken which are not really necessary to protect the local, regional or national environment. These issues will be discussed below. It still remains, however, that there are no specific, autonomous criteria for assessing whether national environmental measures are necessary (proportionate) or not. It is up to Member States to establish the degree of environmental protection at local, regional or national level which they consider appropriate. In this, however, Member States must take into consideration the state of science at international and EU level, such as the statements of the World Health Organisation or the EU scientific committees; the greater the scientific certainty about the risk of a substance is, the more reduced is the discretion of the Member State. The attempts by the Court of Justice to limit this discretion by an extensive use of the proportionality principle are to be considered with caution. Indeed, also the national legislature has a large amount of discretion as to the measures which are to be taken in order to protect the environment and humans. The Court of Justice only can control the obvious exceeding of this discretion.

3–15   *Non-economic grounds.* The discretion of Member States is limited by the provisions of the Treaties. When establishing its jurisdiction on the mandatory requirements which justified, under art.34 TFEU, a restriction on the free circulation of goods, the Court of Justice stated that such measures were not allowed to be discriminatory or disproportionate and had to be applied indistinctively to national and to imported products. As can be seen, the two criteria of non-discrimination and proportionality are taken from art.36(2) TFEU,[18] but apply both to measures which are examined under art.36, and to measures assessed, under the *Cassis de Dijon* jurisdiction, under art.34.

To these limits has to be added the proviso that art.36 TFEU itself only refers to non-economic criteria, as can be concluded from art.114[19]; this limitation also applies under art.34 TFEU, as the Court of Justice has clarified: "aims of a purely economic nature cannot justify barriers to the fundamental principle of the free movement of goods". With this argument, the Court of Justice rejected an argument by the Dutch Government that restrictions to the shipment of waste were necessary to enable a Dutch waste recovery installation to operate in a profitable manner with sufficient material at its disposal and to ensure it a sufficient supply of recoverable waste.

3–16   *Discriminating measures.* A discrimination or, as art.36(2) puts it, an arbitrary discrimination exists when goods from other Member States are subject to conditions which are, directly or indirectly, stricter than those on domestic goods. Since the Court of Justice also takes into consideration indirect discrimination,

---

[18] See para.3–04, above.
[19] *Dusseldorp* (C–203/96) (fn.7, above), para.44.

practically every national environmental measure will have to be weighed in the balance as to whether it factually leads to a different treatment of domestic or imported goods or not.

In case 302/86[20] the Commission had tackled the Danish deposit-and-return system by arguing that the mandatory use of reusable containers for drinks and beers indirectly discriminated against imported goods: reusable containers— mainly glass bottles—were considerably heavier in weight than containers made of plastic or other material. Therefore, the costs of transporting them to Denmark and, in their empty state, back to the country of origin, were higher than necessary and created indirect discrimination. If a foreign producer or trader wanted to avoid transport, it had to set up a deposit-and-return system of its own in Denmark which would be costly.

The Court did not discuss questions of discrimination. Since it rejected the Commission's application, it must be presumed that it did not consider the increased transport costs or the difficulties involved in the setting-up of a deposit-and-return system to be sufficiently relevant as to constitute indirect discrimination. In cases C–309/02 and C–463/01 which concerned German legislation on packaging, the question, whether the German mandatory deposit system constituted a discrimination, was not discussed any more.[21]   **3–17**

In case C–2/90,[22] the Wallonian Government's import ban on waste from other Member States was tackled by the Commission, which argued that waste from other Member States was not more harmful than waste generated in Wallonia. The Court rejected that argument. It held that waste, while coming under art.34 TFEU, had special characteristics. As there was an obligation to dispose of waste as close as possible to the place where it was produced in order to transport waste as little as possible, which followed from art.191(2) TFEU,[23] the different treatment between Wallonian waste and imported waste did not constitute, in the opinion of the Court, an arbitrary discrimination.[24]

Another case, which was finally not decided by the Court, as Denmark repealed its national legislation, was the Danish ban on metal cans, introduced in the early 1980s. The Commission had considered that this measure was taken in order to protect the (Danish) environment, and had therefore not attacked this ban before the Court of Justice; the attempts of the United Kingdom, as a third-party intervenor, to have this ban discussed in case 302/86, failed for procedural reasons, since a third-party intervenor may not enlarge the object of litigation before the Court beyond the limits which the main applicant has established by its application.[25]

If it is correct that a Member State, in the absence of EU provisions, itself establishes the necessary degree of protection of the environment which it wishes to achieve at national level, then it is in principle up to the Danish authorities to decide whether they wish to have metal cans in their environment. Such metal cans made from aluminium or steel take more natural resources to produce than   **3–18**

---

[20] Case 302/86 (fn.9, above).
[21] Court of Justice, *Commission v Germany* (C–463/01) [2004] E.C.R. I–11705; *Radlberg* (C–309/02) [2004] E.C.R. I–11763.
[22] C–2/90 (fn.11, above).
[23] See para.1–30, above.
[24] See for a critical comment L. Krämer, *European Environmental Law Casebook* (London, 1993), p.77.
[25] 302/86 (fn.9, above).

glass or cardboard containers, are not reusable, constitute litter in the environment when they are thrown away and reduce the efficiency of reuse systems, which a Member State may have set up.

Compared to the Danish general ban, however, might be an Irish draft regulation of 1988, which aimed at prohibiting metal cans, however, only for beer.[26] In this case, many of the environmental arguments in favour of such a ban are not really valid, since they would apply, in the same way, to metal cans for soft drinks. The Commission was therefore of the opinion that environmental reasons could not have caused the Irish Government to consider a ban on metal cans for beer, but that this ban constituted an attempt to reduce the import of British beer. Confronted with this argument, Ireland withdrew its draft regulation.

In Denmark, the ban of metal cans was limited to beer and some soft drinks. Other soft drinks, such as iced tea, were allowed to be marketed in metal cans; also, of course, metal cans are used in Denmark for fruit and vegetable preserves and other food products. While fruit and vegetable containers might not really be comparable to drink containers, this is certainly the case with, e.g. iced tea or chocolate drinks. It is thus very much a question of weighing up the different aspects of the Danish ban in order to come to a decision whether or not it is discriminating. Also, it should be pointed out that, in 1994, an EU Directive on packaging and packaging waste was adopted, which provides for the free circulation of packaging containers that comply with the requirements of this Directive.[27] Any decision on the Danish ban would therefore take into consideration that Directive and no longer an article of the TFEU. In view of this new legislation, the Commission appealed, in 1999 to the Court of Justice and Denmark repealed its ban, before a judgment was given.

3–19   In 1993, the Netherlands set up a national Covenant on Tropical Hardwoods, which provided that, after 1995, only timber from sustainably managed forests was to be traded or processed in the Netherlands. The Covenant, an environmental agreement, was signed by the Dutch Government, the timber trade and timber processing industry, trade unions and environmental organisations. It was intended to introduce a Dutch approval mark in order to distinguish sustainably produced timber from other timber. Since the Covenant was actively supported and signed by the Dutch Government, it must be considered a national public measure[28] and therefore be assessed under art.34 TFEU.

The discrimination problem lies in the fact that the Covenant refers to timber imports from tropical timber only; other hardwood-producing countries, such as Canada and Russia (Siberia) are not covered. It is not really clear why such differentiation is made; environmental reasons require the same treatment in both cases. The Dutch Covenant therefore seems to be discriminatory. It must be mentioned, though, that it never became effective, because no agreement could be found on what constituted a "sustainable forest management".

3–20   Some German Länder had adopted, in the 1980s, smog regulations which provided for restrictions on the use of private cars in the case of smog. Cars equipped with catalytic converters could, during the first stage of smog alert, circulate whereas cars without a catalytic converter could not. The Commission

---

[26] See L. Krämer, *E.C. Treaty and environmental law* (London, 1998) para.4.58.

[27] Dir.94/62 on packaging and packaging waste [1994] OJ L365/10; see also para.10–49, below.

[28] Private measures would have to be assessed as to their compatibility with the TFEU, against arts 101 and 102 TFEU.

stated that this measure discriminated against car producers from other Member States, since the EU provisions valid at that time had considered the emissions from cars to be equivalent, whether or not the cars were equipped with catalytic converters. According to the Commission, foreign manufacturers were more severely affected by the German measures than German producers.

In the 1980s, there was no EU legislation on smog and, therefore, Member States were free to decide on measures in the case of an extraordinary situation such as smog. Since cars with catalytic converters emit fewer pollutants than cars without such converters, and since all manufacturers were producing, at the time of the German measure, cars with catalytic converters, no discrimination can be seen in the smog regulations, which, in each case, were measures to deal with a temporary situation. When the Commission changed its policy in 1987 and began working towards EU emission limit values which required catalytic converter equipment, it ended the case against Germany.

These examples might show how much depends, in an assessment upon whether a Member State's measure constitutes an arbitrary discrimination of products, on the concrete, specific circumstances of a case. This is confirmed by the jurisdiction of the Court which appears to differentiate between measures that are discriminating and those measures that constitute an arbitrary discrimination.[29] Thus, in several cases, the Court accepted national discriminating environmental legislation which it considered to be environmentally oriented, without discussing, in the majority of these cases, much of their discriminating character. This could mean that national measures which pursue a legitimate environmental objective, may also be justified under arts 34/36 TFEU, where they discriminate against products from other Member States.[30] A detailed case-by-case analysis of each specific case is therefore necessary.

Disproportionate measures. The second requirement set up by the Court of Justice is the proportionality requirement: where it must be examined whether there are other measures available which restrict the free circulation of goods less severely than the measure which was taken.

3–21

The proportionality requirement became relevant in case C–131/93 where Germany had prohibited the import of living crayfish in order to protect the health and life of indigenous crayfish species.[31] The Court did not contest Germany's right to take such measures; however, it argued that Germany could have taken other, less restrictive steps, such as health controls for crayfish imports from other Member States, or licensing requirements for putting living crayfish into German waters. The Court also came to this conclusion because Germany had been rather generous in granting derogations from the import ban and shown that a licence system, together with strict conditions, did ensure a sufficient protection.

In case 302/86[32] the Court considered the Danish measure on only allowing approved drink containers to be part of the Danish deposit-and-return system to be incompatible with art.34 TFEU; a Danish measure to allow some derogations for importers of small quantities was considered disproportionate. The Court did

3–22

---

[29] J. Jans-H. Vedder *European Environmental Law* 3rd edn (Groningen, 2008), p.247, consider that "differentiation" is allowed, but "discrimination" not; this distinction is not quite clear.

[30] See in this regard F.Jacobs, "The role of the European Court of Justice in the protection of the environment" in *Journal of Environmental Law* 2006, 185.

[31] *Commission v Germany* (C–131/93) [1994] E.C.R. I–3303.

[32] 302/86 (fn.9, above).

not explain what other, less restrictive, measures Denmark could have taken; its judgment is instead confined to the statement that "a very considerable degree of protection of the environment" was not really necessary to protect the environment. This seems to have the hallmark of a political statement.

In case C–2/90,[33] the Court did not discuss at all whether or not the Belgian measure to ban waste imports was disproportionate: as Belgium had argued that the measure was taken in order to react to a suddenly increased import of waste and as the judgment was given nine years after the taking of the measure, there would well have been reasons to discuss the proportionality requirement.

In its Decision 98/523,[34] the Commission considered the limitation of access to Karlstad airport to less noisy aeroplanes disproportionate, except as regarded a night curfew between 22.00 and 07.00 hours. The Commission argued, amongst other things, that the airport was situated in a sparsely populated area away from the city centre and that it accounted for a rather low traffic volume. The Commission requested that the Swedish authorities demonstrate the need to take the noise-restriction measures.

In case C–320/03[35] the Court had to decide on a regional Austrian legislation which prohibited, for environmental reasons, the transport of certain non-perishable goods on the Brenner Autobahn. The Court did not discuss the question of discrimination. It held that the Austrian measure was disproportionate, because Austria had introduced it at extremely short delay and had not provided for possibilities to transport the goods otherwise.

3–23   There is a lot of discussion on questions of the burden of proof or the burden of evidence. However, this rule of procedure simply means that in a dispute attempts must be made from the Commission, other parties, private bodies and Member States to clarify the facts as far as possible. The more substantiated the arguments from one side are, the more detailed those from the other side have to be. Only at the end of this process, where factual aspects remain open, can there be a question of who is to have the charge that a factual aspect has not been clarified.

It has already been pointed out that environmental protection reasons are, under the EU Treaties, not subordinated to considerations of free circulation of goods. In an assessment under art.34 TFEU, whether the consideration of free circulation of goods or the protection of the environment prevail, Member States have an amount of discretion as to the degree at which level they wish to fix the protection of the environment. It is difficult to understand why a night curfew should comply with the principle of necessity and proportionality but a limitation on access to the airports to less noisy aeroplanes does not. This issue cannot be solved by shifting the burden of proof.

3–24   Also, how difficult the proportionality principle is to apply in practice may be demonstrated by the question of product bans. Member States have pronounced a considerable number of bans of products; besides those mentioned on metal cans (Denmark) or pesticides (Netherlands), one could mention the restriction on phosphates in detergents (Italy–1988), or the Austrian ban of polybromated biphenyls (PBB), non-biodegradable plastic bags (some local authorities in Italy),

[33] C–2/90 (fn.11, above).
[34] Dec.98/523 (fn.16, above).
[35] *Commission v Austria* (C–320/03) [2005] E.C.R. I–9871.

lead capsules for alcoholic beverages (Germany, Netherlands), waste shredding machines (Germany) or lead-containing ammunition (Denmark, the Netherlands) and PVC.

The argument that a ban is not allowed where other means are available which less restrict the free circulation of goods must not be overused. Indeed, as has been already mentioned, the Court of Justice had expressly recognised the right of Member States to ban pesticides which had not been the subject of EU secondary legislation.[36] It would theoretically always be possible to argue that a strict licensing system together with control and surveillance mechanisms would reach more or less the same result, but would be less restrictive than a total ban. The Court's jurisdiction to allow the complete ban of pesticides by Member States means in practice that the Court grants them a considerable amount of discretion to decide on what measures they consider appropriate. Following the same line of reasoning, the Court of Justice accepted that the fixing of noise emission limit values for aeroplanes was the most effective and most appropriate means of combating noise emissions from aeroplanes; indeed, investments in construction around airports were normally very cost-intensive. Establishing noise emission limit values was therefore not disproportionate.[37]

This reasoning also applies to the German ban on waste shredding machines, which the Commission accepted. Waste shredding machines cut biological waste into small pieces, which are then disposed of together with ordinary waste water. German law provides that waste must first of all be recovered; this conforms to the EU waste hierarchy which is laid down in Directive 2008/98.[38] Disposing of waste by shredding it and discharging it into the sewer system contradicts this principle. Furthermore, the pipes for waste water would be charged with the mud, filtering would become more difficult and costly, waste water treatment stations would incur increased costs, and so on. It would therefore certainly be possible to prohibit waste disposal together with waste water without banning the shredding machines. In order to find out whether the marketing of waste shredding machines might be prohibited as well, the import of such machines into Germany would have to be considered and the possibility of controlling the ban on using these machines and of disposing of the waste via the waste water flow. Since such a ban could probably never be effectively controlled, a ban on marketing shredding machines appears not to be disproportionate. **3–25**

Italy, the United Kingdom, Denmark and Sweden took measures, in 1996–1997, to prohibit the marketing of self-chilling cans. These are metal cans for drinks which contain hydrofluorocarbons (HFCs), a cooling gas, which is spread between the wall of the can and the drink, in such a way that the can functions as a mobile mini-refrigerator, chilling the content of the can. **3–26**

HFC is a greenhouse gas, used as a substitute to CFC; it is considered, in global warming terms, to have a global warming potential of 11,700 (CO_2 has a global warming potential of 1).[39] It was in the mid-1990s not yet regulated by international agreements or EU legislation, but was identified, under the Kyoto Protocol (1998), as one of the greenhouse gases. Its extensive use would undermine efforts in other sectors to reduce CO_2 emissions and thus combat

---

[36] 125/88 (fn.17, above).
[37] *Aher-Waggon* (C–389/96) [1998] E.C.R. I–4473.
[38] Dir.2008/98 on waste [2008] OJ L312/3, art.4.
[39] See para.9–05, below.

climate change. Therefore, national bans on HFC or on products and equipment that contain HFC are justified under art.34 TFEU.

As regards the Italian ban of phosphates in detergents, it is not clear what less restrictive measure could reduce the eutrophication of rivers, lakes and coastal waters. The same applies to the Danish and Dutch ban on lead-containing ammunition which aims at reducing the presence of lead in the environment. If Denmark and the Netherlands consider that there is too much lead in the environment, and that ducks and birds might eat that ammunition, then a ban appears appropriate since equally effective measures, which restrict the free flow of goods less, are not available. The Commission has not taken any legal action against these three Member States. Similar considerations apparently also influenced the Commission in the case of the ban of non-biodegradable plastic bags, which was also accepted.[40] In the case of lead capsules for alcoholic beverages, the European Union thought it appropriate to adopt EU regulations in order to provide for a complete EU-wide phasing-out of such capsules.[41]

3–27   In 1999, the Netherlands issued draft legislation which considerably restricted the use of chlorinated paraffins. This measure was a follow-up of a decision taken within the framework of the Paris Convention of 1995,[42] aiming at progressively reducing paraffin in order to prevent marine pollution. The Commission did not object to this restriction on the free circulation of goods.

A similar case is the Austrian ban on PBB. PBB is suspected to cause serious health or environmental problems; however, the definitive scientific evidence on the risk of PBB has not yet been determined. The Commission considered that the OECD had recommended, at international level, that the marketing and use of PBBs be stopped and decided to accept the Austrian ban. This example shows that in the case of conflict between the free circulation of goods (art.34 TFEU) and environmental protection, the precautionary principle of art.191(2) TFEU may apply and lead to preference being given to measures which aim at environmental protection.

As mentioned in paras 1–28 et seq., above, there are attempts, in particular from economic operators, to limit the application of the precautionary principle also as regards national measures and to require, for its application, that there is a possibility of severe and irreversible hazard, a need to adopt measures urgently and that national legislation is of a provisional nature only. These attempts to reduce the application of the precautionary principle are unacceptable, as they try to interpret into this principle aspects which it does not contain. The Austrian PBB ban demonstrates well that Member States' discretion under the precautionary and the proportionality principles, is wider.

3–28   The precautionary principle may also be relevant in cases which concern national measures to restrict or ban the use of PVC. PVC is a plastic product which is mainly used in construction materials, packaging, cars, toys and office equipment. When incinerated, however, it generates dioxins and furans; its recycling as well as its disposal is particularly difficult. The question is whether

---

[40] An Italian judge had asked the Court of Justice whether such a ban was compatible with EU law, but omitted to ask for its compatibility with art.34 TFEU. The Court therefore only assessed its compatibility with Dir.75/442—now replaced by Dir.2008/98 (fn.38, above) and found no problem with this Directive, *Enichem v Cinisello-Balsamo* (380/87) [1989] E.C.R. 2491.

[41] See, e.g. Reg.3280/92 [1992] OJ L327/3.

[42] Paris Convention for the protection of the marine environment in the North-East Atlantic (OSPAR), see Dec.98/249 [1998] OJ L104/1; see also para.7–38, below.

Member States may, in view of the complications of waste incineration and disposal, restrict the use of PVC products or of certain substances (phthalates or heavy metals) in PVC. In application of the precautionary principle and in the absence of EU measures, it is well within the discretion of Member States to restrict or prohibit the use of PVC; it is not clear what less restrictive measure would be available.[43]

In another case, Greece prohibited the import of diesel cars for private use, arguing that the heavy air pollution in Athens and Thessaloniki required such a measure. It seems obvious that a total import ban on private diesel cars in order to combat air pollution in two regions is disproportionate. Upon the request of the Commission, Greece amended its legislation and prohibited the use of diesel cars in Athens and Thessaloniki. Such a measure may be proportional, if the air pollution in these two regions is primarily due to the use of diesel cars. However, it seems rather unlikely that the air pollution is caused more by diesel and petrol-driven cars, than, for example by industrial emissions, other economic activities and household heating. As long as a significantly higher participation of diesel cars emissions is not established, the restriction on the use of diesel, but not on petrol-driven, cars is discriminatory; furthermore, the measure as such is disproportional, since it appears that it is not capable of reaching the objective, i.e. the reduction of environmental pollution.

In 1998–1999, Denmark announced and adopted draft national legislation which intended to limit considerably the marketing of lead in Denmark, and of products which contained lead; these products were expressly listed in an annex. Products which complied with EU directives were exempted from this ban. The essential question in this case is whether Denmark was entitled, in the absence of EU law, to decide that it does not wish to see lead in its environment. In my opinion, this is indeed the case and it cannot be argued, in the name of proportionality, that less restrictive measures could be taken. The Commission did not object to the Danish legislation.   3–29

In 1998, Sweden prohibited the export of mercury containing products, including dental amalgams, for reasons of human health and of environmental protection. The Court of Justice held[44] that this export ban was incompatible with Directive 93/42 concerning medical devices,[45] though this Directive aims at the protection of human health, but not at the protection of the environment. Article 34 TFEU would thus have allowed Sweden to provide for this export ban.[46]

Protecting the environment outside the national territory. It has been argued in legal texts that a Member State's environmental measure under art.34 TFEU may also be taken in order to protect the environment outside its own jurisdiction. The Court of Justice has not yet formally decided on this issue. The first argument which is relevant in this context is the fact that the requirements of environmental protection are not limited to the EU territory. If the point of departure defended in this Chapter is correct—that in the absence of EU measures, the task of ensuring environmental protection is with Member States—it cannot seriously be argued   3–30

---

[43] As regards PVC, see also para.6–52, below.
[44] Court of Justice, *Kemikalieinspektionen* (C–288/08), judgment of November 19, 2009; see note L. Krämer, *Journal of European Environmental and Planning Law* (2010), 124.
[45] Dir.93/42 concerning medical devices [1993] OJ L169/1.
[46] In 2008, the EU adopted Reg.1102/2008 on the banning of exports of metallic mercury and certain mercury compounds and mixtures, [2008] OJ L 304/74. This Reg. exempts dental amalgams from the export ban. The Swedish ban was incompatible with this Reg.

that such measures are not allowed under arts 34 or 36 TFEU. Indeed, measures to combat climate change or to protect the ozone layer, tropical forests, elephants, whales, tigers or rhinos do affect the environment outside the EU territory—and yet have been taken by the European Union, without ever having seriously been questioned under art.34.[47] In the absence then of any EU measures this competence is with Member States.

The possibility of protecting the environment outside the national jurisdiction of a Member State finds its limits in the general Treaty provisions, in particular in that of art.4(3) TEU which lays down the principle of sincere cooperation.[48] Thus, the protection of the environment in another Member State will normally have to be left to that other Member State. However, the individual case will have to be weighed carefully. For instance, where a Member State decides to enact a national import ban on ivory in order to protect the African elephant,[49] this measure also affects the imports of ivory from other Member States. And yet this measure may be upheld under art.34 where the principles of non-discrimination and proportionality have been respected.

A similar reasoning may apply for the protection of an endangered species that lives in another Member State. Normally, it would be, under art.4(3) TEU, up to that Member State to protect this species. But there may be circumstances where such a measure is not taken, for political, economic or other reasons. In such a case, another Member State may decide to take measures to protect that species. An example is the German ban of the mid-1980s on imports for products made from corallium rubrum: corallium rubrum is a coral which lives in the Mediterranean and which is used in some Member States to produce jewellery. Weighing the arguments, the Commission did not see in that import ban a breach of Germany's obligations under arts 34–35 TFEU.[50]

The Court of Justice has not accepted export restrictions which France and the Netherlands[51] had introduced for specific wastes and for which they had invoked, amongst other arguments, the necessity of protecting the environment in other Member States. The Court considered that nothing indicated that the other Member States did not or could not protect themselves and their environment. In case C–203/96,[52] the Court was of the opinion that a Dutch provision which allowed the export of specific waste was not permitted, unless the processing of such waste abroad was "superior" to the processing in the Netherlands, was

---

[47] In *Safety Hi-Tech* (C–284/95) [1998] E.C.R. I–4301, the Court of Justice assessed the validity of EU measures to protect the ozone layer against art.34 TFEU, but found no breach of the Treaty provisions; see also paras 9–21 et seq., below.

[48] art.4(3) TEU: "Pursuant to the principle of sincere cooperation, the Union and the Member States shall in full mutual respect, assist each other in carrying out tasks which flow from the Treaties... The Member States shall... refrain from any measure which could jeopardise the attainment of the objectives of this Treaty."

[49] Reg.2496/89 [1989] OJ L240/5 introduced an EU-wide import ban on ivory. However, a number of Member States had already decided, at national level, to introduce such a ban prior to the EU action.

[50] Since then, corallium rubrum has been the subject of Community measures to restrict its trade, see Reg.338/97 on the protection of species of wild fauna and flora by regulating trade therein [1997] OJ L61/1.

[51] *Inter-Huiles* (172/82) [1983] E.C.R. 555: "The environment is protected just as effectively when the oils are sold to an authorised disposal or regenerating undertaking of another Member State as when they are disposed of in the Member States of origin"; *Nertsfoederfabriek* (118/86) [1987] E.C.R. 3883; the case concerned poultry waste.

[52] Court of Justice, *Dusseldorp* (C–203/96) [1998] E.C.R. I–4075.

illegal; the Court considered that the treatment methodology in both countries was equivalent, and that therefore the export restriction was not justified.

In case C–169/89,[53] the Court decided that the Netherlands could not lawfully prohibit the marketing of a bird which had been legally marketed in the United Kingdom. The details of this judgment appear questionable: as the EU legislation expressly required to protect *all* birds and constructed national hunting provisions as exceptions to that rule; however, this case will not be discussed here,[54] since the judgment mainly dealt with the interpretation of Directive 2009/147 on the conservation of wild birds.

In 2007/2008, Belgium and the Netherlands adopted legislation to prohibit the trade in seal furs and seal products. The measures also affect the trade with other EU Member States; they are envisaged to counteract the large-scale and frequently inhumane killing of seals which the Canadian government had authorised. Canadian seals are not an endangered species. Nevertheless, as measures to protect wild animal welfare are environmental measures (see para.1–03, above), such measures could be justified, as well under EU law as under WTO-law. In order to preserve the unity of the EU market, the European Union introduced legislation to regulate trade in seal products for the whole of the European Union.[55] Canada and Norway brought a case against this legislation before the WTO; there are also proceedings pending before the Court of Justice.

In conclusion, Member States may, in the absence of EU provisions on specific products, take those measures to protect the environment against the risk arising from the products which they consider appropriate. However, arts 34 and 36 TFEU and the very sophisticated and detailed case law of the Court of Justice require that a very careful assessment is made between the environmental advantage and the restriction of the free circulation of goods. Any national measure which restricts the circulation of goods must be based on non-economic considerations to protect the environment. It may not constitute an arbitrary discrimination between national producers and traders and producers or traders from other Member States. The national measure must be capable of reaching the envisaged aim and not go beyond what is necessary to reach it (proportionality). The different criteria—arbitrary discrimination, proportionality, a non-economic objective—leave a considerable amount of discretion to the Court of Justice, which is the final place for deciding on the legality of the national environmental measure. Therefore, a case-by-case assessment is necessary, which carefully considers all aspects of a national measure.

3–31

National measures affecting exports

Similar requirements apply to measures which concern the export of products. Article 35 TFEU prohibits quantitative restrictions on exports as well as measures having an equivalent effect; art.36 constitutes an exception to this principle and allows export restrictions, amongst other things for reasons to protect life and health of humans, animals or plants. The Court of Justice interpreted art.35 in a way that this prohibition "concerns all national measures which have as their

3–32

---

[53] *Gourmetterie van den Burg* (C–169/89) [1990] E.C.R. 2143.
[54] See for a detailed discussion L. Krämer (fn.24, above), p.149.
[55] Reg.1007/2009 on trade in seal products [2009] OJ L286/36.

specific object or effect the restriction of patterns of exports and thereby ...
provide a special advantage for national products or for the domestic markets".[56]

A frequent way of prohibiting exports is the requirement to deliver waste to
specific (national) plants. The Court of Justice considered that such an obligation
constituted an indirect export ban and was therefore incompatible with art.35.[57]
In some contradiction to these judgments is the decision in case C–422/92 where
the Court of Justice declared that the requirement to dispose waste generated in
Germany only in that country was compatible with EU law.[58]

It should be noted that on the one hand waste is a product of a specific nature
which may have as a consequence that different provisions apply.[59] On the other
hand, the European Union adopted, in 2006, new and specific provisions on the
shipment of waste within the European Union, which have been substituted for
previous provisions.[60] Member States may, under these provisions, oblige waste
generators or holders to deliver their waste to specific plants, provided that the
activity is a disposal activity. However, where waste is shipped for recovery to
another Member State, it is not possible to prohibit such a shipment by a
provision which obliges the waste holder to supply it to a specific waste disposal
or recovery plant. Such a provision contradicts art.35 and the abovementioned
Regulation on waste shipments.[61]

In particular in Germany, local authorities which have set up waste treatment
(incinerators) or disposal installations, often try to prohibit the export of
municipal waste to other municipalities or abroad, establishing an obligation to
deliver the waste to the local installation (Anschluss-und Benutzungszwang). The
compatibility of such measures with art.35 TFEU is doubtful, in particular, where
waste is exported for recovery purposes.[62] Apart from waste issues, there has not
yet been any Court decision to allow or disallow export restrictions for
environmental purposes. In practice therefore, the export ban for environmental
purposes does not play a significant role.

Measures under other policies

Agricultural policy

3–33　　Since the entering into force of the Lisbon Treaty at the end of 2009, agricultural
policy is no longer the exclusive competence of the European Union; rather, the
competence is shared (art.4(2d) TFEU). Member States' measures in environmental matters that would affect the common agricultural policy and its
legislation which were, in the past, not allowed, are now permitted, provided they
follow the general lines which were indicated above.

---

[56] Case 172/82 (fn.51, above).
[57] Cases 172/82 (fn.51, above); *Vanacker* (C–37/92) [1993] E.C.R. I–4947; *Nertsvoederfabriek* (118/86) [1987] E.C.R. 3883.
[58] *Commission v Germany* (C–422/92) [1995] E.C.R. I–1097; in that judgment, the Court did not expressly discuss art.35 but examined the German legislation under Dir.84/631 on the shipment of waste [1984] OJ L326/31.
[59] See para.2–76, above.
[60] Reg.1013/2006 on shipments of waste [2006] OJ L190/1.
[61] See, however, now Dir.2008/98 (fn.38 above), art.16(1), where Member States were authorised to restrict imports of waste for recovery, in order to protect their national incineration network.
[62] See for more details paras 10–36 et seq., below.

Thus, Member States may only take measures to the extent that the European Union has not taken action; such measures are under a permanent threat of being replaced by EU action. An example is the setting up of national criteria for organic farming and food therefrom: as the European Union has regulated this matter,[63] there is no competence for national measures in this area.

Measures which had been taken in the past include, in particular, the ban on certain agricultural pesticides. Since 1991, this subject has been regulated at EU level, presently by Regulation 1107/2009[64]; however, since the implementing provisions have not yet all been elaborated, the European Union de facto accepts that Member States continue to maintain national bans or restrictions of the marketing or use of pesticides. Once the EU system is fully established, this practice will have to be abandoned.

Environmental measures which Member States may take under these restricted conditions concern, for instance, the handling of manure, the limitation of the size of industrial feedstock installations, irrigation measures, action on the management of water resources and limiting the use of fertilisers or the number of cattle per km^2.

Transport policy

Transport policy (arts 90 to 100 TFEU) has also become, under the FEU Treaty, a common policy with shared competence (art.4(2g) TFEU), though EU measures are much less comprehensive than the common agricultural policy. For this reason, Member States have a much greater possibility of adopting environmental measures affecting transport. An important limitation, however, is art.92 TFEU, which prohibits direct or indirect discrimination of carriers from other Member States. In 1992, the Court of Justice had to decide on a tax on the use of roads by heavy goods vehicles which Germany had introduced.[65] While this road tax was the same for all carriers, Germany had, at the same time, provided for a reduction in the motor vehicle tax to the same amount; thus, the charge of the tax on the use of roads only affected carriers from other Member States. The Court did not accept the German Government's argument that the tax on the use of roads had an environmental objective because it was intended to increase the rate of goods transported by railway. Instead, it was of the opinion that there was no encouragement for German carriers to move to railway transport and that, therefore, the effect of the German measures contradicted art.92 TFEU. The Court came to a similar result in case C–205/98. Austria had raised, in 1995 and 1996, the toll rates for use of the Brenner motorway, but had provided that Austrian hauliers were charged less than foreign hauliers who were thus, in the opinion of the Court, discriminated.[66]

Member States may therefore take, in the absence of EU measures, non-discriminatory environmental measures, as regards, for instance, provisions on night flights at airports, taxes or charges on the use of roads of all types of cars

3–34

---

[63] Reg.834/2007 on organic production and labelling of organic products [2007] OJ L189/1; see for more details para.6–58, below.
[64] Reg.1107/2009 concerning the placing of plant protection products on the market, [2009] OJ L309/1; this Reg. replaced Dir.91/414 [1991] OJ L230/51.
[65] *Commission v Germany* (C–195/90) [1992] E.C.R. I–3141; see also *Commission v Germany* (C–195/90R) [1990] E.C.R. I–3351, which dealt with interim measures.
[66] Court of Justice, *Commission v Austria* (C–205/98) [2000] E.C.R. I–7367.

or provisions on ships. Since the European Union has, up until now, not taken many measures to integrate environmental requirements into the transport policy, arts 90 et seq. leave, in theory, large scope for national measures, although Member States do not seem inclined to make extensive use of this possibility.

State aids

3–35   Under the FEU Treaty, a State aid is a measure which provides a company or business with an economic or financial advantage, which must be granted by the State or through State resources; it must favour certain undertakings or the production of certain goods and it must affect the trade between Member States (art.107 TFEU). State aids are in principle prohibited. The intention of granting State aid has to be notified to the Commission (art.108(3) TFEU) in order to allow the assessment of its compatibility with the FEU Treaty, as art.107(2) and (3) TFEU allows State aids under certain conditions.

The connection with the Treaty's provision on competition needs to be underlined. Indeed, where consumers or users receive financial advantages to buy environmentally better products, there is normally no question of a State aid, since financial benefits are not given to particular firms.[67] Where this is the case, aid may be authorised where it is granted without discrimination and does not exceed 100 per cent of the extra environmental costs. Small amounts of aid—up to 100,000 € per firm over a period of three years—are considered not to affect trade and need not be notified to the Commission.[68]

3–36   In the same way, financial assistance which is granted to every undertaking is not aid, but may, of course, be seen as such where the receiving companies are in competition with other companies that do not have access to this assistance. Environmental aid, between 1996 and 1998, accounted on average for only 1.85 per cent of total aid granted to the manufacture and service sectors.

The Commission has, since 1974, established guidelines for national aid with environmental objectives,[69] which were reviewed and published several times, last in 2008.[70] Legally, these guidelines are not rules of law, but a communication to Member States and the other institutions, which indicate the criteria which the Commission uses to exercise its discretion for authorising national aids; they limit the Commission's discretion, as the Commission may not depart from them without reasons that are compatible with the principle of equal treatment.[71]

---

[67] See for example Court of Justice, *Preussen Elektra* (C–379/98) [2001] E.C.R. I–2099. The case concerned price advantages which were granted to small German producers of renewable energy.

[68] Commission, 26th report on competition policy (1996) (Luxembourg, 1997), p.59.

[69] Commission, Fourth report on competition policy (Brussels and Luxembourg, 1975), para.175; 10th report on competition policy (Brussels and Luxembourg, 1981), para.222; 16th report on competition policy (Brussels and Luxembourg, 1986), para.259; Guidelines 1994 [1994] OJ C72/3.

[70] Guidelines for state aid for environmental purposes [2001] OJ C37/3; Community guidelines on State aid for environmental purposes", [2008] OJ C82/1.

[71] Court of Justice, *Archer Daniels Midland v Commission* (C-397/03P) [2006] E.C.R. I–4491, para.91: "whilst rules of conduct designed to produce external effects as it is the case of the Guidelines [Guidelines on the method of setting fines in competition law, L.K.] which are aimed at traders, may not be regarded as rules of law which the administration is always bound to observe, they nevertheless form rules of practice from which the administration may not depart in an individual case without giving reasons that are compatible with the principle of equal treatment".

The basis for authorising national environmental aid is now art.107(3c)[72]; however, in specific cases, arts 107(3a) or (3b) might be applicable.

Aid for investment—in land, buildings, plants and, under certain conditions, technology transfer—may be authorised up to 70 per cent of the eligible costs where aid is given in order to help firms adapt to new mandatory standards. For small enterprises, the normal investment aid is 70 per cent, but may reach up to 100 per cent. For medium-sized enterprises, the normal investment aid is 60 per cent, for large enterprises 50 per cent. In specific circumstances, this aid may even be increased. The guidelines differentiate between aid for undertakings which go beyond or which anticipate EU environmental standards, environmental studies, waste management, renewable energies, energy saving, district heating with conventional energy, the remediation of contaminated sites – here the aid for any enterprise may reach 100 per cent—and the relocation of undertakings.

3–37

Member States shall report annually on the environmental aid which they grant. The Commission publishes this information on the internet.[73] These provisions thus open up a very large range of possibilities to financially assist companies which invest in clean technologies or otherwise improve the environment. Examples of state aids concern investments in the reduction of CO_2 emissions and in renewable energies,[74] aid for the development of a new, cleaner car,[75] industrial waste management,[76] energy saving measures[77] and alternative energies.[78]

Taxes and charges

Member States' possibilities of adopting environmental taxes and charges are equally great. They find their limitation in art.110 TFEU which is limited to goods and which prohibits any direct or indirect discrimination. The very existence of this provision shows that national fiscal measures are not to be assessed under art.34 TFEU. Indeed, art.110 is *lex specialis* to art.34.[79] The essential difference between the two provisions is that art.110 prohibits discriminating taxation measures, but does not refer to disproportionate taxes; and as the primary function of taxes is to ensure income there cannot be question of environmental taxes only being allowed for non-economic reasons. Hence, Member States may fix taxes on whatever topic they wish and at whatever level they wish, as long as they do not discriminate against products from other Member States. No notification of a national measure to the Commission is necessary under art.110.

3–38

Denmark had fixed the registration tax on new vehicles at between 105 and 180 per cent of the net sales price. The Commission was of the opinion that this

---

[72] art.107(3c) TFEU: "[The following may be considered to be compatible with the common market:] aid to facilitate the development of certain economic activities or of certain economic areas, where such aid does not adversely affect trading conditions to an extent contrary to the common interest."
[73] Commission, Community guidelines 2008 (fn.70, above), no.195.
[74] *Bulletin of the European Union* (1996) 5, para.1.3.42.
[75] *Bulletin of the European Union* (1996) 7–8, para.1.3.74.
[76] *Bulletin of the European Union* (1997) 4, para.1.3.83.
[77] *Bulletin of the European Union* (1997) 9, para.1.2.36.
[78] *Bulletin of the European Union* (1997) 11, para.1.3.77 and (1998) 4, para.1.2.50.
[79] Court of Justice, *Iannelli and Volpi* (74/76) [1977] E.C.R. 557; *Compagnie Commerciale de l'Ouest* (C–78–83/90) [1992] E.C.R. I–1847.

provision was incompatible with art.110, since it impeded the free movement of goods. However, the Court of Justice decided that art.110 only applied where tax measures were meant to protect domestic production; and since Denmark did not have a national car production industry there was no question of a breach of art.110.[80] Article 34 could, in such a case, become applicable only where a tax is so high that the import of products from other Member States would be effectively barred. Even in such cases a national tax may be compatible with art.34, namely in those cases where a Member State has legitimate environmental or other grounds for raising such a tax. Where for instance, a Member State would not like to see a *Concorde* aeroplane, a pesticide, metal cans or other products on its market or in its environment, it would be entitled, instead of prohibiting the use of that product, to levy a high, disuasive tax on the product.[81]

3–39   National eco-taxes, on CFCs, energy use, packaging, groundwater and so on, are to be examined initially under art.110, not under art.34. Besides the objective of creating income, they aim at influencing economic operators', users', consumers' and tax-payers' behaviour to reduce pollution, ensure prudent use of natural resources and encourage a preference for environmentally friendly products. In 1993, Belgium adopted legislation providing for an environmental tax on a number of products, in particular packages for drinks, disposable cameras and razors, batteries, pesticides and paper. Products on which the tax was levied had to carry a distinctive sign, showing that they were eco-taxed. The Court of Justice considered the tax to come under art.110[82]; however, since the distinctive sign was to be applied on the products, it directly affected the circulation of goods and had therefore to be assessed under art.34.

In 1996, France informed the Commission of its intention to introduce tax exemptions for biofuels. The Commission at first refused to accept the French measures, since they advantaged French products and thus were in conflict with art.110.[83] France then amended its legislation; the Commission was of the opinion that the new system eliminated any discrimination between the types of vegetable matter or crops which produce the biofuel and between French producers and those from other Member States. It therefore approved of the system. However, the General Court considered the French measures incompatible with EU law, as they gave competititve advantages to French producers.[84]

3–40   A number of German local authorities taxed single-use packaging, in order to promote reusable packaging. The Commission, seized with complaints from several economic operators, decided in 1996, that no infringement of the Treaty provisions was visible. In the meantime, these taxes were held to be incompatible with internal German law. In 1997, the Commission made a communication to the other institutions, in which it discussed environmental taxes and levies in the internal market.[85] The Communication examined several aspects of eco-taxes,

---

[80] *Commission v Denmark* (C–47/88) [1990] E.C.R. I–4509.
[81] As regards metal cans, see paras 3–15 and 3–16, above. Sweden had introduced a rather high tax for such cans. And while the Commission had tackled the Danish ban, it had not taken measures against Sweden.
[82] *Bic* (C–13/96) [1997] E.C.R. I–1753.
[83] Dec.97/542 [1997] OJ L222/26.
[84] General Court, *BP v Commission* (T–184/97) [2000] E.C.R. II–314 para.13: "That decision was adopted without any communication being published in the Official Journal to allow interested third parties to submit their comments... the decision was not published in the Official Journal".
[85] Commission, COM (97) 9, [1997] OJ C224/4.

with the implicit intention of bringing as many of the national taxes and levies under the control of art.34 TFEU as possible. This is understandable since with the progressive elimination of technical barriers to trade by art.34, barriers with similar effect may result by virtue of the introduction of national taxes and charges.

Since the mid-1990s, Germany tried to promote alternative energies. National legislation obliged to electricity companies to buy electricity from alternative energies produced in Germany at a fixed price which was determined by legislation, and to put the electricity into their grid. Seized with the question, whether this legislation was compatible with EU law, the Court decided[86] that the measures did not constitute State aid, as no public funds were made available to competitors. And it also decided that in view of the present state of integration of the electricity market, the German legislation did not contradict art.34 TFEU. The discriminative character of the measure, which aimed at the promotion of German alternative energy, but excluded electricity produced from alternative energy from other Member States, could not really be put in doubt. The only explanation of this is that the Court considered the legislation to be a discrimination, but not an arbitrary discrimination. It is clear that such a differentiation can only be made by the Court—which does not increase transparency and legal certainty.

Eco-taxes are a useful tool in the promotion of environmentally sound behaviour; they help to keep environmentally unwelcome products off the market.[87] Member States have always used taxes to influence the behaviour of economic operators or private persons; examples are the taxation of petrol and diesel, of spirits and cigarettes, water, electricity and heating. Examples of past eco-taxes are differential taxes for leaded and unleaded petrol, tax relief for nuclear energy, natural gas, lignite or coal, or landfill taxes. Since eco-taxes are being used increasingly in the north of the European Union, but have until now been used only rather infrequently in the south,[88] their divisive effect increases EU differences rather than promoting integration and cohesion.

3.   Existence of community legislation and the taking of national measures

General aspects

As mentioned above, Member States' competence to deal with environmental   **3–41** measures does not end once the European Union has adopted an environmental measure. However, it is "superseded" by the EU measure, as far as the EU measure reaches. Member States' possibility of acting therefore depends both on the content of the EU legislative act, and on the legal basis on which that legislative act was based.

---

[86] Court of Justice, C–379/98 (fn.67, above).
[87] See also European Environment Agency, *Environmental taxes, implementation and environmental effectiveness* (Copenhagen, 1996).
[88] The annex to COM (97) 9 (fn.85, above) listed, for October 1996, 22 eco-taxes in Denmark, 20 in Sweden, 19 in Finland, but only four in Greece, seven in Italy and eight in Spain.

In order to assess the legal content of an EU measure, it is important to examine exactly what the measure intends to cover. For instance, the EU measure might, for product standards, cover only the standards for those products which participate in the trade between Member States, but leave the standards for products which remain on the national market to Member States. EU terminology speaks, in such cases, of optional harmonisation, since Member States may decide to set up two different types of standards for products.[89] In contrast to this, total harmonisation exists where an EU measure intends to set standards for all products which are put into circulation within the Union, whether they cross a border or not.[90] Partial harmonisation only concerns some products, but not all of a given type.[91] Minimum harmonisation sets standards at EU level, but leaves the possibility to Member States to fix more stringent requirements.[92] Combinations of these types of harmonisation are possible; thus, an EU directive may well fix standards for some products only (partial harmonisation), deal with all products that are on the EU market (total harmonisations) and leave Member States the possibility to adopt more stringent standards (minimum harmonisation).

The different approaches find their source in the EU Treaties themselves. Indeed, the FEU Treaty provides for differences in Member States' rights according to the legal basis on which an EU environmental measure is grounded. For this reason it is important to examine what the objective of a specific EU legislation is, in order to determine the possibilities for Member States to legislate.[93]

Rights under art.193 TFEU

3–42   Where an EU measure was based on art.192 TFEU, the relationship between the Member States' and the Union's right to legislate is governed by art.193.[94] The provision only refers to protective measures and it may thus be doubtful whether measures that aim at preserving or improving the quality of the environment (see art.191 TFEU) are also covered. However, such a differentiation would make no sense, all the more since no clear distinction can be drawn between protective, preserving and improving measures. "Protective measures" must therefore be interpreted as including all measures adopted under art.192, even where only the main objective of a measure—say 55 per cent—is environmentally oriented and a considerable part—say 45 per cent—is aiming at the achievement of internal market objectives.

Article 193 says nothing about the form which the EU provision under art.192 must take. It is therefore irrelevant whether the provision is set out in a directive, a regulation or a decision—for instance, whether to adhere to an international convention—whether the measure was adopted unanimously or by majority vote, whether it is a partial or an optional or a total harmonisation measure.

---

[89] Examples are the limit values for noise emissions from construction equipment, see para.8–39, below.

[90] Examples are the limit values for air emission from cars since 1988, see para.8–47, below.

[91] An example is Reg.1102/2008 (fn.46, above).

[92] Examples are standards for waste incineration plants, see para.8–34, below.

[93] See, e.g. Court of Justice, *VAG Sverige* (C–329/95) [1997] E.C.R. I–2675.

[94] art.193 TFEU: "The protective measures adopted in common pursuant to Art.192, shall not prevent any Member State from maintaining or introducing more stringent protective measures. Such measures must be compatible with the Treaties. They shall be notified to the Commission."

Article 193 only allows stricter measures to be taken. Consequently, the   **3–43**
Member States may not adopt different measures from those adopted by the
European Union. On the contrary: the more stringent national measure must
follow the same direction and come closer than the European Union to attaining
the objectives of art.191(1) TFEU. It is important that the rules adopted by the
individual Member State are of the same type as the EU provisions, because then
the European Union and other Member States have the possibility of catching up
and aligning with the more protective measure taken by one Member State,
re-establishing in this way uniform legislation throughout the European Union.[95]

For example, if the European Union decides in a measure based on art.192, to   **3–44**
halve the production and consumption of chlorofluorocarbons (CFCs) because of
its ozone-depleting potential, any Member State may still propose an outright ban
on the production and consumption of CFCs. However, it may not ban, on the
basis of art.193, the use of aerosol cans which contain CFC gas: this is not a more
stringent protective measure, but another, different measure: an *aliud*. The
legality of such a measure is therefore determined according to general Treaty
provisions, in particular by arts 34 and 36 TFEU.

If the European Union introduces a system of strict, unlimited liability for
environmental damage, but excludes the compensation of bodily injury, each
Member State may impose strict liability and provide for the inclusion of
compensation for bodily injury of individual persons. However, it may not
provide for unlimited liability only for damage that was caused by negligence
instead, since this is a different system. Nor could the Member State in that case,
argue that experience had shown that certain industrial activities too often give
cause for environmental liability and then prohibit that specific industrial activity
altogether.

When the European Union introduced an eco-label for products and took a
flower as its symbol, it expressly allowed Member States to maintain their
national ecolabel systems.[96] Without this express authorisation, Member States
would not have been able, based on art.193, to maintain their national systems.
Indeed, the symbols as well as the selection and assessment criteria being
different, these national systems are not "more protective" systems under art.193,
but rather different systems.

A more protective system is a system which establishes stricter limit values for
the emission of pollutants into the environment, which reduces emissions more
quickly than the EU measure or which regulates, for emissions from an industrial
plant, more pollutants than the EU measure.

The nationally more protective measures must be compatible with the Treaties.   **3–45**
Consequently, they may not conflict with any provision of the Treaties,
particularly with the provisions on the free circulation of goods or on undistorted
competition. The measures must not constitute a means of arbitrary discrimination or a disguised restriction on trade between Member States (arts 34 and 36
TFEU). Reference to the Treaties means, of course, reference to the interpretation
given to the different Treaty provisions, by the Court of Justice in particular.
Therefore, a national, more protective measure may neither be discriminatory nor

---

[95] See also Court of Justice, Case C-6/03 *Deponieverband Eiterköpfe*, [2005] E.C.R. I–2753, where
the Court requires the national measure to pursue "the same objectives".
[96] Reg.66/2010 on the Community ecolabel [2010] OJ L27/1, art.11 and Recital 15; see para.6–56,
below.

disproportionate with regard to the objective that is pursued with it. Protectionism is still protectionism, even if the aim is to protect the environment.

3–46   "Treaties" refers also to secondary EU law, since this is based on the FEU Treaty.[97] This theory is contested mainly by German writers[98] who argue that otherwise the right to take more protective measures would be undermined by EU secondary legislation and become meaningless. However, this opinion does not take into consideration the fact that EU secondary legislation is also based on the Treaties. As regards art.36 TFEU, it is well established Court jurisdiction, and in the meantime is no longer contested, that this provision no longer applies where the European Union has adopted secondary legislation—whether such EU measures were based on arts 114, 192 or any other provision.

Furthermore, it has already been discussed above[99] that the Council considers arts 114 and 192 as being equally valid grounds on which to base environmental legislation and that it differentiates the legal basis, supported in this by the Court of Justice and the Commission, according to the "centre of gravity" of a measure. This means that up to 49 per cent of a measure that is based on art.192 may be provisions which deal with internal market issues. In such a case, Member States may also take more protective measures with regard to the provisions concerning the 49 per cent of the measures. An example is Directive 2000/53 on end-of-life vehicles[100] which prohibited, in new cars, the use of certain heavy metals. Member States are allowed, under art.193, to provide for further restrictions, of course, under the conditions that these measures were also justified under other Treaty provisions, in particular arts 34 and 36 TFEU. In order to prevent Member States from taking such measures, the legislation on electrical and electronic waste was split up: the ban of heavy metals was regulated in Directive 2002/95 which was based on art.114,[101] whereas the other provisions concerning such waste were regulated by Directive 2002/96 which was based on art.192[102] and thus allowed to recur to art.193. The opposite example is Directive 94/62 on packaging and packaging waste which is based on the present art.114.[103] In order to allow Member States to fix more demanding recycling targets than those provided for by the Directive, art.6(6) of that Directive had to introduce an express provision allowing Member States to adopt more stringent targets.

3–47   The problem is of considerable practical importance. For example, Regulation 66/2010, based on art.192, introduced an EU ecolabel.[104] The EU criteria for attribution of an ecolabel are set for product groups by EU decisions which are based on Regulation 66/2010 and, finally, on art.192 TFEU. The specific decisions, to grant the ecolabel for a specific product, are made at national level.[105] It seems an impossible idea to establish EU-wide criteria for specific product groups and then, when a producer asks a national authority to obtain the

---

[97] In this sense also Pagh, E.U. *Miljoeret* (Copenhagen 1996), p.242; *contra* Epiney, *Umweltrecht in der Europäischen Union* (fn.20, above), p.126 quoting other German authors.

[98] Also see on this point, para.1–15, above.

[99] See paras 2–60 et seq., above.

[100] Dir.2000/53 on end-of life vehicles [2000] OJ L269/34.

[101] Dir.2002/95 on the restriction of the use of certain hazardous substances in electrical and electronic equipment [2003] OJ L37/19.

[102] Dir.2002/96 on waste electrical and electronic equipment (WEEE) [2003] OJ L37/24.

[103] Dir.94/62 on packaging and packaging waste [1994] OJ L365/10.

[104] Reg.66/2010 (fn.96, above).

[105] For more details see para.6–49.

ecolabel, inform him that the Member State in question has adopted more protective provisions so that he could not obtain the ecolabel. Such a solution would be all the more contradictory as the same producer could obtain the ecolabel in another Member State that had not adopted such "more protective measures" and could then circulate his product freely within the European Union. Thus, within one and the same Member State, products could circulate with the same ecolabel, but with different eco-criteria: this result is absurd.

Another example is the regulation on the shipment of waste, which is based on art.192.[106] The Regulation establishes lists of non-hazardous and hazardous waste, for which different surveillance and control systems as regards shipments apply. Non-hazardous waste may be shipped practically without restriction. The question is whether Member States are allowed, under art.193, to classify a non-hazardous waste as hazardous and then apply stricter controls to such shipments. I am of the opinion that this is not allowed.

A last example again concerns the shipment of waste. Regulation 1013/2006, differentiates, for hazardous wastes, between shipments that are made for disposal and shipments that are made for recovery purposes. While Member States may prohibit shipments of hazardous waste for disposal altogether,[107] they may object to shipments for recovery only in specific cases which are listed in art.12 of Regulation 1013/2006.

Article 12(1.g) allows objection to shipments:

> "if the ration of the recoverable and non-recoverable waste, the estimated value of the materials to be finally recovered or the cost of the recovery and the cost of the disposal of the non recoverable fraction do not justify the recovery under economic and environmental considerations."

Could a Member State, invoking art.193, also generally prohibit shipments of waste for recovery?

The answer must be in the negative. Indeed, there is no sense in differentiating between waste for disposal and waste for recovery at all, if Member States could adopt provisions which would lead to an equal treatment of waste in both cases. Why should there be the necessity for very carefully considering environmental and economic aspects of a waste shipment under art.12 of Regulation 1013/2006, if a Member State could ensure, as a general rule, that shipments of waste would be prohibited even if the weighing up of arguments showed that such a shipment was environmentally sound? Listing specific grounds for objecting to waste shipments in art.12(1) and then admitting an unlimited number of supplementary objections does not really make sense.

3–48

This question was, under the previous Regulation on the shipment of waste, Regulation 259/93, submitted to the Court of Justice in case C–203/96[108]. The Court found that neither Regulation 259/93 nor Directive 75/442 on waste[109] allowed the application of the principles of self-sufficiency and proximity to shipments of waste for recovery. However, it did not answer the question of

---

[106] Reg.1013/2006 on shipments of waste [2006] OJ L190/1; this Regulation replaced Reg.259/93 [1993] OJ L30/1.

[107] Reg.1013/2006, art.11(1).

[108] *Dusseldorp* (C–203/96) (fn.7, above).

[109] Dir.75/442 as amended by Dir.91/156 [1991] OJ L78/32. This Directive is now replaced by Dir.2008/98 (fn.38, above).

whether art.193 allowed such an application and, thus, whether Member States could go beyond Regulation 259/93 by invoking art.193. Instead, it examined the grounds invoked by the Dutch Government for its national measure which went beyond Regulation 259/93 and found that the justification—to ensure the continuity of supply of Dutch undertakings and increased risks for the environment by waste shipments—did not justify, in this specific case,[110] the restriction under art.36 TFEU.

3–49   This judgment might well be claimed by both sides. Indeed, if a Member State could have have recourse to art.193 and generally object to waste shipments, an examination of whether such a restriction is contrary to art.35 TFEU would not have been necessary. On the other hand, if the objections listed in art.12(1) of Regulation 1013/2006 were exhaustive, should the Court have entered into an examination of supplementary objection grounds?

In my opinion, it should first of all be noted that the problem only appears as regards product standards, where the EU principle of free circulation of goods interferes. Indeed, where EU secondary legislation establishes limit values for emissions from installations, or quality standards for concentrations of pollutants in water, there is general agreement that Member States may, on the basis of art.193, set stricter provisions at national level.

3–50   As regards product-related secondary EU legislation, the solution lies in the necessity of reading the two criteria of art.193 together—i.e. "more protective measure" and "compatible with the Treaty": any EU environmental legislation, including the legislation that is based on art.192 must respect the provisions of arts 34 and 36—this is established case law of the Court of Justice.[111] Thus, EU legislation also has to respect the principles of non-discrimination and proportionality,[112] although the EU legislature enjoy a large degree of discretion as to how to draft legislation in a specific case. The more the EU legislature has weighed up the different economic, ecological, social, political and other arguments in detail and has elaborated detailed, balanced and sophisticated provisions (such as decisions on ecolabel criteria, waste lists, objection grounds) the more the principles of arts 34 and 36 are "filled up"; in such a case of total harmonisation—on this notion see para.3–41—there is thus no room left for the principles of arts 34 and 36. Therefore, when a Member State, based on art.193 TFEU, wants to take more protective measures, its legislative discretion is reduced in proportion to the concretisation which EU secondary legislation has given to the balance between environmental and economic interests in a specific situation. A national measure which deviates from the solutions set by EU secondary legislation would thus be disproportionate and therefore not compatible with the Treaties.

This means in the concrete case of waste shipments that Regulation 1013/2006—and its predecessor, Regulation 259/93—constitute, as regards objects to waste shipments for recovery—total harmonisation measures. Member States may not go further than Regulation 1013/2006 and invoke other grounds for objecting to shipments.

---

[110] It is not clear why the Court entered into the discussion of this specific case, although it was a question which was put to the Court under the procedure of art.267 TFEU.

[111] *Denkavit Nederland* (15/83) [1984] E.C.R. 2171; *Meyhui* (C–51/93) [1994] E.C.R. I–3879; *Safety Hi-Tech* (C–284/ 95) [1998] E.C.R. I–4301.

[112] The proportionality principle is also laid down in art.5(4) TEU.

The problem has only been seen in practice in one case up until now. Directive 87/416 allows Member States to prohibit the use of leaded petrol, but requires that the intention of such a ban be published and notified to the Commissions six months in advance.[113] Germany wanted, based on art.193, to disregard the six-month delay and ban leaded petrol four months after notification. Finally, however, it accepted the Commission's request that the six-month delay be respected, which safeguarded the interests of producers, importers, traders and users of petrol and cars.

Another example is that of sewage sludge in agriculture. Directive 86/278 on protecting the environment and soil against the use of sewage sludge[114] fixed maximum permitted concentrations of some heavy metals in sewage sludge and in the soil. Where these concentration values are exceeded, the use of sewage sludge is prohibited. In view of the accumulation of heavy metals in the soil and the possible residues in food, Austrian and German regions prohibited the use of sewage sludge on or in soil altogether. In my opinion, such a measure is justified under art.193 TFEU. Article 34 does not stand against this solution, as sewage sludge may nevertheless be traded within the European Union. It is not forbidden to trade in sewage sludge, only to use it on or in soil. And as sludge contains heavy metals, it must remain the decision of Member states to fix themselves the degree of protection which they want to apply for their soils.

When the European Union introduced a greenhouse gas emissions trading scheme, it amended Directive 96/61 and provided that industrial installations which participated in the trading scheme, were not obliged to apply, with regard to CO^2-emissions the best available techniques.[115] The question is, whether a Member State may, on the basis of art.193 TFEU, introduce the requirement of using the best available techniques at national level. This is, in my opinion, well the case. Each Member State is entitled to discriminate against its own national installations.[116] If the Council and the European Parliament wanted to provide for a total harmonisation, they should have based the legislation on industrial installations on art.114 TFEU, instead of art.192 TFEU.

Measures adopted under art.193 must be notified to the Commission. There is   **3–51**
no time limit for such notification and the measures need not be notified to the Commission in draft form; the Member State is not either obliged to wait for a certain period after the notification, before adopting the measures. However, the situation is different, where the national measure comes into the field of application of Directive 98/34.[117] Indeed, that Directive provides that all product-related measures shall be notified to the Commission in draft form in order to allow an examination of whether or not they could create new barriers to trade. Therefore, where a more protective measure could have an influence on

---

[113] Dir.87/416 [1987] OJ L225/1.

[114] Dir.86/278 on the use of sewage sludge in agriculture [1986] OJ L181/6.

[115] See now Dir.2010/75 on industrial emissions [2010] OJ L334/17, art.9(1): "Where emissions of a greenhouse gas from an installation are specified in Annex I to Directive 2003/87 in relation to an activity carried out in that installation, the permit shall not include an emission limit value for direct emissions of that gas, unless necessary to ensure that no significant local pollution is caused".

[116] Jans-Vedder (fn.29, above), p.108 appear to deny such a right of a Member State under art.193. They hold that the EU legislature could make such a "self-binding" commitment to exclude such a possibility. This would mean that the legislature could make a commitment to prohibit the application of a provision of the EU Treaties.

[117] Dir.98/34 laying down a procedure for the provision of information in the field of technical standards and regulations [1998] OJ L204/37. This Directive replaced Dir.83/189 [1983] OJ L109/8.

art.34 TFEU, the Commission must be notified of it in draft form. Under Directive 98/34, there is then a standstill period of at least three months during which the Commission and all other Member States may question the compatibility of the draft measure with art.34 or secondary EU legislation. Omitting to notify the Commission of the draft makes the national provision unenforceable.[118]

Article 193 does not contain any procedural provisions for checking whether the national measure fulfils the conditions that are laid down in this provision. Where the Commission is of the opinion that a national measure is not a more protective, but a different measure (an "*aliud*"), or where it believes that the measure is not compatible with primary or secondary EU law, it has, in the last instance, to recur to procedures under art.258 TFEU. The same possibility is open to any Member States under art.259 TFEU, though Member States never used that provision.

Rights under art.114(4)–(8) TFEU

General aspects

3–52   Article 114(4)–(8) TFEU deals with the right of Member States to maintain existing or introduce new legislative measures where the Union has legislated on the legal basis of art.114.

The present art.114 was introduced, as art.100a, into the Treaty in 1987. Its para.4 allowed Member States, in the case of decisions according to that provision and under certain conditions, to "apply" diverging national legislation. Between 1987 and 1997, the Commission took three decisions under art.95(4)[119]; in one case, the Court of Justice issued a judgment,[120] where it stated in particular that the national measure would only become applicable, once the Commission had authorised it. However, this created problems, because the Commission sometimes did not take a decision for several years: on two notifications from the Netherlands, dated 1992 and concerning restrictions on the use of cadmium and pentachlorophenol, the Commission took more than six years for a decision, though it tolerated the application of the restriction in the Netherlands; this was not quite in line with the Court's judgment in case C–41/93.

In case C–319/97[121], the Court decided that where the Commission failed to take a decision within a reasonable time, a Member State could only take court action against the Commission under art.265 TFEU, but had, in the meantime, to apply the EU measure. The Amsterdam Treaty then solved this problem, by introducing art.114(6) according to which the Commission had to take a decision under art.114 within six months; otherwise, the national measure would be deemed to have been approved.[122]

The Amsterdam Treaty modified art.114 considerably, and, in particular, explicitly provided for the possibility for Member States to *maintain or introduce*

---

[118] Court of Justice, *CIA Security International* (C–194/94) [1996] E.C.R. I–2201.

[119] [1992] OJ C334/8 (*Pentachlorophenol Germany*); [1994] OJ L316/43 (*Pentachlorophenol Germany*); [1996] OJ L68/32 (*Pentachlorophenol Denmark*).

[120] *France v Commission* (C–41/93) [1994] E.C.R. I–1829.

[121] *Kortas* (C–319/97) [1999] E.C.R. I–3143.

[122] See for a case, where the six-month delay had been exceeded, General Court, *Poland v Commission* (T–69/08) judgment of December 9, 2010.

national measures after the European Union had adopted a measure under art.114. This ended the extensive legal discussion on the former wording, whether "apply" was to be understood as "continue to apply"—this had always been the Commission's understanding—or was equivalent to "maintain or introduce". In 2003, the Commission resumed its practice under art.114 in a communication[123]; it also started to report on its decisions under that provision, but gave up this initiative again.[124]

Maintaining national legislation (art.114(4))

For a Member State to maintain national environmental legislation, according to art.114(4) despite EU legislation, a number of conditions must be fulfilled: **3–53**

1. the European Union must have adopted a harmonisation measure;
2. a Member State must deem it necessary to maintain its national legislation on grounds that relate to the protection of the environment;
3. the Member State notifies the Commission of these provisions as well as of the grounds for maintaining them;
4. the Commission approves of the national measures (art.114(6)).

These different conditions will be examined one by one.[125]

Adoption of a harmonisation measure. The express inclusion of measures   **3–54**
taken by the Commission clarifies that the adaptation of EU measures to scientific or technical progress or by other means of delegated or implementing acts (arts 290 and 291 TFEU), may also lead to the right of Member States to maintain national legislation; such cases may well occur where technical annexes of directives are adapted to technical progress.

"Harmonisation measures" are measures adopted under art.114 TFEU. Such a measure need not have been adopted by majority decision; even in the case of a unanimous decision, the right of a Member State to maintain its national legislation exists. It is not contradictory to vote in favour of an EU measure and then decide to maintain more stringent national legislation. Indeed, a Member State may well vote in favour of an EU measure because it wishes to see the level of environmental protection increased throughout the European Union, even if the EU measure does not go as far as its own national legislation.

---

[123] Commission, Communication concerning Article 95 (paras 4, 5 and 6) COM(2002) 760 of December 23, 2002.

[124] See Commission, 19th annual report on monitoring the application of Community law (2001) COM(2002)324; 27 the report, COM(2010) 538.

[125] The Commission has, in the meantime adopted a number of environmental decisions concerning the application of art.95(4), in particular: Decision 99/831 (Netherlands—PCP) [1999] OJ L329/15; Dec. 99/832 (Netherlands—creosote) [1999] OJ L329/25; Dec.99/833 (Germany—creosote) [1999] OJ L329/43; Dec.99/834 (Sweden—creosote) [1999] OJ L329/63; Dec.99/835 (Denmark—creosote) [1999] OJ L329/82; Dec.2000/59 (Belgium organo-stannic compounds [2000] OJ L205/7; Dec.2002/3999 (Sweden—cadmium in fertilizers) [2002] OJ L138/24; Dec.2006/347 (Sweden—cadmium in fertilizers), [2006] OJ L129/19; Dec.2006/348 (Finland—cadmium in fertilizers) [2006] OJ L129/25; Dec.2006/349 (Austria—cadmium in fertilizers) [2006] OJ L129/31; Dec.2006/390 (Czech Republic—cadmium in fertilizers) [2006] OJ L150/17; Dec.2007/955 (Netherlands—paraffin) [2007] OJ L148/17.

3–55   *Necessity of maintaining national legislation.* It is doubtful whether any national legislation may be maintained. These doubts stem from art.114(7),[126] which demonstrates the aim of the Treaty legislature to ensure that uniform legislation applies throughout the European Union. Therefore, the EU measure shall, if at all possible, be adapted to that of the derogating Member State in order to ensure the continuous free circulation of goods in the Union's internal market.

These questions will be discussed below, when the Commission's options are examined for approving or of refusing the Member State's maintaining its national legislation. It is certain that a Member State may notify any national measure under art.114(4); it is not necessary that the legislation is adopted at national level; regional measures may also be notified.[127]

3–56   *Notification and justification of the national measure.* The Member State which wishes to maintain its national legislation must formally inform the Commission of its intention to do so. There is no time limit for this notification; terms that require such notification to be addressed to the Commission within a specific time-span after the adoption of the EU legislation or within the time-span which was provided for in the EU measure for transposition into national legislation, have not been retained. Usually, therefore, a Member State is free to notify the Commission when it seems fit to do so.

However, it is clearly in the self-interest of the notifying Member State to notify as early as possible. On the one hand, provisions of EU law prevail over national law and may have a direct effect, even where they are not transposed into national law; this means in practice that national law which is in conflict with an EU provision may not be applied—and not be enforced either.[128] On the other hand, the notification puts into operation a six-month delay within which a decision on the national measure must be taken (art.114(6)).

3–57   And, finally, the Court of Justice has decided[129] that a Member State may only apply its national legislation which deviates from the EU harmonisation measure, once it has received an approving decision from the Commission. It is doubtful whether this decision, which was taken at a time, when the Treaty text did not yet differentiate in art.114, between "apply" and "maintain/introduce", is of much relevance now. Indeed, it would constitute a considerable disturbance of economic operations and administrative practice if a Member State would have to suspend the application of national legislation which might have existed for years, and wait for a Commission decision. The reasonable, and largely logical, consequence is therefore to consider the Court's statement remaining valid only for the cases of art.114(5), i.e. for cases where new national legislation is introduced. Anyway, the uncertainty of the described legal situation suggests that

---

[126] art.114(7) TFEU: "When . . . a Member State is authorised to maintain or introduce national provisions derogating from a harmonisation measure, the Commission shall immediately examine whether to propose an adaptation to that measure."

[127] See, for example, the legislation referred to in General Court, *Austria v Commission* (T–366/03) [2005] E.C.R. II–4005, which originated from the Land (region) Ober-Österreich. The appeal was rejected, *Austria v Commission* (C–439/05) [2007] OJ LI–7141.

[128] Case C–41/93 (fn.120, above), para.30.

[129] See Case C–41/93 (fn.120, above), para.30, Opinion of Advocate General Tesauro, para.9, who argued that this interpretation is the only one which is compatible with the supremacy of EU law and which avoids legal insecurity.

the Member State has a strong interest in trying to obtain the Commission's decision as quickly as possible and before the transposition period for the harmonisation measure has ended.

The notifying Member State will also have to give the grounds for its decision to maintain national legislation. It has to indicate the factual and legal aspects in sufficient detail to allow the Commission to reach a decision on the notification within six months. The requirement of providing the grounds for the decision is new and constitutes, without doubt, a considerable supplementary burden for the notifying Member State.

Commission approval. The Commission must "approve" of the environmental measure; this wording of art.114(6) is more precise than that of the previous version of the Treaty which provided that the Commission should "confirm" the national measure, since it is now—since the judgment in case C–41/93, quoted above—clear that the approval must be made in the form of a decision under art.288 TFEU.

3–58

Approval has to be given if the national measure does not constitute a "means of arbitrary discrimination or a disguised restriction on trade between Member States". This wording is identical to that of art.36(2) TFEU. Thus, the interpretation of art.36(2) may be used to interpret this provision. Arbitrary discrimination or disguised trade restrictions are cases of abuse, where a formally legitimate objective—the protection of the environment—is used to discriminate against goods from other Member States or to pursue protectionist goals.

To these two goals, which were already contained in the previous versions of art.114, a third one has been added: the national measure "shall not constitute an obstacle to the functioning of the internal market".

3–59

It is clear that any national measure which is maintained, despite a harmonisation measure taken by the European Union, constitutes an obstacle to the functioning of the internal market; the two bans on pentachlorophenol in Germany and Denmark, on which the Commission had decided, constitute a clear example, since products containing that substance were not allowed to circulate in these countries. It is thus not quite clear what the provision intends to achieve.

Where, for instance, the European Union decides to create a uniform ecolabelling system throughout the European Union, such a measure would have to be based on art.114. Supposing that Germany then wanted to maintain its national eco-symbol, which is a blue angel—and not a flower, as is the EU symbol—could this be done by invoking art.114(4)? The answer seems clearly to be in the negative. Indeed, it is possible to have either a system based on the flower or on the blue angel, but one cannot have both systems inside an internal market. In fact, the German system, in this example, would be a different system. Also, it is not clear what the environmental grounds would be which would make it "necessary" to maintain the blue angel system; greater efficiency cannot be a valid ground, because the EU system is just meant to create an equivalent system. In conclusion, thus, the maintaining of the blue angel system would be a different system where the environmental grounds that would make its maintenance necessary are not visible.

3–60

Where the European Union provides for certain limit values for noise emissions from coaches, any more stringent national limit value would, if properly enforced, create an obstacle to the free circulation of coaches and would thus have to be disallowed. This solution could be avoided where the Member

State that wishes to maintain the more stringent national emission limit values would at least allow the circulation of coaches on its territory, which are registered in other Member States and only occasionally circulate within the Member State with the more stringent values. This consideration demonstrates that the assessment of whether the maintaining of a national measure is necessary, requires a detailed consideration of the pros and cons under internal market and ecological auspices. Sevenster[130] goes so far as to generalise this position: she is of the opinion that the necessity of considering whether the national measure constitutes an obstacle is a badly drafted expression of the proportionality principle.

3–61   In conclusion, the new addition to art.114 does not mean that the national environmental measure may not, under any circumstances constitute an obstacle to the free circulation of goods. It is only meaningful when it is completed by a word such as "inadequate", "inappropriate" or "disproportionate".[131] This would mean that, in each individual case, the Commission would have to weigh up the protection of the environment against the proper functioning of the internal market. Thus, a national measure must be proportional to the objective pursued by it; where a less restrictive measure is available, the Member State may be asked to recur to that measure even where this would mean a change in its national rules. Also, a measure that constitutes a significant obstacle to the functioning of the internal market and where the environmental advantage is insignificant, could be rejected by the Commission.

This interpretation would bring the principle of proportionality from art.5 TEU into the assessment process of art.114(6): while it is legitimate to protect the environment and not to see the national level of environmental protection lowered by a harmonisation measure from the European Union, the national measure must not go beyond what is necessary to achieve appropriate environmental protection.

3–62   *Procedure.* The Treaty does not fix a delay, when the national measure has to be notified or approved. As mentioned, it would make sense to have it notified after the adoption of the EU measure, but before the period for transposing the EU measure into national law has expired. However, it will be impossible not to approve a national measure exclusively with the argument that it was notified too late, though the Court of Justice stated that the principle of sincere cooperation of art.4(3) TEU obliges Member States to notify a national measure "as soon as possible".[132]

The Commission is required to approve—or reject—the national decision to maintain national legislation within six months of notification; in particularly complex cases it may prolong this period by a maximum of six months more. As mentioned, this provision was introduced by the Amsterdam Treaty as a reaction to the fact that some national notifications under art.114(4) had not been decided upon for several years.[133] It is not possible to prolong this delay, for instance when the Commission argues that the Member State's decision has not been sufficiently argued. The Commission may then refuse to authorise the measure; but it may not ask for further documentation, evidence or other justification, since

---

[130] H. Sevenster, *European Yearbook of Environmental Law* (Oxford, 1999), p.116.

[131] See in the same sense Commission, Dec.1999/831 (fn.125, above) para.23.

[132] Court of Justice, Case C–319/97 (fn.121, above) para.35.

[133] For an example, see Dec.2001/59 [2001] OJ L210/46.

this would introduce supplementary conditions for the application of the six-month period, for which the Commission has no mandate in the Treaties.[134]

The time given for approval may appear short. It should be noted, however, that the legal and environmental situation in the different Member States has normally been discussed at EU level during the elaboration of the harmonisation measure. The subject-matter of national legislation is thus not entirely new to the Commission.

The sanction for failing to decide within six months is tough: the national measure "shall be deemed to have been approved". The national measure has, in such a case, an effect on all other Member States as well as on all economic operators, even though they did not have the possibility of influencing the speed of decision-making within the Commission. Where a Member State is of the opinion that the Commission has made a wrong decision, either by approving or rejecting the national measure within six months or by letting the six-month period elapse, it may bring the matter before the Court of Justice directly (art.114(8)). The procedure is governed by art.263(2) TFEU if the action is directed against the Commission, and by art.259 TFEU, if the action is directed against another Member State. The two-month delay of art.263(6) TFEU starts, in the case of the absence of a Commission decision within six months, at the end of this six-month period. Until the end of 2010, no Member State ever took such an action against another Member State or against the Commission.

3–63

Private operators may take action against the Commission under art.263(4) TFEU if they are directly and individually concerned by the decision, for instance when their exports or imports are affected. They may also try to conform to the EU harmonisation measure and, where they see their trade affected, bring the matter before the competent national court and then ask for a preliminary ruling by the Court of Justice under art.267 TFEU, in order to have the Commission's decision checked.

Introducing new national legislation

The new provision of art.114(5) clarifies that Member States may, under certain conditions, introduce new legislation in cases where the European Union has adopted a harmonisation measure.[135] The possibility of introducing new measures exists only for measures relating to the environment and the working environment. The different grounds of art.36 TFEU which allow Member States, under art.114(4) to maintain existing more stringent national provisions, may not be invoked for the introduction of new measures.

3–64

The conditions for introducing new national environmental measures are relatively strict. They are the following:

1.   the new national measure must be based on new scientific evidence;

---

[134] See General Court, Case T–69/08 (fn.122, above).

[135] art.114(5) TFEU: "… if, after the adoption of a harmonisation measure by the European Parliament and the Council, by the Council or by the Commission, a Member State deems it necessary to introduce national provisions based on new scientific evidence relating to the protection of the environment or the working environment on grounds of a problem specific to that Member State arising after the adoption of the harmonisation measure, it shall notify the Commission of the envisaged provisions as well as the grounds for introducing them."

2.   the problem must be specific to the Member State that wishes to introduce the measure;
3.   the problem must have arisen after the adoption of the harmonisation measure.

The three conditions must be fulfilled cumulatively. Their likely effect will make it very rare for a Member State to demonstrate the necessity to opt out of the common EU measure, although the acting Member State has a certain amount of discretion to assess whether the new situation requires the opting out of the EU measure ("deems it necessary"). Its decision is, in turn, assessed by the Commission and, in case of litigation, by the Court of Justice.

3–65   *New scientific evidence.* New scientific evidence may consist of studies, reports or other documentation, showing that there is a real risk to the environment and that, therefore, it is necessary to introduce a more protective national measure. It is not easy to comply with this criterion. For instance, the fact that benzene, an additive in petrol, is carcinogenic, has been known for years; thus, a Member State would not be allowed to lower the maximum admissible content of benzene in petrol below the level that was fixed by the European Union. It might be argued that the cancer statistics which show the effects of benzene, constitute "new evidence". This seems doubtful, though, in the end, acceptable; in any case, however, such a discovery would not be specific to an individual Member State, but would concern the whole of the Union. For such cases, the new formulation of art.114(3) suggests that the Commission make a new proposal for a harmonisation measure "taking account in particular of any new development based on scientific facts". To take another example: the continuing global climate problem would not justify a Member State introducing national standards for air emissions from cars which deviate from EU standards; again, this is neither a "new" scientific evidence nor is the problem specific to one Member State alone.

Scientific evidence is new where the EU legislature was not able to take it into account at the moment of adopting the harmonisation measure. The word "evidence"[136] will, also in the light of the precautionary principle, have to be interpreted broadly and will be considered to include data, the accumulation of existing studies which bring to light a specific problem, and other factual aspects which allow to conclude that there is the probability of environmental risks. It is not to be understood as requiring "proof" of new risks or damage.

3–66   *Specific problem.* The condition that the problem must be specific to a Member State is probably the most difficult to comply with. Indeed, since art.114 refers to the internal market and thus mainly to product-related measures, it is difficult to imagine the effects of a product causing environmental problems that are specific to the national territory of a single Member State. Neither would the effect of a product on global warming, on the ozone layer, or on water or fauna and flora be sufficient, since, normally, all these effects affect more than one Member State.

When the Commission decided to allow Denmark to apply more restrictive measures on the use of the biocide pentachlorophenol (PCP), it declared that PCP easily migrated to groundwater, that Denmark took most of its drinking water

---

[136] At least in some EU languages the word which is used has the connotation of "findings", such as in Dutch (*gegevens*), German (*Erkenntnisse*), Portuguese (*novedades*) and French (*preuves*).

from groundwater and that therefore Denmark should be allowed to deviate from the EU harmonisation measure.[137] The decision to allow Germany to deviate from the harmonisation measure was essentially justified by the argument that Germany had built a lot of buildings after 1945 and had extensively used PCP for wood preservation.[138] This may be the case; however, in most Member States drinking water is taken from groundwater, and the use of PCP for wood preservation was widespread in the European Union, although not necessarily as widespread as in Germany. Taking the criterion seriously would mean that in either case, the new art.114(5) would not have allowed the introduction of new national legislation in derogation from the EU measure. More generally, a derogation under that provision could not be granted where an environmental problem appeared in several Member States.

The result is not as strange as it might appear at first sight: indeed, under art.114(7) the Commission is obliged to examine whether a new proposal for EU action shall be made; furthermore, where a concrete risk for man or the environment becomes apparent, national action under the safeguard clause of art.114(10) remains possible.[139]

In 2005 the Netherlands wanted to introduce legal requirements to reduce the emissions of particulates from diesel cars, in deviation from Directive 98/69. The measure would have required, under the present state of technical knowledge, to equip diesel cars with specific filters which are presently not required under EU legislation. The Commission accepted that the numerous studies which had been published on the problem, constituted new scientific evidence. However, it compared the emissions of particulates in the Netherlands with those in other Member States and, furthermore, the number of diesel cars in the Netherlands. On that it concluded that the health problems caused by diesel particulates were not particularly acute in the Netherlands, but existed also in other Member States.[140] This decision is bitter and absurd: Overall, the annual number of premature deaths in the European Union due to diesel particulates in the air is estimated to be more than 100,000. Filters for diesel cars are available on the market since years and are in particular offered by French car manufacturers. However, the Commission hesitates to propose amendments to the existing legislation and prescribing their use, because it made arrangements, in the 1990s, with the car industry, according to a time plan for air pollution reduction: And then, in the name of law, it even prevents individual Member States to take measures.

The Commission furthermore rejected a number of attempts by Member States to prevent the cultivation or placing on the market of genetically modified products, arguing that the national environment was not specifically different from the environment in other Member States. It was confirmed in this interpretation by the Court of Justice.[141]

---

[137] Commission, Dec.94/783 [1994] OJ L316/43.

[138] Commission, Dec.96/211 [1996] OJ L68/32.

[139] See para.3–72, below.

[140] On appeal, the Court of Justice quashed the Commission's decision for formal reasons: the Commission had not examined all data that had been submitted by the Netherlands, *Netherlands v Commission* (C–405/07P) [2008] E.C.R. I–8301.

[141] Commission Dec.2003/653 (Austria) [2003] OJ L230/34; Dec.2006/255 (Cyprus) [2006] OJ L92/14; Dec.2008/62 (Poland) [2008] OJ L16/17; Dec.2009/828 (Portugal) [2009] OJ L294/16. Court of Justice, *Austria v Commission* (C–439/05P) [2007] E.C.R. I–7141.

3–67   *New problems.* The condition that the problem must have arisen after the adoption of the harmonisation measure may concern cases in which environmental effects of a specific problem become evident, such as the effect of a biocide, a pesticide or another chemical product which suddenly shows serious environmental problems in a specific region to have been caused. A simple change in the environmental policy in a Member State would not justify the introduction of new legislation. In the same way, this condition would not be fulfilled where an environmental problem—gradually or suddenly—appears before the adoption of the harmonisation measure and the Member States wishes to introduce "opt out" legislation after the adoption of the harmonisation measure.

3–68   *Procedure.* The procedure for measures under art.114(5), including the time delays, verification, approval or rejection of the national measure, is the same as in the case of the maintaining of a national measure. In the case of the introduction of new legislation, however, the standstill period stipulated by the Court of Justice will apply; thus, a Member State may only introduce its legislation after the Commission has approved of it. For the rest, reference is made to para.3–62, above.

3–69   In Decision 1999/836,[142] the Commission rejected a German request to introduce new national legislation on the classification and labelling of certain hazardous chemicals. The Commission held that the scientific and technical grounds, on which Germany had based its request, had been discussed during the elaboration of the EU legislation in question, and did thus not constitute new evidence. The Court rejected the German appeal against that decision, arguing that Germany had not submitted "new" scientific evidence.[143] By Decision 2001/570,[144] the Commission rejected another German request to introduce new national legislation on organo-stannic compounds that went beyond Directive 1999/51,[145] arguing again that Germany had not submitted new scientific evidence. The Commission maintained, amongst others, that in the framework of art.114(5) only human health arguments related to the working environment are relevant. This opinion overlooks the fact that art.191 TFEU explicitly states that environmental measures also aim at protecting human health.[146] Furthermore, the concept of the "centre of gravity" to determine the legal basis for a measure would exclude the mentioning of a human-health related Treaty provision next to art.192, where the EU measure covers, for instance, 60 per cent environmental matters and only 40 per cent health protection issues. Refusing Member States in such cases the recourse to art.114(5), as the Commission suggests, cannot therefore be correct.

In Decision 2002/570,[147] the Commission approved for the first time the introduction of new national legislation under art.114(5). This decision concerned a request by the Netherlands aiming at the ban of creosote-treated wood. The Commission considered that detailed studies made in the Netherlands on the effects of creosote constituted new scientific evidence. It stated that the

---

[142] Commission Dec.1999/836 [1999] OJ L329/100.

[143] Court of Justice, *Germany v Commission* (C–512/99) [2003] E.C.R. I–845.

[144] Commission Dec.2001/570 [2001] OJ L202/37.

[145] Dir.1999/51 [1999] OJ L142/22.

[146] An example is Dir.98/83 on the quality of water intended for human consumption [1998] OJ L330/32. This Directive is based on the present art.192 TFEU; it clearly aims at the protection of human health.

[147] Commission Dec.2002/59 [2002] OJ L23/37.

environmental concerns were *not* specific to the Netherlands, but was of the opinion that the extent to which the problem existed in that country—which is rich in groundwater and surface water—allowed the conclusion that the conditions of art.114(5)were complied with.

Rights under other Treaty provisions

Where an EU environmental measure is based on Treaty provisions other than arts 192 or 114, it is doubtful whether Member States also have the possibility of maintaining or introducing stricter national environmental measures. This applies in particular to measures based on arts 43 for agricultural policy measures, 91 or 100 on transport policy measures, 113 on tax measures or 207 TFEU on commercial policy measures.

3–70

German legal writers have developed, since 1987, a concept according to which the EC Treaty contains a legally binding principle according to which environmental protection within the European Union must be optimised. The reasoning is based on several provisions and principles of the Treaty, in particular arts 175, 95(4), 100b(2) EC Treaty which has been deleted in the meantime, and art.6 EC Treaty. The definition varies. Zuleeg, who later acted as judge at the European Court of Justice and who "invented" that principle, defined it as "the right of Member States to maintain or introduce more protection of the environment, even where the EU has adopted a measure to protect the environment".[148] Other authors, while following Zuleeg in his approach, go even further; some declare that in the case of conflict between environmental objectives and objectives under other policies priority should, in the case of doubt, be given to the environmental objective. Others even suggest that, for EU environmental measures, the Treaty provision which optimises environmental protection should be used as a legal basis, and this is usually art.192.

For the question with which we are here concerned, these writers suggest that, generally speaking, Member States be granted the rights under art.193, whatever the legal base was on which the EU measure had been based. However, the legal concept is unconvincing. Indeed, it is not clear why the principle of optimising protection should just apply to environmental protection and not to the protection of human health, the respect of human rights and fundamental freedoms or to any of the values which are mentioned in art.36 TFEU. If ever the authors of the EU Treaties had in mind to establish such a principle, they could have inserted it in the Treaties at one of the Treaty amendments in 1993, 1999, 2003, or 2009.

3–71

Furthermore, where an EU environmental measure in the sector of agricultural policy is based on art.43 TFEU it is not clear at all, whether art.193 is a more protective provision than art.114(4) and (5) and, following, which of these two provisions should apply for a measure adopted under art.43. The concept of optimising environmental protection is incapable of explaining why Member States' residual rights have been organised differently under arts 193 and 114, although there would have been the possibility of finding a single, optimising solution. Also, the concept is more motivated, it seems, by concerns about

---

[148] M. Zuleeg, *"Vorbehaltene Kompetenzen der Mitgliedstaaten der Europäischen Gemeinschaft auf dem Gebiet des Umweltschutzes"*, *Neue Zeitschrift für Verwaltungsrecht* (1987), p.280 (my translation).

national powers to legislate than about environmental optimisation, since it cares little for those Member States which do not have an elaborated, consistent, national environmental policy.

As none of the Treaty provisions on which an environmental action can be based contain provisions similar to those of arts 193 and 114, the conclusion must be that these provisions are exceptions to the general rule that EU measures cannot be derogated from by Member States, unless EU law expressly so provides. Their application to measures which had been adopted by virtue of arts 43, 91, 113 or 207 TFEU is therefore not possible, all the more so since it would not be clear whether arts 193 or 114 should apply in a specific case. Article 11 TFEU is of no help either, as the possibilities which Member states have under art.193, are not "requirements"; if one were adopting another position, one would also have to consider art.114 an environmental requirement—which again would raise the question which article should apply in a given case. As discussed in paras 2–69ss above, it will still have to be decided by the Court which are Member States' residual rights when an EU legislation was adopted on a double legal basis, such as arts 114 and 192—no such decision exists as yet—or arts 207 and 192.

Rights under safeguard clauses

3–72   The safeguard clauses of both arts 191(2) and 114(10) TFEU apply where secondary EU legislation expressly contains a provision which enables Member States to take safeguard measures. However, both provisions require a specific provision in secondary EU legislation; they do not directly give rights to Member States.

The specificity of safeguard clauses is that they allow Member States to object to the marketing or the circulation of goods even in those cases where these products comply with the requirements which were laid down at EU level. This basic consideration leads to the consequence, expressed in both provisions of arts 191(2) and 114(10) that the national safeguard measures may only be provisional, limited in time and subject to a decision by the Union as to its compatibility with EU law. In practice, safeguard clauses hardly play a role at all.

3–73   Safeguard clauses in EU environmental legislation existed long before arts 191(2) and 114(10) were introduced into the Treaty. A considerable number of EU directives or regulations contained safeguard clauses which allowed Member States to deviate, for health or environmental reasons, from EU standards. The conditions for having recourse to a safeguard clause were practically always the same:

- an express provision in the corresponding EU directive or regulation;
- a formal notification by a Member State that it had evidence that a product, while complying with the requirements of the directive/regulation, constituted a hazard for man or the environment and that therefore the circulation of the product was restricted or suspended;
- justifications for the national decision taken.

The Commission then had to proceed to consultation with the other Member States and to take, on a regular basis by the committee procedure instituted by virtue of art.202 EC, an EU decision. Such a decision could consist of adapting the EU harmonisation measure to the requests of the notifying Member State, or in informing the Member State that his safeguard measure was not justified and had to be abandoned.[149]

In the highly controversial area of genetically modified organisms, a number of Member States recurred to the safeguard clause and prohibited the marketing and/or cultivation of genetically modified plants, though the Commission had authorised them. The Commission did not take legal action against this obvious misuse of the safeguard clause, but rather tried to find policy solutions.[150]

---

[149] See, e.g. Dec.90/420 [1990] OJ L22/49, informing Denmark that a specific substance which Denmark had declared carcinogenic by way of a safeguard measure, was in reality not carcinogenic.
[150] See for more details paras 6–43 et seq., below.

CHAPTER 4

Horizontal Measures

1. The right to a clean environment

General remarks

The Treaty on European Union and the Treaty on the Functioning of the **4–01**
European Union do not contain a catalogue on fundamental rights. However,
art.6(1) of the Treaty on European Union states:

> "The Union recognises the rights, freedoms and principles set out in the Charter of
> Fundamental Rights of the European Union of 7 December 2000, as adapted at Strasbourg on
> 12 December 2007, which shall have the same legal value as the Treaties...
> The Union shall accede to the European Convention for the Protection of Human rights and
> Fundamental Freedoms...
> Fundamental rights, as guaranteed by the European Convention for the protection of Human
> rights and Fundamental Freedoms and as they result from the constitutional traditions common to
> the Member States, shall constitute general principles of the Union's law."

Prior to the adoption of the Lisbon Treaty, all Member States had adhered to
the Convention for the Protection of Human Rights and Fundamental Freedoms;
however, the European Union had not adhered to the Convention, in particular for
institutional reasons.[1]

At the end of 2000, the European Parliament, Council and Commission
proclaimed a Charter of Fundamental Rights of the European Union[2]. The
Charter is not meant to create legal rights of citizens, but by "making these rights
more visible".[3] Its application within the Union is nuanced by a Protocol and
some declarations annexed to the Treaties.[4]

The discussion on a fundamental right to a clean environment at EU level had **4–02**
some antecedents. In 1989, the European Parliament adopted a resolution on
fundamental rights and fundamental freedom which formulated that the
preservation, protection and improvement of the quality of the environment was
an integrative part of all Community policy.[5] In 1990, the Commission, in a
contribution to the discussions on the Maastricht Treaty on European Union,

---

[1] See Court of Justice, Opinion 2/94 on the accession of the EC to the European Convention on
Human Rights [1996] E.C.R. I–1759.
[2] Charter of Fundamental Rights of the European Union [2000] OJ C364/1.
[3] Charter (fn.2, above), Preamble.
[4] Protocol 30 on the application of the Charter of Fundamental rights of the European Union to
Poland and the United Kingdom [2008] OJ C115/313; Declarations no.2 [2008] OJ C115/337; no.53
[2008] OJ C115/355; no.61 [2008] OJ C115/358; no.62 [2008] OJ 115/358.
[5] European Parliament, Resolution of April 12, 1989 [1989] OJ C120/51 art.24.

suggested the insertion of such a right into the Treaty,[6] but remained unsuccessful. In 1997, the European Parliament adopted another resolution on the respect of human rights within the European Union where it submitted for discussion a catalogue of about 150 provisions concerning fundamental rights.[7] As regards the environment, the Parliament abstained from formulating a provision that gave rights to individuals, and limited itself to confirm that the right to live included a responsibility for present and future generations, that public authorities should guarantee a healthy environment for everybody and grant the possibility to influence decisions on his/her environment. National legal provisions should be harmonised and sanctions for impairment of the environment should be strengthened, according to the polluter-pays principle. Finally, Parliament asked that the export of all materials, food, drugs, etc. which were forbidden to be marketed in the European Union, should be prohibited.[8] This Resolution did not lead to any concrete consequences.

4–03   The Charter that was adopted at the end of 2000 did not create a right to a healthy environment. It limits itself to formulate, in art.37:

> "A high level of environmental protection and the improvement of the quality of the environment must be integrated into the policies of the Union and ensured in accordance with the principle of sustainable development."

This provision is rather misleading, as it is not clear in what sense such a formula which largely corresponds to art.11 TFEU, creates "rights". The European Parliament, though, was satisfied with the Charter.[9]

In landmark decisions of 1991, the Court declared that air quality standards were adopted in the interest of protecting human health.[10] Therefore, a citizen must be entitled to ensure in court that the air-quality standards are actually complied with. This interpretation comes close to giving individuals which are affected by polluted air or water, a right to clean air or to clean water. Unfortunately, though, environmental organisations and individual citizens hardly ever tested the potential and the limits of this jurisprudence in other cases. Thus, the judgments of 1991 are practically being ignored by the administration.

The academic discussion on a fundamental right for a clean and healthy environment which had started already in the 1970s, had made it soon clear that a meaningful enforceable right to a clean environment could not be introduced into the constitutions of Member States or into primary EU law and where some constitutions had tried nevertheless, the contours of such a right remained unclear. The discussions therefore concentrated on formulating *procedural* rights

---

[6] Commission, Contributions to the Intergovernmental Conference COM (90) 600 of October 21, 1990, art. 7: "Every Union citizen shall have the right to enjoy a healthy environment and the obligation to contribute to protecting it. To this end, he shall have the right to information and the right to consultation where appropriate."

[7] European Parliament, Resolution of April 8, 1997 [1997] OJ C132/31.

[8] European Parliament (fn.7) nn.161–164.

[9] European Parliament Resolution of November 14, 2000 [2001] OJ C223/74.

[10] Court of Justice, *Commission v Germany* (C–361/88) [1991] E.C.R. I–2567, para.16: "the obligation imposed on the Member States to prescribe limit values not to be exceeded within specified periods and in specific circumstances...is imposed 'in order to protect human health in particular'. It implies therefore, that whenever the exceeding of the limit values could endanger human health, the persons concerned must be in a position to rely on mandatory rules in order to be able to assert their rights". See also *Commission v Germany* (C–59/89) [1991] E.C.R. I–2607. In 2008, the Court confirmed this jurisdiction, *Janecek* (C–237/07) [2008] E.C.R. I–6221.

to a clean environment which consisted of three parts, a right of access to information on the environment, the right of participating in decision making on the environment and the right of access to the courts in environmental matters. Though the idea of a human right to a clean environment—be it procedural—was not popular with the European Commission, some elements of such procedural rights were taken up in the context of the European Union which also transposed the requirements of the Aarhus Convention on access to information, participation in decision-making and access to justice in environmental matters. The Aarhus Convention[11] was signed and ratified by all EU Member States except Ireland.

Access to environmental information

National level

In 1990, the European Union adopted a Directive on the "free access" to information on the environment.[12] In 2003, the Directive was substituted by a new Directive which gave "public access".[13] This Directive "guarantees the right of access to environmental information" (art.1) to any natural or legal person which is held by public authorities or by any person performing public administrative functions. The applicant does not have to prove an interest in the information or state the reason why he wishes to obtain the information. The notion of "environmental information" is very broad; it even includes "the state of human health and safety, including the contamination of the food chain" which brings a good part of food legislation into the field of application of the directive. Nuclear elements are not expressly mentioned, with the exception of radioactive waste; however, as "energy" is enumerated, information on nuclear energy, including permits, programmes, releases, etc. is covered by the Directive.

4–04

The right of access to information is given against public authorities and all bodies that perform public functions; this includes transport or agricultural authorities, public research institutes, agencies, etc. The authorities need only supply information which is "available", but are not obliged to start collecting information themselves; with regard to the earlier Directive 90/313, though, the obligation for active information to be disseminated by authorities has considerably been increased (art.7). The authorities may charge reasonable costs for the supply of the information—but not for the refusal of it[14]; not all authorities resisted, in the past, the temptation to charge prices at a level that was deterrent for applicants.

4–05

---

[11] Aarhus Convention of 25 June 1998. The EU adhered to the Aarhus Convention by Dec.2005/370 [2005] OJ L124/1. The text of the Convention is reproduced in the annex to that Decision.

[12] Dir.90/313 on the freedom of access to information on the environment [1990] OJ L156/58; see also Commission, Report on the experienced gained in the application of Directive 90/313, COM (2000) 400 of June 29, 2000. As regards the discussion of the transposition of this Directive, see also Commission Annual Report on Monitoring the Application of Community law, 17th Report (1999), [2001] OJ C30/43; 18th Report (2000) COM (2001) 309 of July 16, 2001, n.2.8.1; 19th Report (2001) COM (2002) 324 of June 28, 2002, n.2.8.2.

[13] Dir.2003/4 on public access to environmental information and repealing Dir.90/313 [2003] OJ L41/26.

[14] Court of Justice, *Commission v Germany* (C–217/97) [1999] E.C.R. I–5087.

Access to information may be refused in certain, explicitly enumerated circumstances (art.4); with regard to the earlier Directive, this catalogue has been enlarged and finetuned. Some of these exceptions are self-evident, such as documents which had been declared confidential by law, further information relating to international relations, public security or national defence. Others might be more difficult to be interpreted with precision; to these belong in particular the possibility to refuse access to "unfinished documents or data", "internal communications" or "the course of justice".

Germany had vetoed the adoption of Directive 90/313 for several months with the argument that access to information should only be granted where the applicant had a legitimate interest to obtain that information; it tried and continues to try to deter applications by charging extraordinarily high prices for granting access. A Commission application to the Court against this practice was rejected for formal reasons[15] and the Commission did not try to assemble a number of concrete cases in order to have the German practice stopped.

4–06   Reasons for refusing access to information must be given in all cases. Where information can be given in part, this must be done. Where the request for access to information was refused, there must be a possibility to address the courts (art.6).[16]

As Directives 90/313 and 2003/4 placed access to information in the context of a human right, the right was not just given to citizens of the European Union, but to everybody, including associations. The omission to require proof of a specific interest constituted for many local, regional or national administrations a change from traditional concepts in their relationships with citizens. Many authorities will need more time before they will fully accept this concept; particular problems of this kind might appear in the twelve new Member States, though Directive 2003/4 is fully applicable also in these countries since their accession.

As with any fundamental right, the problem with the rights flowing out of the Directive lie in their day-to-day application. Indeed, there are numerous attempts not to grant access to information in individual cases. The most frequent issues concern the charging of prohibitively high prices, wide interpretations of the exceptions, such as the concept of "commercial and industrial confidentiality", the commencement of enquiries or investigation procedures or the simple omission to give an answer to an application; the threat of terrorism is beginning to be used as a reason to refuse access to data on industrial emissions and similar information. Citizens rarely go to courts in order to enforce their rights; the Commission rarely examines individual cases, it rather refers complainants to the national judiciary.

European level

4–07   Directive 2003/4 is addressed to Member States and therefore does not apply to EU institutions. When making the proposal for a Directive in 1988, the Commission announced that it would take initiatives to apply the Directive's principles to the EU institutions.[17] Based on a joint Code of Conduct,[18] the

---

[15] Court of Justice, *Commission v Germany* (C–217/97) [1999] E.C.R. I–5087.
[16] See also paras 4–18 et seq., below.
[17] Commission, COM (88) 484.

Council and the Commission[19] had adopted, in 1993/1994 decisions concerning the access of the public to documents; almost all the other Community bodies and agencies had subsequently adopted similar decisions. In 1997, the Amsterdam Treaty included a new art.255 on access to EU documents into the EC Treaty (now art.15(3) TFEU) which became effective in 1999.[20]

Subsequent to that, the EU institutions adopted Regulation 1049/2001 on access to documents which intended to make art.255 EC operational and which became effective at the end of 2001.[21] The Regulation referred to the "right of access" established by the present art.15(3) TFEU and endeavoured to "ensure the widest possible access to documents" (art.1). The Regulation was built along the content of Directive 90/313. In 2006, the Union adopted Regulation 1367/2006 which adapted EU law to the requirements of the Aarhus Convention.[22] It is marked by the Council's efforts to amend the original Regulation 1049/2001 as little as possible. As it applies to a supranational organisation, it is normal that Regulations 1049/2001 and 1367/2006 have a number of specificities, of which the most relevant are the following:

4–08

1. Regulation 1049/2001 gives a right of access to documents to citizens of the European Union and to residents: Thus, a professor in Switzerland would not have a right of access to documents. Regulation 1367/2006 extends this right, in environmental matters, to everybody, in line with Directive 2003/4 which also gives a right of access to information to everybody[23];

2. The possibilities to refuse access to internal documents, suggested by the Commission,[24] was not retained by Regulation 1049/2001. In contrast to that Directive 2003/4 allows Member States to refuse access to "material in the course of completion or unfinished documents or data."(art.4(1.d))[25];

3. Except for the basic grounds for refusal—public security, defence and military matters, international relations, financial, monetary or economic policy and privacy—all other grounds for refusal must be balanced against the public interest in disclosure. This requires a case-by-case weighing of the different interests at stake. Regulation 1367/2006 provides in art.6(1) that "an overriding public interest in disclosure shall be deemed to exist

---

[18] Code of Conduct concerning public access to Council and Commission documents [1993] OJ L340/1.

[19] Dec.93/731 on public access to Council documents [1993] OJ L340/43; Commission, Dec.94/90 on public access to Commission documents [1994] OJ L46/58.

[20] art.15(3) TFEU: "1.Any citizen of the Union, and any natural or legal person residing or having its registered office in a Member State, shall have a right of access to documents of the Union institutions, bodies, offices and agencies, whatever their medium, subject to the principles and the conditions to be defined…"

[21] Reg.1049/2001 regarding public access to European Parliament, Council and Commission documents [2001] OJ L145/43.

[22] Reg.1367/2006 on the application of the provisions of the Aarhus Convention on access to information, public participation in decision-making and access to justice in environmental matters to Community institutions and bodies [2006] OJ L264/13.

[23] Dir.2003/4 (fn.13, above), recital 8: "It is necessary to ensure that any natural and legal person has a right of access to environmental information held by or for public authorities without his having to state an interest".

[24] Commission proposal for a regulation on access to documents [2000] OJ C177E/70.

[25] Directive 2003/4 (fn.13, above) requests Member States to indicate, when material is in the course of completion, the estimated time needed for completion.

where the information requested relates to emissions into the environment". In other cases, the fact that the information relates to emissions into the environment "shall be taken into particular account" when the environmental interests are weighed against other interests.

4.	The Commission's proposal not to give access to letters of formal notice and to reasoned opinions under art.258 TFEU was not accepted by the Council and the European Parliament, when they adopted Regulation 1049/2001; the Commission now applies the exception "inspections, investigations and audits" to refuse such access; this practice is not compatible with the Aarhus Convention, as will be explained below[26];

5.	The right of access to information on the environment exists, following the amendment in art.3(2) of Regulation 1367/2006 with regard to all documents that are held by any "Community institution or body"; this includes access to those documents, of which the Member States or other persons are authors. The author of the document has to be consulted on a possible disclosure, though the EU institution has the final decision (Reg.1049/2001, art.4(4)).[27] Directive 2003/4 does not contain similar provisions;

6.	Where access to documents is refused, the applicant may first ask for a confirmatory administrative decision (Reg.1049/2001, art.8). Against that decision the applicant may address the Court of First Instance under art.263 TFEU.

4–09		Administrative practice shows that compliance with the letter and spirit of the Aarhus Convention and the Regulation is a process which only will progressively be realised. The most striking practices are:

●	the Commission interprets the exception that access to documents for "the purpose of inspections, investigations and audits" may be refused extremely largely. This significantly contributes to the fact that a considerable number of applications are still being rejected, mainly because the decision-making process is not yet finished, there is a commercial interest invoked or the correspondence—in particular internal e-mails—is considered not to be "information on the environment"; in a proposal for a review of Regulation 1049/2001, the Commission suggested that access to all documents be refused which relate to "dispute settlement" procedures.[28] This would even further enlarge the number of documents which are not released.

---

[26] See also L. Krämer, "Access to letters of formal notice and reasoned opinions in environmental law matters" [2003] *European Environmental Law Review*, p.197 as regards the procedure under art.258 TFEU.
[27] The Commission interpreted art.4(5)—"A Member State may request the institution not to disclose a document originating from that Member State without its prior agreement"—as giving a right of veto to a Member State, and was supported in this by the Court of First Instance, but not by the Court of Justice, see *Sweden v Commission* (C–64/05) [2007] E.C.R. I–11389. For access to information on the environment, Reg.1367/2006, art.6(3) now clarifies that the Commission has the final decision and that there is no veto right.
[28] See Commission, COM(2008) 229, art.4(2.c); the Commission also proposed to considerably restrict the notion of "document".

- the Commission also refuses access to documents concerning comments which it makes towards Member States in reaction of the notification of draft national legislation under Directive 98/34,[29] though there is no inspection or investigation visible.

- Regulation 1367/2006 did not take up an amendment which the European Parliament had suggested and which consisted in giving access to information on "sustainable development" issues. Council's reasoning is remarkable: "sustainable development is outside the [Aarhus] Convention and not in line with Article 174 of the EC Treaty with regard to the objectives of environmental policy".[30] At least, this remark is revealing: sustainable development is not an element of environmental policy! This is in line with the efforts to promote, at EU level, the objectives on economic growth and social cohesion. But it is neither historically correct nor compatible with arts 3(3) TEU[31] and 11 TFEU which are both based on the assumption that the environment is an integrated part of sustainable development and that sustainable development cannot be reached without appropriate environmental protection.

Article 2(6) of Regulation 1049/2001 clarifies that the provisions of the Aarhus Convention on access to information which are part of EU law, prevail over the provisions of Regulation 1049/2001.[32] This is in line with settled case-law by the Court of Justice.[33] The provisions on the exceptions to the right of information provided by the Aarhus Convention are considerably narrower than the exceptions provided for under Regulation 1049/2001: under the Aarhus Convention, authorities *may* refuse access, when one of the exceptions applies; under Regulation 1049/2001, they *must* refuse access in such a case, at least where general interests are at stake. The Aarhus Convention does not provide for an exception to protect the "financial, monetary or economic policy of the Union and of Member States" which Regulation 1049/2001 foresees.[34] The Aarhus Convention does not contain an exception of "legal advice" which is foreseen in Regulation 1049/2001. The Aarhus Convention allows not to disclose information, in order to protect "the ability to conduct an enquiry of a criminal or

---

[29] Directive 98/34 laying down a procedure for the provision of information in the field of technical standards and regulations [1998] OJ L204/37.

[30] Council, Common Position 31/2005 [2005] OJ C264E/18 (p.25, no.III.2).

[31] Article 3(3) TEU: "The Union shall establish an internal market. It shall work for the sustainable development of Europe based on balanced economic growth and price stability, a highly competitive social market economy, aiming at full employment and social progress, and a high level of protection and improvement of the quality of the environment. It shall promote scientific and technological advance."

[32] Reg.1049/2001 (fn.21, above), art.2(6): "This Regulation shall be without prejudice to rights of public access to documents held by the institutions which might follow from instruments of international law or acts of the institutions pursuant implementing them".

[33] Court of Justice, *IATA and ELFAA* (C–344/08) [2006] E.C.R. I–403, para.35: "Article 300(7) EC (now Article 216(2) TFEU, L.K.) provides that 'agreements concluded under the conditions set out in this Article shall be binding on the institutions of the Community and on Member States'. In accordance with the Court's case law, those agreements prevail over provisions of secondary Community legislation".

[34] In *IFAW v Commission* (T–362/2008) judgment of January 13, 2011, the General Court upheld a Commission to refuse disclosure of a document on the destruction of a natural habitat by an airport on grounds that the document served to protect Germany's economic policy. As this exception does not exist under the Aarhus Convention, the Court erred in referring to Reg.1049/2001.

disciplinary nature", whereas Regulation 1049/2001 allows this exception in order to protect "the purpose of inspections, investigations and audits".[35] The Aarhus Convention allows to protect "a legitimate economic interest where protected by national law"; Regulation 1049/2001 generally refers to the protection of "commercial interests". And the Aarhus Convention allows to protect "personal data relating to a natural person"; Regulation 1049/2001 provides for the protection of the "privacy and the integrity of the individual, in particular in accordance with Community legislation regarding the protection of personal data".

To what extent the amendments brought to Regulation 1049/2001 by Regulation 1367/2006 and the Aarhus Convention will align the Union's practice to the letter and the spirit of the Aarhus Convention, remains to be seen. In the past, the practice by the Commission, the numerous agencies, but also, for example of the European Investment Bank was marked by the effort to disclose as little information as possible. The general problem at EU level is that there is no European public opinion and not sufficient private groups or individuals who would try to get access to information on the environment which is held by the EU institutions and bodies.

Participation in environmental decision-making

National level

4–10   EU involvement concerning participation in decision-making in environmental matters first dealt with participation in environment impact assessment for specific projects which come under Directive 85/337.[36] Article 6 of this Directive provided that where an impact assessment is made, the public must be informed and the "public concerned" must have the possibility of expressing its opinion on the envisaged project and its environmental impacts. The Directive lays down in detail, how this participation can be made operational.[37] In 2003, Directive 85/337 was amended further, in order to adapt its provisions on participation in decision-making to the requirements of the Aarhus Convention.[38]

4–11   As regards permitting of industrial installations, Directive 2010/75 provides that with regard to applications for permits for industrial installations, the decision on such an application and the results of the surveillance of emissions from industrial installations shall be available to the public.[39] According to those

---

[35] The Commission also applies this exception to environmental letters of formal notice and reasoned opinions under art.258 TFEU, though that procedure is neither an investigation nor an enquiry of criminal or disciplinary nature.

[36] Dir.85/337 on the assessment of the effects of certain public and private projects on the environment [1985] OJ L175/40, as amended by Dir.97/11 [1997] OJ L73/5 and by Dir.2003/35 [2003] OJ L156/17.

[37] Dir.85/337(fn.36, above), art.5(2): The operator must submit a non-technical summary of his examination of the impact and must report on the alternatives which he studied; a consultation of the nature protection administration is mandatory, whose opinion must be publicly available (Court of Justice, *Mecklenburg* (C–321/96) [1998] E.C.R. 3809).

[38] Dir.2003/35 providing for public participation in respect of the drawing up of certain plans and programmes relating to the environment and amending with regard to public participation and access to justice Council Directives 85/337 and 96/61, [2003] OJ L156/17.

[39] Dir.2010/75 on industrial emissions [2010] OJ L334/17.

provisions, the public shall have the possibility of commenting on applications for a permit. The public is, furthermore, to be informed of the results of surveillance of the installations.

As regards *plans and programmes*, Directive 2001/42 which became effective in 2004 requires an environment impact assessment for plans and programmes that are likely to have significant environmental effects.[40] The Directive covers such plans which lead, at a later stage, to projects that have to undergo an environmental impact assessment under annexes I or II of Directive 85/337 or under arts 6 and 7 of Directive 92/43.[41] The impact assessment under the Directive mainly consists in the elaboration of a written assessment and of extensive public consultation of such plans; it allows the public concerned the possibility to give its opinion on the plan in question. Directive 2003/35[42] provides for participation of the public in the elaboration and updating of a number of expressly enumerated plans and programmes, in particular in the waste area.[43] And in water management, Member States have to promote the participation of the public in the elaboration, monitoring and updating of water management plans.[44]

However, it is clear that these different specific measures do not give a general right to individuals to participate in environmental decision-making. First, Directives 85/337, 2010/75, 2000/60 and the different waste Directives which are mentioned in Directive 2003/35 do not cover all decision-making in environmental matters. Rather, these Directives concern some (larger) industrial installations and projects. Most of medium-sized and small projects and installations are not covered by EU legislation but come, as regards environment impact assessment and permits, under the responsibility of Member States.

4–12

Secondly, environmental decision-making not only deals with the permitting of projects and installations and the authorisation of plans and programmes. There are many other decisions which affect the environment, such as decisions on the authorisation of products and processes, management decisions, monitoring methods and processes, derogations, omissions to decide, etc. These very diverse and different means of the administration which affect the environment have not been the subject of the Aarhus Convention which is thus far from granting a general right of participation. In the same way, EU law does not provide for a general right of participation, but limits it to certain projects, plans and programmes. Also, EU law very generally speaks of the "public concerned" which will be entitled to participate in the decision-making, but leaves the determination of the public concerned in any specific case to the Member States. As it is, for instance, obvious that the "public concerned" is different for the construction of a 1,000 km motorway and a waste incinerator, there is a necessity to determine before-hand what a "public concerned" is.

---

[40] Dir.2001/42 on the environment assessment of the effects of certain plans and programmes on the environment [2001] OJ L197/30.

[41] Dir.92/43 on the conservation of natural habitats and of wild fauna and flora [1992] OJ L206/7.

[42] Dir.2003/35 (fn.38, above).

[43] Annex I of Dir. 2003/35 (fn.38, above) enumerates the following plans and programmes which are covered by its provisions: waste management plans, plans for the recycling of batteries, plans for reducing nitrate inputs into waters, plans for hazardous waste management, plans for packaging waste and plans for the improvement of air quality.

[44] Dir. 2000/60 establishing a framework for Community action in the field of water policy [2000] OJ L327/1.

Furthermore, the question how much time should be given for the consultation process is not clear, and only exceptionally has EU law laid down obligations for the administration to give an account what it has done with the opinions that were expressed during the participation process.[45]

4–13   Furthermore, the different directives do not specify how the opinion of the participating public is to be assembled (hearing, written submission, attributed time for oral representation) and how the administration shall manage the collected information: the best would probably be to require a written paper accompanying the final administrative decision which lists the results of the participation process and explains the reason of the administration for following or not the opinion. Administrative practice in Member States at present shows little result improved citizens' participation. An Irish provision which charges citizens to pay a fee for participating in the decision-making on projects, plans and programmes, was declared compatible with EU law by the Court of Justice[46]; in my opinion, this contradicts the character of the participation right as a fundamental right.

European level

4–14   In 2002, the Commission published two communications on public participation[47] which were not limited to environmental issues. According to these communications, the consultation of interested groups should allow at least eight weeks for reception of responses to written public consultation and 20 working days' notice for meetings. However, the consultation principles referred to by these communications constitute internal instructions for Commission officials, but do not create any rights to participate for the "public concerned". The Commission expressly stated that it was opposed to giving citizens the right to participate, as this would interfere with formal consultations which were taking place after the adoption of a proposal by the Commission; this remark alludes to the participation of the European Parliament, the Economic and Social Committee and the Committee of the Regions in the legislative process. In contrast to that, there is no doubt that the Aarhus Convention requires contracting parties to give *rights* to citizens, not to create obligations for the administration only, though this is limited to projects, plans and programmes.[48]

Regulation 1367/2006 which intends to make the principles of the Aarhus Convention applicable to the EU level, was adopted in 2006,[49] endeavours to give a right to participate in EC environmental decision-making. The Regulation defines plans and programmes relating to the environment as:

---

[45] See now Dir.2010/75 (fn.39. above), art.24(2) concerning the information which has to be made available once a decision on a permit has been taken; see also at para.4–40ss., below.

[46] Court of Justice, *Commission v Ireland* (C–216/05) [2006] E.C.R. I–10787.

[47] Commission, Towards a reinforced culture of consultation and dialogue—proposal for general principles and minimum standards for consultation of interested parties by the Commission. COM (2002) 277 of June 5, 2002 and COM (2002) 704 of December 11, 2002.

[48] Aarhus Convention art.1: "In order to contribute to the protection of the right of every person of present and future generations to live in an environment adequate to his or her health and well-being, each Party shall guarantee the rights of access to information, public participation in decision-making and access to justice in environmental matters in accordance with the provisions of this Convention."

[49] Reg.1367/2006 (fn.22, above).

"plans and programmes

which are subject to preparation and, as appropriate, adoption by a Community institution or body;

which are required under legislative, regulatory or administrative provisions; and

which contribute to, or a likely to have significant effect on, the achievement of the objectives of Community environmental policy, such as laid down in the Sixth Environment Action Programme, or in any subsequent general environment action programme.[50]"

However, it also states in the same provision: **4–15**

"This definition shall not include financial, banking or budget plans and programmes, namely those laying down how particular projects or activities should be financed or those related to the proposed annual budget... or emergency plans and programmes designed for the sole purpose of environmental protection."

This provision clearly contradicts the provisions of the Aarhus Convention. This Convention does not exempt any plans and programmes. There might be some wisdom in not including budget plans as such plans do not "relate to the environment" (Aarhus Convention art.7). However, the exemption of financial or banking plans and programmes which lay down how particular projects or activities should be financed, cannot be based on the Aarhus Convention, where such plans relate to the environment. The provision mainly aims at exempting activities from the European Investment Bank for which the FEU Treaty provides that EU provisions on access to documents—not on participation rights!—shall only apply where the Bank is performing administrative tasks.[51] For an exemption of participation provisions, no reason can be found. The same applies to the emergency plans of civil protection, though there has to be a line struck: it might be understandable to exempt emergency measures in the case of an actual disaster such as an industrial accident or a flood catastrophe, where no time may be wasted to save humans or property; in such cases, participation normally would take too much time. Another question is, for example, the restoration plan or programme after a forest fire or a flooding: here, the same urgency does not exist and an exemption from participation cannot be justified.

EU plans and programmes are only those that are *required* under legislative, regulatory or administrative provisions. This wording is ambiguous. Indeed, the Sixth Environment Action Programme and also the Thematic Strategies under this Action Programme constitute "plans and programmes", but art.192(2) TFEU does not *require* the elaboration of EU environmental action programmes. Also, when the Commission decides to launch a programme to promote alternative energies, to promote human health in environmental matters or to co-finance model projects in coastal zone management, this is an initiative of the Commission itself, and there is no requirement laid down anywhere to elaborate such plan or programme. Whether in such cases the Commission really will make the public participate in the elaboration of the plan or programme, remains to be seen.

It is difficult to see, what the Regulation means by "participation": it limits   **4–16**
itself to state that the public shall have early and effective opportunity to participate during the preparation of the plans or programmes. It does not contain any indication of what the EU institution or body is to do with the information

---

[50] Reg.1367/2006 art.2(e).
[51] art.15(3) TFEU.

received from the public[52] and no general principles are laid down in the Regulation in this regard. In this way, Regulation 1367/2006 in practice declares "participation" synonymous to "consultation"—which it is not. The Aarhus Convention provides in this regard that the public shall be allowed to submit in writing or, as appropriate at a public hearing, its comments or opinions; that in the administrative decision due account is taken of the outcome of the participation and that, after the decision has been taken, the text of the decision shall be made available to the public along with the reasons and considerations on which the decision is based (art.6(7) to (9) Aarhus Convention). Participation is thus a bilateral concept, whereas consultation is unilateral: it leaves the administration free to decide what it wants to do with the information received through consultation, and no explanation is to be given to the consulted persons or bodies.

The transposition of the Aarhus Convention is thus only partial. Much will also depend on how the provisions of the Regulation are put into practice by the EU institutions—and how active citizens and environmental organisations will make use of their participation rights.

4–17   In the past, neither products nor production processes were authorised at EU level; rather, EU law normally determines which substances—heavy metals, chemicals, additives etc.—may be used in which quantities in products. The permits then are issued by Member States. From this general statement, dangerous chemical substances[53] and genetically modified products constitute an exception, as it is now the Commission which authorises a genetically modified product to be put into circulation within the European Union; its decision is valid for all Member States.[54] The Aarhus Convention was only concerned with projects, plans and programmes; however, in view of the political sensitive nature of permits for genetically modified organisms, a clause was inserted in the Convention that Contracting Parties should take care of participation in such permitting procedures (art.6(11)). In 2005, the Convention was modified in order to provide for participation also in this area.[55] The Council was of the opinion that this amendment did not require any changes of existing EU legislation and ratified the Convention's amendment.[56] This appears legally wrong, because at least Regulation 1829/2003 on genetically modified food and feed[57] does not provide for any participation of citizens; under this Regulation, an application for the release of GMO food or feed goes to the European Food Safety Authority (EFSA) which examines the application and is obliged to make the application available to the public. Thus, members of the public may send observations—provided, they know of the application: however, this has nothing to do with

---

[52] Council, Common position (fn.30, above): "it should be left to institutions and bodies to determine how they want to take account of public participation results, on the basis of general principles laid out in the regulation".
[53] Reg.1907/2006 [2006] OJ L396/1.
[54] Dir.2001/18 on the deliberate release of genetically modified organisms into the environment [2001] OJ L106/1; Reg.1829/2003 on genetically modified food and feed [2003] OJ L268/1.
[55] Aarhus Convention (fn.11, above), art.6bis: "1. In accordance with the modalities laid down in Annex I bis, each Party shall provide for early and effective information and public participation prior to making decisions on whether to permit the deliberate release into the environment and placing on the market of genetically modified organisms..."
[56] Dec.2006/957 [2006] OJ L386/46.
[57] See Reg.1829/2003 (fn.54, above).

participation. EFSA's proposal for a decision is submitted to the Commission which must decide on it within a specific time-span. No public participation is foreseen.

Under general interpretation rules, it is not possible either that EFSA simply amends its practice and now follows the principles of Regulation 1367/2006. Indeed, according to the Court of Justice—which referred, of course, to situations in Member States—such a change would have to be laid down expressly in a legislative text, in order to give legal security to the citizens. And at least from the appearance, there is a contradiction between Regulation 1829/2003 and Regulation 1367/2006.

Nothing different applies in general cases of the deliberate release of genetically modified organisms. Article 9 of Dir.2001/18[58] provides for a consultation of the public. And art.24 introduces the obligation to inform the public of applications and to allow it to comment to the Commission. Nothing is said about any participation rights of the public and on the subsequent treatment of the comments of the public.

Access to Justice

National level

There are almost no EU provisions on access to national courts or to EU courts in environmental matters. The Commission's announcements in the fifth environmental action programme and the 1992 working programme[59] to submit a proposal for a Directive on access to justice was followed by a proposal for such a directive only in 2003.[60] There is a Directive on access to justice for consumer organisations in consumer matters[61] which is limited to trans-national aspects and appears to have limited effects.

4–18

EC provisions on access to justice to national courts in environmental matters exist in the following cases:

1.   Where the right of access to environmental information under Directive 2003/4[62] was not respected (art.6 of Directive 2003/4). Instead of giving access to a court and in conformity with the Aarhus Convention, Member States may provide access to an "independent and impartial body established by law", whose decisions may become final and which are binding on public authorities. These provisions aim at allowing decisions to be taken by bodies such as an ombudsman, though it is doubtful whether the different environmental ombudsmen which exist in the different Member States, really fulfil all the conditions laid down in the Directive;
2.   Where the right of participation in decision-making concerning an environment impact assessment under Directive 85/337 or a right to participate in decisions concerning permits for industrial installations

---

[58] Dir.2001/18 (fn.54, above).
[59] Fifth environmental action programme [1993] OJ C138/1, Ch.9: "Individuals and public interest groups should have practicable access to the courts".
[60] See para.4–20, below.
[61] Dir.98/27 [1998] OJ L166/51.
[62] See paras 4–04 et seq., above.

(Directive 2008/1 and its successor, Directive 2010/75) was not respected by an authority in a Member State.[63] Such a right to address courts implicitly existed already by virtue of these two Directives. However, it is useful that Directive lifted any ambiguity concerning such a right.

3. Directive 2001/42 concerning an impact assessment for plans and programmes[64] does not contain a provision on access to justice, where consultation or participation concerning a plan or programme is refused. This question is left to national law: as the Aarhus Convention does not provide for access to justice in cases, where the right of participation of participation in the elaboration of plans and programmes is not respected—art.7 of the Convention is not mentioned in its art.9(2)[65]—Member States are free to regulate this question.

4. Where environmental damage was caused by one of the activities and under the conditions mentioned in Directive 2004/35 on environmental liability, a citizen or an environmental organisation may draw the attention of the public authorities to the damage and ask for remedial action. Where the file is substantiated, the administration will have to take a decision on that request. This decision may then be challenged in court in view of its procedural and substantial compliance with Directive 2004/35.[66]

4–19   Similar considerations to those of Directive 2001/42 apply with regard to Directive 2003/35 which also provides for the participation of "the public" in the elaboration of certain plans and programmes under EC environmental legislation. Again, "the public" is not defined. By virtue of art.2(b), it is "entitled" to participate. The Directive does not indicate, whether the public has access to the national courts in the cases, where its entitlement is disregarded. However, it should be remembered that the Aarhus Convention contains, in art.9(3), a general clause on access to courts[67] which also refers to access to the courts in cases of art.7. As it is the declared objective of Directive 2003/35 to implement the Aarhus Convention,[68] and the Aarhus Convention intends to give rights to individuals, there is a right to look for judicial remedy for all those whose participation entitlement is not respected. The details of this right to access to the courts are determined by national law.

4–20   In 2003, the Commission made a proposal for a Directive on access to justice in environmental matters.[69] The proposal intended to put the relevant pillar of the Aarhus Convention into EU law. It suggested to give environmental organisations a right of standing in courts, where EU environmental law is breached.

[63] Dir.2010/75 (fn.39, above).

[64] Dir.2001/42 (fn.40, above).

[65] Aarhus Convention art.7 on participation in plans and programmes, and art.9 which only refers to art.6.

[66] Dir.2004/35 on environmental liability with a view of prevention and remedying environmental damage [2004] OJ L143/56, arts 12 and 13.

[67] Aarhus Convention art.9(3): "In addition and without prejudice to review procedures referred to in paragraphs 1 and 2 above, each Party shall ensure that, where they meet the criteria, if any, laid down in its national law, members of the public have access to administrative or judicial procedures to challenge acts and omissions by private parties and public authorities which contravene provisions of its national law relating to the environment".

[68] See the recitals of Dir.2003/35 (fn.38, above).

[69] Commission, proposal for a directive on access to justice in environmental matters, COM(2003) 624.

Environmental law was defined in a rather broad way. The proposal, which was based on art.175 EC (now art.192 TFEU), was supported by the European Parliament which even wanted to further strengthen it.[70] However it met, in Council, considerable objections from Member States which were of the opinion that access to national courts was, under the principle of subsidiarity, their competence and that the European Union should not interfere in this area. They hardly discussed the proposal which has, in the meantime, become obsolete.

In 2011, the Court of Justice decided that the Aarhus Convention, including its art.9(3), were part of EU law.[71] However, the Court declared that art.9(3) was not directly applicable, because members of the public or environmental organisations only had access to the courts, where they complied with the requirements that were laid down in national law. The Court continued by inviting the national courts to give the fullest possible effect to art.9(3) with regard to standing of members of the public.

This decision is certainly also politically motivated. It would have been possible to declare the provisions of directly applicable and give standing to every member of the public, until the Member State in question had not laid down conditions to restrict such an *actio popularis*. The Court of Justice preferred to ignore that the burden of legislating was with the Member States and that it allowed them practically to take advantage of their own passivity to lay down specific conditions; in other cases on the direct effect, the Court had argued that a Member State should not be allowed to invoke its own omission to act and then oppose the direct effect of an EU provision.

The judgment means in practice that in each individual case, applicants will have to persuade local, regional or national courts of the wording the objective and the spirit of art.9(3), in order to obtain standing. As courts are, by nature, conservative, this means that in practice, not much will be changing in future. Article 9(3) will remain nice in words, but not very relevant in practice. Also, it is not likely that the Court of Justice will change its opinion, as it decided, in case C–240/09, in the composition of a Grand Chamber (13 judges) which gives a particular weight to the judgment.

European level

EU law gives persons a right of access to the European courts, where an EU measure is addressed to that person or where the person is directly and individually concerned by the measure.[72] This right was enlarged, as mentioned above, by giving persons, in Regulation 1049/2001 a right to ask for access to documents. In such a case, the EU institution is obliged to formally respond to that person, to comply with the conditions of art.263(4) TFEU.   **4–21**

As far as participation in environmental decision-making at EU level is concerned, there was, prior to the adoption of Regulation 1367/2006, only soft law which obliged Commission officials to involve individuals in measures which they are preparing. A breach of this obligation did not lead to the

---

[70] European Parliament, Legislative Resolution [2004] OJ C103E/626.

[71] Court of Justice, *Lesoochranárske zoskupenie* (C–240/09), judgment of March 8, 2011.

[72] art.263(4) TFEU: "Any natural or legal person may … institute proceedings against an act addressed to that person or which is of direct and individual concern to them, and against a regulatory act which is of direct concern to them and does not entail implementing measures".

possibility to recur to the application of art.263(4) TFEU. Regulation 1367/2006, adopted in 2006, now gives citizens a right to participate in environmental plans and programmes which are elaborated at EU level (see paras 4–11 et seq., above). If this right is not granted, there is a possibility for the affected public to apply, under art.263(4) TFEU, to the Court of Justice. The same applies, in my opinion, where the EU institutions and bodies only provide for consultation of the public, instead of a full participation—and this difference requires a definition of the two notions. Participation clearly goes further than a mere consultation. It gives the participating persons a guarantee that his/her opinion is received, weighed and considered during the decision-making process and that the administration explains, once a decision has been taken, for which reason it followed or did not follow the opinion which was issued.

As regards access to the European Courts in other areas, Regulation 1367/2006 introduced the possibility for environmental organisations to "make a request for internal review to the Community institution or body that has adopted an administrative act under environmental law or, in case of an alleged administrative omission, should have adopted such an act" (art.10(1)). In such a case, a written reply shall be given within a specific time-span. The environmental organisation then may institute proceedings before the Court of Justice "in accordance with the relevant provisions of this Treaty" (art.12).

The Council's Common Position which was not changed by the final adoption of Regulation 1367/2006, expressly stated that "the Common Position carefully sticks to the provisions contained in Articles 230(4) and 232(3) of the EC Treaty, which are sufficient to ensure compliance".[73]

This means in clear terms that there is an internal review procedure, but that access to the European Courts has not changed in substance. Contrary to the Council's opinion, I consider this not to be compatible with the Aarhus Convention. Article 9(3) of the Convention gives members of the public, including environmental organisations, a possibility to adequate remedies against acts and omissions which contravene environmental law and with the means to have existing environmental legislation enforced and made effective. The Compliance Committee, set up under the Aarhus Convention, considered that Contracting Parties of the Convention were not obliged to introduce an actio popularis. However, it was of the opinion that they were not either entitled to "introducing or maintaining so strict criteria that they effectively bar all or almost all environmental organisations from challenging acts or omissions that contravene national law relating to the environment".[74]

At present, access to the European Courts is practically barred for environmental organisations and very largely also for citizens. There is no case, where an environmental organisation was given standing in environmental cases until now—except, of course, under the provisions on access to information. The Court is extremely restrictive in its interpretation in this regard.[75] And the introduction of an internal review procedure under Regulation 1367/2006 does not change the rules on access to justice. It can only be hoped that the Aarhus

---

[73] Council, Common position (fn.30, above).
[74] Aarhus Convention, Compliance Committee, Compliance by Belgium, Doc.ACCC/C/2005/11 of June 14, 2005.
[75] See the leading case *Greenpeace v Commission* (C–321/95P) [1998] E.C.R. I–1651.

Convention Compliance Committee soon will find the opportunity to assess the provisions of the TFEU and of Regulation 1367/2006 in the light of the Aarhus Convention.

Furthermore, the internal review procedure is not sufficient to comply with the requirements of art.9(3) of the Aarhus Convention, in particular because no possibility is foreseen to take action against private persons that do not respect EU environmental law and because the internal review procedure is limited to some environmental organisations. Furthermore, it follows from art.9(4) of the Aarhus Convention which requires the procedure under art.9(3) to "provide adequate and effective remedies, including injunctive relief as appropriate, and be fair, equitable, timely and not prohibitively expensive", that art.9(3) intends to introduce court procedures, not internal review procedures by the same body that adopted or should have adopted the incriminated measure. A review by the same body is just neither fair nor equitable; and no injunctive relief is foreseen.

2. Funding

General remarks—Environmental Fund

The European Union has not set up a general environmental fund. Attempts to introduce such a fund failed in the beginning of the 1980s. In 1987, a clause was inserted into art.175(4) EC Treaty (now art.192(5) TFEU) that as a rule, "Member States shall finance... the environment policy." The reason for this basic decision were more economic than legal. Title XVIII TFEU (arts 174–178) mentions economic and social cohesion; however, it is not clear why this Title does not read "Economic, social and environmental cohesion" which would parallel the objective of "sustainable development" of art.3(3) TEU. Indeed, if one looks at the three pillars of sustainable development, the European Union has established funds for economic—Agricultural Fund (art.40(3) TFEU), Regional Fund (art.176(1) TFEU), Cohesion Fund (art.177(2) TFEU)—and social problems (art.162 TFEU). One might well reflect whether, under the auspices of the European Union, this basic decision remains justified: for damage caused by the sea transport of petrol and by nuclear accidents, systems are set up under public international law which provide for funds solution in order to ensure that in any case, the damage caused to the environment is compensated—at least as far as the liability system reaches.

The absence of an EU Fund for the environment would be less dramatic, if at the level of Member States, financial means were made available to address the environmental problems. This, however, is almost never the case and the result is that environmental damage is frequently not repaired or compensated. The infrastructural inferiority of environmental protection with regard to the protection of economic and social interests becomes all the more visible by this constellation. As the environment disappears in silence, the issue raises only a limited amount of concern.

An EU Fund for the environment would certainly need an amendment of the TFEU, as all existing funds are explicitly mentioned in the Treaty. In substance, a Fund would have a potential of a great number of areas to cover, such as aspects

4–22

4–23

of climate change, renewable energies, contaminated land remediation, environmental catastrophes, natural habitat protection and monitoring, awareness-raising
for environmental matters, clean technologies, implementation of environmental
legislation.[76] The problem of a Fund for the environment is that Member States
might cede to the temptation and ensure environmental protection only to the
extent that EU finances are made available. This was the main reason, why in the
1980s, the creation of an EU Fund had been rejected.

Weighing all the pros and cons of a Fund, it seems more appropriate to use
existing funds—the Regional Fund and the Cohesion Fund—to support the
protection of the environment. The reason for this is that the environment cannot
hope to be protected "by its own". Rather, environmental concerns must be
integrated into all kinds of human and economic activities such as energy, leisure,
transport and the corresponding EU policies (art.11 TFEU). Greening other
policies seems, in the long term, more promising to achieve environmental
objectives than letting environmental policy try to fight its own fund. Financial
instruments which are concentrating on specific environmental aspects such as
habitat protection or environmental catastrophes will continue to be necessary.
The sheer amount of financial means that would be necessary for the protection,
the preservation and the improvement of the quality of the environment at a high
level—these are the requirements of art.191 TFEU—will exceed the means of
any environmental fund that could be set up.

Following a major flood in parts of the European Union in 2002, the European
Union decided on the establishment of an EU solidarity fund.[77] The Fund is to
intervene in cases of "major disasters, mainly natural disasters" which have
serious repercussions on living conditions, the natural environment or the
economy. The damage shall normally exceed 3 billion €. Next to flooding, one
might think, in the area of the environment, of droughts, forest fires, major
industrial disasters or pipeline incidents The amounts which are available under
the Funds are rather limited.

Structural Funds and Cohesion Fund

4–24   In the context of the EU Regional Policy which takes about one-third of the
overall EU budget, financial means under the structural funds are made available
to Member States for agricultural, social and regional concerns. The funds
distribute, between 2007 and 2013, 308 billion €, which means about 43 billion €
per year.[78] The general priorities for the different funds are laid down in the
relevant EC regulations.[79] Under the regional policy, programmes for the
different measures are elaborated by Member States which follow the priority
objectives that had been laid down at EU level. These programmes are in some

---

[76] A Commission study of 2003 estimated that about 110 billion € would be necessary to ensure the
application of existing legislation in the accession countries and in spring 2003, the Commission
published a study which indicated that the habitat network Natura 2000 set up under Directives
79/409 and 92/ 43 (see para.5–10, below) would cost between 3.4 and 5.7 billion € per year till 2013,
see Commission COM(2004) 431 of July 15, 2004.

[77] Reg.2012/2002 establishing the EU solidarity fund [2002] OJ L311/3.

[78] See Reg.1083/2006 concerning general provisions for the structural funds [2006] OJ L210/25.

[79] Reg.1080/2006 on the Regional Development Fund [2006] OJ L210/1; Reg.1081/2006 on the
Social Fund [2006] OJ L210/12; Reg.1082/2006 on the European grouping of territorial cooperation
[2006] OJ L210/19; Reg.1084/2006 on the Cohesion Fund [2006] OJ L210/79.

form approved by the Commission which has, however, neither sufficient time nor sufficient personal resources to make a serious assessment. The individual projects are then decided by Member States. How many environmental projects are co-financed by the structural funds, is also dependant on the definition of "environmental project". With this proviso, the Commission estimated that some 10 per cent of the measures that are co-financed by the Regional Development Fund and 50 per cent of the Cohesion Fund were in the past spent for environmental purposes[80]; the 10 per cent figure appears to be much too optimistic. For the coming years, Regulation 1080/2006 on the Regional Funds mentions the possibility to finance the following environmental projects:

> "measures connected with water supply and water and waste management; waste water treatment and air quality; prevention, control and fight against desertification; integrated pollution prevention and control; aid to mitigate the effects of climate change; rehabilitation of the physical environment, including contaminated sites and land and brownfield redevelopment; promotion of biodiversity and nature protection, including investments in Natura 2000 sites; aid to SMEs to promote sustainable production patterns through the introduction of cost-effective environmental systems and through the adoption and use of pollution prevention technologies.[81]"

Elsewhere, the prevention of risks, including the development and implementation of plans to prevent and cope with natural and technological risks, sustainable tourism and sustainable urban development are mentioned. How much of the sums which are available, are spent for the construction of roads or other infrastructure projects and how much is spent for the environment, is decided by the Member States. Long-term effects of the regional policy—impacts of motorway construction or other infrastructure projects—on the state of nature such as biodiversity or land use are difficult to assess, as many other factors also play a role. However, it seems obvious that many projects in Member States which would never have been realised without the support of EU funds, are detrimental to the protection of the environment. Environmental organisations often tried to stop such projects, normally, though, without success.[82]

The Cohesion Fund,[83] established under art.177(2) TFEU did, until 2006, not **4–25** work with programmes; rather, it made money available for specific transport and environmental projects in countries which have a gross national product per capita of less than 90 per cent of the EU average. Till the year 2006, these conditions applied to Spain, Greece, Portugal and Ireland.[84] As of 2007, the Cohesion Fund no longer co-finances projects, but follows the model of the other funds: Member States which benefit from the Cohesion Fund, elaborate programmes and then obtain sums to implement these programmes. Which projects are then co-financed, is up to the Member States.

Article 177(2) TFEU only provides for the co-financing of trans-European transport and of environmental measures. The new Regulation 1084/2006 states that the Fund shall finance:

---

[80] Commission, COM(2004) 621.

[81] Reg.1080/2006 (fn.79, above), art.4(4) and art.6(2).

[82] See for example the facts underlying Court of Justice, *An Taisce* (C–325/94) [1996] E.C.R. I–3727; C–321/95P (fn.74, above); *WWFUK v Council* (C–355/08P), Order of 5 May 2009; General Court, *Apiculteurs v Commission* (T–403/07), Order of November 3, 2008.

[83] Reg.1164/1994 on the establishment of the Cohesion Fund [1994] OJ L130/1, amended by Reg.1264/99 [1999] OJ L161/57.

[84] Reg.1084/2006 (fn.79, above), art.2(1.b)

"the environment within the priorities assigned to the Community environmental protection policy under the policy and action programmes on the environment. In this context, the Fund may also intervene in areas related to sustainable development which clearly present environmental benefits, namely energy efficiency and renewable energy and, in the transport sector the trans-European networks, rail, river and sea transport, intermodal transport systems and their interoperability, management of road, sea and air traffic, clean urban transport and public transport."

This provision is clearly ultra vires: the management of road, sea and air traffic has nothing to do with the protection of the environment; the same applies to rail, river and sea transport—imagine the oil transport by sea—and to most of the other measures which are listed. Article 11 TFEU precisely shows that transport projects which have an environmental dimension remain transport projects. The provision obviously tries to go beyond art.177(2) TFEU and finance energy and transport projects under the heading of "environment".

The Member States that benefit from the Cohesion Fund between 2007 and 2013 are Czech Republic, Greece, Cyprus, Latvia, Lithuania, Hungary, Malta, Poland Portugal, Slovenia and Slovakia. Furthermore, Spain obtained access to the Fund till 2013 "on a transitional and specific basis"—whatever that means. Estonia and Ireland lack in this list, obviously, because their national income was already close to the EU average.

Regulation 1164/94 provided in art.8 that all projects which are co-financed with EU money, must be in keeping with the provisions of EU law, in particular with EU environmental law. A similar clause was found in all earlier regulations concerning the Structural Funds. However, the European Union normally relied on the affirmation of the national authorities that a project conformed with EU environmental legal provisions. Local groups and environmental organisations often protested, arguing for example that no environment impact assessment had been made before a motorway project was started. A general provision was inserted into art.9(5) of Regulation 1083/2006 according to which the measures which are co-financed by the European Union must be in compliance with EU law; however, the provisions on the retention of EU funds, where there is no compliance, have been deleted (arts 99ss of Regulation 1083/2006). This means in clear terms that now the Commission would have to start proceedings under arts 258 TFEU, when a Member State infringes EU environmental law, but would not be allowed to retain funds, when, for example, a motorway is being built without an environment impact assessment. The underlying idea was presumably that protesters might go to the national court. However, there is some value in a legislative provision that the European taxpayer's money should only serve to finance projects which are in compliance with the European legislation.

Overall, regional policy goes more and more into the direction that Member States receive lump sums and spend them at their discretion, being loosely fenced in by the national priority programmes which they fix and which are a little bit controlled and then approved by the Commission. This trend makes the financing of environmental policies and projects increasingly dependent on the political rank that environmental policy has within the different Member States. And as the environment is not voting in elections, this rank is not high in many Member States. For a politician, who wants to be re-elected, it is much more popular to build a new road than a waste water treatment installation, to protect farmers and hunters rather than the soil and the birds. European regional development policy is quite problematic for the European environment.

LIFE—Financial Instrument for the Environment

Following earlier measures to support environmental projects in the Mediterra-   **4–26**
nean, Baltic and North Sea regions, a financial instrument, LIFE was created in
1992 in order to support some environmental activities in Member States and
beyond. Between 1992 and 2006, some 2,500 projects were financially supported
with an overall value of 2,5 billion €, half of this sum coming from EC funding.[85]
For the period 2000–2006, 640 million € were available which co-financed three
types of projects: first, nature protection measures, in particular under Directives
2009/147 and 92/43 (47 per cent); second, innovative and integrated techniques
and procedures on pilot or demonstration projects, on the integration of
environmental requirements, clean technologies and other measures (47 per cent);
and third environmental projects in non-EU countries that border the Mediterranean or the Baltic Sea (6 per cent).

Following the study about the financial needs for the Nature 2000 network,[86]
the Commission tried to shift the financing of Natura 2000 to the general regional
policy funds mentioned above; its proposal for LIFE which covered the period
between 2007 and 2013 only provided for two lines of measures which were to be
supported, implementation and governance on the one hand, information and
communication on the other hand.[87] However, Parliament and Council did not
agree on this approach. The new Regulation, LIFE+ which covers the years 2007
till 2013 re-introduced a third line on nature and biodiversity, for which 40 per
cent of the 2.1 billion €—thus 840 million €—that are earmarked for the period
2007–2013, are reserved.[88] At the same time, the new Regulation is also destined
to ensure the financing of environmental organisations—see para.2–29, above,
and of several other financing activities of the Commission.

A critical look at this result must begin with the sums that are made available
for the protection of nature and biodiversity. The policy target of the European
Union, laid down in the 6th environmental action programme, was to stop the
loss of biodiversity by 2010. As mentioned, the Member State experts on nature
protection estimated that alone for the setting up of the Natura 2000 network,
between 3.4 and 5.7 billion € per year would be needed. Even if one takes the
lower figure and considers it to be exaggerated, the difference of the amount
which Regulation 614/2007 provides—840 million € for seven years, which
means 120 million € per year—remains enormous. It is likely that the
Commission will argue in future that Member States should provide for the
financing of nature protection measures under the regional policy funds, and that
Member States will argue that LIFE+ has to finance the protection of aspects of
nature and biodiversity. The loser is the environment. And it also must be pointed
out that the protection of nature and biodiversity cannot be limited to the
designated habitats of EU interest, the Natura 2000 network.

There are other problems with LIFE. Member States take great care to ensure
that every Member State gets an equal share of the money. Thus, it is not the best
project that is supported. The Commission cannot set priorities for specific

---

[85] Commission, COM(2004) 621.
[86] Commission, COM(2004) 431.
[87] Commission, COM(2004) 621.
[88] Reg.614/2007 concerning the Financial Instrument for the Environment (LIFE+) (2007) OJ
L149/1.

projects or encourage several—or even all—Member States to concentrate on a specific type of projects, such as on renewable energies. Furthermore, it is obvious that the method of project approval leads to some concerted practices among Member States. Finally, there was a limited pilot effect of the specific project in the past: the innovative measures were not easily made operational in the whole of the European Union. It remains to be seen, to what extent these problems of the past will continue to exist under the new LIFE+ instrument.

3. Planning and land use

Town and Country Planning; Land Use

4–27   Article 192(2) TFEU provides that measures concerning town and country planning and land use require unanimous adoption in the Council. The provision thus parts from the idea that such measures may also be adopted at EU level, though problems of subsidiarity are of particular relevance here. Until now, though, almost no such measures have been taken. The Commission issued some communications which concern basic aspects of town and country planning,[89] the urban environment,[90] integrated coastal zone management,[91] and wetlands.[92] On coastal zone management, the European Parliament and the Council adopted a recommendation which gives guidelines for an "environmentally sustainable, economically equitable, sociable responsible and culturally sensitive management of coastal zones".[93] Despite these words, the individual recommendations are of a very general nature and not really operational. And a look at coastal zones in the European Union shows that the Recommendation is largely ignored, the most obvious example being the destruction of the Spanish coast by construction projects.

4–28   In execution of Decision 1600/2002 on the Sixth Environmental Action Programme the Commission published in early 2006 a thematic strategy—i.e. a sectoral action programme—on the urban environment[94] which addressed in particular problems of transport in urban agglomerations. This thematic strategy which had not been suggested by the Commission, but introduced into Decision 1600/2002 by the European Parliament and the Council, does not suggest legislative actions. Concrete action on implementing the strategy lacked almost completely. Under the Regional Policy, some pilot projects are financially supported, greater cooperation among agglomerations is promoted and awareness campaigns were initiated; the main activities, however, stem from interested

---

[89] Commission, Europe 2000: perspectives of future town and country planning of the Community COM (90) 544; Commission, Europe 2000: outlook for the development of the Community's territory COM (91) 452.

[90] Commission, Green Paper on the urban environment, COM (90) 218; Council Res. of January 28, 1991 [1991] OJ C33/4; see further, Court of Auditors, Special Report on urban environment in the European Union [1994] OJ C383/1; Commission, Communication on urban development in the European Union, COM (97) 197.

[91] Commission, Communication on integrated coastal zone management, COM (95).

[92] Commission, Communication on the wise use and conservation of wetlands, COM (95) 189.

[93] Rec. 2002/413 concerning the implementation of integrated coastal zone management [2002] OJ L148/24.

[94] Dec.1600/2002 laying down the sixth environment action programme [2002] OJ L242/1 art.7(2.g), and Commission, COM(2005) 718.

cities themselves. In general, though, problems of the urban environment are much too large and too diversified to be handled at EU level.

Article 12 of Directive 96/82[95] requires Member States to ensure that the objective of preventing major accidents and limiting the consequences of such accidents are taken into account in their land-use policies. In the long term, there will have to be appropriate distances between such establishments and residential areas, areas of public use and natural value and interest. The implementation of these provisions is to be ensured by consultation procedures. Industrial accidents in Enschede (the Netherlands) and Toulouse (France) in 2000 demonstrated the necessity of such measures, though it is rather difficult to relocate industrial installations, once they come too close to urban agglomerations or newly built residential areas. In practice, art.12 of Directive 96/82 is hardly enforceable. When the Frankfurt airport wanted to enlarge, work was upheld in 2004/2005, because a chemical plant was located exactly in the projected new landing line. After years of negotiations, the plant was relocated.

Apart from these few measures, the different communications aim at focusing the attention on some specific aspects of development within the European Union or showing the environmental problems of specific areas, rather than determining legal measures for town and country planning or land use. Indeed, these measures do not announce or propose new legal measures at all to contribute to the solutions of problems. They have to be viewed alongside the European Union's policies which affect planning and land use, in particular regional, transport and agricultural policy. Sometimes the communications also serve to start a discussion whether EU financial assistance for some specific topics should be envisaged, notably in the framework of the Structural Funds. Also, measures concerning the protection of the architectural and natural heritage of the European Union[96] increasingly come under the provision on culture of art.167 TFEU.[97]

Environment Impact Assessment

Projects

National level. A Directive on the assessment of the effects of certain public and private projects on the environment was adopted in 1985 and substantially amended in 1997[98]. According to that Directive, public authorities, before they give a permit (development consent) for specific public and private projects, shall make an assessment of the direct and indirect effects which the project may have on humans and the environment. Specific procedural provisions are laid down for such an assessment, such as the requirement for the developer to submit factual information on the project and its likely impact, the participation of administrative bodies dealing with nature protection and the possibility for the public

4–29

---

[95] Dir.96/82 on the control of major-accident hazards involving dangerous substances [1997] OJ L10/13, art.12.

[96] See Rec.74/65 on the protection of the architectural and natural heritage [1975] OJ L21/22; Res. of the Council and of Member States meeting in Council on the conservation of the European architectural heritage [1986] OJ C320/1.

[97] Dec.2228/97 on an action programme for the conservation of cultural heritage [1997] OJ L305/11.

[98] Dir.85/337 (fn.36, above).

concerned to express an opinion. The administrative decision on the application shall take into consideration all these comments.

For a first group of projects listed in annex I to the Directive, such as large refineries, large thermal power stations, radioactive waste disposal installations, motorways, lines for long-distance railway traffic, larger airports, an environment impact assessment always has to be made. For a second group of projects (annex II) an impact assessment has to be made where the project is likely "to have significant effects on the environment by virtue, in particular, of its nature, size or location" (art.2). Member States have a large amount of discretion in deciding whether a project has such a significant impact or not. Legally, the Court of Justice has considerably narrowed down this discretion, by requiring, de facto that for any project that is likely to have a significant impact on the environment, an environment impact assessment is necessary.[99] In daily practice at local and regional level, this jurisdiction is rather frequently ignored, though.

Commission attempts in the 1980s to have an environmental impact assessment made for any project co-financed by EU funds—in particular the Structural Funds or the Cohesion Fund—failed, as the main involved Member States from Southern Europe successfully argued that this would be discriminatory. This is not convincing, since the taxpayers in the different Member States, which contribute to the Funds are certainly entitled to be assured that their money is properly used in the distribution of EU funds.

4–30   Directive 85/337 has been implemented in all Member States, although in some States with considerable delay; not all legislation conformed to the Directive's requirements and the amending Directive 97/11 had the same problem.[100] A particular problem is the practical application of the Directive: even after a number of years of the Directive's application, most of the EU complaints, petitions and infringement procedures under art.258 TFEU deal with Directive 85/ 337.[101] The main concerns are the policy decision to realise a project independently from its, potentially very negative, impact on the environment; furthermore, the exclusion of annex II-projects from an impact assessment; the poor quality of the impact assessment[102]; the start of realising the project before the end of the impact assessment procedure; arbitrary exclusions of making an assessment for an annex II project; and omissions to properly consult the public concerned.[103] The transboundary effects of a project are, under the

---

[99] Court of Justice, *WWF* (C–435/97) [1999] E.C.R. I–5613; C–72/95 *Kraaijeveld* [1996] E.C.R. I–5403; *Commission v Germany* (C–431/92) [1995] E.C.R. I–2189; *Commission v Belgium* (C–131/94) [1996] E.C.R. I–2323; *Commission v Germany* (C–301/95) [1998] E.C.R. I–6135; *Commission v Ireland* (C–392/96) [1999] E.C.R. I–5901.

[100] On the date required for implementation of Dir.85/337—July 3, 1988—five Member States had adopted the necessary legislation. When Dir.97/11 had to be implemented on March 14, 1999, only the Netherlands had done so completely, Commission, Annual Report on monitoring the application of Community law, 17th Report (1999) [2001] OJ C30/1 at p.44.

[101] Commission, Monitoring the application of Community law, 13th report [1995] OJ C250/1 at p.175; 17th report [2001] OJ C30/1 (p.45); 19th report, COM(2002) 324, p.22.

[102] See, e.g. Commission, Joint Research Centre: An analysis of environmental impact studies on installations for the treatment and disposal of toxic and dangerous waste in the EU (Brussel, Luxembourg, 1996) which examined 28 impact studies.

[103] See the cases mentioned in fn.99, above and further Court of Justice, *Bund Naturschutz Bayern* (C–396/92) [1994] E.C.R. I–3717.

Directive's provisions, to be discussed and solved in a way which deals with international co-operation more than the attempt to optimise planning processes in the European Union.

Directive 85/337 has undoubtedly influenced the development of permitting procedures in all Member States, by imposing the taking into consideration of environmental aspects into this procedure. In a number of regions, it was possible to limit and reduce the almost total discretion given to local or other authorities to decide on a project. **4–31**

The main problems of the Directive are:

- its loose drafting and the large discretion given to administrations often lead to the non-application of some of its principles;
- the Directive does not oblige a developer to study or have studied alternatives to the project for which he looks for a permit[104];
- the administration is not in any way obliged to avoid and/or minimise the negative effects of a project on the environment, but may give development consent also where serious negative effects are to be expected;
- the impact assessment need not, according to general understanding, be made in writing, though it is difficult to see how one can "describe" (art.3) the effects of a project otherwise than in writing;
- no regular national reports and no Commission report on the application of Directive is foreseen[105];
- the Directive does not provide for consequences when an environment impact assessment has not been made. This leads to large differences. While, for example, in the United Kingdom the planning consent is void and the whole procedure has to start anew, where an environment impact assessment has not been made, German courts consider the omission to make an environment impact assessment an administrative error which is normally irrelevant for planning consent.

European level. The Commission does not itself authorise projects which are realised at national level. There are thus no provisions at EU level corresponding to those of Directive 85/337. There is considerable discussion, whether there should be an EU assessment, before the Commission agrees to co-finance Member States' projects. This idea was rightly rejected, as this would inevitably lead to two environmental impact assessments being made; and there is no reason to duplicate these assessments which are expensive and time-consuming. The problem would probably be less big, if Member States were required to make **4–32**

---

[104] See Dir.85/337 (fn.36, above) which provides in art.5(3) and Annex IV n.2 that the developer has to submit, together with his application "an outline of the main alternatives studied by the developer". However, this clause is generally understood in the sense that the developer is not obliged to study alternatives; only where he has done so, he must submit information on them. Under the Espoo Convention which has also been concluded by the EU (see para.4–35, below), the developer of a project which has impacts on another State, must examine "reasonable alternatives". This provision is binding on EU Member States.

[105] Dir.85/337(fn.36, above) only provides in art.11(3) that the Commission shall publish an implementation report five years after the adoption of the Directive. This report was published in 1993 (COM) (93) of April 2, 1993. The Commission occasionally published further reports, at an interval of about five to eight years. Dir.91/692 standardising and rationalising reports on the implementation of certain directives relating to the environment [1991] OJ L377/48 omitted to provide for regular reports on Dir.85/337.

such an assessment for all projects that are co-financed out of the EU budget, and if the Commission were more systematically checking, whether a necessary national environmental impact assessment was made.

Plans and programmes

4–33   *National level.* Directive 2001/42[106] requests Member States to make an environment impact assessment for plans and programmes which are likely to have significant environment impact effects. Plans and programmes for which such an impact assessment is always required, are listed in art.3(2).[107] For plans and programmes which determine the "use of small areas of local level" and minor amendments to existing plans and programmes an assessment is only necessary, where Member States determine that they are likely to have significant environmental effects. For other plans which "set the framework for future development consent of projects", Member States shall determine, whether they are likely to have such effects, either through case-by-case examination or by specifying types of plans and programmes. Plans for national defence, civil emergency and financial or budget plans or programmes are not covered by the Directive.

The definition of "environment assessment" is different from that under Directive 85/337. Under Directive 2001/42 it means "the preparation of an environment report, the carrying out of consultations, the taking into account of the environment report and the consultations in decision-making and the provision of information on the decision" that is finally taken. The environment report must describe and evaluate the likely environmental impacts and reasonable alternatives. Consultation[108] must be made early and in any time before the adoption of the plan or programme or its submission to the legislative procedure. It must include consultations on the draft plan and on the environmental report. The public which is to be consulted includes the public affected, or likely to be affected by, or having an interest in the decision, "including relevant non-governmental organisations, such as those promoting environmental protection".

4–34   Once a decision on the plan or programme has been taken, (a) the public that was consulted shall be informed, (b) the relevant plan or programme and a statement must be made available, summarising how environmental considerations were taken into consideration, as well as the results of the consultation and "the reason for choosing the plan or programme as adopted". The Directive also covers plans and programmes that are co-financed under the EU structural funds, though the wording is not entirely clear in this regard.[109] The Directive will hopefully ensure that public discussions on the environmental effects of plans and

---

[106] Dir.2001/42 (fn.40, above).

[107] Dir.2001/42 (fn.40, above), art.3(2): "… an environmental assessment shall be carried out for all plans and programmes, (a) which are prepared for agriculture, forestry, fisheries, energy, industry, transport, waste management, water management, telecommunications, tourism, town and country planning or land use which set the framework for future development consent of projects listed in Annexes I and II to Directive 85/337, or (b) which, in view of the likely effect on sites, have been determined to require an assessment pursuant to Article 6 or 7 of Directive 92/43."

[108] Dir.2001/42 uses the words "participation" and "consultation" synonymously. As to the difference between these notions see paras 4–16 and 4–21, above.

[109] Dir.2001/42 (fn.40, above), arts 3(9), 11(3) and 12(4).

programmes take place and it may be hoped that this progressively benefits the environment. The necessity to explain, why a specific solution for a plan was taken, might also reduce the administrations' discretion which, in some parts of the European Union, is in need of more democratic discussion. It is problematic, though, whether enough interested persons will participate in the impact assessment and how an interested public or an environmental organisation will be able to assess the environmental impact of any such plan.

European level. In the context of the international Convention on Environment Impact Assessment in a Transboundary Context, signed in Espoo (Finland) in 1991, and to which the EC adhered in 1993,[110] a Protocol was signed in May 2003 in Kiev (Ukraine) which provides for a strategic environmental assessment of plans and programmes which will come into effect in the coming years; the Protocol was signed by all EU Member States and by the European Union itself. The Protocol's content is very similar to that of Directive 2001/42.[111] The most important difference is that plans and programmes for which a strategic environmental assessment is required, are those that are required by legislative, regulatory or administrative provisions and are subject to preparation or adoption by an authority (art.2(5) of the Protocol). 4–35

The problem of the Protocol's application to the EU institutions is, whether there are plans or programmes elaborated by the EU institutions—not just co-financed by them, as these remain Member States' plans and programmes— that would come under the field of application of the Protocol. This is indoubtedly the case. Indeed, already the different thematic strategies which are to be elaborated under the Sixth Environmental Action Programme[112] fulfil the conditions of art.2(5) of the Protocol. Other plans and programmes which exist and which will be covered by the provisions of the Protocol are plans for energy-saving, programmes in the agricultural sector, on trans-European networks under arts 170 et seq. TFEU, etc. At the end of 2008, the Council approved the Protocol which entered into force in July 2010.[113]

Policies and Legislation

National level. There are no specific EU provisions which require Member States to make (environment) impact assessments of national policies or legislation, before such policies or legislations are adopted. The abovementioned Aarhus-Convention mentions public participation in policies and legislations, but in a form of soft law which does not provide for an obligation of Contracting Parties to take implementation measures. 4–36

A certain form of consultation obligation for national legislation is created by EU law, however, not for environmental, but rather opposing purposes. Directive 98/34[114] which is based on the actual arts 114, 337 and 43 TFEU, aims at the removal or reduction of any barriers which national legislation might create to the free movement of goods. It requests Member States already to notify the Commission of draft product-related legislation. Where a restriction on use or a

---

[110] Dec. of October 15, 1996. The Decision appears never to have been published.
[111] See on that Directive para.4–33, above.
[112] See para.2–21, above.
[113] Dec.2008/871 (2008) OJ L308/34; the Protocol is published on p.35.
[114] Dir.98/34 (fn.29, above).

ban of a substance or a product is in question, the Member State is asked to add, "if available", data on production, substitution products as well as "in appropriate cases" the conclusions of a risk evaluation made in accordance with the principles of Regulation 793/93.[115] The national draft measure is sent to all other Member States and the notifying Member State may adopt the draft measure only after a period of three months following notification. Where the Commission or another Member State indicate that the draft measure may create barriers to the free movement of goods, the standstill period is extended to six months. Where the Commission indicates its intention to propose a legally binding Community measure or where there is already a proposal on the subject-matter in question before the Council, the standstill period is 12 months.

4–37   Where a Member State adopts a national measure without having complied with the procedure under Directive 98/34, the national provision is unenforceable on economic operators, and national courts are obliged not to apply the national provision in question.[116] This "sanction", which follows from the direct effect of the Directive's provisions,[117] is very effective, since penalties, fines or other sanctions which were pronounced under the national provision, could not be enforced either. Directive 98/34 affects numerous environmental measures[118] and has de facto replaced a standstill agreement in environmental matters which was adopted in 1973 in the form of a gentlemen's agreement.[119] The decisive criterion for the Directive's application is, whether the national measure may, directly or indirectly, influence the free circulation of goods; EU environmental considerations do not really come into this assessment, and hardly any weighing of the different interests takes place. With this proviso, measures which fix air or water quality standards normally do not come within the field of application of Directive 98/34. Likewise, nature protection measures, provisions on the storage of products or on the establishment and operation of industrial installations normally are not affected.

    The public is not consulted during this procedure, though it may be assumed that Member States which are informed of draft legislation of another Member State, consult their economic operators to see whether there is a potential impact on the free circulation of goods. The Commission considers the procedure to come under the "enquiry and investigation" exception of Regulation 1049/2001[120] and tries not to grant access to the comments which are made under the procedure of Directive 98/34; in my opinion, this is not correct.

4–38   *European level.* There are no binding provisions concerning impact assessments for policies and legislation at EU level. During the inter-governmental discussions on the Maastricht Treaty on the European Union, the United

---

[115] Reg.793/93 on the evaluation and control of the risks of existing substances [1993] OJ L84/1. This Reg. is now substituted by Reg.1907/2006 (fn.53, above).

[116] Court of Justice, *Security International v Signalsson* (C–194/94) [1996] E.C.R. I–2201.

[117] See para.12–27, below.

[118] In 1997 out of 900 national draft regulatory measures that were notified by Member States, 63 might be qualified as environmental measures. Commission Communication [1998] OJ C281/3.

[119] Agreement of the Representatives of the Governments of the Member States meeting in Council on information for the Commission and for the Member States with a view to possible harmonisation throughout the Communities of urgent measures concerning the protection of the environment [1973] OJ C9/1; amended [1974] OJ C86/2.

[120] See Reg.1049/2001 (fn.21, above) and paras 4–07 et seq.

Kingdom suggested that EU legislative measures should undergo an environmental impact assessment; the suggestion was taken up in a declaration to the Final
Act of the Conference. The Inter-governmental Conference for the Amsterdam
Treaty 1997 adopted another declaration on this question, without immediate
consequence.[121] The Commission had, until then, made assessments of the impact
of its proposals on small and medium-sized companies and on the EU finances.

Since 2002, it submits to an impact assessment:

- legislative proposals that have an economic, social or environmental
  impact;
- non-legislative initiatives which define future policies;
- certain implementing measures which are likely to have significant
  impacts.[122]

This impact assessment is not limited to the environmental impact, but
examines the economic, social and environmental impact; it focuses on the
examination, whether the impact of a proposal "is sustainable and conform to the
principles of Better Regulation".[123] The impact assessment examines, possibly
with the help of studies, the impact of a project, and provides for consultation
with interested parties and relevant experts, including consultations on ethical
and political issues. The results of the assessment which also have to include an
assessment of alternatives, are laid down in an assessment report which forms a
basis for the Commission's decision on the proposal. The assessment reports are
made available by the Commission in the form of SEC-documents.

Practice since 2003 shows a limited value of the assessments. The main issue
of the examination is the cost of the planned measure for economic operators. In
the area of agriculture, internal market, industry and regional policy, the impact
assessment procedure often just gives a rubber-stamp to political decisions which
were taken elsewhere; here, the environmental impact is rarely examined and
assessed in any detail. In contrast to that, most proposals in the environmental
sector are very strictly scrutinised as to their impact on vested interests—
frequently in the name of "better regulation"—and then watered down or
completely rejected, before they even reach the Commission's decision-making
level. To take two concrete examples: Regulation 1080/2006 on the Regional
Development Fund did not undergo an impact assessment, though its impact on
the environment within the European Union is enormous; an examination of the
likely environmental impact of the Regulation would require detailed studies
which the Commission is neither able nor ready to finance and for which there is
not either time. And the Commission decision not to allow Netherlands to
prescribe particle filters for diesel cars—see on that issue para.3–66, above—was
not based on an assessment of how many lives could be saved by such a measure
and how much illness and environmental pollution prevented, thus on general

---

[121] Declaration No.12 [1997] OJ 340/133: "The Conference notes that the Commission undertakes to
prepare environment impact assessment studies, when making proposals which may have significant
environmental implications."
[122] Commission, Communication on Impact Assessment. COM (2002) 276; see also the
Commission's website on impact assessment, *http://ec.europa.eu/governance/impact/index_en.htm*.
The impact assessment reports are published on this site, once the Commission has adopted a
proposal.
[123] Commission (fn.122, above) n.1.3; as regards "Better Regulation" see COM (2002) 278.

social and environmental considerations, but on legalistic arguments which hid the protection of interests of the car industry.

Such examples could be multiplied. The impact assessment requirement, though acceptable in its theoretical concept, thus turns in practice into an instrument of environmental deregulation. This is further strengthened by the fact that the impact assessment is made, under the political responsibility of the Commission's President, by the Secretariat General. In this way, the Secretary General can easily signal to the different departments that this or that legislative proposal is unwelcome and would receive a stiff reception with the Secretariat General. Examples in the past were the proposals for a directive on soil protection or considerations to have a directive on biodiversity elaborated. The assessment process thus strengthens centralising activities inside the Commission, a tendency which is not favourable to the protection of the environment.

4.   Measures concerning industrial installations

Corporate environmental responsibility

4–39   In 2001 and 2002, the Commission published two communications on corporate social responsibility.[124] It expressly stated that the responsibility of companies not only included social, but also environmental matters. The main signal of the Commission was that it did not intend to provide for any binding legislation in this regard, but that it expected companies to assume their responsibility on a voluntary basis. In 2006, a new communication followed which tried to stimulate greater commitment from companies to corporate social responsibility issues.[125]

As companies are, within the European Union, submitted to legislative requirements with regard to their emissions, waste generation and treatment, waste water requirements etc., the corporate environmental responsibility aims in particular at EU companies that are active in developing countries. I would consider it normal that no EU-based company would anywhere in the world eliminate its waste in other places than authorised landfills, even if the political, economic and environmental situation in the host country does not require or enforce such behaviour; in the same way, any company should not discharge its waste water into rivers, lakes or coastal waters without prior treatment, wherever its installation is located. This kind of example could be multiplied. Whether, however, voluntary measures are really sufficient, is rather doubtful. An international convention on corporate social-environmental responsibility appears necessary and, pending, EU binding measures with regard to EU companies' environmental behaviour, wherever they act, highly desirable. Politically, though, there is little chance of seeing any initiative from the EU institutions in this regard for the next years. And no development in this issue took place since 2006.

---

[124] Commission, Green Paper: towards a European framework for corporate social responsibility, COM(2001) 366; Communication concerning corporate social responsibility, COM(2002) 347; see also Council Resolutions [2002] OJ C86/1 and [2003] OJ C39/3.
[125] Commission, Implementing the partnership for growth and jobs: making Europe a pole of excellence on CSR, COM (2006) 136.

Permitting

Directive 76/464[126] provided that EU-wide emission limit values for the   **4–40**
industrial discharge of some dangerous substances into the water were to be
fixed, based on the "best technical means available". As regards air emissions
from industrial installations, Directive 84/360 stipulated that for new installations
permits should be issued for preventing air pollution, based on the best available
technology not entailing excessive costs; for existing installations, Member States
had to "implement policies and strategies, including appropriate measures, for the
gradual adaptation of existing plans . . . to the best available technology."[127]

The putting into operation of the principle of introducing the best available
technology largely failed, among other reasons, because no consensus was
reached as to which technology, in a given case, was the best available
technology. Under Directive 76/464, the EU-wide emission standards were fixed
by way of a political compromise, not by having recourse to an analysis of the
application of the best available technology. Furthermore, Member States were
allowed to use, instead of emission limit values, EU quality standards.[128] Under
Directive 84/360, technical notes were elaborated and published to determine
what constituted, for specific sectors of industry, the best available technology.
However, these notes did not have any significant impact, since they had no
binding legal nature and it was neither controlled nor publicised, whether they
were complied with or not. Both Directives, therefore, did not lead to a
significant change in technologies used in industrial installations. Furthermore,
Member States did not really favour uniform emission standards for industrial
installations, but rather proposed a non-harmonised approach within the
European Union.

In an attempt to accommodate this concern, improve at the same time the   **4–41**
present situation and deregulate, decentralise and take into consideration the
subsidiarity principle of the EC Treaty, the Council adopted Directive 96/61
concerning integrated pollution prevention and control,[129] which became
applicable, for new installations, in 1999; existing installations had to comply
with its requirements since 2007. In 2008, this Directive was replaced by
Directive 2008/1 which, in turn, was replaced by Directive 2010/75.[130] Directive
2010/75 concerns a number of large industrial installations, the categories of
which are listed in an annex I. It also covers large combustion plants, waste
incineration and co-incineration installations and activities using organic solvents
and installations producing titanium dioxide; these activities were, until 2010,
regulated in different specific directives. Directive 2010/75 is thus a real
framework directive on industrial emissions. It will enter into effect in the
beginning of 2013, though the entry into effect of several provisions will be
postponed until 2014, 2015 and even 2016.

---

[126] Dir.76/464 on pollution caused by certain dangerous substances discharged into the aquatic
environment of the Community [1976] OJ L129/23, art.6(1). This Dir. will cease to exist in 2013.

[127] Dir.84/360 on the combating of air pollution from industrial plants [1984] OJ L188/20, art.4 and
art.13.

[128] Dir.76/464 (fn.126, above) art.6.

[129] Dir.96/61 concerning integrated pollution prevention and control [1996] OJ L257/26.

[130] Dir.2008/1 concerning integrated pollution prevention and control [2008] OJ L24/8; Dir.2010/75
(fn.39, above).

For some time the Commission had also pursued the idea of a similar, though less stringent, directive for smaller industrial installations. However, in 1997, environmental ministers of Member States concluded that from an environmental point of view, there was no reason to apply environmentally less stringent standards to small enterprises,[131] and shelved such plans.

Despite its rather ambitious title, Directive 2010/75 essentially lays down framework rules for the national permitting systems with regard to large industrial installations. It provides that as a rule emission limit values are to be fixed in the individual permits. Permits for installations must include emission limit values for pollutants which are likely to be emitted from the installation into water, air or land. The emission limit values "shall be based on the best available techniques". A technique is available when it is:

> "developed on a scale which allows implementation in the relevant industrial sector, under economically and technically viable conditions, taking into consideration the costs and advantages, whether or not the techniques are used or produced inside the Member State in question as long as they are reasonably accessible to the operator. (art. 3(10))."

Thus, the best available technique depends also on economic considerations. Furthermore, the conditions in the permit on emissions into the environment may be less strict than according to the best available technique, and take into consideration the geographical location, the local environmental conditions and the technical characteristics of the installation concerned (art.15(4)).

The requirement to use the best available techniques does not exist for the emission of greenhouse gases, when the installation participates in the EU emission trading scheme; the reason for this is that it was considered that it was impossible to ask installations to use the best techniques and at the same time give them the possibility to buy rights for emitting more greenhouse gases than the best technique would allow. This amendment will, though, not be able to eliminate Member States' rights under art.193 TFEU to fix such emission limit values for greenhouse gases at national (or local) level, as a directive cannot amend the TFEU.[132]

4–42   In order to find the best available techniques, the Commission has to organise an exchange of information with Member States, the industry sectors concerned, environmental organisations and the Commission. This exchange is to take place in a forum. The opinion of the forum shall be taken into account for the drafting of a "best available technique reference document" (BAT reference document) which shall contain, among others, emission limit values for the sector concerned (art.13).[133] Under the present legal system of Directive 2008/1, such documents—called BREFs (Best Available Technique Reference Document)— are elaborated by a Bureau which is part of the Commission's Joint Research

---

[131] President's conclusions, informal meeting of EU Environmental Ministers, Amsterdam, April, 18–20, 1997, para.3: "Environmental requirements should be related to the nature and magnitude of environmental pollution and not to the size of the enterprise. Therefore, in principle similar requirements should apply to larger and smaller enterprises". The conclusions are not published. The reference is taken from M. Pallemaerts, "Production, toxics and transnational law; an inquiry into the effectiveness of international and European Community environmental law", (Oxford, 2003) p.337.
[132] This opinion is, obviously, heavily contested.
[133] art.11(6) of Directive 2010/75 provides that the BREF document shall be published after the adoption of BAT conclusions. This provision contradicts the provisions on access to environmental information, in particular those of the Aarhus Convention, see paras 4–04ss., above.

Centre and is based in Sevilla. Working groups, composed of experts from industry, administrations, research institutes and non-governmental organisations elaborate these documents. At present, BREFs are produced only in English and are published on the internet. By the end of 2010, 35 BREFs had been produced for iron and steel, cement and lime, pulp and paper, non-ferrous metals, glass, textiles, tanning of hides and skins, refineries etc. Several other BREFs were being elaborated.

On the basis of the BAT reference document, a committee, composed of Member States and the Commission, shall decide the so-called "BAT conclusions" which contain, among others, "the emission levels associated with the best available techniques" (art.3.12). This wording seems to indicate that the emission limit values are not decided on by a legally binding measure, but rather in a form of non-binding frame, eventually also in the form of a recommendation.[134]

The fixing of binding emission limit values in the individual permit had led, under Directive 2008/1 to different emission limit values being fixed for the same type of industrial installation, according to its location, economic situation (costs and benefits) and other circumstances. The possibilities for the competent authorities in the Member States to deviate from BAT conclusions in this regard and fix less stringent requirements, have been made more difficult, but continue to exist. Therefore, the present situation will probably not change under Directive 2010/75. For example two cement kilns in a distance of 5 miles, might still have different emission limit values fixed in their permits. Also, the bargaining on less stringent conditions for emission limit values for the location of new installations is likely to increase, since the installations are able to threaten that they will look for a site elsewhere with more favourable permit conditions. The words of Recital 3 of Directive 2010/75 that the chosen approach "will also contribute to the achievement of a level playing field in the Union by aligning environmental performance requirements for industrial installations" rather are wishful thinking, as long as the different emission limit values are not fixed EU-wide. **4–43**

Instead of fixing emission limit values for individual installations, Member States may also provide for "general binding rules", provided that the same results are achieved (arts 6 and 17). This possibility which was inserted into the text especially at the request of Germany is of limited assistance; indeed, competition among industrial installations within the European Union and its internal market is likely to be effective also across national frontiers, not only within the individual Member States.

Member States must send to the Commission "representative data on emissions" and on emission values which were fixed (art.72); the frequency and other details of reporting are to be decided by comitology decision. The Commission shall, every three years, submit a report on the implementation of the Directive which also assesses the need for setting minimum requirements for EU-wide emission limit values and is accompanied, "where appropriate" with a legislative proposal (art.73).

---

[134] The Commission, in COM(2010) 593, p.4, stated that the BAT conclusions will have legal effects, without further specifying this comment. The statement was made before Directive 2010/75 was adopted.

4–44   Under art.16 of Directive 2008/1, the Commission set up a European Pollutant Release and Transfer Register[135] which required Member States to report, for some 25,000 individual industrial installations the emission of some 80 pollutants into the air and the water; releases to land and noise emissions are not part of the Register. The emission data are regularly published. Environmental organisation, local authorities and individuals though, have not yet linked the available data on emissions to the (non-)use of the best available technique by a specific installations, an approach which had been very successful in the United States.

4–45   To what extent Directive 2010/75 and its predecessors, 96/61 and 2008/1, will lead to a high level of protection of the environment as a whole, an objective which is announced several times in Directive 2010/75,[136] will have to be seen; since 1996, the date of adoption of Directive 96/61, progress was limited in this regard. It is to be welcomed that all installations covered by the Directive must have a permit and that this permit must fix emission limit values, and the provisions of Directive 2010/75 have become significantly stricter than those of Directive 2008/1.

The Directive does not provide that there be at least a central register for all permits and their conditions, although such a register would have been easy to set up in the computer age. Individuals could themselves set up a register of permits and conditions, since the decision on a permit, the reasons for setting the emission limit values and a considerable number of other information must be made available to the public (art.24). The organisational capacity for such a private register would, however, only be available within environmental organisations, environmental agencies and institutes.

4–46   In 2005, the Commission published a first, and in 2010 a second implementation report regarding Directive 96/61–2008/1.[137] It reported that some 50,000 installations came under the Directive. Member States had been late—as usual—in transposing Directive 96/61 into national law[138]; furthermore, the Commission had initiated action under art.258 TFEU against 16 Member States for incorrect transposition of the Directive. The same situation was repeated, when, in October 2007, Directive 96/61 became applicable to existing installations: the Commission started legal action against Belgium, Denmark, Estonia, Greece, Spain, Italy, Lithuania, Malta, Portugal, Slovenia, Austria, France, Ireland and Sweden; by the end of 2010, action against Lithuania and Estonia continued.[139] Generally, the Commission stated that more than half of all permits were not based sufficiently on BAT. The Commission proposal to replace Directive 96/61—2008/1 by a new directive—which later was adopted as Directive 2010/75—was made at the end of 2007,[140] thus before any experience was available with permits for existing installations.

---

[135] Reg.166/2006 concerning the establishment of a European Pollutant Release and Transfer Register [2006] OJ L33/1.

[136] See, for example, Dir.2010/75 (fn.39, above), arts 1, 3(10), 15(4), and 73.

[137] Commission, COM(2005) 540; COM(2010) 593.

[138] Spain, United Kingdom and Greece were found of not having transposed the Directive in time, see Court of Justice, *Commission v Spain* (C–29/01) [2002] E.C.R. I–2503; *Commission v United Kingdom* (C–3901) [2002] E.C.R. I–2513; *Commission v Greece* (C–64/01) [2002] E.C.R. I–2523. Austria was found to have incorrectly transposed the Directive, *Commission v Austria* (C–78/04), judgment of November 18, 2004.

[139] Commission, COM(2010) 593, p.3.

[140] Commission, COM(2007) 843.

Individual industrial sectors

At the launch of EU environmental policy in the 1970s, there was a general   **4–47**
consensus on the necessity of regulating environmental emissions from specific
industrial installations.[141] Although the general usefulness of this concept was
confirmed in 1987,[142] it did not lead to many concrete results.

Titanium dioxide (TiO₂). In 1978, the Council adopted Directive 78/176 on
waste from the titanium dioxide industry[143] which was followed by a directive on
monitoring of TiO_2 installations[144] and another one on the uniform reduction of
waste discharges from such installations.[145] The origins of these Directives go
back to discharges of waste in the early 1970s, from a Montedison factory at
Scarlino (Italy) into Mediterranean waters, which caused concern in Corsica and
led to discords between Italy and France.

The Directive's main aim was the progressive reduction of pollution caused by
waste from the TiO_2 industry. The manufacture of TiO_2 which is a white pigment
used principally in paints, normally results in a larger quantity of waste than of
the product.

The implementation of the different Directives raised problems and was   **4–48**
poorly monitored by the Commission. The Commission was incapable of
checking the actual discharges, and soon abandoned the attempts to have regular
national reports and an EU-wide horizontal report on waste from the TiO_2
industry. The progressive reduction of the discharge of TiO_2 waste into sea and
coastal waters was influenced more by debate from international conventions, the
North Sea conferences and in particular by the technological possibility of
recycling TiO_2 waste which has progressively developed over the past twenty
years.

In 2010, the provisions of the three Directives were incorporated into
Directive 2010/75. TiO_2-producing installations need a permit, but are not
obliged to apply the best available technique. Instead, the discharge of solid waste
into waters was prohibited, and limit values were fixed for air and water
emissions. These emission limit values differentiate according to the technical
process being used (sulfate or chloride process), a clear sign that the economic
concerns prevail, not the environmental concerns.

Other industrial sectors. In 1975, the Commission submitted a proposal for a   **4–49**
Directive on the reduction of water pollution caused by wood pulp mills.[146] The
proposal limited itself to proposing emission limit values for some pollutants.
Since the United Kingdom and some other Member States were opposed to the
fixing of EU-wide limit values for emissions into the environment, the proposal
was not discussed in Council and has in the meantime become obsolete. A

---

[141] See first environmental action programme [1973] OJ C112/1 at p.20, where measures for the
paper and pulp industry, the iron and steel industry and the manufacture of TiO_2 are announced and
measures for the chemical, leather, food and textile industry are envisaged.
[142] See fourth environmental action programme [1987] OJ C328/1 at no.3.4.
[143] Dir.78/176 on waste from the titanium dioxide industry [1978] OJ L54/19.
[144] Dir.82/883 on procedures for the surveillance and monitoring of environments concerned by
waste from the titanium dioxide industry [1982] OJ L378/1.
[145] Dir.92/112 on procedures for harmonising the programmes for the reduction and eventual
elimination of pollution caused by waste from the titanium dioxide industry [1992] OJ L409/11. This
Directive took nine years between its proposal and adoption.
[146] [1975] OJ C99/2.

Commission announcement on a Directive concerning environmental pollution by the paper industry, was not followed by concrete action.[147]

The sector-oriented approach was partly used with the adoption of "daughter" directives for Directive 76/464,[148] such as discharges by the chlor-alkali electrolysis industry. However, these Directives all provided also for quality objectives, thus leaving it to Member States not to follow the sector-oriented approach. Since 1991, legislative initiatives for "daughter" directives under Directive 76/464 were stopped.

In other parts of environmental policy, indications of sectoral approaches were found in air pollution, where legislation on large combustion plants was adopted in 1988 and confirmed in 2001.[149] It is noticeable that the 2001 Directive repeated emission reduction targets for 1998 and 2003 which were thus already outdated, when the Directive entered into effect; the reason for this erroneous approach was the objection in particular by France, to have new targets fixed for large combustion plants. France rather preferred to see such plants also coming under the system of Directive 2008/1 which required "best techniques" instead of precise emission targets. In 2010, the provisions on large combustion plants were incorporated into Directive 2010/75. Emission limit values for sulphur dioxide, nitrogen oxides, carbon monoxide and dust were maintained, according to the type of installation and the fuel used. Very extensive transition periods and derogations were fixed, also, for installations which used indigenous coal or fuel and could, therefore, not respect the emission limit values.

Emissions from waste incinerators were originally grouped in several directives, later placed in one piece of legislation, as the objective was to limit the emissions into air and water , whether they came from installations for municipal or hazardous waste.[150] In 2010, these provisions were incorporated into Directive 2010/75. Waste incinerators and co-incineration installations need a permit. Directive 2010/75 maintained the system of emission limit values for such installations. A permit is also required for waste disposal facilities.[151]

Safety measures for nuclear installations that come under the Euratom Treaty, are regulated by Decision 99/319/Euratom, by which the European Union adhered to the international Convention on nuclear safety and Directive 2009/71.[152] While Recital 3 of directive 2009/71 recognises that the provisions of art 31 and 32 Euratom Treaty, on which the Directive was based, aim at protecting workers, the general public *and the environment* against risks of nuclear installations, there was not one single provision in the Directive which concerned the protection of the environment. Generally, the Directive remained extremely general. It asked Member states to ensure a high level of nuclear safety, while recognising that Member States had already done so to a very large

---

[147] See Written Questions 1491/91 (Van Hemeldonck) [1992] OJ C242/4 and E–2849/95 (De Coene) [1995] OJ C109/11.

[148] See, for example, Dir.82/176 on limit values and quality objectives for mercury discharges by the clor-alkali electrolysis industry [1982] OJ L81/29.

[149] Dir.1988/609 [1988] OJ L336/1; Dir.2001/80 on large combustion plants [2001] OJ L309/1; see also para.8–27, below.

[150] Dir.89/369 [1989] OJ L163/32; Dir. 89/429 [1989] OJ L203/50; Dir.94/63 [1994] OJ L365/24; Dir.2000/76 on waste incinerators [2000] OJ L322/91; see also para.8–29, below.

[151] Dir.1999/31 on the landfill of waste [1999] OJ L182/1.

[152] Commission Dec.99/318/Euratom [1999] OJ L318/20; the Convention is published on p.21. Di.2009/71 establishing a Community framework for the nuclear safety of nuclear installations [2009] OJ L172/18.

extent. No provisions on the participation of the public in the authorisation of nuclear installations was foreseen. No measures on accident prevention—for example on the model of Directive 96/82, providing for internal and external emergency plans—were foreseen. The only concrete measure introduced was the requirement to set up a competent national authority which was responsible for nuclear safety of installations—a measure which all Member States that had nuclear installations, had already put in place. Member States were responsible for ensuring a high level of safety of nuclear installations, but the Directive underlined that the primary responsibility in this regard rested with the licence holders. The added value of this Directive to nuclear safety is not easily seen.

Unless there is a new policy approach, the sector-oriented approach can now be considered to be no longer pursued as a central part of EU environmental policy. The trend rather goes into the direction of fixing permit requirements, asking for the use of best available techniques and fix, where unavoidable, emission limit values at EU level. This trend would not exclude that specific activities might require fine-tuned provisions to address the risks for humans and the environment. Examples of this approach are safety measures for nuclear installations—measures which also would be destined to make this technology more acceptable mining activities, pipeline activities or oil platforms.

Asbestos. Asbestos was the subject of EU legislation since the early 1980s   **4–50** which, based on the present art.114 TFEU, restricted the use of a large number of asbestos fibres which are classified as carcinogens. Though several Member States decided on a total ban on asbestos fibres, the Commission did not take action against them. Instead, it prepared for a larger ban at EU level which finally was adopted in 1999.[153] As regards asbestos which is already on the market and in the environment, Directive 87/217 tried to establish integrated provisions.[154] Member States must use the best available technology not entailing excessive costs and take general measures to reduce asbestos emissions into the air—where a general emission limit value of 0.1mg per cubic metre is fixed—and the water; here, a complete recycling of waste water is required, unless this is "economically not practicable", which makes this provision unenforceable. Measures shall also be taken during the demolition of asbestos-containing buildings and transport as well as at the disposal. The Directive's loose drafting and the absence of constant monitoring of its application in and by Member States had as a consequence that its real impact is limited.

Environmental Auditing

In 1993 and after a rather short discussion, the Council adopted Regulation   **4–51** 1836/93 which established a voluntary system of eco-auditing for industrial installations.[155] In 2001 and 2009, the system was revised and opened also to any form of organisation, such as administrations, universities, funds, etc. which

---

[153] Dir.1999/77 on asbestos [1999] OJ L207/18.

[154] Dir.87/217 on the prevention and reduction of environmental pollution by asbestos [1987] OJ L85/40.

[155] Reg.1836/93 allowing voluntary participation by companies in the industrial sector in A Community eco-management and audit system [1993] OJ L168/1.

wishes to improve its environmental performance (EMAS).[156] An organisation that intends to participate in the scheme for its sites—one site at a time or all together—must establish an environmental policy for that site which must provide for the respect of all existing environmental provisions and a continuous improvement of the environmental performance. The site must then be submitted to an environmental review which concerns the environmental conditions such as water and energy use or waste treatment. The organisation then has to develop an environmental programme for all its activities on the site in order to reach its policy objectives and must ensure that at management level the necessary measures are taken to realise the programme. The site then shall be audited, either by auditors belonging to the organisation or by external auditors.

The organisation finally has to report (environmental statement) on its activity, its policy programme, strategy and management system. This report is validated by an independent, accredited verifier and published; following that, the site is listed in a register. The organisation is allowed to inform, in its correspondence and papers—though not on products, in product advertising and packaging—of its participation in the EMAS scheme.

4–52   Although participation in the scheme is voluntary, an organisation which decides to join in must comply with all the requirements of EMAS. Since the end of 1998, the EMAS scheme has been fully operational in all Member States. On January 1, 2010 participation—mostly of industrial installations, as the system, until 2001, was open only to industrial installations—was as follows[157]:

Country Participation	Participation in EMAS	Participation in ISO ISO 14001
Belgium	49	530
Denmark	93	808
Germany	1379	5800
Greece	69	300
Spain	1159	11205
Finland	25	991
France	17	3629
Ireland	8	294
Italy	1037	9825
Luxembourg	2	267
Netherlands	7	1132
Austria	243	550
Portugal	79	564
Sweden	75	4865
UK	65	5400
Estonia	2	182

[156] Reg.761/2001 [2001] OJ L114/1; Reg.1221/2009 on the voluntary participation by organisations in a Community eco-management and audit scheme [2009] OJ L342/1.
[157] For EMAS: *http://ec.europa.eu/environment/emas/index_en.htm;* for ISO 14001 *http://www. iso.org/iso/catalogue_detail?csnumber=31807*

Country Participation	Participation in EMAS	Participation in ISO ISO 14001
Lithuania	–	267
Latvia	6	101
Poland	19	597
Czech Rep.	31	1315
Hungary	20	1140
Slovakia	6	340
Slovenia	3	351
Malta	1	5
Cyprus	5	47

About 40 per cent of all organisations are small and medium-sized companies, though the costs of participation are sometimes significant. Ideas to have less stringent requirements for small companies, are not being pursued. For the participating organisation, there are clear advantages in participation, in particular better motivation of the personnel and improved competitiveness and, generally, better environmental performance. Furthermore, credit institutes and insurance companies have started to consider of making their intervention dependant on the existence of an auditing scheme. Some governments of Member States started to adapt their control system of companies to whether or not they take part in EMAS, or to relieve them from reporting or other obligations.

At international level, EMAS is competing with ISO 14001, an Environmental **4–53** Management Standard, developed in 1996 by the International Standardisation Organisation ISO. This voluntary standard differs from EMAS in particular in that it applies worldwide, that it is open to the participation of all economic sectors—the EMAS revision of 2001 eliminated this difference—and also refers to products, not only to sites. Furthermore, there is no necessity for an organisation to comply with all environmental legislation, a requirement that exists under EMAS. Finally, the publication of an environmental statement is not necessary; the organisation needs not respect transparency as regards its environmental performance. The Commission recognised some elements of ISO 14001 to be equivalent to EMAS.[158] Thus, an organisation may use ISO 14001 as a first step towards adherence to EMAS and thereby avoid duplication of work.

Generally, EMAS is seen as an effective tool where an organisation tries to improve its environmental performance; its impact on the competitiveness of companies appears limited. Companies which adhere to the system feel, though, that their efforts are not sufficiently rewarded by the EMAS-system, for instance by a sort of rebate during the permitting or operating process. As the ISO-system is less ambitious, less demanding, but also less expensive and less exposing, but almost as well capable as EMAS to be used for image purposes, the ISO-system is clearly favoured by economic operators, as the table above demonstrates.

---

[158] Commission Dec.97/265 [1997] OJ L104/37.

Accident Prevention

4–54   In 1976, a serious industrial accident occurred in Seveso (Italy), where dioxin was emitted into the air; some 600 people had to be evacuated from their homes and about 2,000 were treated for dioxin poisoning. Subsequently, the European Union drew up and adopted, in 1982, a directive on accident prevention from industrial installations.[159] Following two major accidents in Bhopal (India— 1984), where more than 2,500 people were killed and Basel (Switzerland— 1986), where a massive pollution of the Rhine occurred, this Directive was amended twice in 1987 and 1988.[160] A complete revision took place in the early 1990s; this led to the replacement of Directive 82/501[161] by Directive 96/82.[162]

    The structure and concept of Directive 82/501 were largely maintained. Directive 96/82 aims at preventing major industrial accidents which involve dangerous chemicals, and at limiting the consequences of such accidents. It concerns installations where dangerous chemicals are present in quantities that are laid down in an annex. The operator of the installation has to produce a safety report which gives details of the establishment, the dangerous chemicals present, major risks for accidents and the management systems which are available. This last requirement is justified by the fact that "analysis of the major accidents reported in the EU indicates that the majority of them are the result of managerial and/or organisational shortcomings".

4–55   Establishments must furthermore have an internal emergency plan and must inform the public authorities in such a way that the public authorities are able to draw up an external emergency plan. Persons inside and outside the installation who are likely to be affected by an accident must be informed of the safety measures and of the requisite behaviour in the event of an accident. After an accident, the operator has to provide comprehensive information to the authorities on the accident and on the measures taken to prevent recurrence.

    Directive 96/82 provides for detailed rules on the inspection of the establishments by competent authorities, which is a rather innovative and unique provision in environmental law. Also, it introduced national and EU reporting provisions, which did not exist before.

    In 1995 a report on the 10-year-functioning of Directive 82/501 was published which reported a total of 178 accidents that had been notified to the Commission between 1984 and 1993. Furthermore, between 2000 and 2008, Member States reported 245 major accidents; the study estimated that 50 to 80 major accidents occurred annually in the European Union.[163] The Commission estimated that there are 20 to 35 major accidents per year in the European Union.

4–56   The Directive which affects about 4,500 installations, does not cover pipelines, which have an estimated length of some 150,000km for gas transmission, 30,000km for oil and 10,000km for chemicals. It also does not cover: transport activities; military establishments; hazards created by ionizing

---

[159] Dir.82/501 on the major accident hazards of certain industrial installations [1982] OJ L230/1.

[160] Dir.87/216 [1987] OJ L85/36; Dir.88/610 [1988] OJ L336/14.

[161] Dir.87/216 [1987] OJ L85/36; Dir.88/610 [1988] OJ L336/14.

[162] Dir.96/82 (fn.95, above).

[163] K. Rasmussen, *The experience with the major accident reporting system from 1984 to 1993* (Luxembourg, 1995); see also C. Kirchsteiger (ed.), *Lessons learnt from accidents* (EUR 17733), (Ispra, 1998). Commission, C(2010)5422.

radiation[164]; mines; quarries; boreholes; and landfills. Since the Directive is based on art.175 EC (now art.192 TFEU), Member States are of course free to extend its application to such installations, but did not, practically, make use of that possibility. Following spectacular accidents linked to mining activities in Aznalcollar (Spain—1988) and Baia Mare (Romania—2000), the Directive was amended in order to have risks arising from storage and processing activities in mining included in its scope of application.[165] A further amendment is under discussion.[166]

Overall, the system which was set up by Directive 82/501 and was improved and fine tuned by Directive 96/82 seems to work well, though it is obviously not possible to assess the exact impact of the prevention measures. The EU accident prevention scheme set up by the two Directives, was taken over by a number of third countries and was at the origin of the International Convention of Transboundary Effects of Industrial Accidents of 1992 to which the European Union and its Member States adhered.[167] A Commission announcement of an accident prevention initiative for nuclear installations, made shortly after the nuclear accident in Chernobyl,[168] was not followed by action.

5. Environmental liability

The efforts of the European Unioin to tackle issues on environmental liability took about thirty years to mature. As regards damaged caused by waste, the Commission submitted proposals in 1976, 1983 and 1989,[169] but none of these proposals was adopted. Whether damage caused by waste comes under Directive 85/374 on product liability,[170] is doubtful. In my opinion, this is the case, as waste material is also deliberately "produced" and put into circulation. Regulation 2027/97 concerns the liability of air companies in cases of accidents, but only deals with personal injury and economic loss, not with environmental damage.[171]

Subsequent to the Sandoz accident in Basel (Switzerland) in 1986, the Council asked the Commission to consider whether it was appropriate to introduce an EU system on environmental liability. In pursuance thereof, the Commission submitted, in 1993, a Green Paper on environmental liability.[172] The European Parliament organised a hearing on the Green Paper and then asked, under art.225 TFEU for the drawing up of a proposal for a Directive.[173] In 2000, the Commission published a White Paper on the question, with options for future

4–57

---

[164] This clause means that nuclear installations which process dangerous chemicals are covered by the Directive.

[165] Dir.2003/105 [2003] OJ L345/97.

[166] Commission, COM(2010) 781.

[167] Dec.98/685 [1998] OJ L326/1.

[168] Fourth environmental action programme [1987] OJ C 328/1, paras 4.3.8 and 4.6.4.

[169] Commission [1976] OJ C194/2; [1983] OJ C186/3; [1989] OJ C251/3, amended [1991] OJ C192/6.

[170] Dir.85/374 on the approximation of laws, regulations and administrative provisions of the Member States concerning liability for defective products [1985] OJ L210/29; amended by Dir.1999/34 [1999] OJ L141/20.

[171] Reg.2027/97 on liability of air companies in case of accidents [1997] OJ L285/1.

[172] Commission, Greenbook on remedying environmental damage [1993] OJ C149/12.

[173] European Parliament [1994] OJ C149/6.

legislation.[174] In 2002, the Commission made a proposal for a directive on "environmental liability with regard to the prevention and remedying environmental damage" which the Council and Parliament adopted in 2004, ten days before the accession of ten new Member States to the European Union. The Directive became effective on April 30, 2007 and only concerns damage which was caused after that date.[175]

4–58   The Directive constitutes a relatively drastic departure from the classical concept of environmental liability including from the Commission's White Paper. Indeed, while liability normally parts from the idea that a person suffers bodily injury or economic damage which he tries to get compensated from the wrongdoer by way of a civil law action, the Directive does not deal with this civil law damage, but leaves legislation on this "traditional damage" (Recital 11) to Member States' law: "This Directive does not apply to cases of personal injury, to damage to private property or to any economic loss and does not affect any right regarding these types of damages" (Recital 14, see also art.3(3)).

The Directive rather deals with environmental damage.[176] Where such damage occurs, it is the public authorities which shall ensure the restoration of the environment. The Commission's proposal had placed the task of restoration on the public authorities, starting from the concept that the environment is a public, not a private interest good; and as the public authorities were mandated to protect, preserve and improve the quality of the environment, the primary task to restore the impaired environment should be incumbent on them.[177] However, the Council did not like this suggestion and amended it. The final text invokes at several occasions the polluter-pays principle and places the obligation of restoration on the polluter (art.8). Where the public authorities voluntarily restore the environment without having an obligation to do so, they may ask compensation of the money which they extended, from the polluter; however, where the polluter does not pay, because he has gone out of business, is insolvent or cannot be identified, there is not any obligation on the public authorities, contrary to the Commission's proposal. This means that in such cases it is likely that the environment is not restored.

4–59   The Directive's concept needs, of course, a number of qualifications, as environmental impairment is ubiquitous. The following limitations to the

---

[174] Commission, White Paper on environmental liability, COM (2000) 66.

[175] Directive 2004/35 on environmental liability with regard to the prevention and remedying of environmental damage [2004] OJ L143/56.

[176] Note that in continental Europe, "damage" normally supposes that there is a damaged person; it is thus considered to be a civil law notion.

[177] Dir.2004/35 (fn.175, above) art.2(1): "'environmental damage' means: (a) damage to protected species which is any damage that has significant adverse effects on reaching or maintaining the favourable conservation status of such habitats or species…; (b) water damage, which is any damage that significantly adversely affects the ecological, chemical and/or quantitative status and/or ecological potential, as defined in Directive 2000/60/EC… (c) land damage which is any land contamination that creates a significant risk to human health being adversely affected as a result of the direct or indirect introduction, in, on or under land, of substances, preparations, organisms or micro-organisms. 'damage' means a measurable adverse change in the natural resource or measurable impairment of a natural resource service which may occur directly or indirectly".

obligation of restoration were introduced:

1.   Not any environmental impairment is to be restored, but only damage which is expressly mentioned in the Directive[178]; Air pollution was excluded, as air contamination sooner or later leads to depositions on the ground—acidification of the soil, fauna and flora damage etc. (Recital 4). Also, the most serious environmental accidents of the past—nuclear accidents and marine pollution by hydrocarbons from tanker accidents— were excluded from the Directive, with the argument that international conventions covered these aspects. However, the international conventions do not provide for restoration of the impaired environment; also the sums which are available under their system, are not sufficient.

    Damage caused by genetically modified products such as seeds, is also included, because the concept starts from the impaired environment, and the deliberate release of genetically modified organisms is expressly mentioned as one of the sources of pollution (Ann III, no.11);

2.   Diffuse pollution, that means pollution caused by a multiplicity of polluting sources is excluded. Indeed, this diffuse pollution is everywhere and it was considered that an inclusion of such pollution would overcharge the public authorities' budgets, all the more as recourse against a specific polluter would not be possible.

3.   The implementing legislation of Member States shall decide, whether polluters who comply with the conditions laid down in a permit shall be liable to compensate public authorities for the restoration of the environment or not.[179] Such a clause would practically introduce polluters' liability for negligence, as exceeding the conditions of a permit is normally due to a deliberate or negligent action.

4.   Member States shall also decide, whether they allow the defence for development risks which intend to limit economic operators' risk in areas of new technologies, in particular for damage caused by biotechnology products.[180]

5.   Finally, it is up to Member States to decide, whether they provide for compulsory insurance in the cases covered by the Directive or not (art.14). Member States were not able to agree on a solution for or against such compulsory insurance.

    Leaving aside the difference of opinions among Member States and the heavy opposition of economic operators to any liability system, the concept of   **4–60**

---

[178] Dir.2004/35 (fn.175, above) art.4(5): "This Directive shall only apply to environmental damage or to an imminent threat of such damage caused by pollution of a diffuse character, where it is possible to establish a causal link between the damage and the activities of individual operators."

[179] Dir.2004/35 (fn.175, above), art.8(4.a): "The Member States may allow the operator not to bear the cost of remedial actions taken pursuant to this Directive where he demonstrates that he was not at fault or negligent and that the environmental damage was caused by: (a) an emission or vent expressly authorised by, and fully in accordance with the conditions of, an authorisation conferred by or given under applicable national laws."

[180] Dir.2004/35 (fn.176, above), art.8(4.b): "The Member States may allow the operator not to bear the cost of remedial actions... where he proves... that the damage was caused by: (b) an emission or activity or any manner of using a product in the course of an activity which the operator demonstrates was not considered likely to cause environmental damage according to the state of scientific and technical knowledge at the time when the emission was released or the activity took place".

compensating for environmental damage seems too far removed from environmental needs. In short, the environment is sick, rather than suffering from specific punctual accidents, pollutions or catastrophes. The liability concept which stems from compensating for physical injury and was extended to economic loss, and later to damages for pain and suffering, only adapts with difficulties to the progressive deterioration, legalised contamination and the disappearance of species.

This is the reason why, until now, national environmental liability legislation had only limited success. The Directive's approach to set up a system which places the restoration of environmental damage in the centre, is a step in the right direction. The future will show whether this direction will be pursued; as neither the environment nor future generations have a lobby or a voice, realism rather than optimism with regard to the effective benefit to the environment—and this is, finally, the objective of environmental legislation—is appropriate.

The Directive enumerates in an annex III those operational activities, the operator of which may be held strictly liable, if they cause environmental damage. This annex lists a number of—mainly dangerous—activities which are regulated by EU directives and regulations. As the EU legislation covers in particular large installations, many small or medium-sized companies do not come under the scope of application of Directive 2004/35, unless they act negligently, as the Directive includes liability for negligent actions (art.3(1.b)).

The Directive does not cover oil pollution damage or damage caused by the transport of dangerous substances by sea or inland waterways which are in force in the Member State concerned (art.4(2) and annex IV) and does not cover nuclear damage either (art.4(4) and annex V).

The overall impression of the Directive is that it has a rather limited field of application. It more aims at the restoration of the environment after an industrial accident—with the exception of the most important cases, oil transport and nuclear accidents—than of restoring the damaged environment, despite the fact that the environment does not suffer mainly from accidents, but from the fact that it is sick. The Directive's actual application therefore risks being rather limited. The numerous exemptions, possibilities for Member States to provide for national different provisions and the absence of regulating the burden of proof—this works in favour of the polluter—make it a directive which does not lead to some sort of unified or harmonised system in the European Union.

4–61 There are a number of efforts at international level to introduce liability for environmental damage which, however, essentially concern traditional damage (physical damage and economic loss). These efforts concern in particular:

- A Protocol under the Basel Convention on the shipment of hazardous waste. This Protocol was elaborated in 1999–2000 and covers personal injury and economic loss caused by hazardous waste. The European Union adhered to the Basel Convention, but has not yet signed the Protocol.
- A Protocol, signed in Spring 2002 under two international conventions which deals with liability that is caused by industrial accidents in international watercourses. The Protocol covers traditional damage and, in supplement, the restoration of the impaired environment.

The European Union did not sign the Protocol, as it is not yet clear, how the dividing line between this Protocol and Directive 2004/35 on environmental liability will be drawn.

● The Cartagena Protocol on Biological Safety[181] which provides in art.27 that a Protocol shall be elaborated on liability for damage caused in particular by genetically modified products. Preparatory work has started, though the international efforts to reach a consensus on a Protocol are hampered by opposition from the United States which are not in favour of such a Protocol.

6. Taxes and charges

Already, the first environmental action programme of 1973 pleaded in favour of economic instruments in the shaping of environmental policy.[182] Subsequent programmes repeated the usefulness of developing economic instruments and the fourth environmental action programme was the first to mention that, besides legal "command and control" provisions taxes, charges and tradable pollution permits could also be an appropriate instrument for improving or preserving the quality of the environment.[183] In order to combat climate change, the Commission submitted a proposal in 1991 for the EC-wide introduction of a combined CO_2 energy tax.[184] The proposal was based on art.93 and 175(2) EC (now arts 113 and 192(2) TFEU), which both require unanimous decisions in Council. This unanimity could not be reached since a number of Member States, in particular the United Kingdom, opposed for principal reasons the adoption of provisions on taxes and charges at EU level. The Commission therefore amended its proposal in the sense that Member States remained free to decide whether they wanted to introduce a CO_2 energy tax; where they so decided, they had to comply with certain conditions fixed in the proposal.[185] This proposal, which again required unanimous adoption in Council, was not adopted either. It is now outdated, though reflections on the introduction of fiscal measures at EU level continue in the context of the discussions on climate change.

4–62

In view of the obvious difficulties linked with this proposal, the Commission has not made other proposals for the introduction of an eco-tax. Scattered in directives or regulations there exist references that taxes or charges will be fixed at EU level[186]; however, such provisions neither introduce such taxes nor do they

---

[181] Protocol on Biological Safety [2002] OJ L201/50.

[182] First environmental action programme [1973] OJ C112/1, p.31: "careful analysis should be made of the economic instruments which can be used in the context of an environmental policy, their various functions, the advantages and drawbacks of using them, their relative effectiveness with regard to the objectives in view and their compatibility with the rules of cost allocation."

[183] Fourth environmental action programme [1987] OJ C328/1, no.2.5.1.

[184] [1992] OJ C196/1.

[185] Commission, COM(95) 172.

[186] See, e.g. Dir.94/62 on packaging and packaging waste [1994] OJ L365/10, art.15: "Acting on the basis of the relevant provisions of the Treaty, the Council adopts economic instruments to promote the implementation of the objectives set by this Directive. In the absence of such measures, the Member States may, in accordance with the principles governing Community environmental policy, inter alia, the polluter-pays principle, and the obligations arising out of the Treaty, adopt measures to implement those objectives."

have any other legal effect or restrict the possibility of Member States to decide
on their own whether to introduce eco-taxes or charges.

4–63   Taxes and charges play a considerable role in the environmental policy of
Member States. Since they aim to influence, via pricing, the economic behaviour
of economic operators and others, their competitiveness and market position, the
European Union cannot remain unconcerned about developments at national
level. Therefore, EU measures with regard to national eco-taxes try to limit their
use, in order to avoid their influence on the circulation of goods.

The most obvious example of attempts to limit national tax initiatives are the
provisions in the car sector. When the catalytic converter for cars was introduced,
the Netherlands and Germany in particular considered encouraging the
introduction of cars with catalytic converters by means of tax incentives. The
objection of other Member States that were afraid of a competitive disadvantage
finally led to a provision which has since become standard for car emission
directives[187]:

> "Member States may make provision for tax incentives for the vehicles covered in this
> Directive. Such incentives shall meet the provisions of the Treaty as well as the following
> conditions:
> they shall apply to all domestic car production and to vehicles imported for marketing in a
> Member State and fitted with the equipment allowing the European standards to be met in 1992 to
> be satisfied ahead of time; they shall cease upon the date set in Article 2(3) for the compulsory
> entry into force of the emission values for new vehicles;
> they shall be of value, for each type of vehicle, substantially lower than the actual cost of the
> equipment fitted to meet the values set and of its fitting on the vehicle."

In 2005, the Commission made a proposal for a directive to restructure tax
bases of the annual circulation and registration taxes in order to make passenger
taxes more CO_2-efficient.[188] This proposal which is based on art.113 TFEU and
therefore requires unanimity for its adoption, would abolish the registration tax
for cars and increase instead the circulation taxes; these would take into account
the CO_2-emissions from cars. By the end of 2010, the Council had not yet
adopted this proposal.

4–64   Another example for the interplay between national and EU rules is that of
Directive 2003/96 which replaced Directive 92/81.[189] This Directive, based on
art.113 TFEU, introduced a minimum rate of taxation on electricity and energy
products. The minimum rates are differentiated according to the use of the
products. As the Directive required unanimity, it contains a long list of
possibilities for Member States to apply reduced rates for specific uses; and
Member States may exempt electricity produced from alternative energies
altogether. The Directive prolonged the possibility for 11 of the then 15 Member
States—except Sweden Denmark, Greece and Netherlands—to apply reduced tax
rates for the use of waste oils in production installations such as cement kilns or
steel or power plants, though such a practice openly contradicted the
requirements of Directive 75/439[190] which gave priority to the regeneration of

---

[187] Text from Dir.89/458 [1989] OJ L226/1 art.3.
[188] Commission, COM(2005) 261.
[189] Dir.2003/96 restructuring the Community framework for the taxation of energy products and
electricity [2003] OJ L283/51, replacing Dir.92/81 on the harmonisation of the structures of excise
duties on mineral oils [1992] OJ L316/12.
[190] Dir.75/439 on used oils [1975] OJ L194/31; amended by Dir.87/101 [1987] OJ L42/43.

waste oils. However, in the past, the Commission did not take action against the national fiscal practices. In order to ensure consistency of EU law, Directive 75/439 was repealed altogether—to the advantage of economic operators, but to the detriment of the environment.[191]

A Commission communication of 1997 tried to determine generally the limits for "environmental taxes and charges in the Single Market".[192] Recommendations for optimising environmental taxes and charges are not given, probably because there are also diverging opinions within the Commission.

---

[191] Dir. 2008/98 on waste [2008] OJ L312/3.

[192] Commission, COM (97) 9; see also Commission, Database on environmental taxes in the European Union Member States, plus Norway and Switzerland. Evaluation of environmental effects of environmental taxes (Luxembourg, 1999); European Environmental Agency, Recent developments in the use of eco-taxes in the European Union (Copenhagen, 2000); European Environment Agency, Market-based instruments for environmental policy in Europe. Technical Report 8/2005 (Copenhagen 2006).

CHAPTER 5

Biodiversity and Nature Conservation

Nature conservation measures within the European Union were, until about the mid-1980s, influenced by the fact that the majority of Member States were of the opinion that nature protection came in their exclusive competence. Since environmental legal acts had, prior to 1987, to be taken unanimously, this attitude considerably influenced the number and the content of the measures adopted; indeed, Member States favoured the negotiation and conclusion of international conventions; another consequence was that all nature conservation measures that the Council was ready to adopt were based on art.308 EC (now art.352 TFEU).

5–01

When arts 191 to 193 were introduced into the Treaty to give an explicit environmental competence to the European Union which included nature conservation, matters only gradually changed. The main reasons were that Member States were very keen to keep their responsibility in land use planning matters, which they saw at least partly threatened by EU nature conservation measures; that transfrontier management of wildlife and nature protection was hardly practised; and that national and EU enforcement mechanisms for nature conservation measures were structurally too weak to properly enforce the different provisions, let alone initiating new measures.

1. General measures

International conventions

The European Union adhered to a number of international conventions which aim, as a general objective, at the protection of nature or of parts of it. For the majority of these conventions, however, the European Union did not take measures of secondary EU law to implement these international conventions. In law, an international convention to which the European Union adheres becomes part of European Union (art.216(2) TFEU)—at least, where the area covered by the convention comes into EU competence—and is thus also binding for those Member States which have not ratified the international convention.[1] As regards the hierarchy, the provisions of the convention rank between primary and secondary EU law, which means that they prevail on EU regulations and directives. The application and enforcement of the provisions of the convention is shared between the European Union and its Member States, according to their internal repartition of competence.

5–02

---

[1] See Court of Justice, *Pêcheurs de l'Etang de Berre* (C–213/03) [2004] E.C.R. I–7357; *Commission v France* (C–239/03) [2004] E.C.R. I–9325.

In practice, the application and enforcement of international environmental conventions to which the European Union adhered, without adopting a regulation or directive to implement its provisions in EU law, does not take place as far as the EU level is concerned; in particular, the Commission does not "ensure" that the legal provisions of the international measure are applied, as art.17 TEU requires. Rather, the Commission leaves it to Member States to apply the provisions of the convention. As a consequence, the decision to adhere to the international environmental convention is marked by the participation of the European Union, but as such does not bring an added value to the protection of the environment.

5–03   The following environmental conventions belong to this group of conventions on nature conservation:

1.   Bonn Convention of June 23, 1979 on the conservation of migratory species of wild animals[2];
2.   Rio de Janeiro Convention of June 5, 1992 on biological diversity[3];
3.   Salzburg Convention of November 7, 1991 on the protection of the Alps[4];
4.   Canberra Convention of May 20, 1980 on the conservation of Antarctic marine living resources[5];
5.   Paris Convention of June 17, 1994 on combating desertification.[6]

On biological diversity, the European Union adopted a communication on an EU strategy for biological diversity[7] which contained four areas of activity: on conservation and sustainable use of biological diversity, on the sharing of genetic resources, on research, control and exchange of information and on education, training and sensitivisation. No specific legislative measures were announced; instead, the objectives of the strategy were to be reached within the context of the different ongoing EU activities.[8] Decision 1600/2002 on the Sixth Environment Action Programme laid down, in art.6(1), the objective of "halting biodiversity decline with the aim to reach this objective by 2010". In 2006, the Commission made a communication suggesting measures to reach the 2010 deadline.[9] It identified a number of possible measures which could be taken, but limited itself largely to appeal to Member States to integrate biodiversity concerns into mainstream EU and national policies. When it turned out, in 2010, that the loss of biodiversity was not stopped, the Commission adopted a new communication, on the basis of which the Council concluded that by 2050 the EU biodiversity and the ecosystem services it provides should be protected and that, by 2020, the

---

[2] Dec.82/461 [1982] OJ L210/10.
[3] Dec.93/626 [1993] OJ L309/1.
[4] Dec.96/191 [1996] OJ L61/31.
[5] Dec.81/691 [1981] OJ L252/26.
[6] Dec.98/216 [1998] OJ L83/1.
[7] Commission, COM (98) 42.
[8] See also Commission, First report on the implementation of the Convention on biological diversity by the European Community (Luxembourg, 1998) European Parliament, Res. of October 20, 1998 on biodiversity [1998] OJ C341/41.
[9] Commission, COM(2006) 216; see also COM(2010) 548 concerning the assessment of implementing this Action Plan.

biodiversity loss should be halted.[10] The announced biodiversity strategy of the European Union was, until the end of 2010, not published.

The Commission recognised that more needed to be done to integrate the biodiversity considerations into other sectoral policies, to make available the necessary funding and to fill the existing policy gaps.[11] It did not consider, though, suggesting a framework directive on biodiversity which could, among other things, transpose the requirements of the conventions mentioned above into EU law, incorporate the provisions of the Council of Europe Landscape Convention, make available the necessary funding and put into binding legal rules the biodiversity targets which had been agreed—included by the European Union and its 27 Member States—in Nagoya/Japan in October 2010, following in this the precise, binding targets on greenhouse gas emission reductions of the Kyoto Protocol.

Forestry is not part of the Common Agricultural Policy, as trees and forestry products do not normally come under the notion of "agricultural products". When the Council tried to integrate forestry measures into the Common Agricultural Policy by basing such measures on art.43 TFEU, the Court of Justice opposed this and declared the measures in question to be part of the EU environmental policy.[12]   **5–04**

In 1998, the Commission submitted a non-binding forest strategy which got a prudent welcome from the Council which underlined the primary responsibility of Member states on forest management.[13] No concrete measures were suggested or decided. The sixth EU environmental action programme announced a number of general actions on forestry, though again in rather general terms.[14] In 2003 a regulation was adopted which brought two earlier regulations on the protection of forests against air pollution and against fire[15] into one single instrument, based on art.192 TFEU.[16] However, already four years later, this Regulation was repealed, and measures for protection forests were integrated into the LIFE regulation.[17]

In 2005, a regulation on the establishment of a Forest Law Enforcement, Governance and Trade (FLEGT) licensing scheme for imports of timber into the was adopted.[18] The Regulation provided that the conclusion of non-binding, voluntary agreements with partner countries identified which "place a legally binding obligation on a partner country to implement the licensing scheme". Under such agreements, only the import of legally harvested timber into the European Union will be allowed. The Regulation tries to progressively reduce the import of illegally logged timber, as at present, it is estimated that between one

---

[10] See Commission, COM(2010) 4 and Council, conclusions of 15 March 2010, Doc.7536/10 of 16 March 2010. See also Commission, The 2010 assessment of implementing the EU Biodiversity Action Plan (2010) 548 and SEC 82010 1164.

[11] Commission, COM(2010) 548, p.14.

[12] Court of Justice, *European Parliament v Council* (Joined Cases C–164/97 and C–165/97) [1999] E.C.R. I–1139.

[13] Commission COM(98) 649; Council Res. of December 15, 1998 [1999] OJ C56/1.

[14] Dec.1600/2002 [2002] OJ L242/1; art.6(h).

[15] Reg.3528/86 [1986] OJ L326/2 (air pollution); Reg.2158/92 [1992] OJ 217/3 (fire).

[16] Reg.2152/2003 concerning monitoring of forests and environmental interactions in the Community [Forest Focus] [2003] OJ L324/1.

[17] Reg.614/2007 concerning the Financial Instrument for the Environment (LIFE+) [2007] OJ L149/1.

[18] Reg.2173/2005 on the establishment of a FLEGT licensing scheme for imports of timber into the European Community [2005] OJ L347/1.

third and half of tropical timber imports into the European Union stems from illegal logging. However, whether bilateral agreements—by the end of 2010, such agreements were concluded with Ghana and the Republic of Congo[19]—can be enforced in the wood exporting country, is not clear; also, an export of Malaysian timber to China which then produces wood products and exports them to Europe, would not be reached by such agreements. In 2010, the Union adopted a Regulation to prohibit the placing on the EU market of illegally harvested timber and timber products.[20] The operators have to apply due diligence measures in order to ensure that timber and timber products come from legally harvested wood. The Regulation will become fully operational in 2013; it considers that timber in countries with which a voluntary agreement had been concluded, was legally harvested.

Furthermore, the Commission tried on several occasions to promote forest protection measures,[21] though with limited success so far, as the interests of the, mainly private, forest owners and those of the protection of the environment do not always coincide.

Land use and soil protection

5–05   There are no general EU measures which directly concern soil protection, although agricultural measures generally may have an impact on land use.[22] A regulation from 1992, several times amended and replaced[23] provided for financial assistance to farmers who voluntarily agree to substantially reduce the use of fertilisers or pesticides, to use organic farming methods, to set aside land—for at least 20 years—for environmental purposes, or to pursue other ways of environmentally acceptable farming practices. At present, more than 20 per cent of EU farmland is covered by such measures, with about 1.5 million agreements.

In the sixth environmental action programme, the Commission considered measures on land use to be necessary in the areas of habitat protection, management of the countryside, of landscapes, the development of forests and soil protection.[24] Measures on a sound use of pesticides were presented in the form of a communication (thematic strategy) in 2006.[25] It suggests in particular that Member States establish national plans to reduce the risks of pollution from pesticides. In environmentally friendly areas, the use of pesticides is to be limited and other accompanying measures are proposed. In 2009, a directive was adopted in this sense which obliged Member States to adopt national action plans for the

---

[19] Agreement with Ghana [2010] OJ L70/3; Agreement with the Republic of Congo [2010] OJ L271/1.

[20] Reg.895/2010 laying down the obligations of operators which place timber and timber products on the market [2010] OJ L295/23.

[21] See, for example, Commission COM(2006) 302 (forest action plan); COM(2008) 645 (forest and climate change); COM(2010) 66 (Green Paper on forest protection).

[22] The Commission's Communication on sustainable agriculture [1999] OJ C173/2 indicates that some 156 million hectares of soil are suffering from water or wind erosion and that soil erosion is increasing (pt 2.3).

[23] See last Reg.1782/2003 [2003] OJ L270/1.

[24] European Environmental Agency, *Environmental Signals 2001* (Copenhagen, 2001) p.11.

[25] Commission, Communication on a Thematic Strategy on the sustainable use of pesticides, COM(2006) 372.

use of plant protection products and to set up targets for the reduction of the use of such products; some accompanying measures also aim to progressively reduce the use of such products.[26]

The use of some pesticides throughout the European Union had already been forbidden throughout the European Commission.[27] In 2009, a new regulation[28] was adopted concerning the placing of plant protection products on the market which repealed, among other things, Directive 79/117. Plant protection products need a national authorisation in order to be put on the market (art.28); the withdrawal of the authorisation is also in the hands of the Member States (art.44).

In 1995, the Commission launched an Integrated Coastal Zone management demonstration programme.[29] This programme, however, only explored ways for an effective management; it did not affect decisions on land use, which are taken at the level of Member States. In 2001 it was followed by a Recommendation with a similar limitation.[30]

In 2006, the Commission presented, in the form of a communication, a thematic strategy on the urban environment[31] which has the ambitious aim of improving the environmental performance and quality of urban areas, where three quarters of the EU population live. The communication provides for integrated management of urban areas, sustainable transport, the exchange of best practices and similar measures. It is doubtful whether it will have any significant impact on the urban environment in Member States.

It is clear that the progressive ban on uncontrolled discharges to rivers, lakes or coastal waters also contributes to the protection of land. The siting of industrial installations or infrastructure measures is decided by Member States at their discretion; eventual negative impacts on the environment, demonstrated for instance by an environmental impact assessment,[32] do not restrict this right.

5–06

Directive 2009/147[33] requires Member States to classify the most suitable territories as special protection areas for some particularly threatened bird species. Within these areas, they shall take "appropriate steps to avoid pollution or deterioration of habitats or any disturbances affecting the birds, in so far as these would be significant".[34] In individual cases, this can lead to restrictions of the use of land: in case C–355/90,[35] the construction of roads and other infrastructure measure within a birds' habitat was declared incompatible with art.4 of Directive 2009/147; that specific habitat had not been classified under

---

[26] Dir.2009/128 establishing a framework for Community action to achieve the sustainable use of pesticides [2009] OJ L309/71.

[27] Dir.79/117 prohibiting the placing on the market and use of plant protection products containing certain active substances [1979] OJ L33/36; this Directive had been updated at regular intervals.

[28] Reg.1107/2009 concerning the placing of plant protection products on the market [2009] OJ L309/1; see also para.6–39ss, below.

[29] Commission, COM(95) 511; progress report COM(97) 744.

[30] Rec.2002/413 concerning the implementation of Integrated Coastal Zone Management in Europe [2002] OJ L148/24.

[31] Rec.2002/413 concerning the implementation of Integrated Coastal Zone Management in Europe [2002] OJ L148/24.

[32] See more closely para.4–10, above.

[33] Dir.2009/147 on the conservation of wild birds [2010] OJ L20/7; this Directive replaced Dir.79/409 [1979] OJ L103/1.

[34] Div. 2009/147, art.4(4).

[35] *Commission v Spain* (C–355/90) [1993] E.C.R. I–4221 (*Santona*).

that provision even though it should have been. In case C–44/95,[36] the United Kingdom had classified a specific area under art.4, but had exempted a specific part, since it considered that at a later stage this part could be needed for the extension of a nearby commercial port. The Court of Justice held that this was not allowed, although, obviously, it did not commit itself on the compatibility of the port extension with the designation of the habitat. A similar provision to art.4 of Directive 2009/147 was introduced in an article of Directive 92/43.[37] However, in reaction to Court jurisdiction, which was considered too restrictive, a provision was inserted that despite its negative effects a measure could be carried out "for imperative reasons of overriding public interest".[38] This provision is likely to facilitate considerably the carrying out of measures even in a classified habitat, in particular in the light of the Commission's wide interpretation of art.6(4).[39]

As regards areas other than habitats, Directive 92/43 invites Member states to "encourage the management of features of the landscape which are of major importance for wild fauna and flora" (art.10); the Directive mentions rivers, field boundaries, ponds and small woods as examples. This invitation is not more than a recommendation to Member States. The European Union has not yet taken any steps to adhere to the Council of Europe Convention on Landscapes which was signed in Florence in 2000.

5–07   Directive 2008/98[40] prohibits the abandonment, dumping or uncontrolled management of waste. Directive 86/278[41] prohibits, under certain conditions, the use of sewage sludge on certain land, in particular where there are overly high concentrations of heavy metals, on grassland or forage crops, on soil in which fruit and vegetable crops are growing and on ground for the cultivation of fruit and vegetable crops which are normally eaten raw.

5–08   There are no specific EU provisions for protecting the soil, in particular against soil erosion although EU funds may assist national measures. The same can be said with regard to questions of desertification. The sixth environmental action programme announced the elaboration of a thematic strategy—thus a sectoral action programme—on soil protection.[42] A first communication, identifying the main problems of the soil within the Member States was published in 2002.[43] The thematic strategy, in the form of a Commission communication and a proposal for a directive on soil protection, was made in

---

[36] *RSPB* (C–44/95) [1996] E.C.R. I–3805 (*Lappel-Bank*); see also *Commission v Germany* (C–57/89) [1991] E.C.R. I–883 (*Leybucht*).

[37] Dir.92/43 on the conservation of natural habitats and of wild fauna and flora [1992] OJ L206/7 art.6(2): "Member States shall take appropriate steps to avoid, in the special areas of conservation, the deterioration of natural habitats and the habitats of species as well as disturbance of the species for which the areas have been designated, in so far as such disturbance could be significant in relation to the objectives of this Directive."

[38] Div. 92/43., art.6(4).

[39] Commission, Opinion of April 27, 1995 [1995] OJ C178/3; Opinion of December 18, 1995 [1996] OJ L6/14.

[40] Dir.2008/98 on waste, [2008] OJ L312/3, art.36. This Directive repealed Dir.75/442 and its later version (Dir.2006/12).

[41] Dir.86/278 on the protection of the environment and in particular of the soil, when sewage sludge is used in agriculture [1986] OJ L181/6, arts 5 and 7.

[42] Dec.1600/2002 (fn.14, above) art.7(2c).

[43] Commission, Towards a Thematic Strategy for Soil Protection, COM(2002) 179.

September 2006[44]; its presentation was delayed, because the industry administration within the Commission tried to water down the content of the proposals as far as possible.

The proposal for a directive was based on art.192(1) TFEU, as the Commission considered that it deals with the protection of the environment and not with land use. It identified as the following eight main aspects of the soil degradation process: erosion, organic matter decline, contamination, salinisation, compaction, soil biodiversity loss, sealing, landslides and flooding. With the exception of flooding, for which the Commission had proposed a separate directive, it suggests that Member States identify areas at risk and draw up national programmes. Of considerable interest was also the proposal to establish a national inventory of contaminated sites and to progressively start remediation work.

The Council discussed this proposal at several occasions. However, a blocking minority of Member States which included Germany, France and the United Kingdom, opposed any legislative measure on soil protection at EU level, for reasons of subsidiarity. There are no signs that this attitude will change in a foreseeable future, though it is not contested that EU regional, agricultural and transport policies contribute to the problems of soil in practically all Member States.

Any land use measure by the European Union would have to be adopted by virtue of art.192(2) TFEU. In legal texts, it is sometimes argued that this provision also applies to amendments of Directives 2009/147 and 92/43.[45] However, both Directives concern general measures which give a specific status to land, but do not directly deal with the use of the land. Indeed, land use is not outlined in a specific way by either directive. The correct legal basis is therefore art.192(1) TFEU.

Habitat protection

The Commission stated in 2001 that: **5–09**

> "Pollution from transport, industry and agriculture continues to threaten natural areas and wildlife... Pressure is coming from the changes in how we utilise land... The building of new roads, houses and other developments is fragmenting the countryside into ever-smaller areas, making it harder for species to survive. All the trends suggest that the loss of open countryside to development will continue in the future... As habitats are degraded or lost, wildlife is frequently under pressure or even the threat of extinction.[46]"

Birds' habitats

In 1979 the Union adopted Directive 79/409 on the conservation of wild birds,[47]   **5–10**
following considerable public pressure in favour of such a measure; in 2009, this directive was renumbered as Directive 2009/147.[48] That Directive aimed at comprehensive protection of all wild birds within the European Union and

---

[44] Commission, COM(2006) 232.
[45] See para.2–89, above.
[46] Commission (fn.21, above) pt 4.1.
[47] Dir.79/409 (fn.33, above).
[48] Dir.2009/147 (fn.33, above).

outlined detailed provisions, in particular on hunting, capturing and trading of birds. Member States were required to take necessary measures "to preserve, maintain or re-establish a sufficient diversity and area of habitats" for all birds (art.3) by the creation of protected areas or biotopes and the upkeep, management and re-establishment of biotopes. For particularly threatened bird species, listed in an annex I, they were asked to classify habitats as special protection areas for the conservation of these species (art.4). The different designated habitats were to form a "coherent whole",[49] which met the protection requirements for birds all over the European Union. Inside these special protection areas, appropriate conservation measures had to be taken.

5–11   The provision of art.3 has, as far as can be seen, not led to any significant change at national level; the provision was scarcely monitored by the Commission.[50] As regards art.4, designation of special protection areas advanced only slowly. While the Directive required the classification to be completed by 1981, the following actual development took place[51]:

1986: 309 areas (10 Member States);
1990: 450 areas (12 Member States);
1995: 1,247 areas covering 71, 679 km² (15 Member States);
1998: 1,842 areas;
2002: 2,885 areas covering 232,062 km²;
2006: 4,523 areas covering 444,108 km² (25 Member States);
2010: 5,315 areas covering 593.486 km² (27 Member States).

The Commission stated in 1991 and in 1998 that only Denmark and Belgium[52] had fully complied with their obligations under art.4 of Directive 2009/147.[53] In 2002, the Netherlands was added as the third Member State,[54] a remarkable change that had obviously been induced by a Court judgment against the Netherlands.[55] In 2010, the Commission indicated that the designation of areas was "largely completed" for Belgium, Denmark, Germany, Estonia, France, Italy, Luxemburg, Malta, Netherlands, Poland, Portugal and Finland.[56] Overall, 9.6 per cent of the EU (terrestrial) territory is protected under art.4 of Directive 2009/147, with variations: the lowest percentage is noted in Malta (2.4 per cent),

---

[49] Div. 2009/147, art.4(3); the French and German texts talk of a "coherent network", which is certainly more precise.

[50] See Commission, *Information sur l'application de la directive 79/409/CEE* (Brussels and Luxembourg, 1990), pp.35 et seq.; Report on the application of Directive 79/409 (1993–1995), COM(2000) 180 of March 29, 2000; Report on the application of Directive 79/409 (1996–1998), COM (2002) 146 of March 25, 2002.

[51] Commission, Information (n.50) p.46; Commission, Second report on the application of Directive 79/409 on the conservation of wild birds, COM(93) 572 of November 24, 1993, p.115; Commission (DG ENV) *Natura 2000* newsletter, May 1996, p.6; *Natura 2000* newsletter, February 1998, p.6; November 1998, p.6; May 2002 p.8; European Topic Centre on Biological Diversity, Nature 2000 Database, June 2006.

[52] As regards Belgium, see however Court of Justice, *Commission v Belgium* (C–415/01) [2003] E.C.R. I–2187, where the Belgian measures were considered as not being legally precise enough.

[53] Commission, Eighth report on monitoring application of Community law (1990) [1991] OJ C338/1, p.220; Commission, *Natura 2000* newsletter, February 1998, p.6.

[54] Commission, *Natura 2000* newsletter, May 2002, p.8.

[55] Court of Justice, *Commission v Netherlands* (C–3/96) [1998] E.C.R. I–3031; WWF, *Spotlight on Natura 2000 No.4/1997*, p.8 reports that the Commission stated during the public hearing before the Court that proceedings had been initiated against the Netherlands, because these had not, contrary to other Member States, "shown any interest in settling the matter bilaterally".

[56] Commission, Natura 2000 Newsletter, June 2010, p.6.

Ireland (2.9 per cent), Lithuania (5.4 per cent), United Kingdom (5.8 per cent) and Denmark (5.9 per cent); the highest percentage is found in Slovakia (25.2 per cent), Slovenia (23 per cent), Spain (18.2 per cent), Hungary (14.5 per cent) and Cyprus (13.4 per cent).

In a number of cases, the Commission tried to ensure through legal proceedings the habitat status of specific zones where it was of the opinion that Member States had not fully complied with their obligations. These procedures are rather time-consuming, in particular where the dispute has to be decided by the Court of Justice.[57] The Commission announced in 2002 that it was developing a strategy to initiate general infringement proceedings, rather that beginning proceedings on a site-by-site basis.[58] This strategy has not led to tangible results.

Generally, however, not much can be said on the practical application of the directive, as the Commission is remarkably—and unacceptably so—discrete in reporting on Member States' failure to transpose or actually apply the Directive's provisions. Its implementation reports became more and more vague and general over the years, and the last one of 2006, mentioned above, does not report on any omission or infringement procedure at all, though it is known that a number of cases are pending before the Court of Justice. The Commission limits itself to suggest that accelerated efforts are necessary in order to make the Directive fully operational. The Commission's annual report on monitoring EC law limits itself to indicate those cases which the Commission has brought to the Court or which the Court decided. The statement that more efforts are needed is, 30 years after the entry into effect of the Directive and as a means to inform and interest the public on the Directive's application, a poor one; it resembles more a non-information.

Fauna and flora habitats

Habitats are also protected by virtue of the provisions of Directive 92/43.[59] This Directive protects 192 different types of habitats of particular ecological value which are listed in an annex I; furthermore, it requires that habitats for those fauna and flora species which are listed in an annex II be designated by Member States. The procedure of designating these habitats is slightly different from that of Directive 2009/147. First of all, Member States have to establish national lists of sites which are important for the conservation of habitat types or fauna or flora species; where the Commission disagrees, the matter is finally decided by a unanimous Council decision. Out of these national lists, the Commission, in agreement with the Member State concerned, establishes a list of sites of EU importance. Member States shall then, within six years, designate the sites on this

5–12

[57] See, e.g. *Commission v Germany* (C–57/89) [1991] E.C.R. I–883; (C–355/90) (fn.26, above); *RSPB* (C–44/ 95) [1996] E.C.R. I–3805; *Commission v France* (C–166/97) [1999] E.C.R. I–1719; *Commission v France* (C–96/98) [1999] E.C.R. I–8531; *Commission v France* (C–374/98) [2000] E.C.R. I–10799.
[58] Commission, 19th Report on monitoring application of Community law (2001), COM (2002) 324, no.2.8.6.
[59] Dir.92/43 (fn.37, above); Commission proposal [1988] OJ C247/3; European Parliament Opinion [1991] OJ C75/12; Economic and Social Committee Opinion [1991] OJ C31/25.

list as Special Area of Conservation, which form, all together, "a coherent European ecological network" or Natura 2000.[60]

By the end of 1997, Belgium, Germany, Greece, France and Finland had not even transposed the Directive into national law. This transposition has taken place in the meantime, and the emphasis has concentrated, over the last years, to see the provisions of the Directive completely and correctly transposed and effectively applied.

The national lists had to be drawn up by June 1995. In April 1996, five Member States had transmitted complete national lists, two others partial lists. In 1999, the Commission warned Member States that if they did not transmit adequate lists for the setting up of the Natura 2000 network, the Commission might not be able to evaluate and co-finance plans and programmes under the Structural Funds; accordingly, it might not be able to attribute the corresponding financial means to Member States.[61] Though this letter raised an outcry in particular in Germany, together with a number of Court judgments it had the effect that the lists of sites under art.6 of Directive 92/43 arrived more regularly. In particular the German *Länder* abandoned their far-reaching opposition to the Directive.

By the end of 2010, the Commission had published EU lists for the bio-geographical areas of Macaronesia (Azores, Madeira and Canary Islands), Alpine (mountain), Continental, Atlantic, Boreal, Mediterranean, Steppic, Pannonian and Black Sea regions.[62] Overall, Member States designated, by June 2010, 22.5290 areas, covering 719.015 km², 12.2 per cent of their terrestrial area.[63] The designations by Belgium, Denmark, Germany Greece, Italy, Malta, Netherlands and Portugal were "largely complete". No Member State had yet proceeded to the definite classification of "special areas of conservation" at national level.

The largest part of the terrestrial area was designated by Slovenia (31.4 per cent), Spain (22.6 per cent), Portugal (17.4 per cent), Greece (16.45 per cent) and Estonia (15.9 per cent); the smallest parts was designated by Poland (4.2 per cent), United Kingdom (6.5 per cent), Denmark (7.4 per cent), France (7.9 per cent) and Cyprus (8 per cent). It should be noted that the designation of a habitat does not say anything about the actual conservation measures which are applied.

5–13   One of the main reasons for the considerable delay in the setting up of national lists was the provision of art.6(2) of Directive 92/43, which requested Member States to avoid:

---

[60] The special protection areas classified under Dir.2009/147 are also included in this network, see arts 6 and 7 of Dir.92/43 (fn.37, above).

[61] *Commission v Greece* (C–329/96) [1997] E.C.R. I–3749; *Commission v Germany* (C–83/97) [1997] E.C.R. I–7191 and Commission, Monitoring application of Community law—15th report (1997) [1998] OJ C250/1, p.178.

[62] Commission, Decisions 2008/966 (Steppic region), [2008] OJ L344/117; 2009/90 (Pannonian region), [2009] OJ L43/1; 2009/92 (Black Sea region) [2009] OJ L43/59; 2009/1001 (2nd list Macaronesian region) [2009] OJ L344/46; 2010/42 (3rd list Alpine region), [2010] OJ L30/1; 2010/43 (3rd list Atlantic region) [2010] OJ L30/43; 2010/44 (3rd list Continental region) [2010] OJ L30/120; 2010/45 (3rd list Mediterranean region) [2010] OJ L30/322; 2010/46 (3rd list Boreal region) [2010] OJ L30/403.

[63] As there might be an overlapping with the percentages which were given for bird areas, these figures may not be accumulated with those given in para.5–11, above.

"the deterioration of natural habitats and the habitats of species as well as disturbance of the species for which the areas have been designated, in so far as such disturbance could be significant in relation to the objectives of this Directive."

Although this provision was completed by the abovementioned provision of art.6(4) and although the Commission decisions even showed a wide interpretation of this exemption, there was considerable concern at local level in many Member States that, on a site which would come under Directive 92/43, economic or leisure activities would severely be restricted. Under pressure from hunters, fishermen, farmers and other groups, France went even so far, in the summer of 1996, as to freeze its work on a national list for several months, arguing that it was neither clear who would finance the managing of the habitats,[64] nor exactly what activities would be forbidden within a habitat; some months later, France abandoned this attitude again.

The question of what is allowed and what is not allowed in a designated habitat is one of the most intricate ones. (Bird) hunting in a habitat is often accepted—although heavily contested by environmental organisations. Other, more relevant economic measures such as irrigation, urbanisation and road construction are often undertaken within habitats without systematic monitoring by local, regional, national or EU authorities. Generally, economic development prevails over conservation, and cases where the development of a project was stopped because of the existence of a habitat or a threatened species, are extremely rare in the European Union. The Commission attempted twice to have a rule adopted that all projects listed in annex II of the environmental impact assessment Directive[65] should, before development consent is given, be preceded by an environmental impact assessment; however, the Council twice rejected this approach.[66] Directive 2001/42 now provides that any plan—though not a project!—which might significantly affect a designated natural habitat or a bird habitat, must be preceded by an environment impact assessment.

The dilemma is that, on the one hand, it is hardly possible to transform designated habitats into nature museums, where no change may take place; this is the reason why local people or authorities so often oppose designation of a habitat. On the other hand, the Commission itself[67] stated that almost everywhere in Western Europe habitats and nature protection sites are shrinking slowly, but dramatically, due to road and other infrastructure construction, urbanisation, intensive farming activity, irrigation and holiday and leisure activities.[68]

5–14

So far, there are only two implementation reports, which are of limited informative value as regards the legal questions of transposition and application of Directive 92/43.[69] The Commission shows a growing disinterest in the

---

[64] Commission, Monitoring the application of Community law, 17th report (1999), p.53.

[65] Dir.85/337 on the assessment of the effects of certain public and private projects on the environment [1985] OJ L175/40.

[66] Commission, proposal for Dir.92/43 [1988] OJ C247/7, art.10; proposal for Dir.97/11 [1994] OJ C130/8; the Council's decision is found in Dir.97/11 [1997] OJ L37/5, recital 10.

[67] Commission, Communication on rational use and conservation of wetlands, COM (95) 189 of May 29, 1995.

[68] Perhaps the most eloquent example is the French habitat Camargue which lost, between 1942 and 1984, about 1,000 hectares per year of its natural surface, see A. Tamisier, *Camargue, milieux et paysages évolution de 1942 à 1984* (Arles, 1992).

[69] Commission, COM(2003) 845 and COM(2009) 358.

practical application of the legislation to specific cases and concentrates on transposition and designation of habitats.

With all the delays and difficulties in designating habitats and conserving them, Directives 2009/147 and 92/43 constitute the first serious attempt in Western Europe to conserve nature protection sites. As such, they go far beyond what individual Member States had done at national level in this area. The experience of 30 years of application of Directive 2009/147, which has neither led to sufficient designation of habitats and adequate conservation measures nor generally stopped the shrinking of individual habitats, does not promote optimism. In Western Europe, which is a small area that is densely populated, that has great economic activity and an impressive transport infrastructure network, nature is in retreat because it conflicts with demographic and economic evolution. For this reason, in almost all cases, where economic interests in building a bridge, a port, an airport, a motorway or a new high-speed train clash with the environmental interests of preserving a habitat, the environmental interests lose. It is not likely that the application of Directive 92/43 will significantly change this situation, all the more as the Commission shows to neglect problems of specific, individual habitats.

5–15   Habitats of wild flora and fauna species are also protected under art.4 of the Berne Convention on the conservation of European wildlife and natural habitats of 1979, to which the Union had adhered by a decision of 1981.[70] However, as is explained above,[71] the Commission does not monitor the application of international conventions to which the European Union has adhered, but leaves their application entirely to Member States: an exception is only made in those cases where the European Union enacts legislation which transposes the convention requirements into Community environmental law. In those cases, the implementation of the transposing act is monitored under art.258 TFEU; indeed, the Commission justified the proposal for Directive 92/43 amongst others with the argument that it transposed the Berne Convention into EU law.

5–16   A specific problem is that of (habitats of) species which are protected under the Berne Convention, but not under Directives 2009/147 or 92/43; an example of this is the badger. Supposing a Member State were infringing the obligation adequately to protect the badger's habitat: would this constitute a breach of the European Union's obligations under the Convention? In my opinion, the European Union undertakes, by adhering to an international convention, to ensure that the convention is respected all over the EU territory. EU Member States are obliged, under art.4 TEU, to take all measures in order to allow the European Union to respect this obligation; such an obligation even exists where a Member State itself is not a contracting party of the Convention, and the Commission has the obligation to ensure, under art.17 TEU, that Member States fulfil their obligations.

---

[70] Dec.82/72, of December 3, 1981 [1982] OJ L38/1.
[71] See para.5–02, above.

Habitats for fish

Directives 78/659[72] tried to protect the habitats of fish. Member States were asked to designate fresh waters to support fish life. For these waters they had to establish programmes which had to ensure that the waters corresponded to specific quality requirements which were laid down in the Directive. A similar approach was followed by Directive 79/923 for shellfish.[73]

5–17

Both Directives completely failed to reach their objective.[74] The main reasons were that Member States were also allowed to designate waters which already complied with the requirements so that no clean-up programme was necessary. Furthermore, the number of waters which were to be designated was not fixed which led several Member States to designate only very few waters; a decision by the Court of Justice in 1988, stipulating that Member States had to designate and clean up waters throughout their territory,[75] did not lead to substantial changes. Finally, the Commission did not monitor the application of these directives closely. Italy was condemned in 1988 and again in 1994, because it had not transposed Directive 78/659 into national law[76]; and in 1996, the Court found that Germany had not designated any waters under both Directives.[77] Both Directives will be repealed, in 2013, by Directive 2000/60[78] which also intends to take over the attainment of the objectives of these Directives, though it deal with water quality, not with habitat protection.

Financial measures to support nature conservation

The different EU financial means, given to Member States in particular in the context of the agricultural or regional policy, may also contribute, as the case might be, to the conservation of nature; examples are the setting aside of land or the construction of walls alongside a road. However, the main purpose of such measures is not the protection of the environment, but rather the achievement of an objective of agricultural or regional policy.

5–18

This also applies to the financial assistance given under Regulation 1698/2005[79] which aims at ensuring income to farmers who practise environmentally responsible farming practices. The regional policy objective is also visible with the financial means which are made available under the Cohesion Fund,[80] which financed transport and environment projects in Spain, Greece, Portugal

---

[72] Dir.78/659 on the quality of fresh waters needing protection or improvement in order to support fish life [1978] OJ L222/1.

[73] Dir.79/923 on the quality required of shellfish waters [1979] OJ L281/47.

[74] See for the factual details Commission, Quality of fresh water for fish and of shellfish water; summary report on the state of application of the Directives 78/659 and 79/923 (Luxembourg, 1995) (EUR 14118).

[75] *Commission v Italy* (C–322/86) [1988] E.C.R. 3995.

[76] *Commission v Italy* (C–322/86) [1988] E.C.R. 3995; *Commission v Italy* (C–291/93) [1994] E.C.R. I–859.

[77] *Commission v Germany* (C–298/95) [1996] E.C.R. I–6747.

[78] See Dir.2000/60 establishing a framework for Community action in the field of water policy [2000] OJ L327/1, art.22(2).

[79] Reg.1698/2005 on support for rural development by the European Agricultural Fund for Rural Development (EAFRD), [2005] OJ L277/1.

[80] Reg.1164/94 setting up a Cohesion Fund [1994] OJ L130/1; Reg.1084/2006 on the Cohesion Fund [2006] OJ L210/79.

and Ireland and which disposed, between 1993 and 1999, of 15.15 billion € and between 2000 and 2006 of 18 billion €; more or less half of which was earmarked for the environment. For the period 2007–2013, the number of Member States which have access to the Fund, has considerably increased, including now all the twelve new Member States—except Estonia—and Portugal, Greece and Spain; furthermore, the Fund now no longer co-finances individual projects, but gives lump sums to the entitled Member States, according to programmes which these States have elaborated and which have been previously approved by the Commission (see details in para.4–22, above). To what extent the Fund will in future co-finance nature protection projects, depends thus on each of the entitled Member States. The overall amount for all regional funds is of 308 billion € (2007–2013, 27 Member States).

5–19   One of the principal objectives of the financial instrument LIFE, which was set up in 1992 and reviewed in 1996, 2000 and 2007, was the protection of "habitats and of nature".[81] LIFE disposed, between 1992 and 1995, of 400 million €, between 1996 and 1999, of 450 million €, between 2000 and 2004 of 640 million € and between 2004 and 2006 of 317,2 million €. For the period 2007 till 2013, 840 million € (27 Member States) are earmarked for the protection of habitats.

Since the time span imposed on Member States to submit national lists for habitats under Directive 92/43[82] elapsed in 1996, LIFE, since then, only co-financed projects for sites which had been listed in these national lists or, in the case of bird habitats, had already been classified under Directive 2009/147. The EU funds were mainly used to buy or to hire the ground—most of the acquisition is done by local or regional nature conservation groups or bodies—to assist in the establishment of national, regional or local inventories or to pay for conservation or improvement measures at the site.[83]

LIFE+ which was adopted in 2007 provides for 2.1 billion €, for 27 Member States, for the period 2007–2013; this corresponds to a sum of about 300 million € per year. While the Commission had suggested to have nature protection measures financed by the Regional Fund and/or the Cohesion Fund, the European Parliament and the Council did not accept this approach and provided that LIFE+ should, with 40 per cent of the available money, co-finance projects to support nature protection and biodiversity measures.

5–20   The European Union also financed measures to protect forests. As regards forests within the European Union, the Council adopted, in 1986, a Regulation on the protection of forests against atmospheric pollution.[84] This Regulation provided for the setting up of inventories for forest damage, a network in order to

---

[81] Reg.1973/92 establishing a financial instrument for the environment [1992] OJ L206/1(LIFE I); the explanatory memorandum, COM (91) 28 of January 31, 1991 contains detailed figures on Community expenditure for the environment prior to 1991. Reg.1404/96 [1996] OJ L181/1 (LIFE II); Reg.1655/ 2000 [2000] OJ L192/1 (LIFE III); Reg.1682/2004 [2004] OJ L 308/1; Reg.614/2007 [2007] OJ L149/1.

[82] Commission, COM (97) 633 of December 12, 1997; *Nature 2000*, February 1999, p.2; see also Commission, COM (95) 135 of April 12, 1995: Progress report on implementation of the LIFE Regulation and evaluation of the action by the Community relating to the environment ACE, MEDSPA, NORSPA and ACNAT; European environment Agency, *Ecosystem accounting and the lost of biodiversity loss. The case of coastal Mediterranean wetlands.* Technical Report 3/2010. Copenhagen 2010.

[83] See para.5–12, above.

[84] Reg.3528/86 [1986] OJ L326/2.

obtain a coherent network of data, regular national reports on that data and for EC financial support for protection measures. Though damage levels have been stabilised from 1995 onwards, the Commission estimated that in 2002 almost one quarter of Europe's trees suffer damage from atmospheric pollution.[85] A Regulation of the same year on the protection of forests against fire provides for technical and financial assistance to prevent forest fire, in particular in the Mediterranean area.[86] Between 1983 and 2003, more than 2 billion € were spent on the conservation, improvement and protection of EU forests.[87] As mentioned above, all measures to finance forest conservation by the European Union, were, in 2006/2007, integrated into the Regional Funds and into LIFE+; it is thus up to Member States to decide on financial means for forestry.[88]

As regards tropical forests, a regulation of 2000 which replaced earlier provisions[89] provided for financial assistance—249 million € for the period 2000 to 2006—in sustainable forestry and generally in sustainable development measures. It also planned to assist in the development of an international labelling system for tropical wood that comes from sustainable forestry,[90] though the later FLEGT Regulation—see on that para.5–04, above—did not take the issue up.

In 2003, a working group set up by the Commission on "Financing Nature 2000" concluded that from 2003–2013, between 6.1 billion € would be needed per year within the then 15 Member States to ensure proper management of the different zones that come under the network of habitats of Nature 2000, established under Directive 92/43.[91] The amount which LIFE+ will make available—for 27, not for 15 Member States!—is about 120 million € per year, not even 3 per cent of the amount which was considered necessary (see also para.4–23, above).

5–21

2. Protection of threatened species

Fauna and flora species

Directive 92/43[92] establishes a general system of protection for European endangered species, which it lists, in Latin only, in an annex; these lists cover 230 animal species, apart from the 182 bird species protected under Directive 2009/147, and 483 plant species; the accession of 12 new Member States has led

5–22

---

[85] Commission, Second Report on Biological diversity; Thematic Report on Forests and Biodiversity (Luxembourg 2003) no.2.6.

[86] Reg.3529/86 [1986] OJ L326/5; this Regulation was replaced by Reg.2158/92 on protection of the Community's forests against fire [1992] OJ L217/3; the Committee of the regions had indicated in its opinion of October 15, 1997 [1998] OJ C64/27 at pt.2.1.18 that out of 300,000–500,000 hectares of forest which burnt every year in the EC, 97 per cent concerned Spain, France, Italy, Greece and Portugal.

[87] Commission (fn.85, above) no.2.7.

[88] See para.5–04, above.

[89] Reg.2494/2000 on measures to promote the conservation and sustainable management of tropical forests and other forests in developing countries [2000] OJ L 288/6; this Reg. replaced Reg.3062/95 [1995] OJ L327/9; both Regulations are based on arts 175 and 179 EC.

[90] See generally on tropical forests, Commission, Communication on the role of the Community in the conservation of tropical forests [1989] OJ C264/1.

[91] Commission, COM(2004) 431.

[92] Dir.92/43 (fn.37, above).

to enlargement of the lists. As the Directive is based on art.192 TFEU, Member States may, at national level, provide for other species to be protected. Deliberate capture or killing, the deliberate disturbance, taking eggs or deterioration or destruction of breeding sites or resting places of fauna species are prohibited. For some particularly endangered species, Member States must provide for supplementary measures, for example, to prevent the unintentional capture or killing (art.12). Derogations from the protection rules are, under relatively loosely drafted provisions, possible (art.16). Reports on derogations granted shall be sent to the Commission every two years; however, the experience with the similar derogation provision of art.9 of Directive 2009/147 does not inspire optimism. And it is surprising to find that the Commission's comments on these national derogations shall only be submitted to the Committee under Directive 92/43, but shall not be published (art.9(2)).[93] The first implementation report of the Commission showed that numerous Member States just enumerate their protection legislation, but do not report on the concrete measures which they have undertaken to protect endangered species; probably, in most cases, Member States satisfied themselves with the legal requirements without trying to make them effective.

The problems with the designation and management of habitats under Directive 92/43 are so considerable that measures to ensure the protection of individual species were hardly taken, apart from measures for big animals such as the bear or the Mediterranean seals which were then financed under LIFE. Reacting to complaints from individuals, the Commission took court action to protect the sea turtle caretta caretta on the Greek island of Zakynthos, the Red grouse in Ireland, the wood pigeon in Spain, the viper in Greece and the wolf in Finland.[94]

Birds

5–23   Directive 2009/147 lists in an annex some 200 particularly threatened bird species which require special protection measures. The most important of these measures are the designation of special protection areas under art.4[95] and the taking of conservation measures within these areas. The list of threatened bird species has constantly been prolonged, in particular due to the subsequent accession of Greece, Spain, Portugal, Austria, Finland and Sweden and then of twelve new Member States in 2004 and 2007 to the European Union. In 1997, the Commission decided for the first time to delete a species, the cormorant, from the list of threatened species, in particular due to pressure from fishermen.[96]

Directive 2009/147, however, does not only protect threatened birds, but all wild birds within the European Union; the reason for this overall protection was most likely the fact that "a large number of wild birds ... are declining in number".[97] The Directive thus provides for restrictive measures such as hunting

---

[93] See also Commission, eighth report on monitoring application of Community law (1990) [1991] OJ C338/1, p.220, where the Commission stated that the reports on the derogations under Dir.79/409 were so general that they did not allow any control.

[94] Court of Justice, *Commission v Spain* (C–135/04) [2005] E.C.R. I–5261; *Commission v Greece* (C–518/04) [2006] E.C.R. I–42; *Commission v Finland* (C–342/05) [2007] E.C.R. I–4713.

[95] See para.5–10, above.

[96] Dir.97/49 [1997] OJ L223/9.

[97] Dir.2009/147 (fn.33, above), second recital.

times restrictions, prohibitions on killing or capturing birds or on the taking of eggs. Furthermore, it bans a number of means for large-scale or non-selective capture or killing of birds (snares, limes, hooks, mirrors, explosives, nets, traps or motor vehicles). Derogations are possible "where there is no other satisfactory solution" (art.9).

Directive 2009/147 meant to improve the conditions of birds in Western Europe. This also implied a considerable change in people's habits. Apart from the designation of birds' habitats, the different provisions, including hunting provisions, proved difficult to enforce.[98] In particular in, but not restricted to, France, Spain, Italy, but also in Malta, hunting is perceived by hunters, farmers and others, as a right. When Malta acceded to the European Commission in 2004, it even obtained a transition period for continue bird hunting with means that are normally forbidden under Directive 2009/147. National hunting provisions often did not correctly transpose the Directive[99]; hunting seasons were generously allowed and little restricted. To what extent the hunting of migrating birds, which art.7(4) of the Directive expressly forbids, has really been reduced, in particular in southern Europe—nobody can argue that it has stopped in reality—is very doubtful.

5–24

In 1994, the Commission gave in to the pressure from (French) hunting interests and suggested an amendment of the Directive's hunting provisions which would have prolonged hunting seasons.[100] As, however, the European Parliament and a number of Member States opposed the proposal, it finally died away. In 1998, the French Parliament adopted legislation which extended the hunting period for birds into the time of migration and breeding, in deliberate and open defiance of Directive 2009/147. In 1999, France was condemned by the European Court of Human Rights because some of its hunting provisions were in conflict with the individual right of property. And in 2000, the Court of Justice gave a judgment on the French hunting rules[101] which once more stated that they were not compatible with EU rules.

Generally, implementation of Directive 2009/147 was slow. The fact that in 2000, 19 years after its entering into effect, the Commission signalled 20 running

5–25

---

[98] *Commission v Belgium* (C–247/85) [1987] E.C.R. 3073; *Commission v Italy* (C–262/85) [1987] E.C.R. 3073; *Commission v Germany* (C–412/85) [1987] E.C.R. 3503; *Commission v Netherlands* (C–236/85) [1987] E.C.R. 3989; *Commission v France* (C–252/85) [1988] E.C.R. 2243; *Gourmetterie van den Burg* (C–169/89) [1990] E.C.R. 2143; *Commission v Italy* (C–334/89) [1991] E.C.R. 93; *Commission v Germany* (C–345/92) [1993] E.C.R. I–1115; *Association des Animaux v Préfet Maine et Loire* (C–435/92) [1994] E.C.R. I–69; *Ministère public v Vergy* (C–149/94) [1996] E.C.R. I–299; *V.D. Feesten* (C–202/94) [1996] E.C.R. I–355; *Ligue belge des oiseaux* (C–10/96) [1996] E.C.R. I–6775; *Commission v Austria* (C–507/04) [2007] E.C.R. I–5939; *Commission v Greece* (C–293/07) judgment of December 11, 2008; *Commission v Greece* (C–259/08) judgment of January 15, 2009; *Commission v Italy* (C–164/09) judgment of November 11, 2010.
[99] See the different cases on national hunting rules: *Commission v Netherlands* (C–339/87) [1990] E.C.R. 851; *Commission v Germany* (C–288/88) [1990] E.C.R. 2721; *Commission v Italy* (C–157/89) [1991] E.C.R. 57; (C–435/92) (fn.73, above); *WWF v Veneto* (C–118/94) [1996] E.C.R. I–1451; *Commission v Spain* (C–79/03) [2004] E.C.R. I–11619; *Commission v Finland* (C–344/03) [2005] E.C.R. I–11033; *Commission v Spain* (C–221/04) [2006] E.C.R. I–4515; *WWF v Lombardia* (C–60/06) [2006] E.C.R. I–5083; *Commission v Italy* (C–503/06) judgment of May 15, 2008; *Commission v Malta* (C–76/08) [2009] E.C.R. I–8213.
[100] Commission [1994] OJ C100/12.
[101] Court of Justice, *Commission v France* (C–38/99) [2000] E.C.R. I–10941; see also the earlier judgment, *Commission v France* (252/85) [1988] E.C.R. 2243.

proceedings against Member States,[102] is significant, but is only one element. Another element is the lack of data transmitted by Member States which has as a consequence that the Commission by 2010 had only published four of the composite reports which it should have published under art.12(2) of the Directive, limiting it largely to reproduce Member States' comments without analysing and assessing the situation itself.[103] The last report of 2006 covered the period 1999–2001, thus came five years late; one might imagine that a report which is delayed for such a long time and then makes an effort only to report on generalities, has not much more than academic value.

The conclusion after 30 years of operation of Directive 2009/147[104] is that it has undoubtedly had positive effects. Its legally binding provisions, which markedly contrast with international conventions that are considered as soft law and are neither enforceable nor enforced, have alerted administrations concerned, public opinion and research and caused them to seriously consider the state of birdlife in Europe. Habitats have been designated and concern for ensuring the survival of the different species of birds has been raised. No international convention was capable of achieving similar results, in particular as the Commission acted and continues to act as a co-ordination and enforcement body. Some species of birds have increased in number. The problems of applying the Directive are the same that apply to nature conservation and to biodiversity generally: the overall decline of birds has not yet been stopped in Western Europe.

Generally, on biodiversity protection by the European Union, the following statement appears pertinent[105]:

> "The absence of a political will, the lack of financial resources, the predominance of traditional interests over ecological interests, outdated systems of criminal law, the inability of environmental associations in many Member States to bring court actions, and the ambiguity of the applicable legal provisions are just a few of the factors undermining the application of harmonised EC rules. It comes as no surprise that despite the number of laws that now exist with respect to nature conservation, and the many positive impacts that they had, these positive steps are falling short of preventing Noah's Ark to sink."

Trade restrictions

5–26   The European Union is not a member of the Convention on International Trade in endangered species of fauna and flora (CITES) of 1973, since that Convention is, at present, only open to states, not to international institutions. A 1983 amendment of the Convention, which would enable the European Union to

---

[102] Commission, 18th report on monitoring application of Community law—2000, COM [2001] 309 of July 16, 2001, annex IV, pt 2.

[103] Commission, Monitoring application of Community law 18th report (2000) COM (2001) 309 no.2.8.5.

[104] See N. de Sadeleer, *"Bilan d'une décennie d'efforts législatifs en droit communautaire de la protection de la nature"* in P. Renaudière and P. van Pelt (eds), *Développements récents du droit communautaire de l'environnement* (Diegem, 1995), pp.199 et seq. (at p.259); C. Mayr, *"Vierzehn Jahre EG-Vogelschutzrichtlinie. Bilanz ihrer Umsetzung in der Bundesrepublik Deutschland"*, *Berichte zum Vogelschutz* 31 (1993), p.13; P. Pagh, *"EU's beskyttelse af vilde fugle og fisk: indgribende betydning for arealanvendelsen"*, *Ugeskrift for Retsvaesen* (1997), pp.511 et seq.

[105] N. de Sadeleer, "EC law and biodiversity" in: R. Macrory (ed.) *Reflections on 30 years of EU environmental law* (Groningen, 2005), p.369.

adhere, has not yet been ratified by a sufficient number of contracting States.[106] The European Union transposed the provisions of that Convention into EU law in 1982 and updated them in 1997 by adopting the new Regulation 338/97.[107]

Regulation 338/97 only deals with conservation measures. Provisions in earlier regulations and also in the Commission's proposal for Regulation 338/97,[108] which aimed at dealing with questions of public safety and animal welfare, were removed from the final version of the Regulation, which led, at the same time, to the taking of art.192 TFEU as a legal basis, rather than arts 114 and 207 TFEU, as proposed by the Commission. The Regulation treats the European Union as one territory. It introduces a differentiated system of protection. Annex A contains all endangered species which are under the total protection of the CITES Convention and, in addition, a number of other species which are considered threatened under the stricter criteria of the Regulation. Trade in these species for primarily commercial purposes is prohibited; also, within the European Union only very narrow derogation possibilities exist. The Commission's proposal generally to prohibit any possession of species listed in annex A was not accepted by the Council.

Annex B contains species which are not actually threatened by trade; however, trade in these species should take place under strict conditions in order to avoid them becoming threatened. Again, the Regulation goes considerably beyond the requirements of the CITES Convention. Importing these species into the European Union requires an import licence from the country of destination, which must be presented at the time of importation.

The import of species listed in annex C into the European Union is subject to the presentation of an import notification rather than a licence. Finally, annex D includes species that are imported into the European Union in such quantities that an import notification is considered necessary.

5–27

Under arts 4(6) and 19(2) of Regulation 338/97, the Commission may, under certain ecological conditions, restrict the introduction of certain specimens of species into the European Union. Several Commission decisions, the last one of 2010, contained a list of species which may not be imported into the European Union.[109] This list and also the amendments to the annexes of the Regulation are drawn up by way of a committee procedure, which allows a speedy reaction to decisions of the contracting parties of the CITES Convention.

Prior to adopting the different CITES Regulations since 1982, the European Union had already, in 1981, adopted a regulation to protect whales.[110] The Regulation strictly prohibited, without derogation, the commercial import of whale and other cetacean meat, bones, fats and oils, leather and furs. Since this ban was in line with international decisions on the protection of whales, this Regulation, which was later largely superseded by the provisions of Regulation 338/97,[111] raised few concerns.

---

[106] CITES Convention of March 3, 1973 [1982] OJ L384/8; see also Written Question E-2183/96 (*Bloch v Blottnitz*) [1996] OJ C365/89.

[107] Reg.338/97 on the protection of species of wild fauna and flora by regulating trade therein [1997] OJ L61/1; this Reg. replaced Reg.3626/82 [1982] OJ L384/1.

[108] [1992] OJ C26/1.

[109] Commission Reg.997/2010 suspending the introduction into the Union of specimens of certain species of wild fauna and flora [2010] OJ L290/1.

[110] Reg.348/81 on common rules for imports of whales or other cetacean products [1981] OJ L39/1.

[111] Reg.338/97 (fn.107, above).

Other measures

5–28   Among the other measures to be mentioned, capturing methods for capturing animals should be particularly noted. Directives 2009/147 and 92/43 both contain a specific annex to prohibit the use of large-scale or non-selective capturing methods, without having been able to stop completely the use of such means within the European Union, in particular for bird hunting.

Regulation 894/97, which replaces a number of earlier legislative acts and which was later replaced by Regulation 1239/98, prohibited the use of fishing driftnets of more than 2.5km in length.[112] This ban applied to most EU waters and outside these waters to ships showing the flag of a Member State or registered in a Member State. Specific provisions applied to the Baltic Sea, where politicians and fishermen jointly successfully lobbied the European Union to obtain the possibility to authorise driftnets up to 21km in length; only in 2004 was there an end made to this practice by 2008. Regulation 894/97 also prohibits driftnets altogether for tuna fishing in Portuguese or Spanish waters, following a ban that these two Member States have pronounced. The reason for these bans is the non-selective character of capturing with driftnets, which may reach 100km in length; originally, the problem started worldwide, when dolphins were captured during the fishing of tuna. Besides this problem, the use of driftnets leads to overfishing and has contributed to the serious depletion of fish resources worldwide and in EU waters.

3.   Animal welfare

Animal welfare and the EU Treaties

5–29   Animal welfare concerns animals as living beings. It tries to protect animals independently from the question of whether a species is endangered or not. It is obvious that such a concept is strongly influenced by ethical, religious and similar considerations. The EU Treaties treat animals differently from goods, as appears clearly in art.36 TFEU, which allows restrictions for the free circulation of goods in order to protect life and safety of animals and plants; furthermore, trade measures for animals are based on art.192 TFEU or, in agricultural matters, on art.43, rather than on art.114 TFEU.

At EU level, the idea that animals could or should have rights of their own, or that trees should be important in their own right, has never seriously been discussed: such considerations appear too distant from the anthropocentric concept of nature, in particular in Roman law Member States. A mention of consideration for animals in the fourth environmental action programme 1987 did not lead to the development of a coherent approach.

5–30   Attempts by animal welfare groups, supported in this also by the European Parliament,[113] to have a specific provision on animal welfare inserted into the EU

---

[112] Reg.894/97 on technical measures to preserve fish resources [1997] OJ L132, p.1, art.11. The Reg. was based on art.43 TFEU. By Reg.1239/98 [1998] OJ L171/1 it was replaced.

[113] Fourth environmental action programme 1987–1992 [1987] OJ C328/1, no.5.1.9: "An improvement in the quality of life also entails respect for animals in the Member States and in the Member States' dealings with the rest of the world. The regular debates concerning the hunting of seal

Treaties, were only successful in 2009. At the conclusion of the Maastricht Treaty, a declaration was made by the Intergovernmental Conference that animal welfare aspects should be taken into consideration in the context of some EU policies.[114] The Amsterdam Treaty on European Union added a Protocol to the Treaty,[115] which provided that EU policy should fully take animal welfare into consideration in its policies on agriculture, transport, internal market and Research.[116] In 2009, this provision was included in the TFEU.[117] It is not quite clear why environmental policy was not also enumerated.

Wild animals are part of the natural resources; measures to protect them, to provide for their welfare when captured and so on, are environmental measures. Indeed, the preservation and protection of natural resources is not limited to protecting endangered species, but applies to all natural resources. Measures regarding wild animals, even where they do not belong to an endangered species, therefore come under arts 191–193 TFEU. This approach was recognised in 1999, when the European Union adopted a Directive on the keeping of wild animals in zoos, based on art.192 TFEU,[118] though it was explicitly mentioned that this Directive intended to protect species of animals, not individual animals. However, it is obviously erroneous to consider all animals in zoos to be part of an endangered species.

The main legal problem is that the rules of international trade, established by the General Agreement of Tariffs and Trade (GATT) and the World Trade Organisation (WTO), are generally interpreted as prohibiting measures which restrict trade because of the production methods used. Debate about these issues is not very thorough, as the examples of products made by working children or those produced in jail demonstrate; indeed, trade in such products may be prohibited under GATT/WTO rules. The discussion on environmentally sustainable production methods—an example is the consideration on import restrictions for tropical wood that does not stem from sustainable production—has only just started. The European Union began, since the early 1990s, to take measures in order to prevent possible conflicts with WTO or trading partners, which might end in formal WTO proceedings.[119] This explains why the full implementation of animal welfare measures is often delayed.

5–31

---

pups should not conceal the many questions raised by the exploitation of animals in Europe: the use of animals for experiments, factory farming, trading in animals and the processing of animals for consumption. The Commission will examine all possible steps which it can take in this connection."

[114] See European Parliament, Res. of January 21, 1994 [1994] OJ C44/206; the European Parliament in particular wanted animals to be no longer called, within the context of agricultural policy, "agricultural products".

[115] [1992] OJ C191/1, Declaration No.12.

[116] [1997] OJ C340/110.

[117] art.13 TFEU: "In formulating and implementing the Union's agricultural, fisheries, transport, internal market, research and technological development and space policies, the Union and the Member States shall, since animals are sentient beings, pay full regard to the welfare requirements of animals, while respecting the legislative or administrative provisions and customs of the Member States relating in particular to religious rights, cultural traditions and regional heritage".

[118] See para.5–38, below.

[119] See also paras 5–35 and 11–34, below.

Tests on animals

5–32   Directive 2010/63[120] limits the use of animals for experimental or scientific purposes, in order in particular to avoid unnecessary experiments and to avoid pain, suffering distress and lasting harm. The Directive is based on art.114 TFEU, but allows Member States to maintain or introduce stricter measures at national level (art.2). It lays down detailed provisions on the authorisation of animal testing, the persons responsible for experiments, the keeping of animals, the establishments, etc.; detailed guidelines for accommodation and care of animals are annexed to the Directive. Particular restrictions apply to endangered animals. The Directive does not apply to non-experimental agricultural practices.

Whether the Directive applies where animals are used to "produce", for instance a secretum, blood or anti-bodies, etc., was doubtful and, since 1986, answered differently by Member States. The limitation of animals for experimental or other scientific purposes (art.3(1)) and the limitation of "procedures" to basic, translational or applied research with specific aims (art.5) indicates that the new Directive 2010/63 does not allow animals to be used for such production purposes.

5–33   Animals may not be used where another scientifically satisfactory method or testing strategy is available (art.4). Endangered species and non-human primates may normally not be used for scientific purposes (arts 7 and 8); animals taken from the wild may not be taken either, though national authorities may grant derogations (art.9).

5–34   Since 1994, the Commission published overall six reports on statistical data concerning the practical application of Directive 86/609.[121] The figures in these reports are not comparable, as the number of EU Member States changed and as the statistical methods for calculation had been amended. The 6th report of 2010, which covers the year 2008, gives for the first time data on all 27 EU Member States.

According to that report, there were about 12 million animals used for scientific or experimental purposes. Mice (59 per cent), rats (17 per cent), cold-blooded animals (10 per cent) and birds (6 per cent, a slight increase since several years) were the most used animals. No Great Apes were used. Some 15 per cent of the animals were used for production and quality control of products.

The European Union adhered to the Council of Europe Convention for the protection of vertebrate animals used for experimental and other scientific purposes in 1998.[122]

In 1993, the Directive on cosmetic products[123] was amended with a view to ban, as of January 1, 1998, cosmetic products containing ingredients or combinations of ingredients tested on animals.[124] Subsequently, this date was extended and only became effective on July 1, 2002.

---

[120] Dir.2010/63 on the protection of animals used for scientific purposes [2010] OJ L276/33; this Directive replaced Directive 86/609, [1986] OJ L358/1.

[121] Commission, COM (95) 195; COM(1999) 191; COM(2003)19; COM(2005)7; COM(2007) 675; COM(2010)511.

[122] Dec.1999/575 (1999) OJ L222/29; the Convention is published in the annex to this Dec.

[123] Dir.93/35 [1993] OJ L151/32.

[124] See Dir.76/768 on cosmetic products [1976] OJ L262/169, art.4(1.i) as amended by Dir.93/35 (fn.123, above) and Dir.2000/41 [2000] OJ L145/25.

Seals

Beginning in 1982, the killing of baby seals, particularly in Canada, attracted **5–35** considerable attention from the Western European media. The European Parliament asked for an import ban on baby seal furs[125] and environmental organisations urged action. Although the Council strongly doubted the possibility of adopting a Commission proposal to ban imports of baby seal furs,[126] it finally adopted such an import ban for two years[127] After an initial prolongation for four years, the import ban was extended, in 1989, for an undetermined time.[128] The Directive did not argue that seals are an endangered species. For that reason alone, the only justification for the import ban on furs and other seal products were the killing methods which were used, thus animal welfare considerations.

Since 2002/2003, Canada allowed the hunting and killing of several million of seal species per year, that were not considered to be endangered species. In reaction to that, Belgium, the Netherlands adopted legislation which prohibited the trade in seals products, pointing to the fact that such a ban was effective in the United States for decades and that Mexico had introduced a similar ban in 2005. Several other Member States considered similar action. In view of this, the Commission proposed a regulation on banning trade in seal products which the European Parliament and the Council adopted in 2009.[129] Canada and Norway submitted the matter to the WTO, arguing that this was an unjustified barrier to the free trade in products; Canadian groups also attacked the Regulation before the Court of Justice, where the case is pending.

In my opinion, such a ban would, for animal welfare reasons, be compatible with art.36 TFEU, as well as with the corresponding WTO/GATT rules. Indeed, public opinion in the European Union does not accept the methods which are used for the hunting of seals which frequently lead to the skinning of live animals. Public morals and animal welfare considerations cannot be the same all over the world; it must be thus a decision of each individual State—or, in this case, the European Union—whether it considers public morals to be affected or not.

---

[125] European Parliament, Res. of [1982] OJ C87/87 and March 11, 1982 [1982] OJ C267/47.

[126] Res. of [1983] OJ C14/1; France, the UK, Belgium, Denmark and Greece were reported to have opposed measures since these would be motivated by purely moral motives.

[127] Dir.83/129 concerning the importation into Member States of skins of certain seal pups and products derived therefrom [1983] OJ L91/30.

[128] Dir.85/444 [1985] OJ L259/70 and Dir.89/370 [1989] OJ L163/37.

[129] Reg.1007/2009 on trade in seal products, [2009] OJ L286/36.

Leghold traps

5–36   Regulation 3254/91 prohibited, as of 1995, the use of leghold traps within the European Union.[130] Leghold traps are considered non-selective[131] and cruel (not "humane"). Bans or restrictions on the use of leghold traps are in use in about 60 states all over the world.[132]

While this ban is undisputed, the Commission had—subsequent to a petition of 272 Members of the European Parliament—proposed and the Council had adopted an import ban on the furs of 13 animal species (beaver, otter, coyote, wolf, lynx, bobcat, sable, raccoon, musk rat, fisher (martes pennanti), badger, marten and ermine) from those countries which continued to use leghold traps.[133] The import ban was to come into effect in 1995[134]; the Council expected that by then internationally "humane trapping standards" would be agreed.

5–37   However, this was not to be the case. In particular, the United States, Canada and Russia heavily opposed the import ban, arguing that it was contrary to the rules of the GATT/World Trade Organisation and disadvantaged indigenous populations. In view of this, the Commission proposed, in December 1995, to replace the import ban by a mandate to be given to the European Union in order to negotiate an agreement with third countries on humane trapping standards.[135] The Council did not adopt the proposal, but agreed to negotiations. An agreement with Canada and Russia was reached in 1997, with the United States in 1998.[136] The agreements provided essentially for the fixing of some trapping standards and the phasing out, within four years, of some leghold traps for two species, without containing a legally enforceable commitment of this kind. In substance, thus, the European Union abandoned its import ban with regard to these three countries. Regulation 3254/91 has not yet been amended. Thus, for other third countries, the import ban entered into effect in 1997.[137]

In 2004, the Commission proposed a directive in order to implement the two international agreements. However, the European Parliament rejected the proposal with its absolute majority, arguing that the proposal intended to consider

---

[130] Reg.3254/91 prohibiting the use of leghold traps in the Community and the introduction into the Community of pelts and manufactured goods of certain wild animal species originating in countries which catch them by means of leghold traps or trapping methods which do not meet international humane trapping standards [1991] OJ L308/1.

[131] According to figures quoted by ECOSOC, Opinion of April 26, 1990 [1990] OJ C168/32, no.1.6.3, about 10 per cent of animals caught in leghold traps are caught unintentionally.

[132] Written Question 1936/88 (Zarges) [1989] OJ C255/15.

[133] The Commission's proposal [1989] OJ C134/5 did not contain a ban on leghold traps, since such a ban had been proposed in the directive on habitats [1988] OJ C247/3; since it thus only contained an import ban, it was based on art.207 TFEU. The Council Regulation is based on arts 207 and 192 TFEU.

[134] Subsequently, there was a controversy whether the ban did indeed become effective. Art.3(1) of Reg.3254/91 stipulates: "The introduction into the Community of the pelts . . . shall be prohibited as of 1 January 1995, unless the Commission . . ." (states that in a third country leghold traps or inhumane trapping methods are forbidden). This wording indicates, in my opinion without any legal doubt, that the ban became effective as of January 1, 1995, since the Commission has not made any such statement.

[135] [1996] OJ C58/17.

[136] Dec.98/487 [1998] OJ L219/24; the Decision was based on arts 207 and 114 TFEU; see also European Parliament [1998] OJ C210/31, which had rejected the agreement.

[137] See Dir.97/602 [1997] OJ L242/64; see also Written Question E–294/98 (Pollack) [1998] OJ C223/160.

the actual practice of Canadian, US and Russian trappers as "humane" trapping methods, without having made scientific research as to less painful trapping methods. The proposal is thus politically dead.

Animals in zoos

In 1991, the Commission proposed a directive on the keeping of animals in zoos,   **5–38**
of which there are about 1,000 within the European Union (EU 15).[138] Following the extensive discussion on subsidiarity and deregulation which followed the signing of the Maastricht Treaty on European Union in 1991, the proposal was listed, by the Edinburgh summit meeting of the European Council and on the pressure from the United Kingdom, as one of the instruments for which the subsidiarity clause should apply; this meant that the European Union should leave the matter to Member States to deal with. The Commission thus withdrew its proposal and replaced it by a proposal for a Council recommendation which contained detailed guidelines on the accommodation and care of animals in zoos.[139]

The European Parliament and the Economic and Social Committee both pleaded in favour of a directive. The Council first agreed unanimously on a common position concerning a recommendation. However, upon the instigation of the United Kingdom, which completely changed its position adopted in 1992 at the Edinburgh summit, it changed the principal objective of the instrument, to make it an instrument for the conservation of biodiversity; the detailed rules on accommodation and care of animals were deleted. Zoos were mainly considered to have a role in the conservation of biodiversity. They had to have a permit and were to be regularly inspected by the national competent authorities. On this basis, a Directive was adopted in 1999 based on art.192(1) TFEU.[140]

---

[138] [1991] OJ C241/14.
[139] Commission, COM (95) 619 of December 12, 1995.
[140] Dir.1999/22 on the keeping of wild animals in zoos [1999] OJ L94/24.

CHAPTER 6

Products

1. General questions

There is no consistent and coherent EU policy on products. Most of the product-related measures adopted meant to establish common rules for the establishment and functioning of the internal EU market and thus enable the free circulation of goods. Aspects of health, safety, consumer protection and, at a later stage, environmental protection, were not systematically tackled at EU level, but were, rather, left to be regulated at Member State level; hence, common rules became necessary in order to ensure a level playing field. The so-called "new approach" to product standards' harmonisation, introduced in the 1980s by a Council Resolution[1], where EU legislation only fixes the essential requirements for a product, leaving the details to industrial standardisation by European standardisation organisations, has not changed this situation. Indeed, these "essential requirements" normally refer to health and safety aspects of a product, but not to its impact on the environment. The Directive on general product safety[2] refers to the "safety and health of persons", but does not mention the environment at all. And legislation on the protection of workers at the working place is limited to that area, but has no general application. In a judgment of 2009, the Court of Justice held that, as regards mercury, references to "health" also included environmental concerns. Thus, where the European Union had regulated health aspects of products containing mercury, Member States were barred from adopting measures at national level which concerned the environmental aspects of mercury.[3] This judgment ignores the dividing line which primary and secondary EU law draw between the protection of health and safety on the one side, on the protection of the environment on the other side.[4]

Different scientific committees, which the Commission had set up in the 1970s, have played some role in determining the effects of products on man and the environment. Only the Scientific Committee on Human Consumption has achieved, in the past, an authoritative reputation; some of the other committees do not seem to have always been completely neutral towards vested interests. In 1997, following the BSE scandal where concern was voiced that the Commission had hidden information on "mad cow disease" and its influence on humans, the

6–01

---

[1] Council Resolution of May 7, 1985 [1985] OJ C136/1.

[2] Dir.2001/95 on general product safety [2002] OJ L1/4; this Directive replaced Dir.92/59 [1992] OJ L228/4).

[3] Court of Justice, *Kemikalieinspektionen v Nordiska Dental* (C–288/08) judgment of November 19, 2009.

[4] See for more details L. Krämer, comment on *Journal of European Environmental and Planning Law* (C–288/08) 2010, p.124.

Commission restructured the different scientific committees, renamed them and placed them under the responsibility of the Commissioner on consumer affairs. Thus, the Scientific Committee for the Toxicity and Ecotoxicity of Chemical Substances became the Scientific Committee for Toxicity, Ecotoxicity and the Environment, without, however, changing its previous responsibilities.[5]

6–02   Product policy inevitably affects health and safety, consumer protection and environmental impairment, aspects which cannot clearly be dissociated from each other. EU efforts concentrate on the attempts to find a balance between health and safety of humans on the one hand, and on the free circulation of goods, their export and import on the other hand. Environmental concerns play a secondary role. The fact that products—in the form of emissions, goods, wastes, residues, etc.—exist everywhere in the environment and present considerable risks to biodiversity, soil, fresh and marine waters, or buildings has not really led to the setting up of a product policy which is less anthropocentric and more integrated.

The Commission's attempt to launch an "integrated product policy"[6] did not really contain what the title promises. The Commission defined integrated product policy "as an approach which seeks to reduce the life cycle environmental impacts of products from the mining of raw materials to production, distribution, use and waste management".[7] This approach was thus limited to try to integrate environmental requirements into product-related aspects. The Commission favoured non-binding instruments under this approach, and published in 2005 and 2006 the results of two pilot projects on mobile phones and teak garden chairs; there was no further follow-up on these projects. Since then, the whole discussion on integrated product policy largely came to a standstill, as also proven by the Commission's poor implementation report of 2009 and a new communication of 2010 which is full of commonplaces.[8]

The discussion on an environmentally oriented product policy at national level is strongly influenced by the Treaty provisions on the free circulation of goods and the interpretation that, under these provisions, a product that is lawfully produced and marketed in one Member State must in principle also be allowed to circulate in the other Member States. It should be noted, though, that this general provision does not prevent the introduction of an environmental product policy at Member State level. Indeed, the Court jurisdiction regarding the interdependency between art.34 TFEU and environmental protection may be summarised in the statement that in the absence of EU provisions concerning a product a Member State may adopt any environmental provision it wishes, as long as there is no discrimination of producers and traders from other Member States and as long as the national measure is not disproportionate to the environmental objective pursued; furthermore, the measures taken by a Member State must be proportionate.[9]

---

[5] Dec.97/579 [1997] OJ L237/18.

[6] Commission, Green Paper on Integrated Product Policy COM(2001) 68; COM(2003) 302.

[7] Commission, COM(2001) 68, p.2.

[8] Commission, Report on the state of implementation of integrated product policy, COM(2009) 693; Commission, An integrated industrial policy for the globalisation area; putting competitiveness and sustainability at centre stage, COM(2010) 614.

[9] See in particular Court of Justice, *Mickelsson and Roos* (C–142/05) judgment of June 4, 2009, and *Sandström* (C–433/05) judgment of April 15, 2010, where the Court laid down the conditions under

Discussions on product policy at Member State level are considerably further advanced. The Netherlands Government formulated its product-oriented environmental policy as[10]:

> "to bring about a situation whereby all market actors—producers, traders and consumers—are involved in an ongoing effort to reduce the impact which products have on the environment."

Germany defined, in 1999, the integrated product policy as "public policy which aims at or is suitable for continuous improvement in the environmental performance of products and services within a life-cycle context". The most advanced approach is, however, that of the Swedish Government which declared as the aim of an integrated product policy[11]:

> "to produce products and services that make the smallest possible impact on human health or the environment at each stage of their life-cycle. Products should be material—and energy—efficient, at the same time as they should not contain or require the use of substances that may involve adverse effects on human health or the environment."

More important perhaps than the conceptual differences are the concrete actions which are undertaken. Almost all depends on the political determination to bring the concept of integrated product policy into reality. An important principle in this concept is the substitution principle, which the EU sixth environmental action programme describes as follows[12]:

6–03

> "Chemicals that are dangerous should be replaced by safer chemicals or safer alternative technologies not entailing the use of chemicals, with the aim of reducing risks to man and the environment."

Though the principle's application is limited, in this context, to chemicals, its application is much broader and applies, it is submitted, to all products.[13] The substitution principle is also expressed in art.4(2) of Directive 2002/95 which limits the use of certain dangerous substances in electrical and electronic equipment and which provides that other substances than those mentioned in the Directive shall be regulated in view of their substitution by environmentally more friendly substances, as soon as sufficient scientific information is available.[14]

In 2001, a judgment of the Court of Justice showed strong sympathy for the substitution principle in environmental law.[15] The new Regulation on chemical products, REACH (see para.6–38ss, below), tries to make the substitution principle one of the cornerstones of the new system on chemicals.[16] Also the new

---

which national measures which restricted the use of personal watercraft on Swedish waters were compatible with arts 34–36 TFEU; these products were, by virtue of EU legislation, allowed to circulate freely within the EU.

[10] (Netherlands) Department of Environmental Affairs (VROM), Policy paper on products and the environment (The Hague, 1994).

[11] Swedish Government Communication 1999/2000:114 (Stockhom, 2000).

[12] Decision 1600/2002 laying down the sixth Community Environmental Action Programme [2002] OJ L242/1, recital 25 and art.7(1).

[13] See also Court of Justice, *Kemikalieinspektionen* (C–473/98) [2000] E.C.R. I–5681.

[14] Dir.2002/95 on the restriction of use of certain dangerous substances in electrical and electronic equipment [2003] OJ L37/19.

[15] Court of Justice (C–473/98) (fn.13, above).

[16] Reg.1907/2006 concerning the registration, evaluation, authorisation and restriction of chemicals (REACH), establishing a chemicals agency [2006] OJ L396/1.

Regulation concerning the placing on the market of pesticides provides for extensive recurrence to the substitution principle.[17]

The integrated product policy approach at EU level has never mentioned the substitution principle as one that would be guiding action in this area. It is not clear either, up till now, which other principles apply and whether there will be any attempt to systematically address environmental issues caused by products. In my opinion, an integrated product policy must base itself, in particular, on the following four principles:

1.   The substitution principle, according to which dangerous substances should not be used in products where substances are available that are less dangerous for humans or the environment;
2.   The precautionary principle, according to which the absence of scientific certainty does not prevent the taking of action, where a presumption of a risk to humans or the environment exists;
3.   The minimisation principle, according to which a product should make the smallest possible impact on humans and the environment;
4.   The principle of producer responsibility, according to which the producer shall be responsible for his product from the selection and choice of the raw materials to the responsibility for the product when it has finished its useful life-time and becomes waste.

Efforts in a product policy are also hampered by the fact that products (goods) are the subject of trade, and EU-wide and international efforts are dominated by the attempt to ensure free trade in goods. From this objective stems the request that the taking of any measure in the product-related area be only allowed where it is scientifically proven that the product or production method that is used presents a risk to human health or safety or to the environment. Free trade in goods should therefore only be affected, where the risk assessment for substances or products demonstrates an unacceptable risk to health or the environment. Where such risk assessment also includes a cost-benefit analysis, the objective is no longer to minimise the impact of products on humans and the environment— see the abovementioned Swedish approach—but rather to minimise the impact of measures on trade in goods.

6–04   At EU level, the attempts to minimise the impact of products on humans and the environment are still at their beginnings and not systematic. The sixth environmental action programme does not mention a policy approach on products. Only in the Chapter on natural resources and waste management is the integrated policy approach mentioned, however, in a rather marginal way. In contrast to that, the attempts to minimise the impact on the free circulation of goods are more systematic: Member States must, before adopting any product-related legislation that might affect the free circulation of goods, transmit their draft legislation together, "if available", with a risk analysis, to the Commission and to all other Member States.[18] For chemicals, Regulation 1907/2006 now requires producers and importers to deliver the results of safety

---

[17] Reg.1107/2009 concerning the placing on the market of plant protection products [2009] OJ L309/1.
[18] Dir.98/34 laying down a procedure for the provision of information in the field of technical standards and regulations [1998] OJ L204/37, art.8(1).

tests to the European Chemical Agency which means that they have to make a sort of impact assessment; the difference to the previous legislation is that it is no longer the public authorities which have to test the safety of chemicals.[19] This is the consequence of the general understanding that risk assessment was slow and resource-intensive and did not allow the system to work efficiently and effectively.[20] In the past, the Commission had committed itself to carry out risk assessments and adequate analyses of the costs and benefits prior to any proposal or adoption of a regulatory measure affecting the chemical industry.[21]

This policy of requiring that any action on the restriction of use of a substance is preceded by a risk assessment contradicts the precautionary and prevention principles of art.191 TFEU, which ask EU institutions to act even in cases where there is scientific uncertainty as to the harmfulness of a substance for humans or the environment. In the case of doubt, these principles suggest EU action, so that, in the case of an error, free trade is affected rather than human health or the environment: where a product or a substance is suspected to be dangerous, it is appropriate to act and not to wait for definitive scientific evidence.

6–05

It is comforting that in the past, the Commission itself has not systematically provided for a risk assessment on specific substances, in particular in those cases either where public opinion was concerned about the risks of a substance for humans or when Member States took action to restrict the use of a substance. Cases dealt with since 1997, where the results of a risk assessment were not available before EU legislative action was started, concern phthalates,[22] asbestos,[23] greenhouse gases,[24] ozone-depleting substances,[25] the restriction of heavy metals in cars[26] or in electrical and electronic equipment,[27] the measures in reaction to the accident of *The Prestige* tanker off the Spanish coast in November 2002[28] or cadmium in batteries and accumulators.[29] Requesting in all cases a risk analysis and a cost-benefit analysis neglects the fact that the environment suffers from the presence of too many pollutants. Accident prevention and remediation procedures are very important for the environment; however, the primary aim of any environmental policy should be to prevent environmental impairment and therefore to reduce the placing of environmentally hazardous substances into the environment.

The Court of Justice in its judgment C–180/96, confirmed the possibility for preventive action, without putting as a condition that a risk assessment or cost-benefit analysis must be undertaken beforehand.[30] Nothing else can apply to

---

[19] Reg.1907/2006 (fn.16, above).

[20] See in more detail paras 6–29 et seq, below.

[21] Commission, White Paper on Chemical Policy (1998) 88, no.2.1.

[22] See para.6–53, below.

[23] See para.4–50, above and para.6–37, below.

[24] See para.9–21, below.

[25] See paras 6–24 and 9–26, below.

[26] Dir.2000/53 on end-of-life vehicles [2000] OJ L269/34.

[27] Dir.2002/95 (fn.14, above).

[28] See Commission, Report on actions to deal with the effects of the Prestige disaster, COM(2003) 105.

[29] Directive 2006/66 on batteries and accumulators and waste batteries and accumulators [2006] OJ L266/1.

[30] Court of Justice, *United Kingdom v Commission* (C–180/96) [1998] E.C.R. I–2265; see also para.1–29, above; see, further, European Parliament Res. of October 20, 1998 [1998] OJ C341/31 on endocrine disruptors.

the protection of the environment, all the more as the Court of Justice, in its abovementioned judgment and in later decisions, expressly referred to the necessity of preventive action, laid down in art.191(2) TFEU.

It is to be expected that the battle will continue between supporters of a wide application of the precautionary and prevention principle in order to promote an active, environmentally sound EU product policy, and the supporters of an unhampered circulation of goods which try to introduce risk analyses, life-cycle assessments, cost-benefit calculations into any decision-making, limit precautionary measures to provisional action, etc.

2.   Composition and marketing of products

6–06   There are only a few EU provisions on the making of products. It is general EU policy that a certain technology for products should not be prescribed in order to reach environmental results and that EU legislation should set targets (results) to be achieved, such as emission limits, and leave it to manufacturers how to achieve these results. Obviously, this principle more applies to machinery than to other products. Indeed, chemical legislation does provide, via the establishment of lists of substances that may or that may not be used in a product, for direct influence on the product; an example is the sector of pesticides, where EU legislation is setting up a list of active substances that may be used in pesticides.[31] Also, the legislation on end of life vehicles and electrical and electronic products which prohibits the use of certain heavy metals in these products belongs to this category.[32]

In contrast to that, the European Union has never applied the principle of art.191(2) TFEU according to which environmental impairment should be rectified at source, to its general product-related legislation. It did not request cars to be equipped, from a certain time onwards, with catalytic converters, but rather fixed emission limit values that could, at the time when they were fixed, only be reached when a catalytic converter was used. In the same way, it is unthinkable that EU legislation would ever require cars to be built in a way that they cannot run quicker than 100km/hour or that they use not more than three litres of petrol per 100km; at least this last legislation is partly in force in California. Within the European Union and in Germany, France, Italy, etc., the car industry is much too influential to ever accept such legislation.

In 2005, the Council and Parliament adopted Directive 2005/32 on the eco-design of energy using products, which was, in 2009, updated by Directive 2009/125.[33] The Directive was based on art.114 TFEU; it was part of the European Union's policy to fight climate change by increasing energy efficiency. It provided for measures at EU level to reduce energy consumption of products, relying to a considerable degree on self-regulation, industrial standardisation, etc. As a first step, stand-by losses and products that offer a high potential for cost-effective reduction of greenhouse gas emissions, such as heating and water

---

[31] See paras 6–39 et seq., below.

[32] See Dir.2000/53 (fn.26, above) and Dir.2002/95 (fn.14, above).

[33] Dir.2005/32, [2005] OJ L191/29; in 2009, this Directive was replaced by Dir.2009/125 establishing a framework for the setting of eco-design requirements for energy-related products [2009] OJ L285/10.

heating equipment, electric motor systems lighting, domestic appliances, office equipment, consumer electronics and heating ventilating air conditioning systems were tackled. Overall, the work programme under this Directive provided for regulations for 57 product groups. The instruments used are Commission regulations, adopted in the form of comitology decisions; obviously, voluntary agreements by producers and industrial standards do not function. Economic operators appear to be too much afraid of free-riders and third country producers who would not be subjected to voluntary provisions. Though the Directive allowed to also tackle other issues of eco-design, such as water consumption, noise levels, or material use, in the recitals it was clarified that the (only) priority would be to reduce the emission of greenhouse gases.

End of 2005, the Commission made a communication on a thematic strategy on the sustainable use of natural resources.[34] The communication underlined the necessity of life-cycle thinking for products, from raw materials to the waste stage. The objective is to reduce the environmental impacts of using natural resources. The measures announced mainly address Member States and do not let anticipate the promotion of legally binding instruments to ensure "ecologically sound and sustainable product design". The Commission expressly clarified that it had no intention to phase out bad materials for the making of products. The announcement of measures to prevent waste generation were not to propose binding instruments either.[35] Overall, the strategy[36] was not really a strategy, but a—rather superficial—description of the present situation and the expression of hope that something will change in the future.

Environmental directives and regulations have established some lists of substances or products[37] that were considered dangerous for the environment, frequently taking inspiration from international environmental conventions.

6–07

Directive 76/464 on water discharges which was, in 2006, codified under the number of Directive 2006/11, created a black list of substances and products, which were selected because of their toxicity, persistence and bioaccumulation; a second list of substances was fixed, which have "a deleterious effect on the aquatic environment".[38] For list I, a priority list of 129 substances was then agreed, which should be regulated by Community emission standards[39]; these measures were brought to a halt in 1991, after only 17 substances had been regulated. Under Directive 2000/60[40] which will repeal Directive 76/464–2006/11 by 2013, a list of hazardous substances was established in 2001 which were to be further examined in view of a prohibition to discharge them into

[34] Commission, COM(2005) 667.

[35] Ibid.

[36] Commission, Communication: Taking sustainable use of resources forward: a thematic strategy on the prevention and recycling of waste, COM(2005) 666.

[37] EU terminology is not consistent. Sometimes, the word "substances" is used, where clearly a preparation, i.e. a mixture or composition of two or more substances, is meant.

[38] Dir.76/464 on pollution caused by certain dangerous substances discharged into the aquatic environment of the Community [1976] OJ L129/23, in particular art.6 and annex, list I; codification of Dir.76/464 by Dir.2006/11 [2006] OJ L64/52.

[39] Council Res. of February 1983 [1983] OJ C46/17. For details on the monitoring of Directive 76/464, see paras 7–24 et seq.

[40] Dir.2000/60 establishing a framework for Community action in the field of water policy [2000] OJ L327/1.

waters.[41] This list included substances—for instance atrazine, benzene, naphta-line, pentachlrophenol or simazine—and groups of substances such as cadmium, mercury, nickel, lead and their compounds. In 2008, a new directive fixed environmental water quality standards and pollution controls for substances which was again different from the 2001 list.[42]

Directive 84/360 on air emissions[43] contained another list of pollutants that were to be considered; no indication was given as to how these substances and products had been selected. The pollutants were not systematically tackled. This list was practically replaced by another list of air pollutants which was laid down in Directive 96/62 on ambient air quality for which air quality standards were to be elaborated[44]; on pollutants in general, Directive 96/61—in 2008 replaced by Directive 2008/1 and in 2010 by Directive 2010/75—on integrated prevention and pollution control laid down a list for air and water pollutants.[45]

The Stockholm Convention on Persistent Organic Pollutants (POP) which was signed in 2001, by the European Union and all its Member States and which was transposed into EU law by way of a Regulation 850/2004, provides for a list of 12 persistent organic pollutants which are to be internationally banned.[46] For existing chemicals, four priority lists were established which list some 120 priority substances which were to undergo a risk assessment under Regulation 793/93[47] in view of a decision, whether to provide for a future restriction or ban or for not taking action.[48] These four lists became more or less obsolete with the adoption of Regulation 1907/2006 and the new assessment mechanisms which it set up.

All these lists had no direct influence on product-related provisions adopted at EU level, but were, rather, aimed at framing EU policy for the limitation of the emission of pollutants into the environment. The EU institutions did not take them as binding either, but were quite loose in working according to the frame which was set by them, sometimes just not following the list and elaborate detailed emission limit or concentration values.

6–08   Restrictions concerning the composition of products had been mainly—but by no means exclusively—inserted into in Directive 76/769[49] which had, up to mid-2006, been amended more than thirty times. This Directive is now replaced:

---

[41] Dec.2455/2001 establishing the list of priority substances in the field of water policy [2001] OJ L331/1.

[42] Dir.2008/105 on environmental quality standards in the field of water policy [2008] OJ L348/84.

[43] Dir.84/360 on the combating of air pollution from industrial plants [1984] OJ L188/20; for more details see paras 8–31 et seq.

[44] Dir.96/62 [1996] OJ L296/55; this Directive was, in 2008, replaced by Dir.2008/50 on ambient air quality and cleaner air for Europe (2008), L 152/1.

[45] Dir.96/61 on integrated pollution prevention and control [1996] OJ L257/26; Dir. 2008/1 on integrated pollution prevention and control [2008] L 24/8; Dir.2010/75 on industrial emissions [2010] OJ L334/1.

[46] Reg.850/2004 [2004] OJ L158/7. The 12 substances are: Polychlorinated biphenyls PCB, dioxins, furans, aldrin, dieldrin, endrin, DDT, chlordane, hexachlorobenzene, mirex, toxaphene and heptachlor. See also Dec.2006/597 by which the EC adhered to the Stockholm Convention [2006] OJ 209/1; the text of the Convention is reproduced there at p.3.

[47] Regs 1179/94 [1994] OJ L131/3; 2268/95 [1995] OJ L231/18; 143/97 [1997] OJ L25/13.

[48] Reg.793/93 on the evaluation and control of the risks of existing substances [1993] OJ L84/1.

[49] Dir.76/769 relating to restrictions on the marketing and use of certain dangerous substances and preparations [1976] OJ L262/201.

the restriction of chemicals will be regulated under the REACH-system for chemical substances and inserted in its annex XVII.[50]

Most initiatives for introducing EU-wide restrictions came from Member States, which introduced bans or restrictions of substances or products in order to protect humans or the environment. This then initiated the procedure under Directive 76/769, since the Commission wished to preserve the unity of the internal market, which requires uniform product standards. It is likely that also in future the majority of initiatives to restrict the use of substances will come from Member States; only gradually will the new Chemical Agency be able to assume itself a leading role and propose restrictions, based on the safety assessments that it receives.

There are only very limited possibilities to provide for interim EU-wide measures that take a substance or a product from the market. When, in 2000, the Commission was of the opinion that six phtalates presented a risk in children's toys and made a proposal for a directive to have the use of these phtalates restricted, it had to recur to Directive 92/59 on general product safety[51] which allowed for interim measures to be taken for a period of three months. As the Commission's proposal was only adopted in 2005,[52] the interim measures had in the meantime been prolonged more than ten times.

Detergents

The first provisions that regulated the composition of products concerned products where diverging national provisions risked the creation of barriers to the free circulation of goods. Thus, from 1973, a Directive prohibited the placing on the market of detergents which were less than 90 per cent biodegradable[53]; since that Directive had to be adopted unanimously and no real consensus was reached as to whether a percentage of 80 or 90 per cent should apply, a compromise was found that the detergent could be placed on the market, as long as the harmonised test methods showed that it is biodegradable by 80 per cent.[54]

6–09

In 2005, a completely new regulation on detergents was adopted which replaced the existing legislation[55] and dealt with the biodegradability of all surfactants in detergents, not only that of anionic and non-ionic surfactants. The Regulation provides for the use of different test standards, which may be used alternatively, as obviously no consensus on the use of one standard exists. The biodegradability must normally be 60 per cent (five test methods, Annex III A) or 70 per cent (two other test methods, Annex III B). Where this biodegradability is not reached, the producer may ask for a derogation, which may, under certain

---

[50] Reg.1907/2006 (fn.16, above); see in particular Commission Reg.552/2009 [2009] OJ L164/7 which transferred the restrictions of Dir.76/769 into annex XVII of Reg.1907/2006; furthermore Commission Reg.276/2010 [2010] OJ L86/7.

[51] Dir.92/59 (fn.2, above).

[52] Dir.2005/84 [2005] OJ L344/40. These restrictions are now found in Reg.1907/2006, annex XVII, no.52.

[53] Dir.73/404 on the approximation of the laws of the Member States relating to detergents [1973] OJ L347/51.

[54] Dir.73/405 on the approximation of the laws of the Member States relating to methods of testing the biodegradability on non-ionic surfactants [1973] OJ L347/53; subsequently, Directives 82/242 [1982] OJ L109/1 and 82/243 [1982] OJ L109/18 completed the provisions for testing methods.

[55] Reg.648/2004 on detergents [2004] OJ L104/1.

conditions, be granted by the EU Commission (comitology procedure), provided the biodegradability does not exceed 80 per cent (Annex II).[56]

Fuels and biofuels

6–10   The combustion of fuels releases pollutants that contaminate the environment—the damage caused by one tonne of sulphur dioxide is estimated at 4,000 €.[57] Measures concerning the composition of fuels concentrated on the reduction of pollutants. As Member States had different perceptions of environmental problems, it is not surprising that such differences reappeared when fuels were regulated.

EU legislation started with regulating the sulphur content of gas oil which was fixed between 0.5 and 0.8 per cent.[58] In 1987, a general level of 0.3 per cent was introduced.[59] However, Member States were allowed to require the use of gas oil with a sulphur content of 0.2 per cent in regions with high pollution or "where damage to the environment or to the national heritage caused by total sulphur dioxide emissions requires" a lower sulphur content than 0.3 per cent; it was clear that such a provision was not really ensuring common standards. As the Commission found in 1991 that Belgium, Germany, Denmark, Luxembourg and the Netherlands applied the 0.2 per cent limit on their whole territory, Directive 93/12, based on the present art.114 TFEU, generalised this approach and applied the sulphur content level of 0.2 per cent throughout the European Union.[60]

Diesel fuels that contain too much sulphur create problems for the use of catalytic converters in diesel cars. In order to remedy this, and to reduce air pollution, Directive 93/12 introduced a level of 0.2 per cent sulphur as of the end of 1994 and 0.05 per cent as of the end of 1996; the Directive stated expressly that this was necessary in order to reach the emission limit values fixed in other EU provisions. However, a directive of 1999 fixed the maximum permissible sulphur content in gas oil at 0.2 per cent as of July 1, 2000 and at 0.1 per cent as of January 1, 2008.[61] Member States were allowed to use, until 2013, gas oil with a sulphur content between 0.1 and 0.2 per cent, if the quality standards of Directive 80/779 were respected and the emissions did not lead to an exceeding of the critical quantities in other Member States; of course, these latter requirements cannot really be controlled: how could the Commission prove, in a litigation under art.258 TFEU, that the quality standards were respected? Furthermore, Spain (for the Canary Islands), France (for its overseas departments), Greece and Portugal (for Madeira and the Açores) were allowed, for an unspecified time, to use gas oil with a higher sulphur content than 0.2 per cent.

6–11   As regards heavy fuels which are used, among others, by ships, the Commission published, in 1997, figures according to which most sulphur dioxide emissions in the European Union stemmed from the burning of coal (62.9 per cent), heavy fuel (18.4 per cent), gas oil/diesel (7.0 per cent) and refinery fuels

---

[56] As to the equivalence of results, see Reg.648/2004 (fn.55, above), Annex IIIB: "It should be noted that the pass criterion of at least 70 percent of these methods is to be considered as equivalent to the pass criterion of at least 60 percent referred to in the methods listed in point A".

[57] Commission, COM (1997) 88, p.44.

[58] Dir.75/716 [1975] OJ L307/22.

[59] Dir.87/219 [1987] OJ L91/19. This Dir. was based on the present art.115 TFEU.

[60] Dir.93/12 on the sulphur content of certain liquid fuels [1993] OJ L74/81.

[61] Dir.1999/32 [1999] OJ L121/13.

(6.5 per cent).[62] As part of the EU strategy to combat acidification, Directive 1999/32 reduced the sulphur content of heavy fuel oils as of 2003 to 1 per cent. However, Member States obtained the possibility of allowing the use of heavy fuels with a sulphur content of up to 3 per cent, provided that the air-quality standards for sulphur dioxide laid down in Directive 80/779[63] and other EU provisions, were respected and that the contribution to transboundary pollution was negligible. It should be noted again that the respect of quality standards under Directive 80/779 are not and cannot really be monitored, as it was not indicated for how much time compliance with standards must have existed, whether transboundary pollution also referred to non-EU regions and how this kind of pollution was assessed.

Directive 2005/33, based on art.114 TFEU, amended Directive 1999/32.[64] It fixed the sulphur level of heavy fuels at 1 per cent as of January 1, 2003—thus retro-actively!—and of marine fuels for ships which sail under a flag of Member States or use Member States' ports at 1.5 per cent. However, this last restriction applied only to the Baltic Sea and, in anticipation of a decision under the Convention on Maritime Pollution (MARPOL), the North Sea. The European Union thus clearly wanted to let sea transport provisions prevail over environmental considerations and leave the decision of generally limiting the sulphur content of marine fuels to the international maritime organisations. For inland waterway vessels the sulphur content was fixed at 0.1 per cent as of 2010, with some exceptions for some Greek vessels.

Directive 98/70[65] fixed the maximum sulphur content of diesel fuel (and petrol) at 350mg/kg; this level was to be reduced to 50mg/kg by 2005. Member States were allowed to introduce more stringent requirements for sensitive areas, subject to Community authorisation. This limit was amended by Directive 2003/17 and lowered to 10 mg/kg as of January 1, 2005.

6–12

Member States were likewise divided on the lead content of petrol. Directive 78/611[66] fixed the lead content to 0.4g per litre, but allowed Member States to lower this level down to 0.15g. Until 1986, Ireland was allowed to apply a level of 0.64g. The reason for this split standard was the fact that Germany had already introduced, as of 1976, a lead content of 0.15g, and was not prepared to go back on this decision.

In the early 1980s, campaigns on reducing the lead content in the air—for health reasons in the United Kingdom, for environmental reasons (Waldsterben—the problem of dying forests) in Germany—led the European Council to ask for the introduction of lead-free petrol,[67] which was proposed in May 1984 and adopted in March 1985, almost a record time.[68] The Directive required Member States to "take the necessary measures to ensure the availability and balanced distribution within their territories of unleaded petrol from 1 October 1989" (art.3). Unleaded petrol was defined as petrol that contained less than 0.013g of lead per litre, leaded petrol as containing between 0.15g and 0.40g of lead per

[62] Commission, COM (91) 154.
[63] Dir.80/779 [1980] OJ L229/30.
[64] Dir.2005/33 [2005] OJ L191/59.
[65] Dir.98/70 [1998] OJ L350/58.
[66] Dir.78/611 [1978] OJ L197/19.
[67] See (1993) 6 *Bulletin of the European Communities*, 1.5.15.
[68] Dir.85/210 on the approximation of the laws of the Member States concerning the lead content of petrol [1985] OJ L96/25.

litre. Member States were also authorised to prohibit leaded regular petrol,[69] which eliminated the free circulation of such petrol within the European Union.

6–13   Other content requirements for petrol concerned the benzene content, which was fixed at 5 per cent, the minimum motor octane number (85) and the minimum research octane number (95) of unleaded petrol. The vague wording of art.3 made any monitoring of the effective introduction of unleaded petrol practically impossible. It was the Member States' policy and the mineral oil companies that determined the speed of the introduction of unleaded petrol. Generally, this introduction advanced more quickly where a Member State had introduced a tax differentiation between leaded and unleaded petrol.[70]

At the end of 1998, Directive 85/210 was replaced by Directive 98/70, which was based on art.114 TFEU.[71] This Directive prohibited the marketing of regular leaded petrol as of January 2000, reduced the benzene content to 1.0 per cent and contained a number of other specifications for unleaded petrol.

6–14   In 2009, Directive 2009/30 further reduced the sulphur content of petrol and diesel[72] which was fixed, as a rule at 10 mg/kg. Some derogations and transition provisions were fixed. Directive 2009/28 required that by 2020, the share of energy from renewable sources in all forms of transport was at least 10 per cent of the final consumption of energy in transport.[73] "Biofuels" were defined as liquid or gaseous fuels for transport, produced from biomass. Biomass "means the biodegradable fraction of products, waste and residues from biological origin from agriculture (including vegetal and animal substances), forestry and related industries including fisheries and agriculture, as well as the biodegradable fraction of industrial and municipal waste". Detailed provisions intended to ensure that such biofuels do not come from "land with high biodiversity value". The Directive enumerates in this regard primary forest and other wooded land; areas designated for nature protection areas or for the protection of recognised rare, threatened or endangered ecosystem or species; highly biodiverse grassland; wetlands; continuously forested areas; forests of more than one hectare; and peatland. Obviously these are also production standards which might constitute, in the eyes of the United States or other protagonists of free trade, obstacles to free trade.

The controversy with environmental organisations how the requirement of the production of biofuels can be ensured, wether the large-scale use of biofuels does not lead to significant environmental impairment, and how biofuels production in third countries can be effectively controlled, is in full swing within the European Union.

---

[69] Dir.87/416 [1987] OJ L225/33.

[70] See European Environmental Agency, *Environmental taxes: implementation and environmental effectiveness* (Copenhagen, 1996), p.30 ("The tax differentiation schemes for fuels have been particularly successful") and p.55 (annex II, where the Agency reports on the Swedish tax differentiation for leaded petrol). The Commission had proposed such a tax differentiation [1984] OJ C178/5, but the Council had considered this to be a question for Member States alone.

[71] Dir.98/70 [1998] OJ L350/58.

[72] Dir.2009/30, [2009] OJ L140/88. This Dir. was based on the present art.114 TFEU and, as regards the greenhouse gas emission reductions and amendments for marine fuels, on the present art.192 TFEU.

[73] Dir.2009/28 on the promotion of the use of energy from renewable sources [2009] OJ L140/16. This Dir. was based on the present art.192 TFEU and, as regards the sustainability criteria of biofuels, their verification and calculation, on the present art.114 TFEU.

The different provisions on diesel and petrol fuel, based sometimes on art.114,   **6–15**
sometimes on art.192 TFEU, and containing numerous derogations, transitions
and authorisations for Member States' derogations, illustrate well the changing
motivations behind the EU approach, which varies between environmental
protection and internal market considerations. Recently, art.192 TFEU seems to
be favoured.

The different provisions do not concern the composition of fuel for cars
generally. There are numerous additives that are added to petrol in order to
influence its quality, which may later, in the form of emissions, enter the
environment. A new art.8a of Directive 98/70, inserted by Directive 2009/30
asked the Commission to establish by 2012, for the first time, a test methodology
for metallic additives. The additive MMT was restricted in use (6 mg per litre).[74]

Cars

There are almost no EU environmental provisions on the making of cars.   **6–16**
However, numerous provisions exist that decide on the air emissions from cars,
although it is left to car manufacturers to decide how they intend to comply with
the emission standards, whether they install a catalytic converter, and use an
electro motor or another motor with a low consumption of fuel and thus generate
only low emissions. Thus, for instance, the noise levels from cars are fixed in the
form of emission-limit values, but do not require the use of particular materials,
designs or tyres, etc., in order to comply with these values.

Sometimes the different objectives pursued in the car sector contradict each   **6–17**
other. Thus, a reduction of the weight of cars, which would lead to less fuel
consumption, might contradict the objective of increased safety of passengers.
The increased use of plastic materials, which make a car lighter, could make the
recycling of end-of-life vehicles more difficult. The use of aluminium in cars
recurs to a material that is produced in a very polluting way, etc.

The European Union never considered imposing certain product standards on
cars, such as, for instance, a maximal fuel consumption, the use of certain
materials or fuels, or an in-built speed limitation for cars. Directive 2009/125 on
the eco-design of energy using products,[75] which allows the European Union to
provide for design requirements, could apply in theory also to cars and lead to
provisions imposing a certain design; however, as the climate change situation is
not yet perceived as being serious enough, this consideration is, for the time
being, purely theoretical, and cars are expressly exempted from the provisions of
that Directive.

The Directive on end-of-life vehicles[76] contained an article on waste
prevention, but suggested measures for promotion and encouragement as regards
car design and production, recycled materials and hazardous substances in cars;
another provision provided for a ban of the use of lead, mercury, cadmium and
hexavalent chromium, though a number of derogations were foreseen. Finally, the
Directive provided for cars to be 85 per cent recyclable by 2015, which again will
have an impact on the composition of cars.

---

[74] See for MMT also Court of Justice, *Afton Chemicals* (C–343/09) judgment of July 8, 2010.
[75] Dir.2009/125 establishing a framework for the setting of ecodesign requirements for energy related
products [2009] OJ L285/10.
[76] Dir.2000/53 (fn.26, above).

Packaging

6–18   Directive 94/62 on packaging and packaging waste[77] provided for a reduction of the total metal content of four heavy metals—cadmium, lead, mercury and polyvalent chromium—in three steps by the year 2001. The Directive did not fix methods for the measuring of this content. Specific requirements for the composition of packaging were not laid down. There was, however, an interesting combination of the new approach system for product harmonisation and environmental requirements: Member States were obliged to accept on their markets all packaging that complied with the essential requirements of Directive 94/62, which were laid down in an annex II. They included the provision that "packaging shall be designed, produced and commercialised in such a way as to minimise its impact on the environment when packaging waste or residues from packaging waste management operations are disposed of", that packaging "shall be so manufactured that the presence of noxious and other hazardous substances and materials... is minimised with regard to their presence in emissions, ash or leachate when... packaging waste are incinerated or landfilled". These provisions would easily allow a Member State, which so wishes, to prohibit PVC packaging, to restrict the use of aerosols or to provide for other restrictions on the use of packaging; this would raise difficulties, since Directive 94/62 is based on art.114 TFEU, which aims at ensuring the free circulation of packaging.

6–19   CEN (see para.6–67, below) was charged with elaborating European standards for the essential environmental requirements for packaging. As the CEN standards did not correspond to the Directive's requirements, but were drafted in a rather loose and vague way, the Commission initially refused, under the procedure of Directive 98/34[78] to recognise four of them as harmonised EC standards[79]—which would have meant that compliance with the CEN standards created a presumption of compliance with the Directive's requirements. CEN then represented the same standards after some time, and this time got the EU approval, as the environmental enthusiasm diminished in the meantime. As no Member State seems to have, at present, the intention to pursue a strong national policy to reduce or prevent packaging waste, the political impact of this failure to set up environmentally strong harmonised EU standards for packaging was limited.

Other products that contain heavy metals

6–20   The European Union regulated the composition and marketing of a considerable number of products, in particular to ensure the establishment and functioning of the internal market. These include foodstuffs, animal feeding stuff, pharmaceuticals, cosmetics, textiles, toys, pesticides, fertilizers, drinking water, batteries, packaging, paints and varnishes, construction material, footwear, not to mention non-consumer goods such as ships, airplanes or office equipment. Scattered in these provisions there are sometimes provisions that prohibit or restrict the use of this or that substance. The following examples may be given. Directive 2006/66[80]

---

[77] Dir.94/62 on packaging and packaging waste [1994] OJ L365/10.
[78] Dir.98/34 (fn.18, above).
[79] Commission Dec.2001/524 [2001] OJ L190/21.
[80] Dir.2006/66 (fn.29, above).

prohibited the use of certain batteries, where the mercury levels fixed in the Directive are exceeded. Lead carbons and lead sulphates may not be used in paints[81]; some derogations are allowed for the restoration of works of art and historic buildings.[82] Mercury, arsenic or organostannic compounds[83] may not be used to prevent the fouling by micro-organisms (plants or animals) of boats, in fish or shellfish farming and in the preservation of wood.[84] Cadmium and its compounds are banned from use as colourants or stabilisers for different products; also cadmium plating is forbidden in a number of expressly defined products.[85] Finally, nickel is prohibited for use in products which come in contact with the human skin.[86] In cars and in electrical and electronic equipment the use of cadmium, mercury, lead and hexavalent chromium is prohibited,[87] in electrical and electronic equipment furthermore the use of polybromated biphenyls (PBB) and diphenyls.[88] The different provisions contain each time a number of exceptions, derogations or transition provisions.

As can be seen, the restrictions are anything but systematic. Most of the provisions concern heavy metals, in particular lead, mercury or cadmium. In recent times, substances that deplete the ozone layer or lead to the emission of greenhouse gases are also regulated. It is true that a small number of products such as PCBs[89] or asbestos[90] were forbidden by the European Union, mainly in reaction to national bans. However, the phase-out periods were extremely long.   **6–21**

Until now, there was only one attempt to systematically tackle the problem of dangerous substances in products; this was the attempt to regulate cadmium. The first environmental action programme designated cadmium, together with other substances, as a substance that should be examined as a priority, because of its toxicity and its effect on human health and on the environment.[91] The Council confirmed in 1975 that an examination into the effects of cadmium on water was already ongoing and asked for an examination of air emissions of cadmium.[92] In 1981 the Commission asked the Consultative Scientific Committee on the toxicity and ecotoxicity of chemical compounds for an opinion on cadmium, which recommended the reduction of cadmium emissions wherever possible.[93]   **6–22**

In 1987, the Commission sent a communication to the Council, in which it listed 20 directives which limited the use of cadmium, suggested an action

---

[81] Dir.76/769 (fn.49, above).

[82] As regards lead, see also Written Question E–0837/96 (Muscardini) [1996] OJ C297/35.

[83] For these substances see Written Question 1139/89 (Adam) [1990] OJ C328/4.

[84] Dir.76/769 (fn.49, above), nos 19, 20 and 21.

[85] Dir.76/769, no.24.

[86] Dir.76/769, no.28.

[87] Dir.2000/53 (fn.26, above).

[88] Dir.2002/95 (fn.14, above).

[89] As regards PCB, Dir.76/769 (fn.49, above) prohibited the marketing in 1983. However, Dir.96/59 on the elimination of PCB/PCT [1996] OJ L243/31 provided for the final elimination of these materials till 2010.

[90] Asbestos was partly prohibited in the EU by Dir.83/478 [1983] OJ L263/33 which amended Dir.76/769 (fn.49, above); in 1999, Dir.1999/77 [1999] OJ L207/18 introduced an almost total ban.

[91] First environmental action programme [1973] OJ C112/1, p.13.

[92] Res. of June 24, 1975 [1975] OJ C168/4.

[93] Scientific Consultative Committee on the toxicity and ecotoxicity of chemical compounds, opinion of April 1981, published in Activity Report 1979–1983 (EUR 9246) (Luxembourg, 1984), p.37.

programme consisting of nine points to eliminate cadmium from the environment[94] and announced that it would, within two years, submit proposals for all nine points. The Council approved the strategy.[95] In 1991, the Council adopted a Directive to reduce the cadmium content as colourant, stabiliser or surface coating for a number of products,[96] and this Directive was to be reviewed "at regular intervals" —though this was never done.

6–23　　Nevertheless, the Commission considered it necessary to include cadmium and its different compounds into its priority lists for existing chemicals,[97] which were established under Regulation 793/93[98] and which are designed to assess the effects of substances on man and the environment. This assessment, for which Belgium was in the lead, started in 1996 and was finished in 2008, thus after 12 years. The Commission adopted a recommendation on cadmium which had a very limited content—resuming 35 years of attempts to reduce the presence of cadmium in the environment.[99]

The main source of the presence of cadmium in the environment is the cadmium content of fertilisers that are used in agriculture. EU law does not contain limit values for cadmium concentrations in fertilisers, but the national legislation of the three acceding Member States—Sweden, Austria and Finland—did. The Accession Treaty therefore provided that this legislation could be maintained for four years; in the meantime, a re-examination of the EU provisions would take place. In 2003, the European Union adopted new legislation on fertilisers, which again did not provide for a limit of cadmium.[100] The Commission announced that it would present a proposal on the cadmium content of fertilisers; until then, it granted Austria, Sweden, Finland and the Czech Republic derogations under art.114 TFEU to continue to apply their limitations; until the end of 2010, this proposal has not been presented. Overall, this transition period thus exists already for more than fifteen years. This sequence of events shows that a systematic EU approach as regards cadmium simply does not exist.

In 2005, the Commission presented, at the request of the Scandinavian countries, a Communication for a strategy to reduce the emissions of mercury. The strategy listed more than 20 actions that could be taken at EU level to reduce the use and the emissions of mercury, among others also to ban its export by 2011. This was finally decided, for a number of mercury containing products, in 2008.[101]

Overall, though, no systematic approach to substitute heavy metals, wherever this is possible, exists until now at EU level.

---

[94] Commission, "Environmental pollution by cadmium. Proposal for an action programme", COM (87) 165.
[95] Res. of January 25, 1988 [1988] OJ C30/1.
[96] Dir.91/338 amending, for the tenth time, Dir.76/769 [1991] OJ L186/59.
[97] See Reg.143/97 [1997] OJ L25/13, nos 2 and 3.
[98] Reg.793/93 (fn.48, above).
[99] Commission Rec. 2008/446 [2008] OJ L156/22; the reference to the Belgian risk assessment is found in [2008] OJ C149/6.
[100] Reg.2003/2003 on fertilisers [2003] OJ L304/1; see also, by way of example, the derogation granted to Sweden, Dec.2006/347 [2006] OJ L129/19.
[101] Reg.1102/2008 on the banning the exports of metallic mercury and certain mercury compounds and mixtures and the safe storage of metallic mercury [2008] OJ L304/75; see also Directive 2007/52 [2007] OJ L257/13 which provided for some restrictions of mercury in products on the EU market.

Products containing ozone-depleting substances

In order to protect the ozone layer, the European Union has adopted a number of measures as regards ozone-depleting substances.[102] The Montreal Protocol[103] deals with such substances, but only indirectly touches the question of products that contain ozone-depleting substances.[104] It is true, though, that art.2(11) of the Protocol allows Contracting Parties to "take more stringent measures" than those required by the Protocol. These provisions, incidentally, also apply to "products produced with, but not containing" ozone-depleting substances.

6–24

The European Union could thus, by virtue of the Montreal Protocol, which has been transposed into EU law by Regulation 1005/2009,[105] take measures to prohibit products that contain ozone-depleting substances or had been produced with the help of such substances, without infringing provisions of the World Trade Organisation.[106] However, it has not yet done so, but has instead limited its measures to the substances themselves. Regulation 1005/2009 also prohibits the use of ozone-depleting substances in air condition installations, refrigerators and fire extinguishers.

Chemical substances and preparations

Chemicals, in the form of substances, preparations, pesticides, fertilisers, pharmaceuticals, cosmetics and food additives, are extensively regulated at EU level, since for all these products uniform rules are necessary to establish a common market. Pharmaceuticals, cosmetics and food additives will not be discussed in this book, since health issues prevail and environmental elements are peripheral in these sectors. EU legislation on substances and preparations (a preparation is a mixture of several substances) is based on art.114 TFEU and tries to achieve total harmonisation; this means that national legislation on chemicals that diverges from existing EU provisions is, in principle, not allowed.[107]

6–25

For legislation on chemicals, four basic steps can be distinguished, which can be found in the different EU measures:

1. data collection on the different chemicals;
2. priority setting for regulating chemicals;
3. risk assessment of the chemical;
4. risk management (limiting use and emissions, etc.).

It is a question of political choice, whether—pending the execution of these four steps for the individual chemical—the chemical is to be allowed to be used

---

[102] See for more details, paras 9–26 et seq., below.

[103] Montreal Protocol of September 16, 1987 on substances that deplete the ozone layer; the Protocol was adhered to by the EU by Dec.88/540 [1988] OJ L297/8.

[104] art.4(3) of the Protocol provides for rules to be elaborated that prohibit the import of products containing ozone-depleting substances from States that are not party to the Protocol; art.9(1b) invites research and development of alternatives to products that contain ozone-depleting substances.

[105] Reg.1005/2009 on substances that deplete the ozone-layer [2009] OJ L286/1; this Reg. replaced the earlier Reg.1037/2000 [2000] OJ L244/1.

[106] The EU adhered to WTO by Dec.94/800 [1994] OJ L336/1.

[107] See as a good example on the discussion about total harmonisation Court of Justice, Case C–473/98 (fn.13, above).

without restrictions, to what extent the burden of proof for the harmlessness of a chemical is on its manufacturer or importer or on the public authorities, to what extent the precautionary principle is to apply, and so on.

The pre-REACH system: existing and new chemicals

6–26　　As regards chemical substances, EU legislation, until 2006, differentiated between new and existing chemicals. Existing chemicals were those that were on the EU market on September 18, 1981[108]; these existing chemicals—exactly 1,001,06 substances—were listed in the EINECS inventory.[109] Their manufacturer or EU importer, by virtue of Directive 67/548,[110] had to classify, pack and label them according to their hazard potential and may then trade them freely in the European Union.[111] The European Union tried, by way of a Committee procedure that is described in detail in Directive 67/548, to provide progressively for a statutory classification of these substances, by assessing their risk for man and the environment; where such a risk was identified, the substance was placed into annex I of Directive 67/548. That annex listed the name of the substance, the category of danger attributed to the substance,[112] the label and indications assigned to the substance, risk phrases, which indicate the nature of the special risk, and safety phrases indicating the recommended safety precautions. Furthermore, it listed the concentration limits of a substance contained in a preparation which was necessary to qualify that preparation as dangerous under Directive 88/379.[113]

6–27　　By the end of 2005, annex I contained some 5,000 substances,[114] a considerable achievement, but small compared to the volume of more than 100,000 substances on the market and the time—some 30 years—which was needed for this classification; 1,500 other substances were considered, after examination, not to be hazardous. In order to accelerate the procedure, Regulation 793/93[115] was introduced. It provided that manufacturers or EU importers had to inform the Commission of which substances they produce or import in quantities of 1,000 tons or more and provide information on those substances, such as on their toxicity or ecotoxicity, carcinogenicity and "any other indication relevant to the risk evaluation of the substance". Overall, it was

---

[108] This date is the date on which Dir.79/831 [1979] OJ L259/10, which amended Dir.67/548 on the classification, labelling and packaging of dangerous substances [1967] OJ 196/1 for the seventh time, entered into effect.

[109] [1990] OJ C146A/4.

[110] Dir.67/548 (fn.108, above).

[111] Commission, Report on the operation of Dir.67/548, Dir.88/379, Reg.793/93 and Dir.76/769, SEC(1998) 1986 of November 18, 1998, mentions on p.13 that a survey with 100 companies had shown that 25 per cent of the examined substances were not correctly classified and over 40 per cent were not correctly labelled.

[112] Dir.67/548 (fn.108, above), art.2 fixed the following 15 categories of danger: explosive, oxidising, extremely flammable, highly flammable, flammable, very toxic, toxic, harmful, corrosive, irritant, sensitising, carcinogenic, mutagenic, toxic to reproduction and dangerous to the environment. "Dangerous to the environment" was defined as "substances and preparations which, were they to enter the environment, would present or may present an immediate or delayed danger for one or more components of the environment".

[113] Dir.1999/45 relating to the classification, packaging and labelling of dangerous preparations [1999] OJ L200/1.

[114] See last amendment Dir.2001/59 [2001] OJ L225/1.

[115] Reg.793/93 (fn.48, above).

found that some 2,500 substances were marketed in the European Union in quantities of more than 1,000 tons per year, and 15,000 to 20,000 substances in quantities between 10 and 1,000 tons.[116]

On the basis of that information, EU priority lists for about 110 substances were established, for which an evaluation of their risk to humans or the environment seemed urgent[117]; a specific regulation laid down principles for the assessment of risks to man and the environment, subdivided into human health (toxicity), human health (psycho-chemical properties) and environmental considerations.[118] For each substance on the priority list, a Member State was appointed rapporteur for the evaluation. These evaluations ended with the suggestion by the reporting Member State that either no risk-reduction measures beyond those already applied were necessary, that there was a need for further information and/or testing, or that the available information justifies an EU ban or restriction of use of the chemical. On the basis of the national report, the European Union was asked to decide, by way of committee procedure, on the "results of the risk evaluation" and, if necessary, on "an appropriate strategy for limiting those risks".

The procedure for the risk assessment was extremely slow and took years, in particular where more controversial substances, such as cadmium or phtalates, were in question. For this reason, only a limited number of risk assessments for the priority substances were completed.[119] This is not really surprising, since the—non-binding—guidance document on how to make a risk evaluation comprised about 700 pages.[120]   **6–28**

Substances which were, on September 18, 1981, not yet placed on the EU market and therefore were not included in the EINECS inventory, were *new* substances. Such substances had to be, subject to a number of exceptions laid down in Directive 67/548, notified to the competent authority of the Member State where the substance was produced or—in the case of a manufacturer outside the European Union—where the notifier was established, at least 60 days before the substance was placed on the EU market. This notification had to be accompanied by a technical dossier, a proposal for the classification and labelling of the substance and a proposal for a safety data sheet. The technical dossier had to include the results from testing the substance; the number and intensity of the tests varied depending on the quantity of the substance to be marketed. The test procedures were laid down in annex V of Directive 67/548, which contained 17 test methods for the determination of physico-chemical properties, 38 for the toxicity for humans and only 12 test methods for testing the (aquatic) ecotoxicity of a substance. Where the notifier learned, after notification, of new effects of the substance on humans or the environment, he had, at his own initiative, to inform the competent authority of this.   **6–29**

---

[116] Commission, SEC(1998) 1986 (fn.111, above).

[117] Regs 1179/94 [1994] OJ L131/3; 2268/95 [1995] OJ L231/18; 143/97 [1997] OJ L25/13.

[118] Reg.1488/94 [1994] OJ L161/3.

[119] See as examples, Commission Recommendations 2002/575 on the results of the risk evaluation and the risk reduction strategies for the substances o-anisidine and 1,4-dioxane [2002] OJ L181/29; 2002/ 576 on ethyl acetoacetate, 4-Chloro-cresol and Dimethyldioctadecylammonium chloride [2002] OJ L181/35.

[120] Commission, "Technical guidance document in support of Commission Directive 93/67 on risk assessment for new notified substances and Commission Regulation 1488/94 on risk assessment for existing substances", Pts I–IV (Luxembourg, 1996).

Upon receipt of the notification the national competent authority checked whether it conformed with the requirements of the Directive, informed the notifier of its conclusions and carried out a risk assessment of the notified substance, which identified the risk for humans and the environment linked to the marketing of the substance.

6–30   In this regard, Directive 93/67[121] stated[122]:

> "the assessment of risks should be based on a comparison of the potential adverse effects of a substance with the reasonably foreseeable exposure of man and the environment to that substance; ... the assessment of risks to man should take account of the physico- chemical and toxicological properties of a substance; ... the assessment of risks to the environment should take account of the environmental effects of a substance."

It also defined "hazard identification",[123] such as the toxicity or carcinogenicity of a substance, and "risk characterisation",[124] which is the likelihood of harm.

The competent national authority had to send information to the European Commission consisting of a summary of the notification dossier, a proposal for the classification and labelling, a proposal for the inclusion of the substance in the European list of notified chemical substances (ELINCS—European List of Notified Chemical Substances) and the conclusions of the risk assessment. The Commission had to forward copies of this information to the competent authorities of all other Member States.

6–31   Any other Member State could ask for details of the dossier or suggest further tests. The final decision on the classification, packaging and labelling of the substance was decided by committee procedure; the Committee could, of course, also decide not to classify a substance as dangerous. By the end of 2005, some 3,000 new substances had been notified and, where appropriate, classified, placed into annex I of Directive 67/548 and registered in ELINCS.[125] The Commission regularly published the list of notified substances.

Restrictions on marketing and use

6–32   Where a Member State considered that a substance or a preparation, while complying with the requirements of Directives 67/548 or 88/379, posed a risk to humans or the environment, the Member State could impose restrictions on its circulation or prohibit it. The Commission had to be notified of such measures. An EU procedure was then opened, which leads to an EU-wide decision, taken by a qualified majority.[126] Where a substance or a preparation which was not yet regulated at EU level posed, according to the opinion of a Member State, a risk to humans or the environment, the Member State could provisionally ban or restrict

---

[121] Dir.93/67 laying down the principles for assessment of risks to man and the environment of substances notified in accordance with Dir.67/548 [1993] OJ L227/9.

[122] Dir.93/67 (fn.121, above), recitals 4–6.

[123] Dir.93/67, art.2(2a): "'hazard identification' is the identification of the adverse effects which a substance has an inherent capacity to cause".

[124] Dir.93/67, art.2 (2d): "'risk characterisation' is the estimation of the incidence and severity of the adverse effects likely to occur in a human population or environmental compartment due to actual or predicted exposure to a substance, and may include 'risk estimation', *i.e.* the quantification of that likelihood."

[125] The Commission indicated (fn.111, above) p.32 that two studies had revealed that between 5 and 40 per cent of new substances had not been notified at all and were thus illegally marketed.

[126] See for this safeguard procedure, para.3–72, above.

its marketing or use. It had, however, to notify its draft measure to the Commission, which examined the compatibility of the national measure with the provisions on the free circulation of goods[127] and checked, at the same time, whether EU measures were necessary in order to preserve the unity of the internal market.

The different measures taken at EU level to ban or restrict the use of chemical substances and preparations, either on the abovementioned "initiative" by a Member State or at the Commission's initiative, were normally[128] assembled in Directive 76/769.[129] The Directive was based on art.114 TFEU. The restrictions were laid down in an annex to the Directive, which was, up to the end of 2005, amended or adapted 33 times, providing for restrictions on some 50 substances or groups of substances and covering about 900 individual substances.[130] The specific bans or restrictions of use were the subject of very complex discussions at EU level, where the various different economic interests frequently had a decisive influence on the outcome of the discussions. Most of the bans or restrictions of use are influenced by health considerations; environmental concerns play only a subordinate role.

6–33

Directive 76/769 had in particular restricted: PCBs and PCTs[131]; several chemical substances that are used in ornamental objects, sneezing powders, artificial snow, etc.[132]; benzene in toys[133]; fire retardants[134]; asbestos[135]; lead in paint and anti-fouling applications[136]; pentachlorophenol[137]; cadmium[138]; Tris and nickel in contact with the skin[139]; carcinogens, teratogens and mutagens[140]; creosotes and some chlorinated solvents[141]; hexachlorethane[142]; organostannic

6–34

---

[127] The procedure is laid down in Dir.98/34 (fn.18, above).

[128] See, however, the restrictions for pesticides (paras 6–40 et seq., below), ozone-depleting substances (para.9–26, below), heavy metals in packaging or in batteries (paras 6–18 et seq., above), etc.

[129] Dir.76/769 (fn.49, above).

[130] This rather large figure should be considered with caution. Indeed, most of the insertions into annex I of Dir.76/769 were placed there because a great number of chemical substances were classified, under Dir.67/ 548, as carcinogenic and the Council took a basic decision that such substances should not be sold to consumers. The number of "regular" restrictions on use of substances is relatively small.

[131] Dir.76/769 (n.49); Dir.82/828 [1982] OJ L350/34; Dir.85/467 [1985] OJ L269/56; Dir.91/339 [1991] OJ L186/64 (which concerned Ugilec 21 and 141 and DBBT, which are PCB substitutes); Dir.89/677 [1989] OJ L398/19.

[132] Dir.79/663 [1979] OJ L197/37; Dir.83/264 [1984] OJ L147/9; Dir.94/48 [1994] OJ L331/7; Dir.97/ 64 [1997] OJ L315/13.

[133] Dir.82/806 [1982] OJ L339/55.

[134] Dir.83/264 (fn.132, above).

[135] Dir.83/478 [1983] OJ L263/33; Dir.85/610 [1985] OJ L375/1; Dir.91/659 [1991] OJ L363/1; Dir.1999/77 [1999] OJ L207/18.

[136] Dir.89/677 (fn.131, above).

[137] Dir.91/173 [1991] OJ L85/34; Dir.1999/51 [1999] OJ L142/22.

[138] Dir.91/338 [1991] OJ L186/59; Dir.1999/51 (fn.137, above).

[139] Dir.79/663 [1979] OJ L197/37; Dir.94/27 [1994] OJ L188/1. Directive 94/27 on nickel has not yet become effective, since CEN has not yet produced the necessary standards for testing methods.

[140] Dir.94/60 [1994] OJ L365/1; Dir.97/56 [1997] OJ L333/1, which listed some 800 carcinogens; Dir.1999/43 [1999] OJ L166/87.

[141] Dir.94/60 (fn.140, above).

[142] Dir.97/16 [1997] OJ L116/31.

compounds[143]; short chain chlorinated paraffins[144]; azocolorants[145]; arsenic[146]; and pentabromodiphenyl and octabromodiphenyl ethers.[147]

6–35 Amendments of Directive 76/769 had to be adopted in the form of a special Council and Parliament Directive, which was a slow and laborious procedure considering the risk that many chemicals pose. Past attempts by the Commission to introduce a simplified procedure[148] only succeeded in so far as existing restrictions could be adapted by way of committee procedure. As mentioned already, the adoption of Regulation 793/93[149] had not led to a quicker decision-making procedure. There was no attempt being made systematically to restrict the marketing or use of harmful chemicals, on condition of the availability of substitutes. On questions from members of the European Parliament, the Commission has de facto admitted this situation.[150] Rather, the Directive's annex was normally amended where the EU measure endeavoured to take up a ban or restriction that had previously been initiated by a Member State at national level, where an accident demonstrated the need to take action or where the results of national research, a new assessment of available data, public concern, etc., made action appropriate. This explains why most of the amendments to the annex of Directive 76/769 appear to be of a patchwork nature and not to deal with the most important substances or products.

6–36 Moreover, the Commission tried, since 1994,[151] to propose amendments of Directive 76/769 only where a "targeted" risk analysis and a cost-benefit analysis ("advantages and drawbacks") justified such action. These conditions de facto slowed down any action for restricting the use of chemicals, particularly as the risk analysis was focused more on aspects of human health and much less on environmental concerns; furthermore, environmental concerns were, by definition, of non-economic nature and all attempts objectively to measure the economic value of environmental assets or impairments have not succeeded so far.

It is impossible to differentiate, as regards measures under Directive 76/769, between measures to protect human health and measures to protect the environment. Indeed, it appears already from the wording of art.191 TFEU that environmental measures also aim at protecting human health. Furthermore, substances may be banned or restricted in use in one Member State because that state mainly considers their negative effect on the environment, whereas another Member State considers their effect on human health; examples of this are lead, cadmium or PCB.

6–37 The EU measures of 1983 for restricting the use of chrysotile asbestos—the only asbestos fibre the use of which had remained permissible at EU level—applied to about 40 per cent of all asbestos-containing products. Since

---

[143] Dir.1999/51 (fn.137, above); Dir.2002/62 [2002] OJ L183/58.

[144] Dir.2002/45 [2002] OJ L177/21.

[145] Dir.2002/61 [2002] OJ L243/15.

[146] Dir.2003/2 [2003] OJ L4/9.

[147] Dir.2003/11 [2003] OJ L42/45.

[148] Commission proposal for a directive, COM (83) 556 and [1990] OJ C30/89.

[149] Reg.793/93 (fn.48, above).

[150] See Written Questions 2098/85 (Staes) [1986] OJ C137/12 (on HCH, lindane and bromophos); 2695/85 (Schmid) [1986] OJ C299/16 (on paradichlorbenzole); 632/88 (Glinne) [1989] OJ C132/31 (on impregnating sprays); 778/89 (Schmid) [1990] OJ C125/14 (on azo-colours); E–2336/91 (Glinne) [1994] OJ C140/1 (on parathion).

[151] Since the adoption of Dir.94/60 (fn.140, above).

some Member States considered these measures insufficient, they progressively banned all asbestos products at national level. Instead of taking action against these nine Member States for not complying with the requirements of Directive 76/769, the Commission prepared a total ban of such asbestos at EU level, which was finally adopted in 1999.[152]

When Directive 91/173 introduced limitations on the use of pentachlorophenol, Germany notified its intention under the old art.100a(4) EC Treaty to maintain a total ban for this product. The Commission accepted this ban; however, on the request of France, the Court of Justice annulled that decision, because it had not been sufficiently justified.[153] The Commission then took a second decision,[154] which was not contested. Similar derogations were granted to pentachlorophenol bans in the Netherlands, Denmark and Sweden. And the EU provisions on the use of creosotes[155] led to a number of derogations granted, under art.114(4) TFEU to different Member States.

Overall, the application of Directive 76/769 remained reactive: the Directive's principal objective was the free circulation of chemicals. Therefore, substances and preparations which presented a risk to humans or the environment were not systematically assessed and subsequently subjected to restrictions. Rather, the EU reacted to national—exceptionally also to international—initiatives and endeavoured and tried to find an EU-wide solution.

The REACH reform

Preceded by a White Paper on a Strategy for a future chemicals policy in 2001   **6–38**
and an internet consultation with more than 6,000 comments, the Commission submitted a proposal for a far-reaching reform of the chemicals legislation in 2003. The proposal was based on art.114 TFEU. The European Parliament tabled some 3,000 amendments, of which only a small part was accepted by the Council. The main discussions went on the question of what economic burden the new Regulation would place on economic operators. Impact assessment studies varied between four and 258 billion euros. Despite these controversies, the proposal was adopted at the end of 2006.[156] The new Regulation which abandoned the differentiation between existing and new chemicals became progressively applicable since 2008; it will become fully applicable after eleven years, thus shortly before 2020.

The Regulation created a European Chemicals Agency, which was established in Helsinki and will have a staff of some 600 persons. As regards *registration*, all chemical substances—some substances, such as polymers, are exempted, though—which are manufactured or imported in quantities of more than one tonne will have to be registered with the Agency. The registration must be accompanied by technical dossier with test results about the risks that the substances might present. Where certain quantities are exceeded, a chemical safety report has to be produced. Some substances also have to be registered, where they are contained in articles, as hazardous substances may be released

---

[152] Dir.1999/77 [1999] OJ L207/18.
[153] *France v Commission* (C–41/93) [1994] E.C.R. I–1829.
[154] Dec.94/783 [1994] OJ L316/43.
[155] See Dir.94/60 (fn.140, above).
[156] Reg.1907/2006 (fn.16, above).

from the article. Manufacturers furthermore have to address the risks of any use that have been identified to them by downstream users. The new element of this Regulation is that at present, knowledge about the properties and uses of existing chemicals often does not exist or is not shared by the manufacturers, as no testing and registration requirements exist for such chemicals. Manufacturers and importers must now accomplish the tests of the substance, identify the potential risks and transmit these data to the Agency.

The *evaluation* will evaluate the dossier that was submitted as regards completeness, quality and the need to prevent unnecessary animal testing. Furthermore, the Agency may require to submit more information on a substance, where it has the suspicion that a risk to human health or the environment might exist.

Substances which are of very high concern, as they have hazardous properties, shall be the subject of an *authorisation* system. This concerns substances that are carcinogenic, mutagenic, toxic for reproduction (CMR substances), persistent, bioaccumulative and toxic or which have endocrine disrupting properties. The applying manufacturer has to demonstrate that the risk from the use of the substance is adequately controlled. According to the Regulation, the application is made to the Agency, whereas the authorisation itself is granted by the Commission, which bases itself on the findings of the Agency.

Restrictions may be fixed, where a chemical presents an unacceptable risk to human health or the environment, which need to be addressed on a EU-wide basis. The dossier is prepared by the Agency, in close consultation with Member States; the decision on any restriction is taken by the European Union. The restrictions that were laid down in Directive 76/769, were taken over by Regulation 1907/2006 and inserted into annex XVII to the Regulation.[157]

During the first years of its existence, the Agency is mainly occupied in registering all the existing chemicals for which manufacturers and importers have progressively to submit the required data. The procedures on the authorisation procedure and on the chemicals that shall be subjected to this procedure, are also absorbing a considerable amount of resources. As all chemicals are affected that are marketed within the European Union, the Regulation has a strong impact on trade in chemicals and products worldwide.

Pesticides and biocides

6–39   Pesticides in EU terminology are subdivided into agricultural (plant protection products) and non-agricultural (biocides) pesticides. As regards agricultural pesticides, of which some 25,000 with about 700 active substances are thought to be on the market, Regulation 1107/2009 which replaced Directive 91/414, deals with the authorisation for their placing on the market[158]; a number of directives deal with pesticide residues on and in fruit and vegetables, cereals and foodstuffs of animal origin.[159]

---

[157] Commission Regs 552/2009 and 276/2010 (fn.50, above).
[158] Reg.1107/2009 concerning the placing of plant protection products on the market [2009] OJ L309/1; this Reg. replaced Dir.91/414 [1991] OJ L230/1.
[159] Dir.76/895 relating to the fixing of maximum levels for pesticide residues in and on fruit and vegetables [1976] OJ L340/26; Dir.86/362 on the fixing of maximum levels for pesticide residues in and on cereals [1986] OJ L221/37; Dir.86/363 on the fixing of maximum levels for pesticide residues

Plant protection products

Regulation 1107/2009, based on arts 43, 114 and 169 TFEU, regulated the   **6–40**
placing on the market of plant protection products (agricultural pesticides). The
Regulation differentiated between products that have to authorised by the
individual Member States and the active substances for such products (which are
authorised by the European Union). An agricultural pesticide may only be
authorised to be placed on the market if it contains an active substance that is
listed—and is thus authorised EU-wide—in Regulation 1107/2009. The Regulation fixed a number of conditions for the authorisation of pesticides, such as the
requirement that the pesticide may not have unacceptable effects on plants, does
not have damaging effects on the health of humans or animals or on the
groundwater or does not have unacceptable effects on the environment in general.

The authorisation of a pesticide is valid for the Member State for which it was
requested. For the recognition of the pesticide in another Member State, the
Regulation divided the European Union in three biogeographical zones, North,
Centre and South.[160] When the recognition is asked for a Member State of the
same zone, this recognition has to be given, subject to some exceptional
situations. For the authorisation in another zone, a new authorisation has to be
requested.

Active substances are assessed, as regards their effects, by an EU mechanism.
Applicants must submit detailed dossiers, and a comprehensive risk assessment
which are examined and assessed, on the basis of a Member State's report, by the
Standing Committee on Plant Health[161]; the substance is, after a positive
decision, registered in annex to Regulation 1107/2009. The programme for
examining existing active substances was to be finished by the year 2003, but was
prolonged; no final decision on active substances—which is normally made for a
period of 10 years—has yet taken place. In the meantime, the Commission and
Member States accept that some pesticides are banned or not authorised in one
Member State,[162] but are permitted to be used in other Member States; this is
clearly not compatible with considerations of free circulation of pesticides, but
also cannot be prevented.

Where the examination revealed that the requirements for an EU-wide
authorisation of the active substance were not fulfilled, the Commission took a
decision, addressed to the Member States, asking them to repeal all authorisation
for pesticides that contain that active substance.[163]

---

in and on foodstuffs of animal origin [1986] OJ L221/43; Dir.90/642 on the fixing of maximum levels
for pesticide residues in and on certain products of plant origin, including fruit and vegetables [1990]
OJ L350/71.
[160] See Reg.1107/2009, Annex I: The zone North includes Denmark, Estonia, Latvia, Lithuania,
Finland and Sweden; the zone Centre includes Belgium, Czech Republic, Germany, Ireland,
Luxemburg, Hungary, Netherlands, Austria, Poland, Romania, Slovenia, Slovakia and United
Kingdom; the zone South includes Bulgaria, Greece, Spain, France, Cyprus, Malta and Portugal.
[161] This Committee was set up by Dec.76/894 [1976] OJ L340/25.
[162] See, e.g. Written Question 2600/88 (Megahy) [1989] OJ C276/30, where the Commission stated
that captan is banned in one Member State, dinoseb in seven, methylbromid restricted for use in three,
parathion in two and phosdrin in four Member States. Another well-known case is that of Atrazina,
which is banned in several Member States, but authorised in others.
[163] See, e.g. Dec.95/276 [1995] OJ L170/22, repealing the authorisation for pesticides containing the
active substances ferbam and azinphosetyle; Dec.98/269 [1998] OJ L117/13 repealing the

In 2009, a directive was adopted on the sustainable use of pesticides which required Member States to adopt National Action Plans in order to reduce risks and dependence on pesticides, to provide for compulsory training of distributors and professional users.[164] The Directive was based on art.192 TFEU.

Biocides

6–41   The Directive on the authorisation of non-agricultural pesticides (biocides), was adopted in 1998, on the basis of art.114 TFEU[165]; a revision, following the orientations of Regulation 1107/2009, is at present being discussed by the EU institutions. The Directive concerns pesticides such as disinfectants, preservatives, pest-control products, anti-foulants and insecticides—overall, some 15,000 products. These products were grouped in 23 product types, which constitute an exhaustive list for the Directive's application.

The structure of this Directive was very similar to that of the old Directive 91/414. New active substances will be authorised by the European Union and inserted into a positive list (annex I). The evaluation will be based on the report of a Member State, which acts as rapporteur and which will receive data from the applying manufacturer. Existing active substances will be assessed as to whether they can be inserted into annex I; it is thought that this review programme will take 10 years. Biocidal products will continue to be authorised by the different Member States, on the basis of common principles that are laid down in the Directive. Authorisations given in one Member State must in principle be recognised by other Member States.

Ban of plant protection products

6–42   Bans and restrictions of use of agricultural pesticides were, until 2006, regulated by Directive 79/117, which was based on art.115 TFEU and which contained a positive list of pesticides that are banned for use within the European Union.[166] This list was regularly updated. Member States were entitled to ban other pesticides where the conditions of arts 34/36 TFEU were fulfilled, as the list of Directive 79/117 was not exhaustive.[167] Member States were also entitled temporarily to authorise the use of the banned pesticides for specific purposes. The list enumerates, among others, aldrin, dieldrin, chlordan, DDT, heptachlor and hexachlorbenzol. The REACH-Regulation 1907/2006 repealed that Directive which means that bans of pesticides are now either decided under the procedures of Regulation 1907/2006 or by way of a specific EU legislation.

---

authorisation for pesticides containing the substance dinoterb; Dec.98/270 [1998] OJ L117/15 repealing the authorisation for pesticides containing the substance benvalerat.

[164] Dir.2009/128 establishing a framework for Community action to achieve the sustainable use of pesticides [2008] OJ L309/71.

[165] Dir.98/8 concerning the placing of biocidal products on the market [1998] OJ L123/1.

[166] Dir.79/117 prohibiting the placing on the market and use of plant protection products containing certain active substances [1979] OJ L33/36.

[167] Court of Justice, *Brandsma* (C–293/94) [1996] E.C.R. I–3159; *Harpegnies* (C–400/96) [1998] E.C.R. I–5121.

Products from biotechnology

EU legislation on biotechnology and products derived from biotechnology, which   **6–43**
started in the mid-1980s, is scattered, because in particular in the areas of
agriculture and food on the one hand, and of pharmaceuticals on the other hand
numerous directives fix specific provisions for certain products; these provisions
are not presented here, since they concern the sectors of agriculture, consumer
protection, health or industrial policy. As regards the environment, two basic
Directives, on the contained use of genetically modified micro-organisms[168] and
on the deliberate release of genetically modified organisms (GMO),[169] were
adopted in 1990; the Directive on the deliberate release was substituted, in 2001,
by Directive 2001/18.[170] A third directive, on the legal protection of
biotechnological inventions, was adopted in 1998, after 10 years of discussion at
EU level.[171] This Directive is based on art.114 TFEU. It provides for the
protection of such inventions by national patent law of Member States and
completes these provisions with a number of common rules. Furthermore, the
European Union adopted legislation on GMOs in food and feed[172] and the
transport of GMOs.[173]

Directive 2009/41 on the contained use of genetically modified micro-
organisms[174] was based on art.192 TFEU. It defined micro-organisms as any
microbiological entity, cellular or non-cellular, capable of replication or of
transferring genetic material; this definition shows that the Directive deals with
living beings, which are, for economic reasons, treated as chemicals. The
Directive divided contained-use operations into those which are for teaching,
research, development or non-industrial or non-commercial purposes and which
are of small scale (type A operations) and other (type B) operations. Before an
installation is used, a notification has to be made to the competent authorities,
which describes the work, the scale of the operation and an "assessment of the
contained uses as regards the risks to human health and the environment that may
occur". The amount of information to be notified depends, furthermore, on the
type of micro-organisms and the operations to be carried out. If new aspects
become known, which might affect the risk, this information must also be
conveyed. Also, information on any accident—"any incident involving a
significant and unintended release ... which could present an immediate or
delayed hazard to human health or the environment"—that has occurred, has to
be given to the authorities.

The competent authorities must examine the completeness of the information   **6–44**
received. In certain cases, operations may not begin before consent is given; in
other cases, a waiting period of 60–90 days must be respected. The authorities

---

[168] Dir.90/219 on the contained use of genetically modified micro-organisms [1990] OJ L117/1; this
Directive was, in 2009, codified under number 2009/41, [2009] OJ L175/75.

[169] Dir.90/220 [1990] OJ L117/15.

[170] Dir.2001/18 on the deliberate release of genetically modified organisms [2001] OJ L106/1.

[171] Dir.98/44 [1998] OJ L213/13.

[172] Reg.1829/2003 on genetically modified food and feed [2003] OJ L268/1.

[173] Reg.1946/2003 on the transboundary movement of genetically modified organisms [2003] OJ
L287/1.

[174] Dir.2009/41 (fn.168, above).

may put conditions for the operations to be carried out, may provide a consultation of "groups or the public" and may generally take all measures that they consider necessary.

Since, in particular, economic operators considered several provisions of the Directive too restrictive—including the "small scale" requirement—a major amendment of the Directive was adopted in 1998.[175] The different procedures were simplified; notably the procedures for the risk assessment of the operation were specified in more detail, and the number of micro-organisms that come into the lower categories of risky organisms was considerably increased.

6–45   Directive 2001/18,[176] which was based on art.114 TFEU, dealt with the deliberate release into the environment of genetically modified organisms (GMOs) and of products that contain such organisms. The Directive replaced Directive 90/220 which had been in force since 1990 and had two sections, on experimental releases of GMOs and on the release of products. Its application had led to more than 1,000 experimental releases and some thirty releases of products containing GMOs.[177]

6–46   A crisis in the application of Directive 90/220 broke out in 1996.[178] The Swiss company, Novartis had applied, in France, for the authorisation to market genetically modified maize (Bt-maize). France examined the dossier that accompanied the application and considered that the risk assessment which was part of the dossier, allowed the placing on the market of the maize. It thus sent the application with a favourable opinion to the European Commission, which transmitted the dossier to the other Member States. The Commission shared France's opinion that the placing on the market should be allowed and therefore submitted a corresponding proposal to the Committee set up under Directive 90/220. However, the great majority of the Member States (13 out of 15 Member States) was of the opinion that the risk assessment did not allow the placing on the market; they held that further research was necessary. Under the committee procedure of Directive 90/220, an opinion of the Committee which differed from the Commission's proposal, needed unanimity; and this unanimity could not be reached as France sided with the Commission. The dossier then went to the Council, which again needed, under art.293 TFEU, unanimity in order to amend the Commission's proposal. As France sided once more with the Commission, the fact that 13 Member States favoured a rejection of the application, was of no help. Under the committee procedure, the dossier therefore went back to the Commission which then decided to give a positive opinion to the application.[179]

This decision led to strong reactions from the Member States. A number of them adopted national provisions, which prohibited the placing on the market of the maize, invoking a safeguard clause of Directive 90/220. As all Member States expressed concern on the procedure and at the same time there was "growing concern on the part of the general public . . . with . . . this new technology", the Commission did not take legal action against Member States. Under this moratorium, no further application under Directive 90/220 was made, discussed or decided at EU level. Rather, the elaboration of amendments to Directive

[175] Dir.98/81 [1998] OJ L330/13.
[176] Dir.2001/18 (fn.170, above).
[177] Commission COM (1998) 85.
[178] Part of the events are described in Court of Justice, *Greenpeace France* (C–6/99) [2000] E.C.R. I–1651, in particular *in* the Advocate General's Opinion.
[179] Commission Dec.97/98 [1997] OJ L31/69.

90/220, was prepared. When the Commission suggested amendments, Parliament and Council agreed that it would be better to have a completely new Directive; this finally led to the adoption of Directive 2001/18. The Directive became effective in October 2002; in 2003/2004, the standstill on the placing of new GMO-containing products on the market ended, at the same time, when new legislation on genetically modified food and feed was adopted.[180]

Directive 2001/18 distinguished between releases for "any other purpose than the placing on the market"—in particular thus releases for research, development or experimental purposes—and the placing on the market of GMOs "as or in products". A deliberate release for "other purposes" must be notified in advance to the competent authority of the Member State in which the release is to take place, and be accompanied by a technical dossier. This dossier must in particular contain information on the GMO, the conditions of release and the receiving environment, a plan for monitoring, information on control, remediation methods, waste treatment and an environmental risk assessment, for which detailed provisions are laid down. The competent authority must, within 90 days, decide in writing on the application, provided the dossier is complete; the authorisation procedure is thus purely national. However, where the competent authority is of the opinion that sufficient experience has been obtained with such a release, it may ask the release to be admitted EU-wide. In this case, all other Member States become involved in the decision. The public "and, where appropriate, groups" (art.9) shall be consulted on deliberate releases. Furthermore, the public shall be informed of all "other-purposes" releases.

6–47

Where GMOs are placed on the market "as or in products", again the applicant has to submit a notification to the competent authority where the product is to be placed on the market for the first time. The application and a summary of the accompanying dossier is immediately transmitted to the other Member States and the Commission. The notification shall contain extensive information and documentation, in particular on the GMO, indications for use and handling, the environmental risk assessment, data on results form research and development releases, the conditions for placing on the market, a monitoring plan as well as a proposal for packaging and labelling of the product. The competent authority must react to the notification within 90 days. Where it decides that it has sufficient information which indicates that a GMO release would not put a risk to humans or the environment, it shall send the dossier to the European Commission, together with an assessment report and an indication whether the GMO product should or should not be placed on the market. The other Member States who also receive the dossier, and the Commission may ask for further information; they may also comment on the application or present reasoned objections to the placing on the market of the GMO (product). The aim is to arrive at a final EU-wide decision on the application within 105 days from the date of circulation of the assessment report. The summary of the notified dossier and of the assessment report must be made available to the public. Comments from the public shall be circulated among public authorities.

6–48

Where objections are raised, the period for decision-making is prolonged to 120 days. The Commission is then obliged to consult the relevant EU Scientific Committee.[181] The Commission also may consult any committee that it has set up

6–49

---

[180] See para.6–50, below.
[181] On this Committee see para.6–01, above.

with a view to obtaining advice on the ethical implications of biotechnology. The Commission shall then elaborate a proposal for a decision, which is submitted to the Committee that was set up, in conformity with Decision 1999/468,[182] under art.30 of Directive 2001/18. Where the Committee agrees with the Commission proposal, the Commission takes the decision. Where the Committee does not give an opinion or disagrees, the Commission's proposal is referred to the Council, which has three months to decide. If the Council opposes the proposal with a qualified majority, the Commission shall re-examine it, re-present it anew to the Council, shall present a modified proposal or present a legislative proposal.[183] Where the Council does not raise objections, the Commission adopts its proposal and sends the dossier back to the Member State that first received the notification. That Member State finally authorises the placing on the market of the GMO (-product).

6–50   In order to further mitigate concerns of consumers and public opinion, the Council adopted a regulation on novel food,[184] which required food products that contain GMOs to be authorised EU-wide or—where the risk is less great—notified and bear a corresponding label, in so far as differences to normal food products can scientifically be detected. Furthermore, Commission Regulation 1813/97[185] and Council Regulation 1139/98[186] fixed supplementary labelling requirements for the labelling of food and food additives that were produced with the help of GMOs.[187]

Regulation 1829/2003 on genetically modified food and feed[188] deviated, for these products, considerably from Directive 2001/18. Applications under this Regulation are now to be made to the European Food Safety Authority (EFSA), seated in Parma; Member States only play a marginal role in the authorisation procedure. It is EFSA which evaluates the application and gives, if possible within six months, an opinion on it to the Commission. The Commission decides within three months and by Comitology procedure, whether to authorise the placing on the market of the product.

The participation of the public is almost not ensured.[189] And it is not surprising that the "club"-attitude of EFSA and the considerable secrecy surrounding the decision-making process has raised considerable suspicion with public opinion in Europe, which remains—including the majority of farmers—sceptical with regard to the new technology. Almost all authorisations that were given since the end of the moratorium were given under the new procedure of Regulation 1829/2003, no longer under Directive 2001/18. A WTO condemnation of the European Union for practising a moratorium and not authorising GMO-products

---

[182] Dec.1999/468 [1999] OJ L184/23.

[183] Dec.1999/468, art.5.

[184] Reg.258/97 on novel food and novel food ingredients [1997] OJ L43/1; see also Commission Reg.1813/97 [1997] OJ L257/7.

[185] Commission Reg.1813/97 [1997] OJ L257/7.

[186] Reg.1139/98 [1998] OJ L159/4.

[187] See also Commission Regs 49/2000 [2000] OJ L6/13 and 50/2000 [2000] OJ L6/15.

[188] Reg.1829/2003 (fn.172, above).

[189] See on participation in the decision-making procedure for authorising GMO-products para.4–14, above.

any more, which had examined the procedure under Directive 2001/18, did thus not raise concerns within the European Union.[190]

Regulation 1946/2003 dealt with the transboundary movement of genetically modified organisms,[191] following a requirement of the Cartagena Protocol on biosafety. The European Union adhered to the Protocol itself by Decision,[192] the Court of Justice having confirmed, at the request of the Commission, that art.192 and not 191(4) and/or 207 TFEU was the appropriate legal basis for that Decision.[193] The Regulation was based on the principle of prior informed consent, in order to promote trade in GMO-products.

In Summer 2010, the Commission proposed to let Member States decide whether they would allow the planting of GMO-seeds in their country, provided that such a decision would be based on other considerations than those of health and the protection of the environment.[194] The underlying consideration was that health and environment aspects were already harmonised at EU level. This proposal appears inconsistent: objections against the planting of GMO-seeds are just based on health or environmental concerns: even where such plants might impair organic agricultural production, the concern is one of health. Indeed, consumers buy organic food, because they consider it to be less treated with chemicals, produced in an environmentally more friendly way, etc. The underlying reason for favouring organic food is thus the concern for health and/or the environment. The correct way of addressing the concern of numerous Member States would have been to suggest either that the legal basis for the EU legislation were changed and art.192 TFEU became the legal basis, allowing Member States to recur to art.193 TFEU and completely prohibit GMO-plants (or GMO-animals), or inserting the provisions of art.193 TFEU into the existing EU legislation which is possible, even where the legislative act is based on art.114 TFEU.[195]

The twenty years of discussion on the placing of genetically modified products on the market of the European Union have thus led to a strong centralisation of the permitting procedure. As the European Union is not a State, many of the democratic safeguards which exist at the level of a Member State, have disappeared or been reduced at EU level, such as full access to the scientific data which accompany the application, a public discussion of the necessity and opportunity to authorise the placing of the market, of the health and environmental risks linked to this placing on the market, etc. Opinion polls show a continued public hostility to the use of genetically modified food, feed and seeds—though much less of medical and industrial uses. An increasing concern is that of a cross-fertilisation of organic farming products by GMO-farming, which would make organic farming—the relevant EU provisions provide that organic farming must be GMO-free—impossible.

6–51

---

[190] World Trade Organisation, Case DS 291 *USA v European Union*, Panel Report of 29 September 2006.

[191] Reg.1946/2003 (fn.173, above).

[192] Dec.2002/628 [2002] OJ L201/48.

[193] Court of Justice, Opinion 2/00 [2001] E.C.R. I–9713.

[194] Commission, COM(2010) 375.

[195] A recent example is Dir.2010/63 on the protection of animals used for scientific purposes [2010] OJ L276/33 which is based on art.114 TFEU and allows Member States to maintain or introduce more stringent national measures; see para.5–32, above.

The health risk of GMO products seems not beyond suspicion, if one considers long-term effects, plant resistance, allergy issues and the uncertainty of animal tests. It is not clear why this technology should be introduced: it is made for industrial agriculture, brings limited benefits to farmers who already produce too much food, does not constitute a solution to the hunger in the world—which is a problem of distribution, not of production—and favours patents on life of industrial companies. The environmental problem with GMOs is that once they are released into the environment, they cannot be taken back. GMO-products in agriculture seem to require the increased rather than the decreased use of pesticides, because plants and pests get resistant to the new product. Also the co-existence with organic food production is, at long term, impossible. From that angle, the public request, based on the precautionary principle, to err on the side of caution, is more than understandable. However, it seems that in view of the worldwide development and expansion of this new technology—in particular in agriculture, food and pharmaceuticals—the large-scale introduction of genetically modified organisms into the environment is no longer reversible, unless new data demonstrate the long-term adverse health and environmental effects.

The difference of approach between public opinion which is afraid of and therefore opposed to biotechnology, and economic operators and EU public authorities which favour it and try to press this technology on the market, cannot be solved by providing for labelling for GMO-products, at least not as long as the European Union does not introduce a label "GMO-free"—which the Commission has rejected until now. A label that informs consumers of the presence of GMOs which is meant to allow consumers to make an informed choice will have little or no effect in many situations (hotels, restaurants, catering, food aid), apart from the fact that labels are not frequently read. And the placing on the market of agricultural GMOs in developing countries is not in the general interest of those countries and their economic development, as it rather increases economic dependence on industrialised countries. Overall, GMO-technology in agriculture seems to be a technology that is superfluous, profitable to few, promoting industrial agriculture and bearing risks for humans and the environment.

PVC

6–52   Polyvinyl chloride (PVC) is a chemical preparation that is at present produced in quantities of about 5 million tonnes per year within the European Union. It is mainly used as building material (about 55 per cent), packaging (14 per cent), and in toys, cars, pipes, etc. More than half of the PVC consists of chlorine, an irritant that is not found in other plastic raw material. In order to ensure the specific properties of PVC, the use of additives—plasticisers and stabilisers—is necessary. The main plasticisers are phthalates, of which several hundred exist. The European Union classified DEHP, the most commonly used phthalate, as not carcinogenic, but did not take a final classification decision on its other dangerous properties.[196] At present, DEHP and two other phthalates are the subject of a risk evaluation of Regulation 793/93. Phthalates are suspected to have long-term negative effects in the aquatic environment and to be endocrine disruptors, which may disturb the hormone system of mammals and humans.[197]

---

[196] Commission Dec.90/420 [1990] OJ L222/49.

[197] See also Commission, Communication on endocrine disruptors, COM(1999) 707.

Stabilisers used in PVC are mainly lead and cadmium (both toxic and bioaccumulative) and organo-tin compounds (which are considered toxic to the aquatic environment). Substitutes, mainly on the basis of barium-zinc or calcium-zinc, exist, but are less often used, for economic reasons.

Manufacturing of PVC creates some environmental problems; however, the main problems occur during its use, incineration (which generates hydrochloric acids, residues with high concentrations of heavy metals and dioxins) and landfill (where a risk of leaching of heavy metals exist). Recycling of PVC proves, at present, extremely difficult.

There is little EU legislation on PVC. Directive 86/280[198] established water-emission limit values of 1.2-dichlorethane (EDC), another additive of PVC; however, no air-emission standards have ever been fixed for this substance or for other componants of PVC. Cadmium is limited for use in many PVC applications. As regards incineration, Directive 94/67 on the incineration of hazardous waste fixes air-emission standards, particularly for dioxins[199]; however, PVC waste is not classified as hazardous waste and no dioxin standards as yet exist for the incineration of non-hazardous waste.   **6–53**

An EU recommendation of 1998 suggested to Member States that they take the necessary measures in order to ensure a high level of health protection of toys destined to be put in the mouth by small children and which contained certain phthalates.[200] Under public pressure, this was turned into an amendment of Directive 76/769 that restricted the use of phtalates.[201]

A number of Member States and third countries have looked into the question whether, in view of its environmental effects at the waste stage, it would not be appropriate to restrict the use of PVC generally. In its proposal on the directive for end-of-life vehicles, the Commission made some remarks on this point, though the adopted directive did not take up this point.[202] Should a restriction on the use of PVC ever come into force, this would constitute the first EU measure with regard to a product in view of its behaviour in the waste stage. Since any restriction of the use of PVC is heavily opposed by economic operators, such EU action is not very likely to succeed. Rather, it may be expected that measures are taken against some PVC additives—cadmium, lead and phthalates—and not against PVC itself.   **6–54**

3. Environmental labelling

The European Union developed a considerable number of labels which refer to environmental aspects of products,[203] without forming a consistent and coherent   **6–55**

---

[198] Dir.86/280 [1986] OJ L181/16.

[199] Dir.94/67 [1994] OJ L365/34.

[200] Rec.98/485 [1998] OJ L217/35.

[201] See Dir.2005/84 (fn.52, above); the restrictions are now found in Reg.1907/2006 (fn.16, above), Annex XVII, no.52.

[202] [1997] OJ C337/3: "the Commission will consider the evidence regarding the environmental aspects relating to the presence of PVC in waste streams; on the basis of this evidence, the Commission will review its policy regarding the presence of PVC in waste streams"; see also Dir.2000/53 (fn.26, above), recital 12.

[203] See also the definition of the International Standardisation Organisation ISO for environmental labels: "A logo or a symbol attached to a product which is awarded by a third-party, agency or

whole. Mainly two groups of labels may be distinguished:

1. environmental quality labels which present the environmental performance or an environmentally "good" composition of products and which want to incite buyers and users to make an informed choice and prefer the environmentally "better" product;
2. labels which warn of environmental risks and dangers of a product.

Environmental Quality Labels

Regulation 66/2010 on eco-labelling

6–56   In 1992, the European Union adopted a regulation on an eco-label award scheme with the aim of promoting products which have a reduced environmental impact during their entire life cycle and which give better information to consumers/ users. In 2000 and 2010, the system was revised, but not significantly modified.[204]

Participation in the scheme is voluntary. The scheme consists of an eco-logo—a flower with a corolla of petals in the form of the 12 EU stars surrounding an "E"—and is granted to products which satisfy certain environmental criteria. These criteria are fixed at an EU level for specific product groups, while the attribution of the label to the individual product is decided by the competent authorities of each Member State. The Regulation fixes selective criteria, organises the consultation with interest groups and other relevant matters for the functioning of the scheme.

In the follow-up of the deregulation move of 1992, economic operators tried to see the system privatised, but met with stiff opposition from the Council, led by the United Kingdom and Denmark.[205] Nevertheless, the system had difficulties to overcome in order to succeed. Indeed, it met with the opposition of economic operators' associations from the very beginning, who opposed the idea that some 15, 20 or 30 per cent of products of a specific product group should be allowed to bear an official label which qualified these products to be "better". Such objections formed themselves at national level in countries that were afraid of competition from other Member States, but reached EU level. Furthermore, procedures for determining criteria for product groups were long-lasting and complicated; consumers barely knew about the logo, so that producers did not have much to gain from using the logo which was not inexpensive. National eco-label systems, in particular the Blue Angel in Germany or the Green Swan in Scandinavia, were well established, better known and accepted and quicker at producing results.

Finally, third countries—first of all the United States, but also Brazil— complained that the scheme created barriers to international trade. Typical controversies concerned questions, whether the use of recycled paper in toilet and other papers should be rated as environmentally favourable: wood-exporting

---

non-governmental organisation and which is based on multiple criteria and lifecycle analysis." A second type of eco-labels includes claims of single attributes, such as "energy efficient".
[204] Reg.66/2010 on the EU ecolabel [2010] OJ L27/1; this Regulation replaced Reg.1980/2000 [2000] OJ L237/1; the original Regulation was Reg.880/92 [1992] OJ L99/1.
[205] Environmental Watch, October 7, 1994, p.1.

countries were, of course, not of this opinion. The United States was of the opinion that, if criteria concerning the production methods were taken into consideration, this would mean that the European Union wanted to impose its production standards on third countries. In contrast, EU producers were of the opinion that production or social standards in third countries were not adequately taken into account and that this privileged imports.

For the review of the scheme, the Commission had suggested to phase out   **6–57**
national and regional eco-labels for product groups which were covered by the EU scheme, to introduce a graded system that would allow products to obtain one, two or three flowers, depending on how environmentally superior they were, and to transfer responsibility for fixing the ecological criteria for the different product groups to an independent body.[206] All these proposals were rejected. The co-existence with national eco-label schemes was solved by allowing the co-existence of the two systems for one and the same product.

By mid-2010, criteria for 26 product groups had been established and 1,073 products had, EU-wide, received the EU eco-label, an infinitely small number. Denmark even turned away from the EU system and back to the Scandinavian eco-label system, while not less than 13 Member States set up national eco-labelling schemes—though often with limited success. The status of the eco-label scheme is still very uncertain; neither economic operators nor environmental or consumer groups are enthusiastic about it. The label is not well known and has not really reached consumer awareness.[207] A recent decision to develop eco-labels for hotels and campsites could make the label better known, provided that specific regions, such as islands, systematically equip their hotels with such a label.

Organic farming

Agricultural products which come from specific ecological production—the   **6–58**
conditions of which have been very meticulously laid down, in order to avoid abuses and, at the same time, make life for traditional farmers easier—may bear the label "organic farming".[208] Products from organic farming reached a market share of about 5 per cent within the European Union, although the differences among Member States are considerable.[209] In 1999, the Council adopted an amendment in order to have animal farming included in the Regulation.[210] And in the same year the Commission created a specific logo which products from animal farming were allowed to display; in 2008, this logo was refined.[211] Products from third countries may bear the statement "organic product", where the production methods have expressly been recognised as being equivalent to the requirements of Regulation 834/2007. The label is not well known, also because

---

[206] [1997] OJ C114/9.

[207] See also Commission Dec.2006/402 establishing the EU eco-label working plan [2006] OJ L162/78 which is relatively ambitious.

[208] Reg.834/2007 [2007] OJ L189/1; this Regulation replaced Reg.2092/91 [1991] OJ L198/1; the labelling details were fixed by Commission Reg.889/2008 [2008] OJ L250/1.

[209] European Environment Agency, Environmental Signals 2001 (Copenhagen, 2001) pt 7.4.

[210] Reg.1804/99 [1999] OJ L222/1.

[211] Commission Reg.889/2008 (fn.208, above); this Regulation replaced Commission Reg.331/2000 [2000] OJ L48/1.

the agricultural policy tries to favour traditional farming and make life for organic farmers as difficult as possible; the refinement of 2008 tried to improve this situation.

Energy consumption

6–59   The EU discussion on the labelling of energy consumption of electrical household appliances started about 30 years ago. However, attempts to obtain solutions via industrial standardisation and voluntary agreements with manufacturers failed.[212] This led the European Union to develop, since 1992,[213] environmental labels for electrical or electronic household appliances, which are somehow too narrowly called energy labels. The labels indicate, according to national standards or other provisions fixed in the annexes and in a graphically fixed scheme the energy and water consumption, performance and noise level.

In 2010, a new directive was adopted on the energy labelling of products[214] which will apply to all products that consume energy. The detailed labelling requirements shall, until 2011, be elaborated by the Commission. It is likely that the system set up by Directive 92/75 will more or less be taken over.

Fuel consumption of cars

6–60   Directive 1999/94, based on art.192 TFEU, introduced a requirement that all new passenger cars at the point of sale bear a label on the official fuel consumption and their average CO_2 emissions.[215] Also, a guide on fuel economy and CO_2 emissions had to be made available to consumers at the point of sale, free of charge, but "on request" only (art.4). Extending the labelling requirement in future also to used cars was under consideration (Recital 6), but abandoned since.

Such a label is not really capable of making the consumer change his intentions and buy a car that consumes or emits less, as there is no yardstick to allow the consumer to measure possible economies. The label requirement was mainly introduced at the instigation of the car industry, which wanted to be seen as contributing to fight climate change. There is general consensus in the meantime that the Directive did not reach its aims.

Recyclable packaging

Under Directive 94/62 on waste and packaging waste,[216] the Commission made a proposal for the marking of reusable or recyclable packaging.[217] The symbols consisted of different round circles. The proposal attempted to create new, EU-specific symbols. As economic operators, however, oriented themselves more and more to the US system for labelling of packaging which is also promoted via international standardisation organisations, the Commission proposal received a

---

[212] See Economic and Social Committee [1995] OJ C155/19, no.2.7.
[213] Dir.92/75 on the conservation of energy and other resources by household appliances [1992] OJ L297/16.
[214] Directive 2010/30 on the indication by labelling and standard product information of energy and other resources by energy related products [2010] OJ L153/1.
[215] Dir.1999/94 [1999] OJ L12/16.
[216] Dir.94/62 on packaging and packaging waste [1994] OJ L365/10.
[217] [1996] OJ C382/10.

cool reception. The Council did not discuss it and the European Parliament suggested it rather take over symbols that had been developed by different sectors of the packaging industry. The proposal is now obsolete.

Forest label

In view of the disappearance of tropical and other forests, discussions have gone on for a considerable amount of time to create a label for wood, which indicates that the wood comes from sustainable forestry. The European Union indicated on several occasions its commitment to such a label. In decisions taken in the context of the EU eco-label scheme, one of the criteria for paper products is that the wood must stem from sustainable forestry. Until now, however, no internationally recognised label for such sustainable forestry exists. The European Union has not either developed such a label. Attempts in the Netherlands to impose such a label failed, because no agreement could be found as to what exactly sustainable forestry meant. At present, illegal logging continues to be practised in numerous countries, without trade in wood products being affected. The new Regulation on timber and timber products did not introduce a label to inform users and consumers that the timber was legally harvested.[218]

Environmental Warning Labels

Chemicals that are dangerous for the environment

Directive 67/548[219] on dangerous chemical substances was amended in 1979 to include a label "dangerous to the environment". The label consisted of a symbol showing a dead fish beached beside a dead tree, both in black on a yellow- orange background; the symbol was accompanied by phrases on the special risks (R-phrases) and on the safe use of the substance (S-phrases). By the end of 2007, some 200 substances were labelled with the symbol "dangerous for the environment". This seems somewhat few substances. However, some thousand substances from petrol refining, such as aromatic hydrocarbons, naphta, extracts and distillates, which are classified "toxic", did not bear this label, though they obviously appear to be dangerous for the environment. The reason for this was that a substance that was labelled "toxic", need not also be labelled "dangerous for the environment" (art.23 of Directive 67/548). The same was true for substances where the indication "may cause cancer" was obligatory.

    In 2008, this labelling system was significantly amended by a new regulation, which adapted the EU labelling scheme to the existing global labelling scheme for the transport of goods.[220] The new Regulation ignored the fact that the risks for the consumer/user and for the environment are very different during the transport of a product and during its use in the home, in the garden, at the working place or in agriculture. The most significant change in the new system is

6–61

---

[218] Reg.995/2010 laying down obligations of operators who place timber and timber products on the market [2010] OJ L295/23.
[219] Dir.67/548 [1967] OJ 196/1.
[220] Reg.1272/2008 on the classification, the packaging and the labelling of chemical substances and mixtures [2008] OJ L250/1.

the abandoning of the yellow-orange background of the label, which was replaced by a white background. This makes the label much less visible. Furthermore, the risk-phrases were limited to indicate risks to the aquatic environment and to the ozone-layer; all other risk-phrases referring to the environment were deleted. Also the number of environment-related safety-phrases was strongly reduced.

Pesticides labelling is not included in the present labelling requirements for dangerous mixtures: there is some pressure from economic operators to see pesticide labelling be more dependent on risks from exposure under field conditions rather than on the product's intrinsic hazards. If this suggestion were followed, this would signify a decisive change in the European Union's legislative approach. However, until now, no specific EU-wide pesticide labelling requirement exists.

Separate collection

6–62   Directive 2006/66 on batteries[221] contains a symbol indicating "separate collection" of batteries, which consists of a roll-out container crossed through, accompanied by an indication of which heavy metal is involved (Hg for mercury, Cd for cadmium or Pb for lead). This symbol is to be placed on batteries only and indicates that they are subject to separate collection, and shall not be put in a normal waste-bin. The same symbol was used in Directive 2002/96 to indicate that electrical and electronic products shall be collected separately.[222]

Labelling of products containing GMOs

6–63   In order to meet public concern within the European Union regarding the placing on the market of products that contain genetically modified organisms, the European Union adopted a regulation[223] that requires food labels to indicate that the food contains genetically modified organisms; however, this requirement only applies to those cases where differences between such food products and normal food products can be scientifically detected. Since this label neither covers all products nor all products that contain genetically modified organisms— estimations indicate that 90 per cent of all food products will not be covered by the labelling requirements—it will not allow consumers systematically to avoid such products. The large-scale introduction of products that contain genetically modified organisms cannot be stopped by such a measure; at best it will be slowed down. Requests from environmental and consumer organisations to introduce a label "GMO-free"—this would be perceived as a quality label, not as a warning label—have so far been rejected by the European Union. Based on a recital of Regulation 1830/2003, a number of Member States introduced, at national level, a label "GMO-free", without the Commission taking action against this practice.

---

[221] Dir.2006/66 [2006] OJ L266/1.

[222] Dir.2002/96 [2003] OJ L37/24.

[223] Reg.1830/2003 concerning the traceability and labelling of genetically modified organisms and of food and feed products produced from genetically modified organisms [2003] OJ L 268/24.

4. Imports and exports of products

There are no general provisions on the import and export of products. In **6–64** particular, the European Union has no general provision which provides that a product which is banned or severely restricted to be placed on the market within the European Union should not be exported, either to any third country or at least to any non-industrialised country. Rather, the European Union follows international trends which are based on the principle that any country should decide for itself, whether it wishes to have certain substances or products on its market or not. International conventions thus follow the principle of "prior informed consent" (PIC): prior to the first export, the importing State is to be informed of the existence of the ban or the restrictions that exist in the exporting country. Then it has to decide whether it allows the import.

If one takes asbestos products as an example: which reasons may exist that asbestos fibres which are known now to cause cancer, are banned within the European Union, but undergo the PIC-procedure only, when they are exported to Africa or Asia? In my opinion, the PIC principle does not offer sufficient protection to humans and the environment in the developing countries, where administrative controls are often insufficient. The EU policy should rather provide that as a rule, a substance or a product that is banned or severely restricted in use within the European Union shall have the same restriction when it is exported to non-industrialised countries.

The European Union follows a different approach. Regulation 689/2008, which replaced the earlier Regulation 2455/92,[224] provided that where a third country notifies an EU Member State of the export to the European Union of a chemical substance that is banned or restricted in use in that third country, that notification shall be sent to the Commission and hence to all other Member States. The Regulation does not provide for any other follow-up; neither does it provide for any systematic notification of third countries to the Commission nor to Member States. In substance, thus, no import requirements for industrial or chemical products exist at present.[225]

In 2002, the European Union decided to ratify the Rotterdam Convention of **6–65** 1998 on the PIC-procedure related to the export and import of chemicals[226] which had been elaborated under the auspices of the Food and Agricultural Organisation FAO and the United Nations Environment Programme UNEP. Regulation 689/2008[227] intended to adapt the EU requirements to the provisions of the Rotterdam Convention. Annex 1 of that Regulation lists different groups of chemicals. The exporter of a first list of some 20 substances or groups of substances—these include arsenic, cadmium, triorganostannic compounds, creosote, hexachloroethane, chloroforme and DBB—shall notify his intention to export for the first time to the competent authority of the Member State where he is established at least 30 days before the export takes place, and 15 days in advance for the first export of the chemical each year thereafter. The competent authority will then notify the European Commission, which has to ensure that the importers receive notification at least 15 days prior to the first shipment.

---

[224] Reg.689/2008 [2008] OJ L204/1; this Reg. replaced Reg.2455/92 [1992] OJ L251/13.
[225] See, however, also para.5–26 as regards import restrictions on endangered fauna and flora species.
[226] Dec.2003/106 [2003] OJ L63/27.
[227] Reg.689/2008 (fn.224, above).

A second group of some twenty chemicals—such as asbestos fibres, nitrofen, Ugilec 121—are subject to additional requirements. The exporter must provide supplementary information on the chemical and the importing country must explicitly consent to the import, before the export may take place. For a third group of chemicals, import countries will receive in advance details on the chemicals and on the bans or restrictions that are in force. Their answers are directed to the secretariat of the Rotterdam Convention, which transmits them to the other contracting parties, including the European Union. The European Union and its Member States are then legally bound to take appropriate measures so that EU exporters comply with the importing countries' requirements. Of chemicals on this list, three include the asbestos fibre crocidolite, further DDT, HCH, lindane, pentachlorophenol, mercury compounds, PBB, PCT and TRIS. The export of persistent organic pollutants,[228] of mercury and some mercury containing products[229] and of substances that deplete the ozone-layer[230] is prohibited altogether.

It will have to be seen, whether these measures are sufficient. Indeed, administrations in third countries do not always seem to be able fully to assess the impact of chemicals that are to be imported. Also, the World Health Organisation estimates that every year a considerable number of persons suffer acute unintentional poisoning as a result of the misuse of pesticides; no figures exist for environmental damage caused by chemicals the use of which is banned or restricted within the European Union.

5. Industrial standardisation

6–66   Environmental requirements for products—as for processes—may be fixed by legislative regulation, such as, for instance, for emissions from cars. They may also be fixed by industrial technical standards, which are elaborated by private standardisation organisations and the result of which is a technical indication for some product characteristics.

Industrial standards are, by definition, not mandatory. Legally, they constitute a recommendation of the authors to follow the indications laid down in the standard. Their degree of recognition depends on the readiness of producers to apply the standard. Public authorities often support the application of standards, for instance by providing in legislation that standards must be complied with or by not laying down specifications in regulations, but referring to (private) standards, etc.

At EU level, there are no specific EU standardisation organisations. Rather, the three organisations that exist are international bodies, which went, right from their beginnings, beyond the borders of the European Union. All three organisations have close relations with national standardisation bodies on the one hand, and with international bodies on the other hand, which include arrangements to avoid the duplication of work.

6–67   CEN (*Comité Européen de Normalisation*; European Committee for Standardisation) was created in 1961. It is an association under Belgian law, the

---

[228] See Reg.850/2004 [2004] OJ L158/7.
[229] Reg.1102/2009 [2009] OJ L304/75.
[230] Reg.1005/2008 [2008] OJ L286/1.

members of which are national standards institutions of Western European countries and, since 1992, associate members in the form of organisations that represent economic and social interests at European level and which fulfil certain conditions as regards representativity and objectives. About half of CEN's budget is provided for by EU funds.

The CEN secretariat is located in Brussels. Since 1989, CEN has had an agreement with the International Standardisation Organisation (ISO), which enables one of the two organisations to allow the other to take the lead on a specific standardisation project. This avoids different standards being elaborated at global (ISO) and European (CEN) level.[231]

CEN standards are prepared by technical committees—at present numbering about 300. Programme committees and technical sector boards have the task of providing for co-ordination among these committees. Since the early 1990s, CEN has established a Programming Committee on the "Environment", which, in turn, has set up a working group on "Environmental Aspects in Product Standards"; this group has the task of looking into the environmental aspects of general product standards and to give guidance and make recommendations to standards writers.

CEN differentiates between direct and indirect standardisation work. Direct standardisation concerns items such as environmental assessment methods; measurement methods for environmental properties of chemicals; pollution control methods and equipment; environmental management tools; and methods for the evaluation of environmental effects of products. Indirect standardisation aspects deal with the environmental aspects of general product standards.

6–68

CENELEC (*Comité Européen de Normalisation Electrotechnique*; European Committee for Electrotechnical Standardisation) began its work in the early 1960s. Since 1972 it has been located in Brussels. Its members are national electrotechnical committees. It elaborates standards in the area of electrical and electronic equipment and roughly one-third of its budget is provided by the European Union. About three-quarters of all CENELEC standards are parallels of international electrotechnical standards.

ETSI (European Telecommunications Standards Institute) was created in 1988 for the telecommunications sector.

For the European Union, industrial standardisation is of growing importance for environmental issues, since the European Union opted, in the early 1980s, for a "new approach" to the approximation of national legal rules,[232] by which the Council—

6–69

"emphasizes the importance and desirability of the new approach which provides for reference to standards—primarily European standards, but national ones if need be, as a transitional measure—for the purposes of defining the technical characteristics of products."

The same resolution laid down four "fundamental principles" for the new

---

[231] In pursuance of this agreement, CEN decided, e.g. not to prepare separate environmental management systems, but to adopt the standards ISO 14001 and 14004 prepared by ISO; ISO has also taken the lead for standards on life-cycle assessments.

[232] The definition of "new approach" was first used in Commission, COM (85) and Council Resolution of May 7, 1985 ([1985] OJ C136/1: On a new approach to technical harmonisation and standards).

approach:

- "legislative harmonization is limited ... to the adoption of the essential safety requirements (or other requirements in the general interest) with which products put on the market must conform;"
- the task of drawing up the technical specifications of products is done by industrial standardisation organisations,
- these technical standardisations maintain their status of voluntary standards;
- products which conform to harmonised standards are presumed to conform to the essential requirements established by a Directive.

6–70   A number of product-related directives have been elaborated since the mid-1980s according to the new approach.[233] However, the essential requirements, laid down in these Directives, practically never deal with environmental issues. Thus, the impact of these directives on the environment is limited: indeed, since the protection of the environment is also an essential requirement of EU policy,[234] the omission of the regulation of environmental issues in the context of essential requirements at EU level means that Member States are free to adopt environmental measures at national level as regards these products.

The new approach is certainly not applied systematically. For a number of areas, European standards do not as yet exist, and large sectors such as food and pharmaceuticals, cars and chemicals are not covered by it at all. Its main area of application is the mechanical sector.

6–71   Up to mid-2006, the only environmental Directive adopted under the new approach has been the Directive on packaging and packaging waste.[235] This Directive, which is based on art.114 TFEU, contains an annex which lays down essential requirements for packaging. Thus, packaging shall be:

- so manufactured that the packaging volume and weight is limited to the minimum adequate amount to maintain the necessary level of safety, hygiene and acceptance for the packed product and for the consumer;
- designed, produced and commercialised in such a way as to permit its reuse or recovery, including recycling, and to minimise its impact on the environment when packaging waste or residues from packaging waste management operations are disposed of;
- manufactured so that the presence of noxious and other hazardous substances and materials is minimised with regard to their presence in emissions, ash or leachate, when packaging or residues are incinerated or landfilled.

6–72   Where the standards do not, in part or in full, comply with the essential requirements of the Directive, the only "sanction" is that the European Union

---

[233] In particular Dir.73/23 on low-voltage equipment [1973] OJ 77/29; Dir.87/404 on pressure vessels [1987] OJ L220/48; Dir.87/378 on toy safety [1987] OJ L187/1; Dir.89/106 on construction products [1989] OJ L40/12; Dir.89/392 on the safety of machines [1989] OJ L183/9; Dir.90/396 on appliances burning gaseous fuels [1990] OJ L196/15; Dir.92/42 on new hot-water boilers fired with liquid or gaseous fuels [1992] OJ L167/17; Dir.94/62 on packaging and packaging waste [1994] OJ L365/11).
[234] *Procureur de la République v Association de Défense de Bruleurs* (240/83) [1985] E.C.R. 531.
[235] Dir.94/62 (fn.233, above).

could refuse to recognise them as harmonised standards. This has as a consequence that the presumption—laid down in art.11(2) of Directive 94/62—according to which a packaging that complies with the standards also complies with the requirements of the Directive would not apply. Member States are then not obliged to admit a packaging on their market that they consider not to comply with their interpretation of the essential requirements, even where the packaging complies with the standards. This would mean that, for instance, Denmark might continue to refuse metal cans on its market with the argument that they do not comply with essential requirements, though Denmark repealed, in the meantime, its national restrictions for metal cans. Other candidates for national measures could be PVC packagings, aerosols or—more generally—plastic or non-biodegradable packagings, where in each case it could be argued that the packaging does not comply with the essential requirements of Directive 94/62.

Obviously, these considerations depend on the determination of Member States to ensure that the essential requirements, laid down in Directive 94/62, really are respected. However, as regards the standards for packaging, this is what the Commission did: it considered the standards that CEN had elaborated of such a poor quality that it refused to recognise them as harmonised standards.[236] As mentioned in para.6–19, above, the Commission accepted, at a later stage the CEN standards, though these had hardly been amended in the meantime.

It remains to be seen, how the packaging policy within the European Union will develop. Few Member States seem prepared to pursue a policy that aims at the reduction of packaging material and the recycling/reuse of packaging material.

The problems of standards for packaging illustrate well the general **6–73** environmental difficulties with industrial standardisation: the problem how industrial standards can be made greener is not yet solved. Indeed, at national level, public authorities can participate and do participate in the working groups that elaborate the technical standard. Their representative may bring into the discussion on the elaboration of a standard environmental aspect and influence the taking into consideration of the general interest to protect the environment. Where they do not succeed in this attempt, they may suggest governmental regulation on the subject covered by the standard, which makes the industrial standard more or less obsolete.

At EU level, the representatives of economic operators in CEN/CENELEC write their own standards and are hardly influenced at all by environmental organisations, which are too weak and financially too feeble to organise themselves structurally at EU level. Commission officials do not, in practice, participate in the working groups of CEN or CENELEC, and written contributions, if they are made at all, do not significantly influence the making of standards. Until now, no horizontal structures have been set up, which would—if instigated in time—change this situation. Despite all discussion on the integration of environmental requirements into industrial standardisation, nothing significant has changed during the last 25 years. Most of the reflections on such new structures aim at the increased participation of environmental organisations in the discussion and decision-making process of CEN and, to a lesser degree, of

---

[236] Dec.2001/524 (fn.79, above).

CENELEC. Other measures discussed are an environmental impact assessment for the subject covered by a standard; the results of this assessment would be incorporated into each CEN standard.

CHAPTER 7

Water Protection

1. European union water policy and law

EU water policy and law is about 40 years old. It was fixed, in the beginning, on **7–01** two objectives; on the one hand, it set quality requirements for specific water uses, such as surface waters, groundwater, bathing or drinking water; on the other hand, it tried to limit discharges of pollutants into the waters. In 1988, an inter-ministerial meeting on water policy endeavoured to lay down the principles of a more coherent water policy[1]; however, the objectives identified at this seminar only very partially materialised.

The European Council in Edinburgh, in December 1992 which tried to start a deregulation process, fixed a number of orientations for EU policy and invited the European Union to simplify, consolidate and adapt EU environmental legislation.[2] Nowhere was this statement taken more seriously then in the water sector, probably also because the United Kingdom, which had presided over the Edinburgh Council, had just received a judgment from the Court of Justice, which obliged it to make considerable investments in cleaning up drinking water.[3] Subsequent to this Council, and on the repeated insistence of the European Parliament,[4] the Commission published a Communication in 1996 on the "European Community Water Policy".[5] This Communication fixed as objectives of EU water policy:

- a secure supply of drinking water;
- sufficient quality and quantity of water resources to meet other economic requirements;
- to protect and sustain the good ecological state and functioning of the aquatic environment and meet the water needs of wetland and terrestrial ecosystems and habitats;
- the management of water so as to prevent or reduce the impact of floods and droughts.

These objectives obviously refer to fresh and coastal water rather than, for **7–02** instance, to oceans. They are targeted to meet, first of all, human needs. The

---

[1] The conclusions of this seminar were never published; a short report is found in (1988) *Bulletin of the European Communities*, para.2.1.175; the Council adopted a resolution on the follow-up of the seminar [1988] OJ C209/3.

[2] See (1992) 12 *Bulletin of the European Communities*, p.18.

[3] *Commission v United Kingdom* (C–337/89) [1992] E.C.R. I–5973.

[4] See in particular European Parliament, Res. of October 23, 1996 [1996] OJ C347/80.

[5] Commission, COM (96) 59.

communication stated that the "environmental quality objectives approach" and the "emission limit values approach" were complementary and not contradictory. It continued by stating that quality objectives could either fix common parametric values applicable in all Member States or could be expressed in a form such that common criteria for the establishment of parameters and values were fixed at EU level, but that the values were established at national level, in order "to allow flexibility to adapt to the very different environmental conditions in different parts of the Community". The Commission clearly indicated that it preferred this approach.

The European Parliament was of the opinion that the Communication failed in its objective to present a coherent overall concept and requested that the review of water policy should in no way lead to a lowering of standards; as a minimum the fixing of strict and uniform emission standards was necessary.[6]

7–03   The first EU water Directives and other measures were regularly based on arts 100 and 235 European Commission which since became arts 115/114 and 352 TFEU, and were adopted at unanimity.[7] Despite the existence of environmental action programmes from the early 1970s, the adoption of these directives did not follow a political strategy; rather, the Directives were adopted, where political or legal opportunities existed. They were often drafted by non-lawyers, and perceived more as guidelines than as legally binding requirements for Member States and water administrations. The Commission did not look closely into questions of their practical application.

Since 1987, art.192 TFEU became the legal basis for all environmental matters, including those on the protection of waters. Such measures continued to request unanimous decisions, until the Maastricht Treaty introduced, in 1993, majority decisions into art.192 TFEU. This amendment of the Treaty, however, brought some uncertainty as to the correct legal basis for EU water legislation. Indeed, while art.192(1) provided for majority decisions, art.192(2) provided for unanimous decisions by the Council for measures concerning "the management of water resources". And while art.192(1) introduced the co-decision procedure with the European Parliament under the present art.294 TFEU,[8] art.192(2) limited the role of the European Parliament to a consultative function.

7–04   The different interpretations on the delimitation between art.192(1) and (2) as regards water measures were solved by a judgment from the Court of Justice.[9] This judgment concerned Decision 97/825, by which the European Union had adhered to the Convention on Co-operation for the Protection and Sustainable Use of the River Danube[10]; the Council had based that Decision on the old art.130s(1) EC—now art.192(1) TFEU. Spain was of the opinion that the Decision should have been based on art.192(2), as it concerned the management of water resources, and applied to the Court of Justice. The Court found that only the Dutch version of art.192(2) used the word "quantitative", and that the French

---

[6] European Parliament, Res. of October 23, 1996 [1996] OJ C347/80; see also Economic and Social Committee [1996] OJ C30/5; Committee of the Regions [1997] OJ C34/30.

[7] Dir.75/440 on the protection of surface waters for the abstraction of drinking water [1975] OJ L194/6; Dir.76/160 on the quality of bathing water [1976] OJ L31/1; Dir.78/659 on fresh water supporting fish life [1978] OJ L222/1; Dir.79/923 on shellfish water [1979] OJ L281/47.

[8] Between the entry into force of the Maastricht Treaty in 1993 and the Amsterdam Treaty in 1999, art.192(1) provided for the co-operation procedure according to art.252 EC Treaty.

[9] Court of Justice, *Spain v Council* (C36/98) [2001] E.C.R. I–779.

[10] Dec.97/825 [1997] OJ L342/18.

version also used expressions which signalled that the quantitative management of water was in question. The Court then referred to the purpose and general scheme of the provision and concluded that art.192(2) was limited to quantitative aspects of water management; this judgment conformed to the overwhelming opinion in legal literature. Two weeks after this judgment, the Treaty of Nice was signed which amended art.192(2). Unanimity is now required, where a measure concerns quantitative aspects of water management.

Until early 2011, the European Union had not adopted water measures that were based on art.192(2) TFEU.

In its efforts to give greater coherence to measures on water protection and, at the same time, to follow the trend towards deregulation and the abandoning of precise provisions, the Commission submitted, in 1994, a proposal for a directive on the ecological quality of water.[11] The proposal suggested a good ecological water quality for all surface water in the European Union. Member States were to identify the sources of pollution and to fix objectives in order to reach this good ecological quality. They were then to elaborate integrated programmes to reach the objectives. The proposal met with little enthusiasm in the European Parliament, which continued to press for a more coherent approach to water policy.[12] The Commission accepted this request and presented, on the one hand, a communication on water policy[13] and, on the other hand, a proposal for a directive "establishing a framework for Community action in the field of water policy".[14] This proposal was adopted in 2000 and came into effect at the end of 2003.[15] It aimed at the protection of all waters, i.e. surface waters, groundwaters and coastal waters, but did not cover marine waters. Article 1 fixed five objectives:

7–05

1.   prevention of further deterioration and protection and enhancing of aquatic and terrestrial ecosystems and halt to further deterioration;
2.   promotion of sustainable water use, based on long-term protection of available water resources;
3.   enhanced protection and improvement of the aquatic environment through the progressive reduction of discharges and the cessation or phasing-out of discharges, emissions and losses of priority hazardous substances;
4.   progressive reduction of groundwater pollution;
5.   mitigation of the effects of floods and droughts.

The Directive requested Member States to organise their waters—including groundwater and coastal water—according to individual river basin districts.[16] Where a river basin covered the territory of more than one Member State, it must be assigned to an international river basin district (art.3(3)); where non-EU

7–06

---

[11] [1994] OJ C222/6; explanatory memorandum COM (93) 680.

[12] European Parliament, Res. of October 23, 1996 (fn.4, above).

[13] See fn.5, above.

[14] [1997] OJ C184/20; explanatory memorandum Commission COM (97) 49; amendment of the proposal [1998] OJ C16/14 and [1998] OJ C108/94.

[15] Directive 2000/60 establishing a framework for Community action in the field of water policy [2000] OJ L327/1.

[16] art.2(13) of Directive 2000/60 (fn.15, above): "river basin means the area of land from which all surface run-off flows through a sequence of streams, rivers and, possibly, lakes into the sea at a single river mouth, estuary or delta".

countries belong to a river basin—examples are the Rhine or the Danube—
Member States were asked to "endeavour to establish appropriate co-ordination".
The river basin administration shall ensure the application of the Directive's rules
in the river basin; for "international river basin districts the Member states
concerned shall together ensure this co-ordination".

These provisions thus obliged, in regionalised or in federal countries, the
water administration to organise itself in administrative units—districts—which it
might not really wish to see being set up. Also, the obligation to a joint
administration in international river basin districts constituted an interference
with political or administrative autonomy that met—for instance in German
regionalised legal literature—some concern. These provisions had, though, a
number of precedents: Directive 91/271 obliged Member States to build specific
waste water treatment installations.[17] Directive 85/337 on the environmental
impact assessment obliged Member States to co-operate among themselves in
those areas, where transfrontier elements of environmental protection were in
question. This obligation to administrative co-operation flows from art.10 EC—at
present art.4(3) TEU—which establishes the basic principle that Member States
have to co-operate. In the last instance, one might ask, what the European Union
is really about, if there were not even the possibility to organise environmental
protection measures—which are, by nature, not limited by a national frontier—
according to reasonable objective criteria such as river basins.

7–07   Article 4 of Directive 2000/60 fixed environmental objectives, separated for
surface waters, groundwater and protected areas. The objective was to reach
"good" surface water (groundwater) status of "good" ecological potential, and
"good" water chemical status. Under certain conditions, Member States may aim
to achieve less stringent environmental objectives for specific bodies of water
which are so strongly affected by human activity that the achievement of the
normal objectives is infeasible or disproportionately expensive (art.4(5)). And
Member states were declared to be "not in breach of this Directive", when certain
new sustainable human development activities or new modifications of the water
body occurred (art.4(7)). The objectives had to be achieved "at the latest" by
2015, though Member States may themselves prolong this date may until 2027
(art.4(4.c)).

The Directive defined what is "good" by reference to criteria that were laid
down in an annex V. This means in practice that each river basin plan fixes itself
the water quality which is to be achieved under the Directive, though the criteria
of annex V may lead to some alignment. Also, the question of whether a water
had a high, a good or a moderate status, whether a water was to be classified as
good, poor or bad—all these classifications are introduced by the Directive—
depended on the decisions taken within the water management bodies and could
thus vary from one water basin to the other.

In order to reach the objectives of the Directive, Member States had to
establish, by 2009, programmes of measures for each river basin district,[18] for
which a considerable number of conditions were set in the Directive (art.11).
Such programmes had to be updated every six years. Furthermore, for each river
basin district, a river management plan had to be produced (art.13(1)). Member

---

[17] Dir.91/271 on waste water treatment [1991] OJ L135/40.
[18] This obligation was, for international river basin districts, limited to the territory of each Member
State.

States were only obliged to produce such a plan for districts that lie entirely within their territory. For international districts, Member States had to co-ordinate such plans among each other and, where third countries were involved, "endeavour to produce a single river basin management plan" (art.13(4)). The "public" had to have the possibility to comment on the production, review and updating of the river management plan (art.14). For groundwater, the adoption of a specific directive was foreseen; this directive was adopted in 2006.[19]

In order to reduce water pollution, art.16 provided that EU measures would be taken for specific pollutants or group of pollutants. These measures aimed, for priority hazardous substances, "at the cessation, phasing-out of discharges, emissions or losses" (art.16(1)). For this purpose, a list of priority substances had to be fixed at level. These substances had then to undergo a risk assessment or targeted risk assessment.[20] For priority substances, EU measures for the control of the progressive reduction of discharges, emission, limits or losses were foreseen (art.16(6)). Discharges, emissions and losses should be completely stopped within a period which "shall not exceed 20 years", after the EU decision on these substances (art.16(6)).

7–08

At the end of 2001, the European Union adopted a list of priority substances.[21] The list contained 33 substances or groups of substances, out of which 25 were identified as priority hazardous substances. In 2008, the European Union fixed quality standards for a number of number of substances, in part different from those of the list of 2001.[22]

Furthermore, Member States had to take measures to control emissions into the EU waters. The authorisations for the emission of these substances would be given by the authorities of the Member States; the emission values would be based either on existing or future EU legislation or on best available technologies. For this purpose, EU emission limit values and quality standards (quality objectives) listed in a number of EU Directives[23] had to be observed at the latest in 2012, though earlier compliance dates in those Directives remained valid.

Finally, Directive 2000/60 repealed a number of existing water directives according to a precise timetable.[24]

---

[19] Directive 2006/118 on the protection of groundwater against pollution and deterioration [2006] OJ L372/19.

[20] A targeted risk assessment focusses solely "on aquatic ecotoxicity and on human toxicity via the aquatic environment".

[21] Dec.2455/2001 establishing the list of priority substances in the field of water policy and amending Dir.2000/60 [2001] OJ L331/1.

[22] Directive 2008/105 on environmental quality standards in the field of water policy, [2008] OJ L348/84. The regulated substances were: Alachlor, Anthracene, Atrazine, Benzene, Brominated Diphenylethers, Cadmium and its compounds, Carbon tetrachlor, C_{10-13}-chloralkanes, Chlorofenvinphos, Chlorpyrifos, DDT, DEHP, 1,2-Dichloroethane, Dichloromethane, Diuron, Endosulfan, Fluoranthene Hexachlorobenzene, Hexachlorobutadiene, HCH, Isoproturon, Lead and its compounds, Mercury and its compounds, Naphthalene, Nickel and its compounds, Nonylphenols, Octylphenols, Pentachlorobenzene, PCP, Polyaromatic Hydrocarbons, Simazine, Tribultyltin compounds, Trifleralin, Trichlorobenzenes, Trichloromethane. See further para.7–29, below.

[23] See for details Annexes IX and X of Directive 2000/60.

[24] The following timetable for repeal was fixed:
- End 2007: Dir.75/440 on surface water [1975] OJ L194/26; Dir. 79/869 on measuring methods [1979] OJ L271/44;
- End of 2013: Dir.78/659 on fishwater [1978] OJ L222/1; Dir. 79/923 on shellfish water [1979] OJ L281/47; Dir. 80/68 on groundwater [1980] OJ L20/43;

7–09   Several Member States were late in transposing the directive into their national law. The Commission took action against France, Belgium, Finland, Germany, Italy, Luxemburg, Netherlands, Portugal and the United Kingdom[25]; the Court of Justice found Belgium, Germany, Luxemburg, Italy and Portugal in breach of their obligations in this regard.[26] The Commission found, in 2008, that transposition of the Directive was poor[27] and mentioned that significant transposition problems existed with 19 out of 27 Member States. Proceedings under art.258 TFEU were initiated against Slovenia, Hungary, Finland, France, Greece, Malta, Poland, Estonia, Czech Republic, Latvia, Slovakia and Lithuania[28]; nothing is known on the content of the Commission's arguments, as the Commission does not publish studies which led to its findings and does not disclose any other relevant information.

Article 4(1)(a.i) of Directive 2000/60 requested Member States to "prevent deterioration of the status of all bodies of surface waters". It does not indicate though, from when on this prohibition of deterioration applies, since 2000 (date of adoption of the Directive, 2003 (date of its final transposition into national law), since 2008 (beginning of monitoring of surface water according to art.8), or 2012 (date of the beginning of measures according to art.12). The Directive does not either define what exactly deterioration means and how significant it must be; a transitory deterioration does not appear relevant (see art.4(6)). Anyway, the Commission did not take any action against any Member State with regard to the prohibition of deterioration.

7–10   The Directive did not clarify whether the good surface status of waters is an objective which Member States shall have to reach, or an orientation which Member States shall endeavour to reach; this last understanding is the point of view of the Netherlands, without the Commission intervening. Furthermore, while art.4(1)(a.ii) indicated that the good surface water status shall be achieved "at the latest 15 years" after 2000, art.4(4) allowed this delay to be extended "for the purposes of phased achievement" by, overall 12 further years. United Kingdom and Netherlands already signalled that the achievement of a good surface water status by 2015 would be too expensive, and prolonged the delay until 2027. The Directive did not clarify what happens, when the good surface water status is not achieved in 2027. This vagueness considerably reduces the relevance of the Directive.

Artificial and heavily modified bodies of water were subjected to less stringent requirements, art.4(1)(a.iii). The definition of such bodies (art.2 no.8 and 9) was not precise. As the designation of such bodies is in the hands of Member States, these may reduce their obligations by designating more waters as artificial or heavily modified.

• specific repeal provisions were fixed for Dir.76/464 on the discharge of substances [1976] OJ L129/23.

[25] Commission, SEC(2005) 1055, p.11.
[26] Court of Justice, *Commission v Belgium* (C–33/05) judgment of December 15, 2005; *Commission v Germany* (C–67/05) judgment of December 15, 2005; *Commission v Luxemburg*(C–32/05) [2006] E.C.R. I–11323; *Commission v Italy* (C–87/05) judgment of January 12, 2006; *Commission v Portugal* (C–118/05) judgment of January 12, 2006.
[27] Commission, COM(2007) 128.
[28] Commission, SEC(2009) 1884/2, s.7.4.

Member States had to adopt River Basin Management Plans by the end of 2009. A Commission map showed that by March 2011, Portugal, Spain, Belgium (Wallonia and Bruxelles Region), Greece, Slovenia and Cyprus did not yet have adopted management plans.

Over the next 20 years, this comprehensive Directive will strongly influence water management within the enlarged European Union and—in particular via the river basin concept—beyond. As it has not even become fully operational, it is too early to assess whether it will reach its objectives. As numerous provisions of the Directive are very loosely drafted[29] much will depend on the political will and the determination of the relevant administrations to work for the improvement of water quality rather than for the administration of the status quo. It is encouraging to see that Member States decided a joint implementation plan for the Directive,[30] even though its monitoring lacks any transparency and democratic control.

7–11

Problems are also to be anticipated in the management of water scarcity. The Directive does not really address this problem. A good example of this problem was the Spanish National Hydrogeological Plan of 2001, which was adopted by parliamentary procedure and which provided for the transfer of about 1.05 billion m^3 of water per year from the Ebro river to Southern Spanish regions which lack water. The Plan included the construction of some 900 dams, the destruction of a considerable number of natural habitats and wetlands and other considerable interferences into more traditional water management and infrastructures; it met with considerable resistance from "water exporting" regions, environmental groups and others, while the "water importing" Spanish regions generally favoured the Plan. General or specific environmental impact assessments had not been undertaken. When the government changed in Spain in 2004, the plan to transfer Ebro water was abandoned—though many of the envisaged infrastructure projects had, in the meantime, been completed. Therefore, the plan might be reanimated in future, when the government changes again.

It is remarkable, that EU water law played hardly any role in the attempt to find, in this or in similar cases—Portugal is planning, in 2010, the construction of a number of water dams—adequate balances between economic interests and environmental concerns, a problem which will become more acute with climate changing in Europe.

Following a series of floods, mainly in Central Europe, the European Union adopted, in 2007, a directive on the assessment and management of flood risks.[31] The Directive was based on art.192(1) TFEU; a suggestion by the United Kingdom, to limit its field of application to transboundary river basins was rejected by the majority of Member States in Council. The Directive covered

7–12

---

[29] A good example is art.9 of the Directive. It asks Member States "to take account of the principle of recovery of the costs of water services, including environmental and resource costs", but allows them "in so doing have regard to the social, environmental and economic effects of the recovery as well as the geographic and climatic conditions of the region or regions affected". It is difficult to see in these provisions more than a policy recommendation addressed to Member States. See generally European Environmental Bureau: *10 years of the Water Framework Directive. A toothless tiger?* (Bruxelles, July 2010).

[30] Common strategy on the implementation of the Water Framework Directive (2000/60) as agreed by the Water Directors under Swedish Presidency, May 2, 2001; *http://ec.europa.eu/environment/water/water-framework/objectives/pdf/strategy.pdf* [Accessed April 8, 2011].

[31] Dir.2007/60 on the assessment and management of flood risks [2007] OJ L288/27.

inland and coastal waters. It mainly provided for three measures by Member States: (1) The making of a preliminary flood risk assessment. This assessment is to be made for each river basin and shall describe the factual situation, the likelihood of future floods and a forecast of their estimated consequences. Where the assessment concludes that no potential significant flood risks exist, Member States have no further obligation. (2) For basins districts with a potential significant flood risk Member States shall, by end 2013, elaborate flood risk maps, in order to increase public awareness, orient investments and strategies and support planning. (3) For these basin districts, flood risk management plans are to be elaborated, for which some orientations were laid down in the Directive.

2. Quality measures

Drinking water

7–13   Directive 80/778, adopted in 1980, five years after the proposal of the Commission, limited the presence of undesirable substances in drinking water.[32] The Directive was based on arts 115 and 352 TFEU. The Directive fixed maximum admissible concentrations for 62 substances in drinking water, and gave non-mandatory guide values for some of them; Member States had to take the necessary measures to ensure compliance with the concentrations. At the request of the UK Government, which had argued that Directive 80/778 only requested Member States to take "all practicable steps" to comply with the Directive's standards, the European Court stated expressly that Member States were not only obliged to make an effort, but were obliged to reach the specific result that was required by the Directive.[33]

The monitoring requirements, laid down in Directive 80/778, were weak. Annex II fixed requirements as to the minimum frequency of and other Directives oblige Member analyses, which depended on the quantity of water distributed and the population concerned; however, for toxic parameters such as lead, mercury and chromium, e.g. the frequency was left at the discretion of Member States.

Member States were given five years (until 1985) to clean up their drinking water; they were entitled to ask for a longer delay, but none did so.

The Directive introduced, for the first time, objective standards for drinking water in all EU Member States, oriented investments and led to a considerable, though slow, improvement of drinking water quality.

7–14   Since there were difficulties in complying with the Directive's requirements, considerable pressure was put on the Commission to lower the standards, in particular as regards pesticides, where the agro-chemical and agro-industrial industry were particularly active. In 1995 the Commission made a proposal for replacing Directive 80/778 by a new directive which the Council adopted in 1998.[34]

---

[32] Dir.80/778 relating to the quality of water intended for human consumption [1980] OJ L229/11.

[33] *Commission v United Kingdom* (C–337/89) [1992] E.C.R. I–6103.

[34] Dir.98/83 on the quality of water intended for human consumption [1998] OJ L330/32; Commission proposal [1995] OJ C131/5 and COM(94) 612.

The new Directive provides that drinking water, at the point of entry into the domestic distribution system, must be wholesome and clean; the consequence of this change from the requirement of water quality at the tap to water quality at the point of entry into the domestic supply system is that individual persons can no longer argue against the water supply companies that their tap water must be in compliance with the EU Directive; they had this right under Directive 80/778.

Drinking water is wholesome and clean, when the water is free from micro-organisms, parasites and substances which may, in numbers or in concentrations, constitute a potential danger to human health, and when the requirements of some 28 parameters, laid down in annex I(A) and I(B) are respected. The parameter for lead was lowered from 50 to 10 microgrammes, with a transition period of 15 years.[35] The European Parliament managed to avoid a change of the pesticide parameter, though the Commission had proposed to delete the collective parameter of 0.5 microgrammes and though there had been strong representations from the agro-chemical sector. Where the parameters are exceeded, Member States have to take remedial action.

Annex I(C) contains a list of 20 indicator parameters for which the Member States need only fix parameters for monitoring purposes; this annex includes, among others, aluminium, ammonium, chlorides and coliform bacteria. When these parameters are exceeded, Member States shall consider whether this poses any risk to human health; if that is the case, they must take remedial action.

The grounds for derogations are no longer enumerated, so that Member States may decide themselves, where and when they derogate; the list of derogations was considerably enlarged. For the 26 parameters of annex I(B), Member States may provide for derogations "up to a maximum value to be determined by them, provided no derogation constitutes a potential danger to human health" (art.9). The derogation may not exceed three years. Where a second, prolonging derogation is intended, the Commission is to be informed—though not consulted. Any third derogation which again may not exceed three years, has to be decided by the Commission. In all cases the affected population must be informed of the derogation.

Member States and the commission must each publish a report every three years on the quality of drinking water. The first national reports were due before the end of 2005, the first EU report in 2006. The last available "synthesis report" on drinking water, available in March 2011, dealt with the drinking water between 2002 and 2004; thus, none of the 12 new Member States was taken into consideration. And one might well ask about the value of a report that informs, in general terms of the drinking water quality six years ago and which refer to Directive 80/778![36]

In substance, the reports only give general data. Though they provide for different reports for each Member State, they do not indicate where parameters were exceeded, which derogations were granted. Parameters which were exceeded in more than 1 per cent of all samples taken, are listed. The information on "trends" is vague and not helpful.[37] To the individual citizen, the report is of no use at all.

---

[35] Dir.98/83 (fn.34, above), art.4.

[36] Commission, Quality of drinking water in the EU 2002–2004 (Bruxelles, 2007).

[37] See, for example, the trend in the United Kingdom: "There is no trend visible in the water quality in the UK, the percentage of non-compliance for the THM parameter is still high" (p.106); Germany:

Bathing water

7–15   In 1975 the Council adopted, on the basis of arts 94 and 308 EC (now, arts 115 and 352 TFEU), a Directive on the quality of bathing water,[38] which fixed, for coastal and for fresh-water zones, quality requirements for bathing waters. Imperative or guide parameters were fixed for a number of pollutants. Member States were given 10 years to comply with the Directive's requirements. In 2009, 13,741 coastal zones and 6,8676,684 fresh water zones (27 Member States) were monitored under the Directive.[39]

All Member States transposed the Directive into national law, though in part with considerable delays. In order not to have to invest too heavily into the clean-up of waters, Member States often did not designate bathing waters that qualified for the Directive, did not sample the parameters or the results were not published. The 2009 report indicated that about 3.9 per cent coastal bathing waters and 14.4 per cent fresh-water bathing waters did not comply with the Directive's requirements.[40] Within its 35 years of existence, the Directive caused a significant improvement of bathing-water quality. To this contributed the fact that annual reports were published; and that a private organisation had launched a "blue flag" campaign,[41] which identified high-quality bathing waters and beaches; and finally that, in general, the data on bathing-water quality found its way into tourism prospectuses, advertising campaigns etc. This also caused local authorities to publish data, invest in water improvement and to make specific efforts to comply with the Directive's requirements.

7–16   In 1994, the Commission made a proposal to replace Directive 76/160 by a new Directive.[42] It justified this by the need to take into account subsidiarity questions, the need to simplify the text and by scientific and technical progress. The proposal was not discussed in Council. For that reason, the Commission published a Communication and, based on the reactions to it, another proposal for a new directive which was adopted in 2006.[43] The Directive which is based on art.192(1) TFEU, entered into effect in March 2008; Directive 76/160 will be repealed as of 2014.

The notion of bathing water concerned water, where public authorities expect a large number of bathers, having regard to past trends and to existing infrastructure for services. Waters in swimming pools and waters for therapeutic purposes were not covered by the Directive. Contrary to requests which were made during the consultations, the Directive did not extend its scope of application to areas concerning the recreational use of waters such as surfing,

---

"Decrease in the number of non-compliant parameters and in the number of wsz that show non-compliance for microbiological parameters" (p.105).

[38] Dir.76/160 (fn.7, above).

[39] European Environment Agency, *Quality of bathing water (2009 bathing season)* EEA-Report 3/2010 (Copenhagen, 2010).

[40] Since 1990, a total of 17.2 per cent of bathing waters had disappeared from the EU list, European environment Agency (fn.39, above).

[41] On the "blue flag" campaign, see Written Question P-1667/02 *Carnéro Gonzalesz* [2002] OJ C301E/208. The Commission indicates in its answer that since 1998 it did no longer participate in the activities of the private body to award a blue flag and did not either grant financial assistance.

[42] Commission, [1994] OJ C112/3 and COM (94) 36.

[43] Directive 2006/7 concerning the quality of bathing water [2006] OJ L64/37.

kayaking etc. The number of 19 parameters which were to be sampled of
Directive 76/160 is reduced to two—Intestinal Enterococci and Escherichia
coli.[44]

The Directive did not provide that bathing waters must comply with certain
quality requirements. Rather, it required Member States to make a "bathing water
quality assessment". This quality assessment is to be made at the end(!) of the
bathing season and shall take the average results of the running and of the four
preceding bathing seasons into consideration. Then the bathing water is to be
classified as "excellent", "good", "sufficient" or "poor". The maximal concentrations for the two parameters are differentiated in Annex I A, with average
methods of calculation ensuring that the results remains positive. Member States
must sample the water quality by means of taking at least four samples per
bathing water season, plus one sample before the season starts. Short-term
pollutions—up to three days—may be ignored, provided Member States have
identified the source of the pollution and addressed the issue. Where a water is of
"poor" quality, it nevertheless complies with the Directive provided, Member
States pronounce a prohibition to bathe or give advice not to bathe. Only where
the water is to be classified "poor" for five subsequent bathing seasons, shall
there be a permanent prohibition to bathe. The first classification of waters is to
be made in 2015; by then, all bathing waters shall attain at least "sufficient"
quality.

Directive 2006/7 very considerably increased the flexibility for local
authorities and makes it almost impossible for citizens and environmental
organisations to get reliable information on compliance issues. The initial
classification of waters and the possible changes during the bathing season cannot
be properly controlled and enforced by others than the (local) administrations
themselves. The average of quality of four seasons is of very limited information
value for the next bathing season. The small number of samples required is
inadequate for bathing waters, where several thousands of bathers dwell. It is to
be expected that the Directive's application will lead to reports with very good
results, without the environmental quality of bathing waters having improved.

Groundwater

In 1979, the Council adopted a Directive on groundwater quality, based on arts   **7–17**
115 and 352 TFEU.[45] The Directive aimed to prevent groundwater pollution and
to eliminate the consequences of pollution, as far as possible. It established a list

---

[44] The levels are for intestinal enterococci per 100ml, in coastal waters: 100 for excellent quality, 200
for good quality and 185 for sufficient quality; in inland waters: 200 for excellent quality, 400 for
good quality and 330 for sufficient quality. For Escherischia coli in 100ml: coastal waters: 250 for
excellent quality, 500 for good quality and 500 for sufficient quality; in inland waters: 500 for
excellent quality, 400 for good quality and 330 for sufficient quality. The fact that the values for
sufficient quality are occasionally stricter than for good quality, is explained by the different
calculation of the average of the sampling. Where the sampling exceeds the level of "sufficient", the
water is of "poor" quality.
[45] Dir.80/68 on the protection of groundwater against pollution caused by certain dangerous
substances [1980] OJ L20/43. As regards implementation and compliance, see Court of Justice,
Commission v Belgium (C–1/86) [1987] E.C.R. 2797; *Commission v Netherlands* (C–291/84) [1987]
E.C.R. 3483; *Commission v Italy* (C–360/87) [1991] E.C.R. I–791. In 1993, Belgium was even

I of substances that were considered toxic, persistant or bioaccumulative, and a list II that groups together substances that "could have a harmful effect on groundwater". The direct discharge of list I substances was prohibited, and the indirect discharge—discharge after percolation through the ground or the subsoil—of that list was subject to investigation and authorisation. Discharges of list II substances were subject to investigation and authorisation. Furthermore, the Directive dealt with details of the authorisation procedure. No provision for informing of the public was provided for and no comprehensive report by Member States on the implementation of the Directive was foreseen. The Directive also regulated artificial enrichment for the purposes of groundwater management—thus, in practice, for drinking water purposes—which were only allowed "if there is no risk of polluting the groundwater" and contained a rather severe provision on the leachates from existing landfills; both these provisions, however, were, in practice, virtually ignored by Member States and not seriously monitored by the Commission.

7–18   The new Water Framework Directive 2000/60 also covered groundwater. Article 17 of that Directive provided that a specific directive was to be elaborated to prevent and reduce groundwater pollution. This new Directive was adopted in 2006.[46]

Directive 2006/118 provided for quality standards for groundwater that are fixed at EU level; the standards shall be for nitrates (50mg/l) and pesticides (0.1 micrograms per pesticide, 0.5 micrograms for all pesticides). Furthermore, Member States were asked to fix national threshold values—these are quality standards—for the presence of hazardous and other undesirable substances in groundwater; the Directive listed, in a non-binding provision, a number of substances for which such thresholds might be fixed. Groundwater is of "good" quality, where the quality standards and the threshold values are either not exceeded or exceeded under the conditions that are laid down in the Directive. The monitoring of groundwater quality is done at national level, mainly in the context of the river basin management activities under Directive 2000/60. Quantitative elements of water management were not covered by the Directive.

The added value of this new legislation for the environment is limited. Indeed, management and monitoring is almost entirely in the hands of Member States, though it has to be mentioned that the Commission did not monitor compliance with Directive 80/68 in any continuous and significant way. The main feature is thus that the new legislation enters into the line of re-nationalising water legislation. The national threshold values for heavy metals show differences of up to 1:1500.[47]

---

censured a second time, under art.260 TFEU for not having complied with the first judgment: *Commission v Belgium* (C–174/91) [1993] E.C.R. I–2275. See also *Commission v Germany* (C–131/88) [1991] E.C.R. I–825.

[46] Dir.2006/118 (fn.19, above).

[47] Commission, SEC (2010) 166, Annex III: the values had a scale between 1:300 for arsenic, 1:1200 for cadmium, 1:1500 for lead and 1:500 for mercury.

Nitrates in water

Directive 91/676, adopted in 1991 and based on art.192 TFEU, tried to protect   **7–19**
waters against pollution by nitrates and thereby to combat eutrophication.[48] It was
almost the first Directive that provided for measures against pollution from
agricultural activity. "Waters" were not defined and thus referred to fresh water as
well as to coastal and marine waters. Member States had to designate vulnerable
zones in their territories according to criteria fixed by the Directive; the decisive
criterion was whether the nitrate content of the water exceeded or risked
exceeding 50mg per litre or whether the waters were eutrophic. For these
vulnerable zones, Member States had to establish action programmes, for which
the Directive fixed some measures, amongst which were the necessity of
prohibiting the use of certain fertilisers during certain periods and restricting the
amount of livestock manure applied to the land per year to not more than 170kg
of nitrogens, though some transitional periods were allowed.

Furthermore, Member States had to establish a code of good agricultural   **7–20**
practice "to be implemented by farmers on a voluntary basis" with the objective
of reducing nitrate pollution, for which the Directive gave a number of possible
("should contain") provisions. Member States had to report on the implementation every four years and the Commission had to establish a summary report.

Member States had to transpose the Directive into national law by the end of
1993. Spain, Italy, the United Kingdom, Luxembourg, Spain and Italy again,
furthermore Germany, France, Netherlands, Belgium and Ireland were condemned by the Court of Justice for not having correctly transposed or applied the
Directive or for not having sent plans, data or reports.[49] On average, Member
States took the necessary measures to transpose the Directive with a delay of five
years.[50]

In its most recent report on the implementation of the Directive which dates
from 2010,[51] the Commission stated that at least 30–40 per cent of rivers and
lakes showed symptoms of eutrophication. Agriculture was responsible for 50–80
per cent of all nitrate inputs into waters. In order to improve this situation,
effective application of the Directive would constitute the most efficient
way—and is, at the same time, the biggest problem. In 2002, Denmark received a
derogation from the requirement of 170kg nitrogen per hectare and was allowed
to provide for an output of 230kg, under a number of conditions; such a decision

[48] Dir.91/676 concerning the protection of waters against pollution caused by nitrates from
agricultural sources [1991] OJ L375/1.
[49] Court of Justice, *Commission v Spain* (C–71/97) [1998] E.C.R. I–5991; *Commission v Italy*
(C–195/97) [1999] E.C.R. I–1169; *Commission v Spain* (C–274/98) [2000] E.C.R. I–2823;
Commission v United Kingdom (C–69/99) [2000] E.C.R. I–10979; *Commission v Luxembourg*
(C–266/00) [2001] E.C.R. I–2073; *Commission v Italy* (C–127/99) [2001] E.C.R. I–8305;
Commission v Germany (C–116/00) judgment of March 14, 2002; *Commission v France* (C–258/00)
[2002] E.C.R. I–5959; *Commission v Netherlands* (C–322/00) judgment of October 2, 2003;
Commission v Ireland (C–396/01) judgment of March 11, 2004; *Commission v Belgium* (C–221/03)
judgment of September 22, 2005; see also *Standley* (C–293/97) [1999] E.C.R. I–2603.
[50] Commission, Implementation of Directive 91/676, COM (2010) 47.
[51] Commission, Implementation of Directive 91/676, COM (2010) 47.

was repeated in 2005.[52] Furthermore, also Netherlands, Austria, Belgium and the United Kingdom applied for and obtained derogations, the Netherlands for an output of 250kg.[53]

Other directives

Surface water

7–21   Directive 75/440, based on arts 115 and 352 TFEU, concerned the quality of surface water that was used for the production of drinking water.[54] It asked Member States to divide their surface waters according to their quality into three classes—class 3 was not allowed to be used for drinking-water purposes— and to identify all sampling points in a given water. At these sampling points they had to set quality values for a number of pollutants that were specified in the Directive. In order to ensure a "continuing improvement" of the surface-water quality which was to be achieved within 10 years, they had to draw up a systematic plan of action, including a timetable. Some derogations and exceptions were allowed. A specific Directive fixed the methods of measurement and frequencies of sampling and analysis for surface water.[55] A requirement to report on the application of the Directive was not foreseeen and was only introduced in 1991. Before any implementation report was published, the Directive ceased to exist, having been repealed by Directive 2000/60 with effect of end 2007.[56]

Generally, it seems not exaggerated to state that most Member States considered the Directive, right from its beginnings, as a recommendation. In particular, the clean-up plans were hardly ever drawn up and never transmitted to the Commission. The Commission, while belatedly taking some legal action against Member States, did not really monitor the application of the Directive, but instead turned its attention to Directive 80/778 on drinking water. Thus, the move to reduce discharges into surface waters was turned into the obligation to treat water in order to obtain drinking water.

Fresh fish water

7–22   Directive 78/659[57] fixed quality standards for fresh fish water. Member States had to identify those waters, which came under the Directive and had then to draw up clean-up programmes in order to make the fish waters conform, within five years, to the quality values of the Directive. The Directive suffered from the

---

[52] Dec.2002/915 [2002] OJ L319/24; Dec. 2005/294 [2005] OJ L94/38.

[53] Dec.2005/880 [2005] OJ L324/89 (Netherlands); Dec.2006/189 [2006] OJ L66/44 (Austria); Dec.2007/863 [2007] OJ L337/122 (United Kingdom—Northern Ireland); Dec.2008/64 [2008] OJ L16/28 (Belgium—Flanders); Dec.2008/69 [2008] OJ L32/21 (Belgium—Wallonia); Dec.2009/189 [2009] OJ L14/28 (United Kingdom—England Scotland, Wales). See also Commission, COM (97). The European Parliament (Res. of October 20, 1998 [1998] OJ C341/35) declared itself "shocked" and concerned about the lack of implementation of the Directive.

[54] Dir.75/440 (fn.7, above).

[55] Dir.79/869 [1979] OJ L271/44.

[56] See Commission statement in COM (96) 59 (fn.5, above), annex point 1.1: "This is an old Directive, adopted before the Drinking Water Directive. The parameters and classifications are now out of date and it makes little or no contribution to the safety of drinking water now that the Drinking Water Directive exists. Its value in protecting future sources of drinking water is unproven."

[57] Dir.78/659 (fn.7, above).

fact that Member States themselves assigned which waters were to be submitted to the Directive; they often designated waters that were unpolluted or did not designate waters that were too polluted. The Commission published, in 1995, a report on the application of the Directive; however, that report limited itself to reproducing the Member States' reports without any assessment and only added a disclaimer: "publication of the report does not mean the Commission accept that the requirements of the directives are being fully met in all Member States".[58]

In 1991, the Commission reported that only three Member States had transmitted clean-up programmes.[59] A judgment by the Court of Justice, that Member States had to designate fish waters all over their territory, not only in some regions,[60] only had limited effect: Italy was, in 1994, condemned a second time and in 1996 the Court found that Germany had not designated any fish water[61]—18 years after the adoption of the Directive! In the absence of systematic monitoring of this Directive by the Commission, its effects remain modest. According to art.22 of Directive 2000/60, Directive 78/659 will cease to exist in 2013. This did not prevent the Community from codifying the Directive which now has the new number 2006/44.[62]

Shellfish water

Directive 79/923[63] had a construction similar to Directive 78/659: Member States had to designate waters to which the Directive applied, then had to draw up pollution reduction programmes in order to make these waters conform to the quality requirements that the Directive had fixed. Again, implementation was slow: in 1991, four Member States had drawn up programmes[64] and the Commission monitoring was neither systematic nor whole- hearted[65]; only Italy was condemned for not having respected the Directive.[66] The Commission is now of the opinion that Directive 91/492,[67] which fixed health conditions for the production and placing on the market of live bivalve molluscs, made Directive 79/923 redundant.[68] According to art.22 of Directive 2000/60, Directive 79/923 will cease to exist in 2013.

7–23

---

[58] Commission, "Quality of fresh water for fish and for shellfish water" (Brussels and Luxembourg, 1995).

[59] Commission, Eighth report on monitoring application of Community law (1990) [1991] OJ C338/1, p.218.

[60] *Commission v Italy* (C–322/86) [1988] E.C.R. 3995.

[61] *Commission v Italy* (C–291/93) [1994] E.C.R. I–859; *Commission v Germany* (C–298/95) [1996] E.C.R. I–6747.

[62] Dir.2006/44 [2006] OJ L264/20.

[63] Dir.79/923 (fn.7, above).

[64] Commission, Eighth report (fn.59, above), p.218; see also the implementation report mentioned in fn.58, above.

[65] See, for instance, Court of Justice, *Commission v Italy* (C–225/96) [1997] E.C.R. I–6887, where the Commission had applied to the Court for absence of legislation in Italy in 1996, 17 years after the adoption of the Directive.

[66] Court of Justice, *Commission v Italy* (C–225/96) [1997] E.C.R. I–6887.

[67] Dir.91/492 [1991] OJ L268/1.

[68] Commission, COM (96) 59 (fn.5, above), annex point 1.6.

3. Reduction of discharges into water

Dangerous substances

Directive 76/464

7–24   Directive 76/464, adopted in 1976 on the basis of arts 115 and 352 TFEU, fixed the framework conditions for discharges of dangerous substances into waters.[69] The Directive established two lists of substances and groups of substances. List I contained substances considered toxic, persistent or bioaccumulative,[70] list II other polluting substances.[71] The Directive required all discharges which contained list I or list II substances to be authorised. The authorisations had to lay down emission limit values for these substances.

Article 6 stipulated that the European Union would lay down emission limit values for list I substances "taking into account the best technical means available". At the same time, the Council was to adopt quality standards on the basis of concentrations in living organisms and in sediment. The emission limit values were to apply all over the European Union "except in cases where a Member State can prove to the Commission . . . that the quality objectives . . . are being met and continuously maintained". The Commission had to report to the Council on cases where the quality standards were used; the Council should review every five years the cases where the quality objective method had been applied.

7–25   For list II substances, Member States had to establish programmes in order to reduce water pollution, and set timetables for their implementation. The programmes had to include quality objectives for water; individual authorisations had to be issued in such a way that these quality objectives could be respected. No publication of the programmes was foreseen; however, they had to be sent to the Commission, which had to make regular comparisons.

The Directive's provisions on emission limit values and quality standards constituted a compromise between the United Kingdom and the other—by then eight—Member States, which was necessary, since the Directive had to be adopted unanimously. The United Kingdom opposed the fixing of EU emission limit values, arguing that local environmental conditions were too different.[72] Rivers in the United Kingdom were short and quick-flowing and, at the coast, the tide would quickly wash away any eventual polluting discharge. While the other Member States pleaded in favour of common measures, they finally accepted the compromise, indicating in a statement that they would introduce only emission limit values.

7–26   Under the Directive, emission limit values and quality objectives were fixed for 17 substances. At least in the beginning, only the United Kingdom recurred to the quality standards approach. At no time, though, did the Commission report to

---

[69] Dir.76/464 on pollution caused by certain dangerous substances discharged into the aquatic environment of the Community [1976] OJ L129/23.

[70] Organohalogens, organophosphorous and organotin compounds, carcinogenics, mercury, cadmium, mineral oils and hydrocarbons and persistent synthetic substances.

[71] In particular, heavy metals, biocides, silicon compounds, cyanides, fluorides, ammonia, nitrites and all list I substances, for which no EU emission limit values had been fixed.

[72] See on the history of this controversy in particular, N. Haigh (ed.), *Manual of environmental policy: the E.C. and Britain* (looseleaf, London), at Chs 3.9 and 4.8.

the Council asking for its review. Rather, the Commission and the other Member States accepted that two different approaches were practised within the European Union. Also, the formula of using the best technical means available, remained a dead letter: instead, the values for the different pollutants were fixed on the basis of a political compromise between the institutions and Member States.

The Directive was a complete failure as regards list II substances. No Member State established programmes for them in order to reduce pollution; no Member State fixed quality objectives, either. Finally, it had clearly been impossible to undertake regular comparisons of Member States' pollution reduction programmes, as such programmes either did not exist or were too vague.

In 1992, the Commission reported that it had started 40 infringement procedures under art.258 TFEU against Member States, for not complying with the requirements of Directive 76/464.[73] The new evolution in water law, which started with the Edinburgh summit meeting,[74] led to a complete standstill in the monitoring of Directive 76/464—except as regards the procedures under art.258 TFEU that were progressively submitted to the Court of Justice.[75] In 1996, the Court of Justice found that Italy had not even yet transposed the requirement of prior authorisation for discharges into Italian law as regards existing installations.[76]

The different judgments against Member States for absence of programmes for List II-substances did not have consequences: the Commission did not systematically start proceedings under art.260 TFEU against Member States which did not submit (complete) programmes. Commission and Member States rather relied on the fact that art.22 of Directive 2000/60 provided that Directive 76/464 will cease to exist in 2013; this date is, in practice, anticipated, all the more, as Directive 2000/60 provided that art.6 was repealed already since 2000.

Daughter directives

Subsequent to the framework that had been set up by Directive 76/464, the European Union fixed emission limit values and quality standards for list I substances. To that end, the Commission established a list of 129 substances under list I, to which the Council agreed in a resolution.[77] A proposal for a directive on quality standards for a list II substance (chromium) was made,[78] but not adopted by the Council.

7–27

---

[73] Written Question 1496/91 (van Hemeldonck) [1992] OJ C202/7.

[74] See para.7–01, above.

[75] The first ever judgment on Dir.76/464 was given on June 11, 1998, 22 years after its adoption; this case, *Commission v Greece* (Joined Cases C–232 and 233/95) [1998] E.C.R. I–3343, concerned the absence of programmes for two Greek waters. Since then the following judgments were given *Commission v Luxembourg* (C–206/96) [1998] E.C.R. I–3401; *Commission v Italy* (C–285/96) [1998] E.C.R. I–5935; *Commission v Spain* (C–214/96) [1998] E.C.R. I–7661; *Commission v Belgium* (C–207/97) [1999] E.C.R. I–275; *Commission v Germany* (C–184/97) [1999] E.C.R. I–7837; *Commission v Greece* (C–384/97) [2000] E.C.R. I–3823; *Commission v Portugal* (C–261/98) [2000] E.C.R. I–5905; *Commission v Portugal* (C–435/99) [2000] E.C.R. I–11179; *Commission v Netherlands* (C–152/98) [2001] E.C.R. I–3463; *Commission v France* (C–130/01) [2003] E.C.R. I–5829; *Commission v Belgium* (C–406/02) judgment of February 12, 2004; *Commission v Ireland* (C–282/02) [2005] E.C.R. I–4653.

[76] *Arcaro* (C–168/95) [1996] E.C.R. I–4705.

[77] Res. of February 7, 1983 [1983] OJ C46/17.

[78] [1985] OJ C351/33.

As regards the list I substances, the emission limit values were expressed either in micrograms or milligrams per litre of water discharged or grams per kilogram or tonne of substances produced. The allowable discharges varied according to the nature of the water (inland surface water, estuary water, coastal water or territorial sea water). Normally, methods for measurements were fixed. Quality standards again varied according to the nature of the water. They were expressed as the arithmetic mean of the results of concentrations in water obtained over a year, but the number of measurements taken was left to Member States. The Commission had to establish comparative assessment reports on the implementation of the daughter directives.

7–28   Emission limit values and quality standards were fixed for mercury,[79] cadmium,[80] HCH (lindane),[81] carbon tetrachloride, DDT, pentachlorophenol, aldrin, dieldrin, endrin, isodrin, hexachlorobenzene, hexachlorobutadiene, chloroform, 1.2-dichloroethane, TRI, PER and trichlorobenzene.[82]

As an example, Directive 83/513 on cadmium discharges[83] may be quoted in more detail. It fixed emission limit values for zinc mining, lead and zinc refining, the cadmium metal and non-ferrous metal industry, the manufacture of cadmium compounds, pigments, stabilisers and batteries, and for electroplating. A footnote requested Member States to fix emission limit values for other industrial sectors and, in particular, the production of phosphoric acid and/or phosphatic fertilisers from phosphatic rocks.[84] Member States had to institute a monitoring procedure to check whether the actual discharges complied with the emission standards. That procedure had to provide for the taking and analysis of samples and for measurement of the flow of the discharge and the quantity of cadmium handled. A sample representative of the discharge over a period of 24 hours had to be taken. The quantity of cadmium discharged over a month then had to be calculated on the basis of the daily quantities of cadmium discharged. These monitoring requirements did not specify whether the industrial installation itself was to monitor its discharges, nor whether public authorities were ever to check the private monitoring system.

The Commission did not systematically monitor the application of the different daughter directives by, for instance, spot checks, asking Member States for data or comparing the monitoring procedures and the actual measuring results reached. Comparative reports were never made; no attempt was made to find out

---

[79] Dir.82/176 on limit values and quality objectives for mercury discharges by the chlor-alkali electrolysis industry [1982] OJ L81/29; Dir.84/156 on limit values and quality objectives for mercury discharges by sectors other than the clor-alkali electrolysis industry [1984] OJ L7449.

[80] Dir.83/513 on limit values and quality objectives for cadmium discharges [1984] OJ L291/1.

[81] Dir.94/491 on limit values and quality objectives for discharges of hexachlorocyclohexane [1984] OJ L274/11.

[82] Dir.86/280 on limit values and quality objectives for discharges of certain dangerous substances included in list I of the annex to Dir.76/464 [1980] OJ L181/6, amended by Dir.88/347 [1988] OJ L158/35 and Dir.90/415 [1990] OJ L219/49.

[83] Dir.83/513 (fn.81, above).

[84] Dir.83/513, annex I, nn.1 and 4: "Limit values for industrial sectors not mentioned [in this Directive] will, if necessary, be fixed by the Council at a later stage. In the meantime the Member States will fix emission standards for cadmium discharges autonomously in accordance with Directive 76/464. Such standards must take into account the best technical means available and must not be less stringent than the most nearly comparable limit value in this Annex . . . The absence of such limit values [for phosphatic rock utilisation] does not release the Member States from their obligation under Directive 76/ 464 to fix emission standards for these discharges."

what kind of emission limit values were fixed for the different industrial installations, whether they were expressly mentioned in the directives or not. Legal action against Member States was only taken where national legislation had not been adopted or where a Member State had transposed the directives by administrative circulars rather than by binding legislation.[85]

Apart from such legal action, monitoring work on these daughter Directives as well as on setting new emission limit values and quality standards came, since 1990, to a standstill, without an express decision by the Council or the Commission. The causes for this are not clear: indeed, all published programmes, resolutions, press releases and communications pleaded instead in favour of accelerating and intensifying work at EU level. It can only be presumed that the subsidiarity discussion which had started with the adoption of the Maastricht Treaty on European Union in 1993 has led the Commission deviate from its obligations and accommodate the wishes of Member States, in particular of the United Kingdom, not to have EU-wide emission standards, but to accept that the best available technique for discharges be applied—whatever a Member State understands by this notion.

Article 22(3) of Directive 2000/60 provided that the priority list of substances that was established in 1982, was to be replaced by a new priority list. A first new list of substances was set up by Decision 2455/2001.[86] It identified 33 substances or group of substances which were considered to be of a particular risk to the aquatic environment (art.16 of Dir.2000/60) and the Commission was asked to come forward with proposals: "of controls for the progressive reduction of discharges, emissions and losses of the substances concerned and in particular the cessation or phasing out of discharges, emissions and losses of the substances.., including an appropriate timetable for doing so" (art.16(6)). Article 16(7) of Directive 2000/60 furthermore stated: "The Commission shall submit proposals for quality standards applicable to the concentrations of the priority substances in surface waters, sediments or biota." In 2006, the Commission submitted a proposal "on environmental quality standards in the field of water policy and amending Directive 2000/60".[87] The Commission proposed quality standards for 33 priority substance and explicitly referred to art.16(7) of Directive 2000/60. The proposal also aimed at repealing all the abovementioned daughter directives by 2012 and explained that, in the meantime, Member States need no longer monitor application of emission limit values of these daughter directives (art.8(2)). With regard to the requirements of art.16(6) of Directive 2000/60, the proposal stated (Recital 5):

7–29

> "As regards emission controls of priority substances from point and diffuse sources as referred to in Article 16(6) and (8) of Directive 2000/60/EC, it seems more cost-effective and proportionate for Member States to include, where necessary, in addition to the implementation of other existing Community legislation, appropriate control measures in the programme of measures to be developed for each river basin in accordance with Article 11 of Directive 2000/60/EC."

---

[85] Court of Justice, *Commission v Portugal* (C–213/97) [1998] E.C.R. I–3289 on failure to transpose Dir.86/280 and Dir.88/347; *Commission v Portugal* (C–208/97) [1998] E.C.R. I–4017 on failure to transpose Dir.84/156.

[86] *Commission v Germany* (C–262/95) [1996] E.C.R. I–5729.

[87] Dec.2455/2001 (fn.21, above).

The proposal was adopted in 2008.[88] It meant in clear terms that the European Union does not have the intention any more to adopt legislation for emission limit values for priority hazardous substances, in view of their complete phasing out in the next twenty years, as was requested by Directive 2000/60. As at the same time the existing limit values for water discharges are repealed—by 2012, however with possibilities of anticipating that date—this Directive signified the departure from EU emission limit values. Thus, after 30 years, the United Kingdom won the battle against EU interference in its national water policy.

The environmental problem is that water (and air) quality standards are not enforced in practice and most likely cannot be enforced. It is of course much easier and more precise to measure emissions at the point, where the leave the discharging installation, and this control of point sources is also more cost-effective. Nobody would consider letting cars circulate with whatever air emissions or noise emissions they might generate, and just measure the pollution concentration or noise levels in the air. There is no difference with regard to water pollution. It is also sure that diffuse pollution sources cannot be subject of emission controls: it is physically impossible to measure the faecal emissions into the water of every cow or pig. For this reason, EU environmental policy, for the last thirty years, has underlined that emission limit values *and* quality standards were necessary in order to ensure an effective protection and reduction of pollution. This basic principle appears to have been abandoned.

Emissions from industrial installations

7–30   The EU measures on emissions, including water discharges, from the titanium dioxide industry were already discussed.[89] As regards water discharges from incinerators for hazardous waste, the Commission proposed a directive where it suggested emission limit values for, in total, 15 pollutants, which it later withdrew.[90] Generally, however, the sector-oriented approach, where emission limit values are fixed for a specific industrial sector, has been abandoned with the adoption of Directive 96/61[91] which requests the application of the best available technique. This policy change, however, created a problem, since Directive 96/61 which was since replaced by Directive 2010/75 on industrial emissions,[92] only applied to certain large industrial installations, whereas water contamination depends on the quantity of discharges, which may also stem from cumulated emissions from smaller plants.

Directive 2010/75 required the fixing of emission limit values in the individual permits for installations that come under the Directive. The pollutants covered are those: "likely to be emitted from the installation in significant quantities, having regard to their nature and their potential to transfer pollution from one medium to the other (water, air and land)". Special attention shall be given to fixing emission limit values for 13 "main polluting substances", which are listed in Annex II.[93]

---

[88] Commission, COM(2006) 397.
[89] Dir.2008/105 on quality standards in the field of water policy [2008] OJ L348/84.
[90] Commission, [1998] OJ C13/6.
[91] Dir.96/61 [1996] OJ L257/26. In 2008, this Dir. was replaced by Dir. 2008/1 [2008] OJ L24/8.
[92] Dir.2010/75 on industrial emissions [2010] OJ L334/17.
[93] Dir.2010/75 (fn.92, above), annex II (water pollutants):
    1. Organohalogen compounds and substances which may form such compounds in the aquatic environment;

Dumping of waste; discharge of offshore installations

Legally speaking, the discharge of waste is no different from any other discharge   **7–31**
into water; the terminology "dumping" stems from international conventions,
which wanted to give a specific definition to the discharge of waste from ships
and called this practice dumping. Under EU waste legislation, the discharge of
waste needs an authorisation; thus, Member States may authorise the discharge of
waste into waters at their discretion.[94]

In 1976, the Commission made a proposal on the dumping of waste at sea; it
made another proposal in 1985.[95] However, these proposals were not extensively
discussed in Council, since Member States preferred to see questions of marine
pollution discussed in the context of international conventions, rather than at EU
level. Waste dumping from ships is now prohibited by Directive 2008/98 on
waste.[96]

Identical considerations apply to the discharge of ships themselves and of   **7–32**
offshore installations. At the end of their useful lifetime, offshore installations
become waste. Their discharge into waters thus follows the same rules. After the
Brent Spar incident—in 1995, an oil company had tried to sink a rig into the
North Sea/Atlantic, but had abandoned its plans after massive public protests in
some (northern) Member States—the Commission considered the elaboration of
a directive on the decommissioning of offshore installations. However, it
abandoned these plans in view of the resistance from Member States; the
decommissioning of offshore installations was then addressed within the
framework of the OSPAR Convention.[97]

In 2006, France wanted to send its airplane carrier *Clemenceau* to South Asia,
in order have it dismantled there. As the ship contained some 30,000 tonnes of
asbestos, it was, legally speaking, hazardous waste, the export of which is
prohibited under EU waste legislation (see para.10–38, below). Nevertheless,
France pursued its action. When Egypt refused the transit of this hazardous waste
through the Suez Canal, it obtained development aid and forgot its objections. In
the Gulf States then, Greenpeace activists entered the ship and protested against
the shipment. At the same time, the French Conseil d'Etat confirmed that the
transport in question was well a shipment of hazardous waste. In view of the

---

2. Organophosphorous compounds;

3. Organotin compounds;

4. Substances and preparations which have been proved to possess carcinogenic or mutagenic
properties or properties which may affect reproduction in or via the aquatic environment;

5. Persistent hydrocarbons and persistent and bioaccumulable organic toxic substances;

6. Cyanides;

7. Metals and their compounds;

8. Arsenic and its compounds;

9. Biocides and plant protection products;

10. Materials in suspension;

11. Substances which contribute to eutrophication (in particular, nitrates and phosphates);

12. Substances which have an unfavourable influence on the oxygen balance (and can be measures
using parameters such as BOD, COD, etc.).

13. Substances which are listed in annex X to Dir.2000/60.

[94] Dir.2008/98 on waste [2008] OJ L312/3.

[95] [1976] OJ C40/3; [1985] OJ C245/23.

[96] See fn.94, above.

[97] Dir.2008/98 (fn.94, above), art.36: "Member States shall take the necessary measures to prohibit
the abandonment, dumping of uncontrolled management of waste". See also para.7–39, below.

public protests, the French President ordered the ship to come back to France. This single case stands out, though European tankers and other commercial ships are regularly shipped to South-East Asia, in order to be dismantled and shredded, under appalling social and environmental conditions. No action has yet been taken by the European Union on this situation.

Waste water

7–33   In 1991, the European Union adopted a Directive on urban waste water,[98] based on art.192(1) TFEU. The Directive aimed at reducing the pollution of surface waters with nutrients, in particular nitrates and phosphates from urban waste water, and thus to combat eutrophication. It applied to domestic waste water and the mixture of domestic waste water with industrial waste water and/or run-off rainwater. The Directive required Member States to provide, by the end of 2005, a sewerage system for all agglomerations consisting of more than 2,000 people; agglomerations of more than 15,000 people have to be equipped with such a system by the end of the year 2000. The Member States which joined the European Union since 2004, obtained, at their request, transition periods.

Before the waste water enters such a collecting system, it must undergo at least secondary (biological) treatment; this requirement was to be complied with by the end of 2005, and by the year 2000 for agglomerations of more than 15,000 people. Furthermore, Member States had to designate sensitive areas for which more stringent treatment requirements were to apply; such areas are waters that are found to be eutrophic, that are intended for the production of drinking water and could contain more than 50 mg of nitrates per litre, and areas where more than secondary treatment is necessary to comply with the Directive. Member States were also allowed to designate their whole territory as a sensitive area. They could also consider certain areas as less sensitive areas (marine waters), for which less stringent requirements applied. The discharge of sludge from treatment installations into waters had to be phased out by the end of 1998.

Member States had to establish programmes for the implementation of Directive 91/271 and to publish, every two years, situation reports on the disposal of urban waste water and sludge. Overall, it was estimated that about 40,000 water treatment plants were to be constructed or renewed for the some 23,000 agglomerations that were covered by the Directive; to this had to be added the construction of sewerage systems.[99]

7–34   The Directive had to be transposed into national law by mid-1993. By the end of 1994, only Denmark, France and Luxembourg had done so.[100] In 1996, the Court of Justice condemned Greece, Germany and Italy for not having transposed the Directive into national) law[101]; Belgium and Italy were also condemned for not having provided for waste water treatment for Bruxelles and Milano,[102] and a

---

[98] Dir.91/271 concerning urban waste water treatment [1991] OJ L135/40; amended by Commission Dir.98/15 [1998] OJ L67/29.

[99] Court of Auditors [1998] OJ C191/1, paras 3 and 5.

[100] Commission, 12th report on monitoring application of Community law (1994) [1995] OJ C254/1, p.128.

[101] *Commission v Greece* (C–161/95) [1996] E.C.R. I–1979; *Commission v Germany* (C–297/95) [1996] E.C.R. I–6739; *Commission v Italy* (C–302/95) [1996] E.C.R. I–6765.

[102] Court of Justice, *Commission v Belgium* (C–236/99) [2000] E.C.R. I–5657; C–396/00 *Commission v Italy* [2002] E.C.R. I–3948.

number of other Member States for incorrect transposition or application or for not co-operating with the Commission in implementing the Directive.[103] In 2004, the Commission reported that there were still 34 infringement proceedings running against Member States; this figure included cases, where Member States did not transmit plans, reports, etc. The Commission stated that frequently only the threat of bringing a case before the Court of Justice caused Member States to co-operate.[104]

4. Oceans and rivers

Oceans

Though the EU environmental policy also has as its aim to contribute to the solution of global or regional environmental problems (art.191 TFEU), it has not developed a consistent policy to address the protection of the marine environment. Until 2008, there was not one single EU environmental measure which expressly protected the marine environment, though a number of the above mentioned directives also apply to marine waters. Even in those directives, the European Union has, in its political and legal activity, only considered the seas adjacent to EU territory, in particular the North Sea, the Baltic Sea and the Mediterranean Sea, and to a lesser extent the Atlantic Ocean. A different approach as regards the environment was only taken in the context of the Common Fisheries Policy, where the Community also took an interest in fish—the "natural resources"—in West Africa, the Caribbean Sea and the Antarctic waters; it was also dealt with within the framework of the Common Transport Policy.

    In 2006, the Commission published a communication on an EU maritime policy.[105] The title, indicative, better explains the ideas behind the communication which does not announce concrete measures, in particular not on environmental issues.

    The sixth environmental action programme provided for the elaboration of a thematic strategy on the protection of the marine environment.[106] Following that, the Commission made a Communication on the marine environment and, in 2005, a proposal for a directive on the marine environment which was adopted in

7–35

---

[103] Court of Justice, *Commission v Spain* (C–419/01) [2003] E.C.R. I–4947; *Commission v Greece* (C–119/01) judgment of June 26, 2004; *Commission v Belgium* (C–27/03) judgment of July 8, 2004; *Commission v France* (C–280/02) [2004] E.C.R. I–8573; *Commission v France* (C–191/04) judgment of June 16, 2005; *Commission v France* (C–280/02) [2004] E.C.R. I–8573; *Commission v Luxemburg* (C–452/04) [2006] E.C.R. I–120; *Commission v Italy* (C–293/05) [2006] E.C.R. I–122; *Commission v United Kingdom* (C–405/05) [2007] E.C.R. I–10; *Commission v Spain* (C–219/05) [2007] I–56; *Commission v Greece* (C–440/07) [2007] I–145; *Commission v Portugal* (C–233/07) [2008] E.C.R. I–79; *Commission v Ireland* (C–316/06) [2008] E.C.R. I–124; *Commission v Portugal* (C–530/07) judgment of May 7, 2009; *Commission v Finland* (C–335/07) judgment of October 6, 2009; *Commission v Sweden* (C–436/07) judgment of October 6, 2009; *Commission v United Kingdom* (C–390/07) judgment of December 10, 2009.

[104] Commission, Third Report on the implementation of Dir.91/271, COM(2004) 248. See also Commission Fifth Report on the implementation of Dir.91/271, SEC(2009)1114.

[105] Commission Communication: Towards a future maritime policy for the Union: a European vision for the oceans and seas, COM(2006) 275.

[106] Commission, Towards a strategy to protect and conserve the marine environment COM(2002) 539 of October 2, 2002.

2008.[107] The Directive aimed at achieving good environmental status of the marine environment in 2021. It limited itself to fix objectives and principles, but omits to provide for measures. It established European Marine Regions as management units which happen to coincide with the areas covered by the three regional water conventions of Paris/Oslo (North East Atlantic), Helsinki (Baltic Sea) and Barcelona (Mediterranean Sea). The Black Sea Region was mentioned in the Directive, but only marginally, as the European Union is not a contracting party of the Bucharest Convention on the Protection of the Black Sea; that Convention is only open to States.

Member States shall develop, for each Marine Region, a Marine Strategy which shall contain a number of measures designed to achieve good environmental status. The Directive did not define what a good environmental status is, or give a description of it. It rather attempted to let the regional conventions' structures take care, elaborate and monitor the future programmes, limiting itself largely to provide for reporting provisions. Other aspects than marine *water* aspects—for instance on the fauna and flora or marine natural parks—were practically not covered.

It is too early to reflect on the impact of the Directive on the marine environment. As the Directive allows or even encourages the existing intergovernmental cooperation within the framework of the regional marine conventions, it is to be expected that not too much will change with regard to the present situation of marine waters surrounding the European Union. Rather, the state of the marine environment, as it is in 2021, is likely to be declared "good", while it will be acknowledged that improvements could still be made here or there.

7–36 The European Union adhered to the following international conventions concerning the marine environment, most of which having been completed by a number of protocols to which the European Union normally also adhered:

- Paris Convention on the prevention of marine pollution from land-based sources[108];
- Barcelona Convention on the protection of the Mediterranean Sea against pollution[109];
- Bonn Agreement for co-operation in dealing with pollution of the North Sea by oil and other harmful substances[110];
- Co-operation Agreement for the protection of the coasts and waters of the north-east Atlantic against pollution[111];
- Helsinki Convention on the protection of the marine environment of the Baltic Sea Area[112];
- Helsinki 1992 Convention on the protection of the marine environment of the Baltic[113];

---

[107] Dir.2008/56 establishing a framework for Community Action on marine water quality in the field of Marine Environmental Policy (Marine Strategy Framework Directive), [2008] OJ L164/19.
[108] Dec.75/437 [1975] OJ L194/5.
[109] Dec.77/85 [1977] OJ L240/1.
[110] Dec.84/358 [1984] OJ L188/7.
[111] Dec.93/550 [1993] OJ L267/20.
[112] Dec.94/156 [1994] OJ L73/1.
[113] Dec.94/157 [1994] OJ L73/19.

- Paris Convention for the protection of the marine environment in the north-east Atlantic (OSPAR)[114];
- Montego Bay Convention on the law of the sea.[115]

With the adhering of the European Union to these international conventions, their legal provisions became part of EU law. However, for each negotiation of a protocol to a convention or any other amendment, the Commission needs a mandate from the Council in order to negotiate in the name of the European Union; for the signing of such a protocol, the same procedure applies.[116]

7–37

The reasons why Member States object to the taking of EU directives or regulations on environmental problems facing the sea, have never been expressly specified. They are presumed to be the following:

1. International conventions are normally adopted unanimously. It is true that, during the last few years, public international law has developed the habit that amendments may, under certain conditions, be adopted by majority decisions; however, this possibility remains largely theoretical. Instead, the principle of international conventions remains based on consensus. Each contracting State thus has the right to veto decisions.
    In contrast to that, EU environmental measures are normally adopted by qualified majority, which allows measures to be taken against the will of an objecting Member State.

2. The initiative for measures at international level is, jointly or severally, in the hands of contracting States. This allows a fairly direct influence of the international agenda. For the Commission to negotiate, in the name of the European Union, at international conventions, a mandate is necessary under art.218 TFEU. In contrast to that, initiatives for measures at EU level are taken by the Commission, which has the monopoly on this.

3. At international level, media attention and the participation of environmental organisations is normally relatively limited. At EU level, the increasing importance of the European Parliament and its co-decision function make quasi-confidential discussions and decisions practically impossible.

4. For years, France and the United Kingdom have also discharged radioactive materials, which stemmed from military or private activity, into the sea. In the name of national sovereignty, such activities were always considered to remain outside the area of EU competence. This attitude has probably caused these two countries, but also other Member States where the situation was similar—though not necessarily concerning radioactive matters—not to accept EU environmental initiatives to protect seas. Generally, a number of Member States continue to consider the seas as a big sewer system, where discharges are all too often allowed to take place.

The statement that the international conventions become, with the adherence of the European Union, part of EU environmental law is legally correct. It is, however, rather theoretical, since the monitoring of these conventions is not ensured by the Commission, but by the secretariat of the different conventions. At

7–38

---

[114] Dec.98/249 [1998] OJ L104/1.
[115] Dec.98/392 [1998] OJ L179/1.
[116] See for details art.218 TFEU.

no time has the Commission tried, with regard to the different decisions incorporating the conventions into EU law, to "ensure the application of the Treaties and of measures adopted by their institutions pursuant to them",[117] and thus to control the effective implementation and enforcement of these conventions. Unless there is a specific EU directive or regulation that reproduces the content of the international convention, it is left to Member States to decide if and to what extent they transpose the provisions of the conventions into their national legal order and apply them. The Commission has never explained why it applies this self-restraint.

In case C–213/03, the Court of Justice confirmed the interpretation given here. It declared that France had infringed EU law, because it did not apply a Protocol to the Barcelona Covention; this Protocol had been ratified by the European Union, but not by France.[118] However, this is up to now the only case, where the Commission took action under art.258 TFEU against a Member State for infringement of provisions of an international environmental convention which had become part of EU law.

The present practice by the EU institutions leads to different legal situations and, hence, to different pollution situations for the different seas. To give some examples: OSPAR took decisions to reduce the discharge of radioactive substances into the North East Atlantic (Decision 2000/1), on the use of organic-phase drilling fluids (Decision 2000/3), a control system for use and discharge of offshore chemicals (Decision 2000/2), on carbon dioxide streams in the water column, on the seabed or in geological formations (Decisions 2007/1 and 2) or on maritime protected areas (Decisions 2010/1 to 5).

7–39　　Most, if not all, of these measures have an impact on the functioning of the European Union. However, it is highly unlikely that in the context of the Barcelona Convention on the Mediterranean Sea similar subjects will be raised at all, not to mention the taking of binding decisions.

At the same time, this list of subjects indicate the impact that OSPAR decisions have or might have on the European Union. Indeed, the ban of products or processes will impinge on the free circulation of goods and the competitive situation of undertakings.

In the case of hexachloroethane, a substance which a decision by the OSPAR Convention had phased out, the potential conflict was solved, not without complications, by the adoption of a EU Directive which took over the OSPAR decision to phase out that substance.[119] Another approach was taken in the Brent Spar incident: while the Commission had first considered making a proposal for an EU directive on offshore installations, it finally rejected this approach with legally unconvincing arguments and left the decision to OSPAR, which took, in 1998, a decision.[120] The Commission then proposed to approve, by way of a

---

[117] art.17 TEU.

[118] Court of Justice, *Commission v France* (C–239/03) [2004] E.C.R. I–9325; see also *Pêcheurs de Berre* (C–213/03) [2004] E.C.R. I–7357.

[119] Dir.97/16 [1997] OJ L116/31.

[120] OSPAR, Decision 98/3 on the disposal of disused offshore installations. See also Commission Communication on removal and disposal of disused offshore oil and gas installations, COM (1998) 49, para.6.2: "The disadvantage of this approach [a directive] is that only EC and EEA Member States would be bound to the common approach whereas other third countries with which we share the Seas concerned would not be bound to implement the same or similar measures without the Community taking the initiative to negotiate and adopt such rules in the relevant regional seas Conventions.

Decision, this decision by OSPAR, without, however, proposing an amendment of EU law, in order to introduce provisions on offshore installations that were binding on all EU Member States.[121] However, the proposal to take over the OSPAR Decision was never adopted by the Council.

It must be assumed that the Commission definitely abandoned its plan for a   **7–40**
directive on offshore installations because any such proposal would have been rejected in the same way as the proposal for a directive on the dumping of waste at sea. However, de facto, this evolution also risks leading to a loss of the Commission's right of initiative for EU action. Rules neither on subsidiarity nor deregulation can solve the problem of decisions being taken by the regional marine conventions which have an impact on the European Union as a whole.

The Commission also submitted proposals to approve other OSPAR decisions, for example on a new annex V to the OSPAR Convention,[122] the disposal of radioactive waste,[123] and on emission limit values from the production of vinyl chloride monomers.[124] However, these proposals were, again, not adopted.

In November 2002, the tanker Prestige which was single-hulled and had   **7–41**
loaded 77,000 tonnes of heavy fuel oil, had an accident off the coast of Galicia (Spain) and sank. A large quantity of fuel oil was released which polluted in particular the Spanish and French coast. Estimation of the damage caused by the accident and the subsequent coastal and marine pollution are for more than 1 billion €. The accident caused a strong activity from the EC to improve the safety of maritime transport of fuel oils and other dangerous substances, and generally to improve maritime transport safety.[125] Similar increased legislative activities had already taken place after the accidents of Braer in the Shetlands 1993 and Erika in France 1999. The Erika accident led to the setting up of a European Maritime Safety Agency[126] which has the task to ensure "a high uniform and effective level of maritime safety and prevention of pollution from ships"; (art.1) the Decision is based on art.90(2) TFEU.

Rivers

The European Union is a member of the following international conventions   **7–42**
regarding rivers:

- Bonn Convention for the protection of the Rhine against chemical pollution[127];

Although this approach would have the advantage of applying to all EC Member States immediately, i.e. also to those Member States outside OSPAR—namely Austria, Greece and Italy—it would only apply to Norway after a Decision of the EEC Joint Committee. It could also be interpreted as prejudicial to Community interest in other OSPAR policies if the Commission were to be seen to press ahead separately for action via EC legislation rather than via the newly ratified OSPAR Convention. Furthermore it could be seen as an attempt to exclude Norway from negotiations on any final policy."
[121] Proposal for a Council decision [1999] OJ C158/10.
[122] [1999] OJ C158/1.
[123] [1999] OJ C158/8.
[124] [1999] OJ C158/19.
[125] Commission, Report to the European Council on action to deal with the effects of the *Prestige* disaster, COM (2003) 105 of March 5, 2003.
[126] Reg.1406/2002 [2002] OJ L208/1.
[127] Dec.77/586 [1977] OJ L240/35.

- Regensburg Agreement on co-operation on management of water resources in the Danube basin[128];
- Magdeburg Convention on the International Commission for the protection of the Elbe[129];
- Sofia Convention on co-operation for the protection of the Danube[130];
- Wroclaw Convention on the International Commission for the protection of the Odra against pollution[131];
- Helsinki Convention on the Protection and use of transboundary water-courses and international lakes.[132]

7–43   The legal situation as regards rivers is similar to that of seas. While the different conventions became, with the EU decisions to adhere to them, part of EU law, they are de facto treated, by the European Union and by the Commission, as instruments of public international law. In particular, the Commission does not monitor the adoption of measures to incorporate the conventions into national law and their application in practice. Thus, the question that was put some years ago, particularly by Dutch lawyers, "Who shall clean up the Rhine river—the Rhine Commission or the European Community?", is in reality answered for the Rhine and for the other rivers that are the subject of conventions: it is not the European Union, but the different secretariats of the conventions, which are in charge of combating river pollution. The question of water resources goes beyond river water, since it might also apply to groundwater resources. To date, though, there has been not one single provision in EU water law which deals with quantitative aspects of water resources.

The abovementioned Directive 2000/60 will also request the elaboration of river basin plans for Rhine, Danube, Elbe and Oder. Member States may use the administrative structures existing for these rivers to fulfil their obligations under Directive 2000/60. To what extent the Commission will play a greater role in the monitoring of compliance as regards these rivers, will have to be seen in future.

---

[128] Dec.90/160 [1990] OJ L377/28.
[129] Dec.91/598 [1991] OJ L321/25.
[130] Dec.97/825 [1997] OJ L342/18.
[131] Dec.1999/257 [1999] OJ L100/20.
[132] Dec.95/308 [1995] OJ L186/42.

CHAPTER 8

Air Pollution and Noise

1. Air policy and law

The first environmental action programmes of the European Union mentioned air pollution, its causes and its effects on the environment, but actions were dispersed, incoherent and limited to specific pollution sources, in particular to emissions from passenger cars. The turning point came at the beginning of the 1980s, when the state of the forests, particularly those in Germany and central Europe, raised considerable concern. The subject of air pollution was discussed, in 1983, by the Heads of State and Governments who suggested effective action against acid rain and air pollution.[1] This led, in the same year, to proposals for a general directive on air pollution from industrial installations,[2] for a directive on large combustion plants[3] and for a directive for quality objectives for NOx.[4] Other measures concentrated on the introduction of a catalytic converter for cars, which had been discussed since 1984 and had been progressively introduced since 1988 for new cars; since 1993, all new cars have had to be equipped in this way.

8–01

Since the mid-1980s, the depletion of the ozone layer and climate change entered more and more into the foreground of discussions. These aspects will not be dealt with here, but in a separate chapter.[5]

EU legislative measures on air emissions from industrial installations were based, in the early 1980s, on the concept of emission limit values which was in use mainly in legislation in Germany.[6] Large industrial installations in specific sectors were to operate on the basis of a permit which was to impose the best available technology not entailing excessive costs. EU-wide emission limit values were to be elaborated.[7] This concept led to the elaboration of directives for large combustion installations[8] and incinerators.[9] However, the European Union went

8–02

---

[1] (1993) 3 *Bulletin of the European Communities*, para.1.5.2.
[2] Commission, proposal for a directive on air emissions from industrial installations [1983] OJ C139/5.
[3] Commission, proposal for a directive on large combustion plants [1984] OJ C49/1.
[4] Commission, proposal for a directive on air quality objectives for NOx [1983] OJ C258/3.
[5] See Ch.9, below.
[6] Dir.84/360 on the combating of air pollution from industrial plants [1984] OJ L188/20.
[7] Dir.84/360 (fn.6, above), art.8.
[8] Dir.88/609 on the limitation of emissions of certain pollutants into the air from large combustion plants [1988] OJ L336/1; this Dir. was since replaced by Dir.2001/80 [2001] OJ L309/1 and, since 2010, by Dir.2010/75 on industrial emissions [2010] OJ L334/17.
[9] Dir.89/369 on new installations for the incineration of municipal waste [1989] OJ L163/32; Dir.89/429 on the incineration of municipal waste from existing plants [1989] OJ L203/50; Dir.94/67 on the incineration of hazardous waste [1994] OJ L365/34. All these Directives were since replaced by

away from this concept and more or less implicitly—at least silently—took the decision that emission standards for industrial installations within the European Union should not be harmonised.[10] This policy found its expression in Directive 96/61—since then replaced by Directive 2008/1 and later on by Directive 2010/75[11]—which was based on the principle that the emission limits for an industrial installation were to be fixed in the permit which were issued for the installation. This Directive which provided for the repeal of Directive 80/360 after a transition period, very largely affected air emissions. Three days after the adoption of Directive 96/61, a new framework Directive was adopted,[12] which established the legal frame for setting quality standards on air pollution and which was, via daughter directives, progressively put into operation.

8–03 Under the Sixth Environmental Action Programme[13] the Commission submitted, in 2005, a thematic strategy on air pollution[14] which intended to provide for a long-term integrated air policy strategy.[15] The non-binding strategy established targets on the reduction of air pollution for sulphur dioxide (82 per cent reduction), nitrogen oxides (60 per cent), volatile organic compounds (51 per cent), ammonia (27 per cent) and fine particulate matters (PM2,5—59 per cent) until 2020, compared to the year 2000. As the binding concentration limits in particular for fine particulate matters were not respected by the majority of Member States, a new Directive which replaced Directive 96/62, was adopted which also brought the different daughter directives back into one single legal text.[16]

8–04 Policies, strategies and measures concerning air pollution are strongly influenced by a number of basic factors which need to be borne in mind.

First, air emissions stem in particular from the combustion of fuels, and the energy policy within the European Union on the use of energy—nuclear energy, oil, gas, coal and lignite—varies considerably, depending also on the national availability of energy sources. Secondly, air emissions cannot be regarded separately from other environmental problems; while, for instance, nuclear energy does not emit significant quantities of air pollutants, it has numerous other environmental and other disadvantages, such as the technological risk, waste treatment and disposal problems, the location of installations and decommissioning of installations, vulnerability to terrorist attacks and acceptance by the population. Also, nuclear energy is not economically competitive within the European Union—with the exception of France, where investments in the past

Dir.2000/76 on the incineration of waste [2000] OJ L332/91. In 2010, the provisions on waste incinerators were integrated into Dir.2010/75 (fn.8, above).

[10] See for a background to this shift in policy, A. Héritier, C. Knill, S. Mingers, *Ringing the changes in Europe. Regulatory competition and redefinition of the state. Britain, France and Germany* (Berlin, New York, 1996).

[11] Dir.96/61 on integrated prevention and pollution control [1996] OJ L257/26; in 2008, this Dir. was replaced by Dir.2008/1 [2008] OJ L24/8, and in 2010 by Dir.2010/75 (fn.8, above); see also para.4–16, above.

[12] Dir.96/62 on ambient air quality assessment and management [1996] OJ L296/55.

[13] Dec.1600/2002 laying down the Sixth Community Environmental Action Programme [2002] OJ L242/1.

[14] Commission, Communication: Thematic strategy on air pollution, COM(2005) 446.

[15] See also Commission, The programme Clean Air for Europe (CAFÉ): a thematic strategy on air quality, COM(2001) 245.

[16] Dir.2008/50 on ambient air quality and cleaner air for Europe [2008] OJ L152/1. For more details see Ch.9.

have been heavily subventioned by State aid. Thirdly, air emission quantities largely depend on the level of economic development, which continues to vary considerably between Member States and makes common solutions difficult. Fourthly, and perhaps foremost, there seems to be no readiness in Western European society seriously to question present lifestyles, particularly private passenger and truck transport. The words used in the early 1990s by a President of the USA that the American way of life is not negotiable, appear also to be true for the European way of life—at least in the eyes of many citizens. Renewable energies have only recently become the subject of concentrated attention[17] and continue to play at present a subordinate role within the European Union.

At the international level, EU participation in the discussions on long-range transboundary air pollution has intensified, illustrating well the global nature of environmental (air pollution) problems. Furthermore, co-operation with the World Health Organisation WHO—mostly represented by its European Centre for Environment and Health—led to a situation, where the European Union oriented its air quality standards on recommendations of the WHO.[18]

It is difficult to assess existing provisions, in particular the scientific, economic, mathematical, technical and political conditions of the different standards, the measuring mechanisms, the monitoring of the standards and of the measures which Member States, regions, local authorities and individual emittors are taking in pursuance of EU law, as these measures are highly complex, only perceptible to initiated experts and not sufficiently transparent. One practical consequence of this situation is that EU air pollution legislation is hardly enforceable: where a Member State is determined to reduce emissions, improve air quality and intensively work[19] with clean-up programmes or reduction measures that are provided in EU legislation, this legislation is a useful yardstick with which the different measures may be aligned, co-ordinated and structured. Where, in contrast, a Member State is attaching less importance to air pollution or where its environmental policy ranks lower in the political priority, EU legislation will only with difficulties, if at all, be capable of leading to a continuous reduction of emissions and an improvement of air quality. This same problem with regard to the enforcement of quality standards had already been observed with regard to discharges into water, see Ch.7, above.

8–05

In the last instance, air quality directives cannot really be enforced. It is true that the Court of Justice had paved the way for an enforcement of air quality directives by individual persons, by providing that whenever the exceeding of the limit values could endanger human health, the persons concerned must be in a position to rely on mandatory rules in order to be able to assert their rights. However, the large discretion for administrations in the fixing of the number and location of measuring stations, of measuring methods, the frequency of measuring, the average values, etc., the publication of data only months or years later, leads de facto to the situation that EU air quality values constitute policy guidance standards rather than legal instruments. This explains the very low number of infringement cases under art.258 TFEU against Member States which

8–06

---

[17] Commission, Energy for the future: renewable sources of energy, Green Paper, COM (96) 576; White Paper for a Community strategy and action plan COM (97) 599.

[18] See in particular WHO, *Air Quality Guidelines for Europe* 2nd edn (Copenhagen, 2000).

[19] Court of Justice, *Commission v Germany* (C–361/88) [1991] E.C.R I–2567; *Janecek* (C–237/07) [2008] E.C.R. I–6221.

are limited to cases of non-transposition of EU Directives or the absence of reporting,[20] but practically never deal with the lack of application in a specific case or in a specific agglomeration. Knowledge about the inter-relationship between air pollution and health—to humans and the environment—is not precise enough to allow the full assessment of these health effects and the transformation of such knowledge into legislative provisions. Generally, the European Environment Agency[21] gives a prudent but positive assessment of the measures taken on air pollution.[22] It sees the biggest ground for concern in the areas of the tropospheric ozone, particulate matters and acidification and signals that there is no EU legislation on the reduction of emissions of ammonia or particulate PM 2.5 matters.[23]

2. Air quality values

8–07   The basic EU instrument on air pollution is—next to Directive 2008/1 and now Directive 2010/75,[24] which only applies to some large industrial installations—Directive 2008/50.[25] This Directive deals with sulphur dioxide, nitrogen dioxide, benzene, carbon monoxide, lead, particulate matters (PM10) and (PM2.5) and tropospheric ozone.

Regarding its field of application, it constitutes a remarkable regress in environmental protection. Unlike previous directives, it no longer required that air quality standards shall have to be respected all over the territory of the Member States: "Member States shall ensure that throughout their zones and agglomerations, levels of sulphur dioxide, PM10, lead and carbon monoxide do not exceed the limit values" (art.13). Zones and agglomerations had to be established by Member States, and it was in those zones and agglomerations that the air quality shall have to be assessed. A limit value was defined as a value that has to be attained within a given period and not to be exceeded thereafter.[26] However, the Directive provided for "margins of tolerance", within which the limit values may well be exceeded; furthermore, the definition of limit value itself provided that it may not be exceeded for more than a certain number of days per calendar year which means that it is not an absolute limit. Furthermore, when limit values are exceeded, Member States are obliged to draw up a clean-up plan which means that they may delay the respect of the limit values until the end of this—or even a second—plan. Finally, the locations where the Member States are requested to measure the concentration of pollutants, are fixed by the Member

[20] The cases *Commission v Italy* (C–92/79) [1980] E.C.R. 1115, *Commission v Belgium* (C–186/91) [1993] E.C.R. I–851, *Commission v France* (C–320/99) [2000] E.C.R. I–10453, *Commission v Spain* (C–417/99) [2001] E.C.R. I–6015 concerned the non-transposition into national law; the cases *Commission v Germany* (C–58/89) [1991] E.C.R. I–2607, *Commission v Germany* (C–361/88) (fn.18, above), *Commission v France* (C–13/90) [1991] E.C.R. I–4331, *Commission v France* (C–14/90) [1991] E.C.R. 4331, *Commission v France* (C–64/90) [1991] E.C.R. I–4335, concerned the transposition into national law by non-binding instruments.
[21] See Reg.1210/90 setting up the European Environment Agency [1990] OJ L120/1.
[22] European Environment Agency, *Environmental signals 2001* (Copenhagen, 2002), pp.72 et seq.; EU emission inventory 1990–2008, Technical Report 7/2010; Copenhagen 2010.
[23] European Environment Agency 2001 (fn.22, above), p.72.
[24] Dir.2008/1 (fn.11, above); Dir.2010/75 (fn.8, above).
[25] Dir.2008/50 (fn.16, above).
[26] Dir. 2008/50, art.2.5.

States themselves. The Directives established criteria; however, these are very general and allow all sorts of measures which might significantly influence the measuring results.[27]

In appropriate cases alarm thresholds—these are values "beyond which there is a risk for human health from brief exposure and at which immediate steps shall be taken by Member States"—were to be fixed; where such values are exceeded, the population has to be alerted. No limit values were fixed for tropospheric ozone and for $PM_{2.5}$.[28]

The following limit values were established[29]:   **8–08**

Pollutant	Time	Limit value	Number of days per year where exceeding is allowed	Margin of tolerance
Sulphur dioxide	Hour	350 microgram/m³	24	150 microgram/m³
	Day	125 microgram/m³	3	
Nitrogen dioxide	Hour	200 microgram/m³	18	
	Year	40 microgram/m³		
Benzene	Year	5 microgram/m³		5 microgram/m³
Carbon monoxide		10 milligram/m³		60%
Lead	Year	0,5 microgram/m³		100%
Particulate matters PM_{10}	Day	50 microgram/m³	35	50%
	Year	40 microgram/m³		20%

Member States may postpone the application of the limit values for benzene and nitrogen dioxide in a given zone or agglomeration by five years, provided they set up an air quality plan for those pollutants which had the objective to

[27] For example the sampling point "shall be between 1.5 m (breathing zone) and 4 m above the ground"—as if children could not be affected by air pollution (annex III); "traffic-oriented sampling probes shall be at least 25m from the edge of major junctions and no more than 10m from the kerbside"(annex III). In earlier EU legislation the requirement was that the measuring station should be placed where pollution was thought to be the worst.

[28] The reason given for this was that tropospheric ozone is not emitted, but is formed by reactions of different precursor substances, in particular under the influence of sunlight. And Member States found it too difficult to respect, be it in future, limit values for $PM_{2.5}$.

[29] Directive 2008/50 (fn.16, above), annex XI. These limit values are in force since the beginning of 2010.

allow them to respect the limit values at a later stage. The same possibility exists for PM_{10},[30] though the respect of the Directive's limit value had to be ensured by June 2011.[31]

8–09   In the zones and agglomerations designated by them, Member States have to monitor ambient air quality. In particular, they have to establish measuring systems for air quality and to assess air quality. These systems vary according to the air pollution in question: in certain places, measurement from fixed stations is required; in other areas, where the limit values are not exceeded, modelling or indicative measurement are sufficient. Member States have then to establish a list of those zones and agglomerations, where the limit values are exceeded. Such an exceeding is based on average concentrations, not on the fact that, for example, the limit values were exceeded in only one street. Member States have then to elaborate an air quality plan in order to keep the period of non-compliance as short as possible (art.23). These plans have to be sent to the Commission, by the latest two years after the discovery of the exceedings. The Commission is given no possibility to influence the content of the plan or monitoring progress in respecting the limit values. Its only way of action would be to start legal proceedings under art.258 TFEU—a very hypothetical option. It is true, though, that Member States have obligations to inform the Commission of details of their national compliance situation (art.27).

8–10   Directive 96/62 had set the framework for the elaboration of limit values for thirteen explicitly enumerated pollutants. Eight of them had been covered by three daughter directives[32] and are now covered by Directive 2008/50. A fourth Directive covering the remaining pollutants from the list of Directive 96/62—cadmium, arsenic, nickel, mercury and polcyclic aromatic hydorcarbons (PAH)—should have been proposed end 1999, but was only submitted in 2003 and adopted end 2004.[33] The problem with these substances was that Directive 96/62 required the fixing of binding limit-values and these substances are, at least as regards their compounds, known carcinogens. Industry which would be most affected by the provisions—oil refineries, cement producers, waste incinerators, chlor-alkali and glass producers, iron and steel processes, non-ferrous metal processes and combustion processes—argued that the economic costs for complying with limit-values were high, while the advantages for human health and the environment would be limited; it could not assume obligations beyond the non-binding provisions which are laid down in the different BREF-documents under Directive 2008/1.[34]

8–11   The Directive therefore went away from the Council decision of 1996, only eight years after this decision had been laid down in Directive 96/62, to fix binding limit-values and limited itself to fix target values which were defined as "a concentration . . . to be attained where possible over a given period" (art.2(a)).

---

[30] Particulate Matter 10 (PM_{10}) is a particulate with a diameter of less than 10 micrometer.

[31] The limit value for PM_{10} had already been fixed by Dir.1999/30 [1999] OJ L163/41; Member States were obliged to ensure that it was, as of January 2005, not exceeded during more than 35 days per calendar year. However, numerous cities had not taken measures to reach this result and were, since 2005, in open breach of EU law. This was the main reason for the EU to replace Directive 96/62 and its different daughter directives by Dir.2008/50—which delayed the requirement to respect the limit values until 2010/2011. See on this Commission, COM(2005) 446 (fn.14, above).

[32] Dir.1999/30 (fn.31, above); Dir.2000/69 [2000] OJ L313/12; Dir.2003/2 [2003] OJ L67/14.

[33] Dir.2004/107 [2005] OJ L23/3.

[34] Dir.2008/1 [2008] OJ L24/8; see on this Dir. in more detail Ch.4.

The justification given in the Recital is in diplomatic language, yet clear: "With a view to cost-effective measures, ambient air concentrations of arsenic, cadmium, nickel and polycyclic aromatic hydrocarbons which would not pose a significant risk to human health, cannot be achieved in specific areas" (Recital 3). For mercury, not even a target value was fixed, with the argument that there would be a general strategy to reduce mercury in the environment; in the meantime, this strategy was published, however, without limiting industrial air emissions of mercury. Rightly so, this turn of policy approach with regard to heavy metals emissions was considered to be a "victory for industry".[35] Indeed, as the different substances are known "human genotoxic carcinogens" (Dir.2004/107, Recital 3), their presence in the environment should be limited as far as possible. And as Directive 2008/1 only covers some industrial installations, a reference to the non-binding provisions of the BREF-documents is not likely to lead to significant emission reductions. A public discussion on this change of policy did not take place.

There are no other air quality values for pollutants that are fixed at EU level. Article 32 of Directive 2008/50 provides that the Commission shall review, by 2013, the situation of $PM_{2.5}$ and other pollutants and make appropriate proposals for legislation.

Also Directive 2001/81 may be counted to belong to the area of quality standards.[36] The Council adopted it in 2001. The Directive had the objective to reduce acidification of the soil and to contribute to the reduction of levels of tropospheric ozone. It fixed national emission ceilings for sulphur dioxide, nitrogen oxide, volatile organic compounds (VOC) and ammonia. VOC is a precursor substance for tropospheric ozone. The other three pollutants are considered to be principally responsible for acidification and eutrophication which may cause damage to soils, aquatic and terrestrial ecosystems, and buildings and materials.   **8–12**

The Directive admitted that it is at present "technically" impossible to reach the guidance values which the WHO established for tropospheric ozone and acidification (Recital 7). Article 5 fixed as an objective to reduce, compared to 1990, the surface of excessive acidification by 50 per cent, reduce tropospheric ozone charges on human health by two thirds and on vegetation by one-third. For each Member State, emission ceilings are fixed which were to be reached by 2010 and may not be exceeded on any year after that date. For that purpose, Member States had to draw up programmes for the progressive reduction of national emissions and prepare national emission inventories. The Commission was to be informed annually on these inventories.

Already the title of the Directive which talked of national emission ceilings, pointed at the provenance of the Directive's concept from public international law. Indeed, the emission ceilings are very similar to those of a Protocol under the 1979 Convention on Long-Range Transboundary Air Pollution which the Member states signed in November 1999 and which is transposed into EU law by Directive 2001/81. The Commission had in vain tried to reach more stringent values; when making its proposal, the Commission had indicated that with its proposal, the overall acidification within the European Union would be halved   **8–13**

---

[35] See ENDS Dails, December 20, 2001, p.2; Environmental Issue Manager (Brussels) *Issue Tracker*, January 2003, p.9.
[36] Dir.2001/81 on national emission ceilings for certain atmospheric pollutants [2001] OJ L309/22.

and that the exposure of the population to tropospheric ozone would be reduced by 75 per cent. These arguments, however, did not impress the Council, where Member States stuck more or less to the figures of the Protocol.[37]

The following emission ceilings were agreed[38] (in kilotonnes/year):

Member State	Commission proposal	Dir.2001/81
Austria	327	367
Belgium	362	488
Denmark	360	336
Finland	409	441
France	2,547	3,015
Germany	2,851	3,116
Greece	1,057	1,201
Ireland	265	278
Italy	2,827	3,043
Luxembourg	24	31
Netherlands	548	623
Portugal	454	680
Spain	2,542	2,608
Sweden	486	513
United Kingdom	2,906	3,248

The Commission had to report in 2004 and 2008 whether it was likely that these ceilings are to be reached. By the end of 2010, no such report had been submitted; however, the Commission announced that it would make proposals for a review of the Directive in 2007. By the end of 2010, such proposals had not been made public.

National emission ceilings for sulphur dioxide and nitrogen oxides had already been fixed at EU level, for large combustion plants, by Directive 88/609.[39] In 2001, this Directive was replaced, with effect from the end of 2002, by Directive 2001/80.[40] This Directive introduced a number of measures concerning emissions of large combustion plants and overall national quantities which had to be reduced; leaving in part the option between the different approaches to Member States. For reasons of presentation, this Directive will be discussed in detail in para.8–33, below.

---

[37] It is a general issue that Member States are very unwilling to change a consensus which they once have reached, be it at international, be it at EU level.

[38] See *ENDS Daily*, June 22, 2000, p.1.

[39] Dir.88/609 (fn.8, above).

[40] Dir.2001/80 (fn.8, above).

3.   Pollution emissions from mobile sources (products)

Pollution emission limit values from products were, historically, the first EU   **8–14**
measures on air pollution. The purpose of these first provisions was, however, not
to combat air pollution, but to ensure the free circulation of products.[41] The
efforts undertaken by the European Union to reduce air emissions from products,
in particular from means of transport, were not at all systematic. They
concentrated on cars, since it became more and more obvious that individual
passenger transport was the main generator of air emissions within the European
Union. Measures to combat air emissions from trucks, from railways, aeroplanes
and ships were much less intense and less systematic. As regards the air polluting
substances contained in fuels—e.g. lead in petrol and sulphur in diesel fuel—see
para.6–10, above.

Air emission from cars

EU measures to reduce air emissions from cars started in 1970. These measures   **8–15**
concentrated on emission limit values, and, since the early 1980s, when the dying
forests signalled the need for more stringent measures, on the fuels used by cars.
Consequently, they were based on art.100, and since 1987 on art.95 EC (now
art.114 TFEU).

The European Union never considered to apply the principle of art.191(2)
TFEU and combat air pollution from cars at its source, e.g. by imposing the
construction of cars that do not exceed a maximum speed limit—for instance,
100km per hour—or which do not burn more than a certain amount of fuels per
100km[42]; the reason is probably that such considerations were considered to be
much too interventionist; it must be repeated that Directive 2009/125 on the
eco-design of energy related products[43] would give the legal competence to the
European Union to impose such construction requirements; however, this
Directives explicitly excluded means of transport from its field of application.
Beginning in the early 1990s, directives also stated that progress in reducing air
emissions from cars was countered by the increase in the car fleet and the number
of kilometres driven by each individual car, so that the overall reduction of air
emissions was, at best, extremely small.

The European Union did, until now, not take measures to introduce taxes or   **8–16**
charges for cars according to their emissions into the environment; neither did it
take any measures for EU-wide tax incentives in order to promote the marketing
or use of less-polluting cars, as basic objections against EU tax measures made
such an approach impossible. A proposal from the Commission to fix the tax for

---

[41] See Dir.70/220 on measures to be taken against air pollution by emissions from motor vehicles
[1970] OJ L176/1, 2nd and 3rd recital: "a regulation of 31 March 1969 on the composition of exhaust
gases emitted from petrol engines of motor vehicles was published in France ... those provisions are
liable to hinder the establishment and proper functioning of the common market; ... it is therefore
necessary that all Member States adopt the same requirements..."
[42] See, however, European Parliament, Res. of April 10, 1997 [1997] OJ C132/170, where the
Parliament requested that new cars do not consume more than 5 litres of petrol (4.5 litres of diesel)
per 100km as of January 1, 2005 and not more than 3 litres of petrol or diesel as of January 1, 2010.
The Commission concluded, in 1998, an agreement with the car industry on these issues, see below.
[43] Dir.2009/125 establishing a framework for the setting of eco-design requirements for energy
related products [2009] OJ L285/10.

individual cars according to their CO^2-emissions, made in 2005, was, by March 2011, not yet adopted by the Council.[44] Since the late 1980s, the European Union has accepted that Member States can grant tax incentives for less-polluting cars, albeit under very restrictive conditions[45] that made this instrument almost worthless. Indeed, only temporary incentives were allowed, during the transition period of the directive that reduced air emissions. Only incentives for new cars were permitted; incentives for the retrofitting of existing cars were not. This, for instance, made it impossible to give incentives for the retrofitting of existing cars with catalytic converters. It is interesting to see that the Commission concluded in 2000 that:

"well-targeted, differentiated taxes are considered to be an effective tool to influence consumer behaviour, and can therefore confidently be expected to provide an effective means of accelerated improved performance in the transport sector, with a very low societal cost.[46]"

This remark, it is true, aims at fuel charges. However, it is not clear why it would not also apply to cars or trucks.

8–17   If one considers that the lifetime of a car is at least 12 years and that standards that required the use of catalytic converters were only made mandatory for all new cars as of January 1, 1993, one can easily see that by the year 2005, when more or less all cars without catalytic converters have disappeared from the market, the resulting reduction in air emissions will have been eaten up by the traffic increase. The Commission predicted that by 2020 all emissions from road transport—except CO2, the greenhouse gas—will have fallen to less than 20 per cent of their 1995 levels, despite the growth in transport; SO2 emissions are predicted to fall to 10 per cent of their 1995 levels in 2005, NOx-emissions to fall to 30 per cent of their 1995 levels by 2010.[47]

8–18   Measures to reduce air emissions from cars have, since the early 1990s, been prepared by the Commission's so-called Auto/Oil Programme, which set up working groups where the European associations of the car and petrol industries were invited to "make available their considerable know-how and expertise".[48] Member States were kept informed of the discussions, in informal meetings. Four specific meetings were organised to inform the "Members of the European Parliament"—thus not the Parliament itself—of the work carried out. Other interested groups were not consulted.[49] The Auto/Oil Programme tried to find combined solutions concerning the emission from cars, the quality and

---

[44] Commission, COM(2005) 261. Tax measures require unanimity in Council for their adoption (art.113 and art.192(2) TFEU).

[45] See, e.g. Dir.94/12 relating to measures to be taken against air pollution by emissions from motor vehicles and amending Dir.70/220 [1994] OJ L100/42, art.3, which repeated the standard formula for such conditions for national tax incentives: "they shall apply to all new vehicles offered for sale on the market of a Member State which comply in advance with the requirements of Directive 70/220, as amended by this Directive; they shall be terminated with effect from the mandatory application of the emission values laid down in Art.2(3) for new motor vehicles; for each type of motor vehicle, they shall be for an amount lower than the additional cost of the technical solutions introduced to ensure compliance with the values set and of their installation on the vehicle."

[46] Commission, Review of the Auto-Oil II Programme, COM(2000) 626 of October 5, 2000, pt.6.2.

[47] Commission (fn.46, above) pt 4.11.

[48] COM (96) 248, p.44; this remark referred to the Auto/Oil Programme which started in 1992 and had the task of developing an "objective assessment of the most cost-effective package of measures to reduce emissions...".

[49] COM (96) 248, p.90.

composition of fuels, and new emission control technologies, on a "cost-effective"[50] basis. Proposals for fixing emission limit values by the Commissions were based on the results of this programme. Of course, these proposals can be—and were—criticised for not being based on an objective assessment, but rather on an assessment which conformed to the interests of these two industrial sectors, i.e. the car industry and the petrol industry. In any case, it seems unlikely that the Commission could develop policies and proposals which would be against the interests of these two industrial sectors. Also, the documents and data published do not really allow for a critical examination as to whether the suggested measures really constitute the best environmental protection potential or whether they are just a compromise between diverging interests.

Auto/Oil II started in 1997 and looked in particular at the development of the air quality measures to be adopted or implemented at EU level till 2010, also in so far as other sectors than the road transport sector were concerned. In contrast to Auto/Oil I all interested stakeholders, including Member States, the European Parliament and non-governmental organisations were invited to participate in the discussions.[51] The discussions of Auto/Oil II considerably influenced not only proposals and legislations in the transport sector, but generally all air pollution measures suggested by the Commission and adopted at EU level.   **8–19**

In 2006, the Commission reviewed the EU transport policy and concluded that "all transport modes must become more environmentally friendly, safe and energy efficient". It paid some attention to the negative environmental impact of cars and announced new measures for cars (Euro V) and trucks (Euro VI), but was mainly interested in increasing transport mobility—and thus quantity, and did not argue itself that the implementation of the different measures suggested would lead to a significant reduction of air pollution from motor vehicles.

In the early 1970s, different directives were adopted for petrol and diesel-driven cars. Later, this differentiation was abandoned, in the same way as was the differentiation between passenger cars, light and heavy commercial vehicles and trucks. Furthermore, recent directives have already announced the adoption of new provisions that are aimed at further strengthening the emission limit values and which enter into details as to what such new proposals shall contain.[52] The numerous overlapping directives and proposals which use numerous acronyms, contain extensive technical details, measurements, control and test rules which all constantly change among themselves, as well as the lack of consolidating texts have led to a situation in which the legal provisions lack transparency and cannot really be checked by people other than specialist experts—which are in industry. This is strengthened by the fact that changes to previous provisions are normally signalled by expressions such as "40 per cent reduction", "70 per cent reduction", and so on; and it adds to confusion that such reductions are calculated by including, in addition, the reduction in the fuel composition or changes in test methods.   **8–20**

---

[50] See the criticism of the European Parliament on the way in which this cost-effectiveness was calculated without taking into consideration social costs and environmental costs: Res. of February 18, 1998 [1998] OJ C80/92.

[51] Commission (fn.46, above).

[52] See, as an example, Dir.94/12 (fn.45, above), art.4.

Directive 70/220 set, in 1970, limit values for carbon monoxide and unburned hydrocarbon emissions.[53] In 1977, limit values for nitrogen oxides were established.[54] The values for these three pollutants were progressively reduced by different directives.[55] In 1989, more stringent emission limit values for gaseous pollutants were introduced and progressively extended to all passenger cars. Emissions from diesel engines were fixed in 1972 and progressively reduced.[56] All emission limit values are the subject of an almost permanent review discussion.

8–21   The present emission limit values (mg/km) for passsenger cars are as follows[57]:

Carbon monox-ide (CO)		Hydrocarbons HC		NOx		Particulates Pt	
Petrol	Diesel	Petrol	Diesel	Petrol	Diesel	Petrol	Diesel
1000	500	100	—	60	180	5	5

The biggest surprise in these values is the absence of an emission limit value for carbon dioxide (CO_2), the gas which is held to be primarily responsible for climate changes and designated as such under the Kyoto Protocol on Climate Change.[58] In 1990 CO_2 emissions from passenger cars accounted for about 45 per cent of transport CO_2 emissions and about 12 per cent of total CO_2 emissions in the European Union; a 20 per cent increase was expected by 2000 and a 36 per cent increase by 2010.[59]

In 1993, the Commission had announced a proposal for a Directive on an emission limit value for CO_2 for cars[60] and found support from the European Parliament.[61] This approach was heavily opposed by the car industry which found some support in Member States, in particular in France, Italy and Germany. In 1996, the Commission suggested not to legislate, but to introduce financial incentives to lower fuel consumption, introduce a labelling scheme for fuel consumption of cars, conclude an environmental agreement with the car industry to reduce CO_2 emissions from cars and promote research and development[62]; at the same time, it started discussions with car manufacturers on an agreement. It is not clear what particular reasons have been pleaded for having an environmental agreement just for CO_2,[63] but not for the other abovementioned pollutants.

---

[53] Dir.70/220 (fn.45, above).

[54] Dir.77/102 [1977] OJ L32/32.

[55] Dir.74/290 [1974] OJ L159/61; Dir.78/665 [1978] OJ L223/48; Dir.83/351 [1983] OJ L197/1; Dir.88/76 [1988] OJ L36/1; Dir.89/458 [1989] OJ L226/1; Dir.91/441 [1991] OJ L242/1; Dir.94/12 (fn.55, above).

[56] Dir.72/306 [1972] OJ L190/1; Dir.88/77 [1988] OJ L36/33; Dir.91/542 [1991] OJ L295/1.

[57] Commission Reg.692/2008 [2008] OJ L199/1, annex XVII.

[58] See para.9–01, below.

[59] See for the overall emission of CO_2 within the European Union, Written Question E-2572/96 (Amadeo) [1997] OJ C83/30.

[60] Commission, Legislative programme 1994, COM (93) 588, para.241.

[61] European Parliament Res. of October 27, 1993 [1993] OJ C315/160.

[62] COM (95) 689; Commission Communication on transport and CO_2; COM (1998) 204.

[63] European Parliament Res. of February 19, 1998 [1998] OJ C80/227, pt.14.

In summer 1998, the Commission announced[64] that it was ready to accept the offer by ACEA (Association des constructeurs européens d'automobiles), which groups together 11 European car manufacturers, to limit the CO2 emissions for new cars which were brought into circulation in the EU from 2008 onwards to 140g per kilometre. This offer was different from what the Council had wished to see reached (120g per km by 2005 or, at the latest, by 2010). The agreement that was subsequently made consisted, in legal terms, of:

8–22

- a commitment by ACEA[65];
- a recommendation by the European Commission, addressed to ACEA[66];
- an exchange of letters between the Commission and ACEA.

The commitment stated that as long as ACEA's promises were kept, ACEA assumed:

8–23

> "that this commitment provides complete and sufficient substitute for all new regulatory measures to limit fuel consumption or CO_2 emissions, and for any additional fiscal measures in pursuit of the CO_2 objectives of this commitment;"

this expressed the expectation that the EU legislature—possibly also the national legislature—would not take regulatory measures to reduce CO_2 emissions from cars during the lifetime of the agreement. The commitment was, furthermore, based on several assumptions—amongst others, that non-ACEA car manufacturers would commit themselves to equivalent CO_2 reduction efforts. The agreement provided for a framework for a future monitoring procedure, which included the statement that the Commission's official reports on the monitoring results will not refer to individual companies' achievements, in order to avoid competition being distorted. The Commission entered into the agreement, once the Council had signalled its endorsement of the reduction targets and the European Parliament had reluctantly accepted the deal. The Committee of the Regions and the Economic and Social Committee had no say in the matter. Furthermore, the agreement was made with ACEA alone, not with the car manufacturers themselves. In the beginning, the agreement was made with ACEA which groups European and USA car manufacturers. Later, similar agreements were concluded with the Japanese and Korean car manufacturers associations.[67]

The agreements referred to the EU market, not to cars which were marketed in other parts of the world, though such a restriction would normally also be the consequence of any regulatory measure.

The Commission published a number of progress reports on the implementation of the voluntary agreements. In its report for 2004, it quoted from a letter which it had received from ACEA and JAMA stating that these associations would not be able to reach the 2008-target by technical measures. In 2006, it

8–24

---

[64] Commission, COM (1998) 495.
[65] Published as annex to Commission, COM (1998) 495.
[66] Commission Rec.1999/125 on the reduction of CO_2 emissions from passenger cars [1999] OJ L40/49.
[67] Commission Rec.2000/303 on the reduction of CO_2 emissions from passenger cars (KAMA) [2000] OJ L100/55; Rec. 2000/304 on the reduction of CO_2 emissions from passenger cars (JAMA) [2000] OJ L100/ 57.

became obvious that all three associations were not comply with their commitment by 2008. The Commission then made proposals for legislating which were adopted in 2009.[68] As of 2013, the average emissions per car fleet of a car producer was progressively limited to 130g per km, with considerable transition periods. This solution mainly favoured expensive cars with high CO^2-emissions. The rules applied only to new cars which were marketed within the European Union. No provisions for trucks were adopted. Overall, the introduction of mandatory provisions was delayed by more than fifteen years.

Air emissions from aeroplanes, ships and machines

8–25   There are no EU emission limit values for ships and aeroplanes. Both sectors are, in part, regulated by global organisations (cartels), the International Maritime Organisation (IMO) and the International Civil Aviation Organisation (ICAO).

In 1998 the Commission submitted, for the first time, a proposal on the limitation of emissions for civil subsonic aeroplanes.[69] The proposal only concerned nitrogen oxides and did not contain an emission limit value, but only a formula for calculating such emissions. The proposal had been submitted, because ICAO had not been able to agree on suggestions for reductions which had been submitted to ICAO bodies and discussed there. The EU proposal was based on art.100(2) TFEU, which is a surprising legal basis since all emission limit values for cars and commercial vehicles have been based on art.114 TFEU. When ICAO finally agreed new limit values which would apply to new engine designs after 2003, the Commission's proposal became obsolete and was no longer pursued.

8–26   There has been, to date, almost no EU provision to regulate air pollution emissions from ships. Internationally, the pollution from ships is discussed in the context of the Convention for the prevention of pollution from ships (MARPOL), to which the European Union is not a signatory. While some measures have been taken in that context, no measures have as yet been adopted at EU level. Directive 2003/55 limited the sulphur content of fuels used in marine shipping in the Baltic Sea and the North Sea.[70] Discussions on the introduction of environmentally differentiated shipping charges according to their emissions have been discussed internationally, but have not led to concrete action at EU level.

For internal navigation, Directive 2004/26 introduced emission limit values for inland waterways vessels, with regard to CO (5.0 g/kWh) HC and NOx combined (7.5–11.0g/kWh) and Particulates (0.4–05g/kWh).[71]

8–27   As regards machines, the European Union adopted, in 1997, for the first time, a Directive[72] which set air emission limit values for machines other than passenger and commercial vehicles, airplanes and ships; it thus concerned machinery such as compressors, forestry equipment, road-maintenance equipment, snow-plough equipment, aerial lifts, mobile cranes and ground supports in airports. The Directive was based on art.114 TFEU and concerned machinery

---

[68] Reg.443/2009 [2009] OJ L140/1.
[69] [1998] OJ C108/14.
[70] Dir.2003/55 [2003] OJ L191/59.
[71] Dir 2004/26 [2004] OJ L146/1.
[72] Dir.97/68 relating to measures against the emissions of gaseous and particulate pollutants from internal combustion engines to be installed in non-road mobile machinery [1998] OJ L59/1.

which was type-approved after 1997; existing non-road mobile machinery was thus not affected. The emission limit values were introduced in two steps (1998 and 2000) and differentiated according to the power of the engine. In 2004, the Directive was amended; for the different machines, further differentiation was introduced.[73] The new emission values range from 3.5 to 5.5 g/kWh for CO, 4.0 to 7.5 g/kWh for HC and NOx combined and 0.2 to 0.3g/kWh for particulates.

Emissions of volatile organic compounds (VOCs)

Volatile organic compounds (VOCs) are generated from the handling of (motor) gasoline; this gasoline is stored before being distributed, which can take place by pipeline, road trucks, rail cars and by barge and ships. After that distribution, the gasoline is discharged to a storage tank. During all these stages of loading/ unloading, the gasoline generates VOCs. VOCs are among the precursors of photochemical oxidants such as tropospheric ozone which also is a potential greenhouse gas.[74] Some VOCs that are emitted are classified as toxic, teratogenic or carcinogenic. The biggest emitting sectors are road transport, solvent use and the extraction and distribution of fossil fuels.

8–28

Directive 91/441 and other directives on motor vehicle emissions[75] had already introduced a number of measures to reduce VOC emissions from motor vehicles, the main source of such emissions, without fixing emission limit values. It is estimated that these measures will reduce VOC emissions from road transport by about one third.

Council Directive 94/63[76] followed the same line; it dealt with the VOC emissions resulting from the storage of petrol and its distribution from terminals to service stations, and required Member States to make sure that the conditions laid down in the Directive and its annexes were complied with. The Directive was based on art.114 TFEU; it also applied to road trucks, which is the reason why it is mentioned in this chapter; yet it also applied to stationary sources and allowed Member States to fix more stringent provisions (arts 3(3) and 4(3)). The discussion of limiting VOC emissions from other stationary sources will be discussed at para.8–50, below. Contrary to what its title provided, this Directive did not contain any emission limit values, but rather laid down requirements for storage installations at terminals (stationary petrol tanks, annex I), for loading and unloading of mobile containers at terminals (annex II), for loading and storage installations at service stations and terminals, where the intermediate storage of vapour is carried out (annex III) and specifications for bottom-loading, vapour collection and overfill protection of European road tankers (annex IV). As mentioned, it was thus a measure that affected both mobile and stationary sources of VOC generation. Interestingly, the emission of VOCs from the charging of ships was only covered by a non-committing statement in a recital.[77]

8–29

---

[73] Dir. 2004/26 (fn.71, above).

[74] See para.8–12, above.

[75] Dir.91/441 [1991] OJ L242/1; Dir.91/542 [1991] OJ L295/1; Dir.93/59 [1993] OJ L186/21; Dir.94/ 12 [1994] OJ L100/42.

[76] Dir.94/63 [1994] OJ L365/24.

[77] Dir.94/63 (fn.76, above), Recital 6: "On grounds of international standardisation and of safety during the loading of ships, standards must be drawn up at International Maritime Organisation level for vapour control and recovery systems to apply to both loading installations and ships, whereas the Community must therefore endeavour to ensure that the necessary provisions are introduced into the

Directive 99/13 dealt with VOC emissions from industrial installation, such as printing, surface cleaning, dry cleaning, manufacture of footwear and pharmaceutical products.[78] The limits ranged from 50 to 700 g/l and 30 to 430g/l as of 2010. Existing installations have to comply with these requirements since October 2007. Originally, the Directive also covered paints and varnishes and vehicle refining products. However, an amendment of 2004 established a separate directive for these two sectors with much more differentiated and—at least for vehicle refining products—much less stringent values.[79] In 2010, these two Directives were integrated into the new framework directive on industrial emissions.[80]

4. Air emissions from installations

Framework provisions

8–30   EU law contains only very few provisions which relate to installations, since it is thought that products that circulate within the European Union should be exposed to uniform rules, but that installations do not circulate freely and therefore do not need uniform rules. Neither has the fact that products which leave installations compete with each other, nor has the knowledge that water discharges and air emissions[81] from installations circulate and pollute transnationally, changed this attitude.

Following the discovery of dying forests in the early 1980s, the European Union discussed air pollution at a summit of heads of State and governments in 1983. In 1984, it adopted a framework directive on air emissions from industrial installations,[82] which it based on arts 115 and 352 TFEU. The Directive introduced a general authorisation procedure for all installations which belonged to a positive list that was defined in an annex. The authorisation could only be given where:

> "all appropriate preventive measures against air pollution have been taken, including the application of the best available technology, provided that the application of such measures does not entail excessive costs"

and that the plant did not cause "significant air pollution" (art.4), in particular from a number of pollutants which were mentioned in an annex.[83] The Council committed itself to fix, "if necessary", emission limit values based on the best

---

Marpol Convention during the current revision of Marpol due to be completed in 1996; whereas in the event that the Marpol Convention is not so revised, the Community, after discussion with its major trading partners, should propose appropriate measures to apply to ships and port installations servicing ships".

[78] Dir.1999/13 [1999] OJ L85/1.

[79] Dir.2004/42 [2004] OJ L143/87.

[80] Dir.2010/75 (fn.8, above); for more details on Dir.1999/13 see para.8–37, below.

[81] Dir.2000/76 (fn.9, above) is the only Directive which also provided for provisions regarding the discharge of pollutants to waters, see art.8. When this Directive was, in 2010, integrated into Dir.2010/75 on industrial emissions, the emission limits were maintained.

[82] Dir.84/360 (fn.6, above).

[83] Dir.84/360 (fn.6, above), annex II: sulphur dioxide, oxides of nitrogen, carbon monoxide, organic compounds, heavy metals, dust, asbestos, glass and mineral fibres, chlorine, fluorine.

available technology not entailing excessive costs. For existing installations, "Member States shall implement policies and strategies, including appropriate measures, for the gradual adaptation" of these plants.

Directive 84/360 was transposed into national law by all Member States, but had a rather limited effect. The very loose drafting did not push for changes in the practice that had existed up to then. The "best available technology not entailing excessive costs" proved to be an empty formula that did not require measures to reduce air emissions. Efforts at EU level to elaborate non-binding technical papers of what constituted, for a specific industrial sector, best available technology, had no visible effect on the permitted practice in Member States, particularly as the cost element remained decisive in each specific case.

8–31

Also, no measures were imposed, by virtue of Directive 84/ 360, on existing installations in order gradually to lead to air emission reductions. Since on the one hand Member States were allowed to take more stringent measures than those laid down in the Directive and, on the other hand, no action was taken against a Member States for lack of action, one here finds another example where the added value of EU legislation to environmental protection is small. Directive 84/360 ceased to exist in 2007, when Directive 96/61—replaced in 2008 by Directive 2008/1—became fully operational and also applied to existing installations.[84] It is significant also for the omission to enforce Directive 84/360 with regard to existing installations that the first ever judgment of the Court of Justice which stated that the Directive contained a legal obligation for Member States to progressively adapt existing installations to the requirements of the Directive, was given in July 2005,[85] 21 years after the adoption of the Directive and two years, before it ceased to exist: as if the Commission could not have enforced art.13 of Directive 84/360 earlier!

Large combustion plants

Combustion plants with a capacity of more than 50 MW account for about 60 per cent of SO_2 emissions and 20 per cent NO_x-emissions in the EC In 2001, Directive 2001/80[86] was adopted which replaced Directive 88/609[87] as of end 2002. However, the new Directive very largely repeated the text of the previous Directive. This repetition went so far as to provide for a derogation for Spain which was valid until December 31, 1999 (art.5(2)). Also, the emission limit values for new installations and the overall emission ceilings of SO_2 and NO_x for existing installations (annex I and II) were hardly amended or updated. Finally, Member States had to inform the Commission of their programmes to reduce emissions under art.3 at the latest on December 31, 1990—this provision was inserted into a Directive that was adopted on October 23, 2001! Directive 2001/80, taking over the previous provisions, provided for emission limit values for sulphur dioxide, nitrogen oxides and dust as regards new installations. For existing installations, the Directive introduced national emission ceilings for

8–32

---

[84] Dir.96/61 (fn.11, above), art.20; Dir.2008/1 (fn.11, above).

[85] Court of Justice, case Commission v Greece (C–364/03) [2005] E.C.R. I–6159.

[86] Dir.2001/80 on the limitation of emissions of certain pollutants into the air from large combustion plants [2001] OJ L309/1.

[87] See in this regard Commission Rec.2003/47 on the guidelines to assist a Member State in the preparation of a national emission reduction plan [2003] OJ L16/59.

sulphur dioxides and nitrogen oxides. Calculated on the basis of emissions of the year 1980, Member States had to lower their total emissions in two (NOx) or three (SO²) stages till 2003. No update was made.

A new provision requested Member States to ensure a significant reduction of emissions until the end of 2007, by either requesting existing installations to respect the Directive's emission limits for new installations, or to make sure that existing large combustion installations participated in a national emission reduction plan which Member States could—not: had to—draw up in view of reducing emissions; thus, where a Member State decided not to draw up a national emission reduction plan, there was no obligation for existing installations![88]

Article 6 provided for an examination of possibilities to introduce combined heat-power equipment at the construction of new installations or a significant enlargement of existing installations. However, the taking of such measures was to depend on the "technical and economic feasibility" of providing such an equipment—which obviously made this provision equivalent to a recommendation.

8–33   The Commission had to report, before the end of 2004, in particular on the necessity of taking further measures to reduce emissions, on emissions of heavy metals by large combustion installations, the cost-efficiency of further measures and the technical and economic feasibility of such measures. This provision—and generally the limited review of Directive 88/609—found its explanation in the argument that operators of installations generally took the view that when they applied the best available technique, they contributed their share to emissions reduction and that a specific directive on large combustion installations had no right of existence any more. The Commission did not establish these reports,[89] but gave some vague assessments of the Directive in its proposal for the new Directive 2010/75.[90]

Directive 2001/80 was, as its predecessor, Directive 88/609, only monitored with very great difficulties. Indeed, monitoring compliance with the overall reductions of pollutants' emissions was practically impossible, as the only information on actual emission quantities stemmed from Member States themselves and the emission quantities only referred to those existing plants that came under the Directive. And the share of existing plants that came under the Directive and other plants in the overall air pollution is not known.

The new Directive 2010/75 incorporated the provisions of Directive 2001/80; it maintained emission limit values for such plants for SO², NOx, CO (carbon monoxide) and dust.[91] For the rest, the chapter on large combustion plants is filled with derogations, exceptions, transition periods and other possibilities not to apply the emission limit values in a specific case.

---

[88] See however Commission, Evaluation of the Member States' emission inventories 2004–2006 for large combustion plants (2008). This report was made by a private company for the Commission; it indicated that 2,779 installations came under Directive 2001/80.

[89] Commission, COM(2007) 843 and SEC(2007) 1679.

[90] Dir.2010/75 (fn.8, above), Annex V.

[91] Dir.94/67 (fn.9, above).

Waste incineration installations

In 1989, the European Union adopted two Directives on municipal waste incineration plants. The Directives fixed general conditions for the authorisation and functioning of such incinerators, such as the minimum temperature (850°C for two seconds). Requirements for the design of installations were rather vague and largely corresponded to the requirements in Directive 88/609. In 1994, the European Union adopted a Directive on installations for the incineration of hazardous waste [92] which was based on art.192 TFEU and entered into effect in 1997. All these three Directives were replaced by a new Directive of end 2000[93] which was based on art.192 TFEU and became effective, for new installations, end 2002, for existing installations end 2005. In 2010, this Directive was then incorporated into the new Directive on industrial emissions.[94]

8–34

The reason for this merger of the different texts was that the Directives on the incineration of municipal waste had to be updated anyway and that the environmental impairment through dioxins, heavy metals or other emissions or discharges was the same, independently from which incineration source the pollutant came. Furthermore, it was considered that the far-spread public resistance against the waste incineration technology could best be overcome by strict standards, effective controls and transparency of permit and operation procedures. Directive 2010/75 concerned, as its predecessor Directive 2000/76, almost all waste incineration installations. It excluded installations which exclusively burn vegetal waste, agricultural waste, radioactive waste, animal waste of waste on oil platforms which incinerated there, finally installations for test or research purposes which burn less than 50 tonnes per year. The provisions of Directive 2010/75 also applied to installations, the principal objective of which is the production of goods or energy and which "use waste as a regular or additional fuel or in which waste is thermally treated for the purpose of disposal" (art.3 no.41) (co-incineration); to this category belong installations such as power plants, steel plants or cement kilns. The emission limit values which were fixed, are less stringent for co-incineration installations[95]—as if the environmental impairment were less relevant in the case of co-incineration.

Installations need a permit for operation. Article 4 fixed detailed conditions for such a permit. For example, the permit must indicate the type of (hazardous) waste which may be burnt, the sampling and measuring methods for air and water discharges or—for hazardous waste—the content of pollutants such as chlorides, PCP, PCB, fluorides, sulphur or heavy metals in the waste. A number of other measures have the objective to minimise environmental impairment. The minimum temperature, including in cases of co-incineration, is 850°Celsius, and, where hazardous waste is burned, 1,100°C (art.50). The installation must be equipped with an automatic system to stop the incineration process, where this temperature is not reached, or where emission limit-values are exceeded, due to a disturbance. The following emission limit-values were fixed in annex VI (daily average):

8–35

---

[92] Dir.2000/76 on the incineration of waste (fn.9, above).
[93] Dir.2010/75 (fn.8, above).
[94] Dir.2010/75 (fn.8, above), annex VI.
[95] [1998] OJ C372/11.

Pollutant	incineration	co-incineration	co-incineration in cement kilns
Dust	$10mg/m^3$	Part 4-formula	$30mg/m^3$
Gases	$10mg/m^3$	Part 4-formula	
HCl	$10mg/m^3$	Part 4-formula	$10mg/m^3$
HF	$1mg/m^3$	Part 4-formula	$1mg/m^3$
SO_2	$50mg/m^3$	Part 4-formula	
NO and NO_2	$200–400mg/m^3$	Part 4-formula	$500–800/m^3$
Cadmium and Tl	$0.05mg/m^3$		$0.05mg/m^3$
Mercury	$0.05 mg/m^3$		$0.05mg/m^3$
Dioxins/furans	$0.1ng/m^3$		$0.1ng/m^3$

However, large transition periods, derogation possibilities, exceptions for small installations and differentiations according to new or existing installations and, for cement kilns, according to the fuel used, were provided.

The Directive also fixed emission limit-values for discharges of waste water from the cleaning of waste gases into the water, in particular for heavy metals (annex VI, part 5). It detailed the measuring requirements and methods and imposes in particular an automatic, continuous measuring of emissions into the air and the water (annex VI, pt 6).

8–36   Overall, the requirements of the Directive which were almost entirely taken over from the previous Directive 2000/76, were rather strict and by far the most stringent requirements of any industrial installation that were laid down at EU level. The apprehension of the population against the pollution emissions from incinerators would therefore appear not to be completely justified—if the installation would permanently function according to the legal requirements. However, breakdowns or deficiencies in the operation, the burning of hazardous materials and other circumstances may easily lead to emissions which are toxic or dangerous. This also applies to co-incinerators, though there is less public concern. For this and other reasons, co-incineration and combined heat-power generation by incinerators are the techniques which are being used more and more, and attempts are permanently made to find new names for the installations, in order to avoid the negative image of waste incinerators.

Volatile organic compounds (VOCs) from stationary sources

8–37   The Commission had planned, in 1993/1994, to submit a proposal for a directive on VOC emissions resulting from refuelling operations at service stations. Since it was not able to submit such a proposal, seven Member States—most of them with a more active environmental policy—adopted national measures.[96] In 1999, the Council adopted Directive 1999/13 on emissions of VOCs from solvent-using industries,[97] which was a follow-up to Directive 94/63.[98] In 2010, the Directive was integrated in the new Directive on industrial emissions.

---

[96] Denmark, Germany, Italy, Luxembourg, the Netherlands, Austria and Sweden.
[97] Dir.1999/13 on the limitation of emissions of volatile organic compounds due to the use of organic solvents in certain activities and installations [1999] OJ L85/1; proposal [1997] OJ C99/32.

As in Directive 1999/13, Directive 2010/75 referred to installations and activities using organic solvents; thus, for instance, coating processes, coil coating, dry cleaning, printing, surface cleaning, manufacturing of pharmaceutical products, fat extraction, rubber conversion, or wood and plastic lamination are covered. For the different activities, thresholds and emission limit values were set, based on the solvent consumption, the emission limit (mg of organic carbon per cubic metre) and the diffuse/total emission limit, expressed as a percentage of solvents input (annex VII, part 2). For vehicle coating installations, no emission limit values were fixed; instead, a formula was to be used by such installations (annex VII, pt 3).

Instead of applying the emission limit values fixed by the Directive, an installation could also recur to a "reduction scheme specially designed for his installation", provided that comparable results were achieved (annex VII, pt 5). When an individual operator was able to demonstrate that the respect of the emission limit values was not "technically and economically feasible", Member States were entitled to grant a derogation from the limit values, "provided that significant risks to human health or the environment are not to be expected" and the operator could demonstrate that he applied the best available technique.[99]

8–38

5.   Noise and electromagnetic waves

General aspects

Data on noise levels within the European Union are limited and fragmented. The Commission estimated in 1996 that almost 80 million people in the European Union "suffer from noise levels that scientists and health experts consider to be unacceptable" (above 65dB(A)) and that an additional 170 million citizens are living in areas where the noise levels are such as to cause serious annoyance during the daytime (55–65dB(A)).[100] The European Environment Agency estimated for the year 2000 that about 50 million people were exposed to traffic noise levels above 65 Ldn dB[101] and some 120 million to traffic noise level above 55 Ldn dB. Traffic noise is the main source of outdoor noise, followed by neighbourhood and aircraft noise.[102]

An EU strategy to reduce noise levels within the European Union was announced about thirty years ago, in the context of the different environmental

8–39

---

[98] Dir.94/63 (fn.76 above). See, para.8–29, above; as mentioned, that Directive also partly covered stationary sources.

[99] Dir.2010/75 (fn.8, above), art.59(2).

[100] Commission, Green Paper on future noise policy, COM (96) 540, pp.1a and 3.

[101] Ldn, a day-night level, is a descriptor of noise level based on the energy equivalent noise levels (Leq) over the whole day with a penalty of 10 dB(A) for night-time noise (22.00–7.00 hours).

[102] European Environment Agency, TERM 2000, *Are we moving in the right direction?* (Copenhagen, 2000), p.32.

action programmes.[103] In 1996, the Commission published a Green Paper, "Future noise policy", where it identified noise as one of the principal local environmental problems.[104]

8–40   In the follow-up of that Green Paper, the European Union adopted in 2002 a Directive on environmental noise.[105] The Directive was based on art.192 TFEU and became effective in mid-2004. It intended to avoid, prevent or reduce environmental noise; such noise was defined as:

> "unwanted or harmful outdoor sound created by human activities, including noise emitted by means of transport, road traffic, rail traffic, air traffic and from sites of industrial activity ... (art.3(a))."

The Directive applied to environmental noise to which humans are exposed, in particular in built-up areas, public parks or other quiet areas in agglomerations, in the open country, near schools, hospitals or other noise-sensitive buildings and areas. Noise which is caused by the exposed person himself, noise from domestic activities, created by neighbours, at the workplace or inside means of transport or in military areas was not covered.

Before 2007 Member States had to draw up strategic noise maps,[106] showing the noise situation in the preceding calendar year. These maps had to be made available to the Commission and the public and be updated at least every five years. They referred to:

- agglomerations with more than 250,000 inhabitants;
- major roads which have more than six million passages per year;
- major railways which have more than 60,000 train passages per year;
- major civil airports which have more than 50,000 take-offs or landing per year.

By 2008, Member States had then to draw up, make publicly available and regularly update action plans to manage noise issues, if necessary. The measures taken were at the discretion of Member States (art.8(1)). By 2012 the maps and plans must also cover agglomerations with more than 100,000 inhabitants, roads with 3 million passages and railways with more than 30,000 passages.

The Directive provided for extensive reporting to and by the Commission, for technical provisions concerning the measuring and assessing of noise, for minimum requirements for strategic noise planning and action plans as well as for the data which are to be sent to the Commission. However, the Commission did not and does not seriously monitor the operation of Directive 2002/49, by publishing, for example, the noise levels found, comparing the action plans, share

---

[103] See second environmental action programme [1977] OJ C139/1, Pts 67 et seq.; Fourth environmental action programme [1987] OJ C328/5, Pt 4.5.

[104] Commission COM (96) 540 (fn.100, above); see also European Parliament Res. of June 10, 1997 [1997] OJ C200/ 28.

[105] Dir.2002/49 relating to the assessment and management of environmental noise [2002] OJ L189/12.

[106] Dir.2000/49 (fn.105, above), art.3: a strategic noise map is a map designed for the global assessment of noise exposure in a given area due to different noise sources or for overall predictions for such an area.

best practices, and push for measures that reduce the noise levels.[107] According to art.11, the Commission should have reported, by July 2009, on the implementation of Directive 2002/49. In March 2011, this report was not yet available.

EU measures to reduce noise levels until now concerned noise emissions of certain products. The main objective of these directives consists in assuring their free circulation within the European Union and to make sure that this circulation is not hampered by different noise standard levels at national level. For this reason, the directives set noise emission levels only for those (new) products that are implicated in intra-EU trade; by contrast, Member States may set independent noise standards for products intended exclusively for the domestic market.[108] They may also provide for specific standards for the use of the products in sensitive areas.   **8–41**

All noise levels fixed in the specific directives are based on the work of international standardisation organisations. They fix noise levels for products that are put on the market for the first time, but contain no provisions on noise emissions throughout the lifetime of a product.

Transport

Motor vehicle noise emissions have been regulated since 1970, when noise emission limit values were introduced.[109] This Directive was based on art.115 TFEU. Later amendments were introduced, mainly when technical progress had already led to a practical reduction of noise levels[110]; since 1987, such amendments have been based on art.114 TFEU. The following standards were fixed (in dB(A))[111]:   **8–42**

Vehicle category	1972	1982	1988/1990	1995/1996
Passenger car	82	80	77	74
Urban bus	89	82	80	78
Heavy lorry	91	88	84	80

This legislation led, in practice, to a reduction in actual road traffic noise levels of 1 to 2dB(A), due mainly to the significant growth in traffic and a slow replacement of older, noisier vehicles; in "addition, the test procedure (ISO

---

[107] See, for example, the Report from the European Environment Agency: towards a resource-efficient transport system. TERM 2009. Technical Report 2/2010 (Copenhagen 2010), where the Agency reported (p.20) that 164 agglomerations were obliged to report on their noise levels; 102 had reported on road noise, 93 on railway noise, 76 on air noise and 94 on industry noise. 82,576 reports were expected on major roads, but only 21,310 were delivered. 12,315 reports should have been made on major railways; 5,310 were delivered. Of 78 airports, 66 reported.

[108] As regards noise emissions from cars, this so-called "optional harmonisation approach" was abandoned by Dir.92/97 [1992] OJ L337/1, which introduced the total harmonisation approach: all vehicles which are put into circulation within the EU must comply with the Directive's requirements.

[109] Dir.70/157 [1970] OJ L42/16.

[110] See, for instance, Dir.77/212 [1977] OJ L66/33, 2nd recital: "whereas for the protection of the general public from noise nuisance, suitable measures are required to reduce the noise level of motor vehicles; whereas such a reduction has been made possible by the technical progress in motor vehicle construction"; similar observations are made in Dir.81/334 [1981] OJ L131/6, 1st recital; Dir.84/372 [1984] OJ L196/47, 1st recital; Dir.84/424 [1984] OJ L238/31, 2nd recital.

[111] Commission, COM (96) 540 (fn.100, above), p.30.

R362) doesn't reflect realistic driving conditions and without a regular inspection procedure to ensure maintenance of the acoustical design features the noise levels of the vehicle may increase over time".[112] For two- and three-wheelers, emission limit values have existed since a Directive of 1978,[113] which was amended several times and provided for a reduction of around 3dB(A). Again, the limit values only apply to new motocycles.

Directive 92/97 called for measures addressing the noise caused by tyres on road, which includes the use of noise-absorbing asphalts. A Directive concerning the admissible noise levels from tyres was adopted in 2001.[114]

8–43   Aircraft noise has, since 1979, been regulated by a number of directives,[115] which were based on art.100 TFEU and which applied, at EU level, standards set by the International Civic Aviation Organisation (ICAO); the ICAO levels depend on the aircraft weight and number of engines. The EU directives did not fix emission limit values, but referred to the provisions laid down by the ICAO. Directive 92/14 provided for a ban, as of 1995, of civil subsonic aeroplanes which did not comply with the ICAO "chapter 3" requirements, or with the "chapter 2" requirements, but were not more than 25 years old.[116] A number of aeroplanes from airline companies from third-world countries were exempted from these provisions, because European airlines had sold these planes to the third world countries prior to 1995. A number of other derogations were also foreseen.

8–44   In 1998, the Commission proposed a ban on registration of aeroplanes which had been modified in order to comply with the "chapter 3" requirements, the so-called "hush-kitted" aircraft.[117] As this requirement hit, in particular, older aeroplanes that were used in the United States or by US companies, there were excited discussions as to whether this requirement de facto discriminated against the United States. Under the political pressure from that country, which threatened retaliation measures and also argued that some hush-kitted aircraft were less noisy than modern aircraft (Airbus), the Council Regulation that finally adopted the proposal,[118] postponed the entry into effect of the measure so that from April 2002 onwards, hush-kitted aircraft were to be prohibited at EU airports, unless they were operated at EU airports before May 2000.

8–45   The terrorist attacks on US cities on September 11, 2001, were used by the United States discreetly to suggest again a withdrawal of Regulation 925/1999. This time, the European Union gave in: in a record time of four months, a new Directive, based on art.100(2) TFEU was prepared; it was adopted in March 2002 and repealed Regulation 925/1999.[119] In its place, the European Union took over the concept of the United States: noise-induced restriction for airplanes had to be airport-specific and had to be limited to the necessary environmental objective which had to be established for each airport (art.4). Hush-kitted airplanes—which were not named as such, but called "marginally compliant aircraft"—received protection in the form of a phased restriction (art.6), hush-kitted airplanes

---

[112] Commission, COM (96) 540 (fn.100, above), p.7.
[113] Dir.78/1015 [1978] OJ L349/21.
[114] Dir.2001/43 [2001] OJ L211/25[1998] OJ C30/8.
[115] Dir.80/51 [1980] OJ L18/26; Dir.89/629 [1989] OJ L363/27.
[116] Dir.92/14 [1992] OJ L76/21, amended by Dir.98/20 [1998] OJ L107/4.
[117] [1998] OJ C329/98.
[118] Reg.925/1999 [1999] OJ L115/1.
[119] Dir.2002/30 [2002] OJ L85/40.

registered in developing countries (sic!) which had used European airports before, received a derogation for 10 years (art.7). Urban airports—annex I listed them as being Berlin-Tempelhof, Stockholm-Bromma, London City and Belfast City—were allowed to adopt more stringent provisions with regard to hush-kitted airplanes.

Instead of creating uniform conditions for airplane noise within the European Union which would be normal under a uniform ("common") transport policy, this approach imposed the burden on each airport to impose noise restrictions. In view of competition problems—aircraft companies which are confronted with the possibility of such restrictions are likely to threaten to use the next airport, where no such restrictions exist[120]—noise rules for individual airports are not very likely. Measures on noise restrictions therefore are likely to follow the example of night-flight restrictions which also can only in theory be introduced by each airport, but which are not introduced—for competition reasons.[121]

An EU White Paper on transport policy of 1992 announced EU measures to fix acceptable noise levels in the vicinity of airports.[122] This announcement remained without any follow-up. No EU provisions exist for railways. A proposal for a directive, submitted in 1983, was withdrawn by the Commission in 1993. The introduction of high-speed trains in the European Union, also promoted by the rules on trans-European networks (arts 170–172 TFEU) since the Maastricht Treaty of 1993, did not lead to a change in this situation.

8–46

Construction machines

At the end of 2000, the European Union adopted a Directive on the noise levels of outdoor machinery, construction plant, garden equipment and equipment used for specific vehicles.[123] The Directive which was based on art.114 TFEU, replaced a number of previous Directives. It applied to new machines and equipment and intended, first of all, to ensure the free circulation of these machines within the EU Member States may not prevent the placing on the market of machines that comply with the requirements of the Directive, but are of course free to determine sensitive areas where the equipment may not be used or where it may be used during certain hours only. For a number of machines and equipment, noise emission limit-values were fixed (art.12) which vary between 96 dB(A) and 109 dB(A); new values apply since 2006 which range from 84 dB(A) to 106 dB(A). Where an EU noise emission limit value was laid down, this must be labelled on the machine; where no level was fixed, the machine only has to be labelled with its noise level (art.13) The Directive also determined

8–47

---

[120] See also Written question E–1021/02 (Hortefeux) [2002] OJ C277/E/132; a good example is the case of a DHL company which had its EU headquarters at Zaventem airport (Brussels/Belgium). Planes from overseas landed at night, the freight was charged on other planes and transported to different European countries. Following extended complaints from citizens over too much noise at night, the Belgian authorities negotiated with DHL on noise reduction measures. These negotiations remained unsuccessful and DHL displaced its EU headquarters to Leipzig/Germany—with a loss of some 20,000 jobs in Brussels.

[121] Commission, White Paper on a Community strategy on sustainable mobility COM (92) 494.

[122] Dir.2000/14 [2000] OJ L162/1.

[123] See, however, Court of Justice, cases C–142/05 *Mickelsson and Roos*, judgment of June 4, 2009 C–433/05, *Sandström* judgment of April 15, 2010; where the Court establishes significant limits on the Member States' discretion to restrict the use of noisy products for environmental reasons.

measuring standards. There was no requirement to maintain the noise level for new machines during the total service life of the machine or for some years at least.

After the adoption of the Directive, it turned out that some manufacturers could not comply with the more stringent values; derogations were introduced, as "the intention was never to restrict the placing on the market of use... of equipment solely based on technical feasibility".[124] In other words, the limit values were not meant to protect the environment.

8–48 New household equipment was subject of another framework Directive, which left Member States the freedom to fix emission limit values, but fixed a frame for such requirements.[125] No specific EU measures have subsequently been taken. Thus, Directive 96/594 was repealed; Member States were allowed to use the provisions of that Directive, until new measures were taken at EU level. The energy labels fixed for certain household appliances provided for an indication of the noise level. Whether this approach will be maintained under the new Directive 2010/30,[126] is as yet uncertain.

The European Union has not so far fixed quality objectives for noise emissions in sensitive areas such as, for instance, urban centres, residential areas, near airports, hospitals or schools.

Overall, observation of the noise levels within the European Union is highly inadequate and the EU measures protecting against excessive noise levels also seem inadequate. This protection, by fixing quality standards, tends to be left to Member States. It will have to be seen whether the new Directive 2002/49 on environmental noise will be the beginning of serious EU-wide measures to reduce noise. The first nine years of existence of this Directive do not inspire optimism.

Electromagnetic waves

8–49 There are no EU provisions on electromagnetic waves from electrical power lines and other sources which are thought, sometimes, to cause problems to the health of people living next to such power lines. The Commission stated that there was no "convincing scientific evidence" of electromagnetic fields causing cancer.[127]

Directive 85/337 on the environment impact assessment of certain projects was amended by Directive 97/11,[128] which now requires an environment impact assessment for electrical power lines of more than 15km in length; however, the competent authorities remain free to decide on such projects, whatever the outcome of the assessment.[129]

8–50 In 1998, the Commission proposed a Council recommendation, based on art.168 TFEU, on "the limitation of exposure of the general public to electromagnetic fields",[130] where essentially Member States are invited to take

---

[124] Dir.2005/88 [2005] OJ L344/44.

[125] Dir.86/594 [1986] OJ L344/24.

[126] Dir.2010/30 on the indication by labelling and standard product information of energy and other resources by energy related products [2010] OJ L153/1.

[127] Written Questions E–1387/97 (Baldi) [1997] OJ C373/115; E–4190/97 (Caccavale) [1998] OJ C196/96; E–1788/98 (Sierra Gonzalez et al.) [1999] OJ C50/93.

[128] Dir.85/337 [1985] OJ L175/40; amendment Dir.97/11 [1997] OJ L73/5.

[129] See generally, paras 4–10 et seq., above.

[130] Commission, COM(1998) 268.

action in order to limit exposures to electromagnetic fields. Electrical power lines are not specifically addressed. The Council adopted this recommendation in 1999.[131]

---

[131] Rec.1999/519 [1999] OJ L199/59.

CHAPTER 9

Climate Change and Ozone Depletion

1. General remarks

Since the Lisbon Treaty came into force on December 1, 2009, climate change issues are mentioned in the Treaties: art.191 TFEU fixes as one of the objectives of EU environment policy "combating climate change". This insertion is not particularly convincing, as climate change policy is a horizontal policy which requires numerous EU policies to re-orient themselves in view of this objective; this refers in particular to energy policy, but also to transport, internal market, commercial, development, agricultural and competition policy. Thus, it would have been wiser to insert the fight against climate change at the beginning of the FEU Treaty, for example in art.11.

9–01

Action regarding climate change attempts to reduce anthropogenic interference with the climate in order to prevent a global temperature increase and greenhouse gas concentrations in the atmosphere that are significantly higher than pre-industrialised levels.[1] The appearance of climate change issues as a topic of EU environmental policy is of recent date. The fourth EU environmental action programme which covered the period 1987–1992,[2] mentioned the "greenhouse effect" of human activities and climate change only marginally[3] and announced that the EU research programme would cover, among others, "climatology and natural hazards, addressing long-term problems, such as potential climate changes due to an increase of the CO_2 concentrations in the atmosphere".[4] In 1989, the Commission submitted a first communication to the

---

[1] See the definition of climate change in art.1(2) of the UN Framework Convention on Climate Change of May 9, 1992, signed in New York: "Climate change means a change of climate which is attributed directly or indirectly to human activity that alters the composition of the global atmosphere and which is in addition to natural climate variability observed over comparable time periods".

[2] 4th EU environmental action programme 1987–1992 [1987] OJ C328/5.

[3] See 4th action programme (fn.2, above) Pt 2.3.20: "Looking further ahead into the future it is clear that difficult problems could arise from the use of fossil fuels if the build-up of atmospheric carbon dioxide levels and the 'Greenhouse effect' are shown (as certain scientists fear) to have serious impacts on climate and agricultural productivity worldwide. In case further scientific research should confirm the likelihood of such impacts, the Community should already be thinking about possible responses and alternative energy strategies. The Commission will continue its studies in this context."

See also Pt 7.2.3: "Tropical forests … have a profound influence on climate and on global natural cycles. Because tropical forests benefit people in so many ways, the alarming rate of forest destruction is a matter of grave concern."

[4] 4th action programme (fn.2, above) Pt 6.3.

Council on climate change and its impact.[5] The Council was quick in reacting: in 1990, it committed itself in a non-binding resolution to stabilise CO_2 emissions by the year 2000 at their 1990 level.[6]

In the fifth environmental action programme (1993–2000), climate change issues played a considerably greater role: the programme dedicated a whole section to climate change. It identified carbon dioxide (CO_2), chlorofluorocarbon (CFCs) nitrous oxide (N_2O) and methane (CH4) as the main agents for climate change,[7] tried to fix objectives:

1.   "no exceedance of natural absorbing capacity of planet earth";
2.   "no emissions of ozone layer depleting substances"—and targets up to the year 2000 and announced a number of actions to be undertaken.

In 1994 the European Union adhered to the UN Climate Change Convention[8] and pursued since an active policy to address the issues of climate change.

9–02   Climate change is not a subject which is included in the list of policies and activities which are mentioned in arts 3 and 4 TFEU. The legal basis for measures addressing climate change issues is, depending on the nature of the measure, arts 43 (agriculture), 91 or 100 (transport), 113 (taxation), 114 (internal market), 207 (trade), 194 (energy) or 192 (environment) TFEU. In the absence of a specific legal basis in the past, energy-related measures, therefore, were normally based on art.192 or 352 TFEU. In particular, art.192 TFEU was of increasing importance in the are of energy policy measures. For example, the abovementioned Decision 94/69 to adhere to the Convention on Climate Change was based on art.130s EC Treaty, the predecessor of the present art.192 TFEU. Furthermore, the Decision to adhere to the Kyoto Protocol[9] and different Decisions on energy saving,[10] and alternative energies,[11] the Decision on a monitoring mechanism of greenhouse gas-emissions[12] and the Directive on the energy performance of buildings[13] were all based on art.192(1) TFEU. Politically and legally the competence of the European Union to deal with climate change issues and to adopt EU-wide measures was not seriously disputed, it being understood that this competence was shared between the European Union and the Member States. It is to be expected that in future the energy related measures on energy saving, energy efficiency will be based on art.194 rather than on art.192 TFEU, though the two provisions are not entirely congruent.

---

[5] Commission, The Greenhouse effect and the Community, COM (89) 656.

[6] (1990) *Bulletin of the European Communities*, October 1990, no.1.3.77.

[7] Commission, Towards Sustainability. A European Community programme of policy and action in relation to the environment and sustainable development [1993] OJ C138/5 Pt.5.1

[8] Dec.94/69 [1994] OJ L33/11; the Convention itself is published at p.13.

[9] Dec.2002/358 concerning the approval, on behalf of the European Community, of the Kyoto Protocol to the United Nations Framework Convention on Climate Change and the joint fulfilment of commitments thereunder [2002] OJ L130/1.

[10] Dec.91/565 [1991] OJ L307/34; Dec.96/737 [1996] OJ L335/50; Dec.647/2000 [2000] OJ L79/6.

[11] Dec.93/500 [1993] OJ L235/41; Dec.98/352 [1998] OJ L159/53; Dec.646/2000 [2000] OJ L79/1.

[12] Dec.99/296 amending Dec.93/389 [1993] OJ L167/31) for a monitoring mechanism of Community CO_2 and other greenhouse gases [1999] OJ L117/35.

[13] Dir.2002/91 on the energy performance of buildings [2003] OJ L1/65; in 2010, this Dir. was replaced by Dir. 2010/31 on the energy performance of buildings [2010] OJ L153/13.

In 1991, the Commission adopted a Communication on measures to combat   **9–03**
global warming[14] which suggested, essentially, three types of measures: energy
conservation and improved energy technology, monitoring mechanisms for
emissions and fiscal measures. These measures were, in later years, prolonged
and adapted and, as regards the first group of measures, clarified to include the
reduction of greenhouse gas emissions. Several conferences of Heads of State
and Governments and environmental and energy Councils dealt with climate
change strategies. Following the signature of the Kyoto Protocol in 1997, where
finally the obligations of the contracting parties were clarified, the Commission
submitted, in 2000, a new draft for an EU strategy.[15] The European Climate
Change Programme's (ECCP) objective was to identify and develop all those
elements "that are necessary for the implementation of the Kyoto Protocol". This
requires a comment on the objectives of a climate change strategy. The
Commission stated that it followed a double concept: on the one hand,
strengthening the EU policies and measures regarding climate change, on the
other hand developing an emission trading scheme within the European Union.
The Council discussed the Communication at several occasions and also adopted
several resolutions concerning climate change policies. However, the Council
was cautious in assessing in detail the Commission's programme and limited
itself instead to request the Commission to submit, as soon as possible, concrete
proposals in order to reduce greenhouse gas emissions.[16] The European
Parliament regretted that the Communication did not contain a precise action plan
with a time plan, but rather a list of potential or desirable activities.[17]

The Commission did not see reasons to change its attitude. It realised that the
other institutions had not really disapproved its approach and continued its policy,
being aware that there was no clear action programme for climate change. The
subsequent discussions showed that all discussions continued to concentrate on
the Commission's approach.

The sixth environmental action programme, adopted in 2002, stated that EU
climate change policy should try to align to the "long term objective of 2°Celsius
over pre-industrialised levels and a CO^2 concentration below 550 ppm".[18] In
2007, the European Council declared that global temperature should only rise by
maximal 2°Celsius and committed the European Union to reduce its greenhouse
gas emissions by at least 20 per cent below 1990 levels by 2020, and by 30 per
cent, provided that other developed countries committed themselves to
comparable emission reductions and economically more advanced developing
countries contributed adequately according to their responsibilities and respective
capacities.[19] This commitment was inserted into a Decision of 2009 which was
based on art.192(1) TFEU.[20]

---

[14] Commission, COM (91) 249.
[15] Commission, Communication on EU policies and measures to reduce greenhouse gas emissions:
towards a European Climate Change Programme (ECCP), COM (2000) 88.
[16] See in particular Res. of March 8, 2001 and June 8, 2001.
[17] European Parliament Res. of October 26, 2000 [2000] OJ C197/397.
[18] Dec.1600/2002 laying down the 6th Community Environment Action Programme [2002] OJ
L242/1, art.2(2).
[19] European Council, meeting of 8–9 March 2007, President's conclusions, Doc.7224/07 Rev.1 of 2
May 2007.
[20] Dec.406/2009 on the efforts of Member States to reduce their greenhouse gas emissions to meet
the Community's greenhouse gas emission reduction commitments up to 2020 [2009] OJ L140/136.

However, at a conference in Copenhagen in December 2009, global negotiations on a follow-up agreement on the Kyoto Protocol failed, and neither industrialised countries nor developing countries made formal commitments as regards the reduction of greenhouse gas emissions for the time after 2012. Subsequently, the EU institutions did not increase the reduction commitment to 30 per cent, but decided to leave it with 20 per cent. No further progress was reached for a new global agreement in 2011 (Cancun negotiations), though several countries made unilateral promises to reduce their greenhouse gas emissions.

2.   The Kyoto Protocol

9–04   The objectives of the Climate Change Convention of the United Nations were[21]:

"to achieve ... stabilization of greenhouse gas concentrations in the atmosphere at a level that would prevent dangerous anthropogenic interference with the climate system."

The European Union's Decision on the Sixth Environmental Action Programme[22] repeated this objective and then continued[23]:

"Thus a long term objective of a maximum global temperature increase of 2°Celsius over pre-industrial levels and a CO_2 concentration below 550 ppm shall guide the Programme. In the longer term this is likely to require a global reduction in emissions of greenhouse gases by 70 % as compared to 1990 as identified by the Intergovernmental Panel on Climate Change (IPCC)."

Thus, while it is clear that "dangerous anthropogenic interference" with the climate system is to be avoided, it is not completely clear, what is to be done to achieve this goal. Almost all depends on scientific data and assessment. In 1999, the Commission was of the opinion that CO_2 emissions had to fall "by at least 35% by 2010, if long-term temperature increases are to be limited to 1.58 by 2100."[24] 14 months later, it was of the opinion that:

"a global reduction of 20–40% (depending on actual rates of economic growth and thus greenhouse gas emissions as well as the success of measures taken to combat climate change) over 1990–2020 will need to be aimed at"

and that "global emissions of greenhouse gases need to be reduced by approximately 70% over 1990 levels in the longer term."[25] As mentioned, the Council cautiously took up the second figure only.

9–05   The implementation of the Kyoto Protocol is seen, under this perspective as an objective for the shorter term. In 1997, this Kyoto Protocol, a protocol under the

---

[21] United Nations Framework Convention on Climate Change (fn.8, above), art.1.

[22] Dec.1600/2002 (fn.18, above).

[23] Sixth action programme (fn.18, above), art.2(2).

[24] Commission, Europe's environment: what directions for the future? The global assessment of the European Community action programme of policy and action in relation to the environment and sustainable development COM (1999) 543, pt 3.1.

[25] Commission, Communication on the sixth environmental action programme of the European Community—Environment 2010: our future, our choice, COM (2001) 31, pt 3.2.

Climate Change Convention, was concluded.[26] It covered six greenhouse gases, carbon dioxide (CO2), Methane (CH4), Nitrous oxide (N2O), Hydrofluorocarbons (HFCs), Perfluorocarbons (PFCs) and Sulphur hexafluoride (SF6). The Contracting Parties listed in an annex to the Protocol—all industrialised countries—committed themselves to reduce the emissions of these six gases[27] "in the commitment period 2008 to 2012" (art.3(1)), compared with 1990, to a percentage that was laid down in an annex. For the European Union which was expressly mentioned in the annex, and its—by then—15 Member States, this figure was fixed at 92 per cent so that the European Union had to reach a reduction of greenhouse gases by 8 per cent. As the European Union decided to approve of the Kyoto Protocol and adopted Decision 2002/358 in this regard; there is thus a legal obligation to reduce greenhouse gas emissions within the European Commission by 8 per cent by 2012 at the latest.

However, the Kyoto Protocol contained another obligation. According to its art.25, it entered into force, once 55 Parties to the Climate Change Convention "incorporating Parties included in Annex I which accounted in total for at least 55 percent of the total carbon dioxide emissions for 1990 of the Parties included in Annex I" had agreed to it. The United States signed the Protocol under the Clinton administration, but recalled this signature under the Bush administration and declared that they would not ratify the Protocol. As the United States was the biggest generator of greenhouse gas emissions worldwide, the complicated calculation method under the Protocol led to the necessity that most of the other industrialised countries that are listed in annex I had to adhere to the Protocol, before this could enter into effect. This led to a lot of horse-trading, in particular also with Japan and Russia. Finally, Russia adhered to the Protocol end 2004, so that it entered into effect on February 16, 2005, more than seven years after its adoption.

9–06

The European Union's strategy, prior to 2005, consisted of deploying enough international activity in order to make the Kyoto Protocol become effective. Worldwide, there did not appear to be other countries to be prepared to play a leading role in the attempt to promote the Kyoto Protocol, except the UN Secretariat; the role of that Secretariat is, however, hardly able to take on such a function, as it lacks the most elementary financial and human resources to do so. And similarly, the European Union is hardly equipped to be the driving force for the promotion of the Kyoto Protocol either. In its external relations with other countries, trade questions are largely predominant. Its climate change department lacks the human resources to play an active role worldwide. And many questions to make the Kyoto Protocol operational—measuring methods, frequencies and stations, legislative and administrative infrastructural measures, identifying sources, introducing technologies, etc.—imply a considerable know-how on technical and scientific details as well as financial means to ensure smooth transition periods, allow the taking into consideration of local specificities or sectoral problems and the approval of policy-makers, parliaments and public opinions in the different countries. The few persons working on climate change

9–07

---

[26] The Protocol is published [2002] OJ L130/4.

[27] The different gases have a different global warming potential (GWP). This potential is calculated on the basis of CO_2, the most spread greenhouse gas. The global warming potential for CO_2 is 1, for methane 24.5, for nitrous oxide 320, for HFC between 97 and 12.000, for PFC 5.700 to 11.900 and for SF6 22.200, see Reg.842/2006 [2006] OJ L161/1, annex I. There are some scientific uncertainties on these figures.

issues within the Commission's climate change department are hardly able to assume such work for the whole of the European Union, though they have very great human, financial and administrative support from EU Member States; they are not equipped to be in the driving seat worldwide, all the more as—mainly due to the "mixed agreement" character of the Climate Change Convention and the Kyoto Protocol—Member States appear, at the international level, autonomously, but do not rally behind the EU institutions or the Commission to speak and act with one voice internationally.[28]

9–08   Within the European Union, the Commission tried, prior to the negotiations which led to the 1997 signing of the Kyoto Protocol, and in particular after that signature, to reach an EU consensus on the strategy to follow.[29] This was only in part successful, as Member States did not wish to see a complete and coherent EU climate change policy. Therefore, Member States agreed among themselves—without a corresponding Commission proposal—how they would organise themselves with regard to the commitment under the Kyoto Protocol. Based on existing emissions, economic development and technical possibilities, they politically agreed to a burden-sharing, which allowed some Member States to increase their greenhouse gas emissions while others had to reduce them. This burden-sharing was, in 2002, made legally binding[30] and provided for the following percentages which were to be respected by 2012 (1990=100):

Belgium	92.5	Luxembourg	72
Denmark	79	Netherlands	94
Germany	79	Austria	87
Greece	125	Portugal	127
Spain	115	Finland	100
France	100	Sweden	104
Ireland	113	UK	87.5
Italy	93.5		

Decision 2002/358 was based on art.192(1) TFEU. A number of Member States had favoured the use of art.192(2) TFEU which would have provided for unanimity; the reason was not that they opposed the Decision, but that they wanted to keep a veto right for future decisions on climate change. However, as the Commission had threatened to have the question of the correct legal basis clarified by the Court of Justice, and there was a strong political interest for the European Union to show at the Johannesburg World Summit which took place in September 2002, that it had complied with its commitments under the Kyoto

---

[28] A confirmation of this point might be seen in the fact that for the global climate change negotiations in Copenhagen, December 2009, the EU Commission did not even ask for a negotiation mandate, which had the consequence that United Kingdom, France, Germany and the other EU Member States all spoke for themselves and the EU as organisation did not play any significant role during the negotiations.

[29] Commission, Climate Change—towards a European Union post-Kyoto strategy, COM (98) 353; see also the preceding Commission communication—Climate Change—the EU approach for Kyoto, COM (97) 481.

[30] See Dec.2002/358 (fn.9, above), annex II.

Protocol and was able to take the global lead in climate change matters, art.192(1) was finally accepted as the appropriate legal basis.

In 2009, a new burden sharing was agreed, for the period 2013–2020 and for the 27 Member States.[31] The Decision was again based on art.192(1) TFEU. The Decision requested each Member State to reduce its greenhouse gas emissions in a linear manner by a percentage fixed in an annex, but put as the reference year no longer 1990, but 2005. Where the annual emissions exceeded the required emissions, corrective measures should apply (art.7) which consisted in increased reduction quantities for the following year, multiplied by an abatement factor of 1.08, the requirement to develop a corrective action plan and the temporary suspension of the possibility to transfer part of the emission allocations to another Member State. In contrast, the Decision neither mentioned what would happen, when a Member State was continuously in delay with reducing its emissions, nor what would happen, if a Member State did not reach the required reduction by 2020. In both cases, the only consequence would be an infringement procedure under art.258 TFEU which is, though, not very effective legally and hardly imaginable politically.

The Decision concerned emissions from fuel combustion, fugitive missions from fuels, industrial processes, solvent and other product use, agriculture and waste, but excluded emissions from installations that were covered by Directive 2003/87 on emission trading (art.1 and Annex 1).[32] Whether the 2005 emission data for these different sectors are really known, is very questionable.

The reduction quota were fixed, according to recitals 8 and 9, on the principle of solidarity between Member States, the objective to reach a fair distribution between the Member States and the gross domestic product of each Member State. However, already the use of the year 2005 as baseline is arbitrary. This Decision favoured those countries which deployed less efforts between 1990 and 2005 to reduce their emissions, such as Spain, Portugal, Ireland, Italy or Greece, as is shown by the following table:

Table: Member States emissions since 1990 and reductions/increases by 2020[33]:

Member State	Quantities emitted in 1990 in Tg[34]	Quantities emitted in 2005 in Tg	Quantities to be emitted in 2020 in Tg	Reduction/ increase quantities according to Dec.406/2009 (%)	Reduction/ increase by 2020 compared to 1990 (%)
Belgium	143	142	120.7	-15	-15

---

[31] Dec.406/2009 (fn.20, above).

[32] Dir.2003/87 establishing a scheme for greenhouse gas emission allowance trading within the Community [2003] OJ L275/32.

[33] For the quantities emitted, the figures were taken which the EU officially sent to the United Nations and which had been approved by all Member States, see European Environment Agency, Annual European Community Greenhouse Gas Inventory Report 1990–2007 and Inventory Report 2009. Technical Report 4/2009, Copenhagen 2009, tables ES 3 and ES 7.

[34] One teragram (Tg) corresponds to one million tonnes.

9–09

Member State	Quantities emitted in 1990 in Tg[34]	Quantities emitted in 2005 in Tg	Quantities to be emitted in 2020 in Tg	Reduction/ increase quantities according to Dec.406/2009 (%)	Reduction/ increase by 2020 compared to 1990 (%)
Bulgaria	118	71	85.2	+20	-27
Czech R.	195	146	159.1	+9	-24
Denmark	69	63	50.4	-20	-27
Germany	1215	969	833.3	-14	-32
Estonia	42	20	22.2	+11	-47
Ireland	55	70	56.0	-20	+1
Greece	106	132	126.7	-4	+16
Spain	288	441	396.9	-10	+37
France	563	554	479.4	-14	-15
Italy	516	574	499.4	-13	-3
Cyprus	5	10	9.5	-5	+90
Latvia	27	11	12.9	+17	-51
Lithuania	49	23	27.0	+15	-49
Luxembg	13	13	10.4	-20	-20
Hungary	99	80	88.0	+10	-10
Malta	2	3	3.3	+10	+65
Netherld	212	212	178.1	-16	-16
Austria	79	93	78.1	-16	-1
Poland	459	387	390.9	+1	-15
Portugal	59	89	97.9	+1	+66
Romania	243	149	177.3	+19	-31

Member State	Quantities emitted in 1990 in Tg[34]	Quantities emitted in 2005 in Tg	Quantities to be emitted in 2020 in Tg	Reduction/increase quantities according to Dec.406/2009 (%)	Reduction/increase by 2020 compared to 1990 (%)
Slovenia	19	20	20.8	+4	+10
Slovakia	73	49	55.2	+13	-14
Finland	71	69	58.0	-16	-19
Sweden	72	67	55.6	-17	-24
United K.	771	653	548.5	-16	-29
EU-27	5564	5111	4088.8	20	-26

If one compares the quantities in this table with the commitments laid down in Decision 2002/358, quoted above, it becomes evident that the reduction efforts by (the 15 "old") Member States between 1990 and 2005 were rather limited. This situation does not inspire optimism for 2020, though the overall objective, if one follows this table, is a reduction of 26 per cent compared to 1990.

The emission picture is completely different, when the emissions per capita are considered, an approach which the European Union has not yet taken; globally, though, such an approach will ultimately be the only equitable approach to reach solutions, with transfer rights and other in-built flexibility mechanisms.

9–10

Emission of greenhouse gases per capita (in kg)[35]:

Member State	Emissions 1990 per capita	Emissions 2005 per capita	Emissions 2020 per capita (according to Dec.406/2009)
Belgium	13.690	13.540	11.574
Bulgaria	15.204	9.148	10.977
Czech R.	19.079	14.285	15.570
Denmark	12.751	11.642	9.310

[35] Own calculation. The data from the previous table were taken and divided by the population of each Member State. The population figures stem from Eurostat, "Total population in 2005", http://epp.eurostat.ec.europa.eu/cache/ITY_OFFPUB/CH_02_2010/EN/CH_02_2010-EN.PDF [Accessed April 8, 2010]. The population of 2005 was also used for 1990 and 2020.

Member State	Emissions 1990 per capita	Emissions 2005 per capita	Emissions 2020 per capita (according to Dec.406/2009)
Germany	14.727	11.745	10.101
Estonia	31.169	14.842	16.470
Ireland	13.385	17.035	13.628
Greece	9.564	11.910	11.369
Spain	6.674	10.247	9.222
France	8.969	8.825	7.637
Italy	8.826	9.818	8.541
Cyprus	6.674	13.348	12.680
Latvia	11.706	4.749	5.580
Lithuania	14.305	6.715	7.867
Luxembg.	28.186	28.186	22.548
Hungary	9.804	7.922	8.714
Malta	4.967	7.450	8.195
Netherld	13.001	13.001	10.921
Austria	9.633	9.633	9.525
Poland	12.024	10.138	10.239
Portugal	5.603	8.453	9.297
Romania	11.220	6.880	8.186
Slovenia	9.511	10.012	10.411
Slovakia	13.557	9.100	10.245
Finland	13.558	13.176	11.068
Sweden	7.990	7.435	6.171
United K.	13.383	13.092	10.473
EU-27	11.328	10.406	8.324

Luxembourg, Estonia and the Czech Republic are predicted to be, in 2020, the biggest emittors, Latvia, Sweden, and France the countries with the lowest per capita emission.

3.   Emission trading with greenhouse gases

In March 2000, the Commission adopted a Green Paper on greenhouse gas   **9–11**
emissions trading[36] which was followed one year later by a proposal for a
Directive establishing a scheme for greenhouse gas emission allowance trading
within the European Union. Without significant amendments, the proposal was
adopted in 2003 as Directive 2003/87.[37] The Directive which, in the beginning,
only covered carbon dioxide (CO_2) gases, established a legal framework for an
emissions trading scheme which was launched from 2005 onwards. The scheme
was limited to installations which were mentioned in an annex I and which
concern, essentially, installations covered by Directive 2008/1,[38] i.e. iron and
steel furnaces; glass manufacturing installations; oil refineries; coke ovens;
smelters and cement kilns; pulp and paper mills of a particular size. Installations
which came under Directive 2003/87 had to receive a permit for the emissions of
greenhouse gases. Overall, some 45 per cent of all greenhouse gas emissions
were covered by the Directive.

In 2009, the Directive was revised.[39] Flights which arrive at or depart from an
EU airport were included and the number of installations covered was increased.
For specific types of installations, also other gases than CO_2 were included.

Applications for the permit had to contain specific information on the
installation, in particular the materials the use of which was likely to lead to
greenhouse gas emissions, the sources of emissions from the installation and the
measures planned to monitor emissions (art.3). Member States were obliged to
draw up a national plan which indicated the total quantity of allowances that were
intended to be allocated (art.9). These plans had to be published and notified to
the Commission. The Commission could reject the plan, if it was incompatible
with the Directive. However, it is the Member States which determined the
quantity of allocations and the calculation method, not the Commission.[40]

At least 95 per cent of the allowances for installations had to be attributed free
of charge for the period 2005 to 2007 (art.10). Each Member State had to decide
on the total quantity of allowances it would allocate for the first three-year period
of the national plan (2005–2007), and then for subsequent plan periods. The
amendment of 2009, provided that the allowance would have to be, as of 2013,
auctioned and no longer be issued free of cost, as the free allocation had, in the
past, led to rather generous attributions of allowances by some Member States.
The auctioning is likely to increase the price of allowances which might make it
more interesting to invest in cleaner technologies rather than buy emission
allowances.

Allowances are transferable between persons within the European Union
without restrictions. Every year, the operator of an installation must surrender a

---

[36] Commission, Green Paper on greenhouse gas emissions trading within the European Union, COM (2000) 87.

[37] Dir.2003/87 (fn.32, above).

[38] Dir.2008/1 on integrated pollution prevention and control [2008] OJ L24/8; this Dir. codified the earlier Dir.96/61 [1996] OJ L257/26. In 2010, it was replaced by Dir.2010/75 on industrial emissions [2010] OJ L334/17.

[39] Dir.2009/29 amending Dir.2993/87 so as to improve and extend the greenhouse gas emission allowance trading scheme of the Community, [2009] OJ L140/63.

[40] See General Court, *Poland v Commission* (T–183/07) judgment of September 23, 2009; *Estonia v Commission* (T–263/07) judgment of September 23, 2009. Both judgments are under appeal.

number of allowances that is equal to the total emissions from that installation; these allowances will then be cancelled (art.12). The Directive also provided for sanctions in cases that the operators of installations did not correctly report on emissions or emitted more gases than allowed (arts 15 and 16). The 2009 amendment of the Directive provided that the total quantity of emission allowances be reduced, as of 2013, by 1.74 per cent per year.

9–12   As Directive 96/61 required installations to conform, as regards emissions, to the best available technology, and as the purchase of pollution emission allowances would enable an installation to emit more pollutants than admissible under the "best available technology", Directive 2008/1 was amended (art.26). This amendment leads to the result that an installation which purchased emission allowances would no longer be obliged to comply with the best available techniques, as regards greenhouse gas emissions.

The proposal for a directive had raised considerable concern: the legal competence of the European Union to legislate in this area and the political opportunity to introduce the proposal were questioned. This criticism overlooked that the Kyoto Protocol had, at the request of the United States, introduced the possibility for international emission trading. While no contracting party was obliged, under the Protocol, to participate in such a system, it was thus clear that a global emission trading scheme could be introduced at international level. Then it is difficult to imagine that the European Union should not be entitled to set up such a system of its own.

9–13   The Kyoto Protocol had not only introduced the emission trading system, but also provided for two other instruments, the Joint Implementation and the Clean Development Mechanism. Both these instruments concern specific projects. Joint implementation projects may be undertaken in developed countries or in countries with economies in transition. For a specific project, two countries may agree to a joint emission target. Special mechanisms ensure that the joint implementation does not lead to a double counting of the emission reductions. This method allowed an investment, e.g. by Denmark, in a clean technology project in Russia or in Ukraine, which would be capable of being realised with less investment costs than in Denmark. Care will have to be taken to avoid double counting of the reduction.

The *Clean Development Mechanism* is permitted in developing countries which were not subjected to targeted reductions of emissions under the Kyoto Protocol. It also concerned specific projects. An investment by a developed country in a developing country would be counted for the emissions in the developed country. In this way, an investment in a developing country could be realised at a lower cost than in the developed country, and would give the developing country the advantage of modern, clean investment, while the developed country would incur less cost than it would have with an investment at home. At the same time, the global quantities of greenhouse gases would be reduced.

9–14   In 2004, the European Union adopted Directive 2004/101 which amended Directive 2003/87 and established "a scheme for greenhouse gas emission allowance trading within the Community, in respect of the Kyoto Protocol's project mechanisms".[41] This Directive, based on art.192(1) TFEU, enabled operators in the European Union to use the mechanisms of joint implementation

---

[41] Dir.2004/101 [2004] OJ L338/18.

and clean development mechanisms. The Commission had proposed that a maximum level of 6 per cent of the total emission allowances which had been issued could be used for Joint Implementation investments[42]; however, the Council did not accept this limitation, in order to avoid too heavy a burden for the installations.

These Joint Implementation and Clean Development Mechanisms may not concern nuclear installations, land use and land use change and forestry; these restrictions were already found in the Kyoto-Protocol. The Commission had originally considered also to exempt installations for the production of hydro-electric power, but had abandoned this idea in view of the strong resistance from interested groups.

The Directive tried to strike a balance between environmental and economic considerations. Indeed, it might be tempting for Member States to fulfil their obligations to reduce greenhouse gas emissions by ensuring non-expensive investments in other countries or in technologies that have, in turn, considerable environmental disadvantages.

Directives 2003/87 and 2004/101 concentrated the attention on the economic instruments in the area of climate change. However, it needs to be underlined that the two Directives do not as such lead to a reduction of greenhouse gases; they only allow cost-effective investments. It is even now, in 2011, not clear, whether the two Directives which require high administrative costs for calculation, registration, transparency, reporting obligations, etc. really were successful in reducing the emissions,[43] though it has to be admitted that they constituted a way to obtain the political consensus of Member States in Council, to jointly commit to the reduction of greenhouse gas emissions.

4.   Energy saving, energy efficiency and renewables

In order to promote better energy conservation and use, the European Union adopted Directive 93/76 which was based on arts 175 and 308 EC (now arts 192 and 352 TFEU) and had as its objective, to improve energy efficiency in housing, cars and industrial installations and to promote public investment schemes.[44] It requested Member States to draw up and implement programmes for: the energy efficiency of buildings; the billing of heating; air-conditioning and hot water costs on the basis of annual consumption; thermal insulation of new buildings; and regular inspections of boilers and energy audits of undertakings with high energy consumption. Details for the drawing-up of such programmes were left entirely to Member States.

9–15

Though it was clear from the beginning that the loose drafting of the Directive would not make it very efficient, it took nine years before the Council agreed the next measure, a Directive on the energy performance of buildings.[45] The Directive was based on art.192(1) TFEU and became operational in the beginning

---

[42] Commission proposal for a directive, COM (2003) 403, new art.11(a)(2).

[43] See G. Winter, "The climate is no commodity; taking stock of the emissions trading scheme" (2010) *Journal of Environmental Law*, p.1.

[44] Dir.93/76 to limit carbon dioxide emissions by improving energy efficiency (SAVE) [1993] OJ L237/28.

[45] Dir.2002/91 on the energy performance of buildings [2003] OJ L1/65.

of 2006; its effects will only gradually be felt, as not too many new buildings are constructed. Member States had to apply a methodology of calculating the energy performance of buildings, according to criteria laid down in the Directive. Member States had then to set minimum energy performance requirements. New buildings would have to comply with these requirements; existing buildings with a used floor area of over 1,000m² had to upgrade their energy performance, should they undergo major renovation and this was "technically, functionally and economically feasible" (art.5). Where a building was constructed, sold or rented out, an energy performance certificate was to be made available to the interested person. Boilers fired by non-renewable liquid or solid fuel, and older heating installations with boilers had to be inspected at regular intervals, in order to reduce energy consumption and limit CO_2 emissions; inspections had also to be provided for air-conditioning systems.

9–16   In 2010, this Directive was replaced by a new Directive.[46] The new Directive was based on the energy provision of art.194(2) TFEU; in order to overcome the fact that in the energy chapter, a provision which corresponds to art.193 TFEU and allows Member States to maintain or introduce more stringent national measures, the Directive itself contained such a provision (art.1(3)). As Directive 2002/91, the new Directive applied to new and existing buildings which underwent major renovation; though the limitation of 1000m² was deleted, the Directive continued not to be applicable to all existing buildings. Furthermore, the Directive introduced a common method for calculating the energy performance of buildings and asked Member States to set minimum requirements for the energy performance of buildings and building elements (such as apartments). These measures were to include also products and appliances— heating, air-conditioning, hot water generation, lighting, etc. which were installed in buildings; for these, technical requirements were to be laid down by Member States.

By 2020, all new buildings and by 2018 all new buildings occupied and owned by public authorities will have to be nearly zero-energy buildings; a nearly zero-energy building was defined as a building that has a very high energy performance, as determined in accordance with Annex I. The nearly zero or very low amount of energy required should be covered to a very significant extent by energy from renewable sources, including energy from renewable sources produced on-site or nearby".[47] Member States were asked to draw up national plans to increase the number of nearly zero-energy buildings.

A system of certification of the energy performance of buildings was to be elaborated by Member States which had to include the energy performance and reference values, in order to allow a comparison of the certificates. The energy performance certificate is to be handed over to a buyer or tenant of a building or building unit. Heating systems, boilers and air-conditioning systems in buildings were to be regularly inspected.

9–17   Several EU decisions aimed at the demonstration and dissemination of cleaner and more efficient energy techniques, or for the promotion of alternative energies. However, the financial means which were made available at EU level were

---

[46] Dir.2010/31 on the energy performance of buildings [2010] OJ L153, p.13.
[47] Dir.2010/31, art. 2 no.2. annex I specifies, how the energy performance shall be calculated.

remarkably insufficient:

- Decision 91/565 (SAVE I) covered a period of five years and provided for energy saving measures for 12 Member States financial support of 35 million €.[48]
- Decision 96/737 (SAVE) again covered a period of five years. It concerned 25 countries and provided for 45 million for energy saving €.[49]
- Decision 647/2000 (SAVE II) increased the sum to 66 million € and was destined for 26 countries for a period of five years.[50]
- Decision 93/500 (ALTENER) made available 40 million € for alternative energy measures, covering five years and concerning 12 Member States.[51]
- Decision 98/352 (ALTENER) concerned 26 countries, covered a period of two years and affected 26 countries.[52]
- Decision 646/2000 (ALTENER II) finally covered a period of five years, concerned 26 countries and provided for 77 million €.[53]

Since 2006, financial resources were made available, for renewables, energy efficiency and the promotion of energy in transport, within a framework programme "Intelligent Energy—Europe".[54] The amount made available for energy was estimated at 724 million €. As also non-EU States participate in the programme—overall some 35 States—this amounts to a sum of about 3 million € per State and year.

In 1997, the Commission adopted a White Paper on renewable sources of energy[55] which suggested, among other things, to increase the percentage of renewable energies from 6 per cent to 12 per cent by 2010. This political intention required a whole series of measures, such as price differentiation between conventional and renewable energy sources, labelling, research and development measures and financial assistance. Most of these measures would have to be taken at the level of Member States.   **9–18**

As the Council and the European Parliament[56] requested the Commission to submit concrete proposals, the Commission submitted, in 2000 a proposal for a Directive on the promotion of electricity from renewable sources of energy, which the Council adopted in 2001.[57] The Directive was based on art.192(1) TFEU and became operational at the end 2003. It provided that Member States should encourage greater consumption of energy from renewable energy sources and fixed, for that purpose, national indicative targets. The Member States had to

---

[48] Dec.91/565 [1993] OJ L307/34.
[49] Dec.96/737 [1996] OJ L335/50.
[50] Dec.647/2000 [2000] OJ L79/6.
[51] Dec.93/500 [1993] OJ L235/1.
[52] Dec.98/352 [1998] OJ L159/53.
[53] Dec.646/2000 [2000] OJ L79/1.
[54] Dec.1639/2006 establishing a competitiveness and innovation framework programme (2007–2013) [2006] OJ L310/15.
[55] Commission, Energy for the future: renewable sources of energy, Green Paper, COM (96) 576; White Paper, COM (1997) 599).
[56] Res. of June 8, 1998 [1998] OJ C198/1; (Council); Res. of European Parliament (1998) OJ C210/215.
[57] Dir.2001/77 on the promotion of electricity produced from renewable energy sources in the internal electricity market, [2001] OJ L283/33.

publish every two years a report on progress to reach these targets, and report whether these national targets are consistent with the:

"global indicative target of 12% of gross national energy consumption by 2010 and in particular with the 22.1 percent indicative share of electricity produced from renewable energy sources in total Community energy consumption by 2010. (art.3(4))"

Member States were allowed to give financial support to producers of electricity in order to achieve the objectives of the Directive.

9–19
Electricity from renewable sources is not required to be labelled. However, a guarantee of origin of electricity has to be issued "in response to a request" (art.5). Member States also had to ensure that operators of transmission and distribution (grid) systems guarantee the transmission and distribution of electricity produced from renewable energy sources (art.7).

In 2003, Directive 2003/30 on the promotion of the use of biofuels for transport was adopted, based on art.175(1) EC Treaty.[58] It concerned liquid or gaseous fuels for transport that were produced from biomass.[59] The Directive set an indicative target for Member States which had to reach a share of 2 per cent share in total sales of petrol and diesel fuels by December 2005, and 5.75 per cent by December 2010; these targets were not reached. Member States were obliged to report annually on total sales of transport fuel and the share of biofuels, as well as on measures taken to boost production of biofuels. The environmental problems of biofuels—extensive land use, use of pesticides and other chemicals, monocultures, problems of biodiversity—were not addressed by the Directive.

9–20
Both Directive 2001/77 and 2003/30 were amended and will progressively be repealed by a new Directive on the promotion of the use of energy from renewable sources which was adopted in 2009.[60] The Directive was based on art.192(1) TFEU, with the exception of arts 17 to 19 which deal with biofuels and for which art.114 TFEU was fixed as a basis. It set mandatory national targets for the overall share of energy from renewable sources in gross final consumption of energy, and also for the share of energy from renewable sources in transport. Energy from renewable sources was defined as "energy from renewable non-fossil sources, namely wind, solar, aerothermal, geothermal, hydrothermal and ocean energy, hydropower, biomass, landfill gas, sewage treatment plant gas and biogases" (art.2(a)); the definition of biomass was slightly changed with regard to the earlier legislation.[61] The national targets together had to reach "a target of at least a 20% share of energy from renewable sources in the Community's gross final consumption of energy in 2020" (art.3). This target is rather ambitious, as in 2005 only Denmark, Estonia, Latvia, Austria, Portugal,

---

[58] Dir.2003/30 on the promotion of the use of biofuels or other renewable fuels [2003] OJ 123/42.

[59] As regards the definition of biomass, see Dir.2001/77 (fn.57, above), art.2(a): "biomass shall mean the biodegradable fraction of products, waste and residues from agriculture (including vegetal and animal substances), forestry and related industries, as well as the biodegradable fraction of industrial and municipal waste".

[60] Dir.2009/28 on the promotion of the use of energy from renewable sources [2009] OJ L140/16.

[61] "Biomass means the biodegradable fraction of products, waste and residues from biological origin from agriculture (including vegetal and animal substances), forestry and related industries including fisheries and aquaculture, as well as the biodegradable fraction of industrial and municipal waste" (art.2(e)); see also fn.59, above.

Romania, Slovenia, Finland and Sweden had a part of renewables in the overall consumption of fuels of more than 15 per cent.[62]

Furthermore, "each Member State shall ensure that the share of energy from renewable sources in all forms of transport in 2020 is at least 10% of the final consumption of energy in transport" (art.3(4)). The different targets for Member States as regards gross final consumption of energy were laid down in an annex I. The repartition was made, as explained in Recital 15, according to the different point of departure for Member States, their past efforts, their gross domestic product, and fairness and adequacy of the allocation; the final result remained relatively arbitrary.

Member States were obliged to draw up national renewable energy action plans (art.4) which shall contain an annual "indicative trajectory" which has to be followed. Where the trajectory was not respected in two years, an amendment of the action plan is required. Other provisions of the Directive dealt with the calculation of the share of energy from renewables, the cooperation between Member States and with third countries, access to and operation of the grids, and reporting requirements. The choice of means was left almost entirely to the Member States. The Directive also addressed, in detail, the problems of biofuels and fixed sustainability criteria for their use (arts 17 to 19), which were, though rather vague and did not appear to solve the environmental problems which are caused by an extensive use of land for the purpose of biofuels production.

The Directive did not provide for any sanctions for the case of non-compliance, leaving this entirely to the—in this regard rather unsatisfactory—procedure under art.258 TFEU.

5. Limiting emissions of greenhouse gases

Until now, the Union was very reserved as regards the limitation of the emission of greenhouse gases, or the ban or restriction to use certain gases. In the area of installations, the European Union left, under Directive 2008/1, the decision to limit or prohibit the emission of greenhouse gases to the national permitting authorities. For products, the most important limitations of emissions concerned the car sector. After the failure of the voluntary agreement with the car industry to limit CO_2 emissions—see para.8–24, above—the Union adopted provisions on CO_2 emissions by cars in 2009 which will progressively become applicable as of 2013.[63] No such limits exist, until now, for trucks, though an emission limit for methane was introduced in 2009.[64]

9–21

Regulation 842/2006, based on arts 192 and, as regards the product-related provisions (arts 7–9), on art.114 TFEU, limited the use of certain greenhouse

---

[62] See Dir.2009/28, Annex I. The share of Germany was 5.8%, Spain 8.7%, France 10.3%, Italy 5.2%, Poland 7.2%, and United Kingdom 1.3%.

[63] Reg.443/2009 setting an performance standard for new passenger cars as part of the Community's integrated approach to reduce CO_2 emissions from light duty vehicles [2009] OJ L140/1.

[64] Reg.595/2009 on type-approval of motor vehicles and engines with respect to emissions from heavy duty vehicles (Euro VI) an on access to vehicle repair and maintenance information [2009] OJ L188/1.

gases in appliances.[65] Directive 2006/40, based on art.114 TFEU, progressively prohibited the use of certain greenhouse gases in air-conditioning systems of cars.[66]

In order to get rid of CO_2, the European Union furthermore adopted Directive 2009/31on the geological storage of CO_2.[67] This Directive which was based on art.192(1) and entered into effect in mid-2011, attempted to set a legal framework in order to allow the underground storage of CO_2, though the technique of such underground storage is not yet sure; with regard to climate change, the directive itself called it "bridging technology", as it meant to give more time to greenhouse gas emitting installations which could, instead of reducing their emissions, put these emissions underground. Member States were given the freedom to allow or prohibit underground storage of CO_2, also in parts of their territory. Each storage needed a specific permit, for which an environmental impact assessment had to be made. The storage sites have to be inspected regularly; when leakages appear, an action plan has to be applied which should provide for the necessary steps to stop the leaking.

After the closure of the site, the operator shall normally remain responsible for 20 years to take the necessary post-closure measures. Afterwards, the State shall be responsible for the post-closure care.

CO_2 which is stored underground shall not be considered waste; however, the CO_2 which is leaking from the storage site has probably to be regarded as waste.

6.   Monitoring mechanisms

9–22   The European Union adopted a Decision to monitor all anthropogenic greenhouse gas emissions.[68] The Commission regularly reported under this Decision, evaluating the national programmes to limit greenhouse gas emissions.

It follows from the last Report, which covered the year 2007,[69] greenhouse gas emissions within the European Union decreased between 1990 and 2007 by 4 per cent for EU-15 and by 27 per cent for EU-27. The Commission projected that EU-27 will, by 2012, decrease its greenhouse gas emissions by 12.8 per cent, compared to 1990, despite a considerable economic growth.

7.   Fiscal measures

9–23   In 1992, the Commission proposed a Directive for a tax on fossil fuels, the tax level to be to 50 per cent of the energy content and to 50 per cent of the carbon content of the energy product; the amount suggested was up to $10 per barrel of

---

[65] Reg.842/2006 on certain fluorinated gases [2006] OJ L161/1.
[66] Dir.2006/40 relating to emissions from air-condition systems in motor vehicles [2006] OJ L161/12. This Dir. became effective after the adoption of Commission Reg.706/2007 laying down the requirements for a harmonised test to discover leakages [2007] OJ L161/33.
[67] Dir.2009/31 on the geological storage of carbon dioxide [2009] OJ L140/114.
[68] Dec.280/2004 concerning a mechanism for monitoring Community greenhouse gas emissions and for implementation of the Kyoto Protocol [2004] OJ L 49/1; this Dec. replaced Dec.93/389 [1993] OJ L167/31; amended by Dec.1999/296 [1999] OJ L117/35.
[69] Commission COM (2009) 630.

oil.[70] The proposal was based on arts 113 and 192 TFEU and thus needed the unanimity of the Council. The proposal indicated that it would only become applicable, if other OECD States also introduced a similar tax or took equivalent measures (art.1(2)). This made the proposal unrealistic, as neither the United States, Japan, nor Australia, the countries in question at that time, ever considered introducing an energy tax.

Since the negotiations in the Council showed that it was impossible to reach unanimity—in particular the United Kingdom and Spain were opposed to tax measures being adopted at EU level—the Commission amended its proposal.[71] Under the new proposal, Member States remained free whether or not to introduce, a carbon/energy tax. If they did so, they were to comply with the structural requirements fixed in the proposal. However, this amended proposal did not either find the approval in Council and is now to be considered as obsolete.

In 2003, the Council adopted, on the basis of art.113 TFEU, Directive 2003/96   **9–24**
on the taxation of energy products and electricity which introduces minimum tax rates on all energy products,[72] including coal, natural gas and electricity, as well as motor and heating fuels. National tax rates are harmonised in three stages of two years' interval each. Energy intensive industries and agricultural, horticultural and forestry sectors may be exempted from the tax, if they enter into national environmental agreements, participate in emission trading schemes or otherwise contribute to reduce energy consumption. Member States were allowed to introduce reduced tax rates for bio-fuels and electricity which was produced from alternative energies. Where bio-fuels are used for local public passenger transport, the excise duty could be waived altogether.

In 2005, the Commission made a proposal for a directive on the taxation of passenger cars according to their CO_2 emissions.[73] Originally, this proposal was thought to bridge the gap between the car industry's commitment to reduce the CO_2 emissions of cars to 140g per km by 2008 and the political objective of the Council to reach car emissions of 120g per km by 2010. However, the proposal was, by March 2011, still not adopted. The main reason is that Member States do not want to adopt EU-wide taxes and prefer to have this residue of national sovereignty remain in their hands. It is thus not very likely that the proposal will ever get into the statute books.

8.   General observations

Overall, the European Union has initiated a very considerable number of   **9–25**
measures in order to reduce emissions from point sources, promote changes in the use of fuels, incite professionals and citizens to change their behaviour or their life-style in order to reach the objectives of the Kyoto Protocol. Not all of these measures were mentioned here. It is likely that the European Union will reach the targets of the Kyoto Protocol and reduce its greenhouse gas emissions by 2012 by

---

[70] [1992] OJ C314/11.

[71] Commission, COM (95) 172.

[72] Dir.2003/96 restructuring the Community framework for the taxation of energy products and electricity [2003] OJ L283/51.

[73] Commission, proposal for a directive on passenger-related taxes, COM(2005) 261.

8 per cent, compared to 1990. The problem of the EU climate change policy lies first in the fixing and complying with targets for 2020 and 2050 which do not only require, within the European Union, measures as "usual" to reduce emissions, but rather the putting into effect of efficient climate-change policies in the different sectors of energy, transport, agriculture, industry, etc. The present measures give the impression that the attitude of "business as usual" continues in large parts of EU and national policies. The 20 per cent target for 2020 is hardly ambitious, and scientists appear to be more and more in agreement that from the point of view of climate change, it is not sufficiently ambitious. The political concessions which are constantly made for nuclear energy, coal-fired installations, petrol and gas only slow down the necessary reconversion of the EU economy and society to a carbon-free status.

The second problem is the global dimension of climate change. No successful global climate change policy can be made without the participation of the United States; this country is too big, too influential and too often imitated by other countries in order to be left aside. And it will not be possible to ask countries such as China or India to reduce their greenhouse gas emissions, without the United States doing the same.

The European Union is not a global power and does not have the weight to lead the world towards a successful climate change policy. Its attempts to influence the climate change negotiations worldwide, were rather harshly brushed aside at the global summit in Copenhagen 2009, by the United States and China, but also by Brazil, Australia, Canada, India and other countries. The inability to speak with one voice, paired with the ambition of the bigger Member States—Germany, United Kingdom, France in particular—to speak for themselves and the lack of a strategy to advance the global discussions were the main reasons for this result. Initiatives such as the making of a new EU Treaty along the model of the Euratom Treaty, but for renewable energies, or a concrete suggestion to conclude an international climate change agreement with the some 80 States of the Cotonou Agreement and test the cooperation between developed and developing countries in this format—no visionary or strategic initiative came from the European Union, though everybody in the European Union knows that the fight against climate change will never be won by measures within the European Union alone.

8.   Ozone depletion

9–26   The depletion of the ozone layer was discovered in the end of the 1970s and was relatively quickly attributed to a number of chlorine and bromine compounds which were of human origin. These substances are mainly used as coolant, aerosol gas, cleaning agents, and fire extinguishers.

At the international level, ozone-depleting substances are regulated by the Montreal Protocol on substances that deplete the ozone layer, which was concluded in 1987 and to which the European Union adhered[74] and which is

---

[74] Dec.88/540 (1988) OJ L297/8. The Montreal Protocol was elaborated in the context of the Vienna Convention of 1985 on the protection of the ozone layer. The EU also adhered to the Vienna Convention by Dec.88/540.

regularly updated. Regulation 1005/2009 which replaced earlier regulations[75] transposed the provisions of the Protocol into EU law, though it went further than the Protocol. The Regulation was based on art.192 TFEU, though art.114 would have been the more correct legal basis, as the Regulation deals with product-related standards.

The Regulation banned the production, placing on the market and use of CFCs, other fully halogenated CFCs, halons, carbon tetrachlorides, 1,1,1-trichloroethanes and hydrobromofluorocarbons. The production, placing on the market and use of methyl bromides was progressively phased out by 2004. The production of hydrochlorofluorocarbons (HCFCs) had to be progessively stopped by 2025. From 2008 onwards, the production was limited to 35 per cent of the production of 1997; from 2014 onwards this quantity is 20 per cent, and from 2020 15 per cent of that of 1997 (art.3(3)). The placing on the market or use of such substances is, since 2009, prohibited (art.4 (3.h)). The reason for this long transition period is that a number of producers had developed these substances as a substitute for CFCs and were not prepared to write off their investments; and they found support in this attitude from their national governments. The Regulation limited the use of HCFCs in a number of substances such as aerosols, sprays, cooling systems, air conditioning, but provided for extensive derogations. Quantities which a producer does not use, may be traded within the contracting parties to the Montreal Protocol.

The European Union reserved the possibility to allow the production of banned or restricted substances for essential use, where no substitutes or recycled substances were available. Detailed rules dealt with the import and export of ozone-depleting substances from and to third countries. The export of such substances to countries which did not adhere to the Montreal Protocol was prohibited, and even of substances other than HCFCs to all countries (art.11). The Commission issues licences for imports of ozone-depleting substances from third countries, where this is still legal; import of such substances from countries which are not party to the Montreal Protocol is forbidden (art.8). Undertakings are obliged to inform the Commission in detail on production, processing, recycling, uses and other data on ozone-depleting substances. The Commission may ask national authorities to make investigations as regards these substances. The Regulation also dealt with the recycling of ozone-depleting substances, the monitoring, Member States' information obligations, controls and sanctions, which must be "effective, proportional and deterrent" (art.21).

9–27

Though the Montreal Protocol provided for less strict production and trade provisions for developing countries than for industrialised countries, it was considered that the ozone layer may recover around 2050, if the present measures continue to be applied.[76]

---

[75] Reg.1005/2009 on substances that deplete the ozone layer [2009] OJ L286/1.
[76] European Environment Agency, Environment in the European Union at the turn of the century (Copenhagen, 1999), p.99.

CHAPTER 10

Waste

1.   Waste management policy and law

Waste management issues played a role in EU environmental policies from its very beginnings. The Commission's communication of 1972 mentioned the necessity of preventing waste generation and to promote waste recovery.[1] The first environmental action programme discussed the question of what action on waste management could usefully be tackled at EU level and announced the harmonisation of legislations.[2] The second action programme declared that a comprehensive waste management policy was necessary, which should include measures for prevention, reclamation and disposal of waste.[3] The third action programme repeated the intentions of the second programme in similar form and announced promotional measures for waste prevention and recovery.[4]

10–01

The EU dimension of waste management problems fully came into the open when the incident of the Seveso barrels occurred in 1982. Forty-one barrels containing highly toxic waste, which stemmed from a major industrial accident in Seveso in 1976, were shipped, with the consent of Italian public authorities, but in contradiction to the provisions of Directive 78/319,[5] from Italy abroad, and disappeared. Numerous EU Member States were afraid that the waste might have secretly been brought to their territory.[6] The European Parliament set up, for the first time, an inquiry committee and, in its final conclusions, criticised the Commission for not having properly exercised its role as guardian of the Treaty and ensured the application of existing EU rules on waste management. It expressly asked for the elaboration of a consistent and coherent EU waste policy.[7]

The fourth action programme confirmed the previous policy objectives and underlined, in particular, the importance of promoting clean technologies and recycling of waste; it also announced a specific communication on a waste management strategy.[8]

10–02

This strategy communication was finally made in 1989.[9] It essentially fixed

---

[1] [1972] OJ C52/1, p.12.

[2] First environmental action programme (1973–1977) [1973] OJ C112/1, Ch.7, s.1.

[3] Second environmental action programme (1977–1982) [1977] OJ C139/1, paras 174–201.

[4] Third environmental action programme (1983–1986) [1983] OJ C46/1, para.29.

[5] Dir.78/319 on toxic and dangerous waste [1978] OJ L84/43.

[6] The wastes were later found back on a non-authorised storage site in France, transported to Switzerland and, it was reported, incinerated there.

[7] European Parliament Res. of June 8, 1983 [1983] OJ C184/50; Res. of March 16, 1984 [1984] OJ C104/147; Res. of April 11, 1984 [1984] OJ C127/67. See also Economic and Social Committee [1984] OJ C206/62.

[8] Fourth environmental action programme (1987–1992) [1987] OJ C328/1, para.5.3.

[9] Commission, A Community strategy for waste management SEC (89) 934.

five strategic guidelines:

1. Prevention of waste generation. The strategy advocated, on the one hand, clean technologies that could by financially assisted by the Commission[10] and, on the other hand, environmentally "better" products, for which it particularly requested an ecological labelling scheme[11].
2. The promotion of recycling and reuse, which should be promoted through research and development, the improvement of collection and sorting schemes, the reduction of external costs and the creation of outlets for recycled and reused products. The Commission announced financial assistance for waste reuse and recycling technologies and proposals for directives on plastic waste and metal packaging.
3. Optimisation of final disposal, where the Commission announced proposals for the dumping of waste and on the incineration of hazardous waste.
4. Transport of waste, where the Commission only referred to existing work at national and international level.
5. Remedial action: the Commission announced research on the clean-up of contaminated sites and studies on financial instruments for remedying the damage caused by waste in abandoned landfills.

10–03   In concluding chapters, the Commission stated the objective that "as far as possible waste is disposed of in the nearest suitable centres", but that the situation was "different with waste to be recycled". Furthermore, it confirmed that "waste arising within the Community which cannot be recycled should be treated within the Community where possible and exported only in exceptional circumstances". These statements constituted the basis of the proximity and self-sufficiency principles, which were later laid down in art.5 of the amended Directive 75/442.[12] The Council and the European Parliament both welcomed and supported the communication and made a considerable number of detailed proposals for future action.[13]

10–04   The fifth environmental action programme referred back to the 1989 strategy[14]; it repeated its guiding principles and announced rather ambitious waste management targets for the year 2000.[15] These targets were made somewhat less ambitious by the 1996 review of the waste management strategy of 1989,[16] which confirmed the hierarchy of principles while stating that, within the recovery principle:

[10] Through financial assistance schemes which were later substituted by the LIFE instrument: Reg.1973/92 [1992] OJ L206/1 and Reg.1655/2000 [2000] OJ L192/1. See also para.5–19.
[11] On eco-labelling see para.6–55 et seq., above.
[12] Dir.75/442 on waste, as amended by Dir.91/156 [1991] OJ L78/32. This Directive was, in 2006, codified under the number 2006/12 [2006] OJ L114/9. In 2008, it was replaced by Dir.2009/98 on waste [2008] OJ L312/3.
[13] Council Res. of May 7, 1990 [1990] OJ C122/2; European Parliament Res. of February 19, 1991 [1991] C72/34.
[14] Fifth environmental action programme [1993] OJ C138/5, para.5.4.
[15] Amongst others, a stabilisation of quantities of waste generated at 300kg per capita and year; a recycling/reuse rate of paper, glass and plastics of at least 50 per cent; markets for recycled materials; reliable EU data on waste generated, collected and disposed; a functioning system of liability for hazardous waste; and an inventory of risks for hazardous waste.
[16] Commission, COM (96) 399.

"where environmentally sound, preference should in general be given to the recovery of material over energy recovery operations. This reflects the greater effect on the prevention of waste produced by material recovery rather than by energy recovery."

The reviewed strategy tried to place waste management concepts into the context of the internal market and introduced the principle of producer responsibility for waste management issues. This strategy review was also the subject of extensive comments from the other EU institutions, which made a number of proposals for concrete EU measures.[17]

The sixth environmental action programme linked waste management to the sustainable use of natural resources. It proposed a significant reduction in the quantity of waste going to disposal and the volume of hazardous waste that was produced (art.8). It suggested the development of quantitative and qualitative reduction targets of all relevant wastes and, by 2005, a thematic strategy on waste recycling.[18]

The Commission identified, in 1995, the following difficulties in the establishment and implementation of an EU-wide integrated waste management policy[19]:

- lack of reliable statistical, technical and economical data[20];
- the imprecision of legal acts, legal definitions and the ambiguity of some of the concepts of waste management; and
- poor functioning of collective consultation.

The collective consultation is not to be discussed here, as this is a governance problem; as regards statistical data, the European Union adopted a regulation on waste statistics,[21] which has been operational since the end 2002. The Regulation which is based on art.338 TFEU will hopefully progressively organise the collection of data on waste and allow the political measures to be based on more reliable data.

The third aspect, the objectives of (EU) waste management policy, the definition of Member States' and European Union's respective responsibilities in the area of waste management and the definition of waste are, even after more than 35 years of EU environmental waste management measures, not uncontroversial.

The different policy statements at EU level have, to date, left open three basic policy decisions which very considerably influence waste management policy and legislation at EU level.

[1] Waste policy and product policy. Waste prevention was and continues to be the first and most important objective in EU waste management policy, confirmed by all statements.[22]   **10–05**

---

[17] Council Res. of February 24, 1997 [1997] OJ C76/1; European Parliament Res. of November 14, 1996 [1996] OJ C362/241; Economic and Social Committee [1997] OJ C89/2; Committee of the Regions [1997] OJ C116/74.

[18] Dec.1600/2002 laying down the Sixth Community Environment Action Programme [2002] OJ L242/1.

[19] Commission, Report on waste management policy, COM (95) 522.

[20] Reg.2150/2002 on waste statistics [2002] OJ L332/1.

[21] Reg.2150/2002 (fn.20, above).

[22] See Council Res., February 24, 1997 (fn.17, above), paras 16 and 17: "Reiterates its conviction that waste prevention should be first priority for all rational waste policy, in relation to minimising waste

Preventing the generation of waste, however, means that a product policy is followed which is more than a curing of symptoms. While it seems neither desirable nor realistic to suggest that the basis of the consumer society should be changed because of waste considerations, a very useful step would be systematically to reduce the presence of dangerous substances in products, wherever alternatives are available.[23] No such systematic attempts exist at EU level at present.[24] Since waste management is an end-of-the-pipe management, its conception and implementation must necessarily be influenced by actions or omissions that are taken "upstream".

10–06 [2] Waste as a renewable source of energy. The waste strategy of 1996 declared that, in principle, material recycling of waste should have priority over waste incineration with energy recovery.[25] This priority was also established in several EU Directives and last in Directive 2008/98.[26] In practice, however, the European Union frequently takes measures to promote waste incineration (with energy recovery) rather than waste recycling. This manifests itself particularly in four areas: as regards energy policy, waste is considered a source of energy which is sometimes available at a low price and used as a substitute for fossil fuels. Examples are Directives 2000/76 on waste incineration and its succession, Directive 2010/75 which exempt certain installations that burn waste, altogether from their field of application and which provide for extensive provisions on co-incineration—which is nothing else than the incineration of waste in production installations.[27]

In its policy on renewable sources of energy, the Commission went so far as to consider the incineration of municipal waste as a renewable source of energy.[28] The Council and Parliament were more restricted; they declared "biomass" a source of renewable energies which they defined as follows[29]:

> "the biodegradable fraction of products, waste and residues from biological origin of agriculture (including vegetal and animal substance), forestry and related industries including fisheries and aquaculture as well as the biodegradable fraction of industrial and municipal waste."

---

production and the hazardous properties of waste; considers that efforts made in this respect need to be increased, inter alia, by improving the environmental dimension of technical standards, by reducing the presence of dangerous substances where less dangerous alternatives are available … ."

23 See also para.6–03, above.

24 See paras 6–01ss, above.

25 See para.10–04, above. See also Council Res., February 24, 1997 (fn.7, above), which is, to say the least, ambiguous: "[The Council] recognises, as regards recovery operations, that the choice of option in any particular case must have regard to environmental and economic effects, but considers that at present, and until scientific and technological progress is made and life-cycle analyses are further developed, reuse and material recovery should be considered preferable where and insofar as they are the best environmental option."

26 Dir.75/442 (fn.12, above), art.3(1)(b)(i) and (ii); Dir.94/62 on packaging and packaging waste [1994] OJ L365/10; Dir.2008/98 (fn.12, above), art.4: "The following waste hierarchy shall apply as a priority order in waste prevention and management legislation and policy: … c) recycling d) other recovery, e.g. energy recovery".

27 Dir.2000/76 on the incineration of waste [2000] OJ L332/91; Dir.2010/75 on industrial emissions [2010] OJ L334/17.

28 [2001] OJ C153/81.

29 Dir.2009/28 on the promotion of the use of energy from renewable sources [2009] OJ L140/1, art.2(e); it is to be noted that Dir.2010/75 (fn.27, above), art.2 no.31, did not include waste of animal origin in the definition of "biomass".

As, however, the notion of "biodegradable" is nowhere defined in EU law and as there is not either any obligation to separate biodegradable from non-biodegradable fractions of waste, one might well imagine, how precise this definition is in practice and how easy it is to incinerate industrial waste under this formula. Generally, agricultural policy is interested in seeing agricultural waste—called "biomass"—recognised as a renewable source of energy, allowing the granting of tax relief or State aid for the generation of biofuels and at the same time see the considerable quantities of agricultural waste reduced by incineration. Furthermore, EU research policy has a tendency to promote high-technology and large-scale projects such as the incineration of (hazardous) waste rather than the small-scale technology of separation, sorting, material recycling or composting of waste. A similar tendency can be observed, finally, in the context of regional policy: the Cohesion Fund has as its aim mainly to finance big projects, which gives an advantage to incineration installations with regard to recycling projects.[30]

[3] EU responsibilities and Member States' responsibilities. A consistent EU waste management policy has also not been developed, because it is not clear to what extent waste management strategies, policies and measures are to be established at EU or at national level. Member States generally prefer to keep responsibility for management options, including questions on investments into cleaner technologies, clean-up and others, at national level, also, because the waste management infrastructure—waste collection and treatment, recycling and recovery installations, the transporting of waste, etc.—is set up and monitored by them, not by the European Union.

10–07

The Court of Justice decided, in 1992, that waste materials are, in the EU terminology, products, though of a specific nature, to which art.34 TFEU applied.[31] This judgment ended a long controversy as to whether waste issues came under the provisions of the free circulation of goods, the freedom to provide services or whether they were not covered by the EU Treaties at all. However, the discussion continued at all levels as to what extent the specific nature of waste justified a limitation of the provisions of art.34 et seq. TFEU, in other words, to what extent Member States were entitled to set national standards for waste. While EU waste legislation between 1975 and 1987 was based on arts 115 and 352 TFEU,[32] the Commission, since 1987, based all its proposals for waste legislation on art.115 TFEU. Only when the Court of Justice declared, in 1993, that Directive 91/156, which amended Directive 75/442 on waste, was rightly based on art.192 TFEU,[33] did this Treaty provision prevail and did the Commission recur to that article. Subsequently, most waste measures were based

---

[30] Reg.1164/94 establishing a Cohesion Fund [1994] OJ L130/1 art.10: "Projects ... shall be of a sufficient scale to have a significant impact in the field of environmental protection ... In any event, the total cost of projects or groups of projects may in principle not be less than ECU 10 million." As the new Reg.1084/2006 on the Cohesion Fund [2006] OJ L210/79, no longer provides for a financing of individual projects by the Cohesion Fund, this provision was not inserted into Reg.1084/2006.
[31] Case C–2/90 *Commission v Belgium* [1992] E.C.R. I–4431: "waste has a special characteristic. The accumulation of waste, even before it becomes a health hazard, constitutes a threat to the environment, because of the limited capacity of each region or locality for receiving it."
[32] An exception was Dir.85/339 on liquid beverage containers [1985] OJ L176/18, which was adopted on the basis of art.352 TFEU alone.
[33] *Commission v Council* (C–155/91) [1993] E.C.R. I–939.

on that provision, except two product-related waste Directives.[34] It is obvious, though, that art.192 TFEU leaves Member States greater discretion for national measures, since art.114 TFEU primarily aims at establishing the internal market which requires uniform rules, while art.192 TFEU primarily aims at protecting the environment; under art.114, national measures are systematically controlled and eventually "authorised", if they comply with the conditions laid down in that article, while art.192 does not contain conditions, etc. This leads, in practice, to measures which are adopted on the basis of art.192 TFEU at a relatively low common denominator, since Member States that wish to see higher provisions adopted can easily be referred to the provision of art.193 TFEU.

10–08   To give some examples of political divergence within the European Union: a number of local authorities has set up installations for the incineration or the landfill of waste; this leads to a clear interest to see the waste which was generated at local level also treated or landfilled in these installations, in order to use the available capacities.[35]

The preference for material recycling over incineration with energy recovery, which was laid down in the EU strategy, was also discussed in Germany and the United Kingdom, but was, in these two Member States, finally not laid down in the relevant political and legal documents. Scandinavian Member States, the Netherlands, France and others, strongly promote the incineration of at least municipal waste.[36] The general scarcity of sites for landfills favours waste incineration, unless a very active waste prevention, reuse and recycling policy is pursued; this again presupposes a product policy, which predominantly comes into the realm of EU policy.[37] Other uncertain aspects concerning the question, whether waste management measures are to be taken at EU or at national level involve radioactive waste, the shipment of waste to third countries, the clean-up of contaminated land and old landfills, provisions on liability and monitoring measures.

2.   Waste installations

Siting

10–09   There are no EU provisions on the siting of waste treatment or disposal installations. The directive on the incineration of waste[38] is silent on the question of siting; the proposal for a directive on the landfill of waste stipulated that landfills had to be placed at a distance from residential areas, waterways, water bodies, etc. of 0.5km in the case of municipal landfills and 2km from residential areas in the case of hazardous landfills.[39] The Directive, adopted in 1999, deleted

---

[34] Dir.91/157 on batteries [1991] OJ L78/38; Dir.91/157 was replaced, in 2006, by Dir.2006/66 on batteries and accumulators and waste batteries and waste accumulators [2006] OJ L266/1. This Dir. was based on arts 114 and 192 TFEU. Dir.94/62 (fn.26, above).

[35] This was the underlying situation in Court of Justice, *Dusseldorp* (C–203/96) [1998] E.C.R. I–4075.

[36] See, next to the Dutch situation which was described in case C–203/96 (fn.35, above) the German situation, underlying *Daimler-Chrysler* (C–324/99) [2001] E.C.R. I–9897.

[37] See on the EU product policy para.6–01, above.

[38] Dir.2010/75 (fn.27, above).

[39] [1997] OJ C156/19, annex I, para.1(1.1.a).

any precise minimum distance requirement and limited itself to general considerations, which had to indicate that the landfill does not pose a serious environmental risk.[40] Finally, no specific provisions exist for the siting of installations for radioactive waste.

EU restrictions for the siting of a waste installation flow from arts 4(4) of   **10–10** Directive 2009/147[41] and 6(2) of Directive 92/43,[42] where such installations could constitute a significant disturbance of the habitats or of the species protected in them. Furthermore, a site may—at least de facto—not be chosen where the operation of the installation would, despite precautionary measures that are eventually taken, lead to a breach of the requirements of art.13 of Directive 2008/98.[43] In extreme cases, the siting of an installation may injure human rights,[44] which the EU institutions and national courts must also safeguard.

Before they are authorised, hazardous waste disposal installations must be the subject of an environmental impact assessment; the same requirement applies to incineration installations for the recovery or the disposal of non-hazardous waste that have a capacity of more than 100 tonnes per day.[45] For other waste installations, Member States must either examine case by case whether an environmental impact is necessary, or fix thresholds beyond which such an assessment is necessary.[46]

The choice of a type of waste installation

The choice of the waste installation—landfill, composting plant, recycling plant,   **10–11** incineration plant with or without energy recovery—is at the complete discretion of Member States. It is true that art.3 of Directive 2008/98 provides for a waste "hierarchy".[47] However, this hierarchy is, legally speaking, a recommendation ("encourage"); indeed, para.2 of art.3 asks Member States to consider, when deciding on a measure, the economic viability and several other aspects. The provision, seen in its general context, does not appear to oblige, for example, the

---

[40] Dir.1999/31 on landfills [1999] OJ 182/1, annex I, para.1(1.1.a).

[41] Dir.2009/147 on the conservation of wild birds [2010] OJ L286/36.

[42] Dir.92/43 on the conservation of natural habitats and of wild fauna and flora [1992] OJ L206/7.

[43] Dir.2008/98 (fn.12, above), art.13: "Member States shall take the necessary measures to ensure that waste management is carried out without endangering human health, without harming the environment and, in particular: (a) without risk to water, air, soil and plants and animals; (b) without causing a nuisance through noise or odours; and (c) without adversely affecting the countryside or places of special interest."

[44] See European Court on Human Rights, *Lopez Ostra v Spain*, judgment of December 9, 1994 (41/1993/436/515), where an installation was established at a distance of 12 metres from a private home.

[45] Dir.85/337 on environmental impact assessment [1985] OJ L175/40, as amended by Dir.97/11 [1997] OJ L73/5; see on that Court of Justice, *Commission v Italy* (C–486/04) [2006] E.C.R. I–11025.

[46] As regards Dir.85/337, see also para.4–29, above.

[47] Dir.2008/98 (fn.12, above), art.4: "1. The following waste hierarchy shall apply as a priority order in waste prevention and managment legislation and policy: (a) prevention (b) preparing for re-use (c) recycling (d) other recovery, e.g. energy recovery; and (e) disposal. 2. When applying the waste hierarchy referred to in paragraph 1, Member States shall take measures to encourage the options that deliver the best overall outcome. This may require specific waste streams departing from the hierarchy, where this is justified by life-cycle thinking on the overall impacts of the generation and management of such waste... Member States shall take into account the general environment protection principles of precaution and sustainability, technical feasibility and economic viability, protection of resources as well as the overall environment, human health, economic and social impacts, in accordance with Articles 1 and 13".

United Kingdom, to abandon its landfills—where about 80 per cent of all waste is presently disposed of—and turn to recovery, recycling or waste prevention measures. This is a policy orientation, but it is unthinkable to bring the United Kingdom to the Court of Justice, for not respecting its obligations out of Directive 2008/98, art.4. Indeed, endless legal disputes could take place on the question whether a Member State really has done enough as regards waste prevention. If waste prevention were a legal obligation, the Commission would be obliged, under art.17 TEU, to take legal action against Member States which did not do enough for waste prevention; the same would apply where a Member State favoured landfills over incineration of waste. In reality, such an action has never been taken or even considered by the Commission.

Permits

10–12   The permitting of waste treatment and disposal plants is, in general, subject to provisions of national legislations. For some[48] installations, Directive 96/61 on integrated prevention and pollution control and its recent replacing directive 2010/75[49] were applicable since 1999; the Directives required the permit to provide for the use of the best available technique and the setting of specific conditions and, in particular, emission limit values for pollutants.[50]

While there are no specific provisions on facilities for the treatment, and in particular the incineration, of nuclear waste, specific requirements apply to (non-nuclear) waste incineration installations, which are laid down in Directives 2000/76 and 2010/75.[51] The Directives set emission limits for certain heavy metals and other pollutants, including emissions of dioxins and furans.[52] They also provided for detailed conditions on the operation of the incinerators, such as minimum temperature of the burner and measures for cases of operation disturbance.

10–13   These two Directives replaced earlier Directives on the incineration of municipal waste, because from the point of view of the environment it was considered to be irrelevant whether the dangerous emissions stem from one or the other type of incinerator.

Directives 2000/76 and 2010/75 do not apply to animal waste. Animal waste is regulated under Regulation 1774/2002,[53] as specific provisions had become necessary when the "mad cow disease" broke out in the 1990s.[54] The Regulation,

---

[48] Essentially, installations for the recovery or disposal of hazardous waste with a capacity exceeding 10 tonnes per day, municipal waste incinerators with a capacity of more than 3 tonnes per hour, installations for disposal of non-hazardous waste (biological and chemical process) with a capacity of more than 50 tonnes per day, landfills with a capacity of more than 25,000 tonnes or receiving more than 10 tonnes per day.

[49] Dir.96/61 [1996] OJ L257/26. In 2008, this Dir. was replaced by Dir.2008/1 [2008] OJ L24/8, and in 2010, its provisions were incorporated into Dir.2010/75 (fn.27,above). See also para.4–40, above.

[50] Directive 96/61 became applicable to existing installations from 2007 onwards. See also para.4–45, above.

[51] Dir.2000/76 and Dir.2010/75(fn.27, above).

[52] See in more detail above, para.8–35 et seq.

[53] Reg.1774/2002 laying down health rules concerning animal by-products not intended for human consumption [2002] OJ L273/1.

[54] Until then, Directive 90/667 was applicable, concerning the laying down the veterinary rules for the disposal of animal waste, for its placing on the market and for the prevention of pathogens in feedstuffs of animal or fish origin [1990] OJ L363/51.

based on the public health provision of art.168 TFEU, laid down detailed provisions on the conditions under which animals and material that come under Regulation 1774/2002, may be incinerated. Incinerators have to either comply with the requirements of Directive 2000/76 or be approved separately. The operating temperature of the incinerator must now at least be 850°C (art.12 and Annex IV), while the earlier legislation of 1990 had only provided for incineration at a temperature of 133°C.

Installations that use waste as regular or additional fuel (waste co-incineration plants)—at present, in particular, power plants, cement kilns and steel plants—are regulated by the provisions of Directives 2008/1 and 2010/75 on incinerators (arts 42ss). Where the main purpose of an installation is the thermal treatment of waste, the specific provisions of Directive 2010/75 apply which differentiate between incineration and co-incineration plants.

Landfills

As regards landfills, the Commission submitted a proposal for a Directive in 1991.[55] In 1996, the European Parliament rejected the Council's common position on the proposal[56] with the argument that it contained too many derogations. The Commission then submitted a new proposal which the Council adopted in 1999.[57] The Directive had the same field of application as the framework Directive 2006/12 which codified Directive 75/442, and the new Directive 2008/98; thus, it also applies to radioactive waste landfills, for which at present no specific EU provisions exist.[58]   **10–14**

The Directive applied to all authorised or non-authorised landfills that are in operation; where existing landfills did not comply with its requirements, they had to be adapted by 2009 at the latest or had to be closed. In principle, any storage of waste on land or into land—thus also under ground—is considered a landfill. However, temporary storage prior to disposal operations that does not exceed one year, or three years prior to treatment operations, is excluded from the definition of landfill. The Directive introduced three classes of landfills: for hazardous waste, for non-hazardous waste and for inert waste. It laid down detailed provisions for the permitting of landfills and the conditions accompanying a permit, and in particular for water control and leachate management, the protection of soil and water, gas control, stability and barriers to free access. Criteria and procedures for the acceptance of waste at landfills were laid down in 2002.[59]

Decommissioning of installations

There are no specific EU provisions on the decommissioning of waste installations or, indeed, other industrial installations such as, for instance, nuclear power plants. The demolition of buildings, structures or installations leads to the generation of (movable) waste, for which the general provisions apply. Where   **10–15**

---

[55] [1991] OJ C190/1.
[56] [1996] OJ C59/1.
[57] Dir.1999/31 on the landfill of waste (fn.40, above).
[58] See para.10–45, below.
[59] Dec.2003/33 [2003] OJ L11/27.

such installations contain asbestos, art.7 of Directive 87/217[60] applies, which provides that the release of asbestos fibres does not cause "significant asbestos pollution"—whatever that means. For the rest, the general provision of art.13 of Directive 2008/98[61] also applies to decommissioning of installations.

The decommissioning of offshore oil platforms was the subject of a decision under the OSPAR Convention, taken in 1998,[62] which provided for a prohibition of putting such installations into the sea or maintaining them there after use; the decision allowed contracting parties to grant, under certain conditions, a derogation. The Commission proposed that the European Union approve this decision.[63] However, the proposal was not discussed in detail by the Council and has become obsolete in the meantime.

There are no EU-wide rules on the decommissioning of nuclear installations. The Commission estimated the costs for decommissioning of about 15 per cent of the investment cost for the installation.[64]

Contaminated land

10–16   The Directive on landfills does not deal with issues of contaminated land, such as closed landfills, unauthorised discharges, abandoned military or industrial sites and so on. No EU inventory of such contaminated land sites exists, but some Member States set up national inventories. Thus, in Germany, the number of suspected contaminated sites registered is about 190,000; this figure does not include military sites and sites for the production of armaments. The total number is thought to be well over 240,000. Austria has a list of 2,584, Finland of 10,400 contaminated sites. In the United Kingdom, estimates go from 50,000 to 100,000,[65] while France sometimes quotes a figure of about 1,000 contaminated sites.[66] Based on Member States' data and estimations, the European Environment Agency estimated the number of contaminated sites in twenty-five Member States to be of "more than two million sites".[67] In its waste strategy review of 1996, the Commission expressed the opinion that the identification and rehabilitation of contaminated sites was primarily the task of Member States.[68] No official work is done at EU level concerning the identification of sites, classification, prioritisation and so on. However, in the context of its research policy, the Commission set up, in 1996, a "Concerted action on risk assessment for contaminated sites" (CARACAS) and two other similar networks, NICOLE (1996) and CLARINET (1998).

[60] Dir.87/217 on the prevention and reduction of environmental pollution by asbestos [1987] OJ L85/40.
[61] See Dir.2008/98, art.13 (fn.43, above).
[62] OSPAR Decision 98/3 on the disposal of disused offshore installations [1998] OJ C158/11. As regards OSPAR in general, see para.7–38, above.
[63] [1999] OJ C158/10.
[64] Commission, Nuclear Safety in the European Union, COM (2002) 605, p.3.
[65] National Westminster Bank, Contaminated land: counting the cost of our past (London, 1992), p.3.
[66] See, for instance, Le Monde, April 7, 1998, p.10: "Le gouvernement relance l'inventaire des sites pollués ... la France compte officiellement 896 lieux contaminés. En réalité, il en existe 200,000 à 300,000, de nature et d'impact différents."
[67] European Environment Agency, The European environment. State and outlook 2005 (Copenhagen, 2005) p.171.
[68] Commission, COM(96) 399 (fn.16 above), para.56.

In its proposal for a directive establishing a framework for the protection of soil of 2006, the Commission suggested the elaboration of an EU inventory of contaminated sites[69] and estimated that about 3.5 million sites in the European Union were potentially contaminated. The proposal was rejected by a blocking minority in Council; it is unclear, if and when it will be adopted.

Port reception facilities

In 2000, the European Union adopted a Directive on port reception facilities for ship-generated waste and cargo residues[70]; the Directive was based on art.100(2) TFEU and became operational at the end of 2002. EU Member States were required to ensure that there are facilities in ports for the reception of waste from ships; for that purpose, each port was obliged to establish a waste reception and management plan. All ships that use a port of a Member State shall deliver all ship-generated waste to a port reception facility. In order to avoid the waste being discharged into the sea, the Directive provided that ships have to pay a fee for the port reception facilities, "irrespective of actual use of the facilities" (art.8). This might start competition among the ports as to the amount of the fee. By 2005, the Commission should have reported on the national fee systems and their impact and proposed appropriate amendments, but has not yet done so. There were no specifications set for the reception facilities. However, Member States have to update the waste management plan for each individual port at regular intervals.

10–17

3.   Waste materials

Framework provisions

Reliable and up-to-date figures on the quantity of waste generated within the European Union are rarely available. Data on the basis of Regulation 2150/2002 on waste statistics[71] have not yet been published. The latest available data concern the year 2006, occasionally the year 2008 (in both cases for EU-27).[72] According to these data, the European Union had generated, in 2004, 2,913,252,000, in 2006 2,953,087,000 tonnes of waste. 88,731,000 tonnes were hazardous waste, the rest (about 2.8 billion) non-hazardous waste. The municipal waste generation per capita and year was in 2001 522 kg, in 2008 524 kg, with different trends in the Member States (Belgium 2001: 471kg, 2008, 493kg; Denmark 2001 658kg, 2008, 802kg; Germany 2001 633kg, 2008 581kg; France 2001 528kg, 2008 543kg; Hungary 2001 451kg, 2008 453kg; Netherlands 2001 615kg, 2008 622kg; Sweden 2001 422kg, 2008 515kg; Poland 2001 290kg, 2008 320kg; United Kingdom 2001 592kg, 2008 565kg). Disposed—landfilled or incinerated without energy recovery—were in 2001 278kg/capita, in 2008 207kg, a slow, but steady diminution (Denmark 2001 47kg, 2008 35kg, Germany 2001

10–18

---

[69] Commission, COM(2006) 232.
[70] Dir.2000/59 on port reception facilities for ship-generated waste and cargo residues [2000] OJ L332/81.
[71] Reg.2150/2002 (fn.20, above).
[72] Data from Eurostat, *http:// epp.eurostat.ec.europa.eu.Eurostat* [Accessed July 2011]. Tables, Graphs, and Maps Interface (TGM) (visit of March 7, 2011).

160kg, 2008 3kg; Hungary 2001 375kg, 2008 333kg; Netherlands 2001 50kg, 2008 7kg; Sweden 2001 99kg, 2008 15kg; United Kingdom 2001 474kg, 2008 309kg).

As regards radioactive waste, the Commission generally differentiates between low-, medium- and high-level waste.[73] About 160,000 tonnes of radioactive waste were thought, in 1994, to be produced annually within the European Union (EU-12), 90 per cent of it low or medium level.[74] Considerable quantities of radioactive waste, including all high-level waste, are placed in what is called "interim storage", sometimes for years or decades, as no final landfill site for high-level waste has as yet been decided upon within the European Union.

10–19 The basic legal instrument for waste materials is Directive 2008/98, which constituted a fundamental review of Directive 75/442, its review in 1991, and its codification in 2006. Directive 2009/98 is the framework for waste legislation at EU level.[75] The Directive defined waste, established a hierarchy for waste management (prevention—recovery—safe disposal) and basic requirements for all waste management activities, introduced a licensing requirement for all persons who are active in waste treatment, disposal and management operations, and requested that Member States draw up waste management and waste prevention plans and regularly report on its transposition and implementation.

10–20 The Directive, which was based on art.192 TFEU, did not aim any more, as its predecessor, to the alignment of waste management policies and provisions within the European Union. Member States were keen to maintain their different national approaches to waste management, whether these were successful or less successful.

Waste management policy within the European Union—at EU level and within Member States—was and is still heavily influenced by the attempts, in particular from economic operators, to deregulate waste policy and submit waste production, treatment, trade and disposal to a minimum of rules only. This goes in part hand in hand with efforts from administrations, not to introduce an EU-wide waste management system, but to leave it to Member States—or regions or local authorities—to decide to what extent they want to allow wastes being traded, treated and disposed of. These policy and/or interest-driven concepts appear mainly in the discussions on the definition of waste on the one hand, on the treatment of waste, the export-import restrictions, and the shipment of waste on the other hand.[76]

10–21 In 1975, an EU definition on waste had been established.[77] However, this definition referred back to the different national law of Member States and was therefore considered not to be precise enough. Thus, in 1991, and in conformity with parallel definitions within the OECD and the Basel Convention on the Transboundary Shipment of Hazardous Waste to which the European Union adhered,[78] it was replaced by a new definition in Directive 75/442 which declared

---

[73] Low, medium and high refer to the concentration of radio-nucleides in the radioactive waste and hence to the intensity of the emitted radiation.

[74] Commission, COM (94) 66.

[75] Dir.2008/98 on waste [2008] OJ L312/3.

[76] See, for this last point, para.10–36 et seq., below.

[77] Dir.75/442 (fn.12, above), art.1 (a): "'waste' means any substance or object which the holder disposes of or is required to dispose of pursuant to the provisions of national law in force".

[78] Dec.93/98 [1993] OJ L39/1.

waste any substance or object in the categories set out in an Annex I which the holder discards or intends or is required to discard.[79] Directive 2008/98 maintained that definition, but deleted the reference to Annex I: "Waste shall mean any substance or object which the holder discards or intends or is required to discard."[80]

As already Directive 2006/12 was structured as a framework Directive, its definition was subsequently used in numerous other EU waste legislation.[81] Directive 2006/12, art.1 had requested the Commission to draw up "a list of wastes belonging to the categories listed in annex I". This list had been established in 1994.[82] In 2000, it was completely revised and merged with the EU list on hazardous waste which had been drawn up under Directive 91/689.[83] Article 7 of Directive 2008/98 referred to that list, though it conceded large discretion to Member States, such as the possibility to consider some hazardous wastes as non hazardous, or to consider that materials which were on that list, were in fact not waste. At present, the list contains some 650 entries.

The field of application of Directive 2008/98 is very broad, though there are **10–22** the following exclusions foreseen[84]:

- gaseous effluents emitted into the atmosphere"; such emissions are excluded, obviously for the reason that air pollution provisions would apply;
- land (in situ), including unexcavated contaminated soil and buildings permanently connected with land[85];
- uncontaminated soil and other material excavated in the course of construction activities;
- radioactive waste[86];
- decommissioned explosives[87];
- faecal matter and non-hazardous agricultural or forestry materials used in farming, forestry or the production of energy through non dangerous processes.

The large exclusion of agricultural and forestry waste can only be explained by successful lobbying from those sectors. In particular, it is not clear, why faecal

---

[79] Dir.2006/12 (fn.12, above), art.1(a). Annex I contained a list of 16 categories of materials which were to be considered waste. The last category referred to "any materials, substances or products which are not contained in the above categories". This meant that the categories did not define "waste" but referred back to the general definition.

[80] Dir.2008/98 (fn.75, above), art.3 no.1.

[81] See, e.g. Dir.91/689 on hazardous waste [1991] OJ L377/20; Reg.259/93 on the shipment of waste [1993] OJ L30/1; Dir.94/62 on packaging and packaging waste (fn.26, above) etc.

[82] Commission Dec.94/3 [1994] OJ L5/15.

[83] Commission Dec.2000/532 [2000] OJ L226/3.

[84] See for details Dir.2008/98 (fn.75, above), art.2.

[85] With this exclusion, a judgment by the Court of Justice, *Van de Walle* (C–1/03) [2004] E.C.R. I–7613, was reversed which had declared that the definition of waste also included unexcavated contaminated soil, as well as parts of buildings that were connected with land.

[86] There is no EU legislation on radioactive waste in general; a proposal for a directive is under discussion, see para.10–29, below. The main difference to general waste legislation is at present that nuclear waste which is recoverable or recyclable is not classified as "waste", but as "product".

[87] Why decommissioned explosives are excluded from the scope of the Directive, is not clear. No explanation is offered in the Recitals.

matter should not be considered "waste". Should they be seen as products? As with nuclear waste, the exclusion is not rational, but the outcome of the EU bargaining process.

Furthermore, some waste materials are excluded "to the extent that they are covered by other Community legislation".[88] This wording solved a problem of the previous Directive 2006/12, where the word "Community" was lacking. The Court of Justice had then decided that "other legislation" could also apply to national legislation.[89] The new wording makes this interpretation impossible.

10–23   It is obvious that the definition of waste is a legal creation and therefore exposed to criticism; as does any definition, it contains an arbitrary element. Whether a corporal object is called a good, product, substance, residue, pollutant, discharge (of pollutants), emission or waste, is a question of legal agreement. From the point of view of environmental protection, the name which is given to a specific object is not very relevant; what matters is the contamination or pollution which that object causes or risks causing.

The criticisms against the—unanimously agreed—definition of waste stem in particular from concepts that look at the difference between product and waste from an economic perspective: under this concept, "waste" should not be applied to objects that have an economic value and could thus may be recycled or recovered; to such materials, product legislation should apply in full. It is no surprise that such concepts are in particular defended by economic vested interest groups. The main weakness of this concept is that every object has an economic value somewhere in the world.[90] If one were following this argument, there would be no waste from precious metals, from steel, copper, iron, etc. as all these materials have an economic value and can be recycled or reused. The contradiction goes even further, as the incineration of material is generally, and rightly so, considered to be a recovery operation, where the energetic part of the material is used, for heating purposes, to generate energy etc. As such incineration with energy recovery gives economic advantages—the use of ordinary fuel is not necessary—all materials that burn and generate heat[91] would have to be considered "products" and not "wastes".

It is not to be examined, whether such a definition of "waste" could be viable. It is, in any case, not that of EU legislation, and in particular not that of Directive 2008/98. Legally, there can be no doubt that the EU concept of waste also includes recoverable or recyclable waste. The enumeration of recovery operations in Annex II to Directive 2008/98 on waste—not on products!—would not make sense, if waste that is destined for a recovery operation was not covered by that Directive.

Germany had adopted, in 1986, legislation that declared in essence that recoverable items were not waste but secondary raw materials. It was only after the Court of Justice stated, nine years later, that this provision was incompatible

---

[88]   See for details Dir.2008/98 (fn.75, above), art.2(2).

[89]   Court of Justice, *Avesta Polarit Chrome Oy* (C–114/01) [2003] E.C.R. I–8725; see also the very critical comment L. Krämer, *Environmental Liability* (2003), 231.

[90]   The notion "economic value" cannot be limited to national frontiers, as economic questions per se are independent of administrative-political considerations and notions: international trade may take place in objects which have no value for one person, but a high value for another one. For example, in South Asia even parts of plastic bags are collected from landfills and sold.

[91]   Technically, the generation of heat is feasible with a calorific value of 5,000–6,000kjoule.

with EU law,[92] that Germany changed its legislation; the Court expressly found that the definition of waste under Directive 91/156[93]—which corresponds to the present definition of Directive 2008/98—would not allow to exclude recoverable waste from the waste definition. A similar provision to the German one was then, in 1996, introduced by Italy, which led to the same verdict by the Court of Justice.[94] Despite that, Italian legislative efforts to exempt certain materials from the application of waste legislation continue.[95]

Since this way of proceeding is not really promising, discussions subsequently concentrated on the concept of "discard" which is not defined in EU law. All products become waste, which normally occurs at the end of their useful lifetime. This question has nothing to do with the economic value that the item eventually still has: where a new television set is, after two months' use, thrown away or dumped on the street, it is discarded, even if somebody passes by, takes the television and uses it for several years. Horse manure might be an excellent fertilizer for the garden: it remains true that where it is left on the road, it constitutes—a real production residue—waste.

10–24

Since recovery (recycling) is considered a waste management activity, it is logical that an item can be discarded, even where it is collected or transported with a view to being recycled or recovered. This is, *de lege lata* and *de lege ferenda*, heavily argued about, in particular where residues of production are at stake.[96] Admittedly, the borderline between residues of production, which the European Union considers waste, and the generation of two products, is not always easy to make. Thus, where steel is cut to make the body of a car, gold is worked on to make a golden ring or wood is cut, the residues—steel scrap, gold dust and wood chips—are discarded and thus constitute waste. Where chemical substances are processed to produce two chemical preparations, one of these cannot be considered the residue of the other; normally, thus, they are both products. As with all borderline cases, the final decision is to be made on a case-by-case basis.

In the end, the Court of Justice will be the final arbiter, and has started, in a number of judgments, to be so.[97] It does not seem to have found the right balance in all cases. Thus, in case C–416/02 it stated that pig manure which can be brought out on farmland, was not waste, but a product.[98] This contradicts the Court's earlier judgments according to which a subsequent use of a material cannot be decisive for the question, whether it has to be classified as product or as waste. And, transferred to industrial production, it means that production residues which *can* be used in production, would constitute products.

---

[92] *Commission v Germany* (C–422/92) [1995] E.C.R. I–1097.

[93] Dir.91/156 (fn.12, above).

[94] *Tombesi* (C–304/94) [1997] E.C.R. I–3561.

[95] See, e.g. the facts of *Niselli* (C–457/02) [2004] E.C.R. I–10853; *Commission v Italy* (C–103/02) [2004] E.C.R. I–9127.

[96] A good example is the Resolution on (steel) scrap, adopted by the Consultative Committee of CECA on October 10, 1997 [1997] OJ C356/8.

[97] *Vessoso and Zanetti* (Joined Cases C–206 and 207/88) [1990] E.C.R. I–1461; *Zanetti* [1990] (C–359/88) E.C.R. I–1509; *Commission v Germany* (C–422/92) (fn.95, above); *Tombesi* (C–304/94) (fn.97, above); *Inter-Environnement Wallonie* (C–129/96) [1997] E.C.R. I–7411; *Beside* (C–192/96) [1998] E.C.R. I–4029; *Dusseldorp* (C– 203/96) (fn.35, above).

[98] Court of Justice, *Vera pig farm* (C–416/02) [2005] E.C.R. I–7369.

10–25   Directive 2008/98 tried to answer these questions politically, by introducing the concept of "by-product" into EU waste legislation. The new art.5(1) reads as follows:

> "A substance or object, resulting from a production process, the primary aim of which is not the production of that item, may be regarded as not being waste referred to in point 19 of Article 3 but as being a by-product, if the following conditions are met: a) further use of that substance or object is certain b) the substance or object can be used directly without any further processing other than normal industrial practice c) the substance or object is produced as an integral part of the production process; and d) further use is lawful, i.e. the substance or the object fulfils all relevant product, environment and health protection requirements for the respective use and will not lead to overall adverse environmental or human health impacts."

Decisions on whether these conditions are fulfilled, will be taken by the comitology procedure at EU level (art.5(2)).

In my opinion, this provision will lead to the consequence that precious metal residues, metal residues in general, and numerous other production residues will, in time, not be considered waste any more, but by-products to which product legislation applies. The "normal industrial practice" which is not further specified, will lead to more pressure from economic operators to have production residues excluded from waste legislation. The notion of "overall adverse impacts" is not really a limitation to the decision-making under this provision. And the political side-effect is, that the amount of waste will decrease.

10–26   Directive 2008/98 introduced another way of limiting the application of waste law. Article 6(1) of that Directive reads:

> "Certain specific waste shall cease to be waste… when it has undergone a recovery, including recycling, operation and complies with specific criteria to be developed in accordance with the following conditions: a) the substance or object is commonly used for specific purposes; b) a market or demand exists for such substance or object; c) the substance or object fulfils the technical requirement for the specific purposes and meets the existing legislation and standards applicable to products; and d) the use of the substance or object will not lead to overall adverse environmental or human health exposure."

Decisions under this provision are again taken by comitology procedure at EU level. However, in the absence of such decisions, Member States may take decisions at national level; they then have to notify the Commission and other Member States under Directive 98/34[99] of their draft decision.

To give a concrete example: there is a CEN-standard which classifies used paper under some sixty different categories, according to its contamination, humidity, quality, and other aspects. Where used paper is sorted into such categories, it may, under this new art.6, be classified as "product", while it was, until now, classified as waste. The differentiation is relevant in particular as regards the shipment—shipment of products which is largely unregulated, or shipment of waste where strict provisions apply—and the export of such materials. Until now, a material was classified as waste, until the recycling or recovery process had been finished—thus, for example, the sorted used paper had been transformed into new paper, so that the transport of used paper was a transport of waste. This situation may now be changed under art.6.

10–27   Directive 2008/98 introduced the concept of extended producer responsibility (art.8) and repeated the polluter-pays principle (art.14). The concept of extended

---

[99] Dir.98/34 [1998] OJ L204/37.

producer responsibility, originally developed by Scandinavian countries, is based on the understanding that the responsibility of the producer does not end with the manufacturing of the product. When the product is on the market, he has labelling, information guarantee, eventually warning and take-back obligations. And when his product ends its useful life-time and becomes waste, he has responsibilities as to the collection and treatment of this waste, since he also had the profit from it. With this reasoning, producers and their associations (including importers) can be made responsible for organising and financing take-back systems, collect waste from consumers and users and ensure that such waste is properly recycled, recovered and/or disposed of.

EU law already provided for such concepts in Directives 2000/53 on end-of-life vehicles[100] and 2002/96 on waste from electrical and electronic products.[101] Directive 2008/98 only gave a framework to the concept, and left it to Member States, to what extent they want to recur to this concept.

As regards the polluter-pays principle, the Directive, repeating the previously applicable EU law, imposed the application of this principle in national waste legislation. This has far-reaching consequences for national legislation. Thus, the Court of Justice had held that a petroleum company could be held liable for damage caused by petrol that had spread into the environment following a ship accident, though the company had excluded all such liability by way of contracts with the shipowner.[102] In another case, the Court held that municipalities in the Member States were not entitled to charge the cost for collecting waste according to the size of the ground from which the waste was taken; rather, the actual quantities of waste which were collected, had to form the basis of charging the cost.[103]

The main instrument of the Directive is the waste management plan which Member States shall have to establish and regularly update (art.28). The Directive gave a number of indications as to the content of such plans. The plans shall have to be sent to the Commission which does not have, though, any obligation to assess, compare or otherwise evaluate the plans. This is consistent with past experience. Indeed, Member States were, since 1977, obliged to elaborate and monitor waste management plans and to inform the Commission thereof. However, never has the Commission made any evaluation of those plans, drawn attention to omissions, inconsistencies or failures. Directive 2008/98 now "invites" the European Environment Agency to annually review progress in the completion and implementation of the national waste management plans (art.30(2)). This is an elegant way of complying with art.17 TEU and ensuring that EU law is applied by Member States!

---

[100] Dir.2000/53 on end-of life vehicles [2000] OJ L269/34.
[101] Dir.2002/96 on waste electrical and electronic equipment (WEEE) [2003] OJ L37/24.
[102] Court of Justice, *Commune de Mesquer* (C–188/07) [2008] E.C.R. I–4501.
[103] Court of Justice, *Futura* (C–254/08), judgment of July 16, 2009.

Hazardous waste

10–28   Council Directive 78/319 on toxic and dangerous waste[104] was substituted, in 1991, by Directive 91/689.[105] This Directive defined hazardous waste, introduced a licensing requirement for installations which process hazardous waste, and requested management plans for hazardous waste to be drawn up and regular information on installations which handled hazardous waste. Member States had to report regularly on the implementation of the Directive. Directive 2008/98 repealed this Directive and incorporated provisions on hazardous waste into its own provisions.

As with the notion of "waste", difficulties appeared as regards the concept of "dangerous waste". The Directive of 1978 gave a definition of dangerous waste[106] that was soon considered to be too vague. For that reason, it was replaced, in Directive 91/689,[107] by a "listing approach": hazardous was a waste which was listed in an EU positive list.[108] Directive 2008/98 changed this approach again and considered waste as "hazardous" "which display one or more of the hazardous properties listed in Annex III" (art.3 no.2). This Annex lists in general terms fifteen hazard categories.[109] As regards the precise decision, whether one of the hazard categories applies to a specific waste, the test methods and possible limit values, the Annex to Directive 2008/98 referred to two EU Directives on chemical substances and preparations,[110] without considering that these Directives had, at the time of application, already been replaced by Regulation 1907/2006.[111] In order to reach a somehow uniform understanding of what constitutes hazardous waste, art.7 of Directive 2008/98 determined that the "list of waste shall be binding as regards determination of the waste which is to be considered to be hazardous waste".[112] Member States may, though, consider a non-hazardous waste as hazardous, or a hazardous waste as non-hazardous; in both cases, they have to inform the Commission, so that the waste list may be

---

[104] Dir.78/319 on toxic and dangerous waste [1978] OJ L84/43.

[105] Dir.91/689 on hazardous waste [1991] OJ L377/20.

[106] Dir.78/319 on toxic and dangerous waste (fn.104, above), art.1(b): "'toxic and dangerous waste' means any waste containing or contaminated by the substances or materials listed in the Annex to this Directive of such a nature, in such quantities or in such concentrations as to constitute a risk to health or the environment".

[107] Dir.91/689 on hazardous waste (fn.105, above); the word "hazardous" was presumably preferred to "dangerous", because the Basel Convention on the shipment of waste used this terminology; in substance, there is no difference between "hazardous" and "dangerous".

[108] Dir.91/689 on hazardous waste, art.1(4): "... 'hazardous waste' means: wastes featuring on a list drawn up ... on the basis of Annexes I and II to this Directive ... These wastes must have one or more of the properties listed in Annex III. The list shall take into account the origin and composition of the waste and, where necessary, limit values of concentration ...; any other waste which is considered by a Member State to display any of the properties listed in Annex III. Such cases shall be notified to the Commission and reviewed ... with a view to adaptation of the list."

[109] See, for example: "H 7: Carcinogenic: substances and preparations which, if they are inhaled or ingested, or if they penetrate the skin, may induce cancer or increase its incidence"; "H8: Corrosive: substances and preparations which may destroy living tissue on contact", "H14: Ecotoxic: waste which presents or may present immediate or delayed risk for one or more sectors of the environment".

[110] Dir.67/548 [1967] OJ 196/1; Dir.1999/45 [1999] OJ L200/1. It had already been mentioned in Ch.6 that Dir.67/548 only provided for test methods on the effect of chemical substances on humans and the aquatic environment, but not on other parts of the environment, such as plants and animals.

[111] Reg.1907/2006 [2006] OJ L396/1.

[112] As to the waste list, see Dec.2000/532 (fn.83, above).

updated.[113] They may also "consider waste as non-hazardous waste in accordance with the list of waste referred to in paragraph 1 (of Article 7)".[114] Normally thus, the principle has been maintained that a waste is hazardous, when it is marked as hazardous in the EU list on waste.

The main problems linked to the EU definition of hazardous waste are that   **10–29** Member States use, in their national legislation, different terminology, such as "special waste", "chemical waste", "specially controlled waste", and so on. These different definitions made it possible to establish national waste lists that are different from the EU list. To complicate things further, the Basel Convention on the shipment of hazardous waste and the OECD have established hazardous waste lists, which are different from the EU list, a legal situation that generates difficulties, inconsistencies, grey markets and illegal practices.

Directive 2008/98 only contained few provisions on hazardous waste. The general provision of art.13 that waste shall be treated without harming human health or the environment, also applied to hazardous waste. Article 18 stated that hazardous waste shall not be mixed with other hazardous or non-hazardous waste or materials and may not either be diluted. However, this provision does not apply to operators which have a licence, where the mixing or dilution corresponds to the best available technique or where the provisions of art.13 are respected[115]; furthermore, the provision does not apply to hazardous household waste.

In 2010, the Commission proposed, for the first time, a directive on "nuclear safety of spent fuel and radioactive waste",[116] based on arts 31 and 32 Euratom Treaty. The proposal is at present being discussed by the institutions. "Spent fuel" is considered either to be a usable resource or—when no further use is foreseen, as radioactive waste (art.2.10). This definition means that recoverable radioactive waste is not considered to be waste but to be a product.

The proposal aims at protection workers and the general public (art.1); the environment, fauna and flora are not mentioned. The directive shall not apply to authorised discharges (art.3), which means that discharges of radioactive waste into waters would neither fall under Directive 2008/98 nor under the future directive on radioactive waste. In substance, the proposal essentially requests Member States to draw up and monitor management programmes for radioactive waste; it does not contain a fraction of the details which are laid down in Directive 1999/31 on landfills; and no word is spent on whether radioactive waste may be disposed on ordinary or hazardous waste-landfills. Member States shall draw up a safety plan for radioactive waste, but all the details which are laid down for accident prevention in Directive 96/82, were omitted.

The proposal does not contain any quality requirement as to the treatment or disposal of such waste. In recital 30, the proposal states that national policy "should respect the relevant fundamental safety principles set by the International Agency for Nuclear Energy". However, these principles are not laid down as such

---

[113] See Court of Justice, *Commission v Austria* (C–194/01) [2004] E.C.R. I–4579, where the Court stated that Member States were not obliged to transpose the waste lists word by word into their national legal system. The consequence of that judgment is that the notions of waste and of hazardous waste will continue to vary from one Member State to the other. While thus between Stockholm and Madrid, everybody has the same notion of what is a car, there are differences with regard to waste.

[114] See for details Dir.2008/98 (fn.75, above), art.7.

[115] See the wording of art.13 (fn.43, above).

[116] Commission, COM(2010) 618.

in the proposal. Article 4 provides that by the management for spent fuels and radioactive waste "no undue burdens are imposed on future generations", without specifying, how this could be organised.

Waste prevention

10–30   Directive 2008/98 fixed as the first priority for waste legislation and waste management the prevention of waste generation (art.4). The aim was "breaking the link between economic growth and the environmental impacts associated with the generation of waste" (art.29). It obliged Member States to set up waste prevention programmes (art.29) and offered, in Annex IV, a list of 16 measures that could form part of such programmes. The programmes shall be regularly updated.

A closer look at the measures which were favoured by Annex IV shows their vague and general character of mainly promotional character.[117] Nowhere were Member States obliged to take binding measures to reduce waste generation. The basic error of the Directive's provisions on waste prevention was, that it does not recognise that in order to prevent waste generation, there must be a product policy, because before a material becomes waste, it was a product. However, there is a basic decision by the European Union not to pursue an integrated product policy, and to limit itself, in the context of its product policy, to non-binding measures. However, such non-binding measures will not reduce the generation of waste. The Commission does not either consider to developing a tax on waste generating products (packaging, PVC, etc.) and is not in any way concerned about waste generation in private households (food, appliances, chemicals, etc.).

The result of the past policy is that waste quantities have constantly risen in the European Union, hand in hand with economic growth. No significant change of this evolution is visible and it must be expected that Directive 2008/98 will not change the trends. The waste quantities might be reduced, though, because of the abovementioned changes on "by-products" and on end-of waste decisions.

Waste recovery

10–31   Waste recovery includes re-use, material recycling and incineration with energy recovery. Directive 2008/98 defined re-use as "an operation by which products or components that are not waste are used again for the same purpose for which they were conceived".[118] However, a material may also be re-used, where it had been discarded: a piece of furniture has been placed on the roadside to be taken away by the waste collection services—its taking up by a person and its continued use constitutes a recovery operation. However, where an object is re-used without having been discarded—a friend, visiting a home, discovers a pair of shoes in a corner which are disused, takes them and wears them—the object has never

---

[117] See for example: Annex IV, no.1: "The use of planning measures, or other economic instruments promoting the effective use of resources"; no.4: "the promotion of eco-design"; no.9: "the use of voluntary agreements, consumer/producer panels or sectoral negotiations, in order that the relevant businesses or industry sectors set their own waste prevention plans or objectives or correct wasteful products or packaging"; no.13: "the promotion of creditable eco-labels".
[118] Dir.2008/98 (fn.75, above), art.3 no.10.

become waste; so no waste recovery operation is involved. The repair of a dress, or the re-use of packaging, such as empty bottles, normally comes into the second category, so the classification of reusable packaging as products by Directive 94/62[119] is correct.[120]

Under the Sixth Environment Action Programme, the EC announced a thematic strategy for the recycling of waste which was presented at the end of 2005.[121] The Commission suggested to create a "European Recycling Society", but has not proposed concrete measures.

Directive 2009/98 enumerated in Annex II a non-exhaustive list of recovery operations. It suggested practical measures to be taken by Member States, in order to promote re-use, recycling and recovery. Where "technically, environmentally and economically practicable, waste should be collected separately" (art.10)—which was not more than a recommendation.

With regard to paper, metal, glass and plastic from households and equivalent waste streams, the Directive prescribed separate collection by 2015; a recycling target of 50 per cent by weight shall be reached. For non-hazardous construction and demolition waste, the recycling target, to be reached by 2020, is 70 per cent (art.11). Details for the calculation methods shall be elaborated by the Commission. This approach will most likely lead to the abandoning of separate collection and recovery targets for packaging waste under Directive 94/62, as it does not make sense to provide, for example, for targets for paper from packaging waste and from other origins.

In the past, the greatest discussions were provoked by the classification as recovery operation the "use principally as a fuel or other means to generate energy". Indeed, several Member States had, in their national legislation, established calorific values below which a waste could not be considered to come under this process. While it might be necessary to specify under which circumstances a waste principally serves as a fuel, it was clearly not legal to set these conditions at national level.

10–32

In a judgment of 2003, the Court of Justice clearly rejected, under Directive 2006/12, the possibility to use the calorific value of waste as a criterion for differentiating between recovery (recycling) and disposal operations.[122] the Court also clarified that the shipment of municipal waste to a waste incinerator could not *normally*—whatever that means—be regarded as a shipment for recovery, even if the incinerator uses the energy from the incineration in part or in full.[123] The Court was of the opinion that in such a case, the waste was not substituting a fuel; rather, the objective of the incineration was the thermal treatment of waste, and not the making of products or the production of energy. These judgments played a considerable part in the discussion on the review of the waste Directive (see para.10–27, above), as there were strong forces which would like to see waste incinerators which burn waste and use the energy to be classified as recovery installations; this would facilitate waste shipments and increase the profitableness of such incinerators. Environmental groups, in contrast, pleaded

---

[119] See Dir.94/62 on packaging and packaging waste (fn.26, above), art.1(5)–(9) where a reusable packaging is not considered to be waste.

[120] See for the notion of re-use also Court of Justice, *Oliehandel* (C–307/00 to 311/00) [2003] E.C.R. I–1821.

[121] Commission, Thematic Strategy on the prevention and recycling of waste, COM(2005) 666.

[122] Court of Justice, *Commission v Germany* (C–228/00) [2003] E.C.R. I–1439.

[123] Court of Justice, *Commission v Luxembourg* (C–458/00) [2003] E.C.R. I–1553.

for a classification as disposal installations, as they prefer composting, recycling and reuse of materials. Directive 2008/98 now introduced a complicated formula in Annex IV, according to which an incinerator which incinerates municipal waste shall be considered a recovery installation when it reaches a certain energy efficiency value.[124]

To date the European Union has not fixed provisions on the quality of recycling: where 10kg of materials out of 1,000 tonnes of waste are extracted and recycled, it is obviously not possible to consider the whole process—shipment, storage, extraction—a recycling operation. EU specifications are urgently required. The formula of Annex IV only applies to waste incineration, not to material recycling operations.

10–33   Since Directive 2008/98 was based on art.192 TFEU, Member States are entitled, under art.193 to identify recovery operations other than those listed in Annex II. They are then obliged to notify the Commission. This leads to a decision by way of a committee procedure under Directive 2008/98 to adapt Annex II to the new situation (art.38).

Disposal of waste

10–34   Directive 2008/98 limited itself to the statement that waste should be disposed of without harming human health or the environment; at the same time, it prohibited the abandonment or dumping of waste (art.36). It also contained in Annex I a list of operations that are classified as disposal operations.[125] The legal status of this list is the same as the list in Annex II for recovery operations, so the reader can be referred to the remarks above, para.10–30. The specific disposal operations are not frequently contested. Germany considered the placing of waste into old mines and other underground cavities as recovery operations, since this disposal would prevent the cavities from caving in.[126] This interpretation contradicted several operations in Annex IIA of Directive 75/442.[127] When the Court of Justice established some conditions under which underground storage of waste could be considered to be a recovery operation,[128] Germany introduced legislation to better delimitate underground disposal and recovery operations.

10–35   At present, EU law contains only a few limitations on the landfill of waste. Directive 1999/31 on landfills[129] banned the landfilling of liquid waste, explosive, corrosive, oxidising, flammable waste, infectious hospital waste and of whole and shredded used tyres; furthermore, the landfilling of biodegradable municipal waste will have to be considerably reduced. Apart from that, Directive 2008/98 prohibited the uncontrolled management of waste. Thus, there is no ban

---

[124] See also the further considerations for interpreting the formula in Annex IV, laid down in art.38 of Directive 2008/98.

[125] It should be noted that Dir.75/442 originally also included recovery and recycling operations in the word "disposal". The differentiation between the two notions was introduced into EU law by Dir.91/156 in 1991.

[126] Between 1994 and 2001, between 1.5 and 2 million tons of waste were placed in old mines in Germany.

[127] Dir.75/442 (fn.12, above), annex IIA, D1: "Tipping above or underground (e.g. landfill, etc.)"; D3: "Deep injection (e.g. injection of pumpable discards into wells, salt domes or naturally occurring repositories, etc.)"; D12: "Permanent storage (e.g. emplacement of containers in a mine, etc.)".

[128] Court of Justice, *Abfall Service Austria* (C–6/00) [2002] E.C.R. I–1961.

[129] Dir.1999/31 (fn.40, above).

on, for instance, shipping the waste into the outer space, burying BSE-infected cattle, or providing for seabed insertions of waste. There are also no restrictions in EU law as regards the incineration of waste; thus, it is unclear why Annex I states that incineration of waste at sea is prohibited under EU law. No such provision exists; only the incineration without a permit is prohibited.

Shipment of waste

Directive 78/319[130] had laid down some general requirements on the shipment of waste. Subsequent to discussions which took place within the framework of the OECD and which also concerned the shipment of waste between the United States and the European Union, the Commission proposed, in the early 1980s, an EU directive on the shipment of waste.[131] This proposal, for the first time, introduced into waste law a differentiation between shipments in the European Union that crossed the frontier of a Member State and other shipments, a clear departure from the concept of the single EU market and of the common transport policy, as laid down in art.3(f), 70 and 94 EC Treaty in its version applicable at that time. The Council adopted the proposal in 1984,[132] and it was then, in 1986, amended in order to cover the shipment of hazardous waste to third countries, too.[133]

    Directive 84/631 introduced a system of prior informed consent for shipments of hazardous waste: the holder of waste had to notify the competent authority of the Member State where he wanted to ship the waste, and to use a standardised consignment note in which he had to specify details of the waste, its destination and details of the shipment. The authority had to acknowledge receipt of the notification before the shipment could be effected. The same procedure was to apply to shipments to third countries, where agreement was necessary from that third country; in such a case, the authority of the Member State of dispatch had, amongst other things, to examine whether the final destination of the waste possessed "adequate technical capacity for the disposal of the waste in question under conditions presenting no danger to human health or the environment"[134]—a provision which would have allowed broad assessments of waste management in third countries but which remained, of course, largely a dead letter.

    The adoption of the 1989 Basel Convention on shipments of hazardous waste[135] followed a number of serious incidents concerning illegal shipments from industrialised to developing countries; this Convention and OECD measures on waste shipments adopted in reaction to that Convention led the European Union completely to review its provisions and to adopt, in 1993, a Regulation

10–36

10–37

---

[130] Dir.78/319 [1978] OJ L84/43.

[131] [1983] OJ C53/3.

[132] Dir.84/631 on the supervision and control within the European Community of the tranfrontier shipment of hazardous waste [1984] OJ L326/31; see also below regarding the question of environmental liability for damage caused by (the shipment of) waste.

[133] Dir.86/279 [1986] OJ L181/13.

[134] Dir.84/631 (fn.132, above) in its version amended by Dir.86/279 (fn.133, above), art.3(3).

[135] Basel Convention on the control of transboundary movements of hazardous wastes and their disposal, 1989; the EU adhered to the Convention by Dec.93/98 (fn.78, above).

that was based on art.192 TFEU and concerned all waste shipments.[136] An important amendment in 1997 largely stopped the export of hazardous waste to third countries. A major change of legislation took place in 2006, when Reg.1013/2006 was adopted.[137]

Waste shipments to and from third countries

10–38   The first distinction to be made is between hazardous and non-hazardous waste. This distinction does not follow the lines of Directive 2008/98 and the lists on waste and on hazardous waste that had been adopted at EU level.[138] Rather, due to historical reasons, the Council, decided to largely follow a listing system which had been developed by the OECD. Therefore the question, whether a waste is hazardous or not, is decided by the lists in the annexes to Regulation 1013/2006 (see art.36 of that Regulation). In this way, EU law in practice has a list of hazardous wastes[139] and another list for the shipment of hazardous waste though this is no longer called "hazardous waste list"; this is a model of non-transparency.

A second distinction is made by the Regulation between whether the shipment is made for disposal or for recovery purposes; for these, the definitions in Directive 2008/98 apply.[140]

10–39   Imports of waste for disposal of any kind into the European Union are prohibited, with the exception of imports from countries that are parties to the Basel Convention or where specific import agreements have been made either by the European Union or by Member States (art.41). The import of waste for recovery is prohibited, but such waste may be imported from countries which apply the OECD decision on waste shipment and from other countries with which specific agreements have been made.[141]

10–40   Export of waste to third countries for disposal purposes is prohibited (art.34). An exception is made for EFTA countries, which are also parties to the Basel Convention. Exports for recovery of wastes which are not hazardous—these are now listed in Annexes III and IIIA, though for the time being, these annexes are empty—are the subject of a complicated procedure (art.37). The Commission has to ask each third country, for all types of non-hazardous waste, whether it was ready to accept such waste, and, if yes, which kind of control procedure it wished to see applied. As there are more than 180 countries which had to be addressed, and with some of these countries not answering at all, giving incomplete answers or subsequently changing their position, the Council only decided in mid-1999 which waste can be shipped to what country and under what control conditions. These decisions continue to be applied, until new decisions are taken.

The delay was also due to the fact that the Commission had based its proposal on the trade provision of art.207 TFEU and had proposed that those third countries that had indicated that they did not wish to receive waste, should nevertheless be able to obtain such waste, though under the control procedure

---

[136] Reg.259/93 on the supervision and control of shipments within, into and out of the European Community [1993] OJ L30/1; amended (export ban) by Reg.120/97 [1997] OJ L22/14.

[137] Reg.1013/2006 on shipments of waste [2006] OJ L190/1.

[138] See paras 10–21 and 10–27, above.

[139] Dec.2000/532 (fn.83, above).

[140] See paras 10–23 et seq., above.

[141] See for details Reg.1013/2006 (fn.137, above), arts 43ss.

which applied to hazardous wastes; the Commission had argued that some of these countries "may not be fully aware of the significance of their decision for those parts of their industrial sector which can use 'green' list waste for transformation and further processing".[142] This approach is now laid down in art.37(2) of Regulation 1013/2006: where a third country does not answer a request, it has to be informed of the intended shipment which may then only go through, where a written agreement by the third country is given.

As regards exports of hazardous waste, all exports for disposal are prohibited, except to EFTA countries which are also party to the Basel Convention. Furthermore, the European Union decided in January 1997[143] that as of January 1, 1998 all shipments for recovery to third countries were also prohibited, with the exception of industrialised countries.[144] This measure was a follow-up to a decision of 1995 under the Basel Convention to ban the shipment of waste for recovery to non-industrialised third countries.[145]

As regards the waste that comes under this export ban, Regulation 1013/2006 established its own lists of wastes (Annex V). Even though, the management of these lists and their daily use are bound to create permanent problems for export controls, customs officers, etc.

Shipments between Member States

Non-hazardous wastes that are destined for recovery may freely circulate between Member States; their shipment need not be notified. Regulation 1013/2006 expressed this principle be referring to wastes which do not come under specific annexes. Regulation 1013/2006 allowed a Member State to take the necessary measures to prevent movement of wastes that were not in accordance with its waste management plans,[146] a provision that has until now not been used frequently.   **10–41**

Shipments of waste for disposal were subject to the principles of proximity and self-sufficiency, principles that, normally, only applied to waste disposal, not to waste recovery shipments. However, Directive 2008/98 added to this the recovery of municipal waste. This means in practice that municipalities could prohibit the shipment of municipal waste to other places, where they wanted to incinerate such waste themselves,[147] a provision which had been favoured in particular by Germany, as German municipalities have large over-capacities. Directive 2008/98 also allowed Member States to object to shipments for recovery which went to waste incinerators, "where it is established that such shipments would result in national waste having to be disposed of or waste

---

[142] Commission, COM (94) 678, para.11.

[143] Reg.120/97 (fn.136, above).

[144] Formally, the exception was made for countries which apply the OECD decision of March 30, 1993 on the shipment of waste for recovery.

[145] See Dec.97/640 adhering to this Basel Convention Decision [1997] OJ L272/45.

[146] Reg.1013/2006 (fn.137, p.352, above), art.12(1)(k).

[147] Dir.2008/98, art.16: "1. Member States shall ... establish an integrated and adequate network of waste disposal installations and of installations for the recovery of mixed municipal waste collected from private households ... 2. The network must be designed to enable the Community as a whole to become self-sufficient in waste disposal as well as in the recovery of waste referred to in paragraph 1, and the Member States to move towards that aim individually ... 3. The network shall enable waste to be disposed of or waste referred to in paragraph 1 to be recovered in one of the nearest appropriate installations".

having to be treated in a way that is not consistent with their waste management plan".[148] Member States may prohibit generally or partially or object systematically to waste shipments for disposal; furthermore, they may also object to individual shipments.[149]

10–42   Subject to the changes which Directive 2008/98 introduced, shipments of hazardous waste for recovery may not be objected to systematically. Rather, the grounds for objection are laid down in art.12 of Regulation 1013/2006 and may also not be extended by a Member State that invokes its right, under art.193 TFEU, to set more stringent requirements.[150] Again, the details of the intended shipment must be notified to the competent authorities, which may, in the case of dangerous waste, give tacit consent, but must agree in writing to the shipment of red list hazardous waste.

Overall, these provisions are rather sophisticated and bureaucratic; the number of possibilities for Member States to object to a shipment for recovery has even increased from five to 11 causes. The provisions must be understood as a reaction to several abuses of previous provisions, in particular those under Directive 84/631, but also reflect the will of Member States, *not* to have an internal EU market for shipments of waste, as well as of some Member States (Germany, Netherlands, Denmark) to allow local monopolies for municipal waste treatment. This is not quite understandable, as the bureaucratic provisions introduced by Regulation 1013/2006 are strict enough to prevent abuses.

Shipments within Member States

10–44   Shipments of waste within Member States are barely regulated at all. Regulation 1013/2006 stated in art.1(5) that only art.33 applies to such shipments. This provision only required Member States to set up a monitoring and control system which is coherent with EU law. There was no change with regard to the previous legislation.

Information on the implementation and practical application of the Regulation is vague; in particular, there is a lack of precise data on shipments between Member States and on exports and imports. A working group of IMPEL—see on this para.2–19, above—reported in 2005 that one out of two waste shipments in the European Union did not comply with the requirements of Regulation 259/93, the predecessor of 1013/2006. No details are known.

Shipment of radioactive waste

10–45   As mentioned, there is not yet general EU legislation on radioactive waste; a proposal for a directive is at present being discussed in the EU institutions.[151] Directive 2006/117 which replaced Directive 92/3, is based on arts 31 and 32 of the Euratom Treaty; it only dealt with the shipment of radioactive waste[152]; it was

---

[148] Dir.2008/98 (fn.75, above), art.16(1).
[149] Reg.1013/2006 (fn.137, above), art.4(3).
[150] See, however, also Court of Justice, *Dusseldorp* (C–203/96) (fn.63, above). The Court did not allow the Netherlands to recur to art.176 EC Treaty (now art.193 TFEU), because the objections which were allowed under Reg.259/93, were not applicable to the case.
[151] Commission, COM(2010) 618, above; see also para.10–29, above.
[152] Dir.2006/117 on the supervision and control of the shipments of radioactive waste and spent fuel [2006] OJ L337/1; Dir.92/3 [1992] OJ L35/24.

largely inspired by Directive 84/631 on the shipment of waste which had, however, been replaced in the meantime by Regulation 1013/2006. Consequently radioactive shipments are dealt with by way of a directive, whereas shipments of non-hazardous and hazardous waste are the subject of a regulation; normally, one would expect the more stringent form of the regulation to apply to materials which present the higher risk.

Radioactive waste is defined as "any material which contains or is contaminated by radio-nucleides and for which no use is foreseen", a definition which implies that recyclable or recoverable radioactive waste is—for shipment purposes—not waste. In that, the definition is not in line with that of Directive 2008/98.

Shipments between Member States require the agreement of the authorities of **10–46** the country of dispatch and of destination; normally, the absence of an answer within two months is considered to show tacit consent to the shipment. Exports of radioactive waste require the authorisation of the authorities of the dispatching country, which have to make contact with the country of destination. No export is allowed to countries of the Lomé Convention, to Antarctica and to countries that are not able properly to manage radioactive waste; the assessment is made by the authorities of the exporting Member State. The Directive does not contain any provision concerning the possibility of Member States adopting a partial or total ban on the import of nuclear waste, though some Member States have banned the import of nuclear waste unilaterally. The Commission proposed in 2010 that radioactive waste should be eliminated in the Member State in which it is generated, unless Member States had made an agreement of its disposal in the other Member State.[153]

Overall, Directive 92/3 is considerably less stringent than Regulation **10–47** 1013/2006. Also, conditions for authorising an export to third countries are less stringent than those for a shipment between Member States. Finally, an export ban of radioactive waste to other than OECD countries, as for hazardous waste, is not foreseen.

4.   Specific waste streams

The European Union has regulated a number of waste streams. The purpose of **10–48** the provisions is to promote waste recycling and recovery, safe disposal of waste and to ensure that different national provisions on waste management do not unnecessarily affect the integrated rules on the free circulation of goods.

Packaging

Packaging waste is thought to constitute up to 40 per cent of municipal waste. As **10–49** early as the first environmental action programme it was announced that packaging issues would be looked at more closely; however, the Commission's initiative met with considerable hostility from economic operators, which were of the opinion that the European Union would be better to abstain from this area. The Directive, which the European Union finally adopted in 1985, was based on

---

[153] Commission, COM(2010) 618, art.4.3.

art.352 TFEU and was limited to liquid beverage containers.[154] It asked Member States to set up programmes for reducing the volume of liquid beverage containers. These programmes could even be implemented by voluntary agreements, which showed the Directive's limited objective.

Implementation of this Directive had only very limited success.[155] A number of Member States had adopted national measures on regulating packaging; attempts to have these measures declared void by the Court of Justice failed.[156] Since Germany, having been urged to do so by the Commission, introduced far-reaching measures on packaging, the Commission proposed a general Directive on packaging waste, which was adopted in 1994.[157] The Directive, based on art.114 TFEU, tried to lay down uniform provisions on the free circulation of packaging as well as on the protection of the environment. It asked Member States to promote prevention, reuse and recycling of packaging, to set up collection systems for packaging waste, and established binding recovery and recycling targets for the different packaging materials.[158] Furthermore, the Directive asked for standards for packaging, limited the content of heavy metals, and requested Member States to draw up management plans for packaging and to report regularly on the implementation measures.

10–50   Most Member States were late in transposing the Directive. As the recycling and recovery targets were fixed relatively low, a number of Member States made use of the possibility under art.6(6) to get higher targets approved by the Commission. For the rest, the integration of the environmental and internal market requirements, only was partly successful: imprecise drafting[159] and a loose reference to standards,[160] which did not fulfil the commitments of the Directive, placed the responsibility of achieving the Directive's objective on reducing quantities and promoting reuse and recycling of packaging back on to Member States which were not too keen to venture the battle with the packaging industry and the retailers. While the Directive allowed (national) environmental

---

[154] Dir.85/339 on containers of liquids for human consumption (fn.32, above).

[155] In 1990, five Member States had not yet transposed the Directive: see Commission, 8th report on monitoring application of Community law (1990) [1991] OJ C338/1, p.160. The Court of Justice gave judgments in the following cases: *Commission v Luxembourg* (C–252/89) [1991] E.C.R. I–3973; *Commission v Spain* (C–192/90) [1991] E.C.R. I–5933; *Commission v France* (C–255/93) [1994] E.C.R. I–4949.

[156] *Commission v Denmark* (C–302/86) [1988] E.C.R. 4607, where a deposit and return system for packaging was attacked; and *Enichem v Cinisello Balsamo* (C–380/87) [1989] E.C.R. 2491, where tax measures on non-biodegradable plastic packaging were in question.

[157] Dir.94/62 on packaging and packaging waste [1994] OJ L365/10.

[158] Dir.94/62 art.6, provided that, by the year 2001, between 50 and 65 per cent of packaging waste had to be recovered and 25–45 per cent were recycled; the minimum percentage for each packaging material was 15 per cent. Less stringent requirements were fixed for Greece, Ireland and Portugal.

[159] See, e.g. art.5: "Member States may encourage reuse systems of packaging, which can be reused in an environmentally sound manner, in conformity with the Treaty"; the relationship to the recycling targets of art.6 is not clear. Another example is art.6 itself, which sets targets but does not establish measuring methods. Under certain conditions, Member States may even fix more stringent targets than those of art.6: see art.6(6) and Commission Dec.1998/3940, [1999] OJ L14/25.

[160] Under art.9, Member States shall admit only such packaging on their markets that comply with all essential requirements of annex II. Annex II provides that packaging shall be designed, produced and commercialised in a way as to minimise its environmental impact when it is disposed of. Furthermore, packaging shall be so manufactured that the presence of noxious substances is minimised with regard to their presence in emissions, ash or leachate when packaging is incinerated or landfilled. This might easily lead to national measures as regards metal cans, aerosols, non-biodegradable or PVC-containing packs, etc. with endless debates about whether such measures are permissible.

measures—for example to restrict the use of PVC packaging, impose returnable bottles, tax packaging and other measures—it does not impose them—this favoured divergency among Member States, not harmonisation.

In two cases which dealt with the German system on packaging, the Court recognised that Germany was entitled to introduce a mandatory system for deposit and return, in order to promote the use of returnable bottles.[161] The Court only disagreed with the short notice which was given, when the system was introduced and also was of the opinion that mineral water which was covered by Directive 80/777 could not be requested to be bottled in returnable bottles; indeed, such water had to be filled at source, in order to avoid fraud, and the introduction of a deposit and return system would have constitute too heavy a burden for this industry.

The target dates for recovery and recycling under art.6 applied until 2001. Targets for the period 2001–2006 were fixed by an amendment to Directive 94/62 in 2004[162] and extended to 2008. Once more, the targets were fixed at a relatively low level. No further amendment of the targets of Directive 94/62 was decided since 2008. This can only be explained by the fact that Directive 2008/98 now introduced recycling targets for paper, metal, plastic and glass[163]; in other words, recycling targets for packaging materials do no longer exist, and Member States will all have to change their collection systems for packaging waste and adopt systems for materials in general. No legal objection could be raised against this more general approach—if it were not that of producer responsibility. Indeed, until now, packaging producers and importers paid for the collection and recovery of packaging waste. They will not pay for the collection of other than packaging materials, and controversies may be expected who shall bear the cost of the system for the separate collection of materials, which the correct percentage of packaging is, whether the collection shall be made by municipalities or by private business, who should bear the eventual economic loss or take the possible economic benefits, etc.

Batteries

A second Directive, based on art.114 TFEU, regulated batteries and accumula-   10–51
tors.[164] The Directive limited the content of some heavy metals—mercury, cadmium and lead—in some batteries. These batteries also had to carry a mark—a crossed-out dustbin[165]—indicating that they should not be thrown out with ordinary household waste; Member States had to organise a separate collection system for the batteries under the Directive. After an amendment of 1998, the use of batteries that contain mercury was almost completely forbidden.[166]

As the Directive only referred to some batteries, Member States had difficulties in getting it off the ground, to elaborate plans and to set up effective

---

[161] Court of Justice, *Radlberg* (C–309/02) [2004] E.C.R. I–11763; *Commission v Germany* (C–463/01) [2004] E.C.R. I–11705.
[162] Dir.2004/12 [2004] OJ L47/26.
[163] See para.10–31, above.
[164] Dir.91/157 on batteries and accumulators containing certain dangerous substances [1991] OJ L78/38.
[165] Introduced by Dir.93/86 [1993] OJ L264/51.
[166] Dir.98/101 [1999] OJ L1/1.

collection systems.[167] A revision was made in 2006, when Directive 2006/66 was adopted and Directive 91/157 repealed.[168]

The new Directive declared that its primary objective was to minimise the negative impact of batteries on the environment, but that it also wanted to ensure the smooth functioning of the internal market. Therefore, it was based on art.192(1) TFEU and, in relation to arts 4 (prohibition to place certain batteries and accumulators on the market), 6 (batteries which comply with the requirements of the Directive, may circulate freely) and 21 (labelling requirements) on art.114 TFEU. It applied to all batteries, except to batteries for security and military purposes and batteries that are sent into space (art.2). Batteries with more than 0.0005 per cent of mercury by weight and portable batteries with more than 0.002 per cent of cadmium may not be placed on the market; an exception applied to button cells with a mercury content up to 2 per cent by weight.

Member States had to set up appropriate collection schemes for portable batteries, but could request producers to do so. Producers and persons acting on their behalf have to bear the costs of the collection schemes (art.16). Such systems may not charge end-users. Article 10 fixed binding collection targets for batteries—25 per cent by 2012 and 45 per cent by 2016—though an export outside the collection Member State or even outside the European Union was allowed and counts for the target, "if there is sound evidence that the recycling operation took place under conditions equivalent to requirements of this Directive" (art.15). The disposal of batteries in landfills and the incineration of industrial batteries was prohibited (art.14).

Used oils

10–52   Directive 75/439, the very first environmental directive,[169] which was based on arts 115 and 352 TFEU, provided for the safe collection, treatment, storage and disposal of waste oils. Member States had to give priority to the recycling (regeneration) of waste oils, "where technical, economic and organisational constraints so allow". The discharge of waste oils into waters and drainage systems was prohibited. Activities concerning the collection, treatment and disposal of waste were to be licensed. Waste oils may not contain more than 50 parts per million of PCB/PCT.

Member States all transposed the Directive into national law, though sometimes with a considerable delay.[170] Its application only had limited success:

---

[167] *Commission v Italy* (C–303/95) [1996] E.C.R. I–3859; *Commission v Belgium* (C–218–222/86) [1996] E.C.R. I–6817; *Commission v France* (C–282 and 283/96) [1997] E.C.R. I–2929; *Commission v Germany* (C–236/96) [1997] E.C.R. I–6397; *Commission v Spain* (C–298/97) [1998] E.C.R. I–3801; *Commission v Belgium* (C–347/97) [1999] E.C.R. I–309; *Commission v France* (C–178/98) [1999] E.C.R. I–4853; *Commission v Greece* (C–215/98) [1999] E.C.R. I–4913; *Commission v Italy* (C–143/02) judgment of April 14, 2004.

[168] Dir.2006/66 on batteries and accumulators and waste batteries and accumulators [2006] OJ L266/1.

[169] Dir.75/439 on the disposal of waste oils [1975] OJ L194/23.

[170] See *Commission v Italy* (C–21/79) [1980] E.C.R. 1; *Commission v Italy* (C–30–34/81) [1981] E.C.R. 3379; *Commission v Belgium* (C–70/81) [1982] E.C.R. 175; *Inter-Huile* (C–172/82) [1983] E.C.R. 555; *Rhone Alpes Huiles* (C–295/82) [1984] E.C.R. 575; *Commission v France* (C–173/83) [1985] E.C.R. 491; *Procureur de la République v Assoc. de Défense de Bruleurs de Huiles Usagées* (C–240/83) [1985] E.C.R. 531; *Commission v Belgium* (C–162/89) [1990] E.C.R. 2391; *Commission v Italy* (C–366/89) [1993] E.C.R. I–4201; *Vanacker and Lesage* (C–37/92) [1993] E.C.R. I–4947.

the recycling clause did not fulfil expectation; most waste oils were incinerated; recycling remained a subordinate activity.

A Court judgment of 1999[171] clarified that Member States were obliged to give to the regeneration of used oils priority over incineration. As a consequence, the Commission introduced procedures under art.258 TFEU against all Member States except Italy and France. However, this only increased Member States' objections which had even introduced reduced tax rates for using waste oils as fuels. In particular, the cement industry was keen to use waste oils as fuels. In view of that, the Commission, basing itself on contested studies, announced that the preference of material recycling was not cost-effective. Despite protests, it proposed, when presenting the proposal to review Directive 2006/12, to repeal Directive 75/439 which was successful: Directive 2008/98 repealed Directive 75/439.[172]

PCB/PCT

Directive 76/403[173] contained provisions to control the disposal of PCB/PCT. As these provisions were considered to be not sufficiently protective, the Directive was replaced, in 1996 and after eight years of negotiations, by Directive 96/59,[174] which provided for the decontamination and disposal of all products containing PCB/PCT. This equipment must be inventoried, labelled and reported. Member States were obliged to set up, by September 1999, disposal plans and ensure that PCB/PCT was removed from the environment by 2010 at the latest. Nothing is known, to what extent this deadline has been complied with, as the Commission did not monitor the disposal plans.

10–53

Sewage sludge

Directive 86/278, based on arts 115 and 352 TFEU, deals with the use of sewage sludge in agriculture.[175] The Directive fixed maximum limit values for concentrations of heavy metals in the sludge and in soil and defines conditions for the use of sewage sludge. Sludge and the soil on which it is used must be regularly analysed in order to make sure that the heavy metal concentrations are not exceeded. Member States were expressly allowed to set more stringent requirements. Presumably in view of that, the values fixed by the Directive were not too severe. Several Member States adopted more stringent requirements at a national level.[176] The use of sewage sludge in agriculture has met increasing objections from farmers and the food industry, who are afraid of food contamination. For instance, the spreading of sludge in land in Tyrol (Austria)

10–54

---

[171] Court of Justice, *Commission v Germany* (C–102/97) [1999] E.C.R. I–5051. Germany was found to have breached EU law, because it had not given priority to the recycling of used oils. Later on, similar judgments were given in *Commission v Sweden* (C–201/03) judgment of March 30, 2004; *Commission v United Kingdom* (C–424/02) judgment of July 15, 2004; *Commission v Portugal* (C–92/03) [2005] E.C.R. I–867; *Commission v Austria* (C–531/03) [2005] E.C.R. I–837.

[172] See Dir.2008/98 (fn.75, above), art.41.

[173] Dir.76/403 on the disposal of PCB/PCT [1976] OJ L108/41.

[174] Dir.96/59 on the disposal of PCB/PCT [1996] OJ L243/31.

[175] Dir.86/278 on the protection of the environment, and in particular of the soil, when sewage sludge is used in agriculture [1986] OJ L181/6.

[176] See also Court of Justice, *Commission v Belgium* (C–260/93) [1994] E.C.R. I–1611.

was expressly forbidden by regional legislation of March 2002. In my opinion, such a ban is allowed under art.12 of the Directive and art.193 TFEU. The free circulation of sludge—arts 34–36 TFEU—cannot be invoked, as the trade in sludge is not prohibited and no discrimination of non-Austrian producers or traders is visible. It cannot either be seen that such a ban would have to be considered disproportionate, as it must be left to each Member state to decide how far it wants to go in the preventive protection of its soil—which is a non-renewable source.

A review of Directive 86/278, required under the Sixth Environmental Action Programme,[177] and favoured by most Member States, has not yet been proposed.

Animal waste

10–55   Directive 90/667 laid down hygienic provisions for the disposal and processing of animal waste.[178] The Directive was an early EU reaction to BSE ("mad cow disease"); it introduced "high-risk" and "low-risk" animal waste and stated that high-risk waste had to be adequately incinerated or buried in order to prevent environmental impairment. The Directive was mainly targeted at ensuring disposal of BSE waste without causing problems for humans or the environment.

After the full outbreak of the mad-cow disease and some other EU-wide scandals linked to animal feed and animal waste, Directive 90/667 was replaced by Regulation 1774/2002 which was based on art.168 TFEU.[179] The Regulation avoided almost entirely the word "waste", though many of the material regulated would come under the definition of "waste" of Directive 2008/98; the Regulation preferred the word "animal by-product".[180] The material was divided into three categories:

- category 1 was mainly high-risk material which was suspected or proven to be infected with diseases communicable to humans or animals;
- category 2 included material which did not belong to the other two categories, and which appeared to present a certain risk; and
- category 3 concerned material which did not present risks.

Material from categories 1 and 2 may only be shipped to another Member State with the agreement of the latter (art.8). Reasons for refusing such an agreement had not be given and were not laid down in the Regulation. The disposal of category 1 material was differentiated according to the risk that was linked to it; some parts could only be incinerated, other parts could also be landfilled or processed. Similar, but less strict conditions applied to material from category 2, whereas for material from category 3, art.13 of Directive 2008/98 applied; this meant that it must be treated or disposed of without risk for humans or the environment.

---

[177] Dec.1600/2002 [2002] OJ L242/1, art.8(2.iv).
[178] Dir.90/667 (fn.54, above).
[179] Reg.1774/2002 (fn.53, above).
[180] Reg.1774/2002 (fn.53, above), art.1(a): "animal by-products: entire bodies or parts of animals or products of animal origin referred to in Arts 4, 5 and 6, not intended for human consumption, including ova, embryos and semen".

The Regulation further contained relatively summary provisions on the approval of intermediary plants, storage plants, processing, oleochemical, biogas and composting plants and in particular rather detailed provisions for EU controls in Member States, inspections, on-the-spot checks, and audits. Its relationship to Directive 2008/98 is not quite clear. Though in theory, the scope of application of both texts is clearly defined, in practice, the Commission hardly deals with questions of animal waste under Directive 2008/98, but considers that all animal waste is excluded from the provisions of Directive 2008/98.

End-of-life vehicles

A Directive of 2000 deals with end-of-life vehicles[181] of which about 8 million per year are generated within the European Union. The Directive was based on art.192 TFEU and became effective in April 2002. It contained a number of provisions to prevent waste generation from cars, by imposing restrictions on the manufacturing of new cars. Cars which were marketed after July 2003 were not allowed to contain lead, cadmium, mercury or hexavalent chromium (art.4); a derogation clause in Annex II which was regularly updated, allowed some exceptions. With the much more industry-friendly approach by the Barroso-Commission, this clause was used, after 2003, to largely cut back the original limitations and to accommodate car manufacturers with numerous more exceptions—though the purpose of the clause was originally to further reduce the number of exceptions.

10–56

Furthermore, the Directive contained recovery and recycling targets for cars which will have to be gradually reached by 2015.[182]

Member States had to establish take-back schemes for end-of-life vehicles which had to allow the last user to give back the car without having to pay costs (art.5(4)). A car could only be deregistered—in particular with the fiscal authorities—where its user presented a certificate of dismantling which was remitted to the user by one of the dismantling bodies. These provisions tried to establish the principle of producer responsibility which make the producer also responsible for his products once they reached the end of their service life and become waste.

Waste electrical and electronic equipment

Directive 2002/96 on waste electrical and electronic equipment (WEEE) followed in its structure the model of Directive 2000/53.[183] It was based on art.192 TFEU and became operational in 2004. The Directive contained a positive list of the categories of equipment which was covered.[184]

10–57

WEEE is to be collected separately; since the end of 2006, a rate of separate collection of at least 4kg on average per inhabitant and per year was to be reached. Collection facilities had to be set up which enable final holders and

---

[181] Dir.2000/53 on end-of-life vehicles [2000] OJ L269/34.

[182] Re-use and recovery of 95 per cent of the car weight, reuse and recycling of at least 85 per cent.

[183] Dir.2002/96 Waste electrical and electronic equipment [2003] OJ L37/24.

[184] Large and small household appliances, IT and telecommunications equipment, consumer equipment, lighting equipment, electrical and electronic tools, toys, leisure and sports equipment, medical devices, monitoring and control instruments and automatic dispensers.

distributors to return WEEE free of cost. Normally, distributors which supply new equipment shall be obliged to take back the old equipment free of charge from private users or owners. Collected WEEE shall be brought to authorised treatment facilities.

Collected WEEE shall be treated, recycled or recovered, according to best available techniques. The Directive fixed detailed recycling and recovery targets, differentiated according to the categories of WEEE—recycling 50–80 per cent, recovery 70–80 per cent (art.7). The collection, treatment, recovery and disposal from private households of material that was put on the market before August 2005—historical waste—was at the charge of producers. After that date, each producer was responsible for financing these operations of the equipment that he put on the market. For that purpose, the producer shall provide a financial guarantee. For WEEE from other than private households similar provisions and differentiations applied. In view of the highly controversial discussion on the financing of the collection, take-back and return systems, the European Parliament, Council and Commission adopted a joint declaration in which they indicated their readiness to clarify any uncertainties as quickly as possible.[185]

In order to inform consumers and users, electrical and electronic equipment had to be marked with a crossed-out wheeled bin.[186] The Directive contained a considerable number of other information obligations for producers and distributors, as well as reporting obligations for Member States and the Commission. As the Directive covered new ground, adaptation of its provisions by Parliament and Council was foreseen, in particular as regards the quantified targets.

The Directive did not contain provisions on the ban of hazardous substances in electrical and electronic equipment. In difference to Directive 2000/53 on end-of-life vehicles which included such provisions, the Council and the European Parliament accepted the Commission's proposal that such restrictions should be enshrined in a separate directive which was adopted at the same time as the WEEE Directive.[187] The reason for this procedure was that this separation allowed Directive 2002/95 to be based on art.114 TFEU. As a consequence, no Member State was allowed to maintain or introduce further bans or restrictions of dangerous substances in electrical and electronic equipment than those laid down in Directive 2002/95, except under the very strict conditions of art.114(4) and (5) TFEU. As with Directive 2000/53, the exception clause in Directive 2002/95 for certain uses of heavy metals was used, since 2004, to considerably increase the number of exceptions.

Member States had some difficulties to set up the collection systems, dismantling and recycling systems at local and regional level, as this required a close co-operation with industry, for which both sides were not always well prepared.

---

[185] [2003] OJ L37/39.
[186] See para.6–62, above; that symbol is also used for batteries which must be collected separately, see para.10–51, above.
[187] Dir.2002/95 [2003] OJ L37/19.

Mining waste

In 2006, the European Union adopted Directive 2006/21 on mining waste.[188] This   **10–58**
Directive was a consequence of the accidents of Aznalcollar in Spain and Baia
Mare in Romania. When investigating these accidents, the Commission found
that mining activities were largely exempted from existing EU environmental
legislation and that the provisions of Directive 1999/31 on landfills did not
always comply with practices in the mining industry.

The Directive tried to lay down basic provisions for the storage and treatment
of mining waste, for the permitting of mining activities and for reducing the strict
standards for landfills under Directive 1999/31 by accommodating the mining
industry.

Other waste streams

Besides these measures, to which asbestos waste questions should be added,[189]   **10–59**
other waste streams are being examined by the European Union; the sixth
environmental action programme mentioned explicitly construction and demolition waste, and biodegradable waste.[190] While construction and demolition waste
is not likely to be subjected the EU provisions in the near future—Directive
2008/98 provided for a recycling target of 70 per cent by 2020—a proposal for
biodegradable waste,[191] which includes provisions on the composting of waste, is
since a number of years, requested by Member States, economic operators and
the European Parliament. As the Commission opposes a new directive, Directive
2008/98 only contained some general observation on bio-waste; the Commission
was again invited to assess the situation and come up with a proposal—if it
considered it appropriate (art.22).

It is unlikely that the Commission will propose, in the years to come, new
legislation for specific waste streams.

A Council Recommendation on waste paper from 1981 tried to promote the
recycling of waste paper,[192] but remained largely unacknowledged. Its impact on
economic or administrative practices was insignificant.

---

[188] Dir.2006/121 on the management of waste from the extracting industries [2006] OJ L102/15.

[189] See para.4–50, above.

[190] Dec.1600/2002 (fn.177, above) art.8(2.iv).

[191] Dir.2008/98 now defines bio-waste as follows (art.3 no.4): "biodegradable garden and park waste, food and kitchen waste from households, restaurants, caterers and retail premises and comparable waste from food processing plants".

[192] [1981] OJ L355/56.

CHAPTER 11

Legal Aspects of Integrating Environmental Requirements

1. General remarks

Article 11 TFEU requires that environmental protection requirements are incorporated into other EU policies.[1] This message has been part of the EC Treaty since 1987, when for the first time provisions on environmental protection were incorporated into the Treaty. Indeed, it was clear by then, and it is now even more evident than ever, that the relatively few environmental regulations and directives which the European Union has adopted since 1975 will neither, in themselves, reach a high level of environmental protection nor protect, preserve and improve the quality of the environment or avoid its deterioration. The use of chemicals, the growth of transport and the use of fossil or nuclear fuels continues and even increases. Directives on car emissions will help little in making transport sustainable, since besides the emissions the cars themselves are also the problem. Without specific environmental provisions the environment would probably be in a much worse state; however, this does not necessarily mean that quality of life, in urban centres or elsewhere, has improved, that the progressive disappearance of fauna and flora species has stopped or that climate change problems, tropical forest decline or other environmental problems generally have become insignificant.

11–01

The concept of sustainable development, now also used in arts 3(3) and (5) and recital 9 TEU, and 11 TFEU, tries to assemble all the opposing interests between environmental protection and economic progress into one formula, in order to find a political compromise to which everybody can agree. This attempt is doomed to fail, because the concept of sustainable development is void of sense and is given a political content according to the political actor who uses it.[2]

The integration requirement of art.11 TFEU is nevertheless the most important of the provisions which govern environmental policy,[3] since it constitutes the bridge between environmental policy and all the other policies at EU level. Any effort to describe the legal achievements of the integration of environmental the policies, not the legal aspects of integration. Since the present book does not try to examine policies themselves, but to describe legal measures, its presentation of the other policies will necessarily remain limited and even rudimentary. Some

11–02

---

[1] art.11 TFEU: "Environmental protection requirements must be integrated into the definition and implementation of Union policies and activities, in particular with a view to promoting sustainable development."

[2] See para.1–11s, above.

[3] See for this and the other requirements, para.1–16 et seq., above.

indication as to the necessity of an approach to integration which combines political, legal, economic and strategic action might appear from the list of criteria which the European Environment Agency established for assessing the integration of environmental actions into sectoral policies[4]:

1. Is there qualitative identification of all environmental costs/benefits?
2. Is there quantification of environmental costs/benefits?
3. Are all external costs internalised into market prices (part of the polluter-pays principle)?
4. Are economic instruments designed to achieve behaviour change rather than just revenue raising?
5. Are environmentally damaging subsidies being withdrawn?
6. Is there an environmental impact assessment of projects before implementation?
7. Is there strategic environmental impact assessment of policies, plans and programmes at different spatial levels?
8. Is environmental procurement a cornerstone of purchasing strategy?
9. Are there environmental management measures within the sector and monitoring of their implementation?
10. Have eco-efficiency targets and indicators been developed and used to monitor progress?

11–03   Legal (binding or not binding) or political instruments for the application of these criteria have, up to now, not been developed at EU level, with the exception of a directive on strategic environmental assessment of plans and programmes.[5] Thus, the list is an accumulation of wishful thinking: neither energy nor transport policy, neither fishery nor agricultural policy ever tried to consciously follow the ten points. For all policies, though, it should be clear that the integration of environmental issues must be conceived of as a process which might take decades to achieve and does not depend on one or the other legal or political measure which is adopted; examples would be changes in transport policy, the renouncing of nuclear energy or the transition to environmentally friendly agriculture, where organic farming would be the rule, not the exception.

The Commission tried, in 1993, to organise its internal administration in such a way so as to allow it better to take into consideration environmental requirements[6]; these administrative measures were reviewed in 1997.[7] However, it is significant that it was not really attempted to give these decisions the widest publicity possible; in this way, any serious control of their implementation by the other institutions, the media or the public was lacking.

---

[4] European Environment Agency, *Europe's environment, the second assessment* (Aarhus, 1998), Ch.14.
[5] Dir.2001/42 [2001] OJ L197/30; see also para.4–33, above.
[6] Commission, SEC (93) 785.
[7] Commission, Press Release IP/97/636 of July 11, 1997; the Commission's (1997) *Bulletin on European Union*, no.7/8 is silent on this issue.

The measures provided mainly for the following actions[8]:   **11–04**

- All Commission proposals were assessed on their environmental effects. Where such effects were likely to occur, an environmental impact assessment was to be made.
- Proposals for new legal measures should, in the explanatory memorandum, describe and explain environmental effects and environmental costs and benefits.
- The Commission work programme identifies with a green asterisk those proposals that will have significant environmental effects.
- In all relevant Commission departments, contact persons for the integration of environmental requirements were designated.
- An environmental network of director generals was set up, which was chaired by the director general for the environment and where the director generals of the most important departments are represented. The emphasis was laid on the total co-ordination of environmental questions and the interdependency between environmental policy and other political measures.
- A specific unit was created inside the environmental directorate general, which was directly placed under the responsibility of the director general and which was charged with the implementation of the environmental action programmes and the integration of environmental requirements into other political measures.
- The Commission's annual report was partly modified; it now contained, for key political areas, an indication of which environmental considerations were taken into account.
- The Commission took a number of measures for its recycling, waste management and purchase policy ("green accounting"). A strategy paper was adopted in December 1995, which set a framework for these activities.
- Progress in better integrating environmental requirements into other policies were regularly assessed. The reviewed version of the fifth environmental action programme contained detailed information on the integration of environmental requirements into other EU measures.

The overall effect of these measures on the orientation of the Commission's   **11–05**
policy seems insignificant. No environmental impact assessment was made for any new Commission proposal. In particular, the administrative (re-)structuring measures were bluntly rejected by the administration itself. And the greater accentuation of environmental requirements for example in the Commission's regional policy at the end of the 1990s was less attributable to the above mentioned measures, than to the more environmentally oriented approach by the Commissioner in charge of regional policy.

The Commission did not ensure the implementation of these measures, but tried, since 2003, to make a new start for integration, by providing for an impact assessment for its major legislative proposals and important communications which defined future policies.[9] Under this policy all such proposals shall be

---

[8] Written Question E-0649/97 (Diez de Rivera Icaza) [1997] OJ C367/33.
[9] See most recently Commission, Impact assessment guidelines, January 15, 2009, SEC(2009)92; see also more closely para.4–38, above.

examined as regards their economic, social and environmental impact; furthermore, intensive consultations with stakeholders—government experts, trade and industry, environmental and consumer protection services—were to take place. This policy led to the elaboration of lengthy documents which accompany legislative and other major proposals. However, generally these impact assessments are written, when the political decision to propose legislation is already taken; they thus serve as a supplementary explanation of the measure which was proposed, not as an objective assessment. Furthermore, the more important a measure politically is, the less precise is the assessment. For example, whether the mandatory introduction of filters for diesel cars will be proposed in order to reduce the emission of particulates, is not made subject to an environmental impact assessment, but depends on the question, whether the Commission is able to persuade the car industry and the car-producing Member States that such a measure should be taken. Once the decision is taken, an impact assessment will announce the environmental and human health-benefits of that measure.

Economists have, until now, not managed to convincingly assess in economic terms—and this is almost the only argument that counts at EU level—the advantages or disadvantages of a specific measure for the environment. The diminution of bird species in Europe or the damage made to soil every day—soil erosion, sealing, pollution, compaction and the other elements are mentioned in para.5–08, above—the particulates in the air which are supposed to cause some 140,000 deaths per year in the European Union and an unknown figure of sick persons—nobody ever has calculated the impact. In contrast, when the cost for industry are in question, each environmental measure leads to an outcry that it would cause the loss of jobs and of competitivity, economic advantages for China and higher prices, and very precise figures are given to prove how dangerous this or that environmental proposal would be for industry. This is the reason, why so many environmental proposals are watered down and watered down even before the Commission presents them as official proposals. And this is the reason, why in practice the Commission's idea of "better regulation" turns against the environmental policy and the concrete measures envisaged under this policy.

Until now, the initiative of 2003 did not significantly contribute to the integration of environmental requirements into other sectors of EU policy. Reversely, it certainly has contributed to slowing down or blocking environmental initiatives for reasons of industry or trade interests. This might in part be due not to the instrument of impact assessment itself, but to the fact that, since the beginning of the twenty-first century, the Commission is more prepared to follow ideas of new liberalism. The Commission seems to see the European Union more as an inter-State cooperation body than a Union, and its own role more as a Secretary than a policy institution. What lacks until now in the system, despite many good words in the Lisbon Treaty on European Union, is openness, transparency, accountability of the arguments which allow the policy makers to make a fair balancing; second, of course, there is a lack of a reliable method of measuring the impacts of a given measure on the environment, but also on the society as a whole. This deficiency cannot be overcome for the time being: how can an environment impact on future generations be measured? At the end of the day, it remains that at the decision-making table—of the Commission, of the European Union—the environment is poorly represented, as it neither votes nor has a voice.

The creation of a directorate-general for climate change issues, in 2010, and the transfer of responsibilities such as biotechnology or animal testing, to other administration within the Commission, rather contributes to further marginalising the environmental issues, administratively, but also politically. More and more the needs of environmental protection are comparable to the role which religion issues play in general policy: nobody openly contests their importance, but in the daily work, the requirements are all too often set aside.

The fifth environmental action programme (1993) had singled out five areas of activity as target sectors where particular efforts were to be made in order to integrate environmental requirements in those policies, namely the manufacturing industry, energy, transport, agriculture and tourism.[10] For three of these sectors—the manufacturing industry, energy and tourism—the European Union did, in 1993, not even have an express competence for action.

11–06

The "particular efforts" turned out to be purely on paper. Neither was there any infrastructure set up—such as a network inside the Commission, regular joint meetings between environmental and the specific ministers of Member States, Council meetings, public conferences, discussions, etc.—nor were there any concrete joint actions launched. The reason for this failure was that the action programme had been elaborated by the environmental Commissioner and later been discussed by the environmental working group and the environmental ministers in Council—but agricultural, transport and energy administrations and policy makers had not been integrated; they had other objectives and priorities and did not pay attention to the words in the action programme.

The negotiations and the signing of the Amsterdam Treaty on European in 1997 led to the transfer of the provision in environmental integration into other EU policies from art.174 to art.6 EC Treaty.[11] As a follow-up, the Luxembourg Council of Heads of State and Governments discussed in December 1997, how this new art.6 could be made operational, and charged the Commission to report on a possible strategy. The Commission prepared a report on the question[12] which the Heads of States and Governments discussed at their meeting in Cardiff in June 1998. That meeting invited the transport, energy and agriculture Councils to elaborate strategies for integrating environmental requirements into their sectors and to report on it. In December 1998, the internal market, industry and development Councils were asked to also elaborate a strategy. And in June 1999, the fisheries, economic and general affairs Councils were invited to develop a strategy.

11–07

Different integration papers were submitted by the Commission[13] and "approved" by the different sectoral Councils. However, these "approvals" were not made in a formalised way; the same is true for the discussions by the Heads

---

[10] Fifth environmental action programme [1993] OJ C138/1, p.28 et seq.
[11] See also para.1–24, above.
[12] Commission, Partnership for integration—a strategy for integrating environment into EU policies, COM (98) 333.
[13] See Commission, COM(98) 716 and COM (99) 640 (transport); COM(98) 571 (energy); COM (99) 22 and COM (2000) 20 (agriculture); COM (1999) 263 (internal market); COM (1999) 36 and COM (2000) 264 (development); COM (2001) 143 (fishery); COM (2000) 576 (economic questions); and SEC (2002) 271 (external affairs).

of States and Governments. They constituted thus at best a sort of political commitment for the different Councils; and also the Commission was not in any way legally—probably not either politically, as differences in the opinions were covered by diplomatic language—bound by the Councils' resolutions or other statements.[14] While the process of developing and discussing "strategies" was never formally brought to a halt, it progressively turned more in political declamation than leading to a work programme with objectives, priorities and timetables. Following a Commission Communication in 2004,[15] the Cardiff process is dead. The only thing that is annoying, is that art.11 TFEU continues to exist and requests to integrate environmental requirements into the other policies.

This integration process crossed with the "sustainability process" which was started in Lisbon 2000 and promised to make the European Union the most performing economy worldwide in then years, ensuring at the same time high social protection. During the Swedish Presidency, the Heads of State and Governments added an environmental dimension to the Lisbon process for employment, economic reform and social progress.[16] The fixing of a target date led to the attempt to develop measurement instruments, in order to assess progress towards 2010; this created the efforts to develop indicators. As the environment did not really have environmental performance indicators, their number remained limited; in particular, these indicators were neither really representative nor were they "filled" with reliable national or regional data.[17] Measuring integration of environmental requirements into other policies thus remains an adventure and, in practice, is largely ignored or selective: environmental arguments are being used, when it suits to support other arguments.

The conclusion of this short description of past and present efforts is that any political and administrative effort to give life to art.11 TFEU at EU level has been abandoned or, in a number of policy areas—consumer protection, competition policy, development policy—even not seriously started. There are some tendencies in "greening" the policy in the area of fishery, agriculture, and, in particular due to the climate change discussions, also on energy. However, these efforts are due to external pressure: the European Union had to react to the problem that fish had disappeared because of overfishing; that the Common Agricultural Policy had become too expensive and too restrictive to imports; and that climate change raised the necessity to take energy-related measures at EU level, though there was no explicit legal competence to do so. The Lisbon Treaty created an EU competence for energy issues and made agricultural and—to a

---

[14] It should be remembered that in 1999, the Commission resigned and was replaced; the European Parliament changed its political majority after general elections; in a number of Member States, governments changed.

[15] Commission, Integrating environmental considerations into other policy areas—a stocktaking of the Cardiff process, COM(2004) 394.

[16] Lisbon Statement: "The Union is to become the most competitive and dynamic knowledge-based economy in the world, capable of sustainable economic growth with more and better jobs and greater social cohesion". The European Council in Stockholm 2001 added to that: "the European Union sustainable development strategy should complete and build on the Lisbon statement by including an environmental dimension".

[17] See more closely para.1–11 et seq., above. There is up to now (March 2011) no general provision on environmental indicators and their representativity in EU policy and law.

large extent—fisheries policies areas of shared competence. As regards the integration of environmental requirements, this constitutional change is not likely to change the present situation.

The integration of environmental requirements into other policies, a legal requirement under art.11 TFEU, will start to become a reality, once the Court of Justice annuls an EU regulation or directive, because it did not respect art.11. Whether the Court will ever give such a judgment, is, of course, unknown. Until that time, art.11 will remain a nice objective that is not taken serious by the EU institutions and administrations.

2. Agricultural policy

Since December 2009, when the Lisbon Treaty on European Union entered into effect, agricultural policy is of shared competence between the Union and the Member States; until then, it had been a common policy, i.e. the Union had exclusive competence. Agricultural policy is based on arts 38–44 TFEU. Agricultural policy pursues the objectives of art.39,[18] which may, in general terms or in concrete measures, conflict with the environmental objectives of art.191 TFEU.

11–08

The Commission's progress reports of 1999 and 2000, on integrating environmental requirements into the agricultural sector, mentioned above, remained relatively general, but recognised that the agricultural policy had not changed much. The European Environment Agency identified the agriculture/ forestry sector as a principal contributor to the environmental problems of climate change, chemicals, soil, waste, acidification, biodiversity, inland waters and marine and coastal zones.[19] The Agency gave this resumé[20]:

> "Overall, fertiliser and pesticide use in Europe has decreased since the late 1980s, owing to improved application methods in the West and reduced agricultural output and incomes in Eastern Europe. The number of cattle and pigs has fallen in Europe as a whole, although animal manure remains a pollution problem in north-western Europe and is causing increasing problems in southern Europe. Water use for irrigation has increased, causing wetland loss and supply shortages in some areas. Soil compaction and other forms of soil degradation caused by agricultural practices (for example desertification and salinisation) are still widespread, especially in southern Europe and in the Newly Independent States.
>
> Habitats and species are under increasing threat from intensive agriculture in all parts of Europe, but particularly in the European Union due to current Common Agricultural Policy priorities that continue to place emphasis on increasing yields. In parts of Central and Eastern Europe, there has been an increase in chemical-free food production, for economic reasons."

11–09

In 2001, the Agency reported that agricultural negative impact on land use, water use, river water quality, eutrophication and biodiversity was still

---

[18] art.39(1) TFEU: "The objectives of the common agricultural policy shall be: (a) to increase agricultural productivity by promoting technical progress and by ensuring the rational development of agricultural production and the optimum utilisation of the factors of production, in particular labour; (b) thus to ensure a fair standard of living for the agricultural community, in particular by increasing the individual earnings of persons engaged in agriculture; (c) to stabilise markets; (d) to assure the availability of supplies; (e) to ensure that supplies reach consumers at reasonable prices".

[19] European Environment Agency (fn.4, above), Ch.14.1.

[20] European Environment Agency (fn.4, above), Ch.14.2.

significant, impacts on water use and biodiversity even increasing.[21] In 2002, it mentioned that nutrient surplusses on agricultural land remained a serious problem, causing nitrate pollution of groundwaters and eutrophication of aquatic ecosystems, furthermore, that specialising farming practices—practices which has been pushed by the common agricultural policy—had a negative impact on biodiversity. The 2005 Report did not address agricultural impacts as such; it reported that the water pollution through nitrates has been reduced between 1990 and 2000, with large regional differences, though.[22] In its latest report so far, the Agency identified soil erosion, greenhouse gas and ammoniac emissions, the increase of irregeable areas within the European Union (12 per cent between 1990 and 2000), the threat of diffuse pollution to ground and surface water, the continued decline of biodiversity loss as of particular concern and made the general observation: "Most environmental objectives and targets are not concrete enough to assess, whether they are realised."[23]

11–10   The objectives of agricultural policy, laid down in art.39 TFEU, have not changed since the beginning of the European Union (1958). Environmental considerations came only very slowly into perspective. A 1985 Green Paper devoted, for the first time, a special section to the environmental effects of agriculture.[24] In 1988 a communication on "agriculture and the environment" followed, which was based on the assumption that the common agricultural policy was already under pressure anyway and did not need supplementary pressure from the environmental side.[25] The general problems of agricultural policy led in 1992 to a substantial reform of the common agricultural policy. Although environmental improvement was not among the main objectives of this reform, increased efforts were taken subsequently to ensure income to farmers by progressively considering them to be nature conservationists, with access to environmental money. In pursuance of this policy, measures were gradually introduced to grant financial aid for environmental services provided by agriculture, such as the production of energy, forest-fire prevention, water protection, stabilisation of carbon dioxide and other greenhouse gas emissions, recycling of organic waste, nature conservation and biodiversity management, tourism and recreation, soil conservation, landscape management, the setting aside of land and less intensive production methods or forestation. The principal objective remained, however, financial aid to farmers.

11–11   A Regulation of 1986 aimed to protect forests against air pollution, by providing for reliable data collection and financial support for forest conservation measures. These provisions were reviewed in 2003, together with a more systematic strategy on forest management which takes environmental concerns into consideration,[26] but repealed in 2007.[27] A Regulation of 1991 established and defined rules on organic agriculture and the labelling of products thereof; in

---

[21] European Environment Agency, *Environmental Signals 2001* (Copenhagen 2001), p.49.
[22] European Environment Agency, *Environmental Signals 2002* (Copenhagen 2002), p.44; *The European Environment, state and outlook 2005* (Copenhagen 2005), p.352.
[23] European Environment Agency, Integration of environment into EU agricultural policy—the IRENA indicator-based assessment report. EEA Report 2/2006, Copenhagen 2007.
[24] Commission, Perspectives for the common agricultural policy, COM (85) 333.
[25] Commission, COM (88) 338.
[26] Reg.3529/86 [1986] OJ L326/5; Reg.2152/2003 concerning monitoring of forests and environmental interactions in the Community (Forest Focus) [2003] OJ L324/1; see also para.5–04, above.
[27] Reg.614/2007 (LIFE+) (2007) OJ L149/1.

1999, it was enlarged to include animal production,[28] and, in 2007, replaced by the actually applicable Regulation.[29] Organic farming has been in increase since the early 1990s. It counts for about 4 per cent of total agricultural land in the EU-15 States, and "far below" 1 per cent in the 12 new Member States; Sweden, Italy, Austria, Finland, and Denmark having more than 5 per cent, Malta, Bulgaria, Cyprus, Poland and Romania having no or almost no organic farm activity.[30] Overall, though, the Commission is not too favourable towards organic farming as it competes with traditional agriculture.

Regulation 2080/92 introduced a system of financial aid for afforestation.[31] Another Regulation of 1992 on agricultural production methods compatible with the requirements of environmental protection and the maintenance of the countryside[32] introduced a system of financial aid which aimed at the reduction of pollution caused by agriculture and at the promotion of farmers as nature conservationists and protectors of the landscape. The Regulation's role became increasingly important for the efforts to integrate environmental requirements into agriculture; in 1998, aid distributed by them covered about 15 per cent of all farmers and 20 per cent of EU farmland, though the number of contracts and the surface covered do not yet mean much with regard to the quality of these agri-environmental measures. This system was progressively extended as a second pillar of the EU agricultural policy: while the first pillar provided for direct payments to farmers and subsidies for agricultural products which were paid completely from the EU budget, this second pillar promoted a policy of rural development which included the promotion of agricultural and forestry competitiveness, the protection of the environment, and the improvement of quality of life in rural areas. The measures under the second pillar were in part financed by the Member States.

Following this new orientation of the agricultural policy Regulations 2080/92 and 2078/92 were replaced by Regulation 1257/1999 which grouped the different financial support schemes for rural development,[33] which was, in turn, replaced by Regulation 1698/2005.[34] Agri-environment support could be given for "agricultural production methods designed to protect the environment and to maintain the countryside". Articles 36 to 49 of this Regulation specified the conditions and amounts which may be granted for farming in mountain areas, in other handicapped areas (25 to 250 €/hectare), for farming activities in Natura 2000 areas, areas which are important under the Water Framework Directive 2000/60 (200 to 500 €/hectare), payments for voluntary animal welfare commitments (500 €) and payments for afforestation measures (up to 700€/hectare). Farmers had to commit themselves for at least five years. The support was to be calculated on the basis of income forgone, additional costs resulting from the commitment given and the need to provide an incentive— which again gives a lot of latitude. The maximum amounts are 700 € per hectare.

---

[28] Reg.1804/99 [1999] OJ L222/1.
[29] Reg.2092/91 [1991] OJ L198/1; this Reg. was replaced by Reg.834/2007 [2007] OJ L189/1.
[30] European Environment Agency 2005 (fn.22, above), p.356ss.
[31] Reg.2080/92 [1992] OJ L215/96.
[32] Reg.2078/92 [1978] OJ L215/85.
[33] Reg.1257/1999 [1999] OJ L160/80.
[34] Reg.1698/2005 on support for rural development by the European Agricultural Fund for Rural Development (EAFRD) [2005] OJ L277/1.

New provisions of 2009 provide for State aid (or EU funding) for farmers who commit themselves to measures on climate change, renewable energies, water and biodiversity.[35]

Support for forestry "shall contribute to the maintenance and development of the economic, ecological and social functions of forests in rural areas". It could be given among others, to the investment to improve and rationalise the harvesting, processing and marketing of forestry products, to the promotion of new outlets for the use and marketing of forestry products, the establishment of associations of forestry holders, etc. The amounts varied between 725€ per hectare for farmers or associations thereof and 185€ for any other private law person (Reg.1698/2005, art.31 and annex). These provisions make it sometimes difficult to see the environmental dimension of such measures.

11–12   EU measures that directly affect agriculture mainly stem from environmental policy, such as the protection of waters against nitrates from agricultural sources,[36] the use of sewage sludge in agriculture[37] or the environmental impact assessment of agricultural projects.[38] The overall results of these measures are not yet impressive.

In 2001, the Commission announced an action plan for biodiversity in agriculture[39] which tried to give priority to:

- the conservation of genetic variety;
- the protection of wild fauna and flora; and
- to life support systems.

No concrete measures accompanied this action plan. It is therefore not surprising that a significant impact of this plan could not be found.[40] The nitrate reduction policy, centred around Directive 91/676, will also reach results in some future only, if at all. And the thematic strategy on the sustainable use of pesticides, submitted in 2005 which led to the adoption of Directive 2009/128 aimed at the establishment of national action plans to promote the sustainable use of pesticides.[41] It can thus be fairly stated that changes as regards the impact of agriculture on the environment are likely not to be forced by the EU institutions, and will occur more by progressive changes in agricultural practice (globalisation, trend towards agro-industry) than be a policy to integrate environmental requirements into the agricultural policy.

11–13   Article 39 TFEU provides that agricultural products shall reach consumers at reasonable prices. This could, in theory, also include the environmental costs which are caused by the production and distribution of agricultural products. However, agricultural prices, which are fixed up to now by the EU institutions, do not reflect environmental costs at all. For a number of years, political pressure tried to align these prices with global prices for agricultural products; however, it is implicitly accepted that a price system for agricultural products could not

---

[35] Reg.74/2009 [2009] OJ L30/100; see also the new art.16*bis* of Reg.1698/2005 (fn.34, above).

[36] Dir.91/676 [1991] OJ L375/1; see para.7–19, above.

[37] Dir.86/278 [1986] OJ L181/6; see para.10–54, above.

[38] Dir.85/337 [1985] OJ L175/40; see para.4–29, above.

[39] Commission, COM (2001) 162, vol.III.

[40] European Environment Agency, 10 messages for 2010 agricultural ecosystems. Copenhagen 2010.

[41] Dir.2009/128 establishing a framework for Community action to achieve sustainable use of pesticides [2009] OJ L309/71.

simultaneously reflect environmental costs and align to world market prices. Hence, the more the polluter-pays principle is applied in agriculture, the greater will be the need to avoid competition with agricultural products from the world market, since products from many regions in the world—quite apart from labour costs—do not take environmental concerns into account. As regards the political strategy, therefore, the European Union should reflect whether there is not a need to export environmental (and social) standards of the agricultural sector, instead of having the global discussion almost exclusively centred on the import of agricultural products into the European Union and on the price barriers which the European Union erected. Not much of such a policy is visible at present.

While it was mentioned in para.11–09, above, that the objectives of **11–14** agricultural policy (art.39 TFEU) have not changed since 1958, the instruments progressively changed. A reform of 1992 started to move away from the policy of price and production support towards direct income aid for farmers and rural development matters. This was intensified by measures decided in 2003 which aimed at decoupling direct payments to farmers from production and to make them more conditional to the respect of good agricultural and environmental practice. However, changes take time. "At present, agricultural support, even the direct payments, is still, in its major parts, tied to the level of (past) agricultural production than the reward of specific environmental services by farmers".[42] Subventioning agricultural products from organic farming to a level that they are not more expensive than products which come from traditional farming has not yet become a policy objective in agriculture. Also, the major recommendations which the European Consultative Forum made in 1998 to reach sustainable agriculture within the European Union were not taken over by the EU institutions.[43] The Court of auditors of the European Union, in a report of the year 2000, was of the opinion that the European Union had not yet reached significant progress in greening agriculture,[44] though the abovementioned efforts in making the farmer the steward of the environment and pay him for that, still continue and are even intensified. This situation has not significantly changed until 2010. The next policy discussion on the greening of the EU agricultural policy is likely to take place, when the budget 2013–2020 of agricultural policy will be discussed.

3.   Fisheries policy

Under the Lisbon Treaty, the competence on fisheries is shared between the **11–15** Union and the Member States (art.4(2.d) TFEU), except as regards the "conservation of marine biological resources under the Common Fisheries Policy" (art.3(1.e) TFEU), for which there is an exclusive EU competence. The basic Regulation concerning the Common Fisheries Policy dated from 2002; it replaced an earlier Regulation of 1992 and required that this Policy should take

---

[42] European Environment Agency 2002 (fn.22, above), p.52.
[43] European Consultative Forum on the environment and sustainable development: towards sustainable agriculture in Europe (Luxembourg, 1998).
[44] Court of Auditors, Special Report 14/2000 on the Greening of the CAP, together with the answers by the Commission [2000] OJ C353/1.

account of its implications for the marine environment.[45] The Commission indicated as the main problems of fishery the overexploitation, the pressure on non-target organisms and on the physical environment, the excessive capacity of the European fleet, the negative impact of aquaculture, in particular as regards water quality, dissemination of diseases and parasites and the introduction of alien species and unsatisfactory implementation of EU measures.[46] It pleaded for an ecosystem-based approach to fisheries management and suggested a series of measures to come closer to this. These objectives are less to be reached by legislative than by political decisions; and those policy decisions are therefore not to be described here.

Concrete EU measures for protecting fish and other marine resources are rare. Provisions on the mesh size, the nets to be used, the minimum size of fish which may be landed—all have some influence on the catches, though these measures are normally not taken in order to protect the marine environment or the fish. The European Union decided an almost complete ban on the use of drift-nets, exempting, though, the Baltic Sea, due to the representation of interests[47] which became fully effective in January 2002; in the Baltic Sea, the ban was only applied as of 2008. Measures under Directive 92/43 to protect natural habitats,[48] the different measures on water policy and management[49] and the integrated management of coastal zones[50] also have considerable influence on fisheries. As regards controls, the Council adopted a Regulation to establish a control system applicable to the Common Fisheries Policy.[51] Satellite surveillance was made compulsory, and from January 1, 2000 onwards, all EU fishing vessels and those of third countries operating in EU waters with a length of over 20m had to be equipped with a Vessel Monitoring System—which allowed them to be localised.

In 2002, the European Environment Agency reported that the over-capacity of the EU fishing fleet had not seriously been reduced; nor had over-fishing been stopped[52] or a sustainable aquaculture been established.[53] Attempts to influence aquaculture are mainly channelled through giving financial support to installations that decrease their environmental impact. The new directive on the marine environment[54] is not likely to have any influence on the Common Fisheries Policy; as it was mentioned above, para.7–38, it proposed first of all to continue the monitoring of the European waters by the same (Convention) structures that exist at present. Also, it mainly dealt with water issues, but not with the fauna and flora of the marine environment. In 2006, the Commission stated:

---

[45] Reg.2371/2002 on the conservation and sustainable exploitation of fishing resources under common fisheries policy [2002] OJ L358/99, replacing Reg.3760/92 [1992] OJ L389/1.
[46] Commission, COM (2001) 143, pt 2.
[47] Reg.1239/98 laying down certain technical measures for the conservation of fishery resources [1998] OJ L171/4.
[48] Dir.92/43 [1992] OJ L206/7; see also para.5–12, above.
[49] See Ch.7 of this book.
[50] Rec.2002/413 concerning the implementation of Integrated Coastal Zone Management in Europe [2002] OJ L148/24.
[51] Reg.2846/98 [1998] OJ L358/5.
[52] European Environment Agency 2005 (fn.22, above), p.54.
[53] European Environment Agency 2005 (fn.22, above), p.59.
[54] See Dir.2008/56 establishing a framework for Community Action in the field of marine environment policy (Marine Strategy Framework Directive) [2008] OJ L164/19.

"Whereas some stocks, like herring and mackerel, are exploited in levels approaching sustainability, catches of many bottom-living European fish stock have declined dramatically in recent decades. There has simply been too much fishing in relation to the productive potential of the stocks.[55]"

The Commission suggested either to reduce the fishing capacity or to keep the current levels of employment at the price of economic inefficiencies, but left the decisions on these options to the Council; and it is remarkable that environmental considerations were not even mentioned in this Communication.

In 2009, the Commission launched large consultations on the review of the Fisheries Policy which is to be decided by the Council in 2012.[56] The Commission itself admitted that the European fishing fleet was too big for the limited quantities of fish that were available, conceding thereby that practically nothing had changed in this regard over the last 10 years, despite all the words on sustainability in Regulation 2371/2002. As the fishing associations loudly invoke the social problem linked to the decline of employment in the fisheries sector, and as a number of Southern European States—France, Spain, Italy, Portugal and Greece in particular—back this concern, any drastic change in the EU fisheries policy will be difficult to obtain. Proposals from consulted bodies or persons go to re-nationalising the policy, introducing a credit system, or seriously reducing State aid. However, the over-dimensioned EU fishing fleet is already by now—and will continue to do so in the future—fishing in third countries' waters, on the bases of so-called partnership agreements with third countries.[57] Overfishing is thus by now a global, no longer an EU problem alone.

Changes with regard to the Fishery Policy are therefore likely to come from inside: when there is no longer enough fish to catch, more care might be taken of the marine environment.

4. Transport policy

With the Lisbon Treaty, the EU Transport Policy (arts 90–100 TFEU) became a **11–16** policy sector of shared competence (art.4(2.g) TFEU), while it had been, until the end of 2009, a sector of exclusive EU competence. However, this construction by the EC Treaty had never been realised; national transport policies continued to exist and were in large areas much more relevant than EU transport policy. The EU transport policy was for a long time targeted towards realising the four Treaty freedoms for goods and services, capital and labour. The introduction of an environmental chapter into the Treaty in 1987 has not yet fundamentally changed this situation.

Transport policy contributes to the environmental problems linked with **11–17** climate change, acidification, tropospheric ozone, biodiversity, urban environment and technological and natural hazards, furthermore to land use, noise, waste generation and marine pollution. Subsequent to the different environmental

---

[55] Commission, Implementing sustainability in EU fisheries through maximum sustainable yield, COM (2006) 360.

[56] Commission, Reform of the Common Fisheries Policy, COM(2009) 163.

[57] In early 2011, there existed about a dozen of such agreements with third countries, see for example the agreements with Morocco [2006] OJ L141/4; Ivory Coast [2008] OJ L48/11; Guinea [2009] OJ L156/35.

action programmes, which mentioned the problems of the environment, the Commission first issued a Greenbook in 1992 on environmental problems linked to transport,[58] which was quite quickly followed by a White Paper.[59] The White Paper denounced the increase of environmental constraints over the last 20 years and proclaimed that the consideration of environmental aspects was an integral part of a common transport policy. In order to reduce the environmental impact of transport, the White Paper pleaded for the adoption of strict standards for exhaust emissions, energy consumption and noise emissions, as well as standards on technical controls for cars, the establishing of noise level limits around airports, and environmental impact assessments for infrastructure plans and projects, including cost-benefit analyses. It pleaded for the promotion of public transport, bicycles and electric cars, the reduction of private car use and the reduction of land use for transport infrastructure projects.

11–18   Sustainable transport was defined by the Council as:

> "a transport system that:
>
> allows the basic access and development needs of individuals, companies and societies to be met safely and in a manner consistent with human and ecosystem health, and promotes equity within and between successive generations;
>
> is affordable, operates fairly and efficiently, offers choice of transport mode, and supports a competitive economy, as well as a balanced regional development;
>
> limits emissions and waste within the planet's ability to absorb them renewable resources at or below their rates of generation, and uses non-renewable resources at or below the rates of development of renewable substitutes while minimising the impact on the use of land and the generation of noise." (Council, Resolution of April 4–5, 2001.)

This definition at least mentions the environment in substance, though in a vague form. And it seems significant that the environmental concerns are mentioned last in the list of objectives; this ignores the fact that the competitive economy and balanced regional development cannot be ensured without appropriate environmental protection, whereas the environment can well continue to exist without competitive economy and balanced regional development. Finally, the objective of promoting public means of transport, so dear to environmental policy, is apparently not an objective of transport policy. And the importance of such a definition should not be overestimated: where it is not followed by practical steps to put it into reality, it remains an empty shell.

11–19   Already in 1993, the fifth environmental action programme which was entitled "Towards sustainability" had stated that:

> "because of the projected increases in the volume of cars used, the mileages driven and increases of road freight traffic, the transport . . . will offset any potential reduction attributable to the introduction of new emission standards."

Its suggestions were to:

> "reduce operational pollution, limit the infrastructural development of land use, reduce traffic and congestion and prevent or reduce risks inherent in the transport of dangerous goods and wastes."

It suggested, in particular, road taxes, road pricing, regulation and fiscal

---

[58] Commission, Greenbook on the impact of transport on the environment, COM (92) 46.
[59] Commission, White Paper on a Community strategy on sustainable mobility, COM (92) 494.

incentives for fuels and vehicles and a change in user behaviour.[60] In 1995, the Commission adopted an action programme on transport 1995–2000[61] and a Green Paper on fair and efficient prices in the transport sector.[62] In 1998, the Commission adopted communications on sustainable transport, transport and CO_2 and the environment and heavy goods vehicles[63]; 1999 followed a communication on air transport and the environment,[64] in 2001 a White Paper,[65] and in 2006, 2008 and 2009 other communications.[66]

Overall, there was thus an impressive number of opinions, statements, resolutions and other political measures on the environmental impact of transport, that have been adopted by the different EU institutions, including statements from a joint environment/transport Council in June 1998.

Legally, the most important measures are the efforts to limit the pollution emissions by cars and trucks.[67] The European Union has only rather recently managed to introduce economic instruments, such as fees for the use of motorways.[68] EU rules on fees for the use of roads or airports, incentives for the use of less-polluting vehicles, fiscal advantages for public transport, or even simply the comprehensive promotion of electric cars do not exist.[69] Also, the recurrence to eco-points, used in the agreement with Austria on the Alpine transit,[70] has never been used as a model for measures within the European Union. There seems to be only very limited political determination, at EU level and at the level of Member States, to introduce the necessary changes in the form of a coherent strategy and legally binding acts. Only a minority of Member States pursue a national transport policy that integrates environmental requirements. Attempts to increase car production and to create a more efficient transport infrastructure—motorways, roads, railway lines, airports and so on—are at the centre of transport policy practically everywhere; the necessity of creating this corresponding infrastructure reduces the efficiency of environmental measures, where they are taken. **11–20**

All policy statements and other measures have not changed the trends. The European Environment Agency stated in 2001 that overall trends for transport policy were negative, in particular the decoupling of transport growth from economic growth, the management of demand for travel, the progress towards more environmentally friendly modes and the improvement of fuel efficiency; only trends in the reduction of resources and outputs that damage the environment, as well as efficient pricing had not worsened.[71] In the same year, a **11–21**

---

[60] Fifth environmental action programme [1993] OJ C138/5, para.4.3.

[61] Commission, COM (95) 302.

[62] Commission, COM (95) 691.

[63] Commission, COM (98) 716; transport and carbon dioxide, COM (98) 204; Environment and heavy goods vehicles, COM(98) 444.

[64] Commission, Air transport and environment COM (99) 640.

[65] Commission, White Paper—European transport policy for 2010: time to decide COM (2001) 370.

[66] Commission, COM (2006) 314; (2008) 433; (2009) 279.

[67] See Ch.8 of this book.

[68] Dir.1999/62 on the charging of heavy goods vehicles for the use of certain infrastructures [1999] OJ L187/42 which replaced Dir.93/89 [1993] OJ L316/19, which had been annulled by the Court of Justice: *Parliament v Council* (C–21/94) [1995] E.C.R. I–1827, only fixes the frame for charges.

[69] See European Parliament Res. of January 22, 1993 [1993] OJ C42/256.

[70] See Reg.3637/92 [1992] OJ L373/1; Dec.92/577 [1992] OJ L373/4.

[71] European Environment Agency (fn.21, above), p.30.

special indicator report from the European Environment Agency[72] indicated that out of 34 trend indicators for transport 19 were negative,[73] 12 were stable[74] and only two[75] were positive. The trend indicator for 2002 did not show any significant improvement; the EEA stated in particular that the trends did not show any sign of breaking the link between economic growth and growth in transport, and changing transport use away from roads. There were increased use of cars and airplanes and freight transport growing faster than the gross domestic product. The result was a growing energy use and increased greenhouse gas emissions. The Communications of 2006, 2008 and 2009 paid some lip-service to the environment, but then discussed in great detail, what measures could be taken to have more roads, more traffic and more mobility. The shift from road to rail ("Modal shift") was not mentioned as a target any more.

In 1996, the Commission concluded that transport in the European Union was not sustainable.[76] Thirteen years later, the conclusions, drawn by the Commission itself, are still the same.[77] In this way, transport policy is a good example of (not) integrating environmental requirements in other policies: the analysis what could and should be done, is made; however, the concrete actions bluntly ignore the environmental requirements. No serious will exists at EU level to elaborate and implement an environmentally sound transport policy.

5. Energy policy

11–22   As mentioned, EU energy policy operated, until the entry into force of the Lisbon Treaty (December 2009). without an express legal basis in the Treaty. Article 3 EC Treaty only allowed the taking of (some) "measures" in the area of energy. The lack of an express Treaty competence on energy did not prevent arts 154–156 EC Treaty (now art.170–172 TFEU) from providing for the creation, under the EC Treaty, of trans-European networks, amongst other things, in the area of energy infrastructure.

According to the new art.194 TFEU, EU energy policy has the following main objectives:

1.   ensure the functioning of the energy market;
2.   ensure the security of energy supply;
3.   promote energy efficiency and energy saving;
4.   promote the development of new and renewable forms of energy; and
5.   promote the interconnection of energy networks.

Article 194 TFEU explicitly stated that these objectives shall be pursued while taking into consideration the protection of the environment. Thus, the

---

[72] European Environment Agency, *TERM 2001—indicators tracking transport and environment integration in the European Union* (Copenhagen, 2001). European environment agency: *Towards a resource-efficient transport system. TERM 2009.* Technical Report 2/2010 (Copenhagen, 2010).
[73] These mainly refer to improving shares of rail and public transport.
[74] Mainly for same emissions and the development of strategies.
[75] Investments in infrastructure and volatile organic compound emissions.
[76] Commission, Progress report on the implementation of the European Community programme on policy and action in relation to the environment and sustainable development, COM (96) 624, p.32.
[77] Commission, COM(2009) 279, p.3.

environment has at least been identified as one of the elements which influence EU energy policy measures, which is not the case in any other EU policy.

Within the framework of these objectives, the Commission identified, in 1997, three vital points on which EU energy measures must act: reduce dependence on supplies from energy sources outside the European Union, ensure more competitive prices for energy products and make energy markets more compatible with environmental objectives.[78] One reason for the slow progress in reaching these objectives is that Member States rely heavily on national sources of energy—oil in the United Kingdom, gas in the Netherlands, nuclear energy in France and Belgium, coal in Germany, for example—and wish to keep national responsibility for energy policy measures, including the responsibility to determine the price of energy.

The EC Treaty, the Coal and Steel Treaty and the Euratom Treaty all provided for energy measures. The Euratom Treaty was conceived in order to promote the peaceful use of nuclear energy, but very largely lost its political raison d'être when in the 1960s France refused to integrate nuclear policy into the EU mechanisms and Germany also went its own way. The Treaty of Lisbon did not include the Euratom Treaty and its provisions; the Euratom Treaty is thus a Treaty that stands on its own—an odd construction, as the main institutions (Commission, Council, European Parliament) are identical under the Treaty on European Union and the Euratom Treaty, and the different policies are, of course, closely interlinked. The construction finds its explanation in the different nuclear energy policies pursued by the Member States and by the determination of the "nuclear countries" (France and United Kingdom in particular) not to suffer any interference from the Union on their national policies and measures.   **11–23**

At present, about half of the 27 EU Member States do not have nuclear energy production on their territory, mainly for environmental reasons. Sweden, Germany and Belgium have taken a political decision to phase out nuclear energy, though national policy changes might reverse these decisions. As the nuclear energy industry is extremely influential—backed also by the French and British government—EU decisions on nuclear matters, including those relating to climate[79] frequently took nuclear energy and its continuity for granted. Nobody dared even raising at EU level, the environmental impact of nuclear installations, the risk of accidents or terrorist attacks, nuclear wastes, decommissioning of nuclear installations and the overall energy balance of nuclear energy. As regards energy decisions which were based on the Euratom Treaty, in particular on arts 30, 31, 34 and 37, they did not discuss the impact of nuclear energy on the environment in any significant way; they mainly considered effects of nuclear energy on human health, but not on fauna and flora or other environmental assets, and even there the approach is not consistent.[80]

The Treaty on Coal and Steel entered into effect in 1952 and ended in 2002. Its functions were taken over by the European Union. It mainly provided for   **11–24**

---

[78] Commission, COM (97) 167.

[79] For climate change issues, see also para.9–01 et seq., above.

[80] See, e.g. Commission Opinion [1997] OJ C291/5 on the discharge of radioactive substances from Sellafield (UK). The Opinion, based on art.37 of the Euratom Treaty, did not discuss at all the impact of such discharges on the Irish Sea, on the UK, environment, or on marine fauna and flora. When the Commission examined the effects of French nuclear tests in Mururoa, it looked at their effects on people in other States (the Pitcairn Islands, UK), but neither on French citizens in Mururoa nor on the environment.

measures on coal, though measures on lignite could also be taken under certain conditions. The function of coal as the main energy resource in the European Union—which had taken over from wood in the nineteenth century—had already, at the end of the 1950s, been replaced by oil. The serious adaptation problems caused by this change continue to exist and have contributed to reducing the discussions on environmental problems linked to coal.

All energy resources with the exception of nuclear energy are thus subject to the provisions of the EU Treaties. Energy use is accounted to significantly contribute to climate change and air pollution, acidification, tropospheric ozone creation, waste generation, soil degradation, marine and coastal zone problems and technological hazards issues, furthermore and use by installations and networks, water pollution and light pollution. As some of these environmental problems do not occur with the use of nuclear energy, the ongoing discussion on climate change leads to certain attempts to promote nuclear energy, although this energy is economically not competitive—except in France, where it has been subventioned for decades—and neither the problems of disposal of nuclear waste nor of decommissioning of nuclear installations have been solved. Furthermore, the population in the EU continues, in its majority, to be opposed to nuclear technology, which leads to nuclear decision-making bodies acting in a very closed-shop manner: openness, transparency, accountability and public participation are notions that cannot be attributed to the nuclear sector. EU measures on the safety of nuclear installations, nuclear waste (proposal) and the shipment of nuclear waste are completely insufficient and not comparable to the measures which were adopted for non-nuclear installations and waste.[81]

11–25   As regards environmental-related energy measures, most provisions were based, in the past, on arts 192 or 352 TFEU. Article 192(2) TFEU expressly maintained a veto right for Member States in important energy matters, by providing for unanimous decisions in such cases.[82] Since the end of the 1980s, a number of political, not legally binding statements were made on the relationship between energy and the environment,[83] including the statement to stabilise carbon dioxide emissions by the year 2000 at the level of 1990, in order to combat the greenhouse effect.[84]

Of the different actions taken in pursuance of the energy policy, measures on energy saving, energy taxes and on renewable energies are—next to the measures to combat climate change[85]—of particular interest here. The following measures on energy saving and on renewable energies were adopted: Directive 93/76 (SAVE I), which aimed at an improvement of energy efficiency in housing, of cars and industrial companies[86]; Decision 91/565, which provided for financial

---

[81] See Directive 2009/71 on nuclear safety of nuclear installation [2009] OJ L172/18; Commission, proposal for a directive on spent fuels and radioactive waste, COM(2010) 618; Directive 2006/117 on the shipment of radioactive waste [2006] OJ L337/1.

[82] art.192(2) TFEU: "[The Council shall unanimously adopt] ... measures significantly affecting a Member State's choice between different energy sources and the general structure of its energy supply." See also para.2–89.

[83] Commission, COM (88) 174; Energy and the environment, COM (89) 369.

[84] Commission, (1990) 10 *E.C. Bulletin*, para.1.3.77; this commitment was made in a form of Council conclusions, i.e. in a political and unpublished form.

[85] See Ch.9, above.

[86] Dir.93/76 [1993] OJ L237/28; see also the Commission's proposal COM (92) 182, which had proposed going considerably further.

assistance for energy saving measures[87]; Decision 93/500 (ALTENER), which promoted, particularly through financial incentives, renewable sources of energy[88]; and Decision 96/737 (SAVE II) to grant further financial assistance for energy saving measures.[89] Generally, the amount of financial assistance that was made available by these measures was modest.[90] The discussion on climate change progressively led to the promotion of bio-fuels as a source of energy and, more generally, to the promotion of renewable energy sources.[91] The European Union succeeded to fix binding targets for the share of renewable energies in the total energy consumption. However, the attempt to fix binding targets on energy efficiency failed, as the Member States claimed that this was a question of national competence (subsidiarity).

As regards taxes, the Commission proposed, in 1992, a tax on carbon dioxide emissions and energy.[92] The proposal was intended, in particular, to combat the greenhouse effect. It provided for an exception of renewable energies[93] and stated that:

> "in order to safeguard the competitiveness of Community industry, the tax arrangements cannot be applied in the Member States until such time as other member countries of the OECD have brought in a similar tax or measures having an equivalent financial impact." (Commission (fn.93, above), 10th recital; it is to be noted that Germany had declared itself ready to introduce a carbon dioxide/energy tax, but only in concert with the other EU Member States.)

11–26

This announcement condemned the proposal, since Japan and the United States, in particular, clearly indicated that they had no intention of introducing a similar tax. The amended proposal,[94] which is in the meantime obsolete, provided for some conditions for the introduction of the tax, but left it entirely to the discretion of Member States whether they wished to introduce an emission/ energy tax. Such a tax has been introduced by Scandinavian states and the Netherlands; several states have signalled that they would be ready to increase the tax, but abstained from it in order not to expose their industry to competitive disadvantages in comparison with other EU Member States. The considerations at EU level about energy tax measures continue, though, alimented by efforts to promote measures against climate change, to promote renewable sources of energy and to help farmers to become bio-fuel/energy producer (and be paid for that).

---

[87] Dec.91/565 [1991] OJ L307/34.

[88] Dec.93/500 [1993] OJ L235/14.

[89] Dec.96/737 [1996] OJ L335/50.

[90] 45 million € for four years for SAVE II (fn.90, above), 22 million € for ALTENER II for two years (fn.90, above).

[91] Dir.2009/28 on the promotion of the use of energy from renewable sources [2009] OJ L 140/16.

[92] [1992] OJ C196/1; see also para.9–23.

[93] Renewable energies were not defined; the proposal provided for exemptions for fuel wood and wood charcoal, products resulting from the distillation or processing of wood, and, furthermore, any product of agricultural or vegetable origin and crude or esterified vegetable oils. Compare to that the definition of renewable energies in Dir.2009/28 (fn.91, above), art.2(a): "energy from renewable non-fossil sources, namely wind, solar, aerothermal, geothermal, hydrothermal and ocean energy, hydropower, biomass, landfill gas, sewage treatment plant gas and biogas".

[94] Commission, COM (95) 172.

11–27   In 2003, the Council adopted a Directive on the taxation of energy products.[95] This Directive repealed earlier Directives; it imposed minimum tax rates on all energy products. Energy intensive industries and the agricultural, horticultural, piscicultural and forestry sectors could request to be exempted from the tax, provided they entered into national environmental agreements, participated in emission trading schemes or in equivalent agreements. The minimum levels of taxation, as of 2010, were fixed as follows (in €):

for industry and commerce use		heating fuels and electricity	
Petrol (1000l)	421		
Unleaded petrol	359	(heavy fuel oil)15	
Diesel	330	21	21
Kerosene	330	21	0
LPG (1000kg)	125	41	0
Natural gas	2.6/gigajoule	0.3 gigajoule	0.3 gigajoule
Electricity	1,0/MKwh		

As can be seen, this table does not show much of the favouring of renewable energy or the promotion of biofuels. The subvention of diesel fuel in comparison to petrol cannot really be explained with environmental considerations. Also, Member States remained free to impose unleaded petrol or not. And as its predecessors, Directive 2003/96 contained numerous transition periods, derogations and exceptions.

The Council also agreed to promote the use of bio-fuels for transport and invited Member States to fix non-binding targets at national level, in order to reach a (non-binding) target of 5.75 per cent of fuels for transport stemming from bio-fuels by 2010.[96] Though these targets were not respected, in 2009, a binding target was fixed, according to which the share of bio-fuels in transport should reach, by 2020, 10 per cent.[97]

11–28   Renewable energies—wood, solar, water, geothermal and wind energy— played, until very recently, a modest role at EU level. This sector accounted for 1.6 per cent of energy supply in 1973 and 1.5 per cent in 1989.[98] Its share has risen since, in particular due to the intense discussions on climate change. In 1996, the Commission adopted a Greenbook and, subsequently, in 1997, a White Paper on renewable energies, where it announced its objective to reach a market share of 12 per cent by the year 2010 and 22 per cent of electricity produced by renewable energies (both figures for EU-15).[99]

[95] Dir.2003/96 restructuring the Community framework for the taxation of energy products and electricity [2003] OJ L283/51.
[96] Dir.2003/30 on the promotion of the use of biofuels or other renewable fuels for transport [2003] OJ L123/42.
[97] Dir. 2009/28 (fn.92, above).
[98] Commission, "Energies for the future: renewable sources of energy": Green Paper, COM (96) 576; White Paper, COM (97) 599.
[99] Commission, Green Paper (fn.100, above).

In 2004, the Commission evaluated the measures and concluded that both the **11–29**
12 per cent target for energy (12 per cent) and electricity (22 per cent) from
renewable sources would probably not be attained.[100] To what extent the targets
of 2020—20 per cent share of renewable energy in the total energy consumption,
10 per cent of bio-fuels in transport—will be reached, remains to be seen. At
present, the traditional energy sources, in particular coal, oil and nuclear energy,
continue to prevail and to absorb most of the State aid and EU funding. Member
States appear prepared to have the EU energy policy move them towards
renewable energies, at a pace which is not too quick. However, the policies on
traditional energy sources remain very largely determined by national decisions.

The trends in energy policy are not positive. The European Union did not
manage to decouple economic growth and energy consumption. Energy prices
generally remained low or even fell, offering little incentive to reduce energy
consumption. And the use of renewable energies did not progress as had been
hoped.[101]

The European Parliament had already since years asked for more measures to
promote renewable energies,[102] amongst others to consider the conclusion of a
new EU Treaty along the model of the Euratom Treaty, but dealing with policies
and measures on renewable energies; to consider spending as much money for the
promotion of renewable energies as was spent for research on nuclear fusion (840
million € per year). To date, such ideas have not found an echo among EU
institutions or among Member States.

6. Trade policy

EU trade policy is mainly based on arts 206ss TFEU, which give exclusive **11–30**
competence to the European Union in matters of commercial policy. The Council
and Member States interpret these provisions narrowly and accept the European
Union's exclusive competence only where no other matters than commercial
issues are discussed which deal with products. This considerably limits the area
of exclusive EU competence, because most international agreements also concern
other issues of foreign economic policy, such as economic co-operation,
investments, financial and technical assistance, and exchange of advisers or
experts; according to the Council, agreements that include such aspects do not
come under arts 131–135 EC.

EU decisions to adhere to international environmental conventions which **11–31**
contain trade elements are normally based on art.192, not art.207 TFEU.
Examples are decisions to adhere to the Montreal Protocol on ozone-depleting
substances[103] or to the Basel Convention on the shipment of hazardous waste[104];
Regulation 338/97 should also be mentioned here,[105] which transposes the
provisions of the CITES Convention on trade in endangered species of fauna and

[100] Commission, Communication: The share of renewable energy in the EU, COM(2004) 366.
[101] European Environment Agency (fn.22, above), p.34.
[102] Res. of January 19, 1993 [1993] OJ C42/31; Res. of May 28, 1993 [1993] OJ C176/216; Res. of
July 4, 1996 [1996] OJ C211/27; Res. of November 14, 1996 [1996] OJ C362/279; Res. of May 15,
1997 [1997] OJ C167/60.
[103] Dec.88/540 [1988] OJ L297/8.
[104] Dec.93/98 [1993] OJ L39/1.
[105] Reg.338/97 [1997] OJ L61/1, see also para.5–26, above.

flora into EU law. The European Union is not a member of the Convention itself, since that Convention is open only to nation States, and an amendment that would allow the adhering of the European Union has not yet entered into force. Following a judgment of the Court of Justice, the adhesion to the Rotterdam Convention on the export and import of dangerous chemicals was based on arts 207 and 192 TFEU jointly.[106]

EU environmental measures are affected more and more by the globalisation of economies. In 1994, a new World Trade Organisation (WTO) was set up, which replaced the General Agreement on Tariffs and Trade (GATT) and has the objective of promoting international trade.[107] The WTO took over the GATT rules, which had been drafted in 1947 and did not expressly address environmental issues; it follows the primary objective of promoting free international trade; environmental measures are mainly seen and treated as being barriers to trade. In a half-hearted attempt to discuss ways for reconciling trade and environmental issues, the WTO set up a Committee on Trade and Environment, which should discuss environmental and trade aspects, though it did not have any power to set up rules or provide for concrete proposals; this Committee has not managed to play any significant role in WTO policy. The WTO statutes also provided for a dispute settlement system to solve conflicts between, amongst others, environment and trade; decisions by the WTO in this area are binding upon the contracting parties and financial sanctions are foreseen in the case of non-compliance.

11–32   As in the case of the relationship between the European Union and its Member States,[108] the questions concerning whether the EU environmental measures affect the rules of free international trade have to differentiate between situations where no international environmental measures have been taken, and those cases where international conventions on the protection of the environment exist.

Where no international environmental agreements exist, an EU measure which endeavours to protect the environment is, in principle, compatible with GATT/WTO rules, if it does not constitute a means of arbitrary or unjustifiable discrimination and where it is "necessary", amongst other things, "to protect human, animal or plant life or health" (GATT Agreement, art.XX(b)) or relating "to the conservation of exhaustible natural resources" (art.XX(g)). Different GATT/WTO panels used the word "necessary" in art.XX to introduce a proportionality test into measures by contracting parties. This thus makes the WTO provisions similar to those of art.36 TFEU—except that the European Court of Justice's interpretation of art.34 TFEU, which also allows legitimate national environmental protection measures to restrict trade, has, as yet, no counterpart in the WTO provisions.

11–33   Of particular concern is the discussion as to whether WTO rules allow contracting parties to take trade-restricting environmental measures which protect the environment outside their own jurisdiction. Such measures may either concern the environment in other contracting States such as tropical rainforests or endangered species (tigers, elephants) or the so-called "global commons" that do

---

[106] Court of Justice, *Commission v Council* (C–178/03) [2006] E.C.R. I–107; see on the double legal basis para.2–69 et seq., above.

[107] The EU adhered to WTO by Dec.94/800 [1994] OJ L336/1.

[108] See para.3–04 et seq., above.

not belong to the jurisdiction of anybody, such as the high sea, its resources and its fauna, the climate, the ozone layer and so on.

In 1991 and 1994, two different GATT panels considered US restrictions on imports of tuna fish caught with so-called purse-seine nets, which also trapped and killed large numbers of dolphins. The United States had prohibited the use of those nets and had, furthermore, banned the import of tuna that was caught with capturing methods which did not correspond to the US legislation. The first panel denied that the measures were compatible with art.XX(b), since they had extraterritorial effects[109]; the second panel expressly stated that GATT also allowed extra-territorial measures,[110] but was of the opinion that the measures were disproportionate. Neither finding has been approved by the relevant WTO/ GATT Council and have therefore remained unofficial.

Until now, EU environmental measures have not, as yet, been examined under **11–34** WTO procedures; the international debate is rather politicised and might well lead, within a short time, to such an examination. Possible measures that might come under such examination are: the EU provisions on eco-labelling,[111] which developing countries, in particular, consider to constitute trade barriers; the import restrictions on fur of animals caught with leghold traps[112]; and also packaging, labelling and recycling, the ban of certain substances, products or production methods and eco-taxes.

In 2006, a WTO panel decided in a dispute between United States, Canada and Argentina against the European Union.[113] The dispute concerned the question, whether the de facto moratorium on the authorisation for the placing on the market of new genetically modified products—see on that para.6–46, above—constituted an unjustified barrier to international trade. The panel held that the moratorium constituted a "measure" and that it could not be justified. To the extent that it continued to exist, the European Union was asked to take measures in order to restore free trade. It may be doubtful, whether this dispute really concerned an environmental matter. However, the case shows the potentially large impact which the WTO rules—including those on dispute settlement—may have on the EU policy.

In 2009, the European Union adopted a regulation that banned the trade in seals products.[114] Canada and Norway brought this case before the WTO, arguing that this was an unjustified barrier to free trade. As the EU measure was based on public morals—in particular the public concern about the inhumane killing of seals in Canada—WTO will have to answer the question, whether animal welfare considerations may justify the restrictions of international trade.

My own opinion is that environmental measures under WTO rules are permitted. The basic justification of this is that life, health and natural resources—which are a short formula equivalent to the environment—are not

---

[109] "The record indicates that the concerns of the drafters of Article XX (b) focused on the use of sanitary measures to safeguard life or health of humans, animals or plants within the jurisdiction of the importing country."

[110] "The panel further observes that, under general international law, states are not in principle barred from regulating the conduct of their nationals with respect to persons, animals, plants and natural resources outside of their territory… ."

[111] Reg.66/2010 [2010] OJ L27/1; see para.6–56, above.

[112] Reg.3254/91 [1991] OJ L308/1; see para.5–36, above.

[113] WTO, DS 291 USA against European Union. Panel Report of September 29, 2006.

[114] Reg.1007/2009 [2009] OJ L286/36.

available in unlimited quantities and cannot really be regarded to constitute trade barriers. Where measures are taken to protect the environment, which are neither discriminating nor disproportionate, such measures are also allowed, under WTO rules, to restrict international trade; and the differentiation between production and production standards cannot really lead to different results in this regard. It seems clear to me that, for instance, the US measures in the abovementioned tuna–dolphin case contained an element of protectionism (discrimination).

11–35   The problem with weighing the interests between trade and environment at international level lies in the fact that trade and economic interests prevail quantitatively and qualitatively in international discussions, particularly in developing countries.[115] There is hence all the more need for tribunals or dispute-settlement bodies where environmental considerations are given the same amount of attention as trade matters—which does not seem to be the case at present. Indeed, if one looks at the different reactions of GATT and WTO panels, where environmental and/or health matters were discussed, environmental matters do not have the same weight as economic or trade matters. In international discussions, outside concrete cases, even the European Union has a tendency to let trade interests prevail over environmental interests, for instance by arguing that measures to protect the environment outside the jurisdiction of the acting State should only be allowed where they are in conformity with internationally agreed measures.[116] The necessity of avoiding, on the one hand, protectionist measures that take the formal appearance of environmental protection (green protectionism) and, on the other hand, of allowing legitimate environmental protection measures, is likely to find some compromise solutions only gradually; it is not surprising that legal writers look particularly to regional solutions, such as the European Union or the North America Free Trade Area (NAFTA), in order to find solutions for the problems of integrating environmental requirements into international trade rules. Article 114(7) TFEU shows a possible future solution: much of the pressure on dolphins, sea turtles and other environmental assets would be avoided if the world community were willing and able to adopt worldwide measures to ensure adequate protection of dolphins, turtles or of marine mammals in general.

11–36   Also where environmental measures have been taken at international level, their compatibility with WTO/GATT rules may nevertheless be contested. In particular there is considerable discussion as to whether the three above-mentioned conventions on trade in endangered species, in ozone-depleting substances and in hazardous waste are in conflict with the general WTO rules. The panel on the GMO-standstill in the European Union which gave its report in September 2006, touched on these questions, in a more general form, though. It held that the rules of WTO prevailed over other conventions, at least as long as not all WTO Member States had adhered to the other convention. This opinion appears to be in conflict with rules of public international law (the Vienna Convention) and can be better explained by motivations to let trade rules prevail than by an attempt to balance diverging interests. The legal question as to which international agreement should prevail—the WTO agreement or the specific

---

[115] This is a matter of human behaviour which goes beyond environmental issues: "Ventre affamé n'a pas d'oreille" (J. de la Fontaine); "Erst kommt das Fressen und dann die Moral" (B. Brecht).
[116] Commission, COM (96) 54; see also the reproach by the European Parliament, Res. of May 24, 1996 [1996] OJ C166/260.

environmental convention—will have to be decided politically. Under the existing rules of international law, it is not possible to solve this question. Since all three environmental conventions have been elaborated under the auspices of the United Nations, it appears to be only consequent to assume that measures which are adopted by States or by the European Union, and which are in compliance with these international conventions, cannot be tackled under WTO rules. The fact that such trade restriction measures are also to be applied against States which have not ratified these specialised conventions, is not decisive.

The Montreal Protocol, the Basel Convention and the CITES Convention all allow the contracting parties to adopt more stringent provisions than those of the conventions, in order to protect the environment[117]; and the European Union has, in the different areas coming under those three conventions, made use of this possibility. The question then is whether such additional domestic measures that are taken at EU or at national level are also compatible with WTO rules. The problem has not yet been discussed in detail in legal literature. My own opinion is that such measures are also compatible with WTO rules, since they rest on an explicit authorisation of the conventions, which expresses the wish to improve environmental protection as far as possible. It is self-evident, though, that here, again, a careful examination has to take place in order to avoid such measures being discriminating or disproportionate.

11–37

The discussions on international trade and the environment are considerably affected by recent events at international level, in particular by the Iraq war of 2003. Already before these events, in particular the USA—in this often followed by Australia, New Zealand, Japan, Canada, Mexico, and South Korea—showed, at international level and in conferences, negotiations or meetings under existing conventions, a very limited interest in environmental protection and acted as the principal proponent of free trade; this attitude might be favoured by the fact that there is no environmental ministry in the US government which leads to the result that international discussions, unless they are purely technical, are led by either the Department of Commerce or the Department of State. Discussions on finding the appropriate balance between trade and environmental interests will not become easier by the Iraq events which have at least clarified to everybody that internationally, the rule of law is not the guiding rule for negotiations: power, political pressure and the promotion of interests are important, if not determining factors. This makes any speculation about the evolution of international environmental law and its relationship to trade law almost impossible.

11–38

7. Tourism and the environment

The Lisbon Treaty enabled the European Union to carry out actions "to support, coordinate or supplement" the actions of the Member States in the area of tourism, (art.6(d) TFEU). Article 195 TFEU specified this possibility, excluding though "any harmonisation of the laws and regulations of Member States".

11–39

---

[117] Basel Convention on the control of transboundary movement of hazardous wastes and their disposal (93) OJ L39/3, art.3(11); CITES Convention [1982] OJ L384/1, art.XIV. The Montreal Protocol is formally a Protocol of the Vienna Convention on the protection of the ozone layer; the EU became a party to that Convention and the Montreal Protocol in 1988 (Dec.88/540 [1988] OJ L297/8); art.2 of that Convention allows additional domestic measures.

Tourism contributes in particular to land, energy and water use, waste generation and, via travelling, to air pollution and climate change. It is developing into the largest service industry in the European Union. Particular areas of attention are coastal zones, the Mediterranean and the Alps.

While the integration of environmental requirements into tourism was considered, under the fifth environmental action programme, one of five priority policy areas, this approach changed rather rapidly. The sixth environmental action programme mentions tourism in half a phrase.[118] and also the European Environment Agency stopped mentioning tourism as a separate sector of its report on environmental trends.[119] Thus, environmental measures on tourism became, within 10 years, a negative priority for the European Union.

11–40   Legal matters on tourism are affected by the lack of an explicit competence on tourism. Hence, objectives of tourism policy are not fixed at EU level—except for the statement that tourism should be or become sustainable. And no legal instruments have until now been adopted or proposed to promote this vague idea. The integration of environmental requirements into tourist policy measures remains thus incoherent, largely based on financial assistance to pilot or demonstration projects.

The idea of eco-labels for restaurants, beaches,[120] villages or other holiday resorts has not led to any EU-wide initiative, though eco-labelling for accommodation has significantly increased in the European Union over the last 20 years. In 2003, the European Union adopted rules for attributing the EU eco-label to accommodations and fixed conditions for that; this was followed by an eco-label for camping places.[121] Both provisions put the emphasis on water and energy saving. To what extent hotels and camping places apply for the eco-label is not yet clear.

There are no attempts until now to address the problems of tourism in coastal zones or in mountainous areas. The European Union adhered to the Convention on the Alps,[122] and its Protocols on mountain farming, tourism, and soil conservation, but not to its Protocols on landscape management, mountain forestry, and transport; and as, anyway, the application of international conventions is not monitored by the European Union as long as there are no internal EU measures, this accession has not changed the situation. It rather appears that the same experience which economic and tourist development has caused to the Alpine environment, is being repeated in other mountainous regions, such as the Pyrenees, the Carpates, etc. It is therefore no surprise that all indicators for tourism which the European Environment Agency has established—modal split in tourism transport, environmental costs as part of tourist pricing, carrying capacity of destinations, reduction of energy use—are negative; only the above-mentioned evolution in eco-labelling is seen as stable.[123]

---

[118] Dec.1600/2002 [2002] OJ L242/1, art.6(2.e): (Priority actions should be) "promoting the integration of conservation and restoration of the landscape values into other policies including tourism, taking into account relevant international instruments".

[119] European Environment Agency (fn.21, above), p.30.

[120] See in this regard the blue-flag system, para.7–15, above.

[121] Dec.2003/287 (tourist accommodation services) [2003] OJ L102/82; Dec.2005/338 (campsite services) [2005] OJ L108/67.

[122] Dec.96/191 [1996] OJ L61/31.

[123] European Environment Agency (fn.21, above), p.24.

CHAPTER 12

Implementation

1. Obligations of Member States to apply EU law

Treaty provisions

The Lisbon Treaties do not contain environmental provisions which Member **12–01**
States would have to transpose into, or to apply in, their national legal order.
Article 4(3) TEU states that Member States shall assist the Union in carrying out
its tasks and facilitate achieving its tasks.[1] However, this does not mean that they
would have to place in their national legislation the objective of attaining a high
level of environmental protection or the aim that environmental requirements are
incorporated into the other policies pursued at national level. In contrast, art.4(3)
TEU requires Member States to abstain from any measures at national level,
which would make it more difficult or impossible for the EU to move towards a
high level of environmental protection or to make the different EU policies
"greener", i.e. environmentally more friendly.

   The environmental provisions of the Treaties are not formulated in such a way
that they are self-executing or, in EU terminology, directly applicable. While
art.34 TFEU prohibits creating or maintaining barriers to trade within the
European Union, art.101 TFEU prohibits trade-distorting agreement between
undertakings, art.102 prohibits abuses of dominant positions and art.107 TFEU
state aids, no corresponding provision exists in environmental law, for instance
forbidding environmental pollution. National enforcement bodies or courts
therefore do not have to align Member States' laws to instructions that come from
EU primary law.

Secondary legislation

The situation is completely different as regards secondary EU environmental law. **12–02**
Under art.192(4) TFEU, it is, in principle, the Member States that have to
implement the different measures which have been adopted in pursuance of EU
environmental policy. This provision is somewhat superfluous, since in other EU
policies, too, where no such provision exists, the implementation of measures is

---

[1] art.4(3) TEU: "Pursuant to the principle of sincere cooperation, the Union and the Member States
shall, in full mutual respect, assist each other in carrying out tasks which flow from this Treaty. The
Member States hall take any appropriate measure, general or particular, to ensure fulfilment of the
obligations arising out of the Treaties or resulting from the acts of the institutions of the Union. The
Member States shall facilitate the achievement of the Union's tasks and refrain from any measure
which could jeopardise the attainment of the Union's objective".

an obligation for Member States which follows from art.4(3) TEU. EU directives and decisions address Member States; EU regulations apply in all Member States without even any transposing act (art.288 TFEU). In no situation is there any decision by a national Parliament or regulating body required or admitted to accept or not to accept EU secondary law provisions. This then is the fundamental difference that distinguishes EU environmental law from public international law, which requires, in order to become valid, an express act by the national legislative body.

Regulations directly apply in each Member State (art.288(2) TFEU); and while environmental regulations frequently contain specific provisions that require Member States to take action—such as the appointing of responsible authorities, the publication of reports or even the taking of executive provisions—their general attribute of being directly applicable remains unchanged; the specific provision then has the characteristics of a directive and needs to be implemented, unless it is, in substance, a recommendation. Similar observations apply to decisions, which normally deal with a specific, concrete situation; where a specific provision in a decision is, in substance, that of a directive, it would require implementation as if it were a directive.[2]

12–03   "A directive shall be binding, as to the result to be achieved, upon each Member State to which it is addressed, but shall leave to the national authorities the choice of form and methods" (art.288(3) TFEU). As EU legislation must be applied by Member States—this follows from arts 4 and 17 TEU[3]—Member States have two main obligations as regards EU environmental directives: they must incorporate the provisions of the directive into their national law and they must ensure that these provisions are actually complied with.

Transposition

12–04   Practically all[4] environmental directives contain a provision that requests Member States to transpose the Directive's provisions into national law.[5] Generally, such a transposition into national law has to be done by an express binding legislative or regulatory provision, "in order to secure full implementation of directives in law and not only in facts".[6] The Court of Justice has, on

---

[2] See, more generally, para. 2–36 et seq., above.

[3] art.17 TEU: "The Commission ... shall ensure the application of the Treaties, and of measures adopted by the institutions pursuant to them. It shall oversee the application of Union law under the control of the Court of Justice of the European Union."

[4] The exceptions are Dir.76/464 on pollution caused by certain dangerous substances discharged into the aquatic environment of the Community [1976] OJ L129/23, where this clause was probably forgotten; and Dir.91/692 on standardising and rationalising reports on the implementation of certain directives relating to the environment [1991] OJ L377/48.

[5] See, e.g. art.23 of Dir.92/43 on the conservation of natural habitats and of wild fauna and flora [1992] OJ L206/7:

"1. Member States shall bring into force the laws, regulations and administrative provisions necessary to comply with this Directive within two years of its notification. They shall forthwith inform the Commission thereof.

2. When Member States adopt such measures, they shall contain a reference to this Directive or be accompanied by such reference on the occasion of their official publication. The methods of making such a reference shall be laid down by the Member States.

3. Member States shall communicate to the Commission the main provisions of national law which they adopt in the field covered by this Directive."

[6] *Commission v Germany* (C–131/88) [1991] E.C.R. I–825, para.8.

numerous occasions, rejected Member States' attempts to transpose the requirements of an environmental directive into national law by means of a multi-annual plan, an administrative circular or a similar instrument.[7] Its main argument was the absence of legal certainty for individual persons and undertakings that was created by such a transposition, as it was not clear which rights and obligations followed out of an EU directive.[8] Since the Court of Justice is of the opinion that directives which fix quality standards also give certain legal rights to individuals, most of the provisions of a directive will have to be transposed into national law by a binding provision. This applies even to the establishment of the requirement to set up clean-up programmes or waste management programmes; indeed, such programmes also contain information for individuals about future objectives, about measures taken and envisaged and so on.

Exceptions apply only to those provisions which provide for obligations of the Council, the Commission or other institutions, and, in addition, to provisions which exclusively concern the Member States' relations to the EU administration and ask them, for instance, to send a report regularly to the Commission. Even in such cases, though, the limits to Member States' obligations are not altogether clear: the Court of Justice held that a provision that requires regional or local authorities in border regions to consult with authorities from the adjacent Member State, had to be transposed into national law.[9] The same applied to a provision where a Member State was allowed to grant a derogation under a directive, but had to inform the Commission thereof; where that Member State delegated the right to grant derogations to regional or local authorities, it had expressly ensured that it was informed of the granting of derogations in order to be able to comply with its own requirements towards the Commission.[10] In the same way, it could also be argued that a Member State's implementation report to the Commission, where the Member State reports, how a piece of EU legislation was transposed into the national legal order and how it was applied in practice, ensures transparency of implementation and compliance, allows individuals to take action themselves or otherwise orient their behaviour, and that it therefore has an external effect which requires its transpositions into legally binding legislation.

12–05

The necessity of transposing definitions in an EU directive into national law probably depends on the subject-matter that is regulated: the more directly individual rights and obligations might be affected by a definition, the greater the need to transpose a directive's definition into national law. Good examples are the

12–06

[7] *Commission v Netherlands* (C–96/81) [1982] E.C.R. 1791; *Commission v Germany* (C–131/88) (fn.6, above); *Commission v Germany* (C–361/88) [1991] E.C.R. I–2567; *Commission v France* (C–13/90) [1991] E.C.R. I–4327; *Commission v Germany* (C–58/89) [1991] E.C.R. 4983; *Commission v Germany* (C–262/95) [1996] E.C.R. I–5729.
[8] See, e.g. C–131/88 (fn.6, above), para.6: "The transposition of a directive into domestic law does not necessarily require that its provisions be incorporated formally and verbatim in express, specific legislation; a general legal context may, depending on the content of the directive, be adequate for the purpose provided that it does indeed guarantee the full application of the directive in a sufficiently clear and precise manner so that, where the directive is intended to create rights for individuals, the persons concerned can ascertain the full extent of their rights and where appropriate, rely on them before the national courts."
[9] *Commission v Belgium* (C–186/91) [1993] E.C.R. I–851.
[10] *Commission v Germany* (C–237/90) [1992] E.C.R. I–5973.

definitions of "waste" and "hazardous waste" under Directive 2008/98[11]: Member States' legislation often does not use the words "hazardous waste", but "specific waste", "waste which is to be controlled", "chemical waste", "industrial waste" and other definitions. These linguistic differentiations have consequences as regards monitoring, surveillance, statistics, customs and police controls and other administrative matters, which impinge in turn on private agents, individuals or administrations. For this reason the Commission has adopted the position that the definitions for waste and for hazardous waste had to be transposed literally into national laws. The Court of Justice required a transposition of a definition at least in those cases, where an omission to transpose created doubts as to the meaning of provisions.[12]

12–07   The transposition of an environmental directive, which contains mandatory requirements, cannot be made by non-binding national measures, in particular by administrative provisions, since:

> "mere administrative practices, which by their nature may be changed at will by the authorities, cannot be regarded as constituting proper compliance with the obligation on Member States to which a directive is addressed." (*Commission v Italy* (C–429/85) [1988] E.C.R. 843; *Commission v Netherlands* (C–339/87) [1990] E.C.R. I–851.)

For this reason, implementation of an environmental directive through an environmental voluntary agreement is not possible, unless an EU directive expressly so provides[13]; such a possibility was foreseen, these last years and for the first time, by some provisions of some waste directives.[14] As environmental agreements only apply to contracting bodies, the equality of citizens with regard to rights or obligations that a directive grants is not ensured. Transposition of a directive by environmental agreements that are not generally binding is therefore not possible.

A transposition is also necessary in those cases where the Member State in fact already complies with the requirements of a directive. The legal certainty that economic operators and individuals are entitled to expect would be completely undermined if the local, regional or national administration could argue that the factual situation corresponds to the requirements of the directive and places the burden of proof that this is not the case on the person arguing that transposition is necessary.[15]

12–08   No obligation to transpose the requirements of a directive exists where it is physically impossible that the problem dealt with by the directive could ever occur in a Member State. Thus, Luxembourg or Austria would not be obliged to transpose requirements of a directive on coastal waters or (sea) port reception

---

[11] Dir.2009/98 on waste [2009] OJ L312/3.

[12] Court of Justice, *Commission v France* (C–443/08) judgment of May 7, 2009; see also *Commission v Luxemburg* (C–32/05) [2006] E.C.R. I–4323.

[13] In the same sense, Commission Rec. 96/733 concerning environmental agreements implementing Community directives [1996] OJ C333/59.

[14] Dir.2000/53 on end-of-life vehicles [2000] OJ L269/34; Dir.2002/96 on waste electrical and electronic equipment [2003] OJ L37/24; Dir. 2006/66 on batteries and accumulators [2006] OJ L 266/1. Dir.85/339 on liquid beverage containers [1985] OJ L176/18, which is often quoted as allowing implementation of directives by environmental agreements, is not relevant: indeed, the Directive required Member States to set up packaging reduction programmes and then allowed the implementation of such programmes by non-binding measures; the Directive has in the meantime been repealed.

[15] C–339/87 (fn.13, above).

facilities.[16] In contrast, these Member States would normally be obliged to transpose the directive on (the sea discharge of) waste from the titanium dioxide industry,[17] even if they had no such industry on their territory, as this situation could change and, furthermore, titanium dioxide waste from other Member States might be transported to States that do not have such an industry.[18]

The transposition measures must cover the whole of the territory of a Member State. This observation sounds more trivial than it is. Indeed, in many Member States responsibility for environmental issues lies at least partly with regional authorities; this is the case for Austria, Belgium, Germany, Italy and Spain. But in other Member States, too, environmental legislation is partially split; thus, environmental regulations in the United Kingdom are partly taken in or for Wales, Scotland, Northern Ireland or Gibraltar, and in Finland, the Aaland Islands have a specific legislative status. Finally, waste management plans in Sweden and the United Kingdom are traditionally set up at local level.

From the point of view of the European Union it is not relevant whether a provision of EU law is transposed by one single act at national level or by a number of regional regulations, as long as the transposition measures cover the whole of the territory.

It is much more difficult to comply with the second substantive requirement **12–09** for the transposition measure; that is, that the EU environmental requirement is correctly transposed. First, a Member State may not rely on the wording in which a specific directive is drafted in the Member State's language—all EU languages have the same legal value (art.55 TEU) and that wording may differ from one language to the other. For that reason, the true sense of a provision has to be discovered, which may well vary between specific linguistic versions.[19] Secondly, it has already been mentioned in para.3–02, above, that EU law is autonomous and has to be interpreted without recurring to identical or similar notions that exist in national law. Thus, the same word might be used in EU environmental law and in national law and yet the two meanings are quite different: this potential conflict is increased by the fact that EU law prevails over national law. However, since EU law stems from a source of law other than national law, it might carry different concepts, theories or structures that do not fit into the national legal or administrative infrastructure. An example is art.9(2) of the Directive on the conservation of wild birds,[20] which provided that local nature protection authorities may give derogations from trading, hunting and other bans under the Directive, after having examined the local situation; however, such local nature protection authorities do not exist in Ireland.

---

[16] See for example Dir.2008/56 establishing a framework for Community action in the field of marine environmental policy (Marine Strategy Framework Directive) [2008] OJ L164/19, art.26(7) which provides that Member States without marine waters are only obliged to comply with art.6 (regional cooperation) and art.7(designation of competent authorities).

[17] Dir.78/176 [1978] OJ L54/19.

[18] See in this sense also Court of Justice, *Commission v Portugal* (C–435/99) [2000] E.C.R. I–11179. In practice, the Commission has accepted that Member States that do not have a titanium dioxide industry formally commit themselves to transposing the Directive as soon as such an industry is established on their territory or where waste from such industry is shipped into their country; for the reasons mentioned, this practice is not in compliance with EU law.

[19] Court of Justice, *Spain v Council* (C–36/98) [2001] E.C.R. I–779; *Kraaijeveld* (C–72/95) [1996] E.C.R. I–5403; the last case concerned the interpretation of Dir.85/337 on environment impact assessment.

[20] Dir.2009/147 on the conservation of wild birds [2010] OJ L20/7.

12–10   Another complication is that EU environmental law provisions normally come
up against a structured and elaborate system of national rules that have been built
up over years or decades, and into which the provisions then have to be
integrated. The EU provision is then perceived—and all too often also
treated—as an immigrant, if not as an intruder.[21]

Where the EU environmental law provision sets numerical values such as
emission limit values, quality standards or targets, national legislation will have
to adopt these numerical values. Economic operators and individuals must have
the opportunity to find in the national statute books what these numerical values
are.[22] The same applies to bans on substances or products. For other provisions, it
is normally difficult to establish fixed rules, since it follows from art.288 TFEU
that a word-by-word transmission of the EU provision is not required.

12–11   A correct transposition also requires the establishing of sanctions for
non-compliance with the EU provisions.[23] It is true that EU directives do not
contain more than very general provisions on sanctions for non-compliance, and
regulations, too, remain very general. The reason for this is that sanctions are in
many countries understood as criminal or quasi-criminal sanctions and that the
European Union has, until now, abstained from providing for criminal sanctions
in cases, where the provisions of a directive or regulation are not respected; even
where administrative sanctions could be used, there is considerable self-restraint
used by the European Union when addressing the details of sanctions. This also
applies to environmental regulations, though it follows from art.261 TFEU that
regulations could contain penal sanctions.[24] The Court of Justice interpreted
art.4(3) TEU to mean that national sanctions for non-compliance with EU law
must be equivalent to sanctions for breach of equivalent national law provisions;
furthermore, that they must be effective and proportionate and dissuasive.[25] This
or a similar formula is used in numerous EU environmental directives or
regulations. The transposition of this formula in the different legal orders of
Member States has, until now, not been the subject of any serious control.

Application

12–12   Finally, Member States are under an obligation to ensure the practical application
of EU environmental law. The transposition itself is only a formal legal act,
whereas the protection of the environment begins when emissions are reduced,
substances no longer put on the market or (the equivalent) into the environment,
habitats protected, and so on. The practical application of environmental
provisions is the most serious problem that national, EU and international
environmental law faces. Even a piece of national legislation that copies a
directive word for word will remain a mere piece of paper unless it is applied.

---

[21] Commission, European governance—a White Paper, COM (2001) 428, [2001] OJ C287/1, p.21:
"the feeling persists that Community rules are 'foreign laws'".
[22] See C–361/88 (fn.7, above): "It is clear that legal certainty also requires the specific transposal of
individual limit-values, maximum permissible concentrations and emission values into national
legislation. A general reference to Community legislation is not permitted."
[23] *Commission v Greece* (C–68/88) [1989] E.C.R. 2965.
[24] art.261 TFEU: "Regulations ... may give the Court of Justice of the European Union unlimited
jurisdiction with regard to the penalties provided for in such regulations."
[25] C–68/88 (fn.24, above).

Some unique features which seriously affect the full application of EU environmental law in practice, must be remembered. Since environmental provisions try to protect the general interest of the European Union, they differ markedly from agricultural, transport or industry legislation, which primarily affects specific vested interests. Where vested interests are in question, law making and law enforcement take place, in Western Europe, in constant public—and sometimes not so public—discussions with the representatives of those vested interests; this discussion also continues within the various administrations, parliaments and decision-making bodies. Vested interest groups are also used to ensure the transmission of knowledge on the specific legislation and in this way contribute either to ensuring compliance with the legal rule or bringing about concerted action against that rule, often even preventing its generation. This lobbying function of vested interest groups has become an integrated factor of decision-making at EU level and at the level of Member States.

The general interest "environment" has no vested interest defender. Environmental organisations in Western Europe are structurally and financially too weak to defend environmental interests effectively over a long period of time. While there is consensus that the environment needs adequate protection and that economic development should be "sustainable", the implementation of concrete, legally binding measures proves difficult wherever other, diverging interests appear. The environment, without a voice and without strong lobby groups, loses out in almost every specific conflict of interests. Since, furthermore, local, regional and national administrations in the 27 Member States are not all convinced to the same extent that EU environmental standards are to be enforced, complied with and applied in practice, practical application of environmental provisions varies within the European Union.

General features also contribute to this situation. In a number of Member States, particularly in the south and in the new Member States, environmental problems are perceived to be the problems of affluent society; hence there is an attitude among economic operators, and also among administrations, that economic progress is of primary necessity and that environmental concerns should be tackled once the economic level of richer Member States has been reached. To this has to be added the different enforcement culture which exists in the European Union, traditional weaknesses of central government in some Member States, the lack of national environmental infrastructures such as adequate administrations at local, regional and national level, and a lack of environmental information and education, of general awareness, of environmental research bodies, laboratories and test or monitoring or enforcement bodies.

2.   Monitoring transposition and application

Implementation reports

12–14   Almost all EU environmental directives have contained, since the mid-1970s, a provision asking Member States to report on the implementation of the directive. Typically, such reports had to be made every three years.[26] The Commission was charged with producing, on the basis of these national reports, an EU report on the implementation of the directive in question; the normal period for these reports was, similarly, every three years.

This system did not lead to the desired result, since neither the Member States' implementation reports nor the Commission's comprehensive reports were drawn up regularly. Only for the Bathing Water Directive[27] were regular reports published; however, these dealt with the state of quality of bathing water rather than the implementation of the Directive. Also, monitoring of a number of parameters was omitted and the data transmitted from the Member States were, until recently, not comparable.

12–15   In order to improve the reporting system, the Council adopted, in 1991, a Directive that restructured the reporting requirements.[28] This Directive introduced the requirement for Member States to report, every three years, on the implementation of the different directives in a given sector (for instance, water, air or waste). The reports were to be based on questionnaires which were set up by committee procedure at EU level, in order to allow the national reports to address the same issues. The reporting period was three years.

The Directive has not significantly improved the situation. The reports on water, waste and chemicals were published with considerable delay; a report on air pollution lacks completely. And those directives that have been adopted since 1991 have only partly aligned their reporting requirements to Directive 91/692. Where Member States submit reports to the Commission, these reports, together with the national implementing legislation which is at the Commission's disposal anyway, allow a relatively clear picture to be gained on the transposition of a directive into national law. However, such reports normally do not contain information on difficulties of practical application or cases of non-compliance, lacunae and omissions on the side of local, regional or national administrations, inspections, sanctions, or on specific interpretations of individual provisions. They report on measures taken and legislation adopted, not on results achieved and the state of the environment.

12–16   Commission implementation reports are, overall, very disappointing, apart from the reports on the quality of bathing waters, which continue to be published annually. Directive 91/692 did not lead to a systematic attempt to improve implementation reporting, despite other announcements.[29] Generally, the Commission's different reports on the implementation of the environmental directives

---

[26] See, however, Dir.2006/7 on the quality of bathing water [2006] OJ L64/37, where art.13 provided for annual reports by Member States and by the Commission.

[27] Dir.76/160 [1976] OJ L31/1. This Dir. is now replaced by Dir. 2006/7 (fn.27, above).

[28] Dir.91/692 (fn.4, above).

[29] Commission, Implementing Community environmental law, COM (96) 500, para.58: "Through the most effective use of the Reporting Directive, and close co-operation with the European Environmental Agency, the Commission will ensure that the best possible information is available on the effectiveness of Community environmental measures and can be used in the formulation of its

have, in the past, been marked by the fact that the information contained therein came almost exclusively from the (central) administration of Member States. For that reason, the EU reports, like the national reports, give a relatively reliable picture on the legal and administrative parts of implementing EU directives—for those Member States that did report. However, less information will be found on, for example, monitoring frequency and intensity, practical non-compliance, gaps and omissions of the administrations and results achieved. In order to address this problem, the EU institutions examine, whether in future, the assistance of the European Environment Agency should be obtained when the EU implementation reports are reported. However, these reflections exist already since about twenty years. A review of the environmental reporting provisions is also announced since several years, but has not yet led to concrete proposals.

The Commission has, it is true, conducted some studies of its own on the practical implementation of environmental directives in the Member States, although inevitably only a limited number of these studies have been undertaken. Their value is limited, though, by the fact that it has proved extremely difficult to gain access to the data held by the national, regional or local authorities on the practical application—and non-application; no administration would be easily persuaded to release data showing that a directive is not properly monitored or applied in practice, whether the failure is found in the frequency and results of inspections, the attitude of economic operators that were controlled, the pollution levels recorded or the respect of the conditions laid down in the permits that the administrations have granted. And the Commission does not even make such transposition studies publicly available, but keeps them confidential—for no legitimate reason; this increases administrative secrecy and makes research into effects of EU environmental legislation significantly more difficult.

The Commission's monitoring function

The Commission has to ensure that EU environmental law is applied (art.17 **12–17** TEU). This provision is the nucleus which has allowed the Commission to develop, over the years, a system of monitoring transposition, application and enforcement, which goes far beyond of everything that is known in the relations between States. It is this monitoring task of the Commission that has caused the Commission to be called the "guardian of the Treaty".

It should, however, not be forgotten that it is Member States which have, according to arts 4 TEU and 192(4) TFEU, the obligation to ensure the implementation of EU environmental law; this then means that Member States have to ensure that EU environmental law is applied. The establishment and functioning of the European Union is also the task of Member States and it is they which have to ensure that "their" constitution—the Lisbon Treaties—including its environmental provisions, is properly applied.[30]

---

policies on environmental measures. The Commission will launch and co-ordinate case studies to evaluate the transposition, application and enforcement of selected provisions of Community environmental law."

[30] Commission (fn.30, above), para.25: "The Commission simply cannot monitor the thousands of individual decisions taken each year ... in the different parts and levels of authority within the Member States. The daily application and enforcement ... must be fully ensured by the authorities in the Member States . . . ."

12–18   The Commission's task is to ensure that all EU primary and secondary environmental law is applied, in particular regulations, directives and decisions. As regards international conventions, it has already been stated that the Commission does not monitor their application within the European Union, not even in cases where the European Union adhered to them. This self-restraint has never been justified or reasoned in public. It is legally unjustifiable. Indeed, where the European Union adheres to an international environmental convention, the convention becomes part of EU law (art.216(2) TFEU). The Commission then has to ensure its application, as art.17 TEU does not differentiate between different parts of EU law. By adhering to a convention, the European Union takes the commitment that it will ensure compliance with provisions of this convention throughout the territory of the European Union. This obligation rests with the European Union as such and pertains to the whole EU territory, even where a specific Member State has not ratified the international convention in question. Once the European Union has adhered to the international convention, Member States are obliged, under art.4 TEU, to take the necessary steps in order to allow the European Union to respect its international commitments. This legal obligation was confirmed, in substance by the Court of Justice in a case against France which had not ratified an international agreement. But the European Union had, and the Court found that France was obliged to respect the requirements of the international agreement.[31]

12–19   In reality, it is clear, though, that the Commission has a particular responsibility of ensuring application of EU environmental law, because the European Union is the source of these legal provisions. The Commission does not have any structures to monitor application of environmental legal provisions; this is ensured, rather, by the general Commission administration. In particular, the Commission does not have any inspection bodies to examine whether and to what extent EU environmental law is actually complied with.[32] Discussions on green inspectors have been emotionalised as being an intrusion on national sovereignty and, furthermore, as being incompatible with the subsidiarity principle. This criticism omits to mention that there are Commission inspectors in the areas of competition, veterinary, customs, regional and fishery policy, without questions of interference or subsidiarity ever having been raised. The Commission is very cautious in considering the setting up of EU inspectors.[33] The Council and Member States are clearly opposed to EU environmental inspectors.[34]

Since 1983 the Commission has published annual reports on monitoring the application of EU law,[35] which include a chapter on environmental legislation; attempts in 1991/1992 to produce a specific environmental report failed. The reports publish some general data and trends on the application of EU environmental law, but do not provide complete transparency, do not establish

---

[31] Court of Justice, *Etangs de Berre* (C–213/03) [2004] E.C.R. I–7357; *Commission v France* (C–239/03) [2004] E.C.R. I–9325.

[32] Rec.2001/331 [2001] OJ L118/41 recommends Member States to provide for inspectors in environmental matters; a corresponding recommendation for the EU institutions does not exist.

[33] Commission (fn.30, above), para.9: "Further consideration would be given as to whether there might be a need for a limited Community body with auditing competencies."

[34] Council Res. of October 7, 1997 [1997] OJ C321/1.

[35] See 24th report on monitoring application of Community law, (2006), COM (2007) 398; 25th report (2007), COM (2008)777; 26th report (2008), COM (2009) 675 [1997] OJ C332/1; 27th report (2009), COM [2010] 538.

data which are comparable over the years, and are not always completely reliable[36]; since about 2001, they have become more and more general and vague and principally report on cases which have been brought to the Court of Justice or where a reasoned opinion had been issued, without giving details and without explaining, where the application of a specific directive stands with regard to a specific Member State. The reports are therefore of a rather limited informative value.

Monitoring by other bodies

The European Parliament does not fulfil any significant function in the monitoring of EU environmental legislation. Members of the Parliament pose, it is true, a great number of written or oral questions, which include issues of application of environmental legislation; however, these initiatives remain non-systematic. Since the year 2000, the European Parliament occasionally organised debates in its Environmental Committee, where the Commission has to lay account on its monitoring of the application of environmental provisions. These debates did not yet lead to any organisational consequences.   **12–20**

Where the European Parliament receives a petition from a citizen within the European Union, it does not—contrary to the practice in most Member States—itself investigate the facts which underlie the petition, but leaves the investigation to the Commission, for which the national administration is the principal interlocutor, to clarify the facts. This is a dubious practice, because the Commission is, since some years, rather selective in its handling of cases, and petitions sometimes also complain on the Commission's passivity.

The European Environment Agency, which was set up in 1990,[37] does not have any role in monitoring the application of EU environmental law. When the Agency was set up, the European Parliament had vehemently requested such a monitoring role, following, in that, the example of the United States Environmental Protection Agency. However, it could not persuade the Council, which only conceded that in art.20 of Regulation 1210/90 a clause should be inserted according to which the Council would check "at the latest within two years" whether the Agency should be allocated tasks in the monitoring of application of EU environmental law. When the Commission submitted the corresponding proposal in 1997, it did not suggest giving monitoring tasks to the Agency[38]; the European Parliament had forgotten its previous insistence and the Council did not take this issue up either.[39]

The EU Ombudsman, set up under art.228 TFEU, has the task of controlling complaints of maladministration in the activities of the EU institutions or bodies. This might include maladministration in the treatment of citizen complaints in environmental matters or general omissions in the monitoring of application of environmental legislation. In the beginning of 2010, his office had a staff of some   **12–21**

---

[36] See H. Somsen, "Current issues of implementation, compliance and enforcement of EC environmental law: a critical analysis", in L. Krämer (ed.) *Recht und Um-Welt, Essays in Honour of Prof.Dr.Gerd Winter* . (Groningen: Europa Law Publishing, 2003) p.415.
[37] Reg.1210/90 [1990] OJ L120/1; see also para.2–19, above.
[38] [1997] OJ C255/9, amended [1998] OJ C123/6.
[39] Reg.933/1999 [1999] OJ L117/1 amending Reg.1210/90 (fn.38, above).

70 persons. His control activities occasionally deal with environmental issues, but try to avoid becoming a complaint instance against decisions taken by the Commission.[40]

The Commission announced, in the fifth environmental action programme, that it would set up an implementation network which would aim "primarily at exchange of information and experience and at the development of common approaches at practical level, under the supervision of the Commission".[41] However, at that time Member States had already started to set up themselves an informal implementation network. As they vigorously opposed any mechanism at EU level that would give the Commission more options to monitor application of environmental provisions, they accepted the Commission as a member of that network, but kept its informal nature, and, since 1993, have called it the "European Union Network for the Implementation and Enforcement of Environmental Law" (IMPEL).[42] At present, the network consists of representatives of the enforcement and monitoring bodies of Member States, and Commission representatives; however, since a number of Member States do not have specific enforcement and monitoring bodies, officials from central or regional administrations take part in the network. IMPEL mainly deals with exchange of experience on practical application and enforcement issues, exchange of staff, and the elaboration of guidelines for different aspects of application. IMPEL is financed jointly by Member States and the Commission. Its impact on the actual application of environmental directives is very limited, since it concentrates on horizontal questions. In 2008, its structure was turned into that of a (private) association—which reveals all the more that its objective is not the monitoring of compliance of Member States with EU law.

Citizen complaints

12–22   As the Commission does not have any inspectors, controllers or decentralised administrations which would inform it on the application of EU environmental law within the whole of the European Union, its main source of information on possible omissions in the application of EU environmental provision is the information that comes from outside the administrations, in particular from citizens.

The Commission instituted, in the late 1960s, a complaint system for citizens, in order to obtain information on non-technical barriers to the free circulation of goods. The Commission offered to intervene with Member States' administration in order to eliminate border controls and other barriers. Since the mid–1980s, the system has developed considerably as regards environmental complaints. The fact that individuals were able to register a complaint with the Commission stimulated EU-wide awareness of the environment, demonstrated to the citizen that the Commission was also accessible to the man in the street and made it clear to the individual that he had some responsibility for his environment, that he could become active in contributing to the preservation and protection of the

---

[40] See European Ombudsman, Annual Report 1996 [1997] OJ C272/1.
[41] Commission, Fifth environmental action programme [1993] OJ C138/5, Ch. 9.
[42] Commission (fn.30, above), para.54 et seq.

environment and that environmental impairment should not be taken as an Act of God, against which nothing can be done. This was particularly important for southern European Member States.

Environmental complaints to the Commission came—and come—from individuals, environmental or professional organisations, national, regional or European deputies, local administrations, political parties, ambassadors and occasionally even from environment ministers of Member States.[43]

12–23

The Commission considered as a complaint any written statement that invokes the breach of EU (environmental) law and asked the Commission to intervene to repair this breach. The formal requirements for such a complaint are very low; the reason for this lies in the fact that the Commission has, under art.17 TFEU, the possibility of starting, even without having received a complaint, an inquiry into possible breaches of EU law by a Member State. Procedurally, such an official inquiry is treated in exactly the same way as a complaint. To facilitate the introduction of complaints, the Commission had even drawn up and published a form.[44]

The complaint is registered in a central Commission register. The Commission stated in 2002 that "all complaints received are registered, without any selection". The registration had as a consequence that the complainant was kept informed as to the evolution of the complaint and that only the Commission as an institution—not an individual official—could decide on the final outcome of it.

12–24

The Commission tries to obtain as much factual information from the complainant as possible, which often overburdens the person who has introduced the complaint. For the rest of the facts, the Commission seeks to obtain factual and legal information from the (central) administration of the Member State against which the complaint is directed. In rare cases, expert advice is taken. Hearings or witnesses' testimony are never taken in environmental cases. Also, inspections in Member States do not take place; in very rare cases, visits to the affected sites in the form of fact-finding missions have been organised, but not more frequently than once per year.

In the 1980s, the Commission committed itself—both on the complaint form and in different declarations towards the public—to instruct each complaint; in 1999, it indicated that its administrations would decide according to the internal rules and priorities whether they would examine a complaint or not.[45] And in 2002, the Commission further reduced its commitment to examine each complaint. Under the Barroso-Presidency, the Commission set up a "Pilot scheme": when a complaint is received, it is registered in a special register. Then, the Commission addresses the Member State in question to find out, what the problem is and how it could be solved. The difference to the complaint system is that the Commission administration co-operates with the national administration in order to arrange things; as this is outside any public participation and no information is released, very often the national administration—which frequently is at the origin of the problem by granting permits, remaining passive on disregard of environmental law—gets away with its practice. Also this practice

12–25

---

[43] The evolution of the number of complaints went from 10 in 1982 to 697 in 2002. Since then, the number of complaints goes back, also because the Commission no longer registers all complaints it receives, voiced its reluctance to instruct individual cases and rather tried to reach arrangements with Member States on breaches of EU environmental law.

[44] [1989] OJ C26/1; reviewed [1999] OJ C119/5.

[45] See the different versions of the complaint forms (fn.45, above).

led, during the last years, to a refusal to register complaints, where Commission officials felt that no breach of Community law was likely, or to similar abuses, a clear contradiction to the Commission's own commitment to register all complaints.[46]

Anyway, no sanction exists against an omission to instruct properly, except for disciplinary measures and, eventually, the intervention of the European Ombudsman. The complainant has no direct rights as regards the omission to examine a complaint or to treat it by way of the arrangement (pilot) procedure. Overall, this change in administrative practice by the Commission led, within five years, to reduce the number of instructed cases for example against Spain from some 480 to 30—though no change in the Spanish environmental policy or practice occurred.

The Commission refused all requests to lay down, in a legal instrument, the procedures for examining potential breaches of EU environmental law. Such a legal instrument exists in competition law, where complaints by private persons or associations, or media reports are taken by the Commission as valuable sources of information for examining potential breaches.[47] The difference of treatment between competition and environmental law is flagrant and cannot be explained.[48]

At the end of the instruction period of a petition, a complaint, or an own-initiative investigation, which shall not, according to the Commission's internal instructions, extend beyond one year, the Commission decides either to file the case or to open formal proceedings, under art.258 TFEU, against a Member State.[49] Upon intervention of the European Ombudsman, the Commission changed its rules in 1997; before it decides to file a complaint, the complainant is heard and has the right to present observations.[50] This procedural guarantee, however, does not give any right to a complainant as regards the final decision which the Commission takes; neither can he oppose the filing of the complaint nor can he oblige the Commission to start legal proceedings under art.258 TFEU against a Member State. The complainant also does not have a right to ensure the Commission makes adequate use of its discretion or, in other words, to see that the Commission's decision is not grossly arbitrary, for instance with regard to previous Commission decisions.

12–26 The Court of Justice has rejected all attempts to oblige the Commission to start proceedings under art.258 TFEU or to close a file.[51] The Court argued that the decision under art.258 is not a decision which can be tackled under art.263 TFEU, since it forms an accessory part of a subsequent Court procedure.[52] Furthermore, a complainant is not in the position of a person entitled to take action before the European courts under art.263(4)) TFEU, since a decision under

[46] See the Commission's own evaluation which is, of course, positive, COM (2010) 70.
[47] Commission Reg.774/2004 relating to the conduct of proceedings by the Commission pursuant to arts 81 and 82 of the EC Treaty [2004] OJ L123/48.
[48] See also L. Krämer, "The environmental complaint in EU law" in 2009 *Journal of European Environmental & Planning Law*, p.13.
[49] See para.12–30, below.
[50] Commission, 15th report on monitoring application of environmental law (1997) [1998] OJ C250/1, p.10.
[51] See Court of Justice, *Star Fruit Company* (C–247/87) [1989] E.C.R. I–291; *Asia Motors* (C–72/90) [1990] E.C.R. I–2181; *Sateba v Commission* (C–422/97) [1998] E.C.R. I–4913.
[52] General Court, *Dumez v Commission* (T–126/95) [1995] E.C.R. II–2863.

art.258 would not be addressed to the complainant. Finally, the Commission has a margin of discretion which cannot be questioned by individual complainants.[53] In particular the latter argument could hardly be called convincing, if one reads art.258 TFEU ("the Commission . . . shall deliver . . .", in contrast to the fact that it "may" bring a case before the Court of Justice).

Practice has shown that an environmental case, a complaint or a petition has a greater chance of leading to a positive result, when the conflict between the environmental interests and the diverging economic interests is discussed in public. The mobilisation of public opinion constitutes an important element of ensuring the taking into consideration of environmental interests and demonstrates at the same time the—at least partly—political character of the complaint procedure; this political character also appears through the lack of control of the Commission's decisions, which facilitates policy interventions in the decision-making procedure.

Complaints procedures in environmental matters normally take a considerable time. Their lack of transparency and the—overall—limited results, in particular as regards large infrastructural projects, have not led to a situation where the Commission is perceived as a true complaint institution.

Direct effect of environmental provisions

In an effort to make EU provisions fully operational for the individual citizen, too, the Court of Justice had, by the early years of the European Union, already developed the doctrine of direct effect. It started with judgments which stated that provisions of the EC Treaty also had direct effects in favour of citizens, who were entitled to invoke these provisions before the courts. Later the Court extended this doctrine to provisions of directives which could also, under certain conditions, be invoked by citizens before national courts.[54] This constituted a deviation from the provision of art.288 TFEU, which states that regulations, but not directives, are directly applicable and that directives must be transposed into national law in order to have legal effect. The Court justified this decision by the fact that a Member State should not be entitled to take advantage of the fact that a directive was not or was not correctly or completely transposed into national law. For that reason this doctrine was only applied in favour of individuals, but never—for instance in criminal cases—against individual persons.[55] Furthermore, the Court did not apply this doctrine in cases where two individuals are in

12–27

[53] Court of Justice, *Star Fruit v Commission* (C–247/87) [1989] E.C.R. I–289 and *Asia Motor France v Commission* (C–29/92) [1992] E.C.R. I–3935.

[54] See, e.g. *Comitato di Difesa della Cava* (C–236/92) [1994] E.C.R. I–483: "The Court has consistently held that wherever the provisions of a directive appear, as far as their subject-matter is concerned, to be unconditional and sufficiently precise, those provisions may be relied upon by an individual against the State where the State fails to implement the directive in national law by the period prescribed or where it fails to implement the directive correctly."

[55] See for example Court of Justice, *Arcaro* (C–168/95) [1996] E.C.R. I–4705: "a directive may not by itself create obligations for an individual and ... a provision of a directive may not therefore be relied upon as such against such a person ... a directive cannot, of itself and independently of a national law adopted by a Member State for its implementation, have the effect of determining or aggravating the liability in criminal law of persons who act in contravention of the provisions of that directive".

dispute.[56] This demonstrates that the direct effect of a directive is construed, by the Court, as a sanction against the deviating Member State.

12–28   The following conditions must be fulfilled for a provision of a directive to be directly applicable:

- the period for transposing a directive into national law has expired;
- a Member State has not, or has not correctly, transposed the provisions of a directive;
- the provision of a directive is unconditional, i.e. the provision "is not subject, in its implementation or effects, to the taking of any measure either by the institutions of the Community or by the Member States"[57];
- the provision is sufficiently precise to be relied on by an individual and applied by the court; this is the case "where the obligation which it imposes is set out in unequivocal terms"[58]; and
- the provision explicitly or implicitly confers rights to an individual as against a Member State. In this regard the Court of Justice held on several occasions that where a provision dealt with the relations between administrations, it did not give rights to individuals.[59] I have defended the argument that, for the test as to whether a provision of EU law grants rights to an individual, the provision has to be constructed in such a way as if it were contained in a regulation; then it would have to be checked as to whether in such a case the provision would confer an improved position, a legal advantage. It has to be admitted, though, that the question of whether a provision confers a "right" to a person is extremely difficult to answer.

12–29   As the Court of Justice constructs the direct effect as a sanction against a Member State which has not, or has not correctly, transposed a directive, it is only logical that it does not apply the doctrine of direct effect in favour of the State, for instance in a criminal procedure against a polluter, or in relations between a citizen and a polluting installation. These limitations and the general difficulties with the interpretation of when a provision has direct effect make this doctrine of rather restricted use.

3.   Sanctions for non-application

Action under art.258 TFEU

12–30   By far the most important instrument at the Commission's disposal when fulfilling its obligation under art.17 TEU is art.258 TFEU.[60] This provision

---

[56] Court of Justice, *Dori* (C–91/92) [1994] E.C.R. I–3325: "The effect of extending that case-law [on direct effects] to the sphere of relations between individuals would be to recognise a power in the Community to enact obligations for individuals with immediate effect, whereas it has competence to do so only where it is empowered to adopt regulations".

[57] Court of Justice, C–236/92 (fn.55, above).

[58] Court of Justice, C–236/92 (fn.55, above).

[59] *Cinisello Balsamo* (C–380/87) [1989] E.C.R. 2491 and *Security International v Signalson* (C–194/94) [1996] E.C.R. I–2201.

[60] See wording of art.258 TFEU: "If the Commission considers that a Member State has failed to fulfil an obligation under the Treaties, it shall deliver a reasoned opinion on the matter, after giving the

provides for a three-stage procedure[61]:

1.   formal notice of breach of obligations to the Member State;
2.   issue of a reasoned opinion; and
3.   application to the Court of Justice.

Steps (1) and (2) together constitute the prejudicial procedure, which has the objective of enabling the Member State to comply with its obligations under EU law or to present its arguments to the Commission on why there is no breach of EU law. For this reason the Commission, which alone may initiate the procedure under art.258, is obliged to specify clearly the object on which it considers the Member State's breach to have occurred (object of litigation).[62]

The formal notice to a Member State that is considered to be in breach of its   **12–31**
obligation does not require a specific form. In practice, however, notice is always given in the form of a letter. The decision to send such a letter is taken by the Commission, after detailed preparation of the Commission services. The formal letter is agreed word by word at administrative, legal and political level, before it is formally notified to the Member State. This careful preparation is also due to the view held by the Court of Justice that the Commission's letter defines the object of litigation for any subsequent Court proceedings.[63] Thus, the Commission cannot, in any subsequent part of the procedure under art.258 TFEU, include any additional point of complaint against a Member State, since the Member State would not have had "the opportunity to present its observations" on such points. Since, however, the factual side of the case is normally not completely clarified, changes in the legal assessment are, of course, possible. Normally, the Member State has two months to reply to the Commission's letter of formal notice. However, since, on average, the Commission discusses and decides on cases under art.258 only once every six months, the time available to Member States for a reply is almost always much longer.

Where the Commission is not satisfied with the Member State's answer, it may   **12–32**
decide to issue a reasoned opinion. The reasoned opinion is produced in the same form as the letter of formal notice. The facts of the dispute are supposed to have been clarified during the procedure preceding the decision to issue a reasoned opinion. The reasoned opinion gives a detailed and comprehensive description of the case as it presents itself in the opinion of the Commission, indicates the legal opinion and describes, in particular, in detail how EU environmental law has been breached. Should proceedings subsequently be initiated with the Court of Justice, the facts no longer need to be clarified and the dispute can normally be confined to legal issues. On average, the time-span between the dispatch of the letter of

---

State concerned the opportunity to submit its observations. If the State concerned does not comply with the opinion within the period laid down by the Commission, the latter may bring the matter before the Court of Justice of the European Union."

[61] The procedural provisions regarding art.258 are not codified, in contrast to the competition provisions of art.108 TFEU, see Commission Reg.773/2004 (fn.48, above). The Commission stated in Written Question E–2496/98 (Watson) [1999] OJ C142/18 that the provisions regarding art.258 had been published in the introduction to the Commission's 10th report on monitoring application of Community law (1992) [1993] OJ C233/1, and that later amendments were published in the successive annual reports. This is simply not correct.

[62] *Commission v Spain* (C–266/94) [1995] E.C.R. I–1975.

[63] *Commission v United Kingdom* (C–337/89) [1992] E.C.R. I–6103.

formal notice and the judgment of the Court of Justice was between:

- 1992 and 1994: 57 months;
- 1995 and 1997: 47 months;
- 1998 and 1999: 68 months;
- 2000 and 2001: 59 months;
- 2002 and 2003: 45 months;
- 2004 and 2005: 47 months; and
- 2006 and 2007: 47 months.[64]

12–33   The Commission occasionally publishes a press release on those disputes which it considers politically or environmentally important. The impact of such press releases is sometimes considerable, depending on the sensitivity of the media to the issue. However, the Commission does not make public either the letter of formal notice or the reasoned opinion. This practice, for which no explanation can be found in art.258 TFEU, is justified with the argument that the confidentiality of the relations between Member States and the Commission would otherwise be disturbed and a smooth solution to the problem made more difficult. This attitude seems to be neither in the interest of the environment nor of the citizen and it is not conducive to an open society; finally, it is not either compatible with Reg.1049/2001 on access to documents held by EU institutions.[65] The Commission has a very large discretion to apply to the Court of Justice and, in practice, less than 10 per cent of cases where the procedure under art.258 was initiated are actually submitted to the Court of Justice. There is no delay required in submitting the application to the Court, nor need the Commission demonstrate a specific legal interest in order to obtain a judgment.

The Lisbon Treaty introduced a sort of sanction in those cases, where a Member State does not transpose the provisions of a directive within the delays provided in that directive (art.260(3) TFEU). In such a case, the Commission, when it brings the case before the Court of Justice, may ask for the payment of a lump sum or penalty payment. The Court of Justice may impose such a payment, but may not go beyond the amount specified by the Commission.

12–34   The Court's decision under art.258 TFEU states that there is a breach of EU environmental law, unless the application is dismissed. The Court neither annuls the national measures that caused the breach of EU law nor does it pronounce on the measures that have to be taken; it is up to the Member State to comply with the judgment and take the necessary measures.

Between 1976 and 2011, the Court of Justice decided about 700 environmental cases under art.258; the average time-span, including the prejudicial procedure, has been, during the last years, almost four years.

---

[64] The procedure before the Court (under art.258 TFEU) takes between 18 and 20 months; the remainder is due to the pre-litigation phase between the Commission and the Member State. See L. Krämer, "Environmental judgments by the Court of Justice and their duration" in 2008 *Journal for European Environmental & Planning Law*, p.263.

[65] See L. Krämer, "*Vertraulichkeit und Öffentlichkeit*", in L. Krämer, *Recht und Um-Welt* (fn.37, above) p.153.

Action under art.259 TFEU

Article 259 TFEU allows Member States to take judicial action against another   **12–35**
Member State which has not fulfilled its environmental obligations under the EU
Treaties. However, no such case has ever been brought before the Court in
environmental matters. Member States instead rely on the Commission to take
action.

Action under art.260 TFEU

Where a Member State does not comply with a judgment by the Court, the   **12–36**
Commission may, under art.260 TFEU, start a new procedure. The justification
for that is probably the continued non-compliance with EU law and, at the same
time, the contempt of the Court that is enshrined in the non-execution of the
judgment. Since the entry into force of the Lisbon Treaty, the procedure is no
longer the same as under art.258 TFEU. Indeed, the Commission only has to send
out a letter of formal notice; if it is not satisfied with the Member State's answer
or if the Member State does not answer, the Commission may go directly to the
Court of Justice, without sending out a reasoned opinion (art.260(2) TFEU). The
second judgment of the Court is again of a declaratory nature.

When a Member States does not comply with a judgment of the Court, the
Commission may make, according to an amendment of art.260(2) TFEU
introduced by the Maastricht Treaty of 1993, a second application to the Court; it
then shall specify the amount of the lump sum or[66] of a penalty payment to be
paid by the Member State concerned. The Court may then impose a lump sum or
a penalty payment. The Commission issued a number of communications
regarding the methods for calculating the penalty payments.[67] For each case, a
basic amount of presently 600 € was fixed. This sum was multiplied with a figure
which assessed the seriousness—ranged from 1–20—and another figure which
assessed the duration of the infringement—ranged 1–3. This sum was then
multiplied with a co-efficient which the Commission had determined according
to the ability of the Member State to pay the penalty.[68]

The Court had, until March 2011, delivered four environmental judgments   **12–37**
under art.260 TFEU. In a case where Greece had, since at least 1986, tolerated
the unauthorised disposal of municipal and industrial waste of a whole city in the
river valley of Kouroupitos (Crete), and where it had ignored a first judgment by
the Court of Justice of 1992,[69] the Court pronounced a penalty payment of 20,000
€ per day.[70] The Court approved the method of calculation of the Commission,

---

[66] The word "or" was interpreted by the Court, in *Commission v France* (C–304/02) [2005] E.C.R.
I–6263, as allowing to impose a lump sum *and* a penalty payment. Since then, this became the general
practice of the Commission and the Court.
[67] Commission, [1996] OJ C242/6; [1997] OJ C63/2; SEC(2005) 1658; SEC(2010) 923; Commission,
[2011] OJ C12/1.
[68] This present co-efficient is—following Commission SEC(2010) 923 (fn.67, above) for Belgium
5.81; Denmark 3.70; Germany 25.40; Greece 4.38; Spain 14.77; France 21.83; Ireland 3.14; Italy
19.84; Luxembourg 1.0; Netherlands 7.85; Austria 4.84; Portugal 4.04; Finland 3.24; Sweden 5.28;
United Kingdom 21.9; Czech Republic 3.17; Estonia 0.58; Cyprus 0.70; Latvia 0.64; Lithuania 1.09;
Hungary 3.01; Malta 0.36; Poland 7.22; Slovenia 1.01; Slovakia 1.45.
[69] Court of Justice, *Commission v Greece* (C–45/91) [1992] E.C.R. I–2509.
[70] Court of Justice, *Commission v Greece* (C–387/97) [2000] E.C.R. I–369.

but underlined that it alone had the right to finally fix the penalty amount to be paid. In a second case, Spain was condemned to pay some 624.000 € per year and for each percent of inland bathing waters that did not comply with the requirements of EU law.[71] Later, the Commission filed the case, in an obviously erroneous interpretation of the judgment.[72] A third case concerned the incorrect transposition of a directive in France which had to pay a lump sum of 10 million €, because it had not transposed a directive.[73] A fourth case, finally, concerned the non-application of the common fishery rules by France which was condemned to pay a lump sum of 20 million € and 57.6 million € for every six months that did not lead to the compliance with EU provisions.[74]

In a number of other cases, which did not concern the environment, the Court pronounced the following penalties:

Member State	Case	Judgment	Penalty payment
France	C–177/04	(2006) E.C.R. I–2461	31.650/day
Germany	C–503/04	(2007) E.C.R. I–6153	—
Portugal	C–70/06	(2008) E.C.R. I–1	19.392/day
Greece	C–568/07	4.6.2009	1 million €
Greece	C–369/07	7.7.2009	2 million € and 16.000/day
Greece	C–109/08	4.6.2009	3 million € and 31.536/day

In case C–387/99, Greece paid about 4.5 million €. Then, it had fenced the unauthorised landfill and operated a temporary other landfill. The Commission closed the case. In my opinion, the compliance with the first judgment is ensured, when also the illegally disposed waste has been removed, as the environmental impairment continues to exist as long as the waste is on the ground.[75]

---

[71] Court of Justice, *Commission v Spain* (C–278/01) [2003] E.C.R. I–14141.
[72] Directive 76/160 on bathing water required that 95 per cent of all samples taken from bathing waters had to conform to the EU requirements. The Commission found that 94.7 per cent of Spanish bathing waters complied with EU requirements and filed the case, because the 0.3 per cent were not relevant. It confounded the overall quality of the Spanish bathing waters with the compliance of the individual water.
[73] Court of Justice, *Commission v France* (C–121/07) [2008] E.C.R. I–9159.
[74] Court of Justice, C–304/02 (fn.66, above).
[75] See also Court of Justice, *Commission v Italy* (C–365/97) [1999] E.C.R. I–7773, where the Court obviously agreed with the opinion defended here.

State liability

According to the Court of Justice, a Member State may also be liable for damages   **12–38**
towards private individuals because it has breached EU law by failing to
transpose an EU Directive into national law.[76] The Court laid down a number of
conditions for such a liability: there must be a serious breach of EU obligations;
the EU Directive must confer rights to individual persons; the content of these
rights is identifiable by reference to the Directive; and there exists a causal link
between the Member State's obligations and the damage suffered by the person
affected. Fault or negligence on the part of the Member State is, however, not
required. Until now, this theory has not been applied to environmental cases,
though there might be some potential for such cases, all the more so since the
theory also applies to cases where a directive has not correctly or completely
been transposed. As the Court also considered that individuals also acquire rights
from quality objectives,[77] the construction of such damages could, in future, be
considerable.

Financial sanctions

Financial sanctions for breach of EU environmental law exist in theory. Indeed,   **12–39**
the different regulations for the EU Structural Funds and the Cohesion Fund
provide that measures which are financed or co-financed by the European Union
must comply with the European Union; the formula that they had in particular to
comply with EU environmental law, was deleted in 2006.[78] Thus, according to
this provision, measures could not be financed with EU funds if they failed to
comply with all the provisions of EU environmental law. As a consequence of
this, each measure which was undertaken in a Member State without respect of
EU environmental law—an example would be the construction of a motorway
without an environmental impact assessment—could, in the past, lead to a refusal
of financial assistance or to the recuperation of the sums paid.[79] Subsequent to an
obiter dictum by the General Court,[80] the Commission considered the procedures
under art.258 TFEU and under the provisions of the different funds that deal with
the recovery of the financial assistance as independent from each other. Thus, the
start of a procedure under art.258 or even a judgment by the Court of Justice did
not automatically lead to the Commission recovering the sums paid; rather, the
Commission reserved the right to examine, in each individual case, what steps
were to be taken. This evolution ended in 2006, when the new Regulations on the
Structural Funds and the Cohesion Fund provided that non-compliance with EU
law did not normally entitle the Commission to retain funds.[81]

---

[76] Court of Justice, *Francovich v Italy* (C–6 and 9/90) [1991] E.C.R. I–5357; *Factortame* (C–48/93) [1996] E.C.R. I–1029.

[77] *Commission v Germany* (C–361/88) [1991] E.C.R. I–2567; C–131/88 (fn.7, above).

[78] See, e.g. Reg.2081/93 [1993] OJ L193/5, art.7 and Reg.1164/94 on the Cohesion Fund [1994] OJ L130/1, art.8. The new formula of art.9(5) of Reg.1083/2006 [2006] OJ L210/25 reads (art.9(5)): "Operations financed by the Funds shall comply with the provisions of the Treaty and of acts adopted under it."

[79] Reg.2081/93 (fn.78, above), art.24; Reg.1164/94 (fn.78, above), Annex II, art.H; see also Commission, 15th report (fn.51, above), p.76.

[80] *An Taisce/WWF v Commission* (T–461/93) [1994] E.C.R. II–733.

[81] Reg.1083/2006 (fn.78, above), art.99ss.

When Germany delayed, in the 1990s, the designation of natural habitats under Directive 92/43,[82] the Commissioners for Regional Policy and Environment wrote, in June 1999, a letter to announce that financial means under the structural funds would not be able to be attributed to Germany, as the sums might serve to realise projects which would be realised within future habitats. This letter considerably accelerated the designation procedure in Germany.[83]

12–40   Since the Commission's decision to recover or not to recover its financial assistance cannot be attacked by any third person, and since the Commission does not publish details of cases where EU environmental law was not respected, nor any information as to how often it has suspended, refused or recovered financial assistance,[84] the main value of the provisions is likely to lie in a preventive effect: where a Member State is asked, prior to the financing of a project, whether it has complied with all EU environmental law provisions; this might lead to a more careful consideration of such provisions. From media reports, it is known that the Commission, in the past, has sometimes refused financial assistance or at least threatened to do so; however, no quantification can be given. I know of no case, and no publicly available document records any case, where financial assistance was ever definitely refused in an environmental case.

Criminal sanctions

12–41   In 2001, the Commission made a proposal for a directive to protect the environment through criminal law[85] for a number of specific bans and prohibitions which are already laid down in EU legislation, Member States were to provide criminal sanctions for cases of intentional or grossly negligent breach of the relevant requirements. These cases concerned, for instance, the unauthorised disposal of waste, the deliberate discharge of solid or liquid waste into waters, illegal trade in endangered species or ozone-depleting substances. Member States were to decide themselves on the kind of criminal sanctions which they wanted to introduce.

The proposal was based on art.192 TFEU. While the European Parliament approved of it, the Council was of the opinion that the EC Treaty did not allow to provide for criminal sanctions and refused to discuss the proposal. Instead, the Council adopted, under art.35 of the Treaty on European Union, a framework decision on criminal sanctions in environmental cases.[86] The main difference between the two provisions was that there was no EU competence for monitoring application of decisions under the third pillar of the Treaty on European Union, as a provision that corresponds to art.258 TFEU lacked in the other Treaty. The

---

[82] Dir.92/43 (fn.5, above).

[83] The letter is mentioned in European Parliament, Res. of March, 16, 2000 [2000] OJ C337/333.

[84] The Commission's 14th and 15th reports on monitoring application of Community law (1996 and 1997) [1997] OJ C332/1, p.70 and [1998] OJ C250/1, p.76 contained for the first time a Chapter on monitoring compliance under the Structural Funds. These chapters were virtually identical, though they concerned two different years, and remained very abstract. For 1996, the Commission stated that EU environmental law was not respected in 23 cases, for 1997 in 25 cases. There is neither an indication on the different cases nor is there any information on whether financial assistance was suspended, refused or recovered. The Commission's 18th (COM [2001] 309), 19th (COM [2002] 324), 23rd Report (COM (2006) 416) and later reports did not give a number anymore.

[85] [2001] OJ C180/238.

[86] Dec.2003/80 [2003] OJ L29/35.

framework decision is thus best compared with an international convention. The Court of Justice declared in 2005, that the Treaty on European Union only applied where no EU provisions applied. Therefore, it declared Council's framework decision void, because legislation on criminal sanctions in the environmental sector could be based on art.192 TFEU.[87] In a later decision then, the Court declared that, while the European Union had the competence to deal with criminal matters, the type and level of the criminal penalties was the competence of the Member States.[88] On this basis, Directive 2008/99 was adopted which requires a number of actions which the Member States must provide for criminal sanctions, when they were unlawful and committed intentionally or with at least serious negligence.[89] Such actions concern the emission or discharge of polluting substances which cause or are likely to cause harm to humans or damage to the environment; waste treatment or disposal which causes or is likely to cause harm to humans or damage to the environment; the shipment of waste in non-negligable quantities; the operation of a plant which causes or could cause harm to humans or damage to the environment; the damaging of fauna or flora; the deterioration of a protected habitat; trade in endangered species; and trade in ozone-depleting substances.

As the Member States fix the type of sanctions and their level, the Directive is not likely to change the status quo and have a significant impact on the protection of the environment.

Environmental crime is a considerable growth industry, within Europe and worldwide. The most important areas are illegal trade in endangered species, in ozone-depleting substances, illegal logging and trade in tropical timber and other wood, dumping of and trade in waste and, finally, illegal fishing. No concrete measures have yet been taken by the European Union to combat organised environmental crime. Article 83 TFEU allows the European Union to adopt directives in areas of particularly serious crime with a cross-border dimension, and enumerates the areas to which this provision applies. The environment does not figure in this list, though the Council may unanimously decide to add other areas the list.

Interim measures

Article 279 TFEU provides that the Court of Justice may prescribe any necessary **12–42** interim measure in cases before it. This provision does not state whether the Commission may also take interim measures as soon as it discovers a breach of EU law. However, it is now generally accepted that the Commission has no such powers and that the decision on interim measures can only be taken by the Court of Justice. The Commission may appeal to the Court to prescribe such measures, but this can only take place where a case is pending before the Court or where it is submitted to the Court together with the request for the interim measure. The

---

[87] Court of Justice, *Commission v Council* (C–176/03) [2005] E.C.R. I–7879.

[88] Court of Justice, *Commission v European Parliament and Council* (C–440/05) [2007] E.C.R. I–9097. It is to be noted that the Court did not explain with one single word, *why* the type and level of sanctions was the exclusive competence of the Member States.

[89] Dir.2008/99 on the protection of the environment through criminal law [2008] OJ L328/28.

Commission has then to demonstrate the urgency and necessity of the measure, in particular if there is a risk of a serious and irreversible damage that might otherwise occur.

Attempts by the Commission to stop the construction of a dyke that would have destroyed a bird habitat were rejected, since the Commission was not able to show the urgency of such a measure.[90] An attempt by an environmental organisation to stop the construction of a tourist information centre in a natural habitat was rejected, because a national court had already stopped the project.[91] The attempt to stop, by way of interim measures, the French nuclear tests in Mururoa in 1995, was rejected as inadmissible, since the private applicants were not directly and individually concerned and thus had no standing.[92] Recently, though, the Court stopped by an interim decision the application of a regional legislation on bird hunting in Italy and Malta and the construction of a motorway in Poland which would have destroyed a Natura 2000 area.[93]

Generally, it can be said that it will hardly ever be possible to demonstrate the urgency and necessity of interim measures under art.258 TFEU, since the pre-Court stage, during which no interim measures are possible, takes almost three years.[94]

Action by individuals

12–43   EU environmental law does not provide for any active role for citizens or their organisations to ensure full application of EU environmental law. The role of monitoring application is given to the Commission, though it is obvious that the Commission is not the owner or the unique stakeholder of the environment; however, in that respect EU environmental law is basically no different from law in most Member States and, indeed, most other industrialised countries. It seems that almost only the United States ensures that there is the possibility for its citizens and private organisations actively to monitor application of environmental law. Within the European Union, the idea of having private citizens actively pursuing general interest matters such as the application of environmental law and, thereby, the protection of the environment, is not strongly developed. Member States in the tradition of Roman law resist it, as the concept of an "open society" and the activation of citizens as law enforcers has no tradition in law. In Scandinavian Member States, a concept of the modern welfare state seems to lead to the conclusion that it is best for public authorities to ensure the application of environmental law.[95] The complaint procedure, described in para.12–22 et seq., above, does not give citizens the possibility actively to pursue any lack of compliance with EU law. Actions against Member States can only be taken by the Commission; its decision to act or not to act under art.258 TFEU cannot be challenged by citizens. Where the Commission itself causes environmental

---

[90] *Commission v Germany* (C–57/89R) [1989] E.C.R. 2849.

[91] *An Taisce v Commission* (C–407/92R), Dec of July 6, 1993.

[92] General Court, *Danielsson v Commission* (T–219/95R) [1995] E.C.R. II–3051.

[93] Court of Justice, *Commission v Italy* (C–503/06R) [2006] E.C.R. I–141; *Commission v Poland* (C–193/07R) judgment of April 18, 2007; *Commission v Malta* (C–76/06R) [2008] E.C.R. I–64.

[94] See para.12–32, above.

[95] See Court of Justice, *Djurgaarden* (C–263/08), judgment of October 15, 2009; Sweden, one of the most advanced countries in environmental protection, had granted access to justice only to environmental organisations with more than 2,000 members.

impairment, there is hardly any possibility for a citizen to take action against the Commission, since that citizen is seen as not being directly and individually concerned. The jurisprudence by the Court of Justice, which grants citizens some "rights" under EU environmental directives, has had no influence whatsoever on individuals'—and their organisations'—right of standing under EU law.

In 1998, the European Union and all Member States signed the Aarhus **12–44** Convention on "access to information, public participation in decision-making and access to justice in environmental matters", which had been elaborated under the auspices of the United Nations. This Convention, which is entered into force in 2001, was ratified by the European Union[96]; it provides for access to justice[97] for "members of the public concerned (a) having a sufficient interest or, alternatively (b) maintaining impairment of a right, where the administrative procedural law of a Party requires this as a precondition". This provision includes environmental organisations. In implementing the provisions of the Aarhus Convention, the Commission proposed, in 2003, a directive to give environmental organisations a right of standing in national courts.[98] Member States considered, however, that access to justice was their exclusive competence and did not adopt the proposal.

In order to avoid being accused of measuring with two measures, the Commission also made a proposal for a regulation to improve access to the European Courts by the environmental organisations. The proposal was adopted in 2006, as Regulation 1367/2006.[99] It did not amend the present provisions of arts 263 and 265 TFEU. Thus, the access to the European Courts has not been improved which is incompatible with the requirements of the Aarhus Convention.

In a judgment of 2011, the Court declared art.9(3) of the Aarhus Convention[100] to be, together with the Aarhus Convention itself, part of EU law. It held, however, that art.9(3) did not have direct effect, because that provision granted access to the courts only, once the conditions which were laid down by Member States, were complied with. The Court encouraged the national courts to interpret art.9(3) broadly and do the outmost in order to ensure, in environmental matters, large access by private persons or environmental organisations to the national court.[101] The judgment did not explain why a Member State should be allowed to invoke its own omission to lay down conditions on access to justice, in order to maintain the national status quo and not fully apply art.9(3).

In March 2011, the Compliance Committee of the Aarhus Convention held that the restrictive practice by the EU Court of Justice, to practically bar any access of environmental organisations to the EU Court, was incompatible with

---

[96] Dec.2005/370 [2005] OJ L124/1.

[97] In the wording of art.9(2) of the Convention, this means "access to a review procedure before a court of law and/or another independent and impartial body established by law".

[98] Commission, COM (2003) 624; see also s.4–20ss, above.

[99] Reg.1367/2006 on the application of the provisions of the Aarhus convention on access to information, public participation in decision-making and access to justice in environmental matters to Community institutions and bodies, [2006] OJ L264/13; see also paras 4–08ss, above.

[100] Aarhus Convention [2005] OJ L124/3, art.9(3): "In addition and without prejudice to the review procedures referred to in paragraphs 1 and 2 above, each Party shall ensure that, where they meet the criteria, if any, laid down in its national law, members of the public have access to administrative or judicial procedures to challenge acts and omissions by private persons and public authorities which contravene provisions of its national law relating to the environment".

[101] Court of Justice, *Lesoochranárske zoskupenie VLK* (C–240/09) judgment of March 8, 2011.

the provisions of the Aarhus Convention.[102] The Compliance Committee rejected in particular the argument raised by the European Union that the possibility to address a national court which could then introduce, under art.267 TFEU a preliminary procedure before the Court of Justice, was sufficient to satisfy the requirements of the Aarhus Convention.

12–45   The extent to which an individual can address national courts and claim there a breach of EU law is governed by national law; no general EU provisions exist.[103] At present, there has been no attempt to improve the possibilities for individuals actively to ensure the application of EU environmental law. A Commission communication of 1996 is silent in that respect[104]; the Council's resolution on that communication is no more explicit.[105]

To what extent the monitoring of application of EU environmental law should be ensured by the EU staff or should be, at least to some extent, externalised, is a question of legal and institutional policy. It is obvious that Member States—and even less actual or potential polluters—do not like to be checked as to their environmental performance. The administrations, the governments and the EU institutions prefer maintaining the quasi-monopoly of the EU institutions and of national administrations to bring public and private polluters before the courts. Whether the environment can indefinitely survive the present monitoring practice, which is often influenced by political or administrative intervention or private lobbying, is not a question to be dealt with here.

---

[102] Aarhus Convention Compliance Committee, Draft findings and recommendations of the Compliance Committee with regard to communication ACCC/C/2008/32 concerning compliance by the European Union, of March 14, 2011.

[103] Under art.267 TFEU, a national court may—and in certain cases must—ask the Court of Justice for a preliminary ruling on the validity and interpretation of Community environmental law; however, this provision only has limited functions in the application of EU environmental law.

[104] Commission, Implementing Community environmental law, COM (96) 500 of October 22, 1996. The communication mainly addresses measures at national level and considers, at EU level, better information, co-operation and consultation.

[105] Council Res. of October 7, 1997 [1997] OJ C321/1.

CHAPTER 13

EC Environmental Law and Policy

1. Introduction

EU environmental policy orientations were first formulated in 1971/1972 and progressively expanded since. They were anchored in the EC Treaty in 1987 by the Single European Act and further fine-tuned by the Treaty amendments of 1993 (Maastricht Treaty), 1999 (Amsterdam Treaty) and 2001 (Nice Treaty). In December 2009, the Lisbon Treaties on European Union entered into effect, after long negotiations on what constitutional basis the Union should rest. This last event only demonstrated that the European Union does not enjoy the prerogatives of a State; in particular, it may act only where it has been expressly so authorised by the Lisbon Treaties. Any comparison with domestic environmental law in the Member States, of which there have been 27 since January 1, 2007, or with the United States is therefore necessarily misleading.

13–01

This becomes obvious in the area of environmental law and policy which is part of European law and policy. It is difficult to determine what the European interest in environmental protection is, how far it goes in specific cases and which measures should be taken at which level in order to protect the environment in Europe. There are no European radio or television stations, no European press and, more generally, no European public opinion which would discuss the general environmental interest of the European Union, and not just the French, German, UK or Spanish interest in the European Union. Lawyers very largely continue to perceive and discuss European environmental law from a national law perspective. One might find some consolation in the remark from Arthur Toynbee that the wheels of a car turn around themselves, and yet move the car ahead; however, when the car is called "European Union" which shall achieve an ever closing union among the peoples of Europe, there is some need to discuss the car's equipment, driving instruments and, most of all, the direction which it shall take and is actually taking.

Law alone cannot answer these questions. Making environmental legislation for some 500 million people in the European Union is possible. However, in view of the diversity of culture and education in the different parts of the European Union, the difference of climate, geography and other environmental conditions, the difference of economic and social development and of policies within the 27 Member States and their regions, such European environmental legislation must necessarily be general in character and leave many details to the local, regional and national level.

Also, law as a tool to protect the environment has its inherent limitations. The European Union might adopt thousands more directives or regulations to protect the environment: if the mentality of humans to impair the environment is not reduced, if the ecological footprint of everyone and of the European society is not reduced, all this environmental legislation constitutes food for lawyers, but does not change the societal reality which is marked by the simple fact that the European environment—and more so, the global environment—is sick and becomes slowly, but continuously worse, not better.

13–02 There is a consensus, expressed in several Council political statements, declarations and resolutions that the present life-style within the European Union is not sustainable.[1] This consensus, though, did not yet lead to significant steps in order to revert the situation—and there are many reasons for this, among them considerations of competitiveness, economic growth, welfare and human greed. No politician at European level or within the 27 Member States has ever dared declaring, as the then President of the United States declared for his country, that "the European life-style is not negotiable", meaning that significant changes in life-style are not acceptable. Yet, in practice, the European Union does not behave differently from the United States, though there are differences, as Europe has another history and culture, is less wealthy and has less geographical space. The emphasis which also the European Union puts on economic growth and the neglect of non economic values—social, environment and culture—progressively flattens such differences and makes forget that one cannot live alone from bread. Policies may influence and change trends, but then political leaders need vision, strategic thinking, leadership capacity and credibility. These are qualities which are rare—everywhere in the world, including in Europe.

2. Primary law

13–03 The structure of the EU Treaties still reflects the preponderance of economic interests over environmental (and social) interests. The EU Treaties deal in detail with internal trade, the four freedoms, transport, agriculture etc. After some antecedents, the integration provision of art.11 was inserted, in 1999, into the Union Treaty to ensure that the three environmental provisions of arts 191 to 193 TFEU influence all other EU policies and progressively "green" them. This concept was to be completed by the overall objective of the European Union to reach a sustainable development (arts 2 and 6 EC Treaty, now arts 3 TEU and 11 TFEU) and to aim at a high level of environmental protection (arts 2 TEU, 114 and 191 TFEU).

However, this concept was and is based on the *political* decision to aim for integrating environmental requirements into other policies, to aim for a high level of protection and for a sustainable development. The legal provisions as such were not sufficient. And as the Court of Justice never decided that art.11 TFEU constituted a *legal* requirement, that a specific measure was not of *high* level of environmental protection or what the precise content of sustainable development was in a given context, the concept of the EU Treaties remained unfulfilled.

---

[1] See, as an example, fifth Environment Action Programme [1993] OJ C38/1, recitals: "The Council and the Representatives of Member States, meeting in Council, agree that many current forms of activity and development are not environmentally sustainable...; agree that the achievement of sustainable development calls for significant changes in current patterns of development, production, consumption and behaviour".

The weight of environmental law is different, if one compares it, for example, with the economic provision of art.34 TFEU which stipulates that there should be no quantitative restrictions on the free circulation of goods or measures having equivalent effect. This provision was not only interpreted by the Commission—and confirmed by the Court of Justice—as prohibiting trade restrictions; it was also interpreted as giving individual persons and companies the right to invoke this clause in courts and have all measures declared void which contradicted it. The interpretation of art.34 TFEU was thus not left to the Commission or to the public authorities alone, but could also be, and was in fact, influenced by citizens.

There is no provision in arts 191 to 193 TFEU which prohibits environmental pollution or impairment. Formulating such a provision would not be too difficult, as the sole prohibition is not less precise than the original wording of art.34 TFEU. And indeed, the Avosetta Group, a group of European environmental lawyers, formulated once a formula to be inserted into the Treaty: "Subject to imperative reasons of overriding public interests, significantly impairing the environment or human health shall be prohibited". However, inserting such a provision into the Treaty would have meant that citizens could tackle provisions or practices which contradicted this rule in courts—which would have broken the monopoly of the administration to decide, by action or by inaction, what is good for the environment, what a high level of protection is and to what extent measures in other policy areas contradicted the environmental requirements. The Avosetta formula has therefore no chance of ever being included in any future Treaty. **13–04**

The other big lacuna in the present Treaty provisions, from the point of view of environmental protection, concerns nuclear energy. Article 11 TFEU applies to the EU Treaties as such, not to the Euratom Treaty. It would have been easy to insert a provision similar to art.11 into the Euratom Treaty. But this has not been done. And it is disappointing to see that nuclear energy policy which has the biggest negative environmental potential of all industrial activities, due to the longevity of radiation, risk of accidents, terrorist attacks, waste issues, etc., is not even contained by any environmental provision, while at the same time the European taxpayer—who has, in about half of the Member States, expressly rejected nuclear energy—pays huge amounts for nuclear research and infrastructure.

Is there a lack of a provision on an individual right to a clean environment in the European Treaties? Human rights generally are formulated in the Charter on Fundamental Rights which has, under art.6 TEU, "the same legal value as the Treaties"; the environmental provision there resembles art.11 TFEU.[2] This, thus, could plead in favour of an explicit human right on the environment. However, experience in Member States shows that not much is won with the insertion of such a human right into the constitution (or, for the European Union, into the Lisbon Treaties), as almost all depends on the concrete, political organisation of protecting the environment—such as the environmental infrastructure and administration, the policy rank of environmental issues, the determination of local, regional and national administrations to take effective action in favour of **13–05**

---

[2] Charter on Fundamental Rights [2000] OJ C364/1, art.37: "A high level of environmental protection and the improvement of the quality of the environment must be integrated into the policies of the Union and ensured in accordance with the principles of sustainable development".

the environment, education of the population—including courts, media, academics, etc. Member States which have an individual right to a clean environment in their constitution do not fare environmentally better than those Member States where the protection of the environment is "only" a constitutional policy orientation provision (Staatszielbestimmung). And the EU Treaties do include, in arts 3 TEU, 11, 114 and 191 to 193 TFEU, already such policy orientation provisions. What would be necessary, though, is a change in the abovementioned situation that under the EU Treaties—including its art.263(4) TFEU on access to the European Courts—the Commission's and Member States' administrations have the de facto monopoly of enforcing the environmental provisions, including those of the EU Treaties themselves. In this regard, an individual right to a clean environment would be of use.

The environmental principles of art.191(2) TFEU—the principles of precaution and prevention, the principle that environmental damage should be tackled at the source and the polluter-pays principle—helped to justify specific legal measures, but were not understood to require a specific solution to a problem or to prohibit this or that measure. To have such an effect, their precise content and their borders are too vague. These principles could be completed by others, such as the substitution principles, though this would raise the same problems: the question when a dangerous chemical substance should be replaced by another, less harmful substance can only be decided in view of the characteristics of both substances, their use, the availability of substitution substances, cost elements and even legal considerations: where the use of a substituting substance would make the EU producers dependant of a third country patent holder, the policy decision on that substance will not remain uninfluenced. This proves that the insertion for example of a substitution principle would not change much of the present situation.

Overall thus, the constitutional frame for the protection of the environment at EU level is satisfying. Some fine-tuning might be necessary or desirable in this or that provision; standing for citizens or environmental organisations could be introduced via secondary legislation. However, the Treaty enables the EU institutions and the EU Member States to lead an active, coherent and consistent environmental policy of and within the European Union—if the political will to do so exists.

3.   Law-making and the quality of EC law

On law-making

13–06   When EU environmental law appeared in the statute books since the mid-1970s, it met, at national level, a largely virgin ground. Few environmental provisions existed at that time; and the progressive development of EU environmental legislation led several Member States—Greece, Ireland, Spain, Portugal, Luxemburg, Italy, in part also United Kingdom, France and Belgium—to take over that legislation rather than develop national rules on the basis of a national environmental policy.

Today, national environmental law consists in numerous Member States in southern Europe, as well as in all 12 Member States, which adhered to the Union since 2004, of more or less 100 per cent of the transposition and incorporation of EU environmental law. And for most of the other Member States, this figure varies between 65 and 80 per cent. In theory, thus, the conditions were very favourable for an intensive consensus-building at European level on the orientation of legislation, its degree of details, on issues to address and on instruments to develop. To this has to be added the overall umbrella provision of art.193 TFEU which allowed Member States to maintain or introduce more stringent national provisions. EU environmental law thus had the potential to be the foundation, on which, according to the ecological, social and economic conditions in the different parts of the European Union, national or regional supplementary environmental provisions were allowed to be built.

Practice, though, developed differently. As the national administration and policy had the de facto monopoly to protect or not to protect the environment, legislation that was made at EU level was frequently perceived as interfering with this monopoly. And while at the political level, Member States regularly agreed, in EU environment action programmes, to objectives, principles and priorities of EU legislative activity, at the administrative level this was not always followed—though it has to be admitted that the two levels cannot always easily be distinguished. As the devil of environmental protection is in the detail and not in great principles such as "sustainable development", "best technique" or "the polluter shall pay", the making of environmental EU legislation gave ample opportunity to protect the national administrations' monopoly. The absence of environmental provisions at national level did not therefore mean that a Member State would be in favour to see such provisions imported from the European Union. In concrete terms, this reluctance manifested itself in various forms, such as the stopping of new legislative initiatives,[3] the changes of approaches to tackle environmental pollution,[4] the watering down of proposals[5] and the establishment of provisions which could alone be monitored and controlled by the national administration[6]; of course, the EU administration was not neutral in this effort, but often contributed to it, also according to the national provenance of the different EU officials. The efforts had the (welcome) side-effect that the administrations' monopoly was also affirmed with regard to national environmental organisations, citizen groups and public opinion bodies.

The problem with this approach was that the individual national administration which pleaded for a reduced EU environmental legislation, had its own national situation in mind; for example, it did not wish to see the European Union interfere—this was frequently the attitude prevailing in the United Kingdom; or it wished to ensure its regional power—this was the prevailing motivation of the German Länder—or it was of the opinion that its own national environmental

---

[3] Examples are the proposals for directives on the dumping of waste at sea, on a permit requirement for all industrial installations, on provisions on airport noise or on access to justice.

[4] Examples are the shift from emission limit values to quality standards in air and water legislation, the substitution of provisions for certain industrial sectors by non-binding BREF-documents or on the producer responsibility in waste management legislation.

[5] Examples are the drinking water directive 98/83 [1998] OJ L330/32, the administrative obligation to clean up orphan damage in Directive 2004/35 [2004] OJ L143/56 and the omission to fix quality standards for heavy metals in air in Directive 2004/107 [2005] OJ L23/3.

[6] Examples are the water Framework Directive 2000/60 [2000] OJ L327/1, Directive 2006/7 on the quality of bathing water [2006] OJ L64/37, the Reg.1013/2006 on the shipment of waste [2006] OJ L190/1 and Directive 2004/35 on environmental liability (fn.5, above).

provisions were better anyway than those which could be generated at EU level; this last attitude was frequently found in the Netherlands. Neither national administration paid much attention to the fact that the alternative to EU environmental provisions was not that there would be national provisions in—now—27 Member States. Rather, the alternative was that some Member States would have national legislation on a specific item, but the large majority would not. This lacking European perspective of national decision-takers has dominated the law-making process at European level for decades, though it has never been openly discussed.

Despite this reluctance, EU environmental law achieved a number of quite remarkable results, in quantity and also in quality. The following list of ten pieces of EU environmental law which would, without the EU legislation, not have been subject of national environmental legislation in the vast majority of—old and new—Member States, serves to illustrate this point; it could easily be prolonged: environment impact assessment, participation in decision-making, accident prevention, integrated pollution prevention and control, drinking water, waste incinerators, end-of-life vehicles, packaging and packaging waste, habitat protection and bird protection.

The Commission's administration was and is not strong enough to ensure the adoption of environmental legislation at a high level against or without the support of national administrations. Its allies are not numerous: public opinion, the best ally of the environment, hardly exists at EU level; environmental scientists are almost not organised at EU level; the European Parliament re-acts, but hardly ever has the historic memory or the scientific support which would enable it to play an active role in environmental law-making; and European environmental organisations lack human and financial resources.

The quality of EU environmental law

13–07   These imperfections of the law-making process affect the quality of environmental legislation. EU environmental law was developed ad hoc, without strategic thinking how to organise a specific sector (water, air, waste). Amendments were also made on an ad hoc basis, often as a follow-up to accidents or incidents. Where framework legislation was created, its basic orientations were questioned and changed after few years, discrediting the nature of a framework legislation; examples are Directives 76/464 on water discharges,[7] 84/360 on industrial air pollution[8] or 96/62 on air quality standards.[9] More recent framework legislation—for fresh water (Directive 2000/60[10]), marine waters (Directive 2008/56[11]), pesticide use (Directive 2009/128[12]) or flooding (Directive 2007/60[13])—are so vague and general in their content that their added value to the protection of the environment appears questionable. Indeed, where a Member State has the will to protect the environment in one of the areas mentioned, it may find useful orientation and support in such framework legislation; however,

---

[7] Dir.76/464 [1976] OJ L129/23.
[8] Dir.84/360 [1984] OJ L188/20.
[9] Dir.96/62 [1996] OJ L296/55.
[10] Dir.2000/60 (fn.6, above).
[11] Dir.2008/56 [2008] OJ L164/19.
[12] Dir.2009/128 [2009] OJ L309/71.
[13] Dir.2007/60 [2007] OJ L284/27.

where this political will does not exist, the improved environmental protection will hardly ever be achieved, as the framework legislation mainly works with analysis, planning and reporting as EU instruments.

The codification of environmental legislation into one or several basic texts **13–08** has never been seriously considered at European level. After the Commission's somehow populistic announcement in 2001, to reduce the volume of EU legislation by 25 per cent, efforts were undertaken to incorporate all amendments of a directive or a regulation into one single text, without touching the substance, though. In this way, overlapping, contradictions and inconsistencies between different environmental pieces of legislation are not reduced, though this form of law-making also sails under the name of "codification".[14] In some Member States, the putting together of environmental provisions in one legal act or code has been successfully brought to an end. For a foreseeable time, such initiatives will not take place at European level.

At EU level either, there is no instrument to measure the quality of environmental legislation. The only reasonable yardstick is, whether the legislation has led to an improved permanent protection or not. On that, it is undoubtedly true that EU environmental legislation has contributed to the adoption of environmental legislation in all 27 Member States. Subsequently, this led to the installation of environmental ministries, the creation of environmental structures—local and regional administrations, environmental groups, environmental education, discussion of environmental issues in the media, creation of specialised institutes, laboratories and others—and to the discussion of environmental issues in national policies. However, this alone does not yet protect the environment. To illustrate this point, an example of a decision by the Court of Justice may be quoted. A citizen had applied to the Court, because his private property had been inserted into the EU-wide list of habitats of European importance under Directive 92/43 and he was of the opinion that this Commission decision was wrong. The Court rejected his application as inadmissible,[15] because he was not directly affected by the Commission decision. The Court held that the selection of habitats in a national list and the subsequent decision and publication of a European list were all preparatory acts which did not affect the private property. This means that the existence of Directive 92/43 since 1992—since eighteen years, thus has not, with regard to habitats, led to concrete protection; rather, this protection of the environment with regard to specific habitats will only begin, once conservation measures have been taken.

The biggest merit of EU environmental legislation is that it exists, and that this **13–09** existence compelled all Member States to have equivalent provisions in their national statute books. On this set of rules, environmental policy can build, where the political will exists.

Also, EU environmental law has not prevented Member States from maintaining or introducing at national legislation more stringent provisions. And no area is visible, where a Member State was prevented from protecting its national environment, because of the existence of EU environmental legislation. One might think of the area of biotechnology as an exception: it is well known

---

[14] Examples are Dir.2010/75 on industrial emissions [2010] OJ L334/17; Dir.2008/50 on ambient air quality and cleaner air for Europe [2008] OJ L152/1.

[15] Court of Justice, *Sahlstedt a.o. v Commission* (C–362/06P) judgment of April 25, 2009; General Court, *Sahlstedt a.o. v Commission* (T–150/05) [2006] E.C.R. II–1851.

that countries such as Austria or Denmark would prefer not to have genetically modified seeds on their land, or fruit, vegetables or meat in their shops which contains GMOs. However, it was explained in Ch.6, above, that the European Union—deliberately—placed legislation on GMOs on the product-related art.114 TFEU, not on the environmental-related art.192 TFEU. Member States agreed to that, at several occasions. Then they have difficulties in arguing that they can no longer protect their environment in the way which they think best.

13–10   EU environmental legislation often lacks the necessary precision and details. Definitions of "renewable energy" which includes the "biodegradable fraction of industrial and municipal waste",[16] of "good environmental status" in Directive 2000/60, Directive 2008/56 on marine waters—where the marine environment is practically reduced to the quality of waters—and of "participation" are loosely drafted and invite to different interpretations or abuses. Environmental "plans" and "programmes", "best available technique", reports and monitoring obligations are not defined with the necessary rigidity. More examples could be given. The often-heard argument, that in an enlarged European Union of 27 Member States this flexibility is inevitable, is simply misleading: between Stockholm and Sofia, Lisbon and Riga, everybody knows what a car is and understands the term in the same sense. Yet, there is no uniform definition of hazardous waste.[17] In contrast to that, the Directive on three-wheel cars has 454 pages in the EU Official Journal,[18] and the number of large, very detailed CEN and CENELEC standards is beyond 15,000, with rising tendency. This demonstrates that a European Union needs EU (uniform) definitions. Vague definitions in EU environmental law appear to be due more to the influence of British administrative law; they make law monitoring and application difficult, if not impossible. Article 193 TFEU which allows Member States to better protect their environment, is not an excuse for not precisely defining what the EU legislation is about.

13–11   The greatest problem as regards the quality of environmental law are those pieces of EU environmental legislation which are, de facto, unenforceable. The issue will be discussed in more detail in sections 5 (Application of environmental law) and 8 (EU environmental law and Member States), though it also affects the quality of law. It had been argued in Chs 7 (water) and 8 (air) that EU quality standards are practically not enforceable against Member States. As the Commission has, in any case, the obligation to ensure that environmental law is not only transposed into national law, but also "applied" (art.17 TEU), it should think over twice, before it suggests the setting of quality standards at EU level. And if it does propose them, its proposals should contain provisions which repair this enforcement problem. This has never been done in the past. The consequence is that quality standards are not enforced in the European Union. And it should be remembered that nothing discredits the legislation in a society more than its non-application.

---

[16] Dir.2009/28 [2009] OJ L140/16.
[17] Dir.2008/98 [2008] OJ L312/3.
[18] Dir.97/24 [1997] OJ L226/1.

Better regulation

For about 20 years, starting with the Edinburgh summit of the Heads of States   **13–12**
and Governments 1991, there have been efforts to deregulate environmental
provisions that had been adopted at EU level. In order to hide their objective,
these efforts sail under the flag of "better regulation". While there were some
efforts in the mid-1990s and by the Prodi-Commission (1999–2004) in this
regard,[19] the Barroso-Commission (since 2004) has made the subject of better
regulation one of its central topics.[20] It believes that deregulating the environment
and other areas will create employment, make the European economy more
competitive and will, overall, strengthen the European Union, internally and
globally (Lisbon process).

This neo-liberal policy orientation which I consider wrong, is not to be   **13–13**
discussed here. The Commission received part of an answer of the European
citizens in the form of the negative referendum on the European Constitution in
France and Netherlands 2004. What is to be mentioned here is, that the
Commission itself declared in 2001, when it presented its political environmental
programme for the next 10 years:

> "Despite improvements on some fronts, we continue to face a number of persistent problems.
> Of particular concern are climate change, the loss of biodiversity and natural habitats, soil loss
> and degradation, increased waste volumes, the build up of chemicals in the environment, noise
> and certain air and water pollutants. We also face a number of emerging issues such as
> pollutants that affect the functioning of our hormone systems. Forecasts suggest that with
> current policies and socio-economic trends, many of the pressures that give rise to these
> problems, such as transport, energy use, tourist activities, land-take for infra-structure etc. will
> worsen over the coming decade." (Commission, COM (2001) 31, p.10.)

It this description is correct—and there is no serious environmental analysis
which ever contradicted it—than there is some need for the Barroso-Commission
to explain to the European citizen in detail, how these trends can be reversed by
the deregulation policy which it pursues.

There are several such basic contradictions. For example, under the "Better
regulation" policy, the Commission announced that it would try to promote the
use of voluntary agreements with industry, including in the sector of
environmental policy. In contrast to that, the Sixth Environment Action
Programme declared quite unambiguously that "legislation remains central to
meeting environmental challenges".[21] No attempt was made to clarify this
difference in approach. In 2001, the Commission announced that it would
promote tripartite contracts between European regions, the Member State
concerned and the European Union, in order to promote environment
protection[22]; there was no follow-up, but no explanation either. "Governance", a
central topic of the Prodi-Commission, has disappeared from the policy agenda of

---

[19] See Commission, European Governance—a White Paper [2001] OJ C287/1.
[20] Commission, Communication: Better regulation for growth and jobs, COM (2005) 97.
[21] See Dec.1600/2002 [2002] OJ L242/1, Recital 12. This statement constituted an answer to the
Commission's proposal for the sixth Action Programme, COM (2001) 31, where the Commission
stated: "In some cases, non-regulatory methods will be the most appropriate and flexible means of
addressing environmental issues. The Commission is currently examining new methods of
governance, including alternative to traditional regulation such as voluntary commitments and
agreements, which could improve the ability of enterprise to innovate and change".
[22] Commission (fn.19, above).

the Barroso-Commission. The Cardiff-process, initiated by the European Council and which also should influence law-making and the quality of legislation, has been buried in silence, without any explanation to the European citizen.

All this leads to a credibility gap: how can the European citizen believe, what the European institutions declare, if this is no longer true a short time afterwards? The Commission is not a government which might change policies after elections that brought new political forces to power. Rather, the Commission has to act in the common European interest (art.17 TEU) and it is difficult to understand why and how this interest changes within short time.

4.   The different environmental sectors

13–14   A look at the different sectors of EU environmental law has to start with the Sixth Environmental Action Programme itself. This was adopted in the form of an EU decision and was thus legally binding. The programme contained a number of binding commitments to legislate in different sectors; furthermore, it contained a number of instructions to the EU institutions and in particular to the Commission to tackle this or that aspect of environmental policy; this concerned for example the issues of environmental requirements of energy, transport and industry policy or the management of natural resources.[23] If the fact that the Sixth Programme was adopted by way of a decision had any sense, then the Commission was obliged to follow the mandates and instructions which the programme contains, and this for the lifetime of the Programme—or at least, until the Programme had been amended. It makes no sense to elaborate a programme, to proceed to extensive consultations with all stakeholders, to discuss it at European level for more than two years, have it adopted by way of co-decision under active co-operation of the Commission, and then ignore its content.

Other environmental *programmes* announced in a less binding form—as communications, thematic strategies, green papers, white papers, strategies or framework legislation—suffered a similar destiny. They were often ignored by the administrative structures in Commission, Parliament and Council which were affected by them and thus were not much more than an accumulation of good words. One principal reason for this is that the environmental programmes were elaborated by the environmental structure.[24] And while they were formally adopted by the Commission as a whole, the industry, agricultural, transport or energy departments, hardly having participated in their elaboration, did not feel committed to follow the programmes' objectives, principles and priorities, as they had, in their respective sector, to pursue their own objectives, principles and priorities. This pattern continued in the European Parliament and the Council. In other words: the integrative part of the EU institutions to make one coherent policy, is limited. The different parts of EU policy—transport, industry, agriculture, consumer, environment, etc.—are horizontally little integrated, but work vertically and rather autonomously.

---

[23] See Dec.1600/2002 (fn.22, above), arts 5 and 8.

[24] Environmental structure is understood as being the environmental directorate general within the Commission, the environmental committee in the European Parliament and the environmental working group as well as the environmental ministers in the Council. Similar structures exist for agriculture, energy, etc.

As regards the *horizontal legislation* which tries to follow the principles of an   **13–15**
open society and give citizens more access to environmental information and
more participation rights in decision-making, it is too early to make evaluations
of different legal instruments which were adopted, as regards the EU institutions,
in 2006,[25] and as regards Member States, mainly in 2003. It is clear, though, that
the EU institutions do not try to be as open, transparent and accountable as
possible.[26] There are different cultures in the European Union in this regard, and
the German, French and British culture which is far away from the openness of
the Scandinavian culture, largely dominates the EU institutions and makes the
phrase of art.1 of the Treaty on European Union, that decisions are to be taken as
openly and as closely to the citizen as possible, rather theoretical for the time
being. At the level of Member States, the spirit of openness and participation
which underlies the Aarhus Convention, influences the daily practice in
Scandinavian Member States and in Netherlands. Elsewhere, much change in
mentality of the administration is still needed, before openness, transparency and
accountability will be the leitmotif of daily work.

Looking at *industrial installations*, it is understandable that the European
Union did not establish conditions for the emissions of all industrial installations;
and it is a policy choice to opt for the best-technique approach, in order not to
have to establish the limitations for the different groups of installations and the
pollutants by way of EU legislation. However, whether there should not be a
general provision which covers *all* industrial installations—80 per cent are small-
and medium-sized companies—and requires a permit for their emissions into the
environment, is arguable. Also general requirements with regard to greenhouse
gas emissions, resource management, waste handling could be imagined. On this,
the European Union relies on the Member States and this aspect will be discussed
below.

There is no comprehensive legislation on *biodiversity*. The two Directives on   **13–16**
birds (2009/147) and fauna, flora, habitats (92/43) are clearly not sufficient to
protect EU nature. Directive 92/43 even applies only to species and to habitats
under threat. If it is correct that nature slowly retreats from the European
continent, a more general legislation which also impacts on transport policy,
agricultural policy, energy policy, the trans-European networks, etc. would be of
use. Such legislation could also usefully include considerations on wild animal
welfare; indeed, animal welfare is one marked feature of differentiation of
European values with regard to other parts of the world.

The absence of an environmentally oriented *product* policy was discussed in
Ch.6, above. Climate change considerations generated the adoption of a directive
on the eco-design of energy-related products[27]; it would have been even more
logical to extend the field of application of this Directive to all products, as it is a
framework directive anyway. This would have been all the more consistent, as the
product safety legislation does not deal with environmental concerns.

In the *water* sector, the European Union has largely given up its attempts to get   **13–17**
a fixed set of minimum standards; it left the determination of "good
environmental status" to the different river basin management bodies and, for

---

[25] This is argued in Reg.1367/2006 [2006] OJ L264/13 and art.1TEU.
[26] In 2001, the Commission indicated that there were some 700 consultative committees,
Commission (fn.19, above), p.14.
[27] Dir.2009/125 [2009] OJ L285/10.

marine waters, to the European regional conventions. Also the other EU directives in the water sector show this retreat from integrated standards.

Air pollution provisions from transport appear to be dictated more by the car industry than by environmental or human health concerns. The growing car fleet eats up reduction efforts made by the legislation, and the car industry's wish for planning security makes it impossible to quickly introduce technical innovations such as the particulate filter for diesel cars. Emissions of point sources such as installations diminished, though the overall air pollution, including its effects on soils, forests and human health is still worrying.

As regards *noise*, a first directive of 2002 will have to prove its efficiency.[28] The European Union is deficient in establishing noise reduction standards from transport vehicles (motorcycles, cars, trucks, airplanes). Here, legislation follows the technical evolution rather than driving innovation by legal standards that would have to be reached within a certain period. Compliance with standards throughout the life-time of the product, and not only at the moment, when it is first placed on the market, is another issue which needs being addressed. Furthermore, noise around airports (night flight ban, noise levels) would urgently require an EU-wide solution; letting the individual airport find solutions, is just inappropriate, since the airports in the European Union are in high competition with each other.

13–18   *Climate change* issues have not yet led to a fundamental rethinking of energy policy issues at EU level. It is thought that the targets of the Kyoto Protocol will be respected with existing measures including some supplementary measures on energy saving and the promotion of alternative energies. This analysis is probably true, though the Kyoto Protocol only contains commitments till the year 2012. The major problems, however, lie beyond that date, and the measures to address emission of greenhouse gases by the year 2020 and beyond would need to be fully complied with and strictly monitored. Here, the lack of political leadership of the European Union is particularly felt. In view of this passivity, time works for the return of nuclear energy.

In the *waste* sector, the announcement of moving the European Union towards a recycling society, has not been followed by concrete action. Waste goes the cheapest treatment or disposal path, and the EU instruments have not yet reoriented the majority of waste streams to economically more useful paths. Resource management, prevention of waste generation, recycling, the departure of the highly unpopular incineration of waste—all this would require an integrated and coherent product policy for which not even the preliminary reflections have started at EU level.

5.   The credibility of the process to monitor application

The monitoring policy

13–19   It follows from arts 5 TEU and 192(2) TFEU that Member States have to implement EU environmental law—which means its transposition into national law, its application and enforcement. This is often forgotten. Member States

---

[28] Dir.2002/49 [2002] OJ L189/12.

frequently implement and apply EU environmental law, because the Commission threatens with legal action under art.258 TFEU, not because they perceive the need to ensure an adequate protection of the environment. This is particularly true of Member States which derive their national environmental legislation entirely from EU environmental law, as the national environmental structure is normally not too well developed and not too influential in the political power game.

The Commission started to shift its monitoring policy and intends to concentrate on the *transposition* of environmental directives, much less on its actual *application*. It has not managed in the past to ensure a transformation in time by the majority of Member States and the problem of incorrect and/or incomplete transposition continues to exist. With regard to the incorrect transposition, the Commission treats different Member States differently, due to unsystematically addressing problems and resource problems.

The Commission's policy of reducing or abandoning of monitoring the **13–20** effective application of EU environmental legislation by Member States has some advantage, but also a number of strong disadvantages. This policy saves resources, avoids disputes and litigation with Member States on individual cases and allows the Commission to better concentrate on transposition questions.

A great legal disadvantage lies in the fact that art.17 TEU is unambiguous: it requires the Commission to ensure that EU environmental law is not only transposed, but actually applied. The Commission is thus not entitled to ignore how the law is applied in practice.

The second disadvantage is perhaps even greater. As Member States have successfully prevented any green police, inspectors and other similar enforcement mechanisms in the area of the environment, the principal source of information for the Commission is the citizen complaint. Such a complaint demonstrates the citizens' interest in environmental as well as in European issues. Where this interest is frustrated, because the Commission does not examine the complaint or arranges fake solutions with the Member State in question, the citizen might rightly ask, why *he* should bother about the European Union. He then must perceive the European Union as a Union for big interests, but not for the man in the street. And where he gets the feeling that the EU environmental law is something for the statute books, but can be breached in practice, without consequences, he will not bother about the environment either. The European Union has considerable difficulties in explaining to European citizens, why they should vote in European elections, what concrete advantage there is for the individual citizen in its daily life to belong to the European Union and what all these costly institutions in Bruxelles and other places stand for. Environment protection is popular with citizens all over Europe, and in particular with the young generation. In this area, thus, the Commission could improve its image and show that it is down to earth, close to the citizen, not just committed to the free trade and other policy areas—which means little for the citizen in the street. Its present approach to environmental issues contributes to alienate the young from the EU concept—probably the most disastrous long-term effect of the present policy.

Administrative secrecy

13–21   Closely linked to these general considerations is the Commission's policy to consider that letters of formal notice and reasoned opinions in the environmental sector which are addressed to Member States, are not accessible to citizens. The reason given is that the confidentiality between the Commission and Member States would otherwise be disturbed. The underlying assumption is that the protection or lack of protection of the environment at national level is a matter between the Commission and the Member State in question—as if the Commission or the Member State or its administration were the owner of the environment. As the Commission decisions are the result of a long and detailed internal process, where all administrative, legal, technical and political arguments are weighed, this secrecy is neither comprehensible nor justified. And it is a poor consolation that the General Court implicitly approved the Commission's practice in a number of judgments.

In policy terms, two observations need to be made. First, Member States with an "open society" approach to administrative secrecy—the Netherlands, Sweden, Denmark, possibly also Austria and Finland—do make the letters of formal notice and reasoned opinions available to the public, apparently without any negative consequence. Second, in other areas such as industrial, internal market, insurance or competition policy, or transport and energy policy, letters of formal notice and reasoned opinions are systematically available to the interested trade and industry associations. There is not even a discussion on the necessity to keep the Commission's opinion confidential. This shows that, overall, the system works with two measures: letters which are of interest to citizens are kept secret, while letters which are of interest to vested interest groups, are accessible.[29] It is difficult to see how this policy increases the credibility of the European Union in the eyes of the citizen in the street.

Environmental inspectors

13–22   It was mentioned that Member States did not accept the idea of environmental inspectors which do not exist, at present, at EU level. Little public discussion has taken place on this during the last fifteen years, though there is a need to explain: when a company makes an illegal merger with a company in another Member State, and the Commission hears of that, the Commission may inspect the site, hear witnesses, seize documents and pronounce, at the end of the day fines against the company, against which the company may appeal to the General Court, and then appeal to the Court of Justice. And when the same company exports hazardous waste, in breach of its EU obligations, and the Commission hears of that, the Commission may send a letter of formal notice to the Member State in question; it has, as source of information, the Member State's answer. At

---

[29] In 1985, E. Rehbinder formulated—in a more general context—on access to the EU decision-making process: "Outside access to this process is generally limited to well organised industry groups" (E. Rehbinder-R.Stewart: *Environmental protection policy* (Berlin-New York, 1985), p.334). This remark remains valid, also with regard to the decision-making process under art.258 TFEU.

the end of the procedure, the Commission may bring the Member State to the Court of Justice, because the company has acted illegally. The judgment states the facts, but does not pronounce a fine.

The comparison of the procedure shows the doublespeak. Where the company wishes to increase its profits by concluding a merger, it may be fined; but where it wishes to increase its profits by exporting hazardous waste instead of having it treated properly, there is no sanction. This difference of treatment cannot be explained to either a citizen in the street or a law student. It just shows that environmental interests are ranking lower. Why can the Commission, in the first example, send inspectors to examine the facts, but not in the second? Why are veterinary inspectors sent to 140 countries worldwide in order to check sanitary conditions of slaughterhouses, why are fishing boats equipped with a satellite system and have, furthermore, their landings inspected? The measuring with two different measures as regards inspections is obvious.

The Commission's own monitoring policy is in need of being controlled.   **13–23**
According to the jurisprudence of the European Courts, the Commission's decision to open or not proceedings under art.258 TFEU, cannot be controlled in court.[30] All the more would it be necessary to have the Commission's practice audited, in order to see, where it is inconsistent, contradictory, where it favours some or disadvantages other Member States or industrial sectors, where the Commission omits to take obvious cases to court which even under its own criteria would be priority cases, etc. This has never happened until now.

International conventions

It is the monitoring policy of the Commission—nowhere laid down in writing, it   **13–24**
is true—not to monitor the transposition and application by Member States of international environmental conventions to which the EU has adhered. An exception is made in cases where the international convention had been transposed into EU law by an environmental regulation or, less frequently, a directive; however, the Commission then monitors the transposition and application of this EU legislation, not of the international convention itself.

Again, this policy is in breach with the Commission's legal obligation under art.17 TFEU: as the international convention becomes, by the adherence of the European Union, part of EU law (art.216(2) TFEU), the Commission has the legal obligation to ensure its application. Article 17 TEU does not differentiate between the different instruments of EU law. The Court Justice's confirmation of this legal situation[31] has not yet led to any change in the Commission's practice.

Credibility

With the enlargement of the European Union to 27 Member States, environmen-   **13–25**
tal law-making has undoubtedly become more difficult. All the more would it be important to ensure that the existing legislation is actually applied. Numerous Council and European Parliament resolutions call on the Commission to ensure a full and complete application of existing environmental rules. And there are also

---

[30] General Court, *Dumez v Commission* (T–126/95) [1995] E.C.R. II–2863.
[31] Court of Justice, *Commission v France* (C–239/03) [2004] E.C.R. I–9325; *Pêcheurs des Etangs de Berre* (C–213/03) [2004] E.C.R. I–7357.

a number of self commitments by the Commission in this regard: as recently as early 2005, the Barroso-Commission declared:

> "The Union should deliver in terms of implementation and reach out to every European. First, the Union must work well, and be seen to work well ... Failure to apply European legislation on the ground damages the effectiveness of Union policy and undermines the trust on which the Union depends ... Prompt and adequate transposition and vigorous pursuit of infringements are critical to the credibility of European legislation and the effectiveness of policies."

This statement is contradicted by the practice of the Commission to drastically reduce the monitoring of effective application of environmental legislation in specific cases.

6.   Institutions

Commission

13–26   The Commission's mission to act in the common European interest, its monopoly of making legislative proposals and the fact that it is the only institutions, whose members are permanently present at the seat of the European Union (Bruxelles) gives it a very powerful position to steer environmental protection policy in the European Union. The Commission has enough financial means to launch studies and research on environmental questions. And it has at its side the European Environmental Agency which supplies the necessary data.

The Commission is not well surrounded with environmental advisers. It has set up no scientific, academic, technical, ecological or socio-economic group of advisers which would advise on medium- and long-term trends in environmental issues, comment on actual problems from a point of view away from vested interests or draw the attention on specific developments that are likely to affect the environment. A Forum on environment and sustainable development which was to advise the environmental Commissioner, was quickly dissolved again and replaced by an industry dominated round table group which advised the President of the Commission.[32] Environmental groups are not convened in a consultative group either. This structure is different from structures in agriculture, industry, transport or energy, where the Commission, often together with the Council, set up formal or informal consultative or advisory groups which discuss sector-related policies trends and evolutions.

A politician who is all of a sudden placed as an Environmental Commissioner or at the top of the administration, is bound to listen to someone, as he simply cannot know all environmental intricacies; he will thus turn either to persons from his home country or to networks which stem from his former activity—whatever that was. The result is less strategic thinking and less long-term reflection; also the relay between top politicians is not ensured, when changes at the political level or top management occur, as each time a net has to be knitted anew.

---

[32] Commission Dec. 93/91 [1993] OJ L328/33 (establishment of the committee); Dec.2001/704 [2001] OJ L120/1 (dissolution).

The only "advisory" group which the Environmental Commissioner meets regularly is the Environmental Policy Review Group, which groups the top officials of central environmental administration of Member States. The group is informal and its agenda, minutes and the results of its meetings are not accessible to the public. Whether the group, from its composition, is willing and capable to give the best advice for the *European environment*, may be doubted; it may be assumed that the interests of Member States are at least not forgotten.

As regards the staff level of the Commission, the policy, introduced during the last fifteen years, to see every official move around after three to five years, increases mobility, but produces officials who think more of their career, do not really become experts in their area and are thus not always able to argue with Member States' officials or vested group representatives. This makes the European civil service too easily prone to adopt solutions which satisfy the interlocutors, without necessarily satisfying the needs of the environment.

Within the Commission, the integration of administrations which would be required by the integration requirement of art.11 TFEU, is not a success. **13–27** Administrations normally work vertically, i.e. with their administrative hierarchy, the respective Parliamentary committee and the Council working group. There are no institutional or otherwise regular meetings between the environmental department and other departments within the Commission. One of the reasons for this situation is the fact that in such a meeting, when it is multilateral, the environmental official would regularly be confronted with a majority of officials who represent growth- and economy interested departments (industry, transport, agriculture, fishery, regional policy, competition, fiscal matters, etc.) and could hardly hope to see his point of view prevail. And there are not enough human resources for regular bilateral meetings. This pattern is found at all levels of the hierarchy, Commissioner, director-general, director, head of unit or desk officer. As there is enough work anyway, in all departments, the temptation is great not to discuss environmental issues horizontally, except in concrete cases of necessity.

This incapacity of the Commission to discuss environmental issues in an integrated way, is felt particularly strongly at sensitive points of policy. Examples are the problems of climate change on transport, which would, of course, require regular, intense discussions among the administrations of transport, but also of energy, industry, trade, regional policy, foreign relations and the environment with a view to conceive a strategy. The Sixth Environment Action Programme had developed some considerations in this regard and measures to adopt, however, without significant input from other vertical structures than the environment; these considerations and the measures proposed are very largely being ignored since 2002. Another example is the question of environment and development policy, where the departments of development policy, economic, industry, trade, agriculture, fisheries, consumer protection, social affairs would be in need to develop an integrated strategy on the European Union's policy with regard to environment and development. This has not been done; therefore, the conclusion of the Court of Auditors of mid-June 2006—20 years after the insertion of the requirement to integrate environmental requirements into the other EU policies!—was quite blunt: "the environment has yet to be effectively mainstreamed into the Commission's development cooperation".[33] Similar descriptions could be made on agricultural policy, product policy, energy policy and other policy sectors.

13–28   As regards the outside contacts, the Commission placed, in 2001, its work under the principles of openness, participation, accountability, furthermore on effectiveness and coherence.[34] The question of openness and transparency will be discussed below, para.13–32ss, in the section on citizens and the EU environmental law and policy. As regards accountability the Commission does not really explain why it takes certain measures or does not take certain measures. Some examples, taken at random, might explain the point:

- Almost all environmental directives require the elaboration, by Member States, of implementation reports and the elaboration, by the Commission, of EU-wide reports. The Commission complies with this obligation in about one case out of two and normally with a considerable delay which diminishes the value of its reports. The Commission does not explain its delays, change its approach or otherwise try to improve the situation.

- The implementation reports themselves report normally on legislative measures that have been taken by Member States, but almost never on results. However, from the point of view of the environment, it is the result that matters. There is almost no attempt from the side of the Commission to explain what the state of the environment is before and after the EU and national implementation measures were taken. The reader of the reports thus learns about the legislation, while it may be assumed that he is interested in the protection of the environment; these two things are different.

- The Commission's practice, mentioned in para.13–24, above, of not monitoring the application of international conventions

- The Marine Strategy Framework Directive does not deal with the marine environment, but only with marine waters which have to reach a good environmental status by 2021.[35] There is no explanation given why the Directive does not address issues of fauna and flora, air emissions from ships, waste dumping and other aspects.

- The Sixth Environment Action Programme requests the elaboration of a directive on biodegradable waste, which means essentially one on compost.[36] For once, there is a consensus among the majority of Member State, the European Parliament's environmental committee, environment and industry organisations that EU-wide standards on compost and, more generally, on biodegradable waste are highly desirable; in particular also for countries in Southern and Central and Eastern Europe, where the soil is in need of nutrients.

- The Commission might have good reasons not to make such a proposal. The presentation of a proposal for a directive on the protection of soil would have been a good opportunity to explain its attitude. However, the

---

[33] Court of Auditors, special Report 6/2006 concerning the environmental aspects of the commission's development cooperation [2006] OJ C235/1, no.84.

[34] Commission (fn.19, above), p.7.

[35] Dir. 2008/56 (fn.11, above).

[36] Dec.1600/2002 (fn.22, above), art.8.

Commission never explained, if and why it considered such a proposal to be inadequate. Directive 2009/98 on waste now charges the Commission again to examine the situation and, eventually come up with a proposal.

The list could be prolonged. The impression is that of an administration which knows best what is good for the environment and does not consider it necessary to lay accounts on its acts and omissions.

The Commission's credibility problem was illustrated at paras 13–19ss., above, in the area of monitoring the application of environmental law. This problem is not limited to application issues. Another example is that of the treating of sustainability issues. The question of whether there has not been given an erroneous interpretation to the notion of sustainability development itself, shall not be treated here again. But it is difficult to understand why the Commission adopts a strategy on sustainable development and establishes guiding principles for it,[37] when in the daily practice, it only takes one part of that strategy, the part on economic growth (Lisbon agenda) and promotes it. This is an inconsistency which signals to the public that the strategy on sustainable development is pure rhetoric.

13–29

A similar rhetoric is found in the Commission's approach to transport problems. The different strategy papers duly mention that transport also causes environmental concerns—and then move on to greater mobility, more traffic infrastructure and more aviation. There is simply no serious attempt to integrate environmental requirements into the elaboration and implementation of transport policy. These examples could be multiplied for other sectoral policies.

European Parliament

The European Parliament has, in particular through its active environmental committee, constantly tried to strengthen legislative proposals on environmental issues which the Commission had submitted. This was and is more difficult, when the majority in Parliament is conservative, as conservative parties are traditionally less committed to environmental questions. Yet, overall, the European Parliament proved to side rather with the environment than with vested interests.

13–30

Parliament's problems are structural. The deputes do not stay permanently in Bruxelles, but share their time between their constituency, Bruxelles, where the Parliamentary committees work, and Strasbourg, where Parliamentary plenary meetings are held. This leads to the result that contact between Parliamentarians and the Commission or the Council are rather more rare than frequent.

The political parties in Parliament are not organised in the same way as at national level. They do not work on the same files as the Commission administration or, indeed, the national administrations in the capitals which then, later, meet in the Council working groups. Parliament's scientific and documentary service cannot rebalance this deficit. The result is that the Commission normally knows the environmental file better than the Parliament, and that Parliament has to re-act to Commission's initiatives, but cannot be pro-active. This institutional deficit of the Parliament is particularly obvious in the conciliation discussions under art.294 TFEU, where the deputes are

---

[37] Council, Strategy on sustainable development, doc. 10917/06 of June 26, 2006.

confronted with the combined experts' know-how of all capitals, who know the specific file often since years. Their opinions therefore regularly prevail.

The Parliament does not systematically control the implementation and application of the environmental legislation which it has co-decided. It cannot be argued that this is not Parliament's task, because the Parliament as co-legislator must be interested to know, whether the European environmental legislation effectively works, and if not for which reasons it does not work. Also, the Parliament has to control the Commission's activity; this requires an active, systematic look at application questions. In this regard the democratic system of checks and balances thus does not work properly.

In its contacts with the public, Parliament is the most open European institution. Its members, also due to some lack of detailed knowledge of the complex subjects which the Commission environmental legislative proposals treat, normally recur to interest groups to receive briefings. The European environmental groups frequently find interlocutors in members of the environmental committee—and so do other interest groups with members of Parliament which are closer to their interests. Systematic consultations in the form of hearings could make the consultation process more transparent, but are exceptional.

As, in general, the European Parliament is not yet a fully fledged Parliament comparable to national parliaments, its role in environmental law-making and in controlling the "government"—if one may call the Council and the Commission together like that—is not fully equivalent.

Council

13–31   The Council's environmental activity is very largely determined by the Commission's legislative proposals. These are discussed in working groups where environmental attaches of the Permanent Representations of Member States and experts from central national administrations meet, together with Commission officials who defend the proposal. Strategic discussions do not normally take place in these working groups which limits themselves to finding concrete solutions on the basis of instructions from the capitals. The working groups do not have outside contacts; whether individual members have, depends on their personal decision.

Strategic discussions may take place at the occasion of discussion on action programmes, under "other business" matters at formal Council meetings, or when the environmental ministers meet at the two annual informal Council meetings, for which the Presidency prepares a topic for discussion. As these informal ministerial meetings do not vote, adopt resolutions or other documents, their capacity of committing all members for the future, and thus their influence on long-term environmental policy is limited.

The Council Presidency regularly holds contacts with the Commission on matters that concern the organisation of the work. These contacts also include more general reflections on the different files, though they do not enter into the political area. As the Presidency changes every six months, no long-term or more general discussions occur. Contacts with the European Parliament are much less frequent.

Outside opinions regarding the Council work reach the Council via the capitals, not directly. This again is cause and effect at the same time for the lack of forming a European public opinion.

If one looks at the institutions, the main charge to develop strategic environmental thinking, long-term orientations and to steer the European environmental policy lies on the Commission which itself is not sufficiently equipped for such a think-tank task and, furthermore, does itself not feel bound by strategies such as action programmes.

7.   Citizens and EU environmental law and policy

EU environmental law and policy is popular with European citizens. Euro-   **13–32**
barometer's regular surveys on the opinion of European citizens thinking on EU issues show since two decades a high percentage—80 per cent and more—of citizens who rank environmental issues as very important and among the three to five top priorities for the European Union. This result is not surprising, if one remembers that for many people in the Member States environmental legislation and the accompanying policy originates at EU level. The citizens in the street rather wish to see more EU legislation and a better protection of the environment, for which they also feel responsible. As the European Union has the objective to be a Union at the service of its citizens and not just a free trade area, one would expect that it tries to associate citizens closer to the making and implementing of EU environmental law and policy.

It had already been mentioned that the Commission has not organised an environmental consultative committee or forum which it could consult. Communication activities by the Commission or by the different Commission offices in Member States are not targeted to inform or consult citizens on environmental matters, to make the administrative and political machinery of the EU institutions more transparent and more comprehensible. The communication activity of the Commission in environmental matters is not impressive, and where the language is not diplomatic, it is unfortunately often closer to marketing or publicity concerns than to neutral information. The Commission environmental reports and communications do not appear to reach the citizen in the street, for reasons of language, too complex contents, and because the problem is not presented and options for solutions not discussed, but a specific solution as the right one is pushed ahead. Environmental information and education of citizens might not be the primary task of the Commission, but networking and more concerns for the receiver of the information, including the young receiver, might be worthwhile. And it is little consolation, that the European Parliament and the Council do not fare better in this area.

Access of citizens to environmental information remains difficult, also in   **13–33**
times of the internet. It was already mentioned that the EU institutions are not yet prepared for openness and transparency. Too much information is declared sensitive, also after the relevant decision has been taken. The Commission shows a considerable sensitivity towards the interests of some Member States and of economic groups to keep studies, surveys, findings and other issues confidential. Key examples are information on nuclear issues and on genetically modified organisms. Risk assessments, cost-benefit analyses, impact assessments, planning

instruments, but also reports on meetings between members of the Commission and vested interest groups, communications on files etc.—the list is long, where a normal citizen has difficulty in obtaining access to documents. Regulation 1367/2006, which transposes the Aarhus Convention into EU law and applies to the EU institution,[38] will hopefully progressively lead to some changes. But it is significant that the Regulation excludes banking activities from its field of application, in order to exempt the European Investment Bank—a derogation which is not foreseen under the Aarhus Convention.

Where the Commission receives a complaint from a citizen that access to environmental information was refused in a Member State, it refers that citizen to the national court. This is another way of disappointing citizens; indeed, art.17 TEU constitutes an own obligation for the Commission to ensure that the law is applied; the general reference to a national court is not a way to comply with this obligation. Other factual difficulties in obtaining access to environmental information—unreasonably high costs, long delays for answers or no answer at all, systematic refusals to grant access, etc.—are not examined by the Commission, as it wishes to have as little to do with practical questions of applying EU environmental law (see para.13–19, above). For the citizen, the Commission is perceived as the guardian of EU law; if then the same Commission does not take up issues of practical application, disappointment is inevitable.

13–34   Not much need to be said about citizen participation in environmental decision-making at EU and national level. The Commission appears to understand consultations as being synonymous to participation—which it is not. Internet consultations are not an equivalent to citizens' participation either. What is lacking in particular is the laying of accounts: the Commission does not explain why the opinions and comments from environmental groups or persons were not taken over or why it preferred a more economic- to a more environment-oriented approach.

As regards citizens' participation at the decision-making process at national level, the corresponding legislation is too recent to be capable of being assessed. At present, the positive elements for citizens that there is such legislation at all, certainly prevail. Practical application, once more, will be decisive.

13–35   Giving citizens and/or environmental organisations the possibility to have environmental acts or omissions controlled by courts was one of the objectives of the Aarhus Convention to which the European Union has adhered. However, the Council was of the opinion that the present provisions of art.263(4) TFEU were compatible with the letter and the spirit of that Convention and that no change was necessary with regard to access to the European Courts. Even if this were legally correct—in my opinion, the Aarhus Convention does require a change of the present state of affairs[39]—the political aspect remains: access to the European courts in environmental matters is de facto impossible for individuals and for environmental organisations. A softening of this de facto monopoly of the Commission—more than 80 per cent of all environmental cases are brought by

---

[38] Reg.1367/2006 (fn.26, above).
[39] See now, in the same sense, Aarhus Convention Compliance Committee, Draft findings and recommendations with regard to Communication ACCC/C/2008/32 concerning compliance by the European Union, March 2011.

the Commission—would also be of particular political importance, as it would also eventually hold EU institutions environmentally responsible.

A proposal for a directive to improve access to national courts was likewise **13–36** not accepted by the Council which invoked subsidiarity reasons. This means that Member States will decide on improved access to justice in environmental matters and all indicators point into the direction that the status quo will largely remain unchanged. Thus, for example, a company which is of the opinion that an environmental legislation of a Member State—including legislation which is based on EU law—impedes the placing on the market of its products, may go to court and challenge that legislation by virtue of art.34 TFEU. However, an environmental organisation which is of the opinion that legislation allows too much emissions into the air or the water, cannot appeal to a court.

The recent example of air pollution by particle matters is a good illustration of this argument. The relevant national and EU legislation is not respected in a number of urban agglomerations. The Court of Justice had declared, already in 1991, that air quality standards also protect human health and must allow citizens to claim their respect in court. This line of judgments was repeated in 2007.[40] However, the legislation continues to be not respected and no application of environmental groups has, until now, led to the result that even the breach of EU law is acknowledged.

Lawyers will explain the difference between the rights of a company and of an environmental organisation in cases like this. Politically, this is more difficult. And it adds to the disappointment which European citizens must feel, that the European Union amended the existing legislation to give Member States further delays in respecting their obligations which existed since 1999.[41]

As one way of assisting citizens in contributing to protect the environment, the **13–37** Commission had instituted the complaint procedure, being however careful of avoiding to formalise the procedural rules in any legal act. While at the end of the 1980s, the Commission promised to examine each complaint as to its merits,[42] it went away from this commitment and now only promises to register each complaint; but it reserves the right to treat or not to treat complaints as to its own priorities; and what is more: the registration takes place in a so-called pilot-register and is submitted to a non-public arrangement procedure between the Member State in question and the Commission. Instead of a formal instruction, the Commission thus looks for arranging things, though it is in most cases the public authority itself which is disregarding EU environmental law.[43] Apart from the fact that there are, in the meantime, clear signs that environmental complaints are not even registered at all, this change of procedure—decided without any participation process of citizens or the public—leads to the fact that individual desk officers decide on how to proceed with complaints. Seen from the point of view of the citizen, who sits in Crete, Madeira, Cork or Tampere, the message which is sent from the Commission when his complaint is not examined, is clear:

---

[40] Court of Justice, *Janecek* (C–237/07) [2008] E.C.R. I–6221.
[41] Dir.2008/50 [2008] OJ L152/1.
[42] See the text which accompanied the complaint form issued by the Commission [1989] OJ C26/1.
[43] Commission COM(2002) 725.

> "It may be that the specific project on which you complain, is breaching EU environmental law. However, your Member State has correctly transposed the relevant EU legislation into national law. Therefore, we decided not to look into your specific case."

If one compares this with the Commission's message of early 2005, mentioned in para.13–25, above, the discrepancy becomes obvious. And it also becomes obvious why the frustration about the EU institutions is growing at local level, not diminishing.

Instead of taking complaints on individual cases as a sampling way which allows it to get an impression, how EU law works in practice, the Commission sees individual complaints as an undesirable practice which should best be abandoned. And the remark has to be made that neither in competition matters nor in internal market affairs, would such a handling of complaints be made.

In conclusion, it may fairly be stated that EU institutions deploy very limited efforts to bring the European Union in environmental matters closer to the citizen. Citizens are rather asked to take the initiative—ask for access to information, file complaints—and see their initiatives often enough unsuccessful.

8.   Member States and EU environmental law and policy

13–38   The EU Treaties' concept of distributing responsibilities between the European Union and Member States is quite clear: there is shared responsibility for the European environment. Member States have the responsibility to protect the environment; and certain measures are to be taken at EU level (art.5 TEU).

The political reality is somehow different. Member States rely heavily on the European Union for environmental measures. It was already mentioned that for more than half of the Member States, "environmental law" is more or less equivalent to "EU-derived environmental law". This means that where the European Union does not take legislative measures, in the majority of the Member States no legislative action will be taken either. This contradicts the objective of the European Union to ensure an economic, but also social and environmental playing field which is more or less at the same level—and this aspect is frequently overlooked by countries with a strong, though not necessarily pro-environmental national policy, such as Netherlands, United Kingdom, Germany and the German Länder, or France.

13–39   The result of this repartition of responsibilities and political practice is that EU environmental policy is squeezed between two different orientations. On the one hand, Member States insist on the application of arts 5 TEU and 193 TFEU, with the consequence that the European Union should only regulate where this is absolutely necessary, and should take a low common denominator, in order to leave Member States the possibility to maintain or introduce more stringent provisions. On the other hand, Member States do not develop themselves national measures to protect, preserve and improve the quality of the environment. Countries such as the United Kingdom, Germany or Austria have even taken, in one or the other form, the decision not to adopt national environmental legislation which goes beyond the relevant EU measure, frustrating thus the concept of arts 5 TEU and 193 TFEU.

There are numerous examples for this. The most obvious is the absence of environmental action programmes in Member States. The EU action programmes concern the EU level; the attempt of the Fifth Environment Action Programme, also to address targets and measures to be taken at national level,[44] was a complete failure. However, protecting the European environment is, under the Treaties, also the task of Member States. From the point of view of the environment, it is not relevant whether it is protected through a local, national or EU measure, as long as it is protected. This simple truth is often forgotten in Member States who just rely on the European Union to provide for the necessary protection.

Other examples range from environmental liability via soil protection, permits for small and medium-sized companies, environmental impact assessments for smaller infrastructure projects, marine water and groundwater protection, to contaminated site provisions, access to justice, coastal zone protection, fights against soil erosion or pollution emission registers. For most of these areas there is some legislation in some Member States; however, the overall perspective for the territory of the European Union, seen from the bird's eye view, is an unsatisfactory degree of protecting the environment. This reflects the different role which the protection of the environment plays in the political hierarchy of the Member States. While it ranks high in some, it ranks very low in others, especially in those, where the environmental legislation is more or less completely EU-derived.

The high degree of environmental protection at which the Treaty aims, is normally ignored during the EU law-making procedure. The same applies to the principle that environmental damage should be rectified at source, that the polluter should pay or that environmental requirements should be integrated into the legislation in other policy areas. These principles of the EU Treaties are perceived as EU principles; but when Member States discuss in Council on a Commission proposal, they do not look at the European Union's (environmental) interest, but at their own (environmental, economic and social) interest. And this conflict of interest cannot easily be solved, as on the one hand, the Commission itself which should have defined the EU environmental interest, might have failed in that, due to pressure from vested interest groups or internal differences of opinion on the right approach; on the other hand, the Commission representative, confronted with representatives of 27 Member States, would have to be an over-flyer to impose his point of view. **13–40**

The Council environment working group does not normally wait for the European Parliament's opinion on a Commission proposal, before discussing it. Rather, discussions in the working group ran parallel with Parliament's discussion. It is normal now, that the working group has reached a political compromise on a Council position with regard to a proposal, before the Parliamentary opinion is delivered. This practice increases the Council's dominance in the legislative process, though it contradicts the objective of art.294 TFEU.

The monitoring of adopted EU environmental law varies considerably from one Member State to the other. Again, this reflects the different degree of environmental awareness in Member States, though there is a second element. Member States' administrations perceive EU environmental law sometimes as imported law, as immigrant law, which stems from an outside source and which is **13–41**

---

[44] Fifth Environment Action Programme (fn.1, above).

different from national law.[45] Such an attitude can be found, for example, in Germany, France or Italy. More generally, EU law is monitored, because the Commission asks for such a monitoring, not because it corresponds to its own conviction. Inevitably, the concept of imported law has practical consequences as regards the frequency and intensity of monitoring, sanctions for breaches, etc.

The national implementation reports which Member States send to the Commission report, as mentioned, on measures taken, not on results achieved. They practically never deal with lacunae, omissions, breaches of provisions, with sanctions pronounced, etc. The implementation reports thus do not give an idea of a EU directive's effectiveness.

13–42   The enforcement of EU environmental law is entirely in the hands of Member States and practically no information is made public on that, not either in the previously mentioned implementation reports. The Commission does not monitor enforcement practices and with all necessary caution, it might be stated that the intensity of enforcement, in particular as regards pollution emissions, permit controls, water and soil contamination, and planning-related measures such as impact assessments or participation provisions varies considerably from one Member State to the other. And the Commission hardly ever monitors the application of regulations; these are directly applicable and thus, Member States often do not feel obliged to monitor their application themselves.

It is difficult to identify different groups among Member States with regard to monitoring deficiencies. Some Member States make it a point of national honour to transpose EU environmental legislation in time. For others, delayed transposition is the rule. Some Member States consider that the provisions of EU law, once they are in the national statute books, have to be enforced; this includes the United Kingdom, the Scandinavian States, also Netherlands. Others do not see a problem in having contradictions between the law in the statute books and the law as it is applied; this attitude is not limited to environmental law.

It is too early to rank the 12 Member States which joined the European Union since 2004, into one of these categories. Generally, however, it can be said that under the former Communist system, the State who produced the environmental legislation, and the State-owned companies were the biggest polluters of all. This created a certain cynicism of citizens: why should a legislation be respected, if it is broken in particular by those who made it? This cynicism partly continues to exist and will be difficult to overcome. It adds to the point which is also true for the 15 "old" Member States, that the placing of environmental legislation into the statute books is easy, but that the real problems appear, when these environmental provisions are to be applied. Application of environmental law remains, also in the new Member States, the biggest of all legal—and political—problems.

9.   The European Union as a global environmental player

13–43   The European Union does not play an active role at global level, when it comes to the elaboration of environmental standards. The jealously of Member States, to appear themselves at the international scene and to be seen as a sovereign State, is too big. Own initiatives from the European Union would probably have to be

---

[45] Commission, European Governance (fn.19, above), p.21: "At the same time, the feeling persists that Community rules are foreign laws".

classified as part of a foreign (environmental) policy and share all the difficulties of an EU foreign policy. The participation in international discussions on new environmental conventions is based, according to the Treaties (art.218 TFEU) on a Council mandate. In practice, Member States are reluctant to give such a mandate, as then the Commission would represent the European Union and this would restrict Member States' negotiation possibilities. It is therefore almost normal that in such international negotiations, the Commission is present without a mandate, discusses and negotiates together with Member States and tries to co-ordinate Member States' positions, in order to make the European Union speak, as far as possible with one voice or at least take similar positions.

All this does not facilitate the role of the European Union as such, but has to be accepted as part of international diplomacy. More relevant is the aspect that the United States, for more than 25 years, has proven to be incapable or unwilling to assume international leadership in environmental matters. As the European Union, for the reasons sketched out above, is not in a state to assume leadership functions either, global environmental issues are at present not properly dealt with. Examples are issues of environmental crime (trade in timber, waste, exotic species, fish, etc.), the provisions of biodiversity, the Convention on hazardous waste, the Arctic Area, the environmental behaviour of multinational companies, chemicals, access to water resources, soil erosion, desertification, the construction of dams and many others.

The global discussions on climate change, where the European Union played a very active role and did assume global leadership, are not a proof of the contrary. In that case, the European Union grew into a leading role due to a change in the United States' attitude towards climate change. However, the European Union—neither the Commission nor the Commission jointly with Member States—is not equipped to assume a permanent global leadership function in climate change. Fossil fuel energy responsibilities are too dispersed within the European Union, human resources too small, the scientific and technical data on the situation worldwide are too scattered, diplomatic services of the European Union itself do not yet exist, the financial tools which such a leadership role requires, are not available, etc. **13–44**

At international negotiations which would require an integrated approach by the European Union, such as combining agricultural with environmental questions, the European Union negotiates under trade-agricultural perspectives alone, as it has not implemented art.11 TFEU. Thus, for example, the proposal to open up EU agricultural markets on the condition that the environmental and health standards of the European Union are taken over internationally, has apparently not even crossed the mind of the EU negotiators. The lack of integrating environmental requirements into the EU development policy[46] also makes the EU position in this area difficult in international forums. Generally, the European Union is much more interested to promote exports of European products and services than to have an international policy which effectively integrates environmental considerations.

The implementation of international environmental conventions within the European Union was already mentioned. Though, overall, the European Union's monitoring process regarding the application of law is quite impressive and could serve as a model for many a regional organisation—Mercosur, Nafta, the Asean **13–45**

---

[46] See the reference to the Report 6/2006 of the Court of Auditors, fn.34, above.

Group, etc.—the European Union behaves internationally as the Member States with regard to the Commission: reports are sent late, they report on measures, not on results, they try to give a positive image of the European Union and to hide imperfections.

At present, thus, the European Union has neither the internal structures nor resources to assume a role as global environmental player. This certainly also has consequences for the present state of the global environment—which is not good, if one thinks of climate change, poverty, biodiversity, chemicals, water problems, etc.

10. Perspectives

13–46   As the environment has no voice, there is a tendency for declaring that things slowly go better. The statement of the European Environment Agency of 2001 that the state of the European environment shows some progress, but offers a poor picture overall,[47] appears to be more appropriate, also ten years later. The European Union state of the environment is not satisfactory, the biggest challenges being climate change, the conservation of nature and biodiversity, the omnipresence of chemicals and the problems of urban agglomerations. And the expectancy that there will be 9 billion people on earth by 2030 who all need food, shelter, water, energy and a job, draws the attention to the fact that the EU problems are even small, compared to the global challenges which lie ahead are in part already the problems of today and require a credible leadership now.

The EU structures to adequately deal with the global and regional challenges could be improved. Active citizen involvement is indispensable, if ever the environmental policy is to produce results. And the European Union will never be able to play an active and positive role on the evolution of the global environment, unless it brings its own house in order.

Environmental legislation is not everything, but is a very important factor to distribute justice in society, to determine rights and obligations and to balance diverging interests. Western society has not found other means to achieve these results than legislation, and I doubt that in modern society with the important role of economics other means can fulfil the same function. "Between the strong and the weak, it is the law which makes free and the freedom which oppresses": these words of La Rochefoucauld of the seventeenth century remain valid today and should warn against the hope that economic instruments can ensure justice in the society.

The European Union will need, for a foreseeable time, environmental legislation and its effective application. More and more, this will become relevant also for the global level. It is hoped that decision-makers at all levels are aware of this and find the vision, the strategy and the capacity to develop legal instruments which effectively protect, preserve and improve the quality of the environment, nationally, Europe-wide and globally. The environment can survive without humans, but humans cannot survive without the environment.

---

[47] European Environment Agency, *Environment in the European Union at the turn of the century* (Luxemburg, 1999).

Index

This index has been prepared using Sweet and Maxwell's Legal Taxonomy. Main index entries conform to keywords provided by the Legal Taxonomy except where references to specific documents or non-standard terms (denoted by quotation marks) have been included. These keywords provide a means of identifying similar concepts in other Sweet and Maxwell publications and online services to which keywords from the Legal Taxonomy have been applied. Readers may find some minor differences between terms used in the text and those which appear in the index. Suggestions to *sweetandmaxwell.taxonomy@thomson.com*.

All references are to paragraph number

monitoring transposition and application
  citizen complaints, 12-22—12-26
  Commission's function, 12-17—12-19
  direct effect, 12-27—12-29
  implementation reports, 12-14—12-16
  other bodies,by, 12-20—12-21
optional harmonisation, and, 3-41
partial harmonisation, and, 3-41
parties
  Committee of the Regions, 2-23
  Council of the European Union, 2-24—2-25
  Court of Justice of the European Union,
    2-26—2-27
  Economic and Social Committee, 2-23
  environmental organisations, 2-29
  European Commission, 2-02—2-19
  European Court of Justice, 2-26—2-27
  European Parliament, 2-20—2-22
  General Court, 2-26—2-27
  individuals, 2-30
  introduction, 2-01
  professional organisations, 2-28
policy objectives
  art.191(1) TFEU, under, 1-15
  general, 1-10
  level of protection, 1-13—1-14
  sustainable development, 1-11—1-12
principles
  general, 1-16—1-18
  integration, 1-24—1-26
  polluter pays, 1-32—1-33
  precautionary, 1-27—1-28
  prevention, 1-29
  rectification of damage at source, 1-30—1-31
  subsidiarity, 1-19—1-23
protective measures, 3-42—3-51
quantitative restrictions on imports
  discriminating measures, 3-16—3-20
  disproportionate measures, 3-21—3-29
  extraterritorial protection, 3-30—3-31
  free movement of goods, 3-08—3-14
  introduction, 3-04—3-07
  necessary for action, 3-08—3-14
  non-economic grounds, 3-15
  proportionality, 3-08—3-14
rights under other Treaty provisions, 3-70—3-71
safeguard clause rights, 3-72—3-73
sanctions for non-application
  action by individuals, 12-43—12-45
  action by member states, 12-35
  applications to Court of Justice,
    12-33—12-34
  art.258 TFEU action, 12-30—12-34
  art.259 TFEU action, 12-35
  art.260 TFEU action, 12-36—12-37
  criminal sanctions, 12-41
  enforcement of judgments of Court of Justice,
    12-36—12-37
  financial sanctions, 12-39—12-40
  interim measures, 12-42

notice of breach of obligations, 12-31
reasoned opinions, 12-32
state liability, 12-38
secondary legislation
  application, 12-12—12-13
  generally, 12-02—12-03
  transposition, 12-04—12-11
sources of law, 1-07—1-09
state liability, 12-38
total harmonisation, and, 3-41
transposition
  monitoring, 12-14—12-29
  secondary legislation, 12-04—12-11
  Treaty provisions, 12-01
Treaty provisions, 12-01
EU legislative process
agricultural sector, 2-93—2-94
choice of legal basis, 2-69—2-82
commercial matters, 2-97—2-98
Committee of the Regions, 2-64—2-65
Council procedure, 2-66—2-68
decisions under art.191(4) TFEU, 2-91
decisions under art.192(2) TFEU, 2-86—2-90
ECOSOC, 2-64—2-65
elaboration of legislation measure, 2-61—2-68
energy matters, 2-90
enhanced co-operation, 2-100—2-104
European Parliament, 2-64—2-65
internal market, 2-96
international co-operation, 2-91
land use, 2-87, 2-89
legal bases, 2-83—2-104
measures under art.192(1) TFEU, 2-83—2-84
nature protection, 2-75
other Treaty provisions, 2-92—2-99
planning, 2-87
programmes under art.192(3) TFEU, 2-85
research matters, 2-99
right to clean environment
  European level, 4-14—4-17
  national level, 4-10—4-13
town and country planning, 2-87
transport sector, 2-95
waste, 2-76—2-79
water conservation, 2-8
EURATOM
energy policy, and, 11-23
EU environmental law, and, 13-04
hazardous waste, and, 10-29
integration, and, 1-24
legal and political instruments, and, 2-31
safety measures fro nuclear installations, and,
  4-49
shipment of radioactive waste, and, 10-45
"European Climate Change Programme"
see also **Climate change**
generally, 9-03
European Coal and Steel Treaty
energy policy, and, 11-23